Design for Ecological Democracy

Design for Ecological Democracy

Randolph T. Hester

The MIT Press   Cambridge, Massachusetts   London, England

MIT Press books may be purchased at special quantity discounts for business or sales promotional use. For information, please e-mail <special_sales@mitpress.mit.edu> or write to Special Sales Department, The MIT Press, 55 Hayward Street, Cambridge, MA 02142.

This book was set in Adobe Garamond and DIN by Graphic Composition, Inc., Athens, Georgia.

Printed and bound in Spain, using paper manufactured from sustainable forests.

Library of Congress Cataloging-in-Publication Data

Hester, Randolph T.
Design for ecological democracy / Randolph T. Hester.
    p. cm.
Includes bibliographical references (p.   ) and index.
ISBN-13: 0-262-0851-5 (alk. paper)
ISBN-10: 0-262-08351-5 (alk. paper)
1. City planning—United States. 2. Urban ecology—United States. 3. Public spaces—United States. I. Title.

HT167.H472 2006
307.1'2160973—dc22

2006041958

10 9 8 7 6 5 4 3 2 1

This is dedicated to Marcia, whose commitment to grassroots democracy has enabled every community she has touched, whose visionary but systematic reasoning has helped cities become resilient in ways never before imagined, and whose beauty impels me in the way that cities of ecological democracy will someday impel others.

Contents

Acknowledgments   *xi*

Introduction   *1*

The State of American Habitation   *1*
Ecological Democracy   *3*
Life, Death, and Rebirth of Ecological
    Democracy   *4*
The Marriage of Necessity and Happiness   *5*
Design of City and Landscape Together   *7*
Enabling, Resilient, and Impelling Form   *8*
Enabling Form: "We Got to Know Our
    Neighbors"   *8*
Resilient Form: Life, Liberty, and the Pursuit of
    Sustainable Happiness   *9*
Impelling Form: "Make a City to Touch the People's
    Hearts"   *9*
The Glocal Design Process   *10*
The Focus Is Design   *10*
This Book Is for Students of Ecological
    Democracy   *12*

**ENABLING FORM: "WE GOT TO KNOW OUR
NEIGHBORS"**   *15*

Centeredness   *21*

Ten Rules for Good Centers   *23*
Sociopetal Places, Forming Open Circles   *32*

Places for Community Rituals   *37*
Nourishing Centeredness Every Day   *40*

Connectedness   *49*

Interdependent Adjacencies: What Goes Together
    and What Doesn't   *51*
Transportation and Communication That
    Unify   *52*
Chains, Webs, Flows, Networks, Cycles, and
    Recycles   *54*
Resource Footprints   *57*
Wildlife Habitats   *58*
Ecological Thinking   *59*
Mutualism and Glocalization   *60*
Outside the Confines of the Box   *62*
Things That Don't Go Together but Might   *63*
Finding Fish Heads and Tails   *64*
The Lost Mountain, the Power Map, and the Dirt
    Contractor   *66*

Fairness   *77*

Accessibility   *78*
Inclusion   *80*
Equal Distribution of Resources and
    Amenities   *82*
Paying Attention to Design   *83*
Mapping Injustices   *85*
Fair Landscapes Empower   *87*

Sensible Status Seeking   *97*

   Forming Communities to Be What They Are   *100*
   Lessons from Poverty   *104*
   Taking Root   *105*
   Small Is Often Beautiful   *106*
   Rare and Commonplace Beauty   *107*
   Conspicuous Nonconsumption   *110*
   Inclusive Heterogeneity   *111*
   Dirty Enough to Be Happy   *112*
   Healthy Status Seeking   *114*

Sacredness   *117*

   Sacredness Expresses Our Essential Nature   *117*
   Uncovering Sacredness   *118*
   Transformative Community Awareness   *125*
   Preservation   *126*
   Design Gestalt   *127*
   Recurring Center   *127*
   Natural Boundary   *130*
   Connections to Community, Ancestors, and
     Spirits   *130*
   Particularness   *132*
   Design Inspiration   *133*
   A Higher Purpose for Vexing Problems   *135*

**RESILIENT FORM: LIFE, LIBERTY, AND THE PURSUIT OF
SUSTAINABLE HAPPINESS**   *137*

Particularness   *145*

   Bioregional Distinction: Topographic Typologies
     and Willful Water   *147*
   Peculiar Forms of Conserving, Recycling, and
     Repairing   *152*
   Meditations, Imaginings, and Similar Someplace
     Else   *160*

   Time Lapse and Previous Catastrophes   *164*
   Particularness Provides Goodness of Fit   *169*

Selective Diversity   *171*

   Biological Diversity   *172*
   Cultural Diversity   *184*
   Global Heterogenization and Glocal Design   *186*
   The Landscape Form of a Diversified
     Economy   *187*
   Social Ecotones of Mixed-Use
     Neighborhoods   *188*
   How Much Diversity Is Enough?   *190*
   Intergenerational and Social-Class Diversity   *196*
   Seeding Diversity   *196*

Density and Smallness   *201*

   Concentrated Density Creates Resilience   *201*
   The Conspiracy against Density   *205*
   Net, Perceived, and Affective Density   *207*
   Making Density Desirable   *208*
   Provide for Privacy   *218*
   Hide Density   *219*
   Green the Neighborhood   *220*
   Acquire Big Nature   *221*
   Access Transit   *221*
   Identify the Neighborhood and the Block   *222*
   Create the Center   *222*
   I Beg Your Pardon: I Never Promised You a Rose
     Garden   *223*

Limited Extent   *227*

   Two Excellencies Make a Singular Resilience   *227*
   From Settlement to Edge City and Fat
     Suburb   *229*
   Three Questions of Size   *230*

Appropriate Size: The Outer Limits of Regional
   Carrying Capacity   *230*
Appropriate Size: Internal Limits on Optimal City
   Size   *231*
Reconfiguring Megacities   *233*
Inside and Outside   *237*
Cities Approaching 250,000 People   *238*
Appropriate Size: Small Towns in Regional
   Form   *240*
Creating a Big Wild Greenbelt for Los
   Angeles   *244*
The Essential Scales for Governing Ecological
   Democracy   *251*
A Mollusk, a Crustacean, a Flat Worm, and
   Tocqueville   *253*

Adaptability   *255*

Flexible City Form from Natural Process   *256*
Landscapes of Adaptability   *256*
Emptiness   *259*
Landscape and Building   *260*
Priority Framework and Piecemeal Intricacy   *263*
Continuous Experiment, Adaptive Management,
   and Windows of Opportunity   *272*
Choice   *275*

**IMPELLING FORM: "MAKE A CITY TO TOUCH THE
PEOPLE'S HEARTS"**   *277*

Everyday Future   *281*

Designing for What People Do All Day   *283*
Integrating Present Experience with Change   *284*
Marking Time   *287*
Inspiring Visionary Futures with the
   Everyday   *289*
Everyday Lessons for Designers   *296*

Naturalness   *301*

Naturopathy   *302*
Naturism   *305*
Naturalization   *308*
The Form to Arouse Naturalness   *310*
The Natural Park   *315*
Naturalness Impels   *323*

Inhabiting Science   *325*

Urban Ecological Illiteracy   *327*
Native Wisdom, Science, and the Language of
   Ecological Democracy   *331*
How Science Is Inhabited   *332*
What We Need to Know   *334*
Learning from the Urban Landscape   *338*
Discovery Landscapes   *340*
Cultivating Landscapes   *344*
Instructive Landscapes   *345*
Scientific Landscapes   *348*
Argumentative Landscapes   *350*
LA96C   *353*

Reciprocal Stewardship   *363*

Stewarding and Stewarded   *364*
Naive Stewardship Meets Freedom to Withdraw
   from Civic Life   *365*
Ecological Necessity and Voluntary
   Stewardship   *367*
Many Places at the Table   *369*
Making Places for Effective Stewardship   *371*
The Garden Patch   *375*
Active Responsibility   *383*

Pacing   *387*

    Light Speed and Snail's Pace   *387*

    Dwelling Pace   *390*

    Learning to Walk   *392*

    Slouching toward Obesity at Car Speed   *393*

    Remedial and Preventive Prescriptions   *396*

    Pathfinders Curb the Car   *396*

    Living Symphonic Sequences   *399*

    Metamorphic Walks   *404*

    Grounded   *408*

    Walk All Over   *412*

Epilogue   *419*

Notes   *423*

References and Suggested Reading   *459*

Image Credits   *487*

Index   *491*

Acknowledgments

Sifting through years of city making, I have tried to separate wheat from chaff. Forty years of practice creates a lot of chaff. I alone have rendered husks and half-baked goods, but in collaboration with others, nourishing kernels have been winnowed. And I have been fortunate in that regard. My primary working associates are my son, wife, and large extended family; colleagues, staff, and students at Berkeley, Penn State, and North Carolina State; colleagues at other universities; Democratic Designers in the Pacific Rim; clients, political allies, and adversaries; my partner and the people who have worked with Marcia and me at Community Development by Design; thousands of community members; and more than my share of natively wise mentors. Each of you will recognize the grains you discovered, the projects you kneaded, and the bread you baked and we broke together. I thank each of you for your singular contribution.

This book is a collaboration with the MIT Press. I thank Clay Morgan, Theresa Lamoureux, and Yasuyo Iguchi for an unusual meeting of the minds. I would also like to acknowledge editors Deborah Cantor-Adams and Rosemary Winfield, and publicist David Cecere.

My work in recent years has been supported by generous gifts from two deceased heroines of landscape architecture—Beatrix Farrand and Gerrie Knight Scott. Funds they left to the Department of Landscape Architecture and Environmental Planning at the University of California, Berkeley, have made this book possible. I hope my effort satisfies their watchful eyes.

Three collaborators are most responsible for this book. Thank you, Rachel Berney. Thank you, Amy Dryden. Thank you, Mary Ann Harrel.

Design for Ecological Democracy

Introduction

This book is about building ecological democracy through design. It is about remaking American cities so that we can better work with our neighbors and others; solve intricate community problems that help us sustain our liberty, our way of life, and the ecological systems on which liberty and life depend; and gain pleasure from the places where we dwell. Places that attract an informed and active citizenry, that are resilient ecologically, and that enhance our lives through their livability are the foundation for an ecological democracy that is essential to our nation's long-term health and to lives that are more rewarding than most of us presently live.

The State of American Habitation

What is wrong with the cities we have created? According to most researchers, the way we presently inhabit the earth is not sustainable. They point to the greenhouse effect, to global economics that create international cities and exploit backwaters, to developing-country inequities, and to the loss of cultural and biological diversity. All are critical issues of urbanity.

For example, one thousand species of plants and animals are going extinct each week, primarily because of habitat destruction, and present city forms are in large measure responsible for these declines in biological diversity. But the problems we face every day are more personal and insidious than the loss of biological or even cultural diversity. If we do not address daily issues of habitation, we have little chance of solving more remote ones.

For the last fifty years, at an ever-accelerating pace, cities, subdivisions, parks, even our houses have diminished our daily lives, often in ways about which we are unaware. Poor city design divides us from others in our communities, undermines our sense of community and place, destroys natural habitats that once gave us immeasurable joy (and provided niches for many of those extinct species, some of whose songs welcomed us each morning), and fails to inspire our spirits. In the name of progress, we destroy the best neighborhoods to build highways that are still unable to relieve traffic congestion. The vehicles that ride on ever wider streets add deadly pollutants to our everyday environments, make neighborhood play unsafe for our children, and turn across-the-street neighbors into strangers. As we improve environments for cars, we neglect walking and grow less healthy. We have subverted the intention of separated land uses to such an extreme that zoning segregation makes it nearly impossible to earn a living and be a parent at the same time. We sanitize our suburbs, but we can't make places where we feel safe. We have lost the balance that makes a city clean enough to be healthy and dirty enough to be happy. We have created pockets of poverty and wealth that cannot be escaped. When people are locked in and locked out, alienated from each other, can these be civilized cities?

In the process of city building, building community has been lost. Traditions of barn raising, through which both physical and social communities were nurtured simultaneously, have been replaced by technical experts, none of whose specialties include making community. They attend to bricks and mortar, street widths and lights, zoning and subdivision rules, contracts and financial bottom lines. Nurturing a sense of community is not a goal, and decisions are made that preclude our ability to work together. A popular downtown post office might be closed and a new one built far from downtown, making chance meetings less likely for downtown business people or shoppers. The budget-saving design of the new post office may further diminish community by eliminating a lobby where people might stop and chat.

We have designed cities that do not take advantage of natural factors. Inspired by their regional characteristics, cities could save billions of dollars in energy, food, drinking-water costs, and waste disposal while providing recreational amenities, local identity, and sense of place. But city makers continue to design urban areas more and more the same and less and less particular to vegetative mosaics, microclimates, air-movement patterns, and hydrologic cycles. We still call resulting urban wildfires, energy shortages, and flood damage "natural disasters." Even innocuous-seeming conveniences of air conditioning, television, home delivery of mail, private swimming pools, the Internet, and underground storm-drainage systems separate us from local environments and render us ecologically illiterate.

I recently worked in a neighborhood where twenty years earlier residents culverted the creek running through their community as part of a city flood-control plan. Although there was no history of flooding on that creek, the underground culvert was seen as a modern improvement, and from that point on, residents were denied access to wildlife along the stream. Today, children in that neighborhood never creek walk or pile rocks to divert water or explore riparian mysteries. They never chase native frogs or dragonflies or marvel at the magic of a tadpole or nymph. In fact, residents of the neighborhood today, adults and children, are unaware that a natural stream ever existed there. Such diminishments of joy have sapped our cities of their ability to nurture us in fundamental ways. We don't know what we've got until it's gone and maybe not even then.

None of these actions—a street widening here, a post office relocation there, air conditioning, stream channelization—seems particularly harmful, but the cumulative effect is devastating on the livability of our cities and on us as human beings. These forces also contribute to environmental and community anomie. From the root *anomia,* meaning "lawlessness," anomie is a diseaselike state of confusion individuals have developed about how to act toward their neighbors, their fellow citizens, and the landscape. Citizens of the United States and other developed countries have gained freedom from environmental constraints through technology, standardization, and specialization. We no longer experience ecological interdependence in our daily lives as, say, a farmer does. This freedom and affluence have freed us from community responsibility because we can so often provide privately what was once attainable only if shared. Facilities like parks, schools, swimming pools, gyms, and movie theaters used to be provided only in the public realm but now are routinely afforded privately, making civic engagement less essential. Independence from the world around us and disassociation from community offer us enormous short-term freedoms, but adverse long-term consequences—not just for human beings but also for cities—have thoughtlessly resulted. Anomie undermines our humanity and cripples our ability to create fulfilling, inspiring cities. Seemingly freed from our dependence on community and environment, we must choose and forge new relationships with both.

Ecological Democracy

The vicious iterative cycle in which insecure and unrooted individuals make insecure and unrooted cities, which make even more insecure and unrooted individuals, was generations in the making and will be generations in the undoing. Shifts that disrupt the unhealthy cycle are essential. This is the great challenge of our time.

Neither applied ecology nor direct democracy alone can overcome these problems, but when combined they offer hope. Ecological democracy is an antidote to the poisons we have inflicted on ourselves and habitation. More important, ecological democracy represents the best possible life we can achieve. It offers no quick fix but rather a path for a long journey.

Democracy is government by the people. It is exercised directly through active involvement in a locality and indirectly through elections, following principles of equality and attending to individual needs and broader community goods. Ecology is the science of the relationships between organisms, including our environments and us. It encompasses the study of natural processes, ecosystems, and interactions of humans with each other, other species, and the cities we occupy. It includes principles of social and environmental function and interconnection. It is also a comprehensive, long-term way to think creatively.

Ecological democracy, then, is government by the people emphasizing direct, hands-on involvement. Actions are guided by understanding natural processes and social relationships within our locality and the larger environmental context. This causes us to creatively reassess individual needs, happiness, and long-term community goods in the places we inhabit. Ecological democracy can change the form that our cities take creating a new urban ecology. In turn, the form of our cities, from the shape of regional watersheds to a bench at a post office, can help build ecological democracy.

Life, Death, and Rebirth of Ecological Democracy

Ecological democracy is almost like wedding apparel, "something old, something new, something *recurring,* something *true.*" The founders of our country articulated a rural version of ecological democracy that underlies our independence and constitution. Thomas Jefferson envisioned a yeoman farmer who was so in tune with the local landscape that rainfall, stream patterns, forests, soil, and crops informed his every action, public and private. Farmers stewarded the land in Jefferson's vision. Likewise, farmers stewarded democracy through native ecological wisdom and direct grassroots participation. This vision—in spite of being flawed at the time and romanticized now—serves as a recurring American ideal. It is part of our unconscious identity, a self-evident truth. Over time, however, citizenship that was grounded in land stewardship and direct democracy declined to near extinction. Agrarian society became urban, mobile, and specialized. For over a hundred years—from the Civil War to the civil rights movement—our government was run increasingly by professionals and less by lay citizens. Representative government freed us from obligations of local involvement. Urban specialization freed us from dependence on local ecology.

Near death, ecology and direct democracy reawakened in the second half of the twentieth century. They were separately rediscovered in forms that are radically more complex than those that Jefferson likely imagined: something old became something utterly new. New and powerful enough to be considered among the most important discoveries of our time, applied ecological science and participatory democracy are two forces that most influenced the shift in the postmodern world view. After Rachel Carson sounded the alarm in *Silent Spring* in 1962, ecological principles slowly reworked their way into our consciousness. It became apparent that the built environment must be formed by applied ecology. At first, this ecological thinking focused exclusively on what wild land to conserve and where not to build. But urban ecological design has evolved into a comprehensive understanding of organisms, habitats, and events—natural and political. Likewise democracy has grown! There are twice as many democratic countries in the world today as twenty-five years ago, and in that time, more than sixty-six nations have made a transition from authoritarian regimes. Around the world, a desire for freedom and the associated expectations of citizens to participate directly in city-design decisions are rising and, in many cases, erupting. But these social movements are only infrequently informed by ecological thinking in local governance or the design of democratic habitation.

Ecology and democracy are powerful but separate entities.

The Marriage of Necessity and Happiness

Applied ecology and direct democracy have seldom been partners in modern life, either in the political landscape or in the mundane details of everyday life. In my own profession of landscape architecture and environmental planning, applied ecology and participatory democracy were formed from different ideologies. Landscape ecology, even with its holistic view, is based in fragmented scientific study that is theoretical, objective, abstracted, leery of human emotion and magic, and confounded by democratic impulses. Those who first applied ecology to city design saw a crisis so immediate and severe that solutions had to be imposed top down with minimal citizen participation. Skeptical of lay people, ecological scientists echo the words of the legalist scholar, Han Fei-Tzu, who claimed that the intelligence of the general public is not to be relied on any more than the mind of a baby. Direct citizen participation in city design did not come of age in the United States until the 1960s era of civil rights, and it did so with religious, not scientific, zeal. A passion for freedom and equality and a disregard for top-down authority were essential ingredients for grassroots success. The adage "Don't Trust the Experts" expresses the reciprocal skepticism that democratic movements have for state and corporate science, which so often is biased against the less powerful—and the less powerful include most of us. Of course, it is not this simple. There are good reasons that the application of ecological science to city design and participatory democracy have developed separately and antagonistically.

Whatever legitimate bases for the schism, applied ecology and participatory democracy must be married, otherwise human habitation and life itself cannot be enduring and joyful. Even when combined, ecology and democracy face formidable challengers in the struggle for centrality in the design of our cities. In this struggle between ecological democracy and ever bigger and unaccountable economies, exploitative oppression, global cultural dominance, and our own status seeking, success will depend in large measure on the strength of the union formed between ecology and democracy.

Urban ecology and active democracy strengthen each other and can make a more vigorous city landscape together. Democracy bestows freedom—the dream of all who do not have it. Freedom can fuel personal fulfillment and, if unchecked, alienation, selfishness, and irresponsibility. Ecology explains our interconnected roles to even the lowliest creatures and makes us think comprehensively and outside narrow confines. In so doing, ecology creates responsible freedom. In a democracy, ecology is the constituency for the future. Ecology provides "the rightly understood" in the political phrase "self-interest rightly understood." It forges the basis for civil society to address a shared public good among fractured interests. Ecological processes also inspire the form of human habitation in ways that are efficient, cost effective, locally distinctive, and minimally consumptive.

In return, direct democracy enlivens ecology with local wisdom and overcomes the alienation, anomie, and bleakness that some see in a world of severe limits. Hands-on participation shows ecology how to recultivate fallow community and environmental caring. Involvement awakens us to the poetry of place and civic creativity. Enhanced by ecological knowledge, active engagement reveals the joys of nature itself. In spite of biological caution, democracy accommodates human passion for security, new experience, recognition, and sensual response. Direct democracy provides the forum through which ecological thinking becomes part of daily life and decision making. Together—and only when integrated—ecology and democracy provide the foundation for making informed choices and better cities and for discovering more fulfilling lives. The union of ecology and democracy is essential for making a sustainable future and providing us with greater happiness.

Design of City and Landscape Together

Ecological democracy will produce radically new forms of habitation, not in extravagant architecture but rather in a search for roots, foundations, and fundamentals—the basics of a satisfying life. First, however, these new forms of habitation must be created to nourish, sustain, and make a fledgling ecological democracy appealing. In this book, I focus on an urban form that encourages us to choose and then create ecological democracy.

I concentrate on the form of the city not because I think that economic and government institutions are less important or that city form determines human behavior but because physical design is what I know best. This book is not about participatory process. I have written about participation elsewhere, and in spite of my commitment to process, I observe that the physical city must be made differently for us to attain the needed social transformation. Form matters to participation. Form matters to ecological democracy. City form influences our daily lives. City form concretizes our values and reflects them back to us. City form can make us a more resilient society and more fulfilled individuals.

Enabling, Resilient, and Impelling Form

There are three fundamental issues of habitation and therefore only three roots to be reformulated to make better cities. To effect the transformation to ecological democracy, our inhabited landscapes need to be attended in these ways. First, our cities and landscapes must enable us to act where we are now debilitated. Second, our cities and landscapes must be made to withstand short-term shocks to which both are vulnerable. Third, our cities and landscapes must be alluring rather than simply consumptive or, conversely, limiting.

This metamorphosis of the inhabited landscape must be guided by three fundamental and interrelated traits that integrate democracy and ecology—enabling form, resilient form, and impelling form. These traits are the building blocks of cities where ecological democracy can flourish.

Each of these three foundations is defined by design principles that are grounded in human values, everyday behavior, participatory actions, and ecological processes. By marrying the concepts of the social and natural sciences that are essential for designing the urban landscape, I have distilled fifteen design principles that form a practical thesis for reforming the landscape—from the region, city, and town to the neighborhood, street corner, garden, and household. These fifteen principles are embedded in enabling, resilient, and impelling form.

Enabling Form: "We Got to Know Our Neighbors"

We need to reform our cities so that we can act as communities and not divide and debilitate our deliberative democracy. Enabling form helps us get to know unfamiliar neighbors and facilitates working with them and others to solve difficult problems. Enabling form provides the centeredness that is necessary for both neighboring and shared experiences. A bench at the post office illustrates. It encourages people to linger in a public setting, meet others on their way to get mail, and share news of the locality. Enabling form reveals how interconnected we are to other people and to our landscape. As connectedness permeates our consciousness, it instills the responsibility to care for others far beyond our circle of family and friends. Fairness becomes not a matter of guilt or altruism but a matter of fact. Enabling form allows us to pursue healthy status seeking through the discovery of what is sacred in our everyday habitation. This develops rootedness and a collective destiny that is tied to place and inspires a shared higher civic purpose.

Resilient Form: Life, Liberty, and the Pursuit of Sustainable Happiness

We need to reform our cities to be ecologically resilient. Rather than being ecologically impoverished and imperiled, constantly requiring a technological fix to right the catastrophe prompted by a previous technological fix, resilient cities derive from the particular character of the surrounding ecology—climate, hydrology, vegetation, and building materials. For example, buildings can be designed to heat and cool themselves naturally and to provide healthy air, water, food, and shelter for human and wilder inhabitants. Good cities deliver buoyant natural processes, promoting biological and cultural diversity while selectively balancing unity and complexity in city design. Resilient form turns density and smallness from scorn to advantage and limits the extent of urbanization within the bounds of a region, thus enhancing sustainability and providing healthy doses of natural magic for everyday life. The city becomes adaptable and more financially secure. Resilient form fuels life, liberty, and the pursuit of sustainable happiness.

Impelling Form: "Make a City to Touch the People's Hearts"

We need to reform our cities to impel us by joy rather than compel us by insecurity, fear, and force. The urbanism of mindless free enterprise compels us through insecurity. Doomsday regulators compel us through fear and force. Neither is appropriate in an ecological democracy. We must, instead, make cities that impel us because they touch our hearts. Even though future habitation may be fundamentally different than today's, it will derive from recognizable everyday patterns. Impelling form invites us to be our natural selves. It inhabits our daily lives with the science that is needed to help us be good citizens and also to enrich us. Good cities make us conscious of our oneness with and distinctiveness within the ecosystem, which results in a sense of identity with the places we live, relatedness, and childlike awe. Impelling form produces multiple avenues for stewardship that make both the earth and the stewards themselves healthier. Impelling form provides a variety of urban tempos from light speed to snail's pace. Such cities exude joy.

They acknowledge grief and despair, but above all, they celebrate lives. An impelling city uplifts us in spite of all else. That is the wonder of good cities.

The Glocal Design Process

Implicit to ecological democracy is a design process that is participatory, scientific, and adventuresome. Because ecological democracy stresses the direct involvement of citizens in local decision making, future habitation will be designed at the grassroots level through direct face-to-face participatory actions. These actions will be holistically informed by local wisdom, attachment to place, and networks of interconnectedness and ecological thinking. They will be neither local nor global but *glocal.* The design process of *glocalization,* in which local decisions are made in the context of external forces and ramifications, is fundamental to ecological democracy. I have articulated this process in previous books, most expressly in *Planning Neighborhood Space with People* (1984) and *Community Design Primer* (1990). This process creates a forum where our best and lesser intentions struggle with each other. It facilitates the uncovering of residents' best intentions and incites them to act on those intentions.

The Focus Is Design

This book is not about the participatory process itself. It is about city form. It emphasizes how the urban landscape can be shaped to encourage ecological democracy. I explain—through the principles of enabling, resilient, and impelling form—what to think about and give priority to in designing the landscape. I explain how to analyze and synthesize the urban landscape in a focused, efficient way. I use case studies to show how to form places that support ecological democracy. These projects are more inspired by local natural processes and traditional culture than most present city design. The designs are idiosyncratic: they are more ecologically diverse, culturally expressive, integrated, contextually responsive, and internally satisfying and less subject to formalistic fads and status-seeking than most recent modern urbanity. These projects demonstrate that ecological democracy is at once both visionary and achievable. Most of the cases were dreams just out of the grasp of a community but were attained via concerted collective action. They and thousands of similar successes around the country and world are indicators that ecological democracy is emerging. But the foundations and principles, not singular projects, are fundamental to designing for ecological democracy because the foundations of enabling, resilient, and impelling form will inspire landscapes of ecological democracy not yet imagined.

How do these foundations relate as theory? My primary thesis is simple. To create settings for ecological democracy, every design action must simultaneously address enabling, resilient, and impelling form, not separately but together. In this regard, successful designers craft all three into a single fabric. The most rational way to do this is to ask if each of fifteen design principles is being optimized as the design takes shape. I find this theory most applicable when I am wrestling with one aspect of the design problem. I make myself pause and in orderly fashion check each principle to see which principles are being ignored. Usually some are. Rectifying those omissions enriches the design. In this way, the principles serve as a theoretical checklist. Any useful theory of city design should serve this purpose foremost.

But are some principles more important than others? There are two answers. Theoreticians address this question by analyzing which principles explain most of a phenomenon, in this case the design of cities to encourage ecological democracy. In this regard the single most powerful principle is sacredness for both content and operational importance. It expresses values held most dear and that influence urban form directly. Sacredness encompasses centeredness, connectedness, limited extent, and particularness explicitly and all other principles indirectly. This does not conclude causality but rather singular interrelatedness. In the same manner, centeredness, connectedness, limited extent, and particularness rank as more interrelated than other principles. Theoretically, they are more important.

The principles exert parallel catalyst influences on each other, but some are exceptional. For example, sacredness triggers stewardship and fairness through empathic connectedness. It also counters unhealthy status seeking, which otherwise has a disproportionate negative influence on various principles. Several principles (notably inhabiting science and stewardship), although less connected to others, forge new relationships with place that are based on an understanding of local ecological processes. Catalyst impacts make less connected principles theoretically vital to ecological democracy. I note these relationships throughout the book.

The practical answer to the question of which principles are most important is that it depends on the context of each city region. For example, centering and limited extent are lacking in most American cities and need to be the first order of business, from both a theoretical perspective and the nitty gritty of city making. But in cities like Boulder, Colorado, and Los Angeles, where limited extent is being addressed, other principles take precedence. Similarly, the lack of density is a first-order priority in most American cities but less so in Honolulu. The fifteen principles should be continually evaluated so that focused attention can be paid to the most critical issues rather than to symptoms of any given region. This must be done without losing sight of the overriding consideration that these fifteen principles are interconnected and must be addressed simultaneously.

This Book Is for Students of Ecological Democracy

I have written primarily for people who want to build a sense of community as they build cities. You are designers—mostly landscape architects, city and environmental planners, architects, engineers, lawyers, resource managers, and students with bold ideas. The book might be useful for anyone involved in making cities. This includes experts in law, real estate, education, health, and finance. It includes mayors, council members, city managers, and others who design and administer cities. Nongovernment organizations, whether focusing on environmental justice or intercontinental ecosystem networks, can be helped to act effectively through an understanding of the ideas discussed in this book. I don't know the language of policy makers in state and federal government, but the principles here probably would be useful to you as well. Each can take action to create enabling, resilient, and impelling form.

The book should be useful to any residents who want to improve or remake their community. If you are discontented with your neighborhood, city, or region or if you are a volunteer, a parent, a teenager, an illegal immigrant, an environmental activist, a NIMBY, or a do-gooder who is discontented with your locality, the principles here may help you envision positive alternatives. This is critical because as a citizenry we have become much better at saying what we don't want than what we do want. Scary ecology and weak democracy have made us pessimistic about change. Doomsday ecology is now part of our mainstream consciousness. But intelligent ecology is what we most need. Free-enterprise democracy has made us irresponsible. Principles of ecological democracy can formulate attractive new choices and show us what we need to know and do to be good citizens. An ecological democracy will not work until all of us are more fluent in the language of enabling, resilient, and impelling form.

I have also written for myself. This is a book that would have helped me immensely forty years ago when I was trying to combine sociology, ecology, and design. It would have helped me last year in my professional work designing parks in the San Fernando Valley and South Central Los Angeles. Oh, how it would have helped when I was a young city council member in Raleigh, North Carolina, lacking a practical vision to guide me in making decisions big and small. It would have helped me as a citizen activist fighting against highways and for endangered species. In each of these, I would have done a better job with these principles in my hand, in my mind, and in my heart. I will use this book to improve my efforts. I hope this book will help each of you create places where ecological democracy can grow and enrich many lives.

This book is for students of ecological democracy. Eventually, that will include all of us.

Enabling Form: "We Got to Know Our Neighbors"

A few years ago, I was working on a park in a Hollywood, California, canyon that stretched from the flat basin near Hollywood Boulevard (an area called Ellis Island West for its multitude of newly arrived immigrants) to the ridge top of the Santa Monica Mountains (where Mulholland Drive passes the dream homes of the movie industry's rich and famous). The participatory design process had overcome many obstacles and resulted in a plan calling for a community center and small-scale watershed management. As the designer, I was excessively proud of the plan. I envisioned lemonade served Hollywood-style on the patio of the community center, exuberant community flower gardens at the park entry, and oaks conversing with sycamores amid small check dams and wildlife pools. In my mind's eye the park was already a Hollywood natural—wild and urbane. In the final community meeting before the plan was formally adopted by the City of Los Angeles, a distinguished movie producer who was also a park neighbor rose to speak in favor of the plan, and his comments conclusively deflated my design ego: "This is a good plan, but the best thing about this project is that we got to know our neighbors." His unintended dressing down haunts me as a designer, but his insight is fundamental to ecological democracy. In Hollywood, the wealthy seemed to have everything except a sense of community. Few knew their neighbors, and there was no shared public interest, only powerful individual interests. The group had great difficulty working together to create a civic vision for the park. At one point in the design process, when a decision was made that he disliked, one adjacent homeowner and rising TV star insisted that he would just buy the canyon for his private use. "Name the price!" he demanded of a public official.

Wealthy residents acted as free agents with few public concerns. They were, in popular academic terms, "bowling alone."[1] Developing shared values required getting to know their neighbors and was the first step in redeveloping their capacity to work together to solve complex problems.[2] They had achieved that and were appropriately pleased.

The movie producer who spoke about getting to know his neighbors was right. To achieve an effective ecological democracy, we must first create places that enable citizens to connect with neighbors in their localities. This may seem counterintuitive to environmentalists, but until we have social environments that enable us to work together, there can be little additional progress in ecological health. Strong democracy cannot blossom without the forum for thoughtful and deliberative cooperation. Creating such enabling form is the focus of this section of the book.

You may wonder about whether Hollywood is an isolated case of a lack of shared experience and civic failure. Is this experience widespread? If so, how did we get to this disabled state, and can these problems be addressed by better city design?

The inability to work together locally to solve complex urban problems has been documented for at least half a century.[3] The research that underlies books such as Robert D. Putnam's *Bowling Alone* and Richard Sennett's *The Fall of Public Man* and an epidemic of NIMBY (not in my backyard) actions describe this normative inability in qualitative and quantitative terms.[4] Exceptions are newsworthy precisely because they are outliers.[5] Although exceptional neighborhoods provide inspiring models, most communities lack the common experience and practice in complex cooperation to address problems they face.[6]

This failure takes various forms. In the Hollywood case, residents did not know each other or their local ecosystem processes, were poorly equipped to solve complex problems, but understood externalities very well. They were worldly but locally unaware. In a contrasting case in another city, the residents knew each other well but were unable to work together because key participants mistrusted each other. In another case, the lack of knowledge of externalities in an isolated rural area was the barrier to effective action. Although these cases of failed cooperation had different causes, they had similar outcomes: residents encountered great difficulties in working well with each other to solve perplexing problems.

Sometimes these problems are blamed on our diversity.[7] Great divisions of income, privilege, race, and tenure contributed to the difficulties in Hollywood, but people there did not know even neighbors who were much like themselves. Prejudice, intolerance, and narrow vested interests explain only part of this problem.[8] Other causes are rooted in the form of our present cities.

The difficulty of working together to improve habitation is exacerbated by at least five powerful and deeply held American values—mobility, affluence, standardization, technology, and specialization, each of which produces side effects that affect city life. Mobility frees us from place and indirectly produces rootlessness.[9] We become less concerned about the place where we live and the other people who live there. If they do not please us, we move on or live simultaneously in multiple locations with commitment to none. Affluence frees us from mutual dependence on community and indirectly produces alienation and public phobia, as some Hollywood residents demonstrated. Standardization frees us from irregularities and produces placelessness. Local identity is lost. Technology frees us from dependence on local environmental processes and produces eco illiteracy. We lose the shared magic of everyday nature. For people who live in a climate-controlled world of mechanical air conditioning and heating, for example, the weather is less relevant in daily life than it is for someone who is dependent on natural forces to cool and heat her home. Specialization frees us from the need for a comprehensive knowledge of place and complex social and ecological thinking. This freedom, in turn, produces helplessness in everyday problem solving, encourages simplistic solutions to city design problems, and foments personal insecurity that in turn makes us ever more susceptible to environmental fads and status seeking.

These indirect effects are powerful forces. On the surface, they seem to be intractable because they are so entangled with values we cherish. It is easy to say that the design of the urban landscape can do nothing to overcome these problems. Overcoming them requires a shift in values and behavior. But the design of the modern city and suburb contributed considerably to the loss of shared experience, local knowledge, and civic mindedness.[10] For example, the land-use-segregated subdivision typically provides only housing and no center of community life. Separation from other subdivisions by high-speed arterial traffic and distance makes it nearly impossible to neighbor beyond a small area, especially for the very young and old.[11] With workplace and residence strictly divided, the time that formerly was available for civic activities is spent on commuting. We become transients in our own homes. Further, in the typical subdivision, standardization and technology prevent residents from experiencing natural processes and exclude children from nature play.[12] Changes in such city form can enable changes in behavior and values.[13] Creating potentially enabling landscapes does not guarantee their effective use, but changes in environment often lead to behavior changes. Traffic-calming devices increase neighboring.[14] Concentrations of adjacent uses intensify informal civic discussions. Access to creeks leads to increased play in riparian habitats, ecoliteracy, and lifelong environmentalism.[15] Additionally, because the built environment reflects our values, city form also makes us self-aware and can help us modify these values.[16] But for our purpose, the question is more limited: can the design of the urban landscape enable us to work together locally to solve complex problems of our habitation? The answer is yes. To return to the park in the Hollywood canyon, the participatory design process there provided a forum for estranged neighbors to gather and make an inclusive plan. Residents prioritized new settings in the park that consciously encouraged strangers to come together. They designed the community center to be a focus of activity for nature study, children's play, gardening, getting information, and hanging out with friends, and these many disparate intentions in one place encouraged interaction. The first step for communities to work together is an inclusive process. The second step is a design that enables the community's members to work together.

The problems are difficult and widespread, and our exasperation is justified. Our retreat from each other is understandable, and the design of the city has contributed to these problems. More important, however, design can help us come together to work collectively and effectively if the urban landscape is formed differently. Enabling form is better served by design that encourages us to spend more time in one place, allows us to live fulfilling lives with limited economic means, replaces standard solutions with ones that are uniquely suited to each locale, limits dependence on unneeded technology that separates us from nature and society, and facilitates through daily experience the acquisition of general skills, not just specialized and isolated ones.

The five chapters in this section of the book focus on the principles of design that are most essential in creating enabling form, one of the three foundations of an ecological democracy. *Enabling form,* first and foremost, creates places where community members work together democratically to solve complex problems and are informed by ecological thinking, locality, and shifting externalities. Enabling form makes places that enhance the sense of community and the working effectiveness that come from shared local experiences and values. It heightens an awareness of interdependence and a respectful caring for other people in our community and for the local environment itself. It makes personal and community life fulfilling enough to free us of destructive status seeking. Enabling form makes places where we can get to know neighbors and build an increasingly capable and empathic civil society.

Enabling form is most shaped by five design principles—centeredness, connectedness, fairness, sensible status seeking, and sacredness. Although sacredness, centeredness, and connectedness are most interrelated, each of these five principles is essential to ecological democracy. In any context, the designer must assess which principles are strengths and weaknesses and formulate a strategy to build on assets and overcome liabilities. All the while, the total fabric of enabling, resilient, and impelling form must be crafted as a totality. The fifteen principles—the five to be described in chapters on enabling form and the ten subsequent ones on resilient and impelling form—should serve as a checklist to evaluate the wholism of the design effort.

Centeredness

For community members to work together, they must share interests and have places that draw them together for face-to-face civic engagement. This aggregate of shared experiences, activities, and interests and of associated settings is called *centeredness*. Centers are essential for economic complexity, local identity, and rootedness. Centers build socio-spatial capital, enhance deliberative democracy, and incubate ideas regarding locality.[1]

Almost every city-design theorist from Lewis Mumford to Suzanne Keller concludes that communities require centers for economic efficiency, physical legibility, primary social contacts, sense of community, and local attachments.[2] At the neighborhood level, many have called for specific facilities—a park, a public neighborhood building, a post office, a school, a library, and local stores. This center consisted of a multiuse civic landscape with a variety of mutually supporting commercial facilities surrounding the open space, all within walking distance of houses and apartments.[3]

Centering green

Shifts in economic patterns, increased mobility, special-interest segmentation, and many other lifestyle changes accompanying modern life diminished such centers in American communities. Mixed-use centers were replaced by segregated ones with highly specialized economies. As one measure of this shift, the state of Vermont was named to the National Trust for Historic Preservation's list of America's eleven most endangered historic places in 1993 and 2004 because factory outlet malls and other pseudo centers were draining life from healthy town centers.[4] The Wal-Mart employee chant "Stack it deep, sell it cheap, stack it high, see it fly, hear those downtown merchants cry" signaled not just mean-spirited profit taking but also the death of town centers.[5] Within five years of a superstore's opening, "Small towns within twenty miles suffer a net loss of sales of nearly twenty percent."[6] Public aspects of traditional centers are privatized. Advanced communication networks allow further withdrawal. Moving and parked cars destroy centers and encourage smatterings of commercial and public facilities spread across the landscape. Even the national megatrend of decen-

Centering event

Park Güell was designed as the center of a developing neighborhood and has remained a focus of community life, local investment, and layered meaning.

tralization, which promised to reinforce local centers, actually diminishes them. Nationwide decentralization, it turns out, is actually spreading out— bypassing existing towns, making frail centers more anemic, and leaving local society more centerless. This is what is referred to as *sprawl.* Every place is the center of its own universe, with no shared focus.

Planning theorists contributed to this decline by declaring that physical design was irrelevant in modern life. They applauded the "liberation from associations imposed by the friction of space."[7] They championed the death of place-centered life.[8] Centers, some claimed, were outmoded and nostalgia seeking.[9] Today a few theorists make the same argument that communication technologies have reduced the need for community centers. Indeed, casual communication has been enhanced by technology. However, communication that is not place-grounded contributes little to local identity, rootedness, and direct experience of place. Advanced technology generally reduces time spent with family and local communities. Advances in communication technology, like many other forms of "progress," threaten place-centered life.

Unwittingly, local identity, local attachments, place knowledge, and the capacity to work together with other community members have been diminished with the loss of centeredness. Restoration of centeredness depends on specific design actions—namely, recreating multiuse centers at the microneighborhood, neighborhood, and regional levels; making sociopetal places that encourage interaction; and creating places for community rituals.

Enabling Form

Ten Rules for Good Centers

Centers are places where people gather to undertake many different activities. They are focal points and nodes of activity and interest that serve as points of orientation and invite investments of time and energy. They provide face-to-face communication and incubate ideas. Good centers are surprisingly easy to create when their importance is recognized and their advantages are embraced. Design criteria for good centers are straightforward.

First, good centers are intense concentrations of different uses—commercial, civic, residential, recreational, transportation, religious, and educational—that attract people from different income levels, gender groups, and life-cycle stages. The activities feed off each other, each inviting more users by proximity to others, and seemingly incompatible uses invite diverse

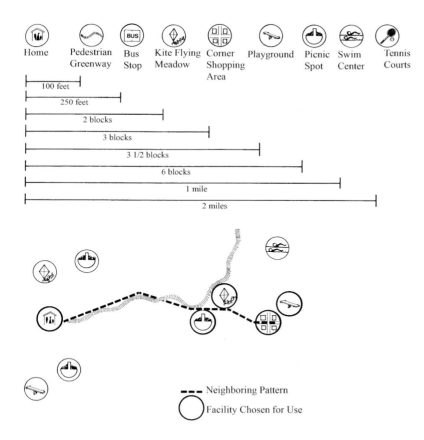

Functional distance—influenced by habit, perception, and neighboring—varies significantly from the actual distance to community facilities.

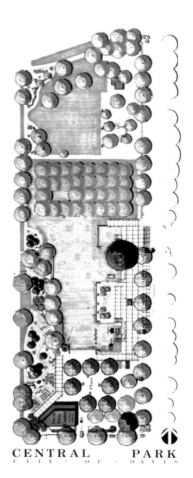

CENTRAL PARK
CITY · OF · DAVIS

publics to the same place. Successful centers do not exclude by subtle design symbols of discrimination. Instead they exude inclusivity.

Mark Francis did precisely this in creating Central Park in Davis, California. First, he convinced city authorities to close a street, which almost doubled the size of an existing downtown park. Then he planned park-centered activities that attracted nearly every segment of the population—a farmer's market (one of the first in California), a teen center, a central plaza with participatory water jets (so popular in heat waves that it is called Davis Beach), gardens, horseshoe pits, a speaker's platform, picnic areas, a carousel, and several children's play areas. Francis intended to "establish it as Davis's central community place," and this he did. The beach alone attracts kids and parents who come with towels and coolers to stay for hours and teens who watch the action. After the farmer's market relocated to the park, sales increased by 30 percent to over $2 million a year. The park's major activities are picnics, festivals, and weekly market days. One researcher found over four thousand people at the park on one day—nearly a tenth of the entire population of Davis.

Such diversity of facilities could easily have created a tossed salad of competing greens, but the activities are arranged around the edge of a simple open lawn that measures 120 feet by 300 feet. Activities are placed in the trees that surround the lawn. This creates a unity among disparate activities by calming the noise of the boisterous and constraining the impulse to over-schedule activities. Equally wise, each art project is integral to the structure of the park. Frequently, public art screams for attention because it is plopped into public spaces without context, but here, artists created the stonework walls that form the central open space. The beautiful walls evoke care, quietly call for lingering attention to the geology, and create places where people can sit, watch, lounge, meet strangers, discuss issues, or just catch up on community news. This center enables.[10]

A cautionary note is needed here. Creating multiple-use settings in centers does not guarantee that people will put them to their desired use. Potential environments become effective only if they match the patterns of local activities or if local values and behaviors change to fit the possibilities of the space.[11]

Second, good centers are easily accessible for everyone in the area—for some by car but for the very young, old, and poor by foot or public transit. Although a good center diversifies access and emphasizes pedestrians, most city design today relies on standards that typically ignore pedestrian access. The Urban Land Institute insists that neighborhood centers must serve the people within a five- to ten-minute "drive" but does not mention access by bike, foot, or transit.[12] Most Americans have become accustomed to this pattern of inaccessibility.

Good neighborhood centers are within walking distance of people's homes. Designers who think critically about accessibility continue to return to the useful neighborhood benchmark of approximately five thousand people who live within a quarter mile of the center. This population with convenient access and local fidelity can support a full range of daily services and a diversity of activities needed to attract a variety of people. To provide ease of walking, good centers usually, but not always, are spatially centered.[13] This depends on perceived distance. The effective quarter-mile radius is elastic depending on functional distance. People form habitual routes to the primary places they visit, such as work, school, and friends' homes. Over time, secondary functions become part of their daily habits, creating clusters of activities along a single route. By careful design, functional distance matches actual distance, which greatly enhances the use of a center. This is accomplished by clustering desired activities and designing routes so pleasant that people will eagerly travel what they sense is a "short" distance.[14]

Third, a good center encourages frequent, preferably daily, use and use throughout the day and evening. The latter allows efficient use of the space and the sequencing of seriously incompatible activities. Attracting people to a center depends on a wide range of factors, but the most powerful is the presence of other people. By staging different activities at different times of the day, various groups can use the same space and form overlapping symbolic ownership of the center. Designers pay far more attention to elite aesthetics, however, and pay little attention to whom their plans will attract, missing the aesthetic preferences of residents, territorial claims, physical comfort, policy on use, and cost to users.[15]

Fourth, a good center provides places for formal and less formal community interaction and for public and private affairs, with a focus on shared activities. Public spaces should encourage shared activities, create settings for multiple and flexible outdoor uses, and provide reminders of their purpose when not in use.

Fifth, good centers help develop local knowledge by providing settings for new ideas to incubate, transform, and spread. They are like nodes of a

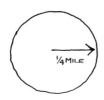

The walking radius

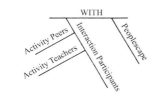

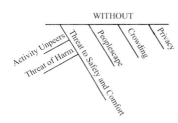

Determinant of use

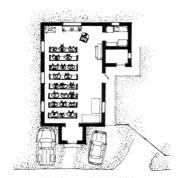

Formal and informal use

Source of local knowledge

plant from which new growth springs, where inklings form into plans and from which seeds disperse. All of these actions are essential for the acceptance of innovations that are necessary to create an ecological democracy.[16] Centers need sources of abstract knowledge and settings for introducing local wisdom and inspiring exploration of nearby nature and society. Good centers have settings where experiments are nurtured. They have places for civic think tanks and local soapboxes. They provide space to spread out plans, to ponder actions together, to refine ideas through thoughtful exchange, and also to protest. Each teaches, communicates, and spreads information.

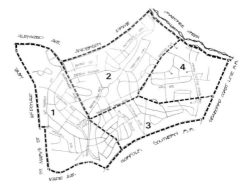

Official city-planning neighborhood boundaries

Residents' neighborhood boundaries

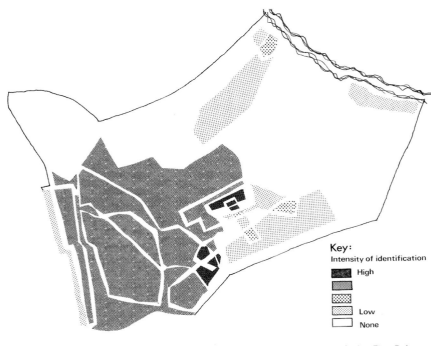

Key:
Intensity of identification

▓ High

▒ Low

☐ None

Intensity of Identification with the Five Points Community Based on Issues

Identity with neighborhood intensifies with political issues, threats of change, and shared interests and use.

Enabling Form

Sixth, good centers, by design, develop shared interests. A center is not only a place but also the mutual values that evolve from common experiences of locality. Mutual concerns are heightened when daily patterns overlap, if even for different reasons. Shared interests may be developed by participating in new activities with people we normally would not know. I recently observed this at bocce courts that were built at a community center. Bocce is a game similar to lawn bowling and can be played by all ages. The courts had been included at the request of elderly Italian American men and had been placed along a major walkway with plenty of places for newcomers to watch and engage with seasoned bowlers. These observations and interactions invited people of all ages and walks of life to take up the game. The bocce courts became a forum for informal civic discussion about topics of local concern, and sharing local concerns develops shared interests like nothing else can. The intensity is especially high during times when the community is involved in political action to enhance the locality. The center and its boundaries often shift when especially important issues are foremost in the community's consciousness.

Seventh, good centers provide a sense of orientation for coming and going and for inside and outside. Centers are starting points in human development because they provide rooted identity in a home place. The Piazza del Campo in Siena archetypally provides all these. There is a *there* in good centers. All these factors are important to psychological health. Additionally, good centers orient us in the local ecology by providing clarity about cardinal directions, sun patterns, rainfall, and topography.

Eighth, a good center reflects its ecological context in its built form. Topography often inspires the location and design of the center, and the natural landscape can be used to dramatize the built environment. By virtue of its human intensity, however, the center is seldom a place where naturalness dominates.

Ninth, a typically successful center presents a consistency of building form that is inspired by the locality and that creates a unified, even spectacular, whole without having any one building dominate. The sense of wholeness is more important than any single structure, but public buildings should highlight special values of the community.

Designers need to be especially cautious regarding the roles of individual projects in creating centers. The primary impetus for the location of neighborhood and other centers resides in communitywide land use decision

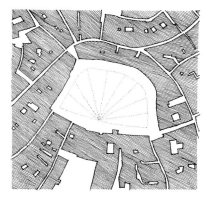

Piazza del Campo, Siena, Italy

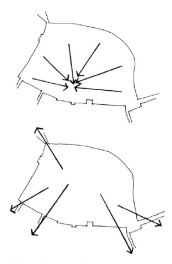

Orientation, in and out

Orientation, up and down

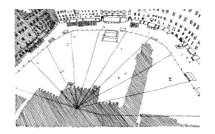

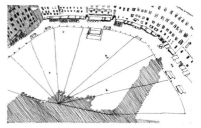

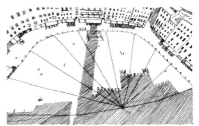

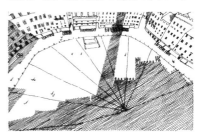

Orientation, time of day

Orientation, topographic context

making and therefore should be included in general or urban design plans. When such plans lack centering policies, they should be challenged and corrected. But many designers work for clients, both public and private, on individual building projects, and often clients have the desire, as noted previously, to make every project the center of its own universe. Avoid making too many centers and centers with segregated single purposes. Most projects need to play supporting roles rather than compete and diminish overall centeredness.

Our impulse to create too many pivots is often supported by observations of everyday urbanism. Careful social observers notice idiosyncratic uses in delightful, unexpected places, and we often want to make more of them. Designers should resist this for two reasons. First, these informal activities do well without embellishment. Second, if successful, such elaborations typically diminish centeredness. Center centeredness; do not diffuse it.

Tenth, good centers are designed to invite commitment. By necessity, they are places of considerable economic investment. Equally important are voluntary investments of time and energy to use, pay attention to, care about, and improve centers. Centers require a concentrated focus of attention and encourage symbolic ownership that is filled with personal and civic meanings. The best centers stimulate the imagination, participation, and stewardship.

Siena's Piazza del Campo provides centering, orientation, and rooted identity through enclosure, slope, landmarks, and local building materials.

The classic center is the downtown common with city hall, post office, churches, school, library, banks, hardware, grocery, and other public, commercial, and residential activities arranged around it. A wide range of face-to-face interactions happen daily among friends and strangers, seemingly by chance but actually because the center has multiple uses and attracts a diversity of people. The small-city Main Street, the New England town square, *plaza mayor,* or *zócalo* come to mind as archetypal centers. But the areas around the Boston Common, Central Park in New York, or Central Park in Davis, California, provide similar centers in a modern context. Reinforcement of such traditional centers is essential for enabling form. Likewise, freshly conceived centers are needed where there are none.

One of the most successful recently invented centers I know is on Matsu Island off mainland China, where a large central park that Westerners might think is the perfect location for a traditional New England common accommodates instead a community garden. Important public and commercial buildings are formally arranged around the active, one-hectare urban farm. This extraordinarily active place is the site of frequent social interactions among merchants and farmers, young and old, rich and poor. After I learned that Matsu has an unusually democratic local government, I tried to make sense of this unusual center. Maybe it was inspired by a temple square or a Chinese courtyard.

Community garden plots are not a standard center in China. The main public building, which is now the centerpiece of civil society, was moved from a remote location to this site near the garden and market buildings. Public buildings were added to create a public center for the emergent ecological democracy. The form cannot be explained in Eastern or Western traditions but is an expression of a strong grassroots democracy that is informed by the local topography, climate, social patterns, and community intentions. The center extends from a small mountain to the sea. The main county government building is nestled into the protection of the sloping promontory and thereby gains the importance of height. It looks over the ocean of Taiwan Strait, a preferred feng shui relationship. The garden is graded to create plots for city farming and gathering. Steps adapt the slopes and enclose the community gardens. Surrounding streets and buildings delimit the center and enclose and focus the view—first inward and then down the axis to the world beyond the sea. Arcaded buildings protect residents from storms and heat and invite them to stop and talk to each other.

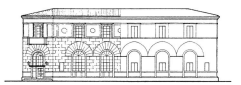

Consistent building form

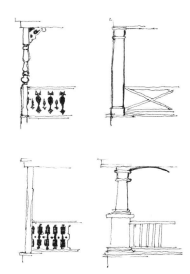

Meaningful detail

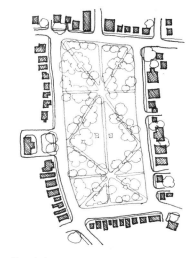

Classic town common

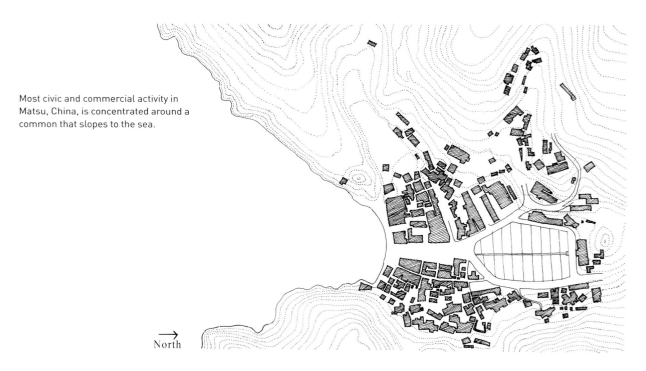

Most civic and commercial activity in Matsu, China, is concentrated around a common that slopes to the sea.

North

Arriving by sea

Arriving by land

Adjacent streets are shared by cars and pedestrians, slowing traffic and adding life and social exchanges. Streets and arcades overflow with commercial and civic life because great diversity is brought together in building functions.

But the brilliance of Matsu's center is its garden. It is located in the center's most prominent spot, surrounded by buildings expressing civic intent and daily needs, and aligned on an axis as orderly as the Forbidden City. It is not a manicured formal garden but a beehive of hundreds of garden plots. Garden plots provide food and also settings where older people teach younger ones about local culture and ecology. Each plot is a gift to the community and is part of a collective living quilt that is fashioned in concert with nature. Garden art includes handcrafted trash cans, play equipment, benches, and gates that are all personalized with touches unique to Matsu. This center expresses almost all the ten rules for good centers that are described above. Many daily uses take place in close, walkable proximity. The site arrangement and garden instruct about local ecology. The center orients in multiple ways. There is an unusual wholeness and no single spectacular

The central common of Matsu is a series of small farm plots, an expression of an emerging grassroots democracy that is grounded in tradition.

architecture. The place generates shared interests and invites investments. What is instructive is that this center has arisen in a culture with no tradition of such a center. Matsu was under martial law until two decades ago and, until recently, was governed by the military. People consciously decided to create a center that supports ecological democracy. For local residents, it represents not a nostalgic past but a bold and centered future.

Closer to home, Pike Place Market offers an American exemplar of centeredness with a farmer's market and hundreds of shops, restaurants, social services, recreation outlets, and housing units clustered in the heart of the city of Seattle. Victor Steinbrueck, a Seattle architect who is credited with saving the market from urban renewal destruction over forty years ago, noted that one single block contained a drug store, a clothes store, a movie theater, a donut shop, a hardware store, a pet shop, a passport photographer, a cabaret, a pawn shop, an antique shop, a barber shop, a shoe shine stand, cafes, hotels, residential hotels, taverns, a tattoo artist, and a view of Mount Ranier in the distance. Such diversity attracts a range of social classes, ages, visitors, and locals. Nowhere else in Seattle does such a broad social mixture go about its business in an uninhibited way. Steinbrueck realized that only here did people of all races, religions, ages, and nationalities come together freely to work, shop, linger, and enjoy themselves. One study counted eighteen nationalities and twenty-six spoken languages among the merchants

Pike Place Market

alone.[17] Pike Place Market, like Matsu, is democratically conceived, taking modern lifestyles into account to create a highly original place of common ground. Over time the seven-story farmer's market has evolved, but unlike many American marketplaces, it provides low-income housing and shopping area for Seattle's poorest residents as well as fresh farm and ocean products that attract gourmets from every economic level. This balance gives Pike Place Market a feel of organic happenstance, but this center is great by careful planning and insightful public design. The market we see today represents the vision of a civic-minded architect who labored for many years to create a place where all of Seattle residents could come together.

Making such new centers requires vision and courage. A controversial policy that requires 70 percent of all retail outlets in the city of Lawrence, Kansas, to be located in the downtown center, for example, is credited with that city's revitalization. Few local governments are willing to take such bold action, but in Lawrence the center has been reinvented. In a celebrated case, a developer who intended to build a suburban pseudo center instead turned a derelict downtown factory into the major Riverfront Plaza retail complex.[18]

At what scales of habitation are centers most needed? They are pivotal at the neighborhood level, the domain of deliberative face-to-face ecological democracy, and in many cases, subcenters for shared civic experiences are needed at the block or tribal level to serve between a dozen and a hundred households.[19] Centers inculcating regional awareness, identity, and loyalty are especially important for ecological democracy.[20]

Sociopetal Places, Forming Open Circles

Environmental psychologists have long known that the form of public places increases or diminishes substantive human contact.[21] Design that facilitates social contact, internal identity, and control (for example, a circle of chairs) creates *sociopetal* space. A circle of chairs is designed to be inclusive and to encourage eye contact, listening to others, and cooperative behavior.[22] In my church, a circle is the smallest unit of social organization—a group of women who support others in times of distress. Consider the difference between circle dancing and partner dancing. Colleagues in Japan who are nurturing participatory design call their effort the *round-table movement,* in reference to the active listening that occurs when people are seated face-to-face at comfortable personal distance around a table. The circle is

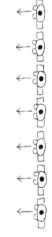

Private space

Social space

powerful metaphor and forceful design element. In contrast, design that discourages social contact creates *sociofugal* space. Sociofugal space provides solitude (for example, benches placed in long parallel rows) but also can discourage communication. For many years, sociofugal space was so overemphasized, that today we need to focus on the creation of sociopetal places[23] that provide for cooperation, accommodation, and acculturation as well as solitude, anonymity, reserve, and intimacy.[24]

We need places that encourage people to listen to one another and to work together. This requires arrangements that facilitate eye contact, physical closeness, equal access to work materials and information sources, and space to work as a whole, as smaller teams, and alone.

Jens Jensen understood these needs. His designs reflect them literally. In every case he could, Jensen incorporated a council ring into public spaces. These council rings—something like campfire circles or outdoor classrooms—were about twenty-five feet in diameter, although their size varied. They most often consisted of a local stone seat wall fit carefully into the topography. Some had a raised circular platform at the midpoint. Most had a single, shared entry and exit. The council rings encouraged community at the small scale by their form. The circles were deceptively complex. Beyond their inclusive and egalitarian shape, the circles frequently absorbed sloping earth and led the eye to the landscape beyond the enclosure. This created subtle distinctions between upslope and downslope divisions and a contrast between inside and outside. The raised midpoint or several large rocks elevated

Sociopetal space

Sociofugal space

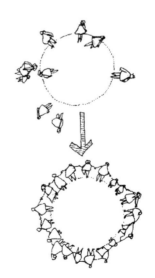

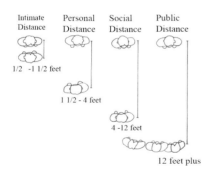

Interaction distances

Shaping the community

Designer's concept

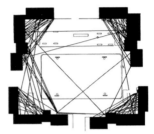

Residents' friendship patterns

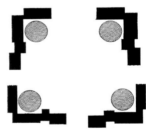

Residents' concept

←N

Courtyard design

above a point on the circumference opened the circle.[25] These nuanced variations of the circle encourage a full range of interactions.

Although democratic interaction is most readily facilitated by the circular form, other shapes can also contribute to sociopetality. Corners, pauses, nodes, bulges, eddies, intersections, and spaces between serve similar purposes.[26] In one embarrassing case in a Cambridge, Massachusetts, public housing project that I was helping to redesign, I noticed frozen clothes hanging on lines in the winter shadows of the courtyard units, but when I proposed clustering all clotheslines in a south-facing sun pocket, residents protested vehemently. The eddies formed by each building had become important meeting places for women. The clotheslines created microcenters of social interaction for the thirty families in each building and fostered friendships and mutual support. Poorly drying clothes were irrelevant compared to these forces. The residents wanted the design to enhance the existing spaces with places to sit around the clotheslines in small clusters where parents could socialize while working or watching children play.[27]

The size of sociopetal space, characterized by an inwardly oriented circle, varies depending on the number of people involved and by type of social interaction. An outdoor place for an intimate exchange between two or three people might be accommodated in a niche three feet in diameter in some cultures; for others, a five-foot circle might be more comfortable.[28] A

Clotheslines in each corner of the Jefferson Park housing court created centers of social interaction that inspired the redesign of the open space.

Enabling Form

larger group discussing a community problem might expand to a circle with a radius no wider than twenty-five feet because loss of eye contact spatially diminishes the sense of group. Few successful campfire circles exceed this dimension. Settings where eye contact can be made and faces recognized are essential for sociopetality.

For years, residents of Yountville, California, wanted to enhance their community center, but every proposal removed the new multipurpose building away from the existing center to accommodate parking needs. These proposed locations precluded eye contact with present users. Designers proposed shoehorning the new building between the existing community hall and the post office, creating a triangle of activity opening to a small town square. By doing this, eye contact is made from each of the three main entries to these buildings. People leaving the post office might recognize a face, make eye contact, and greet someone in the doorway of the community hall and new building. Chance encounters were increased by over 30 percent and encouraged thousands of stopping-to-chat interactions. This triangulation of eye contact breaks down if the distance between entries is farther than about 100 feet or if the entryways are parallel instead of triangulated. In Yountville, the town square is purposely small, eight thousand square feet, which accommodates about seventy people. It sacrifices big events to make a sociopetal space for everyday use.

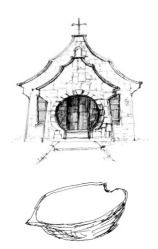

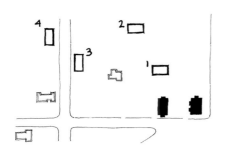

Bad locations for eye contact

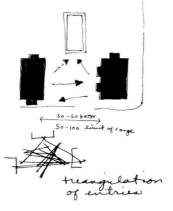

Good location for eye contact

Triangulated social interaction

The new building was shoehorned between the community hall and the post office to maximize eye contact and chance social interactions.

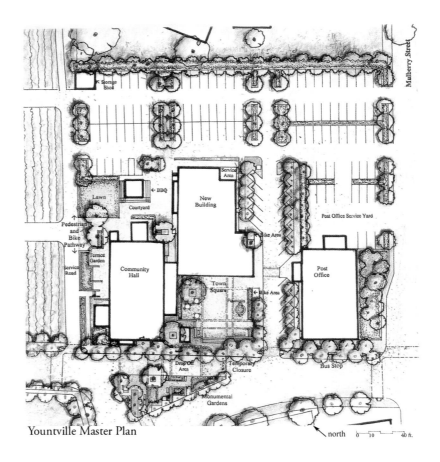

Yountville Master Plan

north   0   10   40 ft.

In larger public outdoor spaces, the public distance may be expanded to over a hundred feet and still provide a sense of shared experience if the space is sociopetally arranged. The Piazza del Campo in Siena slopes downward, creating an amphitheater effect. Eye contact and facial recognition are lost, but from any one point you can see people throughout the space. Slope and amphitheater compensate sociopetality.

Sociopetal space is important even for activities that may seem to be entirely solitary. Most dog walkers, for example, exercise the dog and themselves, privately contemplate, and avoid other people. However, many dog walkers stop to chat and block paths in a spider web of leashes and dogs. When paths are widened at key spots (say, eight-foot semicircles at switchbacks and view spots), comfortable sociopetal space is provided for dog walkers to have longer conversations, increasing the ease of informal exchanges. Seemingly private activities often beg for sociopetal places.[29]

All of these sociopetal forms are important to centeredness. They are a key enabling design element. As basic as this seems, making sociopetal places is a design fundamental for ecological democracy.

Places for Community Rituals

Another effective way to build capacity for thoughtful action among citizens is to provide places for cross-class and -generational rituals. Such rituals, daily and episodic, bring people together in common pursuits, celebrations, and observances. They build trust and effective working relationships. Rituals heighten the uniqueness of a community's culture, landscape, and natural processes.

Mundane activities—like going to the grocery store, the post office, the laundromat, the bank; playing and cheering at Little League games; and gardening in the front yard—offer routine opportunities for shared experiences. To maximize enabling benefits, the environment must be designed to accommodate interactions as previously described. Unfortunately, many ritual places do not. Most grocery supermarkets have narrow aisles and standardized high shelf heights that preclude stopping to chat in or across aisles.[30] In contrast, a farmer's market with wide walkways and niches adjacent to the main circulation paths encourages socializing. As a result, there are more casual social interactions at farmers' markets than at supermarkets.[31] As we have become more modern in technology and services, we have become more backward in community relations.

Many traditional daily rituals that enhanced community have been discarded and replaced by modern conveniences whose developers never considered consequences such as loss of shared experiences. Running water in every home and door-to-door mail delivery serve as examples. In some towns without these conveniences, the daily rituals of water and mail collecting were shared at a common well and post center. In one North African town, French colonists installed a water-distribution system, but women shunned its convenience. They continued to gather water at the common well, largely because their desire for daily socializing was too important to abandon.[32] The long campaign by Representative Earl Blumenauer in the U.S. Congress for local control over postal services is grounded in similar thinking—his desire to maintain the shared rituals of centralized post offices. Many Americans choose postal boxes over home delivery so that they can socialize at the post office, but because post office locations are a federal matter, their design seldom considers such factors.

A group of designers labeled one activity pattern "newsing at the post office." During this daily ritual, over half the postal patrons spent more time socializing than doing postal business. Almost all said hello or waved to other patrons. Most stopped to chat either at the front door or along the sidewalk and street (street conversations averaged approximately five minutes). Conversations were about personal business or community issues. Many of the postal patrons who entered the post office alone left with another person, and they headed for a nearby coffee shop or restaurant or the waterfront. The seemingly straightforward ritual of picking up the mail had multiple purposes, many of which created the social capital required to solve community problems.

Although I favor post office boxes, not everyone can give up the convenience of home mail delivery (or water distribution). Rather, I am pointing out that daily rituals often have values that are essential to an ecological democracy. In those cases, voluntary inconveniences should be accepted to gain community-building capacity.

Equally important are rituals that occur periodically throughout the year, such as Fourth of July parades, local sports tournaments, and music festivals. Some of these heighten awareness of local ecology and culture in addition to providing shared experiences. Harvest fairs, just as farmer's markets, show off locally grown crops. In Gloucester, Massachusetts, the blessing of the fishing fleet seeks heavenly protection for fishermen and calls attention to the fragility of the ocean ecosystem. Likewise, the Roman Catholic pilgrimage from Las Cruces, New Mexico, into the nearby mountains where mass is conducted celebrates the spirit and connects people to their landscape. (This is doubly true for those who make the pilgrimage barefoot.)

The tulip festival in Mount Vernon, Washington, features the uniqueness of the Skagit Valley microclimate, soils, and hydrology along with the beauty of hundreds of acres of flowers. Flower viewing in Washington, DC, was established by a gift from Japan, where a centuries-old tradition allowed entire communities to pause to celebrate when the cherry trees bloom. Fall leaf viewing in New England likewise calls attention to the local landscape.

Blessing the fleet

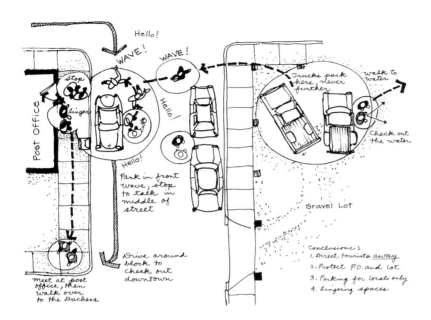

Newsing at the post office enables community. Like many unnoticed daily rituals, it can be encouraged by design.

In Brady, Texas, the Barbecue Goat Cook-Off celebrates the life of that community. In Casper, California, the gorse festival is directly ecological, raising awareness of the native vegetative mosaic and removing invasive gorse plants that threaten local ecosystems.

Many rituals celebrate diversity and teach about subcultural differences. In Monterey Park, California, the first city in the United States to have a majority of Asian American residents, local festivals were exclusive and highlighted cultural tensions, but over time the various cultures accommodated differences. Ritual celebrations became more inclusive and at times confusing. Speaking for many of us in a postmodern society, one Hispanic resident asked, "What's that New Year's dragon doing in our Cinco de Mayo parade?"[33]

For the designer who seeks to build a sense of community, a number of considerations are foremost. One is to inventory existing rituals, grand and small, by drawing the social and spatial dimensions of each. Diagrams like that of newsing at the post office reveal patterns of sociopetality and provoke community introspection when introduced into public discussion.

Imagine what rituals might be developed given culture and ecology. Replicating the community gardening rituals of Matsu, for example, might be appealing to me but absurd to residents in a different city. But flower viewing might be appropriate, and bull riding and rodeo might be more so. Although most celebrations build community, envision and focus energy on the ones that have the greatest potential to do so.

Identify small spaces for intimate rituals. For large festivals, identify large public space that is centrally located. An idea of how major events will grow and change is also needed. Relocating a community ritual because of inadequate space can undermine the centeredness it has fostered. For many ritual celebrations, preparation becomes as important a ritual as the event itself, enabling the community through heightened cooperation. The location and design of areas that are used to prepare for the event are just as important as the event space. The preparation area should be in the center to invite people to observe and participate. Making the ritual makes community. Also consider how that space will be used throughout the year. Spaces for large, public rituals can be discouragingly vacant when they are not carefully programmed for daily life. This is an important responsibility of the designer.

Look for opportunities to create rituals that attract a broad diversity of community members. If a parade excludes some neighborhoods, redesign its route to include parts of the community previously left out. Rituals that address cultural or other social tensions and connect directly to the natural ecology can be particularly enabling.

Always try to direct rituals to existing centers and create sociopetal settings as part of the design. In many communities, a committee evaluates the success of major annual celebrations, which offers an opportunity to introduce changes in the layout of staging areas, preparation spaces, vendors, exhibits, routes, and main performance areas to enhance centers and to create places for informal socializing or conscious collaboration.

Nourishing Centeredness Every Day

Diminishments of centeredness dominate our landscape. Cities have been decentered in much the same way that movie theaters have been displaced by home videos. Communities where centeredness is nourished are themselves nourished by it. But centeredness doesn't just happen. People have to create it and maintain it. We need to be aware of what we give up when we neglect centeredness. Every conscious public action should enhance centeredness. Consider three settings in one town.

The coastal village of Westport, California, has worked to create centeredness. This is reflected in many places in town, but the post office, the church, and the annual volunteer barbecue typify the commitment of townspeople to enabling form.

Westport, California

In a compact village nestled along a California coastal terrace, Westport residents nurture their center through daily life at the store, at the post office, and in special rituals.

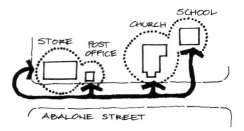

Symbiotic locations

Westport has only one general store, and the center of town gathers around the store. The church, other businesses, and the post office cluster around it. A century ago, there were stores and a school, but as the economy declined, businesses and the school closed. A recent effort to resecure the elementary school succeeded. There were many potential locations, but with little debate people decided the school must be in the center. It was built adjacent to the church, and they share parking, kitchen, restrooms, and outdoor play space. School location is the type of decision that every community faces.

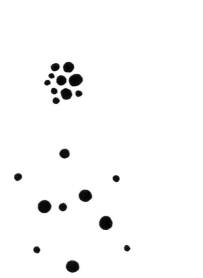

Clustering center versus dispersal

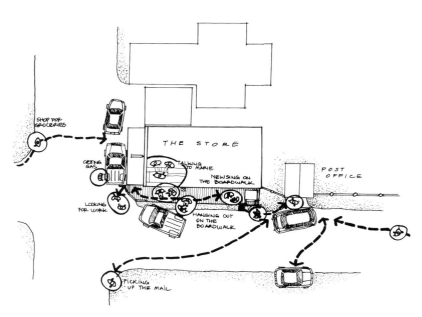

The proximity of the store to the post office, and the microclimate of the connecting boardwalk encourage impromptu social gatherings and exchanges of local news.

Enabling Form

The Westport post office also enables by design. Attached to the store, its policy and form encourage chance encounters. No one has home delivery, so everyone stops by daily to pick up mail. The public service area is about sixty square feet, so if two or more people are in the post office at the same time, they have to acknowledge each other. Because most congregate at prime times to pick up mail, well over three-quarters of the residents are likely to see a dozen other members of the community inside the post office in any given week. More people meet outside because the doorway connects to the store via an outdoor deck facing south to catch the sun and block the wind. It is the perfect microclimate to sit for a time in the otherwise chilly fog of the coast. This is the conjoint of pedestrian traffic—to school, store, deli, church, and post office itself. This concentration explains why the five-minute chat recorded in another city is extended to fifteen minutes in Westport.

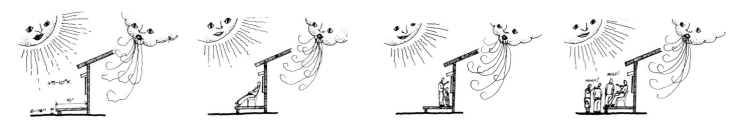

The connecting boardwalk

THE CHURCH AS A COMMUNITY WORKSHOP

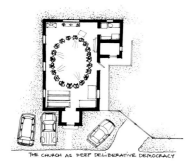

THE CHURCH AS DEEP DELIBERATIVE DEMOCRACY

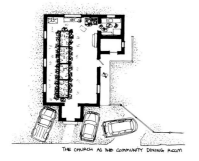

THE CHURCH AS THE COMMUNITY DINING ROOM

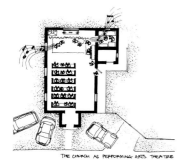

THE CHURCH AS PERFORMING ARTS THEATRE

Moveable church pews

The church was relocated from a distant site to the center two decades ago, another conscious clustering action. It was built through the voluntary efforts of hundreds of local people. It is officially the Westport Community Church, is decidedly multidenominational, and also serves as a community center. Official business of government, as well as the spirit, is conducted there. One small, seemingly inconsequential action is a vital lesson in sociopetal space. The community decided at the outset that the pews should not be fixed to the floor in rows oriented toward the pulpit, as in most Christian sanctuaries. Instead, moveable pews are arranged in a clumsy circle for community meetings. There is eye contact; faces cannot be avoided or impersonalized. Everyone sits at an intimate distance and faces inward as an inclusive covey. In debates that divide the community and normally fill a town with venom, the circle discourages meanspiritedness and encourages cooperation, even if it is shouted. The moveable pews allow many activities, but the sociopetal shape makes a union of disparate parts. Many times, when the community has faced overwhelming issues, residents have gathered in a circle, each person taking a turn to voice opinion—a tribal council of elders, except here every age is voiced. It could not function thusly if the pews were fixed in a sociofugal hierarchy.

A third archetype of centeredness is the annual barbecue, a fund-raiser for the volunteer fire department. It is typical of many small-town annual ritual celebrations, anticipated and planned throughout the year. The week of the barbecue brings heightened activity and excitement. In Westport, all preparation is centered and engages all segments of the community—professionals and laborers, youth and elderly, men and women. With no formal home, the barbecue is staged at different locations depending on the generosity of private landowners. However, one characteristic never changes: there must be a gently sloping field in the center of town with an open view to the Pacific Ocean. The ritual is tied to both its immediate and larger ecological context. Equally constant is the layout. The overall arrangement is a U-shape, with the western end open to the ocean and a large, open field in the middle surrounded by various activities. Usually, the cooking area occupies one perimeter, picnic tables and benches another edge, and games and sales the other edge. A stage for the band terminates either the northern or southern flank downslope closest to the water. Dancing, soccer, football, baseball, volleyball, frisbee, chasing, and other activities occur in the central open space. From the picnic tables, all is in view in layers of activity down to the band and the ocean beyond. The intergenerational dancing is juxta-

Enabling Form

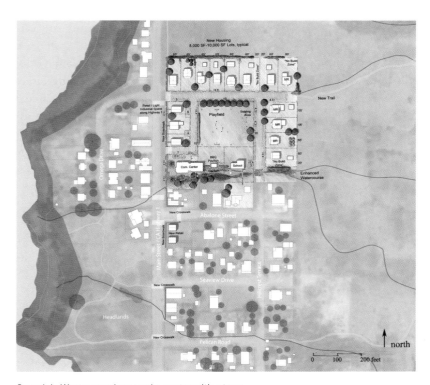

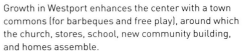

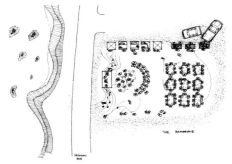

Growth in Westport enhances the center with a town commons (for barbeques and free play), around which the church, stores, school, new community building, and homes assemble.

Seasonal rituals on the common

+ Hillcrest extension

+ new Community Center

0   25 fe

The new community center reinforces existing center functions and strengthens the town's relationship with the mountains and the ocean.

posed with the mass of waves, sea, and sky, dispels disagreements, and creates a shared image that lasts a full year. This simple design—which is quite similar to the Matsu City Center, the Davis Central Park, or even Siena's Piazza del Campo—reminds residents of a shared destiny. It connects people to people and to the surrounding landscape.

In 2004, villagers purchased land near the existing post office to make a larger community center. Not surprisingly, the final design diversifies the existing center. A larger community hall is located next to the store, and the school expands from the church site. New buildings and community gardens huddle around a new town common that accommodates soccer, free play, and the annual barbeque. This design fulfills almost all of the criteria for making good centers. Each action enhances the point around which daily life revolves. People in Westport have consistently nourished it, made it accessible to everyone in town by foot, made it a place of daily use, and provided formal and informal places to gather. The center is the focus of knowledge. The clustering of school, church, store, and new community building encourages the personal exchange of information and news both local and from the outside world. It is the starting point of most days and often the conclusion. The design speaks of its ecological niche. The buildings blend together into a whole. The center is a place of voluntary investment.

For those of us involved in creating cities that support ecological democracy, the Westport post office, moveable pews, ocean-oriented barbecue, and expanded community center speak softly but carry a powerful message. The design of places matters. Location matters. Arrangement matters. Detail matters. If carefully crafted, design can enable centeredness. Someone once remarked after a meeting in the Westport Community Church, "If you want your town to be centered, you have to tend it every day."

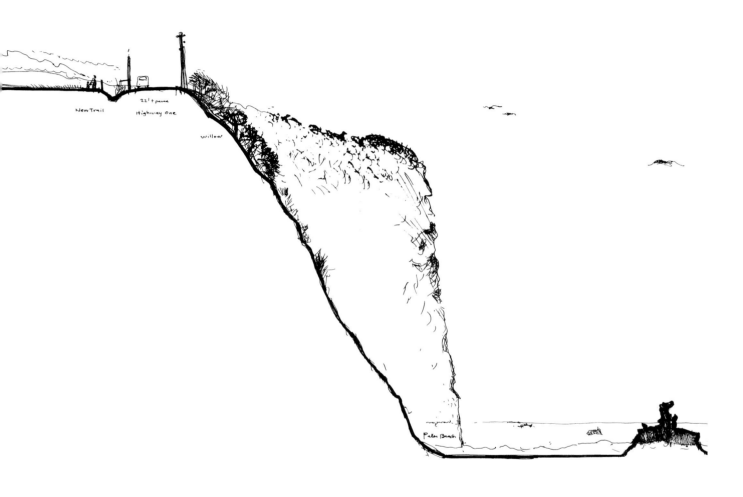

New Trail

22't pave
Highway One

Willow

Palm Beach

Connectedness

A primary lesson of ecology is that everything is interconnected in one single web of life.[1] To work together to solve difficult problems, we need to be aware of, experience, and understand the interrelationships between multiple aspects of the inhabited landscape.[2] Every action in the urban landscape causes an opposite equivalent and many secondary reactions and side effects, which may be invisible, unknown, and harmful to us. This is especially true in making land-use, city-design, and site decisions. Once we comprehend these reactions and side effects, we become aware that we have a single destiny with other people and every part of the earth. This awareness provides us with an incentive to work with others, and these interconnections can be the basis of unusually creative design. Such is the case of recycling, in which one person's waste can become another person's treasure.

Connectedness, the second operating principle of enabling form, encompasses the mutual dependence and appropriate relationships of parts of

A violin

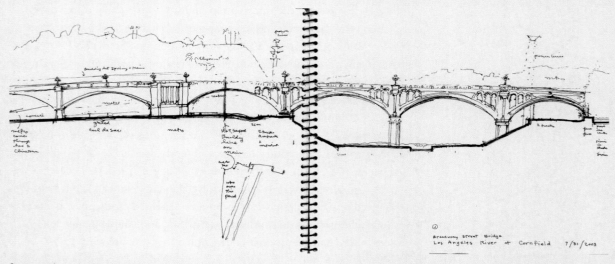

Connectedness is a particular way of design thinking that maximizes mutual benefits by expressing fundamental associations between parts of an urban ecosystem.

an ecosystem, including human and nonhuman aspects, which need to be reflected in physical arrangements. Connectedness is a particular way of design thinking that maximizes mutual social and ecological benefits by expressing fundamental associations—often unknown or unseen locally— between the parts of an ecosystem, a city, or an individual site. Connectedness enables. Disconnectedness disables.

Connectedness in city design counters disjointed and piecemeal environmental decision making. It is fundamental to the survival of ecosystems. Heightened public understanding of how interrelated we are with the entirety of our urban ecosystems underlies comprehensive democratic decision making about nearby and faraway landscapes. Yet the holistic, long-term thinking this requires is alien to prevailing exploitation for short-term consumer satisfaction and economic profit.[3] But demand-side economics is only the most obvious culprit. When ecological process conflicts with individual desire, desire prevails. Equally menacing is simplistic, single-purpose, and non-place-based thinking that accompanies technology-dependent culture. Overly specialized in our work, each of us does narrow, simple tasks very well, but we have lost our capacity for generalized thinking and systemic problem solving. This affects us as individuals and as a society.[4] Our independence from subtle ecological couplings in daily life, especially the indirect and invisible ones, blinds us to their long-term import. And our belief in technology—whether it is convenient appliances, chemical products, landscape fixtures, or the information highway—is equally dim witting.[5]

Recently, Jane Smiley gave a wake-up call personalizing the tragedy of Carson's 1962 *Silent Spring.* On the Iowa farmland of Smiley's 1991 novel, *A Thousand Acres,* the invisible side effects of chemical fertilizers and pesticides eventually poison the ground water and drinking water, producing a cancer cluster that decimates a family and a community. On the surface, crops, farms, and family appear to be thriving, but invisible secondary effects are killing the land and its inhabitants.[6] Similar unseen connections between technology and habitation produce sick landscapes and sick-building syndrome, in spite of fifty years of warnings about such hidden dangers.[7]

Design alone certainly cannot solve these and other problems of disconnectedness, but design can reconnect disjoined landscapes, make sick buildings healthy, reknit sundered city fabrics, and couple people with each other and the natural processes from which they are divided.[8]

In designing the built environment, there are multiple ways to form connectedness, ranging from the physical to the conceptual. The following sections discuss elements that are essential to good city form: interdependent adjacencies; transportation and communication that unify; chains, webs, flows, networks, cycles, and recycles; resource footprints; wildlife habitats; ecological thinking; mutualism and glocalization; outside the confines of the box; things that don't go together; and finding fish heads and tails.

Interdependent Adjacencies: What Goes Together and What Doesn't

Determining the activities that need to be located near each other is primary in efficient design. For example, it is logical to make closets adjacent to bedrooms and to place stores for daily shopping within residential areas. Many public activities simply will not occur without proper adjacencies. Others are greatly enhanced. For example, pickup basketball can be played on a simple concrete slab with two hoops, but teenagers say the best basketball courts have a place to sit, watch, wait your turn, and hang out. A really great basketball court has additional space to work on cars and watch the game. A corner grocery store across the street completes the perfect court. Smaller children need additional hoops that are within viewing distance of the main courts so that they can play unharassed and also imitate the moves of advanced players. Just as this process of acculturation depends on proper spatial adjacencies, so too does the design of the entire city.

Consider this example of recycling household waste. When my family began full-scale recycling twenty years ago, it was inconvenient because our house and city had been designed to disconnect trash and garbage from daily life. Our kitchen had no room to store bins for compost, plastics, glass, aluminum, newspaper, and other paper. The city's recycling center was miles away and accepted only a few highly valued recyclables. Eventually, we had ecological architects redesign our house to make recycling a central part of everyday life. Our kitchen now has special spots for plastic, glass, metals, and newspaper. Other paper is collected in a sculpted wooden drum that makes recycling a visual treat. Significantly fewer materials now go to the city's landfill. Since the city decentralized its recycling centers, we have been able to walk to one that accepts a wide variety of recyclables. City and residential designers created adjacencies that are supportive of sustainable actions.

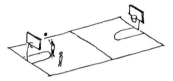

Regulation basketball court

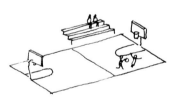

Court with a view

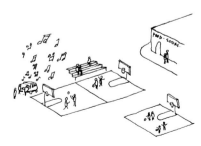

Dream court

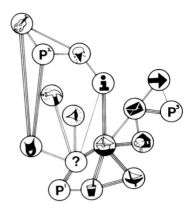

Adjacency requirements

Architectural connections

Some functions do need to be separated. On a farm, the well for drinking water needs to be several hundred feet from the septic field. But as farmers learned in Smiley's novel, the water system is interconnected, even over a distance of a thousand acres. Connectedness means that the most remote is never far away.

We need to rethink what truly must be distanced in the city design. There are serious ramifications whenever we put anything out of sight and out of mind. Just as garbage dumps and landfills were pushed as far away as possible from the homes of the affluent, making recycling seemingly unnecessary and burdening the less powerful in whose neighborhoods the dumps were located, almost every decision to distance ourselves from our toxic by-products puts them temporarily out of our minds at later peril. Good cities of the future will locate and design unpleasantness close rather than faraway. Imagine how much less toxic waste and spent nuclear fuel we would produce if they had to be stored in every neighborhood rather than on reservations thousands of miles away.

Transportation and Communication That Unify

Transportation and communication systems connect, but divisive secondary impacts accompany these systems.[9] Consider, for example, the effects of streets and highways. They generally discourage pedestrian movement, disrupt water and wildlife patterns, and divide neighborhoods into fragments. Isolated from previously adjacent areas, neighborhood fragments suffer island effects, disproportionate pollution, and loss of services. Over time, disinvestment creates concentrated pockets of poverty. City designer Shelby Harrison warned us of this nearly a hundred years ago, long before we destroyed urban neighborhoods with highways and traffic corridors. We did not heed Harrison's warning that the streets and superhighways built throughout the twentieth century would not be like old main streets, which, with modest and slow traffic, unified trading centers along street frontages. Rather, Harrison pointed out that wide streets and highways were lines of severance that divided the city and often destroyed it.[10] The divisive impacts are related to scale, speed, and specialization. Typically, the bigger, faster, and more specialized the street, the more disruptive, disenabling, and costly its side effects. But by careful design, streets can be places of social interaction again.

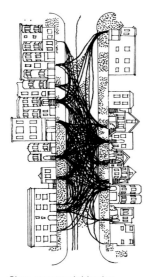

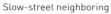
Slow-street neighboring

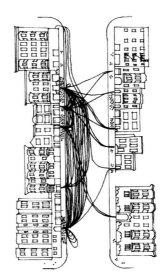
Fast-street neighboring

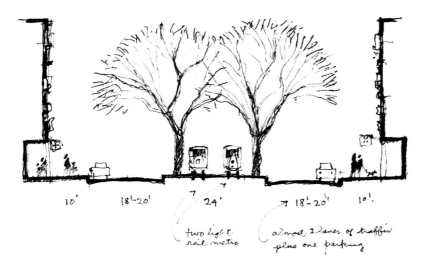

Studying precedents like Milan reveals streets that carry large volumes of traffic with multiple modes and also are comfortable for pedestrians.

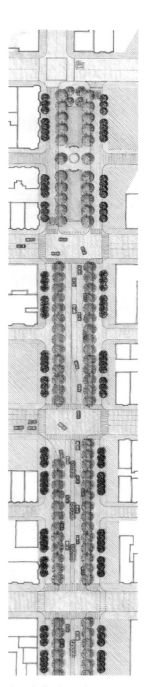

Octavia Boulevard

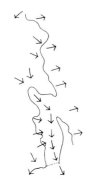

1900 Water flows unobstructed.

1985 Road causes flooding.

1986 Fill gullies, replant eroded areas.

In San Francisco, for example, earthquake-damaged freeways were reconsidered during the 1990s. A battle ensued. Opposing ballot measures to rebuild the Central Freeway or take it down were passed and repealed by citizen votes in 1997, 1998, and 1999. Allan Jacobs and Elizabeth Macdonald developed a plan to remove the overhead freeway that divided the Hayes Valley district. The freeway had long created a dark, uninhabitable corridor that separated neighborhoods. Their plan for Octavia Boulevard was an at-grade boulevard, a smaller and multipurpose street with faster-moving traffic in four central lanes and slower local traffic in access lanes close to the sidewalks. These access lanes are also used by bicycles. Gracious fifteen-foot sidewalks with closely spaced trees invite pedestrians to the street. Even though traffic will move somewhat slower overall, the new boulevard accommodates a greater variety of modes of travel than the old freeway and maintains comparable traffic capacity. The new boulevard provides a pleasant pedestrian environment and reunifies neighborhoods that had long been divided by physical barriers, noise, and visual blight along the freeway route. Reknitting the community with a multimodal boulevard became the alternative candidate in another citizen vote. The boulevard won.[11] After years of study, Jacobs concludes that urban freeways simply cannot be built without severing neighborhoods and causing blight. In contrast, boulevards can accommodate through traffic as well as local traffic and thousands of pedestrians. They form social and economic nodes instead of divisive barriers.[12]

Chains, Webs, Flows, Networks, Cycles, and Recycles

Connections in both social and ecological systems are invisible.[13] Intricate, inconvenient, and not readily observed in a single view, they are frequently disrupted when cities are constructed. These disruptions are extraordinarily costly to repair after the fact. Such is the case of food webs, nutrient flows, drainage networks, and hydrological cycles.

Consider one of the most widespread and costly—drainage networks. In most natural systems, rainwater percolates into the soil or is dispersed across a landscape. As cities develop, soil is paved for streets, parking lots, homes, and other buildings. Rainwater cannot infiltrate where it falls. Storm runoff is concentrated, destroying the fine-grained water network. When and where it is overly concentrated, water creates erosion and flooding. Each building, sidewalk, and street contributes to these problems.[14] Typically, water is culverted to reduce flooding, the most visible and immediate problem. This, in turn, speeds the flow, creates worse flooding downstream, destroys riparian vegetation, and leads to a loss of fish.[15] Small actions cumulatively destroy.[16] Secondary impacts are worse. Culverted streams preclude access to natural water play, so that children grow up without experiencing one of childhood's greatest joys.[17] In many cities, such as Los Angeles, this disruption to the drainage network is further complicated by other more subtle and invisible effects. Storm runoff that is concentrated in areas of steep slopes with highly erodible soils causes disastrous landslides, destroying homes, roads, and other essential infrastructure. Even a leaking swimming pool can saturate soils, overwhelming the dispersed natural drainage network. Local landslides result. The cost of not designing with the natural drainage network in mind averages over $800 per house.[18] When Los Angeles was first being developed, a leading landscape architectural firm recommended creating a framework of natural drainage patterns. That plan called for preserving small canyons and arroyos for storm-water retention, recreation, and wildlife habitat; limiting development on steep slide-prone hillsides; and directing the most intensive growth to flat uplands in basins or above palisades.[19] The recommendation was ignored. Over the next eighty years, the drainage networks were continually attacked and disrupted.

By the 1980s, when we began work on the Runyon Canyon Park in Hollywood (the park where residents said that the best thing about the planning process was that they got to know their neighbors), the natural storm water was so artificially concentrated in the canyon that landslides had destroyed nearby houses, mud flows had damaged downhill apartments, runoff from roads had formed deeply eroded gullies along the entire western side of the canyon, and water-dependent vegetative mosaics had been distorted.[20] The city favored a dam and debris basin at the mouth of the canyon. That was opposed by a few citizens who wanted to maintain the connectedness of the watershed that the debris basin would sever.

Ecological hydrologists calculated how to disperse the water into sub-watersheds with small check dams to prevent flooding. Still, most people wanted the quick technological fix. Site tours were held to explain the natural surface hydrology. Participatory techniques engaged citizens directly in measuring and evaluating the impacts of the choices. After protracted public discussions, an alternative plan was approved.[21] Revegetation parties were held by local volunteers to replant riparian vegetation and engage others in

1988 Check dams control peak flows.

1989 Restore riparian vegetation.

1992 Return 90% of water to origin.

reconnecting the broken network. As a result, neighbors got to know each other and became aware of the critical ecological connections, and the Friends of Runyon Canyon has worked continuously to restore the hydrological system of this watershed.[22] Within a decade, the dispersed stormwater network should be reestablished and function to control flooding and landslides naturally.

From this example, we see that some disrupted networks can be reconnected. Other examples in the chapters on Inhabiting Science and Reciprocal Stewardship support these conclusions. Use a participatory design process to raise public awareness of the importance of obscure chains and flows. Invent effective ways to reconnect broken connections. Standard methods, like large debris dams, are difficult to overcome. Only with sound, practical alternatives can harmful technologies be replaced. Make reconnected chains, flows, networks, and cycles visible in the everyday landscape.[23] Engage citizen volunteers directly in making and maintaining the reconnections so that they will have a deeper understanding of natural functions.[24] Use natural chains, flows, networks, and cycles to give overall structure to city form.[25] These actions enable more informed public decision making.

Dispersing water into subwatersheds and creating check dams saved Runyon Canyon from a concrete flood-control basin, creating a beloved wilderness above Hollywood Boulevard.

Enabling Form

Resource Footprints

Another invisible disconnect is the ecological and social footprint of the products that we use in everyday lives. Those who make cities are increasingly alarmed by interconnections between building products and their environmental impacts. Seemingly harmless landscape actions may contribute to the demise of an ecosystem or culture thousands of miles away.[26]

However, designers can reduce building footprints by employing proper adjacencies, reducing hidden costs (especially of transportation), and attending to local chains, flows, networks, and cycles. The example of the carrot and its larger urban agricultural context can illustrate. The average carrot travels two thousand miles before it reaches the American dinner plate.[27] Its production is completely severed from its consumption. A carrot from a local farmer's market might travel only two miles, and one grown in your backyard travels a fraction of a mile, mostly by foot. In one well studied residential lot, a small, urban farm plot connected to domestic activities minimizes the resource footprint of carrots and other food-related products. It works like this. About three hundred square feet of garden space is located to receive prime sun. Immediately adjacent is a slightly larger barnyard (four hundred square feet) for chickens, ducks, and rabbits. There is a worm box to make soil. Nut trees create a canopy wildlife habitat. (At the top of the food web, hawks window shop above the chicken run.) The residents grow about half the vegetables that they consume, including carrots. Leafy greens grown year round make up the bulk of the harvest. The barnyard animals eat leftovers, produce fertilizer for the garden, and provide eggs and meat for household consumption. Baby rabbits are bartered at the neighborhood pet store for animal feed. (The near worthless cat gets the free lunch, so to speak.) The energy footprint of backyard food is only 1 percent of the footprint of the equivalent commercially produced food.[28] The well-traveled carrot's footprint extends far beyond the gasoline that is consumed to move it, leaving an unhealthy track in distant regions. The untraveled carrot and other locally grown foods, while not worldly, leave hardly any footprint at all.

City design that incorporates urban farming on residential lots (in many regions, the only prime agricultural land that is left is in backyards) or community plots, preserves farmland at the urban edge, and provides in-town farmer's markets can reduce the energy footprint of eating. Similar attention to other urban systems and their complex interactions can reduce catastrophic impacts on resources and communities that are continents away.

Water-resource awareness

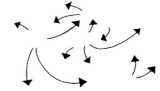

Household food web

U.S. resource footprints

1980 April Cowlitz River attracts hundreds of bird species.

1980 May Eruption destroys riparian habitat.

1980 June Habitat is covered with 30 feet of mud flow debris.

1990 Debris is regraded to create habitat.

1995 Birds return to the vegetative mosaic.

In many cases, the footprints of resources like energy, food, and building materials have such obscure interconnections that they seem to be impossible to unravel. The challenge to city makers is to uncover and apply hidden connections to reduce footprints of human habitation.[29]

Wildlife Habitats

Like other systems, wildlife survival depends on connectedness. Food, water, cover, migrations, reproduction, and species are always strikingly intertwined. Typical urbanization disrupts these connections. Maintaining and recreating these connections through core habitat and corridors in city design are essential for species survival.[30] This is not just about wild species but about the pleasure that humans derive from wildlife every day. Wildlife viewing is a fundamental measure of the quality of life for most Americans.[31] The impact of habitat loss on one community is unforgettable. When the Mount Saint Helens volcano erupted in Washington state in 1980, the debris flow scoured the Cowlitz River of riparian vegetation all the way to the Columbia River, destroying the only available habitat for multiple riparian species. In Castle Rock, Washington, a city that was partially destroyed by the volcanic eruption, one woman spoke at a community meeting about plans to recover the town. She suggested that the town suffered collective psychological depression. She claimed, "The worst thing is that the birds don't sing here anymore." Eerie silence gripped the room. Tears could be seen in the eyes of many residents. It was a moment of catharsis and revelation. Indeed, riparian bird species had not returned ten years after the eruption because there was no riparian habitat. Although not as dramatic as the Castle Rock situation, habitat loss in most cities is leading to a decline of cherished species. In Castle Rock's case, the riparian zone has been revegetated, and other areas have naturally regenerated, returning the habitat and the songs of birds.

City makers can take a number of actions to create connectedness on which urban wildlife depends. They can concentrate urban development to prevent habitat loss and direct urbanization to locations that will least disrupt the habitats of endangered species and rich diversity of species. Each site must be assessed not just internally but within the regional context for import to the creation of core habitat. Large core habitats and connective corridors cannot be compromised: trade islands for connectivity. By using critical wildlife patterns to inspire overall city form, a natural skeleton structures the city, restricts only the most essential habitat, and encourages intense urbanization within the framework. Consider the complexity of species interactions in designing even the smallest site. Although most cannot, some species can be supported adequately in backyard habitats. With careful zonation and creation of specific habitat, mobile species like butterflies and birds thrive in limited fragments in a neighborhood mosaic.

The interactions of other wildlife are more complicated. For example, in California, ground birds like quail and towhees are among bird watchers' favorites, but as habitat is reduced, ground birds precipitously decline. Predation by domestic pets—dogs and cats—hastens the decline. If corridors are created to large core habitats, ground birds recover because, in part, coyotes, bobcats, and mountain lions reduce pet predation. Yes, they kill pet cats. Ground birds have a complex relationship with larger predator mammals. If quail are to be present, a habitat that is suitable for coyotes, bobcats, and mountain lions must be provided. Such intricate connections between species must be recreated to attract treasured urban wildlife.

Thinking like a quail

Ecological Thinking

Connectedness in the urban environment requires holistic, systemic thinking. This is the most fundamental contribution of applied ecology to city design. "Ecological think" is not simply about natural ecology. It also is about considering the consequences of urbanization actions and the interrelationships that create vibrant, self-sustaining habitats. In this sense, "ecological think" is proactive and creative, not just reactionary and prohibitive.[32] In fact, it requires us to challenge a widely used city-design tool—the environmental impact statement (EIS), a primary means of environmental protection that focuses exclusively on the mitigation of negative consequences of individual projects. In the United States, the EIS is effective at maintaining the status quo and stopping the worst, immediate site-scale environmental calamities, but it is ineffective in creating the regionwide connectedness that is necessary for healthy experimental urbanization. Project-by-project impact reviews for subdivisions continue to produce sprawling, low-density suburbs that disconnect people from centers and sever critical regional wildlife patterns. Expanding streets and highways is frequently a mitigation requirement, but it is a self-defeating action.

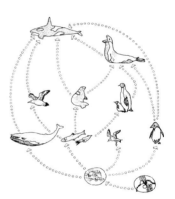

Food-web ecology

An ecological democracy requires positive design thinking to produce systemic connectedness in the inhabited landscape. What is most needed in urban areas is an inviolable regional framework based on a thorough environmental analysis of overlays and a synthesis of development desires and consequences. This should guide urban growth rather than react to it. Within large-scale ecological thinking, smaller decisions can be evaluated for connectedness outcomes. The next sections discuss some techniques that underlie "ecological think."

Mutualism and Glocalization

Even as we become fragmented as a citizenry, our loyalties have been simultaneously stretched by the globalized economy. These forces create debilitating local social rifts that can be addressed through ecological thinking. Two actions are especially important in city design—creating settings of social mutualism and giving form to glocalization.

Social mutualism is an association between groups that typically are in opposition—by age, race, religion, social class, and interest group. In his 1963 "Letter from Birmingham Jail," Martin Luther King Jr. describes this social intricacy thusly:

> I am cognizant of the interrelatedness of all communities and states. I cannot sit idly by in Atlanta and not be concerned about what happens in Birmingham. We are caught in an inescapable network of mutuality, tied in a single garment of destiny. Whatever affects one directly affects all indirectly.[33]

This charge was not lost on residents in Raleigh, North Carolina, who learned that proposed highways would have disastrous impacts on their neighborhoods. As described above, these would be lines of severance that would divide and destroy the city. At first, neighborhood groups simply watched as highway projects uprooted the less powerful, but they soon realized that the thoroughfare plan would cause widespread disruptions. These groups—black and white, affluent and less so—represented separate interests, certainly not King's "single garment of destiny." Destructive road projects continued until a coalition of previously antagonistic groups joined as Goals for Raleigh to create an alternative transportation plan.[34] Attention focused on a highway that would sever black neighborhoods and an historic district. The coalition of mutualism mounted a movement that stopped the highway in a five-to-three city council vote.[35]

Another example of social mutualism that successfully joined traditionally conflicting interests is the wildlife-habitat coalition. Historically, conservationists and bird watchers opposed hunters and sportspeople, but their conflict over recreation preferences was minor compared to the issue of habitat loss. If habitats were not preserved, wildlife viewers, photographers, and hunters would all lose their pursuits. These groups formed cooperative campaigns to preserve wildlife habitats and created one of the most effective lobbying efforts in the nation. Ducks Unlimited, for example, now has over 750,000 members, including hunters and environmentalists. As a comparison, the National Association of Realtors also has about 750,000 members. Combined with other likeminded associations, Ducks Unlimited undertakes significant lobbying efforts at the local, state, and national levels. Wildlife coalitions raise between $3 million and $5 million dollars each year for lobbying purposes. Although not as much as the $8 million that the mining industry spends or the $31 million and $60 million that the real estate and oil industries spend, the wildlife coalition is successful precisely because of its diverse mutualism. As a result, there are now 93 million acres of wildlife refuges around the country. Increasingly, these shape city form.[36]

On a smaller scale, community gardens produce similar mutualism. One that has been particularly successful in bridging racial, class, and generational divides is described in the chapter on Reciprocal Stewardship. In spite of encouraging examples, healthy social mutualism is rare in city making.[37] We need to devote more design attention to this matter. Designers will be rewarded because such mutualism leads to unusually creative innovations in urban landscapes.

Glocalization can create positive social connections if the effects of global standardization, dominance, and exploitation—social relations with harmful effects—can be neutralized. Glocalization is the design process whereby mutualism is extended from locality to locality across continents. Cross-cultural association among grassroots groups with mutual respect, comparable benefits, and a commitment to strengthen idiosyncrasies of local culture can create exceptional enabling form. The International Rivers Network has been especially effective at doing this. They provide technical support and mutual aid for far-flung, previously isolated groups that fight dams that would destroy local cultures. Simultaneously, this protects endangered rivers the world over.

Outside the Confines of the Box

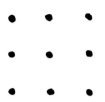

Holistic thinking requires city designers to look beyond the narrow confines of site projects and boiler-plate standardization. Most children obediently color within the lines until they discover the joyful authority that can be gained by choosing to color outside the lines. A delightful exercise illustrates. Visualize three rows that each contains three evenly spaced dots. Now connect the dots with the fewest possible continuous straight-line segments.[38] Connecting the dots with five line segments is easy. To connect them with just four without lifting the pen requires extending the lines beyond the boundaries of the problem. The design of the inhabited landscape is similar.[39]

A landscape architect typically is hired to design a small project, such as a park with distinct property boundaries and a predetermined program of activities (such as a tot lot and parking) proscribed in square feet. The site usually presents enough difficulty that the designer is blinded to important connections just outside the dictated boundaries. Some consider the surrounding context.[40] Others enjoy the freedom of the individual site to create an artistic jewel that outshines its context, often sticking out like a sore thumb and diminishing the whole.[41]

The best design solutions require thinking far outside the lines and making connections beyond the commission. How a city designer does this is described in the chapter on Limited Extent. Consider as a first step the surrounding landscape, context, and adjacencies. This should include the unseen natural systems and the less obvious chains and flows discussed earlier. But there is more to thinking outside the confines. The designer needs to question the program and never assume that the client has thought it out carefully. Often parts of the program are unnecessary. It may have serious omissions. Many projects that are intended to solve a problem address only a symptom. For example, numerous neighborhood park projects are undertaken to keep teenagers out of trouble, assuming that their lawlessness is due to a lack of proper recreation. That is infrequently the case. Working with teenagers to design parks repeatedly reveals that their first priority is not recreation but employment. The park is welcomed but is successful in the

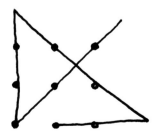

Thinking outside confines

long term only when youth are employed in its construction and maintenance or when they find jobs in related sectors.[42]

In other cases, to produce an elegant city design requires planners to challenge the rules that govern a site. Rigid, long out-of-date standards regarding street widths, parking, setbacks, low density, and segregated land use are often barriers to design for ecological democracy.

As one example, architect Dan Solomon found that in a community where he was working, the city plans called for 2.2 cars per residential unit and 2.8 library books per 1,000 residents. For the 4,000 homes he was designing, that would translate into 8,800 parking spaces and 30 books.[43] Counterstandards offered by new urbanists challenge the absurdity of such rules.[44] Only by thinking outside narrow confines can genuine problem solving be achieved.

Tyree Guyton's art of hope

Things That Don't Go Together but Might

To think outside the dots, try connecting things that do not obviously go together. We often see these connections in our most creative acts. Imagine when the tastes of oil and vinegar were first combined. Such odd couples may become eternally sublime, give us a moment's smile, or solve significant city problems.

The same thinking that Robert Rauschenberg employed in creating his combines (artworks that incorporate canvas, paint, and collage) or that folk artist Leland Holiday employs in creating spirit figures from found objects in his New Mexico desert frequently leads to innovations in the design of our inhabited landscape. Artist Tyree Guyton's *The Heidelberg Project* calls attention to land-use changes and drug infestations in Detroit as nothing else does. Using junk found throughout the city, he has made unthinkable art. He has occupied abandoned houses, driven drug dealers away, and turned the houses into expressions of hope and despair. Combining art and abandoned land, not typically thought of together, has provoked numerous city actions to repair rundown neighborhoods.

Wildlife scientists failed in their attempts to preserve endangered species by setting aside inviolable protection areas that excluded use by local people until conservationists began to connect species protection to local economic development. When local usufructuary rights, ecotourism, and controlled hunting are allowed, preservation follows.[45] The Monarch Butterfly

Wishing pole

Biosphere Reserve west of Mexico City illustrates. The single winter roosting area for butterflies migrating between Mexico and the United States is key to species survival. But roosting trees are threatened by 200,000 mostly subsistence farmers who live within the preserve and cut trees to construct their homes, fuel their fires, and clear land for crops. Residents resent the attention that outsiders pay to the butterflies at their expense. Although traditional logging rights were curtailed, in the last thirty years, over half the intact forest has been degraded by illegal logging. Nothing worked to preserve the disappearing habitat until two biologists teamed with two local farmers to put "implausible ideas" into practice. Rather than preaching restricted use, the team Alternare built a house from a type of adobe that requires only one tree instead of the usual twenty-five trees. They introduced a low-technology oven that replaces open fires. It cooks with scraps, not firewood. Using compost of corn stalks, grass, and manure, they eliminated tons of expensive chemical fertilizers. This reduced to two and a half acres the amount of crop land needed to support a family. They replant degraded forests with seedlings. Only when other farmers inquire do they spread the innovations. Little is said about butterflies. Yet this grassroots effort focusing not on butterflies but on people could save thousands of acres of essential forest where butterfly-focused efforts have completely failed. Some outsiders question whether this is an appropriate habitat-conservation strategy. But for the first time, local people are enthusiastic about saving butterflies. They can improve their lives and protect the forest at the same time. The experiment joins incompatible forces to work together.[46] Such necessities are often the mothers of invention in an ecological democracy but only when someone thinks far afield of the conventional.

Finding Fish Heads and Tails

In every region and neighborhood, resources have been exploited. Using a fishing analogy, to produce the fillet, fish heads used to be discarded as a useless by-product. Today, fish heads, guts, and tails can be made into value-added products like organic fertilizers and specialty foods and the costs of waste-water treatment and waste disposal can be reduced.[47] In one example, a rural entrepreneur makes a pricey salmon spread from fish waste. He dismisses praise for his creativity by saying that you can sell anything to people in San Francisco. Discovery of resources previously considered trash is key to recycling, closing loops, conservation, and creative city making. In one of the largest-scale uses of recycled waste, the 80 million cubic meters of debris that was produced during the destruction of Berlin during World War II were used to build ten hills around the city. These hills today provide outdoor recreation in cherished spaces.

At the city-design level, projects stuck in inertia can be activated by fish heads without degradation and with environmental benefits. If the newly discovered resource has economic value that previously was unaccounted, it provides capital to make a tenuous project feasible. Finding fish heads requires paying attention to interconnectedness. We must consider the absurd and make the strange familiar and the familiar strange. Finding fish heads asks a lot of "what ifs?" and "why nots?" and risks ridicule. In a city-design situation, fish heads might be abandoned buildings, obscure historical events, neglected space, scenic beauty, retired people, or everyday real work.[48]

In one port city, for example, tourists come to see the boats being built and to visit historic attractions. In another city with a strong fish-processing industry, visitors are attracted to machines that separate the fish heads, tails, and guts from the meat to be canned. Americans like to observe real work, even when it is gory. Because work in white-collar professions seldom exposes us to work other than the copier and fax machine, some say that we are eager to experience physical labor (such as fish processing) and undiscovered resources (such as the original fish heads and tails). When designers proposed a secondary tourist industry that focused on fish processing, local people thought they were crazy. Making the familiar strange made the designers objects of local jokes, but urban visitors were enthralled by the fish heads and tails.

Consider a dramatic example of how a somewhat desolate area was transformed into a thriving economy. Along the Columbia River, howling gale-force winds last for weeks, making the gorge inhospitable, agriculture marginal, and daily life miserable. But wind surfers saw those winds as ideal for the most exciting surfing conditions in the world. As wind surfing on the river increased, local leaders promoted the air currents around Hood River, Oregon. Entrepreneurs reused failed industrial buildings for surfing-related products and services. The public sector retrofitted facilities to provide river access and encouraged manufacturing related to wind surfing. The wind turned declining economies into multimillion-dollar industries and renewed local communities. This is the power of connectedness.

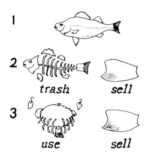

Finding fish heads

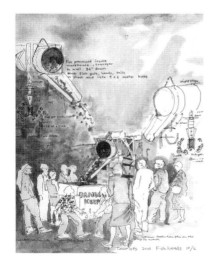

Fish-head tourist attraction

The lost mountain

Neighborhood fisticuffs

Removing Reseda Ridge

The Lost Mountain, the Power Map, and the Dirt Contractor

Reseda Ridge once was a summit in the mountains between central Los Angeles and the San Fernando Valley. Its peak 1,100 feet above sea level was treasured by local people. I never saw it except on a U.S. Geological Survey map. By the time we began working on a plan for a 1,000-acre park surrounding what had been Reseda Ridge, its lower ridges had been removed to fill an adjacent valley for housing development, and its upper ridges were being leveled to make way for a new cross-mountain highway, Reseda to the Sea, from the San Fernando Valley to Sunset Boulevard. Hikers and environmentalists protested unsuccessfully, and protests divided neighbors who supported or opposed the highway. A bloody fistfight exposed the level of neighbors' hostility. Even before completion, the highway was divisive, but after completion, it would sever neighborhoods and isolate many. It would divide wildlife corridors for large mammals and possibly lead to local extinctions. It would reroute two watersheds and culvert streams. Multiple destructive disconnections were concentrated in one action. The highway fight dragged on for years.

As earth-moving equipment approached the highest elevations, even neutral observers mourned losing the mountain. The mountain was disappearing before their eyes. Just days before grading would reach the summit, an agreement halted construction of the freeway. State legislation eventually stopped the highway altogether, but not before extensive damage had been done to topography, vegetation, habitats, and hydrology. The highway fight had also destroyed neighborhood cooperation. The design of the park became the forum for hostility.

Competing neighborhood groups could not work together after their divisive battle. Without a spirit of mutualism, only mistrust and anger lingered. Neighborhoods east of Reseda Ridge still supported the highway and hoped that it would relieve the cut-through traffic that clogged their small residential streets. Neighborhood groups west of Reseda Ridge joined with environmentalists to oppose it to save wildlife habitat and hiking trails. On the surface, that seemed to be the gist of the conflict. Planning a park with these discordant parties was impossible, but there were hints that the hidden battle was over larger stakes. Were the neighborhoods mere pawns to unseen parties?

Someone suggested making a power map as a way to understand the conflict. A simple diagram showed the Encino Traffic Safety Committee on one side supporting the new highway and the Friends of Caballero Canyon on the other side fighting it. Conciliatory neighbors were added to the diagram to get the warring groups to work together to plan the park. In public, the conflict indeed focused on the Safety Committee and others who sought to free their neighborhoods from traffic. They were supported by various city agencies and Los Angeles City Councilman Marvin Braude's office. Neighbors added the names of individuals whom we did not know. The Friends of Caballero Canyon, on the other hand, were joined by dispersed neighborhood associations and environmental groups. More people opposed the highway than supported it. Some claimed the real fight related to a large development project on nearby land owned by Bob Hope. It seemed plausible that real estate deals fueled the neighborhood battle. A confidential memorandum surfaced at the Encino Traffic Safety Committee. Rumors of sexual intrigue filled the power map. Residents worried because they recalled the 1974 film *Chinatown* (in which a conspiracy involving water, real estate, and corrupt government officials is revealed). Few feared for their personal safety, but because they felt that they were prying into a secret world, they were cautious when they added names to the power map.

Within a year, more details became transparent. The real conflict was not between local groups. Rather, L.A. City Councilman Braude was pitted against agencies that were trying to preserve wildlife habitat and park land—including the Santa Monica Mountains Conservancy, the California state parks, and the California attorney general. Curiously, Braude, who had long supported environmental causes, was now pushing for a highway in an area he once had envisioned as an urban wilderness. Braude was bewildered by the controversy, but a key staff person was not. Key staff supported the project against any detractors. One staff member was central in the new geometry of the power map, which revealed personal and political lives that were tied to major land developers and real estate speculators. It appeared that Braude's office was leading the effort to build the highway in spite of him because it would create access to land that was otherwise undevelopable, which would produce millions of dollars of personal profit. This explained why the pro-highway neighborhood groups were well funded. A maze of go-betweens, facilitators, and expediters for real estate speculators was supporting unsuspecting but appreciative neighborhoods.

Power maps revealed that the conflict between neighborhoods was fueled by real estate speculation far beyond the locality.

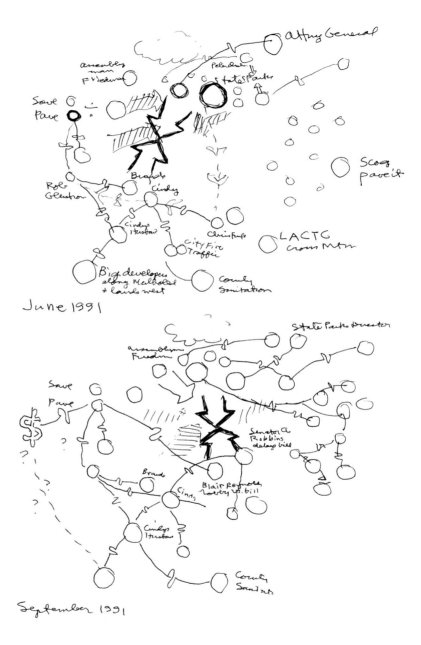

June 1991

September 1991

Enabling Form

Several months later, the power map shifted again. State Assemblyman Terry Friedman introduced legislative bill AB1152 to stop the highway. Suddenly, the entire Los Angeles City Council dropped its plans for the highway and endorsed AB1152. Unanimous support from local government made the bill a consent calendar item, and it moved swiftly through the legislature until opposition arose unexpectedly on the floor of the state senate. The neighborhood groups who wanted the highway had mysteriously raised enough money to pay a lobbyist to lead an organized charge to defeat AB1152. Then a powerful state senator inexplicably delayed the bill, even though it did not apply to his district. Why was he interested in it? The trail led back to real estate interests via the pro-highway neighborhoods and indirectly through Councilman Braude's office. The senator who delayed the bill had long been supported by real estate interests and reportedly had land investments with someone on Braude's staff. Unbeknown to any of these people, the state senator was under investigation and cooperating with law enforcement authorities. His conversations were being electronically recorded. The lobbying effort against AB1152 coincidentally was becoming a part of criminal evidence. In spite of delays, AB1152 passed and was signed into law. The highway was stopped. The senator was convicted.

What have sex, lies, and real estate got to do with connectedness? The power maps for the Reseda Ridge project revealed the true relationships fueling the confrontation between supporters and opponents. One critical piece of information emerged. Many residents of neighborhoods that were leading the public effort to complete the highway were, in fact, against it. When they realized that the battle was about real estate development and was not a neighborhood disagreement, they could work together to plan the park. For residents on opposite sides of the issue, a common enemy emerged—real estate interests with undue power to influence public action. Power maps, the most important drawings made during this design process, revealed unsettling political domination. They helped to diffuse local animosity. Power is one expression of connectedness and is fundamental to city design. Power should be mapped—just like topography, vegetation, and traffic—as part of any initial project inventory.

Plans for Reseda Ridge Park progressed rapidly in a more cooperative atmosphere. There was an overwhelming desire to restore topography where mountains had once risen and to recreate wildlife habitat along routes cleared for the highway. Citizens wanted to rebuild the mountains and restore the

native chaparral landscape. From a technical point of view, the restoration of the topography was unfathomable. The mountain had been removed for over a mile, side canyons had been filled, and arroyos culverted. Caballero Canyon, the largest watershed, had been partly filled and was subject to flooding due to diversions. Flash floods scoured the main arroyo, uprooted mature sycamore trees, and destroyed stream banks in less than a year. To accomplish community goals would require removing recent fill, stabilizing Caballero Canyon, and finding millions of cubic feet of earth to rebuild the mountains. An early estimate for restoration exceeded $50 million. That cost was prohibitive.

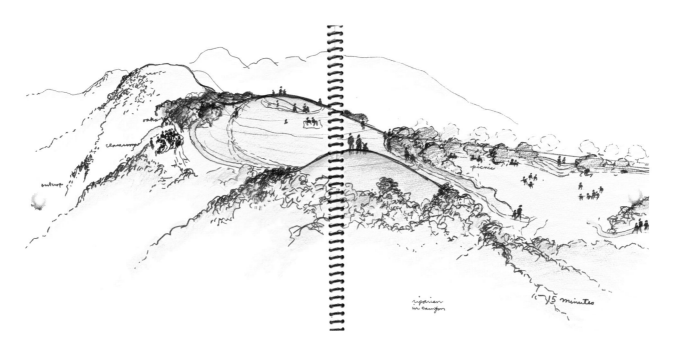

Neighbors previously for and against the freeway agreed that the lost mountain should be recreated, but their vision was prohibitively expensive.

Enabling Form

Planning proceeded with unjustified optimism. The final design called for rebuilding the mountain peaks to approximate historic elevations while meeting city standards for engineered fill. The city required the steepest natural areas be graded with maximum 2:1 slopes and to have soil compacted by construction criteria. The plan specified re-creation of preexisting microwatersheds, rerocking, and revegetating watercourses to naturalize flooding and erosion in Caballero Canyon. Other principles of the plan included fitting topographic forms seamlessly into surrounding mountain ecology and reshaping land to create dramatic settings for urban wilderness recreation.

The watershed restoration and stabilization of Caballero Canyon was accomplished quickly because it was relatively inexpensive. The costly topographic restoration languished. Where once 1,100-foot peaks had risen above Los Angeles, the flat and lifeless plain remained after several seasons. Some citizens wanted to revegetate the flattened mountain.

One day, someone at the Conservancy contacted Paul Burns, a dirt contractor. The scale of operations of dirt contractors in Los Angeles surprised us. Dirt contractors are big business. Burns agreed to haul fill from nearby construction sites to rebuild Reseda Ridge. He had just signed a contract to remove landslide debris from the Pacific Coast Highway, and the Reseda site was more accessible than any of his other disposal sites. The landslides had resulted from a Malibu fire that in the summer of 1993 burned thousands of acres and that in the winter allowed the bare mountains above Malibu to become saturated with rain. With no vegetation to hold the soil in place, catastrophic landslides had occurred, and some of these earthslides closed the main coastal artery through Los Angeles. Removal of the landslides had to be done on an emergency basis. Burns won the contract. Because he cut his hauling costs by three-fourths by disposing of the slide debris on Reseda Ridge, he was able to compact the fill and sculpt the earth to our specifications at no charge. He completed the first phase of the mountain restoration, which had been estimated at $7 million, at no cost whatsoever to the public. One man's trash is another's treasure, and evidently one woman's landslide is another woman's mountain.

For over two years, Burns dumped landslide dirt at Reseda Ridge. As the mountains grew back, geologic time seemed to move in fast-forward motion. Ed Lasack, one of Burns's foremen, oversaw compacting and grading for the bases of new mountains and then for the peaks themselves. Detailed

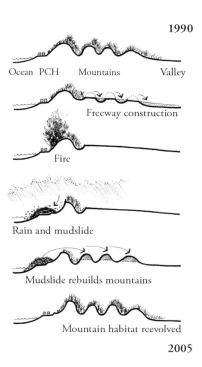

1990

Ocean PCH   Mountains   Valley

Freeway construction

Fire

Rain and mudslide

Mudslide rebuilds mountains

Mountain habitat reevolved

2005

The ecology network of dirt

Compacting the new mountain

Native planting

Restored habitat

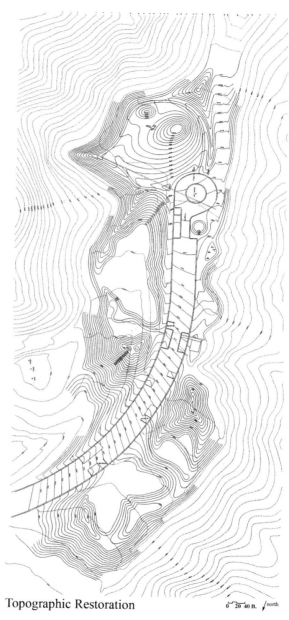

Topographic Restoration

0 20 40 ft.   north

The topographic restoration plan guided rebuilding
the lost mountain, satisfying city slope standards
and providing accessible trails, recreation space,
unparalleled views, and lepidopteran earth art.

Enabling Form

plans for topographic and vegetation restoration served as a guide, but only Lasack knew the specific earth-shaping capability of his machinery. His inspiration came increasingly from the land itself. On a bulldozer, he created land flows that were more in harmony with the surrounding landscape than the working drawings were. A series of peaks memorialize the ones that had been lost and offer extraordinary views. They play against the geometry of the San Fernando Valley grid. Meadows grow in bilaterally organic shapes and are edged with natural vegetation, providing butterfly and ground-bird habitats and flat areas for free play. Native oak and walnut groves provide shade for picnic areas. Parking spaces, teen hangouts, and staging areas for hiking and mountain biking are absorbed on a seventy-four-foot wide section of pavement, a remnant of the abandoned highway. The new mountains were replanted in native plant communities, creating a mosaic that reflected aspect and use.

The park consists of nothing but topographic form, vegetation, and rock, and each serves multiple and sometimes contradictory purposes. The landforms create height and depression. Concavities hide all of the world but the big-sky canopy. Landforms mimic the natural context but, when slightly deformed from natural flows, provide settings more suitable for the informal soccer play and large-group picnics favored by Hispanic immigrants. Native plants enclose wheelchair-accessible trails that lead to spectacular gridded views. There are easy walks favored by the elderly, open trails where women feel safe to walk alone, and peaks too steep for anyone but hardy climbers.

There are no benches, unless you count rocks. A treasure trove of large sandstone slabs and spherical concretions was unearthed from earlier road construction. They make perfect benches, sofas, view spots, mazes, and markers. Each rock was picked for size and shape, numbered, and clustered by use. Ed Lasack placed each rock to create private spots and public gathering places, as well as unnatural geometric swaths through the topography and vegetation. Rocks form bastions perpendicular to Reseda Boulevard, celebrating the defeat of the highway. Rocks also provide picnic tables, benches, and play areas for children.

Reseda Ridge Park never would have been created had connectedness not guided the process. The fill dirt is an archetypal fish head. A creative staff person at the Santa Monica Mountains Conservancy discovered the connection between our need and the needs of Paul Burns, the dirt contractor,

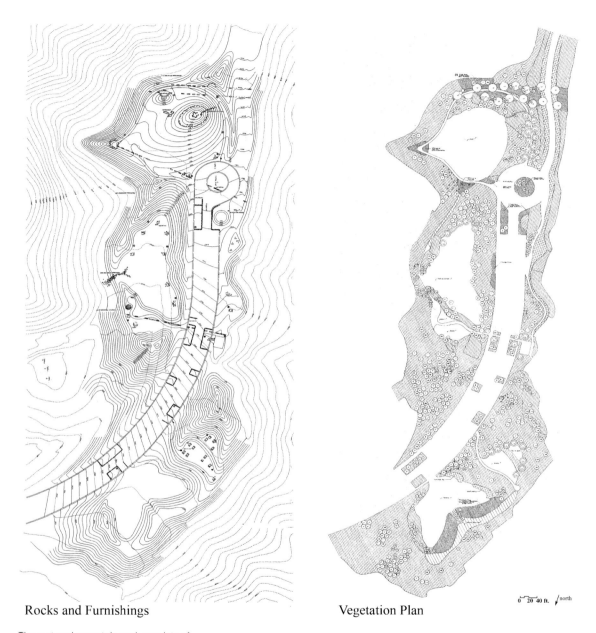

Rocks and Furnishings

The restored mountain park consists of
topography, vegetation, and rock that are
native to the immediate locale.

Vegetation Plan

0 20 40 ft.   ⇗ north

Enabling Form

by thinking about the entire network of construction in Los Angeles. That staff person ventured way outside the box to put together things that typically do not go together. Dirt contractors are not seen as environmental stewards in Los Angeles, and for a dirt contractor to restore hundreds of acres of despoiled landscape is unheard of. Ed Lasack, the foreman, shortened the miles traveled to remove landslide debris and reduced the ecological footprint by over 75 percent.

The rocks were another resource discovered and reused with little cost of energy. A Conservancy ecologist created a vegetative mosaic that supports a full range of species—from riparian skinks to upland birds, raptors, deer, and mountain lions—and makes a complete food web. He did this by using only the native species that he found within a quarter mile of the site. Adjacency helps.

In a different realm, the power map exposed the divisive impacts of the highway before it was built. Mapping the names of those who held power revealed the hidden hands of financial interests. This enabled people from various warring neighborhoods to recognize common concerns and develop a mutualism for creative thinking to flower. In all these ways, connectedness supported ecological democracy.

Native playground

Urban wilderness trails

Picnic and soccer green

Fairness

Urban habitation where ecological democracy can flourish requires fair design processes and a fair final form. Fairness is fundamental to lasting democracy. Either citizens must perceive laws to be clear, impartial, and equitable, or they will resort to the time-honored American recourse of disobedience. In an ecological democracy, citizens are responsible for obeying just laws and disobeying unjust ones.

As citizens participate in the day-to-day aspects of city design, subtle questions of equity arise. Who has information? Who does and does not understand and have access to local government agencies? Who typically participates in the design process, and who doesn't? Who lacks power to influence decisions that affect locality? Mundane compared to the excitement of civil protest, such issues are central to enabling meaningful participation and contributions. Equal access to information is critical for creating legitimate involvement and a well-informed public. In this regard, city designers play a central role by developing better ways to communicate complex information.[1]

Design Precedent, I'd like you to meet Environmental Justice.

The ongoing tension between justice and the formal ordering that is needed to design a city momentarily concretizes the gains and losses in fairness.

De jure exclusion

Omissive exclusion

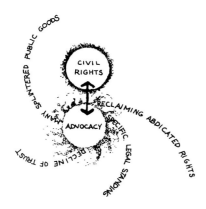

Side effects of civil rights

Fair process must be matched with fair city form. American city form contributes to racial, economic, gender, and age segregation and discrimination. In the words of an old proverb, cities make some citizens feel like sparrows near a hawk's nest. This was obvious during the civil rights movement of the mid-twentieth century.[2] Freeway construction and urban renewal, which were favored city-design strategies, destroyed neighborhoods and uprooted primarily black and poor people.[3] Urban renewal earned the nickname "negro removal" because it condemned poor neighborhoods, bulldozed homes, forced residents to move, and used the land for development to serve wealthier citizens.[4] This racism and exploitation of the poor eventually met fierce and often violent resistance. Over time, the injustices became less blatant.[5] Today, three formal considerations are directly related to fairness in city design—accessibility, inclusion, and equal distribution of resources and amenities. They apply not just to poor African Americans but other minorities and groups.

There are ongoing tensions between justice and the formal ordering that is necessary to plan any city. This was powerfully stated by Martin Luther King Jr. in his "Letter from Birmingham Jail." There he concluded that the great stumbling block for fairness is not the Ku Klux Klan but the white moderate "who is more devoted to order than to justice." King cast order and justice as opposing forces, saying that order without justice becomes a dangerously structured dam that blocks the flow of social progress.[6] The designer of the urban landscape must be constantly conscious of the tensions among the order given to a landscape, the fairness it concretizes, and the injustices it embodies. Through a predictably iterative process, injustices resurface and attack newly created landscapes to make just the unjust order that has been imposed.

Accessibility

To enable more citizens to participate, cities must be designed to provide access to the necessities of everyday life, to appropriate information, and to places for public decision making.[7] Land-use segregation, the remote location of important facilities, and the high cost of transportation make accessibility a debilitating problem for the powerless.[8] Home and work are increasingly separated by zoning that specializes land use, creating commuting annoyances for millions of Americans. For the poorest citizens, this

Enabling Form

combination of land-use and transportation design prevents them from competing for jobs. This is exacerbated by the shift of postindustrial employment centers to green fields with service jobs that are too far distant for the less mobile poor to benefit.[9] As most of us eschew public transit, lack of access to the private car increasingly divides our society. This escalated from a daily handicap to a matter of survival in the aftermath of Hurricane Katrina when the poorest citizens were abandoned as the affluent evacuated New Orleans by private vehicles. These patterns of city design deny access and not just for central-city minorities. Many low-density bedroom suburbs deny mothers access to jobs and deny children access to diversity.[10] Inaccessibility most affects the poor, minorities, new immigrants, women, the very young, and the elderly.[11]

Similarly, transportation costs and remote locations make many facilities like national parks and forests inaccessible. When nearby, as in the Angeles National Forest in Southern California, the urban poor are consistent users.[12]

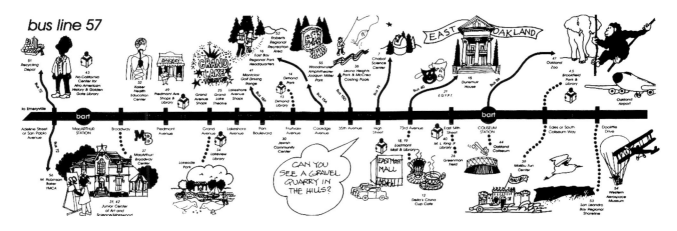

After Oakland teens described inaccessible places they wished to visit in the city, Michael Southworth designed easy-to-read bus maps that helped open new venues for youth.

In one particularly innovative approach to increase access to urban resources, Michael Southworth worked with low-income teens in Oakland to identify the places that they wanted to visit but were difficult to reach. Southworth notes that he was able to predict only half of these places. He offered more suggestions to broaden the possibilities, and those that appealed to the youth were mapped. The teens figured out transit routes that provided easy and inexpensive access to desired locations. Since Southworth had found that 70 percent of the Oakland youth age nine through sixteen used the bus, compared to 49 percent who used the subway, they focused on accessing places by bus. Southworth had also found that teenagers read some types of maps more easily than others. Linear maps, the plan view that designers use most frequently, allowed teens to plan desired routes. Teens found pictorial maps more useful in locating places accurately. Southworth created the landmark map that provided both easy route planning and accurate place location. In Oakland, forty-thousand maps for teens were published, overcoming many obstacles of access and opening the city to new users.[13] Attention to the special needs of those lacking access to the city is essential in overcoming inequities.

Inclusion

Visual integration

Visual separation

Fairness is diminished by city design that explicitly or implicitly excludes certain citizens. Although "whites only" signs have been replaced by economic barriers and city-design policies, segregation by race, income level, and life-cycle stage deepens. Exclusion results from overt policies, such as the resident-only policy for parks in Dearborn, Michigan (where Detroit residents were forbidden from using Dearborn parks with fines up to $500) and the pass and permit policy for beaches and parks in Greenwich, Connecticut (where out-of-towners were required to purchase a $308 season pass and a $100 parking permit to use beaches and parks there).[14] Such exclusionary policies are common. In many cases, exclusion is a by-product of policies like zoning restrictions, large-lot subdivisions, and environmental protection.[15]

Exclusive policies are reinforced by design—from land-use designations to the placement of doorways. Architecture makes manifest the power of property.[16] Community gardens with locked gates, with uniformed guards, or without benches give an unspoken message: do not enter. Both

Enabling Form

physical and psychological barriers are intimidating forces. Exclusion in design typically is directed at the poor, disenfranchised, and marginal, parks that are overtaken by criminal activities or undesirable groups prevent children and the elderly from using the public landscape. By thoughtful design, many of these problems can be mitigated.

Lafayette Square in Oakland was long known as Old Men's Park because seniors met at the park daily. Over time, homeless people and drug users and sellers changed the park's image from a friendly meeting place for old men to a fearful place that scared away many would-be users. About ten years ago, the square was revitalized in an effort by some to rid the park of undesirables, but landscape architect Walter Hood was determined not to exclude any users. His process was compellingly inclusive. A series of spaces serve different users around the edges of the square and along a major walkway through the square. A hillock separates users who might not want to interact. Hood created settings that accommodate all the existing users and a wide array of new users. Young children, old men, middle-income Koreans, lower-income African Americans, concert-goers, and the haircut man and others who engaged in an informal economy all report that the park is theirs. Hood's design is striking because it reverses the topography of inclusion. Typically, a democratic park has a large flat and slightly lower shared plane in the middle; different users collect around the edges, separated but within view of each other. Here the hillock prevents distant eye contact.

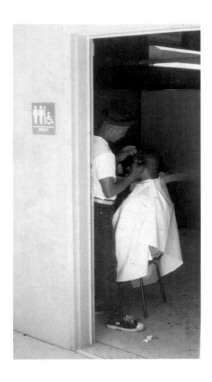

Lafayette Square Park is inclusive by design with topography that is shaped to separate settings visually for multiple users who play, linger in the shade, or cut hair in the toilet.

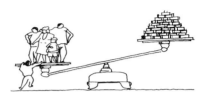

Unequal distribution of resources

Equal Distribution of Resources and Amenities

Uneven distribution of resources prevents healthy development. It precludes the active public participation of millions of citizens. It may be understandable that the wealthiest Americans disproportionately control private resources, but inequities in the public distribution of clean air and water, open space, education, other public facilities, pollution, flooding, and toxic wastes are unconscionable. Generally, public resources are dispersed inversely proportionate to need. The wealthy get most public goods and few public liabilities. The powerless get few public goods and most of the public liabilities.[17]

Consider the disposal of toxic wastes. Robert Bullard and his colleagues found a consistent pattern of waste disposal in the poorest neighborhoods and cities. In one area, deadly PCB-laced oils were disposed of by being spread along roads in predominantly black communities. Such locally unwanted land uses predominate in the poorest communities.[18] You may think that this is true only elsewhere, but consider your own community. Where are the undesired land uses like heavy industry, incinerators, the sewer plant, and landfill located?

Then consider a desired public amenity, such as public open space. Where is most of it located? In Los Angeles, a majority of the city's parks are in wealthy neighborhoods, referred to as "movie-star habitats." The city's west side, which includes Bel Air and Beverly Hills, has 13,310 acres of public open space, compared with seventy-five acres for the entire southeastern section of the city where most poor people of color live.[19] Without access to parks, many Los Angeles youth grow up without their healthful benefits. Consequences include ecological illiteracy and increased domestic violence.[20] Your city may not have movie-star habitats or such disproportionate amenities, but chances are the resources are not fairly shared.

From time to time, these environmental inequities lead to deadly urban rebellions. More often, they cause sickness and arrested development and prevent the less powerful from contributing fully to their communities. Exposure to high levels of toxics causes cancer and preoccupies time otherwise available for civic action.

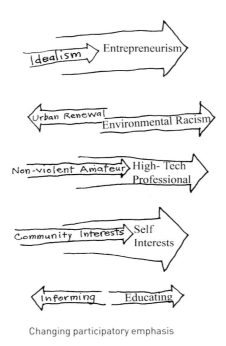

Changing participatory emphasis

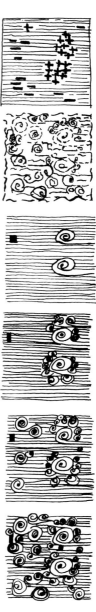

Concentrating positive community energy

Paying Attention to Design

City designers address these issues with subtle actions. Inaccessibility can be rectified by the location of public facilities, well networked public transportation, and integrated land uses. For example, in a highly desirable single-family neighborhood in the East Bay, a designer integrated small, six- to eight-unit apartment buildings at each street corner. Slightly bulkier than adjacent houses, they are small and unobtrusive and fit into the overall character of the neighborhood. Usually, rental apartments would have been segregated into a large complex with fewer amenities and more liabilities than the single-family neighborhood. The integration provides renters access to public facilities and enhances cross-class interactions. Mike Pyatok and Peter Waller have made an art of integrating low- and moderate-income housing into neighborhoods in Oakland and nearby cities. The secret seems to be small projects that are so well designed that they serve the needs of the users yet add architectural value to the surrounding community. In the case of Gateway Commons in Emeryville, designers snuggled seventeen new units of housing into an established neighborhood using a grid pattern that

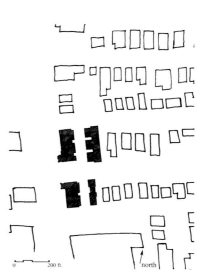

0   200 ft.   north

Creating small, well-designed projects integrates low and moderate-income people into existing neighborhoods, adds value for residents, and overcomes NIMBY actions.

Gateway Commons neighborhood

reflects the existing community. By making the central driveway a pedestrian court and creating a landscaped open space, the plan provides generous places for young children to play, a primary concern of new residents and surrounding neighbors. Every unit has a deck accessible from the kitchen, a valued extension of everyday life in the Bay Area, where only houses for the wealthiest people integrate indoors and out. Although neighbors had opposed earlier plans, they welcomed this project for low-income first-time homebuyers. The high-quality layouts and design elements overcame the usual resistance to higher-density and lower-income residents.[21] Such inclusive design actions require answers to difficult questions. How can land uses that segregate and discriminate be creatively integrated? How can design for poorer citizens be of high enough quality to overcome prejudice? How can activity settings for excluded people be included? Advocates for low-income housing often spend all their energy organizing and ignore design. Both are essential. The brilliance of architects like Pyatok and Waller is paying attention to both.

In a modest but dramatic case, architects listened carefully to senior citizens in San Francisco's Chinatown. They realized that ten thousand elderly Chinese Americans lived in single-room apartments. The apartments—small, cramped, and overstuffed with lifelong possessions—posed immediate earthquake and fire threats to residents' lives. Working with seniors, the design team created multiuse furniture that allowed storage in every nook and cranny. The table structure stores food, and the bed frame stores clothing. By attending to the residents' most critical needs, the designers helped them change depressing rooms into livable space. On seeing her room transformed by the furniture, one senior said, "My life has begun anew."[22]

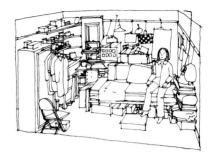

Chinatown apartment before

Mapping Injustices

Most injustices are consciously entrenched. Powerful parties benefit and do not want them addressed. The rest of us are not keen enough to recognize the injustices and often contribute to the inequities. I find myself uncomfortable when I think about Louise Mozingo's research that found that women are often excluded from downtown San Francisco plazas that I like. Men enjoy the bustling corners where they gawk at passing women, but these places make many women uncomfortable. They pass the gawkers only if they must and seek comfortable, quiet places to sit. Mozingo also found that most plazas do not provide seating where a woman wearing a dress can sit modestly.[23] Designers must analyze injustices just as we inventory housing conditions or vegetation patterns.

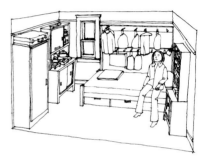

Chinatown apartment after

Fundamental to fairness is accurate accounting of resource distribution. One objective way to assess equities is to map the distribution of various public resources and compare different areas of a city or region. Maps of environmental justice allow scrutiny. They force frank public discussions of critical, controversial inequities. Mapping powerful and powerless places, places that are unloved, and places that are particularly democratic or exclusive may also provoke change. Noting who dominates or is absent from a particular place may likewise be useful.[24] Mapping that shows who is missing from a place may make injustices visible in the landscape.[25] Redressing environmental injustices requires strong technique and determination.

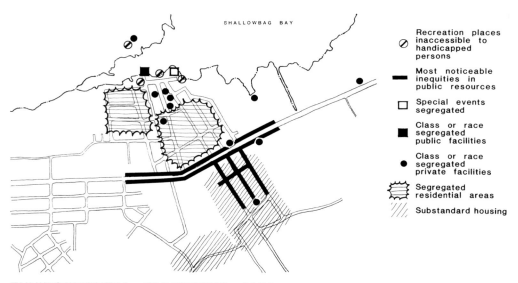

ENVIRONMENTAL INJUSTICES 1980
Most noticeable inequities in public resources

Legend:
- ⊘ Recreation places inaccessible to handicapped persons
- ▬ Most noticeable inequities in public resources
- ☐ Special events segregated
- ■ Class or race segregated public facilities
- ● Class or race segregated private facilities
- Segregated residential areas
- Substandard housing

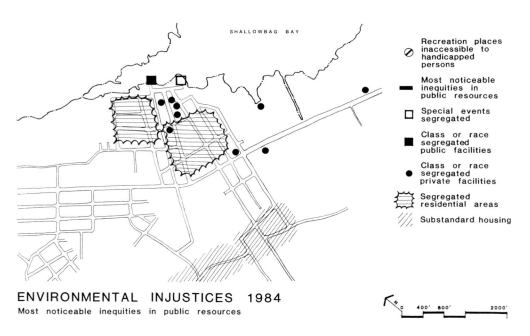

ENVIRONMENTAL INJUSTICES 1984
Most noticeable inequities in public resources

Legend:
- ⊘ Recreation places inaccessible to handicapped persons
- ▬ Most noticeable inequities in public resources
- ☐ Special events segregated
- ■ Class or race segregated public facilities
- ● Class or race segregated private facilities
- Segregated residential areas
- Substandard housing

N   0   400'   800'   2000'

Mapping injustices over time calls attention to them, makes them undeniable, forces frank public discussion, and allows changes to be monitored.

Enabling Form

Fair Landscapes Empower

The Fruitvale District is one of the most densely populated areas of Oakland. It is the most diverse and one of the poorest. It has the greatest concentration of children of any district in the entire city. Fruitvale and the adjacent San Antonio District have the highest proportion of neighborhood-bound residents and the least open space. Only 13 percent of residents are adequately served in terms of the city's own standards for open space: there is less than two-thirds of an acre of local parkland per thousand people. Oakland districts in the more affluent hills have over nine acres of parkland per thousand people, plus larger lots with private open space and access to thousands of acres of regional parks. A 1999 study concluded that Fruitvale needed at least sixty-four acres of additional open space to reach parity with city standards. The report warned that the lack of recreation and open space had moved beyond a matter of quality of life: "This is a crisis that requires immediate action to avoid grave consequences to health and child development."[26]

For years, leaders had been aware of this inequity, but until it was mapped, the disparity was easy to ignore. Although many unsuccessful attempts had been mounted to acquire more open space, the Lila Wallace Urban Parks Initiative, a national nonprofit foundation, spurred unusual cooperation among local groups. The Fruitvale Recreation and Open Space Initiative (FROSI) was formed between the Spanish Speaking Unity Council, the Trust for Public Land, the University of California, and the City of Oakland. The goal of FROSI was to identify issues, raise awareness of the injustices, and prod various authorities into action to acquire open space and develop recreation facilities in Fruitvale.

They first did joint fact finding to define the existing circumstances, compare those to other areas of the city, and uncover undiscovered assets that might lead to success where uninformed outrage had previously failed.

The research revealed that ten times as much open space was available in affluent areas than in Fruitvale's neediest neighborhood. With few opportunities to gain more, open space was being lost to other high-priority actions. Portable classrooms, added to accommodate overcrowded schools, reduced open space in schoolyards. School gardens, taken for granted throughout the region, were paved over in Fruitvale. New Latin immigrants competed for the few athletic fields and other places to play soccer. Informal play places were in short supply.

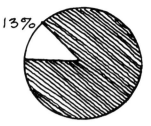

Adequately served residents

Arnstein's ladder in Fruitvale

The open-space distribution map for Oakland revealed enormous disparities in the provision of parks. Some neighborhoods had over nine acres per thousand residents, and some in Fruitvale had less than half an acre per thousand residents.

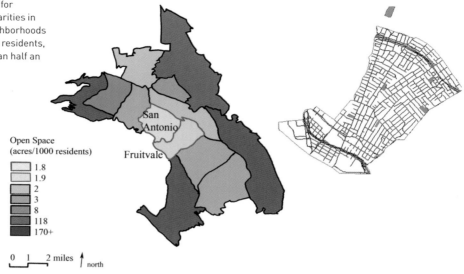

Open Space
(acres/1000 residents)

1.8
1.9
2
3
8
118
170+

0   1   2 miles   ↑ north

Open Space Distribution Map

On the other hand, FROSI uncovered unusual resources. Of twenty miles of waterfront in Oakland, much in transitional industrial land uses, two miles are in Fruitvale and offer the potential for both new economies and open space that reconnects people to the inaccessible estuary. Waterfront lands could readily add thirteen acres of open space. Two major streams, the Sausal and Peralta creeks, run the length of Fruitvale and, although culverted, still provide native vegetation and flood-control projects where recreation could be incorporated, adding fifty-one acres of open space. There are also a few vacant lots and railroad rights of way at strategic points where an additional five acres of open space could be developed. Several schools and existing parks are close enough to each other that they could be linked by green streets and shared recreation facilities, adding another thirteen acres. A vibrant neighborhood shopping district could be enhanced by claiming about 2.5 acres of open space from unnecessarily wide streets. An industrial shift to high technology, coupled with zoning changes, could add seven acres of open space as part of new employment centers and implement a continuous Bay Trail through the Fruitvale waterfront.

Such a detailed accounting of possible resources had never before been done, in part explaining why earlier efforts to secure open space had faltered.

Step One: Identify Schools and Parks

Step Two: Connect Waterways

0   .5 mile ↑ north

One strategy in Fruitvale uses green streets to link schools with nearby parks, streams, and the bay, adding thirteen acres of neighborhood open space and a potential for shared recreation and education.

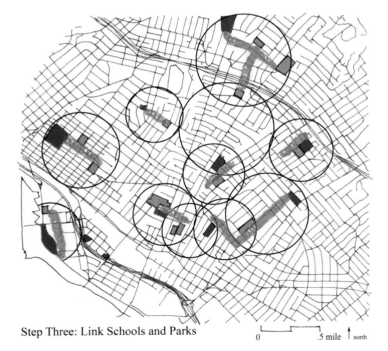

Step Three: Link Schools and Parks

0   .5 mile ↑ north

Inaccessible water

Fact finding exposed embarrassing injustices. It highlighted realistic solutions. While endorsing this multifaceted approach, FROSI partners realized that implementation would occur in fragments. Small parcels would be improved bit by bit. Two strategies, a long-term dream and short-terms actions, were employed simultaneously. Eight varied demonstration projects were proposed. The linking of Sanborn Park with Hawthorne-Whitton School has already begun. Union Point, a nine-acre former industrial site, ranked as a top priority for open-space acquisition because its size and location offered the potential for opening the inaccessible estuary. The purchase of vacant lots at three strategic sites and the development of the Sausal Creek Flood Control Easement and the railroad right of way were other demonstration efforts.

Armed with an undeniable analysis of inequities, a long-term plan, and a handful of immediate actions, FROSI partners moved forward. With the Spanish Speaking Unity Council leading, the FROSI team mounted a campaign—Let's Dream It! Let's Build It!—to create the first major new open space, Union Point Park. The first obstacle was that the land was owned by the Port of Oakland, which has no recreation mandate. But the Unity Council is one of the most effective nonprofits in the Bay Area—well grounded in the grass roots of Fruitvale and well connected to institutions far beyond its borders. Arabella Martinez, the Spanish Speaking Unity Council director, worked the politics behind the scene. Organizers collected three thousand petition signatures for the park and one hundred letters of support from community-based groups. Residents staged acts of protest and solidarity. The City and Port of Oakland agreed in 1998 to dedicate the land for park purposes. The Port of Oakland and the California Coastal Conservancy joined the FROSI partnership. Dedicated staff assumed stewardship roles in making the park a reality. Friends of Cal Crew, a group that supported the rowing team at the University of California, Berkeley, also joined the FROSI partnership to help build a new crew facility in the park.

The next hurdle was to develop a master plan for the park that satisfied the multiple partners. Since the primary intention was to overcome the inequity of recreation facilities in Fruitvale, it was logical to find out precisely what local residents considered most essential. The Unity Council knew that to reach the diverse community would require an unusual participatory design process. Not the typical middle-class neighborhood, Fruitvale consists of many enclaves of new immigrants, many of whom do not speak English. Every meeting had to be conducted in Spanish, Vietnamese, and

Enabling Form

English. Many residents are newcomers with questionable residency status and are reluctant to attend public meetings. FROSI sponsored informal block-by-block gatherings and met with over fifty community organizations and one thousand individuals. The Spanish Speaking Unity Council leader insisted on involving youth not in a token manner but as legitimate, fully empowered participants.

In the spring of 1998, boat and walking tours of the site were organized to introduce community members to the future park and to solicit their ideas about the most important activities that should be included. Hundreds of people toured, and groups were conducted in multiple languages. Preliminary plans were developed based on the goals of the leaders, residents, and FROSI partners.

Overcoming the acute shortage of recreation facilities while not over-filling the open space with structures required careful prioritization of activities. Many were culture specific. Latino groups wanted fields for informal soccer that were in view from picnic groups. The picnic areas, they said, should be as natural as possible, should accommodate extended families and other large groups of up to one hundred people, and be close enough so that picnickers could watch family soccer events. They also wanted play areas for small children.

The Vietnamese strongly urged a public pier for fishing, a community room for their cultural events, and storage facilities for celebration decorations. They also wanted safe places for children to play near the community room.

Adults from various ethnic groups wanted a large, grassy field for community events and their own cultural celebrations. Older people asked for parking spaces that were close enough to the estuary to let them sit in cars and watch the water even in bad weather. Youth argued for public transit to serve the many carless residents and insisted on a bus stop with a roofed shelter.

After the site tour, the top priority for all groups was to provide wildlife habitat and places to watch birds. This had not been a priority until people came to Union Point and saw terns, scaups, and cormorants. More than any other activity, nature observation transcended cultural differences.

These activities and dozens more had to be evaluated for appropriateness. As in most underserved communities, there was pressure to meet all the expressed needs in the little available space, which almost always leads to conflicts. When too many activities are jammed into one place, the result is not just increased playground accidents and tension between users but also

A shared vision

Site tour by boat

Youth questioned the original Union Point Park plan in which Cal Crew privatized the prime location within the site.

the cluttering of the open space. The psychological benefits of open space are lost. At Union Point, residents and professionals prioritized what best fit this waterfront park and what could be located at other sites.

The FROSI partners, while supportive of community empowerment and the program that local people articulated, had their own agendas. For example, the Coastal Conservancy wanted public access along the waterfront, part of a much larger Bay Trail; Cal Crew chose the prime park spot for its building and later acknowledged its intention to prevent public access along "its" waterfront. This conflict over public access along the shore damaged the partnership. The arrogance and heavy-handedness of crew leaders betrayed the spirit of cooperation, exposing their lack of interest in open-space injustices in Fruitvale.

Youth first questioned the appropriateness of the Cal Crew facility. In the fall of 1998, the Spanish Speaking Unity Council organized a workshop for teens to prioritize their objectives. Youth participated in a boat adventure tour, Cal Crew boat rides, and a walking tour to analyze the site. In small groups, they evaluated the activities proposed by adults and made their own programs for the park. They built models to showcase their visions for Union Point Park.[27] More than half of the teen groups questioned why Cal

Crew should occupy the place with the best views and best access to the estuary. Several groups wanted to eliminate the building and said that it was inappropriate in a public park. Most of the teens wanted facilities that were currently unavailable to them—a youth center that would sponsor recreation and job training, open fields for free play and informal sports, a hard-surface multipurpose court, picnic and barbecue areas, a high-quality bus shelter, boat rides, and wildlife areas. One ninth grader described her goals: "I am from a big family. There are ten of us, so my parents don't have lots of time to spend with each child. I want to see activities at Union Point so my brothers and sisters have something to do, so they stay out of trouble."[28] After their priorities were adopted as part of the master plan, teens volunteered to present the proposed plan to community groups. Others organized a leadership forum to lobby for funds in Oakland and Sacramento. Eventually, one of the groups that had been most difficult to engage became full members in the city design process and wielded unusual power. When Cal Crew withdrew from the partnership six months later, the youth could see firsthand the results of their authority. The final master plan reflected all the youth priorities, and construction on the first phase will be completed before this book is published.[29]

Youth design workshop

The final plan replaced Cal Crew facilities with public access to the water and a hilltop from which the entire estuary can be viewed.

The promise of change

Supportive Change

Counterproductive Change

Transformative Change

Fruitvale groups avoided the downward spiral that often dominates poor communities; this enabled them to achieve transformative change.

The several demonstration projects that have been undertaken will not alone rectify the past inequities in the distribution of open space in Oakland, but it is a beginning. For our purposes, the Fruitvale effort is instructive. It shows the extraordinary energy that is required to achieve a modicum of fairness. Partnerships far outside the locality are needed, and they may come with agendas that are not necessarily in the best interests of the local community. In Fruitvale's case, local-use partners prevailed. Some of the difficulties associated with creating an inclusive design process could not be overcome. In this instance, the Spanish Speaking Unity Council had the contacts and resources to reach out to many different groups, all of whom participated. However, some people who speak less well represented languages were not involved at all. Some of the most serious needs of various ethnic groups were met by the park plan, but many remain to be incorpo-

Hills and valleys were constructed as part of toxic remediation. They, in turn, made microclimates for wetland ecologies and nodes for activities protected from the wind.

Union Point Park added nine acres of badly needed open space and created a common ground for the cultural festivals of the many ethnic groups of Fruitvale.

rated elsewhere. This is a painful reality for designers who seek fairness. Clear priorities were set to avoid overbuilding Union Point and ruining its primary purpose—open space. Most dramatic was the success in empowering youth. The process was organized and transparent. Information was shared. Residents acted with knowledge—about the relative need for open space and also about the priorities of various ethnicities and age groups.

Creating a city that expresses fairness in its procedures and form enables more citizens to participate meaningfully and contribute to a strong ecological democracy. For those most interested in appearances, fairness creates more aesthetically pleasing urban landscapes. Whereas inequitable exploitation of resources produces isolated pockets of beauty, such unjust beauty leaves concomitant areas of desperate ugliness. No landscape can be more beautiful than it is just.

PARKER
CRAIGIE
BERKELEY ST
HASTINGS
FOLLEN
WATER-HOUSE
KIRKLAND
GARDEN ST
JAMES
FOGG ART MU
QUINCY
PRESCOTT
FOSTER PL
WILLARD ST
BRADBURY
DINSMORE
ACACIA
ASH
HILLIARD
BRATTLE
FARWELL
CHURCH
FULLER
STORY
MIFFLIN
PALMER
LINDEN ST
CHATHAM
ROSS
MT AUBURN
NUTTING
UNIVERSITY
BEN-NETT
ELIOT
BOYLSTON ST
WINTHROP
DUNSTER
HOLYOKE
SOUTH
PLYMPTON
BOW
ARROW
GRANT
MIDDLESEX
COWPERTHWAITE
Charles
FLAGG
SOLDIERS
BUSINESS
FIELD
SMITH
STADIUM
WESTERN
ST
Smith Plg

Sensible Status Seeking

Many communities suffer from inferiority complexes. They compensate by being something they are not. Misguided status seekers lose their collective identity and increase wasteful public consumption of scarce resources but never achieve the prestige they desire.[1]

For years, Astoria, Oregon, a port at the mouth of the Columbia River, compared itself unfavorably to Seaside, a charming oceanfront resort nearby. Astoria residents felt ashamed of their blue-collar history of fish-processing plants, shipping, and port activities and wished to become a tourist destination like Seaside. Susceptible to planners who preyed on the community's poor self-image, city leaders approved a plan to bulldoze much of the downtown and port and replace them with a highway, parking, and oversized resort projects. Waterfront businesses, the town's considerable history, and fine historic buildings were scheduled to be razed, and a placeless resort—not at all like charming Seaside, without any relationship to Astoria, and undistinguished from hundreds of other chain hotel complexes all over the world—was scheduled to be built. Worse, the waterfront would be severed from downtown and accessible only by car, creating segregated tourist enclaves.

Some years later, Astoria leaders had second thoughts and, with the help of the Oregon Downtown Development Association, reversed their course. Their alternative reinvestment strategy embraced the working port as both primary industry and attraction for visitors. Public investment is stabilizing and, in some cases, expanding port businesses. Abandoned port buildings are being repaired for a wide variety of new uses, and pedestrian improvements (including sidewalks, flowers, and street furnishings) encourage people to walk from downtown to the waterfront. In stark contrast to the highway proposal, this action has helped reconnect the port and Main Street businesses and has stimulated economic activity in both. Local people have rediscovered the special pleasures of their own town. Visitors come not for staged tourist experiences but rather for the working waterfront that was once a source of local embarrassment. Yes, the fish processing is of major in-

Astoria's authentic attraction

People place

Industrial reuse

People places attract visitors and locals to safe areas where they can view exciting tugboat and cargo exchanges on the river.

terest to tourists. It is real work and authentic entertainment; it allows the city to be what it is. Tourists and local sightseers enjoy the port activity from "people places"—specially designed viewing *aediculae,* which are small, raised, partly enclosed towers. Located not to interfere with the working waterfront, they are close enough so that visitors feel that they are a part of the fish-processing, cargo-loading, and tug-boating activities that usually are hidden from everyone but the laborers. Within walking distance through the waterfront is a one-of-a-kind maritime museum that reinforces the ambiance of the working port. By reversing its ill-placed status seeking, Astoria is revitalizing its economy through an appropriate strategy that is grounded in its traditional, if modest, identity. Its new prestige is a model of place-appropriate economic development.

Status, a measure of one's standing relative to others, is as essential to communities as it is to individuals or chickens. Status lets one city know its place in society just as the pecking order tells chickens in what sequence they eat. Status gives order. It satisfies the need for recognition. There is a blurred line between healthy self-expression and unhealthy striving.[2]

Status seeking is complicated and often intertwined with a desire for community improvement and deeply rooted concepts of progress. We must separate positive from negative progress, never accept it blindly, and always consider the consequences of "progressive events."[3] Just like individuals who try to keep up with the Joneses, we often are motivated to seek progress not because of a genuine need but because of communitywide insecurity—the fear of being looked down on by striving cities nearby.

In less rooted and more mobile societies, social status is dependent on the display of visible signs of prestige.[4] House, neighborhood, car, and landscape become primary expressions, evidence, and measures of social standing, often with disastrous consequences for self, community, and the environment.[5] The environments we inhabit become other-directed, less for personal satisfaction and more to impress other people.[6] Predominant forms of status symbols undermine community and consume the landscape, thereby debilitating ecological democracy. In the following discussion, I describe healthy alternatives for forming the landscape. These constitute sensible status seeking. The intent is not to outlaw status objects but rather to redirect harmful expressions toward positive actions that still fulfill our needs for distinctive recognition. The positive patterns are like sensible shoes: they serve the purpose but are not ostentatiously wasteful; they do not

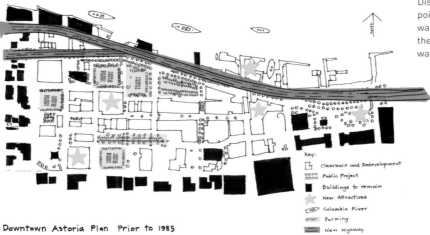

Disregarding its own assets, Astoria was poised to remove much of its working waterfront and sever its downtown from the water by building a highway because it wanted to emulate a resort town nearby.

Key:

⌐ Clearance and Redevelopment
○○○○ Public Project
■ Buildings to remain
★ New Attractions
〜 Columbia River
▥ Parking
▬ New Highway

Downtown Astoria Plan Prior to 1985

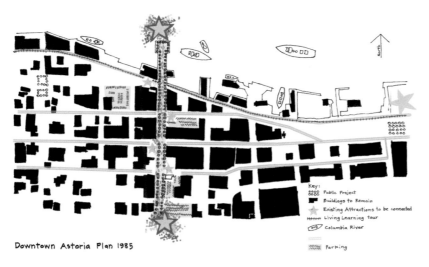

A wiser strategy maintained the industrial waterfront buildings and connected the downtown to the Columbia River via green streets and people places.

Key:

○○○○ Public Project
■ Buildings to Remain
★ Existing Attractions to be connected
⊹⊹⊹ Living Learning tour
〜 Columbia River
▨ Parking

Downtown Astoria Plan 1985

disfigure our feet. Sensible status seeking provides individuals and communities with benefits that have few harmful side effects.[7] Eight healthy forms of status seeking are discussed in the following sections.

Forming Communities to Be What They Are

Unhealthy status seeking originates in feelings of inferiority. Overly consumptive status seeking is often traced to humiliating childhood experiences, deprivation of caring, and the undermining of self-worth.[8] Housing developers have long played on the resulting insecurities of what they describe as "striving, frightened people" to promote sales.[9] The house purchase buys upward mobility and a momentary sense of entering a social class that was previously and possibly still out of reach. For the profoundly insecure, the house in the "right" neighborhood compensates for, although it cannot overcome, emotional abuse and poor self-image. Since nearly everyone is part of the illusionary act of moving on up, the satisfaction is temporary, addicting the status seeker to frequent house purchases in neighborhoods of slightly higher status. The aspiration is to achieve what is perceived to be the possessions of the social class just above through incremental mobility and not dramatic jumps.[10] This is due to fear and housing cost. Status seekers seek prestige but also acceptance by new neighbors. Fear that the "better" neighbors will look down on them dictates striving upward in small steps and learning to blend in.[11] The same process is at work for individuals and cities, as we see in Astoria.[12] As with an individual who works with a psychologist, the design process can be therapeutic for a community with low self-esteem. Only through painful self-examination did Astoria overcome its envy of the charming neighboring town.

In such cases, the designer must make an accurate assessment of local resources and liabilities, show the consequences of various alternative futures, give special attention to assets that might be lost through status seeking, and help the community work from their strengths, not weaknesses. The community must discover its inherent and unique internal form because this allows the community to be what it is. This leads to the creation of new landscapes based on the particular form of the place (see the chapters on Sacredness and Particularness). Designers first became aware of this process when they worked with central-city minorities whose neighborhoods were threatened with urban-renewal clearance. The dominant society declared those neighborhoods to be slums with no redeeming qualities. Many residents accepted these harsh judgments from influential outsiders. They came to view negatively some aspects of their own communities that they had always enjoyed and valued. One critical role for community designers was to help these residents articulate their special assets and distinguish those from things they wanted to change. This was not just an issue for the poor but affected every city-design process.

Let me illustrate. During a participatory process at the Harvard Law School Child Care Center in Cambridge, Massachusetts, a survey of parents revealed a collective desire for a facility that was dramatically unlike the comfortable but funky, converted two-story house that the center occupied at the time. The desired facility envisioned by the parents was sparkling new, a sprawling suburban complex with on-site parking and all the latest plastic play equipment. The staff was suspicious of these survey results, partly because the center was known for its loving atmosphere and somewhat run-down appearance. It was a source of self-deprecating pride for families with children there. It was Harvard, after all; it could be funky. Additional funds almost always went for staff, creating an enviable ratio of one teacher for every three children but frequently deferring maintenance. Staff members readministered the survey by asking the same questions to parents but in small groups using a guided-fantasy technique that is similar to self-hypnosis. They wanted to elicit answers on a subconscious level from the parents about the kinds of environments that were most important from their own childhoods. Many parents agreed to answer the same questions again under hypnotic instructions. The results of the surveys were so at odds they seemed to have been answered by two different groups of people. In a parent-staff meeting, one parent acknowledged his insight. His responses to the first survey described a day-care center in a nearby affluent suburban community. There was embarrassed laughter as other parents followed with similar admissions that they were somewhat ashamed of the appearance of their center when compared to the one used by their wealthier friends. After some reflection, parents refocused their goal for the center to remain a caring, unpretentious place.

The results of the guided fantasy described settings that were consistent with the center—slightly dilapidated, loving, with a rich diversity of experiences for the children. This revealed the inherent internal form of the center and allowed parents to make significant but compatible improvements. The

The Harvard Law School Child Care Center

Nurturing daily life

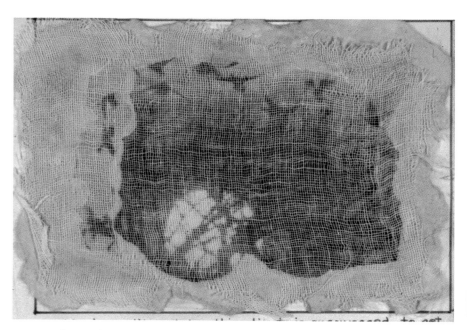

Group self-hypnosis revealed that the day-care parents and staff preferred their plain but loving center; they wanted only a tree that was big enough to climb and more places for nature play.

Enabling Form

single most important change, based on their own childhood memories, was to plant a tree large enough for children to climb. Similarly, parents wanted their children to have frequent experiences in wild nature that could not be provided on the day-care center site itself. An inventory of open spaces nearby revealed resources that had not previously been used. A flowing creek to catch frogs and build dams, flower gardens, and vacant land with wildlife habitat were all within easy walking distance. The natural environments found near Harvard Square were amazing, and excursions to these places became a new feature of the center. Modest changes were made to the building itself, such as more secret lookouts and hiding places on the second floor and enlarged cubbies for children. The cubbies were a practical matter of overcrowding. The idea for the lookouts came from repeated childhood memories of places that provided both prospect and refuge.[13] Sometimes the form of status seeking is not clearly exposed or readily distinguished from the genuine internal form of a place, but is always worth the effort to uncover the internal form because that leads to economical solutions, expresses the spirit of a place, and enables the community to see uniqueness as a matter of pride, even in the face of more prestigious alternatives.

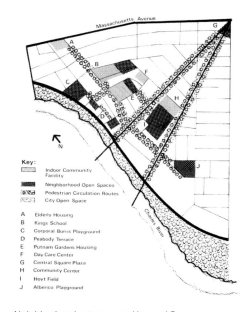

Neighborhood nature near Harvard Square

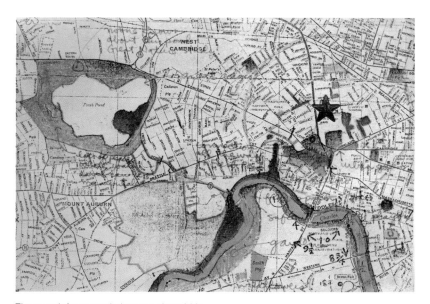

The search for natural places to play within walking distance of the center revealed urban wilderness around Harvard Square to which frequent excursions could be made.

Lessons from Poverty

Status seeking forces people to look constantly upward—not toward heavenly intervention but at the people in the social class above. Moreover, specialized society forces successful people to have a narrow, expert view. This combination greatly restricts the available precedents for habitation from which the community can choose. When the only homes available are within a short, neck-straining gaze into a funnel, the consequences are far more serious than shortsightedness. One way to overcome this status-seeking blindness is to learn consciously from poverty, which is everything considered below one's own social standing, including childhood and other environments of our past, especially when we came from unstatusful places. To status climb, one must cover up previous behavior, speech, and the very environments on which we once relied. These environments, which we reject because we see them as inferior, are often storehouses of precedents that could enable ecological democracy to flourish.

Such precedents are embedded in the environments of new immigrants, people from farm and other backgrounds that require a generalized adaptation to environmental factors, and enclaves of urban and rural poverty. In these cases, mixed land uses, live-work arrangements, multigenerational housing, places of informal socializing, and the aesthetics of repair create a splendid, enabling form in everyday lives.[14] In poorer communities, there is an ethic of "waste not, want not" that is a matter of necessity but can easily become a source of pride, rediscovery, and inspiration. Necessity informed by wisdom leads to inventive improvisations to solve problems of scarcity. In Kenya, this is called *toti toti*. A New York City variation, "available materials, possible ideas," uses wacky thinking to envision and make something from nothing.[15] In rural North Carolina, these improvisations are called "making do." For poor farmers, crazy quilts made of leftover scraps of material not only keep us warm in winter but also are art. My grandmother's crazy quilt is a prized expression of making do. My grandfather's versions of making do were wooden peg planters sculpted from light wood knots, a hay hook shaped into usable form from a broken axle rod, and buzzard wing plows made from discarded metal.

The aesthetics of repair is taught in lesson 184 of *The Tsurezuregusa,* the classic Japanese treatise on beauty. A high-ranking governor was about to visit the humble hermitage of the Zen nun Matsushita. In preparation for

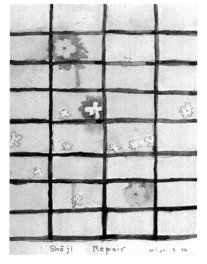

Aesthetics of repair

the official's arrival, the nun repaired the paper windows of the sliding doors in the hermitage. Instead of repapering the whole door, the nun carefully patched each torn pane of the shoji. Her brother, feeling that patching windows was inappropriate for a royal visit, asked the nun if she thought that her patched work was ugly. She replied that she had purposely done it so that the royal visitor would realize it is possible to continue using things by repairing the broken parts.[16] Such self-awareness can remove the blinders that force us to see only what is above us, enabling communities to see possibilities around and below them.

Taking Root

Another form of status-seeking dissatisfaction is busy mobility: the grass is always greener on the other side of the fence. When I was growing up, Coca-Cola was sold only in returnable bottles, and each bottle had the name of the town of its origin imprinted on the bottom. When my friends and I bought Coke, the one with the bottle made closest to home had to buy drinks for the others. The big winner would likely have a bottle from as far away as Roanoke, Virginia, or Spartanburg, South Carolina. The loser would get Roxboro, North Carolina, our hometown. Status increased with mobility, especially to faraway places. And so it has been with most Americans: there is prestige in mobility, especially when it is upward and outward. Since we must keep moving, "leaving any place that doesn't pay off, it's better to pretend that place doesn't matter."[17] This attitude is accompanied by a loss of center, rootedness, and identity.[18] In most communities, there are some people whose actions continually root them and their neighbors in place. In Manteo, North Carolina, Jules Burrus was such a person. In the midst of a terrible economic downturn when many people were seeking fortunes elsewhere, Burrus kept his own business alive and spent years creating new parks for the town through his own labor. He reminded others that this was a place worthy of their roots. Jules's Park testified his commitment to place at a time when few others had faith in Manteo's future. Today the town has made a dramatic turnaround inspired by the work of people like Jules who set their roots deep and resisted easy flight.[19] Design to counter unhealthy status seeking raises the value of a place where one truly belongs, a place that ties the self to a landscape and gives the mind somewhere to go with its thoughts.[20] Every design should help people take root.[21]

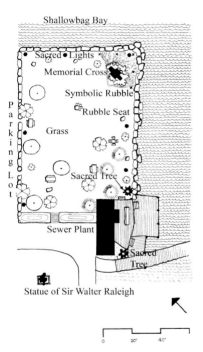

Jules's Park

Easter sunrise at Jules's Park

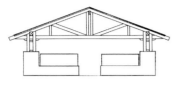

Type 1

Type 2

Type 3

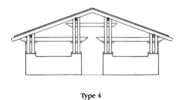

Type 4

Dan Solomon's small houses

Small Is Often Beautiful

An important measure of American status is bigness. This preoccupation, the idolatry of giantism, dominates nearly every aspect of our lives from the fruit we eat and cars we drive to the places we live and work.[22] At work, power is reflected in the largest corner office in the tallest building with the grandest views. Executives note that privileges of an office sometimes are as important as a raise.[23] Bigness is the main perk. Bigness is also essential in the home. Although the automobile is a central status symbol to Americans, the home has been the single most important means of expressing our rank. Home builders have long known that the house is a symbol of success and snob appeal an essential ingredient in marketing.[24]

One key is making the house big and seem even bigger from the street view of passersby. An architect pointed out to her client that the house in one alternative seemed too big for the lot, creating awkward relationships to the neighbors. The designer suggested this alternative be abandoned. The client spontaneously clapped his hands with glee and said, "No, it's perfect!" He actually wanted the house to appear intimidatingly large. Sadly, that house will probably be exchanged for a larger one on a larger property in rapid succession. The size of the American house increased from an average of 1,170 square feet in 1955 to 2,266 square feet in 2000, even as the size of the American household has decreased from an average of 3.4 to 2.6 members.[25] The desire for larger properties is one force in the conversion of agricultural lands and loss of critical wildlife habitats at the suburban fringe. Impulses for bigness have unhealthy consequences for community and the landscape. Perhaps worse, giantism diminishes our happiness because once we become preoccupied with the big, we are blind to small joys. Expelled from a little, friendly world and engaged in the expanded "scale of events in a big alien redefined world," we no longer see virtue in the small.[26]

The plans for the headquarters of a major corporation were presented as a waterfront revitalization strategy at a recent conference. The architects made it clear that the most important aspect of the proposal was that one of the buildings in the megacomplex was to be the tallest in the entire country. There was no discussion about how this project was going to revitalize the area, how it would contribute to the surrounding community, or how it would affect the workers in the building, but it was to be the biggest building. My colleague, Allan Jacobs, passed me a note on a scrap of paper.

Enabling Form

Within a half-inch square, the message was written in his excellent small penmanship: "I aspire to design the world's smallest building."

The Chinese scholar Chuang Chou noted that great knowledge "does not belittle what is small or make much of what is big."[27] E. F. Schumacher saw in smallness just this intelligence. He detailed the humanistic advantages of smallness in every aspect of life. Although he focused on the fallacies of large-scale production, his economic principles relate directly to city design. He insisted that there are inherent thresholds in the scale of human activity that, when surpassed, produce second- and third-order effects that subtract from and usually destroy the quality of life. He called for allowing appropriate decentralization, establishing decision making at the face-to-face level, and building in increments of the small unit of neighborhood. He felt that a land ethic of small ownership would create health, beauty, and permanence and concluded by calling for small cities no larger than 500,000 people.[28]

Restraining the status-seeking impulse for bigness and demonstrating the advantages of smallness in many aspects of human habitation are fundamental to healthy cities. Generally, houses, buildings of other types, and cities themselves can be smaller. Wilderness should be bigger. This is not difficult to do when there is the will. Our best designers have already shown us the advantages of smallness.[29] Dan Solomon's small houses offer one example. As benefits to sustainable happiness become better known, smallness of home and city will become the new status symbols, first of the contrary and then of mainstream culture.

Rare and Commonplace Beauty

Possessing the rare confers status, whether the object is a diamond, a one-of-a-kind car, a new product, or an unusual landscape. In the city, there is a tendency to privatize the most precious landscape resources—hilltops, views, waterfronts, and areas of extraordinary beauty—partly for their expressions of status. Cities, however, are much more fulfilling for their residents if these precious resources are available for public use. Generally, the resources that most distinguish the community should be in public ownership to give overall form to the city. Rare or ecologically fragile landscapes—for example, waterways and steep hillsides—should be protected.[30] The most cherished,

The design for neighborhood open space in Apollo Heights was resolved only after residents found a location for a swimming pool that appeared to be near everyone's backyard.

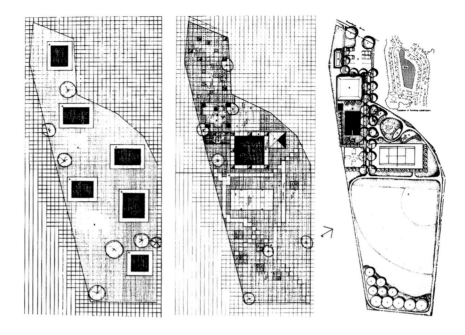

Setagaya's everyday beauty

Enabling Form

distinctive, and fragile aspects of a place, then, become unavailable for individual status consumption.

Public facilities themselves frequently are matters of prestige. During the design process for the central open space in the modest Apollo Heights neighborhood in Raleigh, North Carolina, a game similar to Monopoly was used for residents to create their visions for the park. With play money representing the total budget, they could buy three-dimensional model parts representing park facilities. Everyone wanted a swimming pool close to home. The game resulted in a plan with no facilities except six swimming pools, each a status object for nearby residents. No one was willing to give up "his" or "her" pool, even though the entire budget was depleted on pools, and other recreation facilities (like a community center, a basketball court, a baseball field, play equipment, and landscaping) could not be included. One location could be seen from almost every backyard. It was chosen for the pool. Other facilities were clustered around it. This satisfied the limited-income residents who wanted statusful swimming pools.[31] The design of the public landscape must carefully incorporate statusful symbolic ownership because the proper management of the commons depends on people's shared sense of jurisdiction over the landscape.

Another important strategy in the design of the inhabited landscape is to draw attention to commonplace beauty and make everyday landscapes matters of local pride. This allows everyone access to aesthetic fulfillment. Building on the belief that there is unusual beauty in the most ordinary and least conspicuous landscapes,[32] community designers sponsored events during which residents of Setagaya, Japan, chose common places in their neighborhood that they felt were uncommonly beautiful. Large, red picture frames were then installed at each most valued landscape, calling out to the whole neighborhood that this everyday place is beautiful enough to be framed as an art object. The project directed prestige to common landscapes and also enhanced residents' knowledge of and pleasure in their neighborhood.

From these vignettes, we can cull three strategies for dealing with the rare as a status object. When the rare is fragile or distinguishes a community, that resource should remain in the public domain to create a defining form for the city. Recognizing the importance of statusful facilities to their stewardship, healthy symbolic ownership should be encouraged by design. By championing the beauty in many unrecognized aspects of the urban landscape, the everyday may be cultivated into symbols of prideful identity.

Zero-runoff swale

Conspicuous nonconsumption

Conspicuous Nonconsumption

Nonrenewable resources frequently are consumed in ostentatious exhibits of conspicuous consumption. Such displays parallel planned obsolescence and result in wasted energy, water, land, wood, and other building products.

Worries about resource depletion prompted Michael Corbett to design Village Homes in Davis, California, for a conspicuously nonconsumptive lifestyle.[33] Recognized as a model solar community, the design of the seventy-acre subdivision encourages resource conservation in many other areas. Solar access dictates the overall neighborhood form: lots are oriented north-south, and streets east-west. Bike and pedestrian paths are emphasized, and streets minimized. The relationship of homes to open space reverses the typical middle-class neighborhood pattern: fenced private yards are on the street side while a common occupies the space between lots. This linear open space is collectively managed by residents with gardens spilling out from homes. Moreover, the common is essential for the natural drainage system because it allows steady infiltration after storms instead of the rapid storm-water discharge that typically causes downstream flooding. Challenging typical engineering solutions that use the street as a storm-water sewer, Corbett directed runoff away from streets and into shallow swales that

Village Homes conserves energy and water and produces food by conscious design, changing residents' lifestyles and serving as a symbolic precedent.

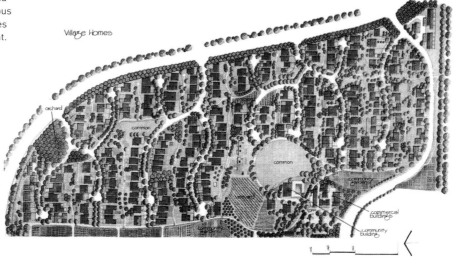

Enabling Form

run between houses. These swales then carry water slowly to larger collector channels that are landscaped as seasonal streambeds. The result is a natural-seeming landscape that is enhanced by a seasonal water element.

The absence of vast, private lawn areas reduces water consumption. Native or edible landscapes replace lawns, and residents integrate vegetable patches into patios and play areas. Wild cherries grow along the drainage channels. Community gardens, orchards, and a vineyard make the neighborhood resource productive. Village Homes allows residents to live modestly on the land and to express nonconsumptive values in their community landscape.[34] Rob Thayer concluded that designers should remember that houses and landscapes are not only for habitation but are symbolic message systems with the power to affect resource-conserving behavior. The medium may be a message of conspicuous nonconsumption.[35] The landscape can be designed to add "status" to healthier and more selective consumption and in many cases nonconsumption.

Inclusive Heterogeneity

For American status seekers, exclusivity is a primary goal. In city design, this is most visibly expressed in residential location.[36] Higher status is achieved by an address in a homogeneous neighborhood that is far from the center of the city, preferably is at a higher elevation than other neighborhoods, is removed from people different from oneself, and guarantees one's exclusivity by a gate that keeps out uninvited visitors.[37] This segregation continues from the upper classes to the lower, nurtured by some city designers.[38] Few people at the top are interested in the convenience or richness that intergenerational and multiple-priced housing offers.[39]

Inclusive heterogeneity

It was not always thus. Until about fifty years ago, most Americans grew up in communities where people from all walks of local life, although often separated by race and class, lived within walking distance of others. One was likely to personally know people from a wide range of professions and ages.[40] Because of personal associations, the disparate groups could work together, when necessary, to address civic issues. Heterogeneous form facilitated this and can again if city design makes inclusivity and heterogeneity desirable, valuable, and prestigious.

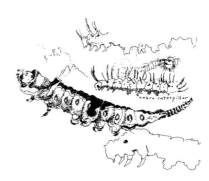

Messy, yucky, gross? Beautiful!

Dirty Enough to Be Happy

In a society in which valued work increasingly emphasizes specialized intellectual professions and devalues manual and farm labor, high status is expressed via sanitized environments.[41] Derived from genuine health concerns, the high prestige of the clean is a main force today. In many places, taboos against those who cultivate the soil or process dead animal products make them society's outcasts. The higher status of "salaryman" is so compelling that the generation just removed from farming rejects every aspect of it in pursuit of "respectable" lives. In the United States, this is complicated by our historic championing, and our now romantic view, of the yeoman farmer as the basis of democratic life. Still, the overwhelming trend is toward an increasingly sterile cleanliness in human habitations that are separated from the labor that invisibly provides food, services, and essential ecosystem functions. Dirty landscapes—and sometimes by association landscapes that are simply disorderly, incomplete, or untidy—get labeled "messy," "yucky," "gross," or worse.[42]

There is a Japanese story about a girl who loved caterpillars, snails, centipedes, and all sorts of other creatures that most people consider disgusting and terrifying. She found them delightful companions and spent all her time in their habitats of muck and overgrown bushes. She was first considered untidy and odd, then wild and barbaric, and eventually queer and stupid. The more she tried to explain how caterpillars would transform into lovely butterflies, the more absurd people considered her. Some pitied her, wishing she would play in proper gardens and not with "nauseous worms" and "nasty insects." In time, people not only scorned her haunts but also shunned her, laughing at her behind her back. Her reply, "If you looked a little more below the surface of things, you would not mind so much what other people thought about you" was a wonderful lesson about status seeking, but it was completely lost on those around her. They simply made more fun of her and the places she found delightful.[43]

Children quickly learn the lowly status of such places from adults and avoid them. This deprives obedient and unadventurous youth some of childhood's greatest pleasures and can even make them susceptible to serious illnesses later in life. Places such as farm yards, junk yards, construction sites, rain forests, swamps, wetlands, mud flats, mud holes, even ponds, creeks, and forests that are sources of joy become stigmatized and off limits.

The landscape we inhabit should be clean enough to be healthy but dirty enough to allow children and adults to hold earthworms in their hands, garden, play in streams, and rummage through junk piles. How can such lowly places be made acceptable in a society prejudiced against them? For those alienated from such places, controlled exposure to their benefits via educational workshops helps overcome the bias. The two most effective design strategies appear to be transparency and framing. Making an undervalued landscape more visibly comprehensible, making its inner workings clear through interpretation, or exposing its functions through revelatory landscape design appeals to intellectual interests of many people.[44] Dirty- and messy-appearing landscapes may also be made more acceptable by framing. A hedge, fence, swale, manicured edge, or other devices give the appearance that the untidiness is contained and the uncontrolled wildness tamed.[45] There are other suggestions for related strategies in the chapter on Inhabiting Science.

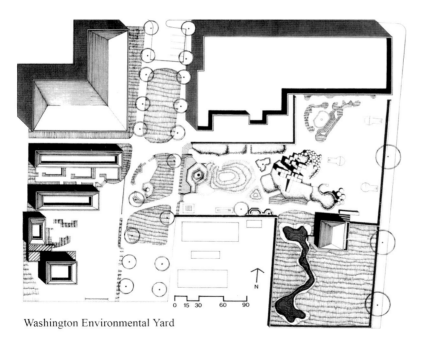

Washington Environmental Yard

Washington Environmental Yard, with overgrown woods and junk piles, has often been perceived by adults to be messy and unsafe, but children consistently view it as an adventureland.

Dirty enough to be happy

In a project that was carefully evaluated for over twenty-five years, messiness has been an ongoing controversy. An innovation in adventure play areas, the Washington Environmental Yard in Berkeley was designed by Robin Moore to be permanently incomplete and open ended and to have a great diversity of settings in which children can play and learn. On what had once been a barren hardscape, hills, forests, and ponds replaced asphalt, and gardens and murals appeared. Parents, children, teachers, and neighbors worked on homemade stages for performances and settings for remarkable summer camps. The Environmental Yard spawned many firsts. Its exuberance showed in overgrown woods, piles of junk, and partially completed projects. To passersby, it looked messy and unsafe. Framing it with murals and evergreen hedges quieted their complaints for a while. Some parents whose children constantly came home muddy called the ponds cesspools, and eventually, the large ponds were removed. There has been a continual ebb and flow of attempts to tidy up that are followed by new experiments. Throughout these years of conflict over the play area's appearance, none of the many children interviewed agreed with adults who advocated neatness. To the children who use the yard, its flexible and indeterminate qualities are both appealing and challenging. It has been an adventureland for a whole generation.[46]

Healthy Status Seeking

Because social class is the single most telling indicator of environmental values and behavior, city designers need to have a sympathetic understanding of the power that class exerts in forming the inhabited landscape—not just in overt power plays but also in nuanced expressions of symbolism. Living in a mobile, fluid, and impersonal world requires more visible status objects to express social standing. Many forms of status seeking are harmful to community and landscape, but eight strategies can help reverse disenabling status seeking—forming communities to be what they are, learning lessons from poverty, taking root, understanding that small is usually beautiful, appreciating rare and commonplace beauty, practicing conspicuous nonconsumption, accommodating inclusive heterogeneity, and allowing people to be dirty enough to be happy. Each has particular remedies for unhealthy status seeking. Each has direct formalistic implications for creating healthier cities and more fulfilling landscapes, not by opposing status displays but by reversing unhealthy patterns and directing our impulses to more productive patterns through self-awareness and creative design.

Sacredness

When form too strictly follows function, form produces lifeless efficiency and spiritless convenience. The modern city, conceived of as a rational, scientific machine for living, results in rational, scientific, machinelike living.[1] This is true of design for ecological democracy, if rules of urban biology are mechanically followed, because function becomes its own primary principle, overwhelming more humanistic intents. Participation, wisely and fairly pursued, interjects our best objectives, among which is the pursuit of the sacred.

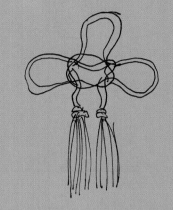

Sacredness Expresses Our Essential Nature

Sacredness manifests fundamental convictions requiring sacrifice, values worth defending, and virtues to be attained.[2] These ennoble humankind and the landscapes that we create because they express our essential nature, our spirit, and the animating force of our existence. They supersede rational function and economy. Sacred landscapes, then, are places that are consecrated by sacrifice and special treatment and endowed by a community with the power of highly revered convictions, values, and virtues. These convictions, values, and virtues are experienced through the ritual use of those places. The qualities of these experiences range from the metaphysical (like transcendence, faith, and hope) to the practical (like empathy, serenity, and charity) and to the earthly (like local wisdom, sense of community, and orientation).[3]

Historical explanations of sacred landscapes were varied. Usually associated with myth and religion, sacred places acknowledged the inexplicable and uncontrollable. Gardens that represented the heavenly prototype, celebrated creation, and were dedicated to ancestors[4] provided a means of transforming mystery into history with comprehensible shape. Likewise, sacred landscapes offered orientation and world views making life coherent through form.[5] In addition to traditionally sacred places, like churches and other religious sites, today prospect-refuge, biophilia, and ecological spiritualism serve contemporary needs for these expressions, often attempting to reconcile paradox and contradiction and reconnecting with primal forces.[6]

Manteo, North Carolina

Abandoned downtown

Sacred boundary

Landscapes may be rendered sacred as embodiments of personal and cultural identity and history.[7] Childhood landscapes, home, peak experiences, and passages provide foundations for sacredness either through symbolism (the landscape represents a virtue or event) or synesthesia (the landscape is like another landscape).[8] Also, needs for rootedness and relatedness make landscapes sacred in and of themselves through the process of topophilia.[9]

Sacred places not only concretize, embody, and symbolize our highest values, convictions, and virtues, but they also make visible our efforts to comprehend mysteries and profess faith. They provide orientation, world view, identity, and rootedness. They express our beliefs in comprehensible form.

At the national level, sacred landscapes include historic buildings and districts, national parks and monuments, national cemeteries and memorials, wild and scenic rivers, wilderness areas, and to a lesser extent wildlife reserves, national forests, military installations, and interstate highways. These extol freedom, equality, wilderness, defense, and mobility among others of our highest values. Nationally sacred places as well as local values impact city design.

Uncovering Sacredness

Let me explain how this works using an example. During the design process to revitalize the central waterfront of Manteo, North Carolina, contentious disagreements erupted because some residents felt that the contemplated changes would destroy their quality of life. This is typical of affluent communities, but Manteo faced 22 percent unemployment, a nearly abandoned downtown, and few prospects for improvement. The designers decided to try to articulate the aspect of community life that was most cherished by residents through a series of interviews and behavior mapping. From the resulting information, they made a list of the places that they thought were important to the social fabric of Manteo.

The list was revised after several community leaders reviewed it. A newspaper questionnaire was developed for townspeople to rank these places in order of significance. The designers also asked residents to state which places they thought could be changed to accommodate tourism and which places they were unwilling to sacrifice to attract tourist dollars. Historic tourism was used as a comparison because that seemed to be the most viable economic development strategy at the time.

Enabling Form

A series of specific tradeoffs were posed, such as whether the respondent agreed that it was more important to leave the Christmas tree in the gravel parking lot downtown than to use the space for parking. Responses allowed the designers to measure the intensity of attachment to places versus the benefits of tourism and to recheck the relative importance of places.

Town launch

Duchess Restaurant

LEGEND
♥ SACRED PLACES
★ SACRED LANDMARKS
▦ SACRED OPEN SPACE
SACRED MARSHLAND
▣ OTHER IMPORTANT PLACES
SACRED NEIGHBORHOODS

THE SACRED STRUCTURE
FOR THE CITY OF MANTEO, NORTH CAROLINA

Jules's Park

Manteo's Sacred Structure—mostly humble places that were essential to the community's daily life, identity, and health—would not be sacrificed even in times of economic hardship.

A ranked and weighted list of significant places resulted. One resident, on seeing how many places ranked higher than the local churches and cemetery, dubbed them the "sacred structures," and thereafter the places were called the Sacred Structure of Manteo. The cemetery and high school provided benchmarks for comparison. They served as cutoff points for the list of places that should not be negatively affected by new development. The places included the marshes surrounding the town, Jules's Park built as a labor of love from the ruins of the local school, a drug store and soda fountain, the post office, churches, the Christmas Shop, front porches, the town launch, a statue of Sir Walter Raleigh, the Duchess Restaurant, the town hall, locally made and unreadable street signs, the town cemetery, the Christmas tree in the gravel parking lot, park post lamps placed in memory of loved ones, and two historic sites.

The newspapers published the results. A map of the Sacred Structure was included with the inventory prepared during the planning process for the town. The map simply showed the places colored with varying intensities based on questionnaire results. It looked similar to other land-use maps. The Sacred Structure touched a subconscious nerve in the community. The residents wanted these places protected. One newspaper editor expressed his concern that the identification of these places meant that the designers were considering changing them to attract tourists. He carefully listed those places that must not be profaned for tourists, stating that they were "perfect jewels" the way they were. His "perfect jewels" referred directly to Jules's Park but included all of the most valued places. Frequently, during the planning process that followed, the editor cornered designers to remind them that those places were sacred and that local people were willing to sacrifice economic gain to save them because they had a higher value than dollars. They did not believe him at first.

What did people mean by this Sacred Structure? The sacred places in Manteo are buildings, outdoor spaces, and landscapes that exemplify, typify, reinforce, and even extol the everyday life patterns and rituals of community life. They are places that are so essential to the lives of residents through use or symbolism that the community collectively identifies with the places. The places are synonymous with residents' concepts and use of their town. The loss of such places would reorder or destroy something or some social process essential to the community's collective being.

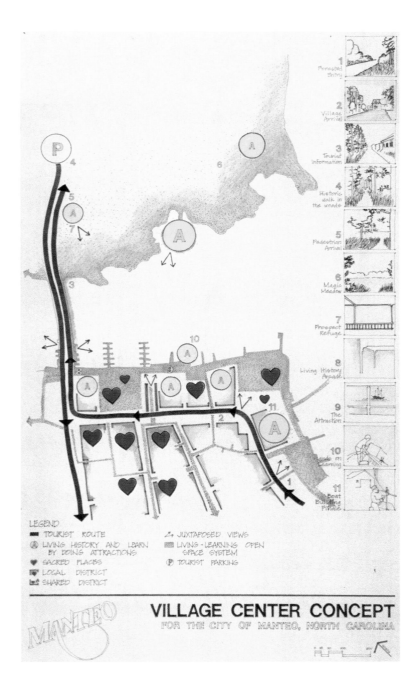

The conceptual plan shows how to reinvent traditional industries, create new ones, and protect the sacred structure by utilizing Manteo's special character and urban form.

Manteo's Sacred Structure, for the most part, consisted of humble places ("holes-in-the-wall") that were the settings for the community's daily routines. No mere places, they embodied the life of Manteo. Although these places expressed Manteo's uniqueness and structured residents' internal images of their town, not one of them was exotic. Each was eloquent in its context, and they were typical (and often rundown) features of what is commonly found along the Carolina coast. They were homey and homely.

These places were almost universally unappealing to the trained professional eye of architects, historians, real estate developers, or upper middle-class tourists. As a result, in Manteo only two places among the sacred structures were protected by historic-preservation legislation. Only a few were protected by zoning laws. Even to locals, the sacred places were outwardly taken for granted. Their value resided in the subconscious but loomed large after four things happened.

First, the places were threatened. Talking about the changes necessary for economic recovery alerted town leaders and then residents that their community was in transition. The dramatic scope of the proposed plans forced people to think about social institutions and environments that mattered most to them.

Second, the places were legitimized. Locals were emotionally attached to many places that they knew did not match media images of good environments. Remember the other-directed environments of status objects? Designers simplify this as the distinction between ordinary vernacular and high-style architecture. Local people contrasted their places with popular-culture stereotypes of success. Because local people were somewhat ashamed of these places, it was important that the outside design experts recognize these places. Otherwise, townspeople would tell them only about places valued by tourists, and truly important places would never have been revealed.

Third, a collective picture of the valued places was presented to the community. Although each person might use and value many of the places, no one knew how much others valued them. Few people knew the separate places created a collective framework. The list of sacred places, the map, and the name "Sacred Structure" overcame this. They provided the townspeople with a gestalt of previously known but separated facts. Neighborhood residents, intimately aware of some parts but not of the total land pattern, acknowledged their piecemeal sense of place. In this case, the map evoked comments like: "I never expected so many people treasured meeting at the post office, and everyone goes to check out the water. I didn't think of them as connected." The map turned special places into a pattern that previously was experienced but not grasped. The name was one resident's way of simplifying the whole. The Sacred Structure became part of the local vocabulary. It was debated at the Duchess Restaurant and Betty's Country Kitchen, along with such topics as job opportunities and the property-tax benefits of tourism. The community's subconscious concern about special places had become part of the collective and now open, conscious expression.

Fourth, the places were consecrated by residents. This required setting aside the most important places from the less valued ones.[10] Townspeople did this systematically by responding to the newspaper survey and refining their list of sacred places throughout the planning process. By the time the design plans were complete, the most valued places had been designated inviolable, not to be changed in any way to accommodate new development. This required sacrifice on the part of townspeople. Economic development suffered to the extent that residents judged projects incompatible with the Sacred Structure. Preserving the Sacred Structure cost the town over half a million dollars each year in retail sales in the 1980s. This sacrifice of financial gain seemed essential in consecrating the places. This was what the newspaper editor reconfirmed when he repeatedly said that these places had a higher value than dollars.[11]

Far from stopping the community revitalization, the Sacred Structure inspired a remarkable economic recovery, preserved cherished landscapes, and concretized the virtues most fundamental to Manteo's identity. The Manteo plan received considerable recognition through awards, books, and movies. It became a model for other cities. In the ensuing years, dozens of other communities systematically identified their sacred structures based on the process developed there. Based on those experiences, there are powerful implications for creating enabling form.

The sacred structure inspired the final plan to revitalize Manteo by enhancing fishing industries, employing traditional skills to craft wooden ships, and making a front-porch-like open-space system.

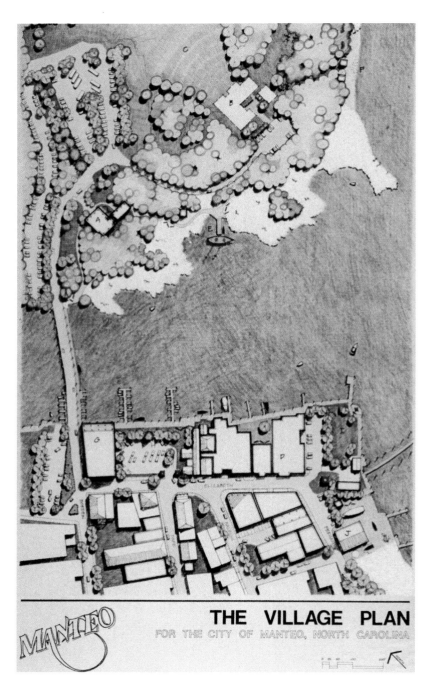

MANTEO

THE VILLAGE PLAN
FOR THE CITY OF MANTEO, NORTH CAROLINA

Enabling Form

Transformative Community Awareness

The process of identifying, mapping, and consecrating sacred places has transformative power for communities. As residents acknowledge sacredness in their locality, they explicate an awareness of the fundamental nature of the community; of the values and virtues they hold dearest; of the direct relationship between the inhabited landscape and orientation, worldview, identity, and rootedness; and of the wholeness of the community. This wholeness includes its social, ecological, and spiritual dimensions.

Sacredness raises the discussion about community form to a high, civic plane. Usually city design is dominated by functional and economic debate. The inclusion of sacred places in the discussion changes the dimensions of decision making. Suddenly, people are invited to discuss the qualities of their community that make life truly worth living. Partly because sacredness embodies the positive, special, and noble within a community, it diminishes petty, selfish concerns that often dominate. And the sacred in a community transcends the traditional vested interests of competing groups; it serves as basis for consensus about highest goals. I am not certain exactly why and how this happens, but I have seen it occur time and again.

Another change that is wrought by sacredness is the inclusion of people with unusual local wisdom. Such people often possess a holistic knowledge of the nature of the community. They may be keenly aware of ecology or social values, for example, but be unable to articulate their wisdom in technical, scientific, or financial terms required in public debate. They may possess the soul of a place, yet they are often marginalized and outcast. Sacredness raises their native wisdom to a central role in community-design discussions. In Manteo, native wisdom was held by many individuals, and each had special knowledge that was embedded in a shared sense of the place. That collective wisdom was joyfully pooled and given life by the sacred-places map. That wisdom has been stewarded for three decades by architect John Wilson, who served as mayor when the plan was developed and has been returned to office recently.

On a practical note, mapping sacred places transforms vague descriptions like "quality of life" that typically fuel emotional disputes into concrete, measurable factors. In Manteo, the Sacred Structure clarified aspects of community that previously had been too hidden in the subconscious and too obscure and imprecise to be thoughtfully debated. The Sacred Structure

Civic front porch

Canoe makers

Wetland walk

Because few sacred places were protected by traditional public mechanisms, creative legislation was required at the state and local levels to maintain the uniqueness of Manteo.

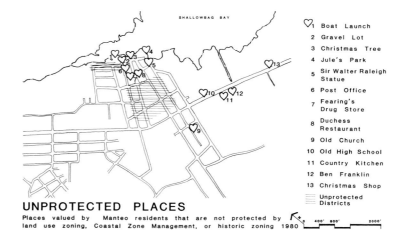

SHALLOWBAG BAY

	1	Boat Launch
	2	Gravel Lot
	3	Christmas Tree
	4	Jule's Park
	5	Sir Walter Raleigh Statue
	6	Post Office
	7	Fearing's Drug Store
	8	Duchess Restaurant
	9	Old Church
	10	Old High School
	11	Country Kitchen
	12	Ben Franklin
	13	Christmas Shop
		Unprotected Districts

UNPROTECTED PLACES

Places valued by Manteo residents that are not protected by land use zoning, Coastal Zone Management, or historic zoning 1980

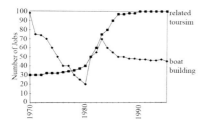

Jobs in boat building and related tourism

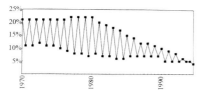

Percentage of unemployed citizens

Launching a wooden ship

map depicted fundamental social patterns and cultural settings more effectively than any other planning document. Less than half of the most valued places in Manteo had been uncovered through traditional inventories such as significant historical architecture, the visual image of the town and culturally important sites as defined in coastal-management guidelines.[12]

If I could make only one map for any community to use as the basis of decision making, I would opt for a map of sacred places. That information most enables community.

Preservation

Making sacredness a part of the community-planning process generally leads to the preservation of aspects of the community that are most important to local people. Typically, this includes historically significant buildings, scenic landscapes, ecologically fragile areas, rivers, mountains, agricultural and forestlands, and wilderness areas, as well as special places of everyday life and rituals. In the communities where sacred places have been mapped, few were protected at the time. In Manteo, for example, less than a third of the sacred places were safe from development.[13]

Equally important, the mapping of sacred places separates those areas that are most critical for preservation from those that are less central to community life and can therefore be altered. This sorting process is fundamental to creating needed change in the face of ossification where residents are fearful of changing anything.[14]

126   Enabling Form

Design Gestalt

A gestalt is a pattern of elements that is so unified as a whole that its properties cannot be derived from the sum of its parts. A foundation of Gestalt psychology is that human life consists of experiential configurations that are more than the various components of sensation and response.[15] As a design parallel, the gestalt is more than a series of overlay maps. Even if there are dozens or even hundreds of maps overlaid, the gestalt is not merely the configuration that is achieved from multiple elements that are added together. More layers—whether ecological, cultural, or economic—will produce a more utilitarian design. Only when a gestalt is synthesized will the design touch the people's hearts. In city design, the gestalt is the essence of community life expressed in a single, irreducible form requiring no elaboration. Every designer knows the pursuit of this essence, this single configuration that simply captures the soul of the place.[16] When a gestalt is achieved, design follows seamlessly.[17] Of various planning approaches, the sacred structure most consistently leads to the formal expression of the gestalt of community life. Although the sacred structures of cities I have studied vary considerably in content and detail, each has repeatedly had four characteristics—center, natural boundary, connectedness, and particularness. Such consistency suggests that these four characteristics are essential for community life and should be pursued above other community actions. I have discussed center and connectedness previously as primary tenets of enabling form and discuss boundary and particularness in the section on resilient form. But several points related directly to sacredness should be made here.

Recurring Center

In every community where we have mapped sacred places, primary centers have been identified by local people as inviolable, frequently as a source of shared experience, personal orientation, and identity. The center considered most sacred is universally of a small area. It may be the center of a village or small city, as in Manteo's case, or a neighborhood in a large city. People articulate center as if it is a nucleus of a biological cell in which their circle of daily life unfolds. In one particularly poignant case, a rapidly developing suburb in Maryland had a sacred structure that included a center that did not exist. It was the intersection of two major roads with no centering public facilities—only a scattering of gas stations, fast-food outlets, and big-box

Repeated sacredness

commercial stores. Community members wistfully described a center that they envisioned much like a European town square but that probably could never exist there. Their low-density subdivisions did not support a center, yet they longed for one.

Hanging out at the docks is a cherished activity in Manteo with explicit spatial requirements.

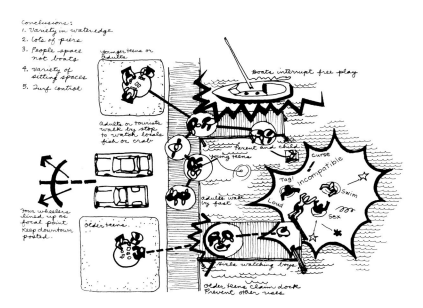

By studying spatial dimensions of behavior patterns, the designers successfully maintained marginal but valued activities (like teens hanging at the docks) while accommodating new economic enterprises.

Front-porch inspiration

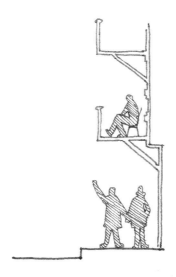

Porch-life design guidelines

The boardwalk serves special rituals but remains a collective front porch through design with intimate spaces, homegrown furniture, and volunteer labors of love.

Natural Boundary

Natural boundary is also repeatedly a part of the sacred structure. These boundaries take different forms. In Manteo, the boundary is created by Shallowbag Bay and wetlands. In Union County, Pennsylvania, the agricultural valleys are delineated by forested mountains. In Oakland, California, the bay, hills, and short creeks create the surrounding geometry. In Haleiwa, Hawaii, and Mount Vernon, Washington, agriculture lands define the boundary. In Raleigh, North Carolina, creeks form edges reinforced by a greenway. These boundaries, like center, provide identity and orientation for inhabitants. Natural edges provide the framework for mental constructs of worldview. They allow residents to comprehend their place. They make each locale distinct from its surroundings. When the natural boundaries are strong enough to withstand development and arranged to maintain small, compact developments, the influence on individual development and community cohesiveness is particularly positive. For small towns surrounded by formidable topography—like Camogli, Italy, the Portuguese hill town of Evora, or the coastal villages of Westport, California, and Matsu, China—this seems a happy accident of geomorphology. Likewise, the big cities of Venice, San Francisco, Honolulu, and Hong Kong benefit from the limits of mountains and water. A few exceptional communities have made conscious choices to create a demarcation where there is no prohibitive natural boundary. Cities in the Napa Valley of California, Boulder, Colorado, and Greenbelt, Maryland, come to mind. Lacking natural boundaries, man-made features like highways and land-use changes form recognizable edges, but these seldom are held sacred by residents.[18]

Connections to Community, Ancestors, and Spirits

Connections to other people, landscape, family and community traditions, God, the metaphysical world, and the mythological past are held sacred, even in contemporary society. Thus, places of worship and burial grounds are designated sacred. More subconsciously revealing is the designation of places of myth and transcendence as sacred. For native people, these connections are embedded in the landscape as sites where rabbit shot the sun or sleeping giant shakes the earth. For natives, distant myths and present science commingle in sacred places, but for most Americans, myths of creation and inexplicable nature were severed long before we inhabited this continent.[19] As a result, few landscapes have been imbued with the continuously supernatural. This was

Enabling Form

just fine as we conquered nature with science and technology. But when people are questioned about their sacred places, they long for connections with places of supernatural power, where myth and transcendence occupy space. We seem to need access to old ways of being—"access to the spirits of land and of place."[20] In Manteo, along some coastal stretches, there have been reported sightings of Sir Walter Raleigh's ghost ship as long as anyone there can remember. Although Raleigh never visited Manteo's coast, myth verifies that he did in some realm, and his spiritual presence inspires community action. Certainly, the connection with God and landscape is felt in the arduous pilgrimage from Las Cruces, New Mexico, to the Tortugas Mountains. The artesian springs deemed sacred on dairy farms in Pennsylvania and on the north shore of Oahu connect believers to history and the spirit of a giving mother earth. In both cases, the spring water that flows continuously from the earth is considered the purest in the world.

I experience this supernaturalism most clearly in Japan, where the ancient nature worship of Shinto is seamlessly incorporated into modern life. In Japan, animistic nature was not altogether abandoned. At Mount Kurama near Kyoto, the god Mao-son came to earth from Venus six million years ago. Mao-son, both the spirit of the earth and the great king of all conquerors of evil, occupied a rock-filled clearing near the summit. Since then, the rocks have emanated Mao-son's spirit, directing the evolution of all humankind and all other living things. Less than a thousand years ago, terrifying red-faced monsters of the Kurama forest, Tengusan, attended to an exiled youth who would become the epic hero of Japanese culture. The Tengu, deformed human figures, who sought only to subjugate evil, trained the young Yoshitsune in the most advanced military arts, discipline, and creative wisdom. Yoshitsune grew into a brilliant leader, epitomizing the best character of humankind. The rocks, tree roots, and springs of Mount Kurama mark his daily encounters with the gods. Kami, the gods of specific places, inhabit each geologic outcrop and vegetative nuance. Their presence is felt throughout the mountain. I have no doubt that Mao-son is in those rocks. Amid the life of technology and science that now defines Japan, the Kami are visited regularly. Visitors communicate with the rocks and trees, the gods embodied in the place. Some seek success in business, love, or even school exams; others beseech the Kami to heal a loved one. Far from diminishing scientific knowledge of the systems needed in a ecological democracy, such worship seems to create the grounds for environmental thinking to be more integrated.

This tiny temple floats above the rocks where Mao-son came to Mount Kurama from Venus 6 million years ago, a continuous connection to ancestors, shared values, and community that is still celebrated today.

Here Tengu, deformed humans with monstrous red faces and pure intentions, trained Yoshitsune to subjugate evil; the place inspires noble action.

Particularness

Particularness, the fourth recurring gestalt of sacredness, is the formal expression of the unique characteristics of a community. People form their societies and landscapes in particular ways and give their place of habitation a special identity. This may come from centuries-old patterns of cultural habit, from everyday life patterns, from differences in virtues most pursued, from the manner in which the forces of nature or technology are mollified or employed, or a combination of these. All are expressed in the built landscape as the best possible life that community can achieve. Like center and boundary, particularness also contributes to individual and collective awareness, orientation, and worldview. But this particularness is often difficult to articulate with language. Like the Chinese poet T'ao Ch'ien says, "In these things is a fundamental truth I would like to tell, but lack the words."[21] In such matters, landscape says what words cannot, and the landscape reflects the gestalt of the particular configuration of the community.

These aspects—center, boundary, connectedness, and particularness—recur as dominant patterns when people map sacredness in their communities. The gestalt emerging from these produces a most powerful framework for community design, mystical yet extremely practical for the designer seeking to create enabling form.

Design Inspiration

Sacredness inspires community and project design. In Manteo, one of the most sacred patterns was sitting on front porches, a cool and neighborly place to do household chores or relax. The gestalt for the overall city plan combined porch life with lines of the local outdoor drama: "Come sit on our front porch; let us tell you of the dreams we keep." The designers realized that the public waterfront spaces could be thought of as the citywide front porch. This produced a distinctive design, unlike other waterfront parks. A series of large spaces front Shallowbag Bay, and they are subdivided and canopied to produce porch-scaled places to sit and watch more public activities. The boardwalk is conceived as a sidewalk promenade connecting the various porch-lined settings for public festivals, parties, and informal gatherings. Each is designed to accommodate civic activities and encourage intimate interactions at a semipublic distance. This is what front porches provide relative to the sidewalk and street. Even the visual quality of details reveals the particularness of Manteo. It looks lived-in like private front porches, partly by design and partly by construction method. To ensure local contractors opportunities to build the public spaces, the overall project was bid as multiple small projects rather than a single, large contract. The boardwalk joins in individualized ways, again as a series of separate porches. This invites participation, interaction, and community pride. Instead of institutionalized furnishings, a local furniture maker created benches and pic-

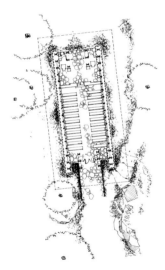

Thorncrown Chapel, Eureka Springs, Arkansas

nic tables for the open spaces. He used vernacular porch furniture as the model for the public landscape. This, too, conveys a welcoming message. Along the boardwalk are a series of living-learning exhibits to teach about Manteo's history. They invite participation. The homey atmosphere has been carefully cultivated to create places that are intimate, sociopetal, small in scale, and porchlike, with the unfinished look of a home-improvement project—faithfully capturing the essence of Manteo.

Sacredness has long inspired some of the world's most emotionally moving landscapes, like the pyramids, the Acropolis, the Duomo cathedral in Florence, and the Kiyomizudera Sando in Kyoto. Just as striking are the thousands of lesser-known expressions of sacredness that exult in and inspire local community values the world over.[22] Each of these built environments is inspired by both its landscape and its community's highest values. Thorncrown Chapel near Eureka Springs, Arkansas, illustrates. Fay Jones made a building so tied to its place, time, and people that it evokes heavenliness. Wood columns rise like tree trunks to hold layered branches that support a gabled roof. The chapel is a temple married to the surrounding Arkansas woodland. It seems part of the forest. Its dappled light makes inside and outside seem one, and it opens to the forest so that leaves, sun, and sky form stained-glass windows where none exist.[23]

Many locally valued places garner sacredness from use of landscape elements arranged in ways to evoke strong emotional response. Mountains, valleys, and forests convey different meanings in different cultures at different times, but they always elicit powerful responses. The association of water with birth and life and of fire with death, eternal life, and ancestors stirs our emotions. A palm tree allee or an almond orchard may give a feeling of purposeful well-being. The apple trees that line the streets of the Japanese city of Iida were originally planted by students after their city was bombed in World War II, and today they express youthful gifts of life, nearly sixty years after they were planted. A shallow creek may stir memories of childhood magic, the headwaters and mouth fueling feelings of awareness and fullness, respectively. A copse of trees on a hilltop provides an aedicula-like prospect and a refuge that evokes feelings of power. It is this language of landscape that allows emotions that are within the community to take shape in the surrounding world.[24] A city designer should capture every opportunity to make simple landscapes of these primal elements.

A Higher Purpose for Vexing Problems

Sacredness has essential roles in creating cities that support ecological democracy. When the urban design process is raised to the level of shared values worthy of respect, petty self-interest is diminished. The design effort, once interjected with the sacred, strives for the noblest, lofty virtues that reflect the best of humankind.[25] This often creates a mutually reinforcing virtuous circle of design whereby each succeeding action builds on the good will and goodness that preceded it.[26] This increases the capacity for residents to work together on complicated community problems.

Sacredness provides wisdom that reorients scientific knowledge and technology toward the organic, gentle, nonviolent, elegant, and beautiful.[27] Sacredness monitors scientific progress, sorting the good and bad through moral filters. In the cases where the heart is more intelligent than the mind, sacredness also intervenes.[28]

In day-to-day actions, sacredness serves the practical purposes of preservation and creates gestalts that express the soul of a place and inspire the details of city form. In all these matters, the designer transforms virtues and convictions that are formless into configurations in the landscape that communicate those values more expressively to the community. Sacredness fills enabling form with goodness, faith, and wonder. These qualities provide the higher purpose that enables people to work together in forums to attack vexing community issues.

Florence, Italy

Athens, Greece

Lofty virtues and local empathy combine to make dwelling meaningful, creating truly great communities of ordinary places like Ciudad Rodrigo, Spain.

Resilient Form: Life, Liberty, and the Pursuit of Sustainable Happiness

A horseshoe crab that is nearly identical to its ancestors 150 million years ago makes its way from ocean to sandy beach to spawn on the coast of my home state. So perfectly fit for survival in its ecosystem, it has changed little since long before this beach was formed.[1] A villager in Haran, Turkey, creates his house with deep clay walls in the same beehive shape that his forefathers did. The design has interior passages that lead to a large courtyard and circulate air to cool the inner rooms. It is so perfectly fit for its extremely hot ecosystem that it, too, has changed little over four thousand years of habitation.[2]

Following a worldwide economic slump in the late twentieth century, Hsin Chu City in Taiwan, which had a specialized high-technology economy, was devastated by over 15 percent unemployment; nearby Tainan City, which had a balanced, diverse economy, weathered the global recession with unemployment that seldom rose over 5 percent.[3]

In midwinter, temperatures in a field remain below freezing for several days, and a lone quail dies within hours in a five-mile-per-hour wind. Nearby, ten quail form a tight circular huddle and survive the life-threatening cold. In the California suburb of San Ramon, which averages 3.2 households per acre, almost all trips to work require driving a car; in denser San Francisco, with 35 households per acre, over 75 percent of the residents walk to work. In the San Francisco neighborhoods, the average family spends $6,300 per year less in car-related expenses than families in low-density suburbs like San Ramon.[4]

Wood snails that inhabit the beech and maple forest on the Lake Michigan dunes have ranges that are limited to the climax dune and never extend their niche into the oak and hickory forest or the beach grass surrounding them. In Napa County, California, an agricultural-preservation ordinance similarly limits urban development from farmlands surrounding the cities of the valley, maintaining niches for both human habitation and grape growing.

A peppered moth in a northern forest is camouflaged with speckled patches of brown on white that blend into the surrounding woodland of light-barked trees. In a heavily industrialized area nearby, the very same species of *Biston betularia* appears to be an altogether different animal. Instead of a white speckled coloration, this one has quickly evolved to a sooty black, matching the darkened vegetation of the polluted forest.[5] Durham was once a center of tobacco production in North Carolina; today outdated tobacco warehouses are being converted to housing and offices for advanced medical research as the city transitions from a dying economy to a city of medicine.

In South Carolina after Hurricane Hugo, three families assess the storm damage: one picks through the few remnants of a mobile home, which is nowhere to be found; another finds a vacation home toppled from its primary dune location and roofless; and a third merely rakes up windblown debris in the yard around an undamaged upland household.[6]

In Masai villages in Africa, via a centuries-old pattern of city making, the most precious community assets—cattle, sheep, and calves—are placed at the center of the communities. Because cattle are essential for subsistence and also a source of wealth, ceremony, religion, and mystical powers, they are protected with successive circles of huts and a thorn fence made of growing trees, brush, and mud, which offer multiple layers of protection to the tribe's treasures.[7]

Each of these vignettes reveals a design of nature or a mimicry of nature that allows human habitation to maintain itself efficiently and compatibly with its surrounding environment through often dramatic changes that threaten survival. Such design with nature is the basis of resilient form that is fundamental to a sustainable urban ecology.

Whether or not you give a hoot about horseshoe crabs, coveys of quail, wood snails, peppered moths, or even villages in Turkey or Africa, you have a vested interest in the lessons they offer us. The principles underlying their perseverance are key to making today's cities healthy. Only resilient form allows us life, liberty, and the pursuit of happiness that can be sustained over many generations. That is why we collectively need to listen up. Resilient urban form may not last as long as the elegant form of the horseshoe crab, but resiliency allows habitation to endure over many centuries. This ability to endure is based on, among other things, having an urban form that continually provides what the community needs, even in times of temporary crises.[8] Resilient urbanity has the internal ability to persist—to recover easily without significant loss from illness, misfortune, attack, natural or social disaster, or other dramatic disturbance. And it can readily absorb change. A resilient city is able to retain the essence of its form even after it has been deformed. In this way, *resilience* seems a better word than *sustainability* for design goals for the city. Resilient form maintains itself efficiently and seamlessly with both the landscape and the cultural networks of which it is a part.

Although the resilient city trends toward relative stability, its form is not static. Fluctuations in urban systems, as in natural ones, are to be expected, cannot be entirely controlled, and, in many instances, are positive.[9] These fluctuations alter the urban form but, in a resilient city, do not cause a catastrophic collapse. Like a defensive team in football, it bends but does not break. In addition, change is necessary to achieve fairness, to become more democratic, to meet new social goals, and, most fundamentally in our present case, to transform the unresilient cities we have created into more resilient ones. Therefore, our cities must change, but Americans are increasingly resistant to change.[10] Because much recent change has been unhealthy and change is rapid, seemingly beyond our control, we want to freeze our communities as they are. We do this to protect our psyches and our investments. Unable to distinguish between healthy and unhealthy change, we simplistically conclude that all change is bad, trapping us in already unfulfilling habitation. Resilience empowers us to change in ecologically healthy ways.[11]

In recent decades, professionals have addressed issues of resilience at a range of scales from regional design to household design, and most of them articulated rules for design most essential to the scale on which they focused. Under the banner of design with nature, Ian McHarg detailed the principles of urban growth to provide regional resiliency.[12] He determined those areas in a region that could be urbanized with the least disruption to ecological function. Patterns of urban growth that are intrinsically suitable for human habitation were to be governed by soils, slope, climate, hydrology, and other natural forces. Urban form would be limited in its extent to provide relative stability. This required maximizing diversity, complexity, symbioses, and interdependencies between ecosystem parts. Urban systems would serve multiple purposes. All these actions would minimize entropy and enhance natural evolution.

At the city scale, Michael Hough comprehensively demonstrates the basic design tenets for retrofitting existing city form to achieve resiliency by following natural process.[13] He calls for a conserver city based on recycling, self-reliance, small-scale enterprises, economy of means, and harmony between urban form and nature. This, Hough notes, can be achieved only by reinvesting in nature to make urban landscapes productive. He, like McHarg, postulates that integrated, multifunctional systems that shun single-purpose specialization and increase diversity are necessary prerequisites for healthy cities. Design of urbanity is derived from large, long-term processes of evolving nature. When designed thusly, human development is actually enriched as the environment is restored. This requires that citizens have an intimate knowledge of their locality through direct contact with nature.

At the neighborhood scale, Michael Corbett creates a more resilient form for everyday life by focusing on the interconnectedness of various parts of the community ecosystem, both social and natural.[14] He integrates energy, water flows, and agricultural production into the neighborhood itself. He curbs harmful technologies, like the car, by narrowing streets and reducing parking. He, too, follows the principle that diversity adds resilience. Like Hough, Corbett depends on recycling and conservation to reduce consumption while creating more fulfilling habitation. He calls for decentralized tribal units within neighborhoods of fifty to a few thousand people, with identifiable architecture, easy access to nature, and an open, democratic process for decision making. Here he begins to intertwine human well-being and environmental design, not just as a matter of ecological necessity but also as a means of self-actualization. He notes that people shape the environment and that, in turn, the environment shapes people. An unfit environment produces stress and illness; a self-sufficient neighborhood increases stability and security.

John Lyle gave form to resilience at the site scale.[15] He let nature do much of the work in creating human habitation. As predators control pests, topography regulates water, and vegetation heats and cools buildings. Nature serves both as model and as context. Just as nature reuses resources, so do his regenerative designs, but the design varies with region. Lyle urged design that aggregates instead of isolates parts of the system, and he sought optimal levels for multiple functions and multiple pathways for resource flows and storage. To Lyle, flow follows form follows flow; his design shaped habitation to guide the flow of natural processes through a site. Form expressed natural processes. All these allowed him to match technology to need. Often this was high-technology water-monitoring or solar-collecting equipment, sometimes it was low technology, but always Lyle's designs employed technology appropriate to the site. He followed the dictate to use information to replace power. If you precisely describe a problem, he argued, you do not need to waste power for contingency. If people are engaged as a key part of this, they, too, replace nonrenewable power usage. He prioritized systems to address the most critical issues on a site and sought common solutions to seemingly unrelated problems.

At the systems scale, Nancy and John Todd apply principles from organic chemistry and biology to design.[16] The living world is the matrix for all design at every scale. Therefore, design should follow, not oppose, the laws of biology. Like Lyle, they see biology as the model for all design. Homeostasis in systems design, then, can be achieved only as biota seek an optimal environment and as designers provide it. The Todds would like design to be grounded in biological equity, bioregional self-reliance, and renewable energy. As others, one of their principles is integration of systems, which they note provides mutually reinforcing advantages. Design should coevolve with the natural world, creating no waste and actually restoring the earth. Finally, design should move humanity toward the divine through an undifferentiated interconnection of human and natural worlds.

Sim van der Ryn articulated the resilient house.[17] House design should not be standardized but should grow from each place and the peculiarities of the site. This entails careful study of the locale. To avoid waste and to account for all the costs of making and maintaining a house require considering the interconnectedness and impacts of every aspect of design. Van der Ryn designs with the patterns and processes of the living world. Enhance diversity. Recycle. Close loops. Use all waste. Make natural processes visible in the design. He urges us to recognize that everyone is a designer. In democratic design, no one individual can claim the solution.

All of these designers, even though working at different scales, share principles about reforming the urban landscape. The following rules of resilient design are held in common across all these scales: (1) increase diversity, (2) integrate parts of urban ecosystems that have been segregated, (3) consider the many and diffused indirect interconnections of urban systems, (4) follow the flows and cycles of biological processes, (5) evolve the design from the intrinsic character of the locale, (6) rely on renewable energy and resources, (7) live and design within the natural limits of the bioregion, (8) solve multiple problems with few actions, (9) reveal natural processes through design, (10) use democratic decision-making processes, and (11) coevolve human development, human habitation, and nature to achieve human fulfillment and the restoration of ecosystems. Most of these dicta speak directly to the physical form of the urban landscape, but some focus on changing behavior and the way that people dwell in the landscape.

A resilient city is dependent on all three—the inherent form of the landscape itself, the way that people relate to the landscape in which they dwell, and the actions of people themselves. After the earthquake in Kobe, Japan, it was discovered to no one's surprise that the parts of the city that were least damaged were built on stable geologic formations. The most damage occurred where design had ignored natural factors such as uncompacted deposits and fill that liquifacted, a clear lesson that resiliency depends on the landscape itself. Less damage also occurred where people had followed stringent building codes in new construction and had retrofitted older housing, respectful of the powers of natural forces. Surprisingly, less damage and fewer deaths also occurred in neighborhoods that had previously organized to fight the government over various issues. Those residents knew the daily patterns of neighbors and were able to save them from collapsed buildings quickly. Additionally, because they had worked together over time, they were better prepared to rebuild after the disaster, so earlier democratic actions contributed to life saving and overall resiliency. These three lessons must not be forgotten when considering resiliency.

What, then, are the fundamental principles that can make our cities more resilient? Urbanity cannot be resilient without enabling form. Centeredness, connectedness, fairness, sensible status seeking, and sacredness underlie resiliency just as fundamentally as do biological principles that are more often associated with natural systems because urban resiliency is distinctively a human endeavor. The urban form must first enable the consideration of designing with natural processes. The impacts of Hurricane Hugo and the Kobe earthquake illustrate the centrality of connectedness as both social and ecological constructs. The aftermath of Hurricane Hugo, like the Kobe natural disaster, indicated there was little natural about the disaster. People were killed and hurricane damage was greatest by design. Vacation homes built astride predictably vulnerable dunes and mobile homes where flood ordinances, anchoring mechanisms, and raised finished-floor elevations were ignored suffered most. In some areas, 90 percent of such mobile homes were damaged.[18] Coastal cities built below rising sea levels will be impossible to sustain as Hugo showed and the 2005 Katrina disaster dramatized. Failure to make connections between the natural forces and the built environment cost many lives and billions of dollars. Just as an increased awareness of connectedness is fundamental to enabling form, the application of connectedness is essential for resilience. Likewise, centering—as in the case of Masai villages, where the least valued resources are located at the periphery and the most valued resources at the center—is equally a social and an ecological foundation. Certainly, urban resilience depends on enabling form, but there is more. Later, we consider how impelling form influences resilience. But here we consider five socioecological principles that are most centrally fundamental to resilient urban form: particularness, selective diversity, density, limited extent, and adaptability. Of these, limited extent is most internally related to others because it influences density and diversity directly and is shaped by particularness. Particularness additionally affects adaptability and diversity. In practice, limited extent, particularness, and density are lacking in most American cities and must be attended to improve resilience.

Particularness

In the not-too-distant past, each landscape produced distinctive cities with different regional configurations, overall urban form, and manner of division into neighborhoods; different patterns of land use, vegetation, and streets; and different systems of drainage and building types.[1] Based on what Charles Darwin might have called "divergence of character"[2] had he studied urban ecology, cities were particular to their landscapes—their geology, soils, hydrology, general climate, specific wind and sun patterns, and native plants.[3] Like the horseshoe crab, cities that fit their environments have historically been more resilient and have outlasted others that were less landscape-compatible. Such cities survived natural disasters and had many other advantages as well. The beehive building complexes of Haran, Turkey, are an example of traditional city form that endures by virtue of its good fit with its ecosystem. The green valleys that were created to clean the air of Stuttgart, Germany, are a contemporary example of how a city can be made resilient through fitness with its surrounding landscape.

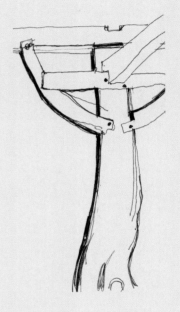

Particularness refers to the distinctive adaptations of human habitation that have been made to fit especially well into the unique natural ecosystem of which that habitation is a part. These adaptations of fitness reduce the destructiveness of natural disasters like periodic fires, earthquakes, hurricanes, floods, and droughts, as well as the disruption of economic shifts and social upheavals. Particularness underlies place-appropriate economic activity, reduces pollution and the use of nonrenewable energy and resources, and gives distinguished form to cities, thus making them imageable, memorable, and well loved.

Traditional settlements possessed an accumulated wisdom about how to build the city in particular ways to make it resilient in its unique setting. Ill-advised experiments became extinct as unfit cities were weeded out and successful ways to build persevered.[4] The knowledge of the particularly fit way to build and dwell in a given ecosystem is a primary component of "native wisdom."

Resilient cities like Evora, Portugal, are built in ways that are particular to culture and place, adapting habitation until they fit the unique ecological niches that they occupy.

In many parts of the United States, this native wisdom has been lost, replaced within a few centuries or even decades with local ignorance of the proper particularness of that ecosystem. The challenge for the city maker today is to find, nurture, and adapt natively wise particularness when it exists and rediscover lost patterns of particularness. In some cases, the prevailing native wisdom, even when it exists, must be supplemented by scientific knowledge and appropriate technologies previously unknown. In such cases, the challenge for the city designer is to invent new patterns of particularness that might make an urban area more resilient. This is the daunting task for New Orleans and the towns along the Gulf of Mexico.

Particularness is revealed in vastly different ways, depending on scale. In making resilient cities, both the macro scale of regional patterns and the micro scale of building form are important. Knowledge of the big patterns avoids building on or depleting aquifer recharge areas, flood-prone lands, and other fragile components. These macro patterns also direct development to locations that maximize agricultural, solar, and wind productivity as well as the economic production of goods needed for urbanity. These patterns provide what McHarg called the intrinsic suitability of human habitation to its ecosystem, which lowers entropy and enhances natural evolution. These patterns have to be identified and managed at the regional level. They are often invisible and so complex and extensive that they are unknown even to natively wise residents, except in a vague, unarticulated way. The tech-

Resilient Form

niques of large-scale overlay mapping that were developed by Ian McHarg, Angus Hills, and Phil Lewis are typically necessary to comprehend these macro patterns. Carl Steinitz, Jack Dangermond, and John Radke have enhanced our ability to see these regional forms via spatial mathematics that synthesize large amounts of complex data through computerized geographic information systems.[5]

At the micro level, specific human adaptation to site and building design manifest particularness in more easily observable ways. These design inventions, like the beehive house, seem to grow from their immediate locale, inspired by the flows and cycles of biological processes that are special to their specific context. Such forces (unconsciously applied in subsistence cultures and consciously applied by architects) make buildings distinctive to the regional resources. These inventions are typically associated with native wisdom; they are revealed more by keen on-site observation than by remote sensing.[6] In the next sections, I consider bioregional distinctions and peculiar micro-scale patterns of conserving, recycling, and repairing.

Bioregional Distinction: Topographic Typologies and Willful Water

One primary lesson of studying traditional settlement patterns is that cities that develop unique local adaptations to live within the limits of their bioregion are typically more resilient than those that do not. Bioregions are most readily identified as distinct areas defined by topography and climate. These two factors—mollified by natural evolution of soils and plant communities over the millennia and cultural choices over centuries—make distinctive types and amounts of local resources available for livelihoods and cities. Historically, it was essential to have enough resources available locally without importing them. Likened to living within your means, the means are limited by the resources in the region. The more resources that have to be imported, the less resilient the city is. By reducing externalities and increasing internalities, the city becomes more resilient. This applies to food, water, air, energy, and any raw or processed materials that are needed in making and maintaining the city.[7] For example, cities like San Francisco and Sacramento, whose nearby watersheds provide adequate water, are more water resilient than Los Angeles and other Southern California cities, which are dependent on cross-basin transfers of water that is imported from watersheds as far away as Wyoming, Colorado, Utah, and New Mexico.

San Francisco drinking water

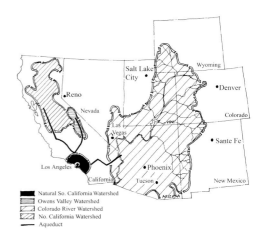

Los Angeles drinking water

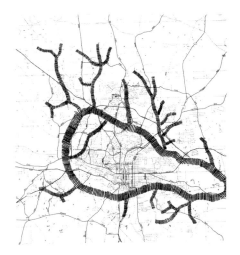

Raleigh greenway

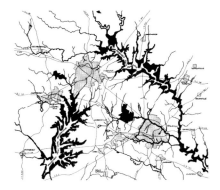

Piedmont greenway

Carefully considered watersheds are key to the resilience of most cities. Raleigh's greenway provides drinking water, flood management, and recreation that is unique to the Piedmont region.

Living within bioregional limits for food production, water provision, or other factors gives distinctive form to the area. This is manifested in the geometries of landscapes that are both built and unbuilt. Frequently, resilience depends on regional open-space systems that are unique to their ecosystems. These systems provide overall form and facilitate the efficient provision of the goods and resources that are needed by the city. The case of Stuttgart, Germany, mentioned above, illustrates one dramatic regional form directed by airsheds. Plagued by air pollution and temperature inversions, as are many other cities that are located in concavities that trap bad air, the city created a network of parks, forests, and agricultural lands that enhance the natural flow of air and help clean and cool the city. The form of the network is derived from the topography, settlement patterns, microclimate, and vegetation particular to the Stuttgart region.[8] As more is learned about the effects and movement of air pollution, regional form will increasingly include open spaces of forest, grasslands, and farms in selected topographies to channel clean air into desired city locations and dirty air away from critical areas. Patterns of strong wind and solar gain will also shape regional form. As one example, the especially expressive pattern of wind farms along the Corteau des Prairies, a region that stretches from North Dakota to Iowa on a hill raised above the flatlands, is creating a distinctive pattern in the landscape near Minneapolis and St. Paul.[9]

Resilient Form

Likewise, when watersheds are carefully considered, they can give dramatic form to a region and offer resilience in terms of water supply, wastewater treatment, and flood management. In the piedmont region of North Carolina, Raleigh was planned as the state capitol in 1792. William Christmas organized the roadways and urban development along a gentle ridge top and protected surrounding streams for water supply. For nearly 150 years, this pattern of development continued. Gentle ridge tops were urbanized. Stream corridors were protected not by law but by wise stewardship. Flooding was minimized, water was safely supplied, and sewage safely disposed. Although Raleigh's urban relationship with topographic form is the opposite of Stuttgart's, both work well in their contexts. Raleigh was urbanized along the convex ridges rather than in a concave valley floor. Because Raleigh is in the temperate forest zone, urban forest regeneration of oak and hickory trees is rapid after urbanization, creating heavily wooded neighborhoods. However, by the 1950s, property owners began to develop flood-plain lands. The region's resilience evaporated. Native wisdom was overwhelmed by greed, growth, and engineering solutions to problems of human ecology. In one particularly notorious act, the then-mayor of Raleigh used his influence and apparently city staff to engineer the creation of a major shopping center at the fringe of the city on land with a long history of flooding; his new shopping center flooded continuously. At the same time, new highways seeking paths of least resistance were proposed along large parts of Walnut and Crabtree creeks. In opposition, residents led by William Flournoy responded by creating the Raleigh Greenway, a series of linear open spaces protecting the floodplain, providing recreation, and giving distinctive form to the city. Related actions to stop the highways proposed in riparian corridors successfully protected additional creeks. Over time, the ridge-top urbanization and natural valley combination became a precedent for a large part of the upper Neuse River watershed. A series of impoundments provide drinking water from within the region, but population growth is testing the resilience of this regional form.[10]

In an extremely different topography along the Yoshino River in Japan, a battle presently rages that will determine the form that urbanization will take in that watershed. The outcome will decide the long-term resiliency of the entire northern Skikoku region. In contrast to the old geology of the North Carolina piedmont, these are younger mountains that were formed by more recent geologic actions. The Yoshino River, which flows north,

Yoshino subregions

makes an abrupt right turn east where seismic activity blocked its once short course to the sea. Today the river runs through three different subregions. The headwaters are in rugged high mountains with steep hillsides that were deforested for military development in the early twentieth century. Habitation is almost exclusively in small cities situated just above the flood level. The midregion begins soon after the river makes its geologic right turn. This is an increasingly wide and flat floodplain of indigo and other crops with small urban settlements that traditionally were protected from periodic floods by walls around the villages, raised floor levels, and floating roofs as last-resort escape routes from the highest waters. The third subregion is an unusual mix of wetlands and mountains. Here the largest city of the region, Tokushima, is located on hills surrounding the mouth of the Yoshino River. The central government of Japan—treating the entire river basin as a uniform engineering entity in spite of vast topographic and cultural differences—intends to build a series of large dams evenly spaced throughout the course of the river. This long-standing strategy of building dams of questionable value as part of local economic stimulus was recently exposed. A grassroots group led by Himeno Masayoshi questioned the proposal and eventually resoundingly defeated one dam in Tokushima via the previously unheard of action in Japan of a citizen referendum. When the government responded by moving the dam several kilometers outside the Tokushima prefecture, Himeno realized that he had to create an alternative plan for the entire watershed. He envisions no big dams but a reordered pattern of regional land use based on the three subregional distinctions. Key is the revegetation of deforested steep mountain slopes with the natural diversity of species that existed prior to World War II. Japanese scientists believe that this would allow enough infiltration in the upper reaches of the river to renew ground-water supplies and reduce downstream flooding. In the broadening floodplain of highly productive farmland, traditional methods of flood-damage avoidance would be reinforced with riparian revegetation to direct flood water into flood-catchment fields that at other times would be planted with secondary crops. Downstream ancient stone dams that once were used to recharge ground water would be refurbished to provide well water for the towns on the hills out of the floodplain. Wetlands at the mouth of the river would clean Tokushima's water. If adopted, the Yoshino River watershed plan would create a regional form from the particular local forces of topography, vegetation, hydrology, and human settlements, creating a

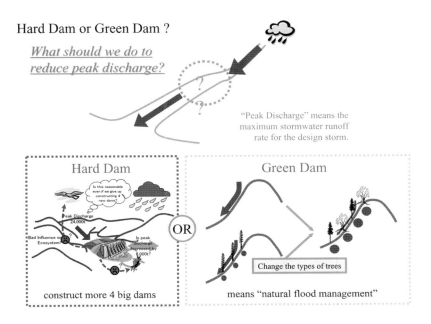

Future city form along the Yoshino River will be determined by how much downstream flooding can be reduced through vegetating deforested mountains, a complex ecological problem about which there is little agreement.

sustainable growth pattern that is unique to the Yoshino River ecosystem and has never before been implemented in Japan.[11]

Although these local adaptations vary from the piedmont of North Carolina to the coastal mountains of Skikoku, they illustrate the importance of designing with the regional hydrological pattern. Of all natural patterns, watershed management offers the most effective way to form distinctive responses that support regional resilience.[12] Defined by typography and flows of surface water, watersheds are more observable than most regional patterns in which aquifers and other ground water are out of sight. Typically, aquatic flows serve as surrogates for many other natural cycles and webs. They predict vegetative patterns and biological diversity and provide for wildlife movement. The quality and health of watersheds underlie our own health directly, and designing with watershed patterns provides the city with far more than the constraints of living within bioregional limits. Topography and water patterns can give lasting form to the city and create a natural framework for neighborhoods. The distinctive forms of each watershed inspire elegant city and architectural patterns. For all these reasons, the first rule of particularness is to derive the bioregional form of habitation from topography and hydrological patterns.

Peculiar Forms of Conserving, Recycling, and Repairing

When looking for macro regional patterns, many details that are essential to resilience escape attention. Usually, the big view imperfectly discerns causal relations of physiography, soils, climate, and vegetation. Particular adaptations of built form that are essential to regional self-reliance may be missed altogether.[13] Switching our view back and forth from the macro to micro scales can be especially informative. If we pick up the story of the Yoshino River watershed again, we can see how the micro reiterates and reveals afresh patterns of fundamental particularness. These small-scale patterns are uniquely useful because local people can see them and visualize how they can be reincorporated into daily life. In contrast to abstract macro patterns, micro ones are locally recognizable precedents, a tangible part of everyday urbanism. They allow implementation at the scale of the individual home.

At the smallest scale of human habitation, the Yoshino River offers instruction on particularness that is worthy of highlighting. As noted above, a distinctive building pattern is still employed today in the broad floodplain of the lower Yoshino valley. Because the flood-deposited soils are prized for agriculture and agriculture is dependent on the floods for replenishment, flood waters are welcomed. No expensive flood-control technologies were traditionally employed. Rather, urban development occurs in the nearby rolling foothills, saving the flood-prone lands for indigo farms. Water is literally walled out of each farmstead, dramatically reducing the materials needed to control the flood, which is allowed to spread silt-rich water everywhere except inside the farmyard. The thick, carefully crafted stone walls of blue rock make a waterproof barrier that generally keeps out flood waters. To protect against damage if the walls are penetrated, floor elevations for functions that must be kept dry, like sleeping areas and crop storage, are raised. In addition, each farmstead has boats specially crafted for navigating local flood conditions; these are stored in the rafters of outbuildings. Old timers recall a few big floods in which boats were used to travel from one village to another for supplies. The final adaptation for flood-damage prevention is in the design of the roofs of farm buildings. These are made of wood and thatch and can be detached if necessary to allow inhabitants to escape the calamitous flood. No one I worked with in the valley remembered having to detach roofs to escape a flood, but the fact that they could be so used convinced me that the floods in the past must have necessitated this design.

Adaptations for Yoshino flooding

The unique way that the Yoshino River communities have adapted to their ecosystem made them resilient over time and gives a distinctive local identity that is readily visible throughout the region. Although these inventions are unfamiliar to most of us, they are keenly conceived and work effectively with an unusual economy of means.[14]

When I was growing up, anyone with an especially odd habit was labeled "peculiar." Miss Ruby was especially peculiar. She would quietly enter our house without knocking and rummage through our refrigerator for leftovers and our trash for things she could use. Apparently, she did this throughout the neighborhood because she almost never went to the grocery store, and she seemed perfectly well fed. She also had a wonderful junk pile behind her house. Miss Ruby fixed broken things—her own and others. Most of these repairs focused on household objects, and she often made exquisite toys from recycled stuff. She also collected discarded plants for her garden. She planted nuts and acorns about the neighborhood in places that

Social activity at low dam

The citizen-generated Yoshino Watershed Green Dam Plan relies on natively wise in-stream interventions like low dams that infiltrate ground water and spread flood waters into adjacent fields.

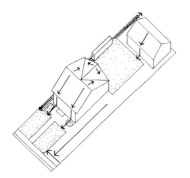

Zero-runoff retrofit

Gravel infiltration

Ground-water recharge

had been neglected or were barren. Her landscaping is a source of beauty today, decades after her death. An oddity to other grownups, she was a source of wonder to the children in the neighborhood. Soon we followed her example, much to the dismay of our parents. She helped me train a chicken, Henny Penny, to follow me around the neighborhood like a pet dog. Miss Ruby's daily patterns of conserving, recycling, and repairing the neighborhood challenged prevailing form in our city but inspired others because her efforts were captivating in our own context. Now I realize that her patterns represent an extremely useful model for an ecological democracy. The landscape she created gave a distinct local precedent for conserving, recycling, and repairing. No faraway abstraction, her peculiar inventions were a recognizable adaptation that was particular to our neighborhood. The memory of it makes me wonder what neighbors in Japan's Yoshino valley must have thought when the first indigo farmer built his roof so it would float and allow him to escape to safety when the Yoshino River flooded.

Such creative patterns exist in almost every community and, if viewed as more than mere oddities, can inspire resilient action in the larger civic landscape. In 1976, Andy Lipkis, a youthful native of Los Angeles, undertook tree planting in his city similar to Miss Ruby's efforts in my town, except his action expanded into a citywide effort called Tree People, which planted over 1 million trees in the three years leading up to the 1984 Olympic Games, changing forever the landscape of Los Angeles and the attitudes of thousands of residents.[15]

Like the idiosyncratic influences of Miss Ruby, the indigo farmers, and Andy Lipkis on the landscape, communitywide patterns that are unique to local cultures reduce the energy that is required to create and maintain the community, use local materials that are replenishable and do not have to be transported long distances, reuse old buildings and landscapes, and reduce waste and toxic side effects.[16] Because they are local adaptations, they also underlie a sense of community distinctiveness.

Consider the case of the Tawo people who live on Pongso-no-Tawo, now called Orchid Island, the northernmost of the Batan Chain in the Philippines. The Tawo developed their house form over centuries of adaptation to the local climate and life patterns. Their home consists of four parts. One, the *vahay,* is constructed of large, local stones and is buried underground to give protection from typhoons. It consists of the family altar, sleeping areas, and a kitchen and is a sanctuary from driving rains and winds.

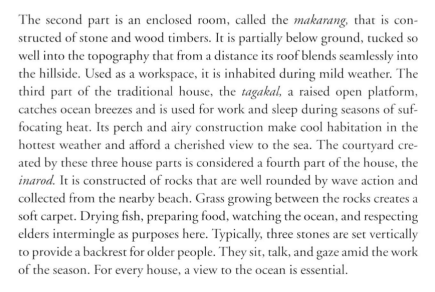

The Tawo people inhabit a house form that is unique to the Batan chain of the Philippine Islands. It is so adapted to monsoons and stifling hot weather that it seems to be part of the landscape.

The second part is an enclosed room, called the *makarang,* that is constructed of stone and wood timbers. It is partially below ground, tucked so well into the topography that from a distance its roof blends seamlessly into the hillside. Used as a workspace, it is inhabited during mild weather. The third part of the traditional house, the *tagakal,* a raised open platform, catches ocean breezes and is used for work and sleep during seasons of suffocating heat. Its perch and airy construction make cool habitation in the hottest weather and afford a cherished view to the sea. The courtyard created by these three house parts is considered a fourth part of the house, the *inarod.* It is constructed of rocks that are well rounded by wave action and collected from the nearby beach. Grass growing between the rocks creates a soft carpet. Drying fish, preparing food, watching the ocean, and respecting elders intermingle as purposes here. Typically, three stones are set vertically to provide a backrest for older people. They sit, talk, and gaze amid the work of the season. For every house, a view to the ocean is essential.

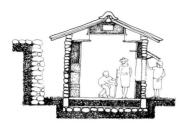

House form and local materials

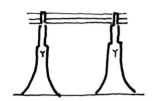

Ancestral soul

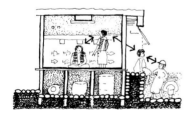

House form and social life

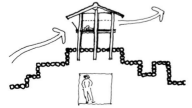

House form and climate

A house like no other in the world, the Tawo house is a peculiar adaptation that is harmonious with and celebrates its landscape setting. Built from local materials, it requires no external energy or resources for construction or use.

The organization of villages is even more remarkable. Each village, consisting of about one hundred dwellings, is located on a gentle slope that is well back from the ocean and away from storm surges. The houses are tightly grouped but arranged on terraces so that every *tagakal* and *inaorod* has a view to the ocean. The harbor, beach, burial rocks, and wood lot below are managed collectively by the village. The taro fields and other croplands on steep terraces above the village are owned by individual families, each with equal water rights that have historically been the limiting force. Every steep mountain watershed provides enough water to sustain only about one hundred families. When a village reached its water-carrying capacity, a new village was started in another small watershed. Today there are six such villages. This idiosyncratic division into new villages when the carrying capacity was exceeded shows an extraordinary local wisdom about the regional carrying capacity.

But all that changed when outsiders declared the houses primitive and unfit for human habitation. The nearby Chinese felt compelled to civilize people they considered to be savages. On a visit to Orchid Island, the wife of the president concluded that something had to be done for the pitiful people living in such deplorable conditions. Soon thereafter, rectangular concrete barracks were built in five long military lines to house the Tawo. As poorly suited to the people and climate as the traditional patterns had been well suited, the ill-fitting housing was just one aspect of destructive cultural domination. The Tawo people had one of the most egalitarian decision-making processes known anywhere, but that culture was largely dismantled.

The new concrete housing was an affront to Tawo daily life and rituals. None of the necessary functions that were so readily accommodated in the old four-part houses could be carried out in the concrete boxes. Food preparation simply did not fit. The indoor toilet was taboo. The concrete barracks were unbearably hot and wet in summer and cold and damp in winter. People tried to add *tagakals* and courts, but the military rows and grid arrangement on flat terrain prevented successful additions. Then the poorly constructed concrete began to fall apart. The salt in the unwashed sea sand that was used in the construction had corroded the reinforcing steel. Roofs

House form and water use

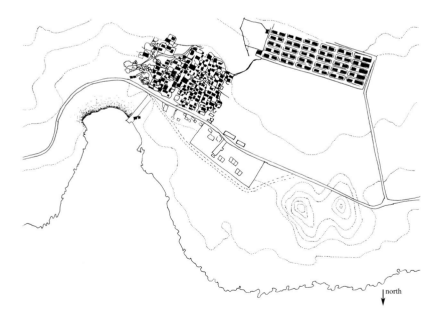

↓north

Organic villages that are sized to watersheds and organized to share clean water and views contrast with the housing blocks that were imposed when government officials declared the Tawo underground homes to be "primitive."

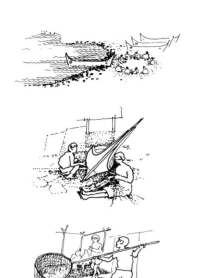

collapsed and walls crumbled. The government had to acknowledge failure. Protest led to a five-year plan to build new housing for the Tawo people. Most local people wanted modern conveniences, but everyone knew that the barracks units had lost many aspects of the traditional house. Some people wanted both.

Working with a group of Tawo who wanted to return to the traditional style but with modern conveniences, John Liu and his associates uncovered aspects of the traditional that could be applied to new housing. By measuring old houses, talking to elders, and observing how people used the traditional houses and the barracks, the architects developed a pattern language that the Tawo could use to discuss future housing. The centuries-old ways

Outdoor household activity

The recent house form combines tradition with modern conveniences, using local materials and techniques that are particular to the Tawo people.

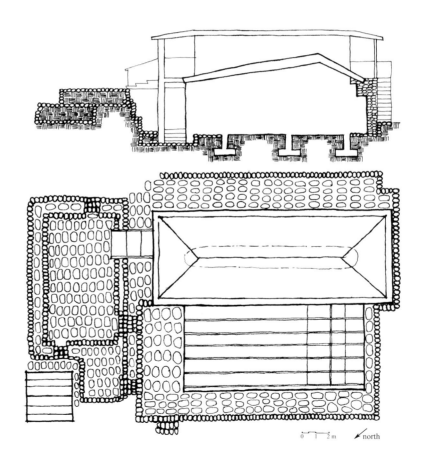

0 1 2m north

of heating, cooking, and keeping the house dry were combined with current lifestyles to create a modern house that, like the traditional four-part house, is particular to its context. It, too, is like no other house anywhere. It is made to suit the local people, the climate, and the site. It has low energy embedded in its construction. It is made of traditional materials—rock and wood. It minimizes the use of concrete. A two-layer roof provides ventilation and creates a draft to cool the house in summer. The new house requires almost no nonrenewable energy to heat, cool, and keep dry. This is due partly to the roof ventilation system and partly to the arrangement of rooms on four different levels, like the traditional house. Even the roofline is kept the same to provide views to the sea without blocking other people's views. Additionally, because the modern house champions the old, daily patterns and rituals, as well as the climatic adaptations of the traditional society, its development has spawned a new appreciation for and revival of the ceremonies and ways of living resiliently with the land that had almost been lost. The Tawo people report that the new house style has reconnected them with their own history. Many envision a cultural renewal that was unthinkable before these new houses showed them how to combine past and future. The new house saves money, reduces energy costs, and is remarkably comfortable—more comfortable than the traditional house—but also more expensive and susceptible to fire than the concrete box.[17]

After the demonstration house was blessed, the Tawo tested its livability and concluded that it fits their life patterns, saves money in maintenance and energy, but is more expensive to build.

Creating the demonstration house rekindled dying cultural rituals that are associated with home making, such as sharing pit-cooked pork throughout the village.

This new modern house that combines traditional values with today's lifestyles and conserves scarce resources now serves as one precedent. It is pitted against seductive new styles that use nonlocal materials and require far more nonrenewable and toxic materials. But it provides a choice.

Less dramatic but powerfully resilient infill projects that are based on traditional row, town, and courtyard house typologies and that use modern solar and water-conserving technologies provide housing particular to climate and topography in multiple American cities.[18] By putting forward such idiosyncratic new forms of habitation inspired by the locality, architects show how ecological reality can be elegantly married with social desire. They may be peculiar, yet they may serve as precedents that become widely accepted.

Meditations, Imaginings, and Similar Someplace Else

Often, the particular patterns of most importance to resiliency are not immediately obvious. Subtle nuances may be undiscovered or hidden by misuse. A landscape architect might say that these types of things should be turned up by good site analysis, but finding details of particularness requires seeing culture and place as one, synthesizing natural and cultural factors, and overcoming the distinctions of observer and observed. The designer must become part of the scene.[19] This takes unconventional effort. I was told as a student that Lawrence Halprin spent days and nights on the California coast before he grasped the way the topography, vegetation, and wind patterns might be orchestrated to create the landscape of the Sea Ranch, which is recognized today as one of the most powerful landscape designs of the last century. Its long, double rows and masses of Monterey cypress and other evergreens (many of which Halprin planted himself) are aligned perpendicular to the rugged coast. By organizing the landscape, they make the entirety and each smaller division of the site immediately recognizable. The rows now control the wind, capture the sun, direct the view, and provide an allee of wildness that lifts the spirit. Halprin's capacity to become part of a place was reinforced when, thirty years later, he and I were developing ideas for the Presidio National Park in San Francisco. After we disagreed about the proper way to connect the main parade ground to the waterfront, he showed up the next morning with dozens of sketches he had done while contemplating the site. When had he found time to restudy the landscape? He had gotten up in the middle of the night and sat through the chilling Golden Gate morning, painting the landscape and imagining on paper how it should be designed. Needless to say, he had found essential idiosyncratic patterns.

Larry Halprin spent a year experiencing and synthesizing the uniqueness of the landscape that became the Sea Ranch and organized the community within the folds of the land and windbreaks of cypress trees.

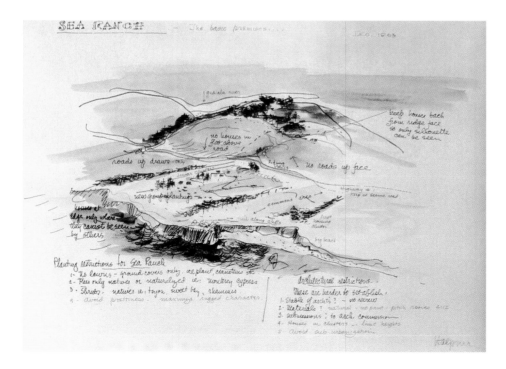

Halprin's cypress windbreaks

When soils, vegetation, wind patterns, and almost anything else you want to know about a site are available via computer, is such time-consuming site meditation necessary?[20] Plain and simple, yes. Pattern discoveries may come from many sources. Computer synthesis reveals forms from complexity, especially at the regional, historical, or contextual scale. When computer data on natural and social systems can be cross-referenced and analyzed, the connectedness of various forces can be made spatially explicit. Invisible forces, like the relationship between ground-water depletion and regional sprawl, can seldom be otherwise made observable. But it is the synthesis of information, not the information itself, that reveals patterns of particularness. One can look at hundreds of single-factor maps, raw data, or even overlays, and nothing of consequence might emerge. Usually, it is the synthesis of multiple factors—how a combination of natural and cultural forces interact—that provides the essential pattern for resilience. In urban contexts, patterns of particularness may be revealed only by mapping the atypical, like barriers to civicness, loved and unloved parts of a stream, or fearful places.

Even though computer maps are easier to create and manipulate, most important insights come from drawing the maps by hand and by on-site meditation. I often discover patterns of particularness as I draw the base in-

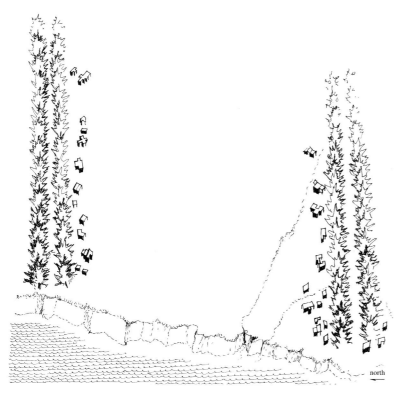

Halprin strengthened existing cypress windbreaks that would protect houses from wind while maintaining views and open space.

north

formation or a synthetic map of various base data. This is because drawing the maps takes more attention, both focused and unfocused, than looking at the same maps that someone else or the computer has made. Similarly, meditation on site, especially when spent drawing or painting, allows for mindful and mindless attention to the place. Thom Alcoze said that you should never begin to design a riparian landscape until you have sat by the stream with your eyes closed and can tell whether a beaver crossing the stream nearby is moving upstream or down. The same is true for any design at any scale, from the region to the arrangement of flowerpots. Patterns of particularness are thus captured for use.

Quiet observation, even in hectic urban settings, provides insights and time for informed imagining and making associations with precedents from similar landscapes. Yet it is sometimes useful to consider particular adaptations of resilient design from places often far away but with similar climate, vegetation, topography, or culture. Recently, my son, Nate, was designing a

Faraway precedent

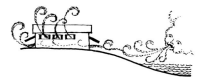

Summer adaptation

Winter adaptation

new barn for our farm in North Carolina. By replacing a pack barn, he intended to create a workshop. His desire to make the workshop fit into its context by mimicking the form of traditional barns conflicted with his desire to have the building light, heat, and cool itself from natural sources. Because of their use for seasoning tobacco before sale, the vernacular pack barns (barns with hand-dug basements walled with red clay and rock) kept the rain out and moisture in. Beyond that, pack barns were never climate controlled: they got extremely hot in summer and very cold in winter. During fall and early winter, seasons of primary use, they were comfortable without elaboration, and their natural moisture prevented tobacco from drying out. They often had only one small door at one end to access loads and few windows. This precluded cross-circulation, which was fine for ordering tobacco but not for an artist's year-round workshop. A local architect insisted that the building should be air-conditioned, arguing that any antique furniture would be ruined without it. "How did antiques get to be antiques since there was no air conditioning before Carrier's 1902 invention?," Nate wondered.

He did not seek architectural advice after that. But Nate was stumped. Maybe he could not keep the form of the old pack barn and cool the building naturally. Then one morning, Nate recalled a building that he had drawn in Haleiwa, Hawaii, where large doors with overhangs at opposite ends of the store provided air circulation through the building. By siting the paired doors perpendicular to the ocean and planting trees around the west end, the Haleiwa building sucked sea breezes through the structure and cooled itself. Nate decided to site our barn to pull up cooling breezes from a nearby lake through paired roll-up doors with deep shade bonnets. The overall mass, roof pitch, bonnets, and shed of his new barn retained the local vernacular style, but the paired doors were borrowed from a building in an entirely different setting with a similar hot summer climate. The new barn fits into its context and cools itself. By borrowing a solution from a similar someplace else, Nate solved the old problem of cooling and could concentrate on new problems, like natural lighting.[21]

Time Lapse and Previous Catastrophes

The search for applicable particularness is often rewarded when both geologic time and periods of recent human habitation are considered. Hikaru Okuzumi notes that "even the plainest most ordinary pebble has the history of the universe written on it."[22] Certainly, present land-use patterns are, in large measure, etched from geologic actions that took place millions of years ago. In the landscape around Chapel Hill, North Carolina, where the above-mentioned barn was being built, most of the forestland has been regularly cut, and few patches of mature oak and hickory woodlands remain, except in fractured rock outcroppings that were too difficult to farm but fertile enough, in time, to grow hardwoods and to cool buildings. Even the wise location of a new barn can be determined by looking at the changes that happened at a small site over geologic time.

At the larger scale, geologic changes have to be imagined to reconstruct the past and predict wise use. When we were doing a plan for the Skagit River Valley in Mount Vernon, Washington, it was impossible to comprehend how much the form of the river might shift in the broad floodplain simply by studying historical maps. It was necessary to speculate on the dramatic movement in the river's course that took place over the millennia before USGS maps were made. The natively wise river dweller Zell Young guided the effort. He was like the holy man who was so aware of ecological change that in his whole lifetime he never sat down but remained crouching.[23] Zell Young understood the likelihood of such continued shifts and periodic jolting changes in the river course. He visualized and described geologic catastrophes. This provided the basis for river management in the Skagit River Valley that was far more respectful of the change than had been practiced in recent years, resulting in a more resilient city form. By thinking about Zell Young's meanders of time, the community understood the current river in a more respectful way. We could see the history of the entire region marked in the river's course. Designing to accommodate change led us to reconsider our heightened levees, concrete revetments, and channelization, which were all efforts to deny the river's past and its inherent nature and, in effect, to make it static. The community wanted a plan to soften concrete embankments, to purchase park land that would receive flood waters at the river's highest flow, and to accept changing patterns of riparian vegetation for nature parks. The latter are unusually dramatic and periodically dynamic parks that allow plants to move about in a pattern like hair braids, depending on shifting flood waters and depositions of silt that vary from one year to the next. Long curving rows, often punctuated in organic bulges of foxglove (*Digitalis purpurea*), show up in different arcing lines, depending on sedimentation patterns, enriched organic decay, and edge conditions of

Momentary stability

sun and shade. The native plants rearrange themselves seasonally, yearly, and episodically. This pattern of shifting vegetation and sediment deposits provides a unique form of park running through Mount Vernon. It is especially powerful when seen juxtaposed against the carefully manicured grid of daffodil, tulip, and Dutch iris farms that extend for miles from the river.

Although lacking both the hydrogeological science and the romance of changes over thousands of years, patterns of response to past stochastic events can provide particular form to increase the resilience of a city. It is certainly informative, although not encouraging, to know that residents in so many cities in fire-, earthquake-, flood-, or hurricane-prone areas never seem to learn from past disasters. When one city does—as in the case of Mount

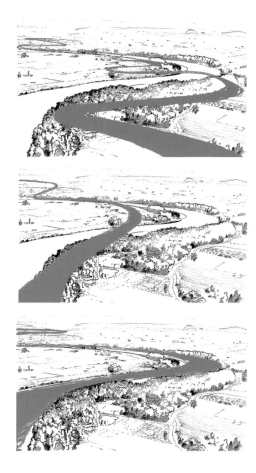

To predict wise future land use for others in his community, Zell Young used his knowledge of the locality to reconstruct shifts in the Skagit River over millions of geologic years.

Expanding sand bar

Considering geologic time, residents developed parks that change seasonally and episodically. Favorites were the expanding sand bar and the digitalis gardens that move with sediment deposits.

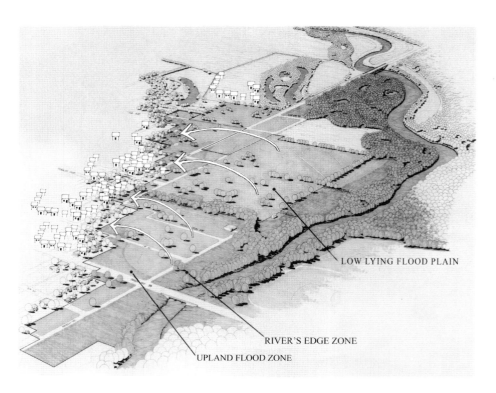

LOW LYING FLOOD PLAIN

RIVER'S EDGE ZONE

UPLAND FLOOD ZONE

After disastrous flooding, residents of Cherokee, Iowa, finally decided to move their city to higher ground, where it snakes along safe topography overlooking 150 acres of flood-prone open space.

Relocating the town

Vernon, Washington, or more radically in the instance of Cherokee, Iowa— it is especially informative.

Residents of Cherokee had long suffered flooding from the Little Sioux River but never before had seen the destruction that resulted from six months of flooding in 1993. Nearly $4 million in damage was done in a city of only six thousand people. Hundreds of houses and businesses were destroyed in low-lying areas. After much deliberation, citizens decided not to repair the buildings in the floodplain. They had rebuilt many times before at great expense. The city took a distinctively different form as it evolved into a more resilient community. Cherokee moved out of flood-prone areas and relocated and rebuilt on higher ground. The new town looks different because its form mimics the topographic flow and soil patterns that are unique to its context. The town snakes along the higher elevations. A great green space—150 acres of native forest and wet prairie—has replaced the relocated buildings. It provides recreational benefits that previously were unavailable to Cherokee residents and protects the town from future flood

Residents visit their old homesite, which is reverting to native forest and wet prairie.

disasters. Although the Cherokee innovation was not cheap, the entire relocation, including the new park, will pay for itself after two more floods.[24]

Particularness Provides Goodness of Fit

Particularness of place can be found in regional topographies, in wind patterns, in stream or underground water flows, in details of architectural heating and cooling, in the arrangement of buildings on sites, in idiosyncrasies of land use, and in the placement of a junk pile. These patterns can sometimes be observed in the landscape at a glance, but often they must be carefully meditated into view by studying a series of maps, evidence of geological history, local oral history, and records of past disasters.

In every case, the discovery of the patterns that are special to a place opens the possibility that a city that is more fit with its ecosystem will be created. The application of particularness is likely to reduce waste, energy use, and demands on nonrenewable resources. Particularness is always less expensive in the long run. Additionally, it decreases susceptibility to ruinous damage from natural and economic disasters and provides an urban form that is more expressive and distinctive.

Selective Diversity

Diversity is variety and difference and is made up of many distinctive components. Diversity possesses multiformity. Diversity means dissimilarity and division.

Few things befuddle Americans about our domestic landscape as much as diversity does. We know from experience that communities with varied economies are less susceptible to catastrophic swings in unemployment. Diversity sounds good. But then the similar industries all flock together and create economies of sameness. Diversity must be bad. We like the idea of our country being born of so many different outcasts, but we sure don't want to live next to them.[1] Where I live, the poetry, biology, and political correctness of diversity fill the air. We're simply not alike; we're different and divided. Is this good or bad? What does diversity suggest for city form?

Urban resilience doubtlessly depends on maintaining or creating diversity in many aspects of urban form. But ecological democracy most critically depends on overcoming landscape fragmentation and shortsighted interest-group divisions. Considering one of our most basic American tenets, *e pluribus unum,* our cities are presently debilitated by rampant pluribusing without consideration for the unum. Reestablishing enough common values so that our cities can be formed as wholes rather than balkanized into segregated districts of mutual unconcern must become a priority. Unity and diversity must be cultivated as balanced partners in an ecological democracy.[2]

This said, sometimes diversity must be pursued with the same vigor that we need to pursue shared values in decision making. Cities that are diverse are more resilient but only when that diversity is within a framework that is delineated by the particularness of the given regional landscape, social respect, and cooperation. Healthy diversity is tempered by limits of locality. Resilient city systems are highly varied and specific to time, place, and people.[3] But the resilient city is neither a botanical garden (which has plenty of variety but no regional delineation) nor single-crop agriculture (which has replaced regional unity with uniformity). Generally, American cities are becoming more and more the same and ignoring local distinctiveness. They are becoming more diverse in a few superficial ways and less diverse in important ways. Therefore, as a rule, the path to urban resilience is a selective diversity by which multiformity is maintained and enhanced within the unifying particularness of a given region. Enhancements should be focused where diversity has been lost or is lacking. For example, consider the loss of wetlands to reclamation projects or the lack of neighborhoods with diverse social classes, ages, and subcultures. However, when a certain urban form—for example, a building type that minimizes the need for nonrenewable energy in its production and maintenance—is developed within the particularness of a given climate and topography, there is little reason to create different building types. So a city's resilience depends most on carefully choosing diversity in those areas that are basic to its long-term sustainability and resisting indiscriminate diversity seeking, which so often plagues designers searching for self-expression.

To design resilient American cities, diversity is critical across a number of landscape scales and social dimensions, including biological diversity, cultural diversity, global heterogenization, mixed economies and land uses, social integration, and the incubation of multiformity. These are the fundamentally important ways we need to make our habitation more diverse.

Biological Diversity

Worldwide, living organisms and habitats are being lost at a rate that is unparalleled, even when compared to times of mass extinctions. Biological diversity—whether measured in genetic distinctness within or between species or in systemic distinctiveness within or between ecosystems—is declining with horrifying human consequences. The easiest measure is species extinctions. On average, over the past five hundred years less than one species became extinct each year. In contrast, some scientists believe that today over fifty thousand species go extinct each year.[4] They estimate that 25 percent of all species in the world will be lost forever within the next thirty years.[5] Some calculate that half of all species may be on the path to extinction.[6] Many of these species will be lost without our ever knowing their essential roles in their ecosystems or to our well-being. Most of these extinctions are caused by the loss of habitat because of human habitation expansion. The extent and form of human habitation are the most important factors in the precipitous decline of biological diversity, and our patterns in the United States are collectively the single worst culprit, placing demands on habitats at home and throughout the world. Long-term solutions require three things: worldwide reductions in the types of consumption that fuel the loss of critical habitats, the control of human population growth, and new forms of human habitation that require less of the habitat that is needed by other organisms.

At first glance, overall biological diversity is negatively correlated with cities in whatever form. Therefore, the first urban design objective for maintaining biological diversity is to protect certain landscapes from human habitation. This can be accomplished by maintaining geographical isolation to encourage natural divergence of character and prevent the spread of non-native exotics that kill or displace native local species, by maintaining temperate habitats where diversity is likely to increase,[7] and by maintaining large unfragmented habitats where interior species can thrive. These can be achieved by avoiding such landscapes when making cities, by designating large remote wilderness preserves, and by incorporating protected preserves into the form of the city.[8]

The plan to maintain the most critical wintering habitat of the black-faced spoonbill (*Platalea minor*) illustrates. One of the rarest birds in the world, it migrates from breeding grounds in North and South Korea and possibly other unknown sites to China, Japan, and the Philippines. The greatest concentration of birds is in the Tsen-wen estuary of coastal Tainan County, Taiwan. The black-faced spoonbill faces immediate extinction due to the loss of its wintering grounds to urbanization. Ten years ago, this winter habitat was about to be developed for the Binnan Industrial Park, one of the largest industrial complexes in the world, a combination of petrochemical refineries, steel plants, and associated factories. After assessing the amount of estuary needed for foraging and roosting, a nonprofit organization called SAVE, International (Spoonbill Action Voluntary Echo) concluded that the black-faced spoonbill faced an extinction vortex from which it would never recover if the industrial complex was built.

Unfortunately, the official environmental impact statement had already concluded that the industries at the Binnan complex would not negatively impact the spoonbill. Could SAVE's preliminary assessment be completely in error, or was the government environmental study flawed? SAVE assem-

Spoonbill migration flyway

Almost the entire black-faced spoonbill population winters in the Tsen-Wen Estuary, where petrochemical industries and related urban development threaten to send it into an extinction vortex.

Daily feeding pattern

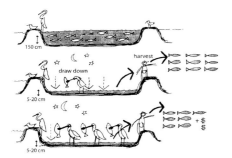

Symbiosis with aquaculture

Habitat-inspired urban form

bled a team of international scientists to evaluate the official environmental impact statement. A six-month study substantiated its worst fears. The first phase of the Binnan complex—which consisted of a naptha cracker plant, an integrated steel mill, and an exclusive industrial port—would require the filling of over 2,000 hectares of productive wetland that was essential for the spoonbill's survival and was a habitat for over two hundred other species of wildlife. Experts—including the cochair of the Specialist Group on Storks, Ibis, and Spoonbills at the International Union for Conservation of Nature and Natural Resources (IUCN) and a dozen other spoonbill scientists— feared extinction due to the loss of habitat to the industrial complex and growth induced by the industries, which would total over four thousand hectares. Then SAVE discovered that the official study had considered only the impact on the roosting area of the spoonbill. Official documents ignored the feeding territory altogether. Because the spoonbill roosts during the day and forages at night, little data existed on the extent of its feeding range. Was this an honest scientific mistake or a sham study? In any case, it was not a mistake that a conservation biologist wants to make. It so happened that the foraging area of the spoonbill would be destroyed by industrial and associated growth, resulting in a poor place to sleep and nowhere at all to eat.

At this point, the lead spoonbill scientist, Malcolm Coulter, pored over the few studies about spoonbills and related species. He described the findings about spatial needs; SAVE's designers drew them on a map. Patterns began to emerge. The daytime roosting area was, indeed, concentrated in one large, open-water estuary just north of the Tsen Wen River. Nighttime foraging, Coulter estimated from related studies, extended north up the coast thirty kilometers. Little habitat remained south of the Tsen Wen River because Tainan City had filled most of it. The habitat most used by the spoonbills for foraging, he hypothesized, was the shallow wetlands, estuaries, and fishponds north and east of the roosting area within ten to fourteen kilometers. These estimates were later confirmed by field studies. Designers drew these radii over a map of potential habitat. Coulter had described the habitat based on his own research: spoonbills are tactile feeders, using their sensitive bills to locate small fish and crustaceans by sweeping bottoms of estuarine waters that are no deeper than twenty centimeters. They need shallow water to feed; windbreaks to protect them from strong ocean winds; large expanses of calm water for roosting, feeding, and safety from predators (mostly domestic dogs and sometimes fishermen); and mud flats and fallow

Resilient Form

Because spoonbills feed at night, little was known of their habitat needs, but field research revealed a symbiotic relationship with aquaculture. This radically altered urban form.

fishponds. SAVE's designers mapped the areas that met these criteria. It was clear the spoonbills could not survive given the Binnan project and present trends of urban growth in the region. This was the most important wintering habitat in the world, and it was about to be ruined.

SAVE began working with local people who wanted to mount a campaign to stop construction of the Binnan industrial complex. Only a few fishermen, local environmentalists, and a lone national legislator, Su Huan-Chi, voiced opposition to the project. But when SAVE's environmental assessment exposed the flaws and chicanery in the official document, others began to question the project. Some were worried about the sixteen thousand jobs in fisheries and related industries that would be lost. Others were concerned because the complex would require 320,000 metric tons of water a day, interbasin transfers from three watersheds away, and multiple dams that would cause extinctions of other species and the destruction of indigenous villages. It was also revealed that the two first-phase plants would produce 27.8 million tons of carbon dioxide annually, 31 percent of Taiwan's total 1990 carbon dioxide emissions.[9]

Habitat loss to Binnan industry

Habitat loss to SAVE plan

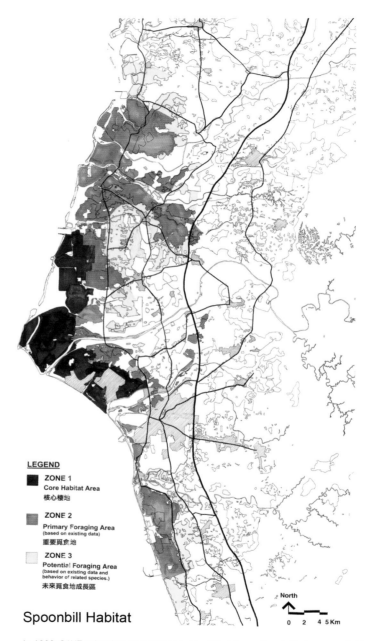

LEGEND

■ ZONE 1
Core Habitat Area
核心棲地

▨ ZONE 2
Primary Foraging Area
(based on existing data)
重要覓食地

▫ ZONE 3
Potential Foraging Area
(based on existing data and
behavior of related species.)
未來覓食地成長區

North

0   2   4 5 Km

Spoonbill Habitat

In 1998, SAVE scientists and planners identified the wetlands that were suitable for spoonbill habitat, ranked the lands that were deemed most critical for species survival, and modeled extinction likelihood in different patterns of urbanization.

Although more people were concerned about the Binnan industrial complex, the local community was still divided. One national leader urged the acceptance of Binnan and said that the area was like an ugly woman who could never get anything better than this industrial complex. Dangerous protests and confrontations ensued. Threats and assaults became commonplace for those who opposed Binnan. In the meantime, SAVE organized an international campaign to force a serious evaluation of the impacts and stop Binnan. International awareness led to outrage, and pressure was applied on the government of Taiwan, but the government was unmoved.

SAVE realized that a new vision was necessary for the coastal Tainan region. Heavy industry had become the only future that most people imagined. For the spoonbill and the fishermen's jobs to survive, a new economy and associated urban form had to be developed. A team from National Taiwan University, legislator Su's office, SAVE scientists, and local people began to develop an alternative plan.

Foundations for healthy new habitation were considerable. Tainan City is a historic area with a diverse economy. There are fledgling high-technology parks in the region. The fishing and agriculture industries remain vibrant. There is potential for expanding green industries and for cultural and ecological tourism. There are dozens of small villages with distinctive economies. After a year of work, SAVE proposed a new regional growth plan. Eliminating the Binnan project and its associated development in a fragile and important wetland habitat, the new plan focused on development of fishing, value-added fish-related industries, tourism, and a research-oriented high-technology industry. When compared to the Binnan complex, this alternative outperformed in almost every category—the environment, long-term job security, and even total number of jobs.

The new form of urban growth is radically different than the wetland destruction of Binnan. The SAVE plan calls for expanded communities around the high-technology clusters and additional compact growth in dozens of smaller villages. The larger cities of Chia-Li and Shuei-Chia, which have particularly diverse economies, are further strengthened with industry that adds value to farm and fish products before they leave the region. Rural growth is being concentrated in small industries, orchid farms, fishing, and tourism villages like Longshan and Pei-men. These villages are now connected by scenic routes. Almost the entire wetland will be maintained for aquaculture, tourism, and wildlife habitat. Less than 2 percent of the critical

Within a framework of natural watercourses and wetlands, the alternative plan directs urban growth to Tainan City and existing villages at the edge of the spoonbill habitat, where local entrepreneurs develop ecological tourism.

Indigenous art center

Salt Mountain proposal

Salt Mountain tourism

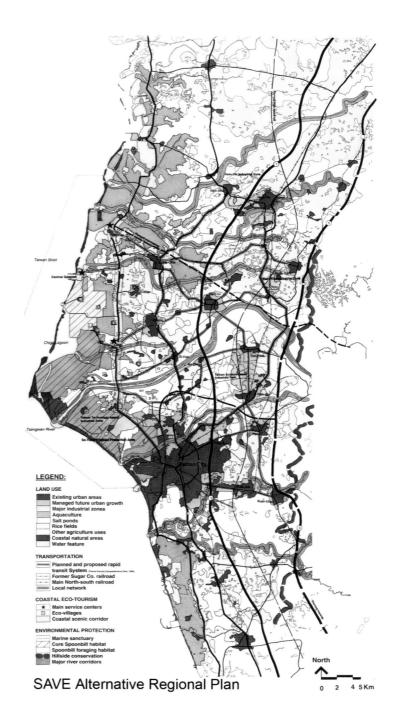

LEGEND:

LAND USE
- Existing urban areas
- Managed future urban growth
- Major industrial zones
- Aquaculture
- Salt ponds
- Rice fields
- Other agriculture uses
- Coastal natural areas
- Water feature

TRANSPORTATION
- Planned and proposed rapid transit System (Tainan County Comprehensive Plan, 1998)
- Former Sugar Co. railroad
- Main North-south railroad
- Local network

COASTAL ECO-TOURISM
- ★ Main service centers
- ☐ Eco-villages
- Coastal scenic corridor

ENVIRONMENTAL PROTECTION
- Marine sanctuary
- Core Spoonbill habitat
- Spoonbill foraging habitat
- Hillside conservation
- Major river corridors

North

0 2 4 5 Km

SAVE Alternative Regional Plan

habitat will be lost in this new urban pattern. The wetland reserve is also an important amenity that will attract skilled employees to the high-technology centers. Integrating the habitat that is necessary for biological diversity into the form of the cities—in fact, shaping the cities into the wildlife habitat framework—serves coastal Tainan well. This reserve creates green boundaries for each city and the overall urban form of the entire region. Seven core areas may be designated exclusively as wildlife preserves within National Scenic Area that was created in 2004 to maintain fishing and aquaculture, promote recreation and tourism, and preserve secondary feeding grounds for the spoonbill.

Beyond preventing extinction for the sake of the spoonbill itself, there is a strong anthropocentric self-interest at play as we preserve biological diversity to make cities more resilient. In fact, there is mixed evidence that natural ecosystems themselves are inherently more resilient if they are more diverse (the exception being cases where diverse species can substitute one for the other in the food web or other functions). The resilience of the human species, however, definitely benefits from biological diversity, not only in preserving genetic structures that may hold the key to our own survival (as in the case of the Pacific yew tree, which produces taxol, the central ingredient in drugs used in fighting breast and ovarian cancer) but also in making more sustainable urban form. In the spoonbill example, the preservation of the estuary and related wetlands saves the spoonbill from extinction, expands the seven thousand jobs in fishing and the sixteen thousand jobs in fishing-related industries, and creates a water-allocation system that maximizes wetlands and fresh-water supply, the single most limiting natural resource in Taiwan's short, highly erodible watersheds.

In such cases, when habitat that is essential for a species or ecosystem's survival is also a part of the urban form, it is important to follow the principle of connectedness, specifically the spatial dictates of conservation biology. In integrating critical wildlife habitat and city form, there is a tendency to diminish geographic isolation and increase fragmentation. In the spoonbill case, and even more so with large-mammal keystone species, there must be areas of isolation and large, uninterrupted interior habitat. This is the reason that the Taiwan plan calls for seven core areas, each of 500 to 750 acres. That provides enough habitat to support a sustainable population during winter if the population ever grows out of the extinction vortex. For comparison, the mountain lion requires approximately 640,000 acres of interior

Lagoon fisherman

Longshan fish market

Longshan fishing fleet

habitat. For both interior species and top predators, the best shape of interior core habitat approximates a circle without urban protrusions penetrating its circumference. The length of circumference must be minimized and an uninterrupted interior maximized to provide the largest area and the greatest distance from urbanization possible. Edges, even with their heightened ecotonal diversity, should be minimized to achieve an adequate interior habitat. The sheer extent required for various species, as well as their many other specific needs, determines the suitability for incorporation into urban form. The spoonbill habitat, for example, has a relatively small core requirement (and a convenient symbiotic relationship with recently harvested fish ponds) and therefore can be incorporated into the city form more easily than the habitat for the mountain lion. In contrast, the habitat of the mountain lion and other top predators can serve only as the boundary to city form. A significant challenge to urban designers is to shape the habitat to provide both the isolation that interior species require and the integration that is needed to form the city and its neighborhoods.

Frequently, the urban habitat for an endangered species may accommodate that species itself but not provide adequate habitat, either in size or quality, for the entire associated ecosystem to survive. For the habitat to provide biological diversity, it must support the entirety of that ecosystem, particularly the top predators that most often are lost with fragmentation. Equally important is the provision of multiple cores that support metapopulations that are essential for healthy genetic diversity and resilience against stochastic events. In the case of the spoonbill, there is a frightening concentration of the endangered bird in the Tsen Wen estuary area. Two-thirds of the entire world population winters in one ten-kilometer stretch. As a result, a single botulism outbreak in the winter of 2002 killed over 5 percent of the population of black-faced spoonbills. Therefore, it seemed important to provide multiple core habitats that are located apart from each other within this one coastal wetland. This is the second reason for the seven distinct core roosting areas that SAVE is trying to establish. This offers the protections of genetic diversity and insulation against human-induced disasters, like an oil spill, that could destroy most of the world's population in one action if the spoonbills were roosting in a single location. The warning for urban designers is that the spatial requirements for each species and associated ecosystems are distinctive and must be thoroughly researched before being synthesized into city form. It is difficult to integrate core wildlife habitat into the city, especially when much of the landscape has already been altered. It

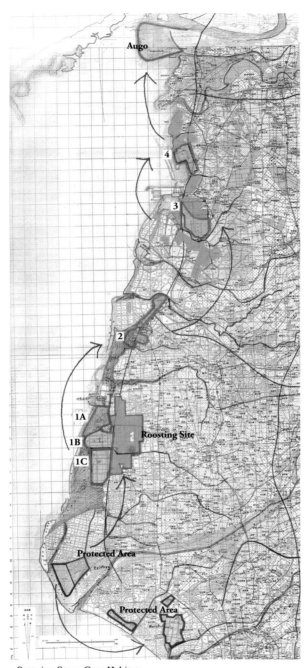

Augo

4

3

2

1A

1B

Roosting Site

1C

Protected Area

Protected Area

Stepping Stone Core Habitats

Only two of the wetlands that are essential for 16,000 fishing-related jobs and spoonbill survival are presently protected. Five more core areas are being considered to allow the bird population to divide and expand.

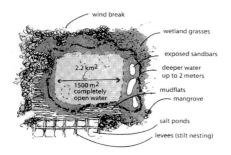

Core roosting requirements

has been easier to make wildlife preserves in remote wilderness. But that strategy was less fulfilling for city dwellers. For selfish, anthropocentric values, not the least of which is to observe wildlife in our everyday lives, the integration of the habitats for some endangered species may well be designed into overall city form. With better science and knowledge about how to translate that science into spatial principles, cities can be retrofitted and regions shaped both to preserve biological diversity and to receive enormous benefits for city dwellers.

In the case of the spoonbill, the benefits to local people have been immediate. The rural villagers have become empowered through their struggle to implement their new vision. In concert with SAVE, local groups drew considerable international attention to the Chigu Lagoon and the surrounding wetland. They defeated the Binnan Industrial Park. Leading environmental organizations now know the irony of this wetland. Scientifically, it qualifies as a hot spot of biological diversity and has been called a wetland

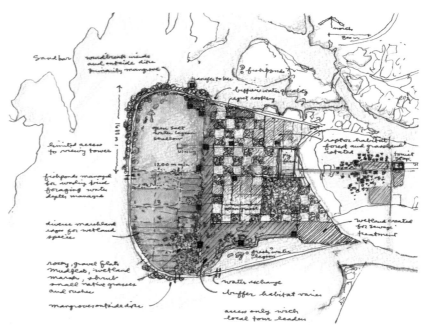

Augo wetland is one of the few areas that are large enough to accommodate a core stepping-stone habitat. It has been designed with local villagers so they control habitat protection, access, and tourism profits.

National Taiwan University designers have created wildlife-viewing centers to fit into each ecological niche, including mangroves, salt flats, and tidal wetlands.

of international importance by criteria of the United Nations Ramsar (Iran) Convention on Wetlands (1971). Any site that is home to 1 percent of an endangered species typically qualifies for designation, and coastal Tainan is the winter home to nearly 80 percent of the entire population of black-faced spoonbills. But because Taiwan is not a member of the United Nations, these coastal Tainan wetlands cannot be officially classified as a Ramsar site. As outsiders became aware of this import, local people gained confidence and pride. Residents immediately implemented ecotourism plans. Within five years, the black-faced spoonbill and related tourist destinations were attracting nearly half a million visitors a year, providing more jobs than had been projected for ten years. Local entrepreneurs and nonprofit organizations have simply developed facilities faster than expected. Thousands of new jobs are being created. Although SAVE has advised on everything from restaurant development and boat tours to ecological education centers and land-use planning, the coastal villages have consistently innovated to capture the benefits of maintaining biological diversity. Local government has constructed ecotourism education centers, designated water and land tour routes, and built multiple wildlife-viewing areas. Four villages have made economic-development plans that incorporate core wildlife. In spite of this success, Taiwan's central government approved the flawed environmental impact assessment, and only the election of Su Huan-Chi as county magistrate stopped the construction of the Binnan industrial complex.

Cultural Diversity

Like biological diversity, cultural diversity worldwide is in a precipitous decline. Consider just one measure, language, which is a good general indication of social diversity. Today there are about six thousand spoken languages, but by the year 2100 the number could drop to three thousand as traditional cultures are globalized. By this measure, in less than a hundred years, our world will be half as culturally distinctive as it is today. In California alone, we expect to lose thirty-four Native American languages that have been spoken for over a thousand years.[10] There is a direct correlation between the form of human habitation and the preservation of cultural diversity. This is especially so because often the distinctiveness of a culture is expressed and embodied in the landscape, whether in the beehive architecture of Haran, Turkey, the tightly terraced rice paddies of mountainous Japan, the spirited *zócalo* in old Mesilla, New Mexico, the spontaneous street theater of Taipei, or the urban agriculture of Hmong immigrants in St. Paul, Minnesota. All over the world, such cultural complexity, both material and nonmaterial, is being lost as city form homogenizes into a universal architecture. Even remote villages with distinct cultures are dazzled by an international culture that dominates via the media in ways that colonialism was never able to do. Loss of cultural diversity is worrisome for the same reasons as the decline of genetic diversity—because any subculture might have specialized forms of habitation key to future resilience.

For example, the Penan people in Borneo have eight different words for sago palm trees, which they use to make flour and dozens of other necessities. For them, the sago is the tree of life. They also have over two thousand names for streams, which they use to place them and to identify subtle distinctions of quality that they feel are essential for their survival. In recent years, their homeland has been largely destroyed by outsiders who are exploiting timber. Only three hundred Penan maintain the traditional nomadic culture. They now have two words for the environment around them. Their world is now divided into either the land of shade or the land that has been destroyed. Loss of forest will doom their culture. These people and their ways will die with their landscape. This matters for many reasons, not the least of which is the lessons the Penan might teach us if they survive. Consider that the Penan people believe that sharing is an obligation; they have no word for *thank you*. They have one word for *he, she,* and *it* and six words for *we*. Imagine what Americans could learn from them about how to cooperate: *e pluribus unum.* They might instruct us in everything we need to know about enabling form.[11]

In the United States, both top-down and bottom-up forces are destroying cultural differences in city form. Urban design is often associated with the acculturation and assimilation of new immigrants into the mainstream culture. Parks display the standards of the dominant mores and have often been a means of teaching new immigrants "how to behave" by reducing deviance, homogenizing the population, and ridding our cities of unwanted subcultures.[12] Urban renewal and federal highways have been even more effective at reducing cultural diversity by simply clearing neighborhoods of poor and ethnic villagers.[13] But the immigrants' own desires are often just as powerful as these top-down forces. Most immigrants are eager to shed old cultural ways and join the mainstream. This is the underlying thesis of the melting-pot culture.[14] Infrequently, has there been resistance to assimilation. Even recent movements in subcultural empowerment appear to be more about getting a fair share than maintaining culture. Is it possible to do both effectively?

In some cases, resistance has preserved cultural diversity through community design, as we saw in the Tawo House in the chapter on Particularness. Cases of resistance can inform the way that future urban landscapes are designed to maintain cultural diversity.[15] A number of spatial characteristics of habitat repeatedly support the preservation of cultural difference. Most important are isolation, a large territory, inaccessibility, design guidelines that support cultural idiosyncrasies, and control of places that are distinctive to the culture.

Isolation by remoteness in rural areas or segregation in urban contexts protects both the idiosyncratic patterns of behavior and environmental adaptations. If either the population or village—rural or urban—is too small, the culture cannot be maintained. A large enough territory to support a critical mass of people is essential. Cultural diversity, like biological diversity, can be maintained only by preventing the island effect, whereby a small population in a small territory typically goes extinct. Isolation and adequate territory are maintained by a lack of highways, and safety and exclusion by inaccessibility. In urban areas, this may be provided by inaccessibility or by a stigma that keeps others out.

Few subcultures can withstand the force and allure of the dominant culture, but some have maintained or rediscovered pride in their unique architectural or community form. This pride and the accompanying sense of identity can be nurtured by responses from city designers who are sensitive to the special spatial characteristics that are necessary for cultural diversity to survive. This requires the relaxation of rules and standards that make environmental expression of cultural difference illegal. These include the most basic city-shaping tools of zoning, building setbacks, and building codes. Regulations that prevent overcrowding, outlaw the use of traditional building types, preclude auto repair in front yards, or prohibit the keeping of small farm animals may seem innocuous on the surface but reduce diversity and resilience.

The subculture needs control over a territory in which their distinctiveness prevails. Public space from street to parks should be formed by the idiosyncrasies of the culture rather than by normative behavior. We see this in genuine Chinatowns in some American cities and in neighborhoods of new immigrants and isolated subcultures where public space is used distinctively by the inhabitants. Rather than a mechanism for assimilation and control, such open space provides the container for diversity with unconventional use of space. In successful cases, these hybrid spaces are uninviting to and sometimes restrictive of outsiders. This creates segregated diversity when considered relative to the surrounding dominant culture, but it has a structure internal to itself. A few settings may be designated by the subculture to provide interaction with and education for outsiders. This connection overcomes the negative impacts that are associated with segregated diversity.[16] By implementing remoteness and uninvitingness, cultural complexity may be enhanced in urban form.[17]

Global Heterogenization and Glocal Design

Globalization reduces both biological and cultural diversity.[18] City designers need to resist homogenization and to create heterogenization in its place, making cities distinctly different in their forms.[19] By this principle, every city would retain a distinct internal unity, a form rooted in and best suited to that ecological context. Without ignoring global connections, local nuances of place making should be the primary forces of design inspiration. Glocal communities use their local distinctiveness and worldly awareness to the advantage of resilience. This is what Wendell Berry calls "local life aware of itself."[20] Self-aware design likely serves biological and cultural diversity in the same actions; it creates internal unity and worldwide diversity.[21]

Does heterogenization encourage conflict? Probably not. Expressing cultural difference in design makes diversity concrete and therefore more comprehensible. With a modest amount of mutual respect, differences can be appreciated, admired, and enjoyed, but design is no match for extreme ethnocentrism or xenophobia.

The Landscape Form of a Diversified Economy

An economically diverse city is resilient over time.[22] The truism is repeated and often relearned when economics are overspecialized, as in Hsin Chu.

Does the form of the urban landscape contribute to business diversity? Certainly. Paul Hawken states simply that biodiversity is the source of all wealth. Then he outlines the criteria for sustainable economies.[23] His primary principle is to create, transform, and consume local products. He notes that the economy must be appropriate to its place and its locality: "A community that can provide many of its necessities locally will be less affected by the roiling national and world economy. It can prosper in good times, but will be more resilient in bad."[24]

Hawken realized that the central problem of the economy is not a management problem but a design problem—"a flaw that runs through all business."[25] The unsustainable economy fails to find a form of habitation that takes resources from the earth to the mouth in the shortest, simplest way.[26] This is, among other things, a matter of design. The most resilient cities and regions are largely self-sufficient. To be self-sufficient, they must have a diversity in landscapes to provide a short, direct transfer of a great variety of resources to the consumer. The more integrated that production and consumption become, the better. The city must be efficiently arranged, without creating conflicts between land uses that are unsuited to each other. Remember the rule of interdependent adjacencies?

In a regional economy that is largely self-reliant, diversity is typically limited by extreme environmental factors or by intense interspecific competition. Therefore, to increase diversity, the landscape should be designed to moderate the extremes and increase cooperative ventures among unlikely partners. In a more typical import-export economy, diversity is limited by

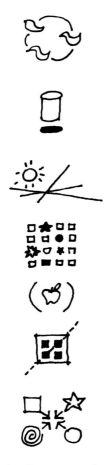

Forming diverse economies

economies of scale, both real and imagined. E. F. Schumacher noted that the scale that is appropriate depends on what one is trying to do. If diversity is a primary goal, aggregations of single economies—whether high-technology production or hog farms—should be limited. Schumacher further argues that for every activity there is a certain appropriate scale but that economies of scale generally can be achieved in much smaller concentrations than corporate business suggests and often require intimate cooperation rather than monoculture aggregation to succeed. The latter suggests the need for an urban form of small-scale ecotones—more precisely, coves and lobes where social edge effects encourage invention between the unlike partners.[27] As a metaphor, important discoveries are more likely to be made when a hog farmer meets a wetlands ecologist rather than another hog farmer.[28]

In sum, a number of design directives can help planners create the landscape that fosters a diverse economy: (1) preserve biological diversity, (2) choose place-appropriate industries that are well suited to the natural resources of the region, (3) moderate the limiting extremes of the region through location and site design, (4) increase landscape and land-use diversity to accommodate a variety of small economies, (5) produce as many of the region's needed goods within the region as is possible, (6) integrate minimally incompatible uses while designing to minimize adjacency conflicts, and (7) make more arenas between land uses for creative interactions.

Social Ecotones of Mixed-Use Neighborhoods

Exclusive, single-use zoning made sense at one time. When home industries expanded a century ago so that neighboring residents were threatened with toxic by-products, a logical reaction was to zone them out. In time, the segregation of such threats to health served as a reason, then an excuse, to separate every land use, even those that had no effect on public health, safety, or welfare. Large districts of single-purpose urban uses—commercial, industrial, and residential—emerged. Today even twenty-acre, single-family residential zones are protected from the "life-threatening intrusion" of one- and two-acre residential zones (even though the health, safety, or welfare threats are no longer apparent). But high property values and status are associated with such segregation in what has been described as "a most limiting concept" of city design.[29] The loss of fine grained diversity is only one problem but is a significant one.

For decades, critical thinkers have urged mixed use as a strategy for healthier cities. This has come from ecologists and urbanists,[30] who in recent years, have articulated precise approaches to intermixing land use. Peter Calthorpe argues for population and land-use diversity at both the neighborhood and regional scales.[31] In most directly confronting land-use segregation, Andres Duany and Elizabeth Plater-Zyberk list some of their principles of design: "the neighborhood has a balanced mix of activities—dwelling, shopping, working, schooling, worshipping and recreating."[32] All of this exists within a quarter mile from home. This fine-grained mix includes a range of housing types for a variety of incomes, especially affordable housing in the form of garage apartments, housing above shops, and apartment buildings.[33]

Richard Register's integral neighborhood has many of the same characteristics. His neighborhood plans are for populations of between five thousand and fifteen thousand people who live within a quarter-mile radius (or five-minute walk) of everything in their district. He includes an open creek and agriculture by increasing housing density slightly. There is animal raising, closed-loop recycling, and solar and wind farms—in short, a self-reliant

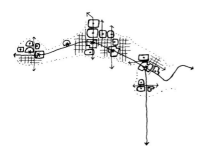

Clusters along a transit line

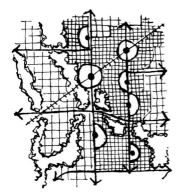

Multimodal transit-oriented development

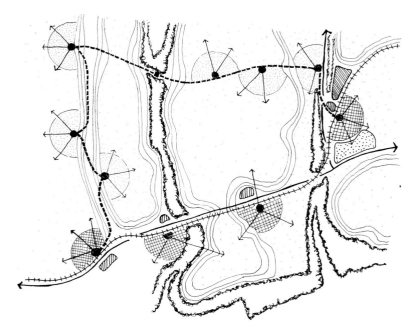

Peter Calthorpe calls for transit-oriented development at least one mile apart to guarantee viable retail and great diversity of land uses within walking distance.

mix of uses at the neighborhood scale.[34] His mixes are diverse and holistic and require no segregated districts in the city. Even in specialized districts, New Urbanists argue for diversity on the basis that the original justifications for land-use segregation seldom exist.[35]

Although some especially toxic industries may justify segregation, I prefer to have them close by so that I can keep my eye on them and feel directly the responsibility of my dependence on their products. Many have the potential to become compatible neighbors.[36] Industries that are so toxic that they cannot be made compatible should be discouraged altogether. That would seem wiser than pushing them off on a poorer neighborhood or nation where some decades from now we will pay the cost to clean up the next generation of superfund sites and the health-care costs of the poisoned.

The integration of social classes into a single neighborhood is more emotionally charged than mixed uses. Most Americans prefer homogeneity—to live near people like themselves and separated from people unlike themselves.[37] This holds true across class and ethnicities.[38] Clustering and segregation, for example, protect cultural diversity. Homogeneous enclaves enhance mutual support, provide agreed-on mores for public life, serve as a defense against stress, and empower.

Some social segregation is by choice, but some is a matter of status, repression, discrimination, and coercion. Socially mixed neighborhoods offer one way to overcome repression, discrimination, and prejudice.[39] Mixed neighborhoods also help us expand world views that are artificially simplified by segregation.[40] Integrated neighborhoods provide the choice for Americans who actually prefer heterogeneity.[41] Cities today suffer from a lack of diversity. Social complexity and multiple and mixed uses increase resilience. Diversity is likely the best assurance a community has that it can minimize social conflict and deal with uncertainty.[42] This requires choice, subcultural enclaves, and integrated neighborhoods. Still, a question lingers.

How Much Diversity Is Enough?

Just as in a natural ecosystem with predictable ratios between a large number of a few species and fewer numbers of many species, the appropriate mix of uses to achieve maximum resilience in a neighborhood is governed by a diversity index.[43] We just do not know what it is. In biology, this creates the balance of unity and diversity. In chaos theory, this is described as reiterative self-similarity. In human relations, this is the desire for both order and free-dom[44] or for both order and justice.[45] In urban design, there are searches for the balance between order and chaos[46] and for unity without uniformity. City designers are confronted with questions about diversity at every scale. For example, how much diversity is enough—say, in the redesign of a pri-marily residential neighborhood?

As in any ecosystem, some species (or in this case, land uses) dominate by sheer numbers or area; others are subordinate. The proportion and dis-tribution of dominant uses and subordinate uses define the neighborhood. When residential uses make up only half the occupied space, they probably cease to be predominant. The neighborhood becomes a gray area.[47] This is a matter of perception. People accustomed to segregated residential living typically are opposed to even slight diversification, some people prefer heterogeneity.[48]

This is only partly a popularity contest where user preferences trump all other considerations. When the full cost of segregated land uses, including health and ecological vulnerability, is better understood, we will have to act to achieve more mixed use, through public education, city design, and regu-lation. This will have to be done in spite of protests from powerful citizens. Long before research is conclusive, professional designers will work with citizens to reform neighborhoods with a resilience-based portion of diver-sity. As has been noted, small enclaves of relative social homogeneity are both desirable and acceptable in some cases.[49] But a judgment must be made in cases such as large-lot single-family zoning that is exclusively segregated. Such large-lot zoning that excludes people of lower income levels is neither desirable nor acceptable in resilient cities.[50]

In a related matter, there is also compelling reason to support jobs and housing balances. Each neighborhood should have approximately the same number of employment opportunities as working residents. Home occupa-tions that turn housing into living and working spaces would be one accept-able way to achieve this balance. This enriches variety and creates an active daily life in neighborhoods that are frequently lifeless during the workday. Garage apartments, granny flats, and other second units, when well designed, can be incorporated into households in single-family residential enclaves, adding diversity with no diminishment of the sense of a homogeneous neigh-borhood. Likewise, rental duplexes and fourplexes that are designed with in-genuity can be placed on corners, and when they comprise about only a

Transit choices

Primary house type

Nature access

fourth of the households in a neighborhood, they do not detract from the feeling of homogeneity in a single-family neighborhood.

Halfway houses that provide social services, on the other hand, can stigmatize whenever they are overly clustered in one neighborhood. In a case in Greenburgh, New York, residents who were concerned that the city was overly concentrating units for homeless forced an agreement from the city to prevent saturation.[51] If they are distributed throughout the city so that no more than 2 or 3 percent of total households are social-service units, then they do not threaten perceived homogeneity and safety.

How much commercial real estate should be a part of residential neighborhoods is a different question. It is less a matter of perception and more a question of how much can be supported. In most instances of mixed use, commercial space will be limited by demand. A walkable neighborhood for five thousand people can support only about fifty thousand to one hundred fifty thousand square feet of commercial real estate. This can readily be accommodated in a single center that holds multiple stores or in several sub-centers. Depending on neighborhood density and topology, commercial space might take up the ground floor, offices might occupy the second floor, and residential units might be above. Many more nonmixed-use residential buildings would result simply because the neighborhood could not support enough commercial space to occupy first floors of all multistory residential buildings.

What other uses are appropriate to be intermixed in the neighborhood, and how much should be allowed? Again, the more everyday necessities that are provided—including local food production, industrial fabrication of everyday hardware, and salvage yards for recycled products for household repairs—the more resilient the neighborhood will be.

Diversity should be pursued but not to the point that subordinate uses overtake the dominant residential ones in a residential district. Yet am I continually amazed at just how much diversity can readily be absorbed. Some years ago, I lived in the Shugakuin neighborhood of Kyoto, where single-family, shop houses, seven-story apartments, and farms intermix. The shop houses manufacture almost all household needs—from tatami mats to kitchen utensils. Farms provide fresh vegetables year round. A hog farm provides pork. Orchards, rice paddies, a nearly wild river, and mountains with wild monkeys all exist within walking distance of residences and define boundaries. This extraordinary diversity still maintains a unified identity as

Orchard in winter

Orchard in fall

Industry and worship

Shugakuin's strong center and boundaries of river and mountain maintain unity and accommodate a rich diversity of housing forms and agricultural and industrial products.

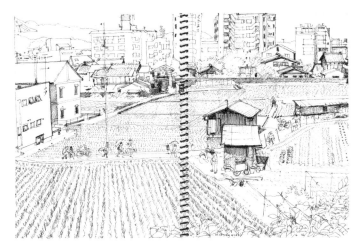

Neighborhood agriculture

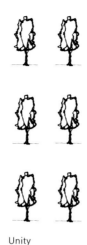

Unity

Diversity

a distinct village within the city. The unity is provided by preserving the forested mountain and the Takano River, by restricting midrise apartments to main corridors at lower elevations, and by everywhere keeping secondary streams and waterways open, providing a distinct sense that the neighborhood is designed with nature. Street trees, gardens, and shrine forests contribute to this unity. Within that strong framework, diversity flourishes but does not compete with the dominant residential quality. In addition to the overall landscape structure, the architecture reinforces the unity. Until recently, only one building type was found throughout the neighborhood— a multistory shop house that was made of local materials by local craftspeople and built adjacent to the street with several tiny gardens within. An entry garden fronts a narrow street, a pattern repeated throughout the neighborhood. In recent years, the unity has begun to break down as parking replaces small residential gardens and international-style single-family homes and apartments demand suburban setbacks. For the present, the unifying landscape remains strong enough to absorb these dissonant diversities, but the discordant variety could soon become dominant. On some streets where front gardens have uniformly been replaced with parking, a pleasant walk has become an obstacle course in a matter of years. The fine balance between unity and diversity has been broken. How much diversity is enough, and what kind of diversity really matters? In city design, these are fundamental questions in every aspect of form making.

Two painfully real examples illustrate. For many years in Berkeley, a single species of tree was designated for each street. This provided identity for each street and diversity because there are nearly 450 streets in the city. Few native plants are suitable for street trees, so experimentation has been necessary. Some designated trees were unable to withstand the dry summer, were susceptible to disease or pests, or simply were objectionable to residents. The little-leaf linden, for example, is vulnerable to aphids and through complex insect relationships creates a sticky dripping on anything below (usually cars). The Chinese tallow invaded riparian zones. The Bradford pear, recently the most popular tree in America, has weak limbs. When such trees had to be removed, entire streets were deforested. This is not the catastrophe of the chestnut blight or elm disease, but in Berkeley it is serious. Jerry Koch, who directs the city street-tree program, has taken an approach to increase diversity to decrease the disaster of a failed species. On

Resilient Form

some few streets, a single successful species is still called for. On some streets, experiments with a mix of natives is being tested. If streets are particularly long, different species may be assigned in each block. For example, on one street, a different species is designated to each of four blocks along one stretch of the street. This increases diversity and indirectly gives more identity to each block rather than to the street as a whole. To some, it might look like a tossed salad. Striking the right balance between achieving healthy vegetative diversity and visual unity is an ongoing issue.[52]

The second case, Yountville, California, challenges the very essence of that Napa Valley community. It was a rural town that had been bypassed by wine-country tourism, but about twenty years ago it was discovered to be the most authentic town in the valley.[53] This stimulated the development of restaurants, hotels, and other tourist-serving facilities. By the mid-1990s, residents began to worry that the town was nearing a tourist takeover, even though it had fewer than two hundred hotel rooms. When they realized that the number of hotel rooms was doubling with projects that already were approved, the town council commissioned a study to determine the financial viability of additional hotels. The market study indicated an unquenchable demand for overnight accommodations because unfettered market forces were creating a monocrop of vineyards and a monoculture of tourists that could soon dominate the town. Landowners—who realized that they could make more profit from hotels instead of residences—sought zoning changes for nearly every residential parcel in town.

In retrospect, the Yountville study asked the wrong question. The question should have explored how much of this subordinate use—hotels—can be accommodated before tourism supersedes the rural residential village. Unless Yountville wants to speciate into a tourist town rather than a residential one, this question must be answered and fast. It is presently the source of debilitating community anguish. Based on the experiences of similar towns, Yountville could readily absorb 10 percent tourist beds and remain a residential town as long as 90 percent of all beds were for permanent residents. If it approached 20 percent tourist beds, it would become a tourist sleepover town and lose its previous identity as a residential town. Long before tourist sleepovers dominate in absolute numbers, local town identity will be lost. How much diversity is enough? In this case, enough diversity is not more than 10 percent of a use that local people consider invasive.

Intergenerational and Social-Class Diversity

Soon after the middle of the twentieth century, most Americans lived in gender-segregated neighborhoods. During the day, women and children inhabited the residential domain, and men occupied special work districts. Today neighborhoods are more specialized. Enclaves of blue-collar workers, lace-collar professionals, families with young children, empty nesters, retired professionals, and the elderly poor are some of the groups that are targeted via advertising and public policy. Resilience suffers from extreme homogeneity.[54] In communities where there is social-class and intergenerational diversity, more of the multiple social rules necessary for every day are efficiently available. Just look at Richard Scarry's *What Do People Do All Day?* for a view of the many roles—dentists, street cleaners, grandmothers, refrigerator repair people, Jason the mason, Sawdust the carpenter, on and on—that create an efficient web of resilience.[55] Does your neighborhood provide housing for all these and the many others that support your daily neighborhood life? Not likely. The single most important design action for achieving intergenerational and social-class diversity is to provide more choice in housing types and arrangements while maintaining overall unity within the neighborhood. Second, the housing choices must be reinforced by services for the diverse population and places shared by the disparate groups. That is a fundamental function of both centeredness and diversity.

Seeding Diversity

John Todd's living machines turn sewage into clean water through exposure to the rich diversity of an aquatic ecosystem. When diversity is enriched, the system removes the harmful toxins from human waste. Since these interactions were unforeseen, Todd seeded the living machines with a great variety of microscopic bacteria, "lower plants," zooplanktons, snails, and eventually fish. Then he observed what happened. Over time, the water-cleansing process designed itself with various bacteria, duckweeds, and cattails that each removed particular pathogens. This thinking can be applied to the design of a building, an entire neighborhood, or the whole region. Ecological architect Sim Van der Ryn describes this way of designing thusly: "Seeding with diversity is a way of catalyzing creativity by providing a diverse repertoire of behaviors for the system to build on."[56] In his design

To achieve resilience, most American neighborhoods need to be seeded with a diversity of housing types, work, and other activities.

work, Van der Ryn has noted, as did Todd, that the environmental processes are more robust when seeded with a wide diversity of elements.[57] A variety of housing types, many mixed uses, and niches for many social classes and life cycle stages seed neighborhood diversity. Creating social ecotones—the coves and lobes previously mentioned—where people with vastly different viewpoints and knowledge come together for civil exchanges is another form of seeding diversity. The settings are not segregated, and uses are not predetermined; rather, they are unsorted. In unsorted situations, new forms of democratic problem solving and habitation are incubated and flourish.[58]

In sum, a number of design imperatives can be derived from the principle of selective diversity. We must be wise about the pursuit of diversity. For cities to function, a heightened sense of shared destiny, values, and unity is essential. Diversity must be balanced with unity in democratic process. We must be selective, discriminating, and intelligent in the pursuit of diversity. We must not confuse diversity, pluralism, multiculturalism, and separatism. We must know when to pursue each. At the global scale, biological and cultural diversity must be enhanced as the most essential acts of city making. Providing enough appropriate habitat to maintain biological and cultural distinctiveness is the first order and can be achieved largely by following the spatial patterns that are derived from conservation biology. At the scale of the regional economy, the city design must accommodate the

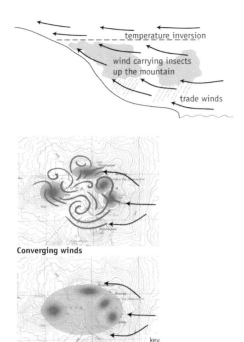

Converging winds

Food dispersal

key

← prevailing winds
● summit cinder cones
✦ converging wind patterns and eddies

The endemic aeolian ecology

The global capital

Telescope development on Mauna Kea promised a diverse economy but has diminished sacred sites and critical habitat and now threatens cultural and biological diversity.

full range of landscapes needed to produce, transform, and consume local products. To be most resilient, this is accomplished with minimum conflict between adjacent economies. This allows the regional economy to produce almost everything that it needs utilizing place-based capital. A wise relative explained the difference between the effects of place-based and global capital by saying she would never live in a neighborhood if the developer was unwilling to live there. She suggested that local capital was less powerful, more committed to the long-term health of the place, and more respectful of local laws than distant investment capital.

The struggle over Mauna Kea, the 13,796-foot snow-capped peak on the island of Hawaii, dramatically illustrates how global capital threatens diversity. Mauna Kea is where Sky Father and Mother Earth created the first Hawaiians. The volcanic peaks embody Papa (Mother Earth), Poliahu (goddess of snow), Lilinoe (goddess of mist), Wai'au (goddess of water), the husband of mist, and the backbone of the whale (a sacred deity), among other gods. The summit region of Mauna Kea is the Realm of the Gods, so sacred to Hawaiians that no permanent structures were ever built there. The cinder cones and the surrounding landscape are themselves the religious temple.

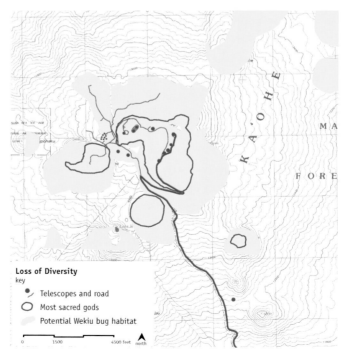

Loss of Diversity

key

●╱ Telescopes and road
○ Most sacred gods
⬚ Potential Wekiu bug habitat

0   1500   4500 feet   ↑ north

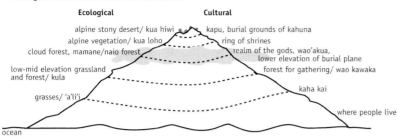

Ecological Zones and Levels of Sacredness

Ecological   Cultural

alpine stony desert/ kua hiwi — kapu, burial grounds of kahuna
alpine vegetation/ kua loho — ring of shrines
cloud forest, mamane/naio forest — realm of the gods, wao'akua,
                    lower elevation of burial plane
low-mid elevation grassland — forest for gathering/ wao kawaka
and forest/ kula
grasses/ 'ali'i — kaha kai
                        where people live
ocean

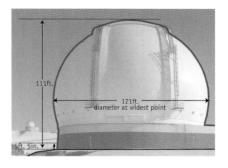

When the KECK telescopes were built into the body of a god, diversity was overwhelmed by single purpose dominance, turning the sacred mountain into an industrial zone.

The aeolian ecosystem at the summit is home to rare, endangered, and endemic species including the wekiu bug. In recent decades, modern astronomy was introduced to the mountain. Native religious practitioners protested, but observatories were approved as a means of diversifying the economy. The telescopes rapidly expanded. There are now thirteen telescopes and more are planned. Fueled by investment from Brazil, Japan, Taiwan, the United Kingdom, France, Canada, and Argentina, among other nations, the summit of Mauna Kea has become a single-purpose industrial zone with little concern for the local environment and cultural practices. Telescopes are built into the bodies of gods and block views essential for religious practices. Roads and telescopes cut through palila bird and wekiu bug habitat. Local diversity has been sacrificed for global dominance with all the characteristics of the real estate investor who does not live in his own development. Both cultural and biological diversity are threatened with extinctions, and the regional economy is dependent on external whims rather than local resilience. When global capitalism dominates the regional economy, diversity suffers and resilience is unattainable. Only resistance can balance the power. Once seeded, diversity must be nurtured.

At the level of the neighborhood, a greater mix of uses is essential—not just more variety of housing to accommodate different classes and generations of people but also a richer mix of food, industrial and energy production, waste removal, and wild nature. Here too the designer must carefully balance diversity to maintain a neighborhood unity through the proportion, structure, and distribution of dominant and subordinate landscapes and structures. Given the resistance to neighborhood heterogeneity, one of the foremost issues in an ecological democracy is to arm the citizenry with an understanding of the critical importance that increased diversity plays in making human habitation resilient.

Density and Smallness

Two seemingly disjointed stories at the beginning of the section on Resilient Form—one about quail, the other about San Francisco residents—tell the same lesson. When the bobwhite quail huddled together in a tight circle to share their warmth against deadly cold temperatures, they produced a similar advantage of aggregation as the residents of compact San Francisco neighborhoods do. The quail are rewarded with survival, and the residents of Nob Hill are rewarded with lifetime savings of hundreds of thousands of dollars per family in car-related expenses. The advantage that is derived from increased density (as W. C. Allee observed nearly a hundred years ago) often significantly increases survival in animals.

In ecology, the Allee principle points out a most critical forgotten lesson for human habitation today. In some cases, most notably among plants, there is value in spreading out to reduce competition for sunlight and food. Sometimes this is true for animals, but concentrated density and the accompanying "intraspecific protocooperation" frequently are more critical. In short, Allee found that for some social animals undercrowding is as detrimental as overcrowding.[1] For those species, resilience depends on a relatively high density of population in a small concentrated space.

The Allee principle

Concentrated Density Creates Resilience

Whether for exactly the same reasons or a combination of reasons, resilient landscape form depends on a concentrated density of human habitation. Concentrated density creates resilience in a multitude of ways—by protecting biodiversity, providing access to nature, creating centeredness, and reducing transportation and health costs.

Concentrated cities with slightly higher density can protect the habitats that are essential for biodiversity. The loss of wild habitat, the primary cause of extinctions worldwide, results from the expansion of human habitation. Increased human population and inefficient city form are pushing farther

Concentrated density in Camogli, Italy, protects biodiversity, provides access to nature and public transport, encourages good health, and creates a vibrant center.

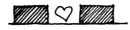

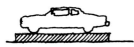

Density tradeoffs

and farther into the habitats required for other creatures. Simply put, we are taking too much of the landscape and leaving too little for hundreds of thousands of other species described in the chapter on Selective Diversity. In one fifteen-year period ending in 1986, cities worldwide expanded by 125 million acres, and associated forestland was reduced by 312 million acres. Critical natural habitat in excess of 250 million acres was lost during the same time period.[2] This is especially critical in the United States, where city form takes a disproportionate amount of acreage. Here 2 million acres of undeveloped land is lost to low-density sprawl each year.[3] The states with the most low-density suburban development have the most threatened ecosystems.[4] The problem is that in spite of slowed population growth, we are taking more and more land per person. Although the United States population grew by less than 50 percent from 1960 to 1990, the amount of land development more than doubled.[5] The Sierra Club reported that the rate of land development more than doubled again between 1992 and 1997. Low-density suburban development takes more than twice as much land per capita as it did less than a decade ago. Species extinctions and ecosystem declines directly result.

Although the loss of biodiversity is the great calamity, an immediate source of human fulfillment is also lost to low-density sprawl. Urban residents have less access to wild nature and significantly fewer opportunities to experience birds and other wildlife as part of their everyday lives. This loss underlies the many illnesses that are associated with nature deprivation.[6]

When low-density sprawl is replaced with slightly higher residential density, access to functioning ecosystems and wildlife is increased.

Concentrated density also underlies centeredness. Clarence Perry first comprehensively studied this in the classic plan for New York neighborhoods. A neighborhood center of multiple public facilities and shopping within a quarter-mile walk of one's home requires a population of between five thousand and six thousand people to justify businesses locating in that center. That requires a minimum density of approximately twelve to fifteen dwelling units per residential acre for enough people to live within walking distance of the businesses. In Perry's model of suburban development, the residential density was 13.8 units per acre.[7] When density drops below that, businesses fail just as the quail die from undercrowding. There simply is not the critical mass of people within walking distance to support the corner grocery, bakery, hardware store, and other neighborhood services.[8] Perry inventoried various cities and concluded that a neighborhood of around five thousand faithful people could justify a grocery store, drug store, furniture store, restaurants, specialty meat market, fruit and vegetable markets, bakeries, plumbers, and auto repair. But seven thousand people were required to make laundry, hardware, clothing, and florist enterprises viable.[9] Details of Perry's study are long out of date, but the underlying principle is fundamental. Today, the Urban Land Institute's *Shopping Center Development Handbook* suggests that neighborhood shopping serves a much wider range of people, between three thousand and forty thousand, because fewer people are faithful to one neighborhood center. The *Handbook* still calls for the same stores Perry described. The ULI now adds videotape rental and photocopy stores, which were unknown a hundred years ago. Further, for the commercial district to be viable it too needs to be concentrated to provide symbiotic shopping. An aggregation of at least ten thousand square feet of commercial is needed for a minimal convenience center and fifty thousand square feet for a neighborhood center. Outside that concentrated area, commerce must be restricted to make the centered shops financially viable.[10] Without a concentrated density of residential and shopping areas, centers with stores and community services are not feasible. This is the unfortunate case for most development in the United States in the last fifty years. We still call them neighborhoods, but in reality, these developments are not neighborhoods. They are, due to their low density, unable to support any neighborhood-center functions. Density of twelve to fifteen dwelling units per acre is essential for centeredness.

Increased density decreases transportation costs. By any measure, transportation is one of the most expensive aspects of American life. Capital outlay usually gets the most attention. Just as one example, the seventeen-mile Century Freeway in Los Angeles cost $3 billion. For many sound reasons, it has been called the last urban freeway. Freeways, of course, are not free. In fact, the government subsidizes highway use by at least $30.7 trillion per year. If external costs are considered, the subsidy may exceed $700 trillion per year.[11] Even a single parking space in a parking garage costs nearly $20,000.[12] Operating and maintenance far exceed capital costs, in recent years, expenses from traffic delays have been added to the balance sheet. The social costs of congestion in the United States are estimated to be $73 billion dollars per year.[13] The best way to reduce overall transportation cost is to shift away from automobile trips to trips via public transit, biking, and walking by increasing residential density.

In moderate-density neighborhoods, 45 percent of all trips are by foot or public transit; in contrast, in low-density neighborhoods, 12 percent are by foot or transit. Low-density suburban residents drive three times as many miles each year as their urban counterparts.[14] By slightly increasing densities, automobile use can be dramatically reduced. Transit ridership increases most sharply when residential densities increase from about seven dwelling units to sixteen units per acre.[15] Doubling density translates into a 20 to 30 percent decline in drive-alone commuting.[16] At somewhere between ten and fifteen dwelling units per acre, investments in public transportation are justified. Peter Calthorpe calls for a minimum of ten dwellings per acre to create public-transit-oriented communities—ten dwellings for local bus systems and fifteen dwellings for light rail.[17] These densities can be achieved in a variety of ways—by mixing single-family housing with duplexes and triplexes,[18] adding garage apartments or second units to large, single-family lots, and providing townhouses.[19] These are not high-rise buildings but simply modest changes from present densities. As Cevero and Bernick conclude, "One doesn't need Hong Kong-like densities to sustain mass transit."[20] In the delightful density of about thirty units per acre, every Paris resident is within a five-block walk of a Métro subway stop that takes them anywhere they wish to go.[21] Even at modest densities of fifteen units per acre, transit pays its way, reducing both public subsidies and individual expenses and providing some of the Paris Métro benefits. Calthorpe calculates that by taking public transit and avoiding the automobile, the average household can save \$8,883 per year.[22] A study in Houston found that the average resident spends \$9,722 annually on car transportation, more than the cost of housing.[23] The crisis of unaffordable housing could be solved by adding a garage apartment to the single-family house on a typical sixty-five by one hundred foot lot.[24] Slightly increasing density reduces the cost of both transportation and housing. In places like San Francisco that are faced with the double threats of congestion and high housing costs, the Allee principle seems to accurately predict the consequences of extremely low density.

Other costs associated with low-density include respiratory illnesses and obesity, pollution, utilities (utilities for a low-density subdivision cost five times those for an in-fill project), and postal delivery (home delivery of mail to a low-density subdivision costs three hundred times more than delivery to an in-fill project).[25] San Jose, California, found that low-density growth costs the city \$4.5 million each year for these subsidies.[26] But the worst costs come in the form of noise, air, and water pollution. Again, the low-density coconspirator is the automobile.[27] Air-pollution costs from automobile use likely exceed \$10 billion annually.[28] Even modest increases in density can reduce air, water, and noise pollution and significantly cut the costs of maintaining a healthy populace.

The Conspiracy against Density

In spite of these significant benefits, Americans find density distasteful. Why are we so antagonistic toward density when it has such benefits and so many other cultures thrive on it? Most people in the United States prefer low density and associate big space with American traditions and the best possible life one can achieve. The partially developed low-density suburb that is adjacent to farmland represents the frontier and freedom. It provides a home on the range for rugged individualists who are accountable only to themselves. Beyond that romantic image, the freestanding house in a low-density residential area today offers enhanced self-esteem, privacy, territory, and ownership.[29] A purchase in a low-density subdivision promises high property values in a segregated neighborhood, a place for children to play in the safety of their yard or cul-de-sac, wide streets, and lots of convenient driving and parking. These latter are among the most important factors for Americans who are shopping for homes.[30] Affordability and schools with homogeneous student bodies, both of which result from public policy, reinforce these immediate reasons.

Government policy and subsidies have reinforced the desirability of low density. Policy to support low density began well over a hundred years ago as central-city residents sought to escape from what were seen as oppressive, unhealthy, and overcrowded cities. Real estate speculators, the highway and building industry, and government decision makers have worked together to champion low-density development. Far more public money has gone to subsidize low-density suburban development than any other single government campaign in American history. If an equal amount of money had been spent in making dense, livable cities over the past century, the overwhelming majority of Americans no doubt would today prefer denser neighborhoods in compact cities.

But city residents were not simply lured out of higher-density environments by government subsidies and the marketing campaigns of real estate developers. Many wanted to escape. Public perception, reinforced by intellectuals and academics, associated density with overcrowding, crime, and physical and mental illness.[31]

The Randy Newman 1978 song "Baltimore," sung by Nina Simone, expresses what so many people felt. A few of the lines describe the emotions felt by millions of Americans at that time:

Hard time in the city, hooker on the corner waiting for a train.
Drunk lying on the sidewalk, sleeping in the rain.
The people hide their faces and they hide their eyes,
'cause the city is dying and they don't know why.

People felt trapped because there was "no where to run to." The song continues to describe the actions taken by many Americans:

Go get my sister Frances and my little brother Ray.
Buy a fleet of Cadillacs, haul them all away.
And we live out in the country where the mountain's high.
Never going to go back there 'til the day I die.[32]

And so suburbanization, once available only to the wealthy, extended its promise of escape to all but the poorest. This was repeated millions of times across the country. Unlike the academic researchers who blamed density outright, Newman's song does not mention it. The scenes that Newman evoked made the suburbs an alluring retreat. People fleeing the city felt, rightly or wrongly, that the culprit for urban ills was density.[33] Their perceptions were corroborated by the leading planners of the time. F. L. Olmsted championed the suburb, as did Frank Lloyd Wright. Even many ecological designers subscribed to Calhoun's pathological togetherness and applied the rat research to human habitation. Some concluded that the heart of the city is the heart of pathology.[34] Thinkers about good urban form have consistently undermined the creation of good cities through their preference for low-density living.[35] Most professional city makers supported the low-density movement with plans, ordinances, and standards that made higher density living nearly impossible. By the 1950s, a density of eight units per acre often qualified a neighborhood as a slum and a health hazard.[36]

Was the perception that density causes illness a poor diagnosis? Yes. Although multiple studies were done in the middle of the twentieth century, they were not conclusive. Gans found that even in slums, solid social networks made for fulfilling lives.[37] In those cases, density may have actually supported social cooperation. Although some studies found high density and illness in the same neighborhoods, it was widely acknowledged that social factors rather than density itself were generally the causes.[38] And the densest American cities are less than one-fifth as dense as most Asian cities, where mental illness, serious crimes, and infant mortality are far lower than in the United States. Conclusions about density and crowding were oversimplified.[39] There is no scientific basis for rejecting sustainable density. In some cases, density is guilty by association; in others, it is a case of mistaken identity. In total, the attack on density is an unfounded and misdirected conspiracy. This conspiracy has produced private fortunes at public expense. It now creates a roadblock to resilient cities that can be removed only with an attitude adjustment.

Net, Perceived, and Affective Density

As is often the case in such matters of academic uncertainty, Amos Rapoport has synthesized incisively much of the research on density. He states that measurable density—usually described in terms of dwelling units per net acre of residential land—is less important than perceived density. The denominator in net density is the acreage in a neighborhood that is used for residential purposes. It excludes streets, open space, and commercial uses. That means that net density is higher than gross density where the denominator includes streets, open space, and commercial uses. For example, a typical gross density of six units per acre might translate into ten units per net acre.

Density may be perceived as high when measurable density is quite low.[40] The presence of such things as tight spaces, tall buildings, signs, lights, noise, traffic, parked cars, and other people may incorrectly increase one's sense of high density. Mixed use increases perceived density, as does social heterogeneity. The same neighborhood with people of a different race from one's self is perceived as higher density than if the people are the same race. Lack of choice and control increases perceived density.[41]

Based on what we perceive there, each environment is assessed. This assessment forms affective density. In neighborhoods with characteristics that make us uncomfortable, the effect is often feelings of crowding and isolation.[42] By association, a place misperceived as high density triggers both feelings and judgments. These feelings and judgments may well become concretized as values that dispose an individual against density as a general idea or as a physical reality. Americans likely have developed a dislike for density as an affective response to something else.

It is perceived density rather than spatial density that is the social force, and our aversion to what we often mistake as dense environments may be caused more by unrelated physical stimuli or even less related factors like stress at work, fear of terrorism, or uncertainty in the world. In total, perceived and affective density are powerful forces that favor continued low-density sprawl. Since density is essential to sustain American habitation, how can both social preference and resilience be achieved? It is not as easy as making your children eat their spinach.

Making Density Desirable

Although Americans generally prefer low density, there are important exceptions. There is significant variation according to social class.[43] Young adults with moderate incomes who currently reside in large apartment complexes are more receptive to higher density.[44] There is also a wide variation by ethnicity and, particularly, recent immigrants.[45] The American LIVES study indicates that single-person households, couples with no children at home, and professionals are more inclined to support higher density along with other strategies to reurbanize our habitation.[46] More important, the

LIVES study found that different market segments can be approached with varying strategies regarding density. They conclude that 20.8 percent of their sample of homebuyers and shoppers were particularly unhappy with low-density suburbs; they are open to a wide range of new urbanist strategies in addition to higher densities. At the other extreme, 30.8 percent like the suburbs the way they are; they are the market segment that is least receptive to high density. The people in the middle (48.4 percent) are unhappy with present suburbs and support centering facilities in town centers and diverse mixed uses but prefer the convenience of the automobile and do not like density. According to the authors of the study, people in this group "like the image of new urbanism but hate the density."[47]

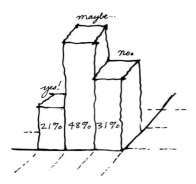

Attitudes about density

Consider the strategies needed for each of these three segments. Those who are positively inclined toward dense neighborhoods may be enticed to density up to thirty-six units per acre through provision of a public park nearby. Cervero and Bosselmann "found some public willingness to accept higher densities, at the level necessary to support rail transit services, in return for public parks, neighborhood shops, and easy access to rail stations."[48] Street trees and other neighborhood greening efforts, pleasant and safe places to walk to shops, reduced local traffic speeds, and controlled noise and visual clutter may make density more desirable.[49] Carefully designed interiors and site relationships may also help.[50]

In planning for the revitalization of Pasadena, California, all these strategies came into play. We had been hired to do a specific plan for its civic center, which housed financial offices and the city government. Like many U.S. cities by the mid-1950s, the city center had been largely abandoned by residents, but what had been abandoned was once a jewel of a classical City Beautiful plan—an extraordinary city hall as the focal point of a grand axis and handsome civic and library buildings on the minor axis. After we had done our analysis, each member of our design team—Donlyn Lyndon, Marvin Buchanan, Marcia McNally, Allan Jacobs, Frances Halsband, and I—independently made lists of what we thought were the most critical actions. Each of us listed the creation of more housing at urban densities among our highest priorities. The citizens with whom we were working were taken aback by our insistence on dense housing as the first and foremost action. They expected, as had we when we began, that the solution to revitalizing the area would be a grand civic gesture in the tradition of the City Beautiful plan. They did not expect so mundane an action as housing. We pointed out that many years ago housing had been intermixed with civic functions and that only recently had the area become a segregated office and institutional district. Because no one lived there, there were no advocates for the area. That alone explained why the civic center was uncared for, poorly maintained, and in serious disrepair. Residents, and lots of them, were needed to restore what had once been the soul of the city. Building new housing on every available site was the only meaningful strategy.

After a two-way educational campaign featuring numerous community workshops and lengthy debate, a blue-ribbon panel recommended a plan with dramatic actions to reintroduce housing. In some cases, zoning had to be changed to allow housing and mixed use. Public land and subsidies had to be offered to attract housing developers. Partnerships were required to provide single-room-occupancy housing for the near homeless and to convince market-rate housing development. The city council adopted a full range of housing strategies. In total, the plan will provide approximately twelve hundred units of housing at an overall density of twenty units per acre, with densities as high as fifty units per acre in some areas. That is an ambitious undertaking, but based on the early success, there is strong evidence that there is a market for higher, livable density in the Los Angeles area.

Pasadena's center, once a jewel of American cities with dense housing surrounding noble civic places, was largely abandoned in favor of lower-density neighborhoods.

Resilient Form

Proposed Housing

The design team, led by Donlyn Lyndon and Allan
Jacobs, concluded that the only way to restore
Pasadena's center was to attract people to live
there. They proposed building dense housing on
every available parcel.

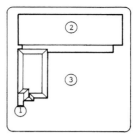

ASSUMPTIONS:
1. County Building will remain.
   If it is removed, arcade remains.
2. Courts Building will remain.
3. Guidelines apply to remainder
   of site.

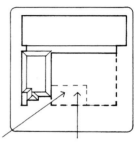

COURTYARD(S)
Views from Garfield and Ramona.

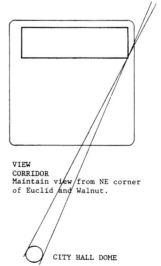

VIEW
CORRIDOR
Maintain view from NE corner
of Euclid and Walnut.

CITY HALL DOME

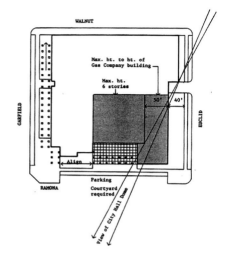

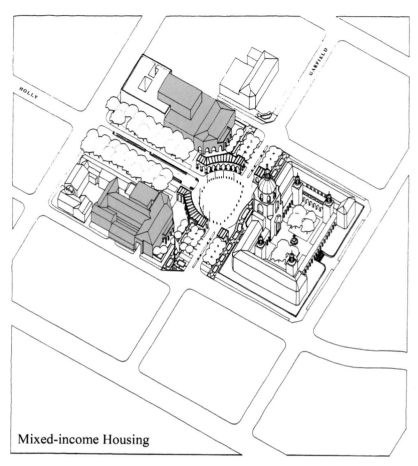

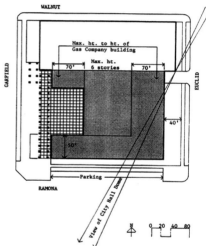

Mixed-income Housing

Around city hall, a great diversity of housing choices (from single-room occupancy for the near homeless to market rate) is provided; each is accompanied by design guidelines to increase civicness.

Resilient Form

However, to attract residents to the higher-density housing, it became clear that other supporting actions had to be taken. This was easier because of the structure that remained from the City Beautiful plan. Several neglected city parks were redesigned. We worked directly with the developer of the first major housing project in the redesign of Memorial Park adjacent to his site. He said that he would not have attempted the project without the park as an attraction. With this same developer, we worked for a year to integrate a light-rail stop under this housing and into the park.

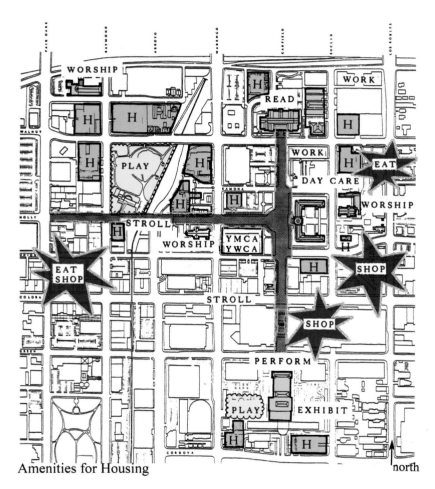

Amenities for Housing

Few developers were initially interested in building housing in Pasadena's center in spite of significant amenities not found in any other Pasadena neighborhood.

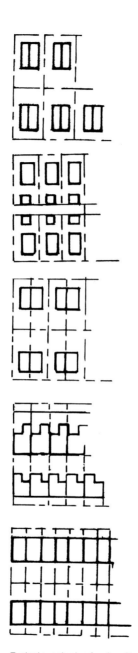

Typical typologies for density

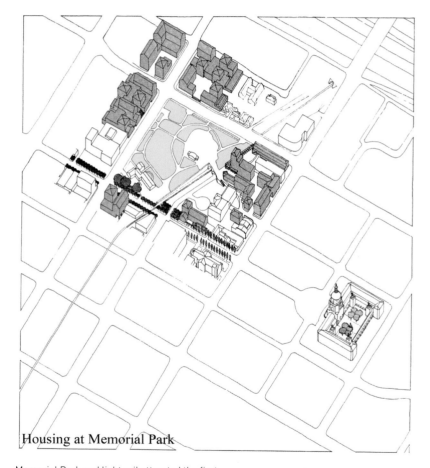

Housing at Memorial Park

Memorial Park and light rail attracted the first developer to make courtyard housing, a dense housing type that was once popular in Pasadena. The developer stated that he invested here only because of the park amenity.

Resilient Form

Along the major axis, Holly Street, street trees and gardens were proposed as part of a districtwide greening effort. We recommended reducing the widths of underused streets to slow traffic and control noise. A wide variety of shops and services were already within short but unpleasant walks of the housing sites. To improve these walking routes, the pedestrian environment has a priority over automobile use. Increased walking resulted.

Guidelines for the development of each site control bulk and mass. To integrate new development into the existing city fabric, Donlyn Lyndon drew detailed designs for entrances and semipublic and private open spaces at the block level. The result is that density is supported by a large amount of green space and interesting architecture. The combination of these actions has made the civic center a highly desirable address for a diverse population in spite of, and possibly because of, the increase in residential density.

Although these design strategies are important, the policy impediments that subsidize low density must be reversed to achieve transit-oriented neighborhoods. Researchers suggest density bonuses, inclusionary zoning, transit-efficient loan programs, and reduced taxes and impact fees for denser projects.[51] Currently, for example, a housing development that is dense enough to support transit typically must provide on-site amenities, provide parking, and pay to widen nearby streets. This adds additional cost burdens for dense projects and undermines the intent of reducing automobile dependence. Such requirements are counterproductive. Reversing such bias against density in public policy is an important strategy for all the market segments.

The 30.8 percent who like suburbs just as they are appear to be a different species altogether and have adapted with great success to the suburban ecosystem. In striking contrast to both other groups, they prefer primarily private gathering places. Many do not value any community places. They prefer uniform suburbs to keep out the "wrong" sort of people and support housing in one price range to keep out the riffraff. They accept large parking expanses for convenience. They do not think that small shops provide better service or opportunities for socializing. They doubt that privacy can be achieved in higher-density neighborhoods.[52] Such attitudes present a formidable barrier to increasing resilience generally. For these people, neighborhood parks and other public amenities, mixed-use neighborhood shopping, and social diversity provide no incentive. In fact, some positive incentives for others are disincentives for this group. But even here, there are windows of opportunity for higher density.

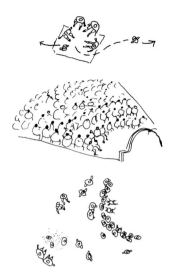

Desired civic activities

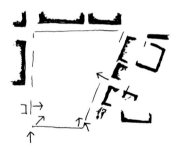

Park as catalyst

Housing over transit

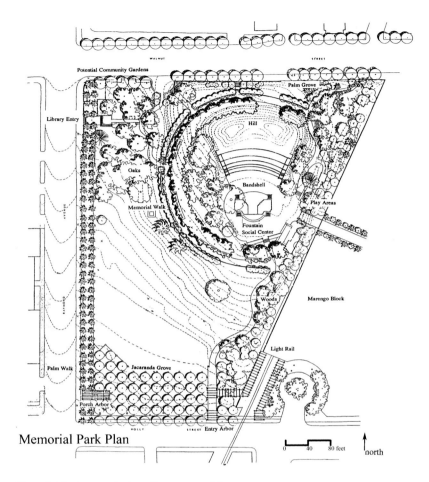

Memorial Park Plan

Memorial Park was redesigned to accommodate
multiple recreational and civic activities and to
provide green views from housing.

Foremost, even among the most ardent advocates of low-density suburbs, 82.39 percent would like to see more greenbelts between towns; they
do not want housing to march to the horizon.[53] One strategy is to use public education to contrast the low-density limitless sprawl with the alternative
of higher density and growth limits to preserve natural green areas. The resulting cognitive dissonance might shift values.[54] This is beginning to occur.
In a striking example of ecological democracy at work, wildlife groups, after
careful deliberation, have begun advocating for higher density for precisely

The band shell attracts a variety of performances, which introduces people to the joys of dense downtown living.

these reasons.[55] However, when the assertive choice for low-density, homogeneous suburbs is a deeply seeded defense mechanism against fear of uncertainty, information overload, loss of identity and status, and avoidance of complexity, the cognitive-dissonance strategy is likely to add more stress.[56] If I am told that my segregated habitation is helping me cope with uncertainty but is preventing greenbelts, it may simply make me more defensive and tense. The LIVES data suggest that this may be the case because respondents who dislike density strongly support the defense of their neighborhoods. They overwhelmingly prefer a neighborhood with a clear boundary, visual uniformity, and social homogeneity—all defensive strategies against overload and complexity. Likely any increase in density might better be accepted by designing clear boundaries between neighborhoods and micro-neighborhoods. To achieve this, some advocate gated neighborhoods.[57] A more resilient solution is to use natural greenways to provide identifiable boundaries. Possibly an overall decrease in complexity and diversity would be a suitable tradeoff to both increase density and satisfy the defense mechanisms. Certainly for this group, design that guarantees privacy and retreat might make slightly higher density acceptable.

Another concern for those most favoring low-density suburbs is the safety of their children.[58] The provision of fenced yards or courts, *woonerf* (Dutch for "street for living") streets, and even street diverters and cul-de-sacs might make increases in density palatable.[59] Designers with skill and patience to help neighborhoods dominated by those satisfied with low-density

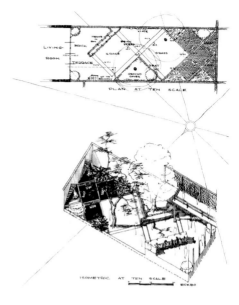

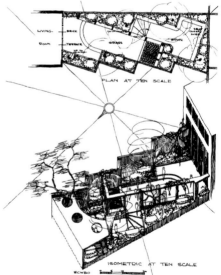

Garrett Eckbo's tiny gardens

life are critically needed—not only because these groups are deeply resistant but also because their transformation is essential.

For the group who likes aspects of new urbanism but "hates" density, there are many more tradeoffs available, largely because this group is less defensive against uncertainty, overload, and complexity. Since these people are even more strongly supportive of greenbelts (90.6 percent favor them), they might positively respond to the dissonance created by the choice between low-density versus a natural greenbelt.[60] Their overwhelming desire (95.1 percent) for a town center suggests that the creation of a strong community focal point with village green, shops, churches, and civic buildings might be incentive for slightly higher density. Creating a small-town ambience (89.2 percent favor) with regional particularness (72.7 percent favor) and traditional architecture, porches, and street trees (83.9 percent favor) should boost the acceptability of higher density. Because this group is positively inclined toward urbanism and open-minded, discussions about tradeoffs should be particularly effective as a way to create innovative design that increases density without appearing to be dense. They might be especially open to moderately increased density that still maintains the single-family household, detached on a smaller lot with a second unit, if those houses and landscapes are exquisitely designed.

Given the complexity of different attitudes, frequent misconceptions of density, and dependence on policy shifts to encourage densification, seven general design strategies for increased density seem most useful.

Provide for Privacy

For most people skeptical of increased density—about two-thirds of Americans—a major concern is that density diminishes privacy.[61] At the household level, density requires houses and lots of smaller square footages. As the amount of space is reduced, architectural and landscape design become more important in creating adequate privacy.[62] This includes design to reduce annoyances like uncontrollable noise and light, to provide for distinctive niches for personal retreat in the dwelling, to make the interior space seem spacious, to create small outdoor spaces that maintain privacy from neighbors, and to make interior views to natural greenery (see the chapter on Sensible Status Seeking).[63] It may also be important to have a clearer distinction between the public and private domains both within the house and at the entry.[64] Privacy satisfies multiple needs, from autonomy and emotional release to self-evaluation and limited communication.[65] The different aspects of privacy cannot usually be satisfied by a single action. Some of these may be accommodated within the home, and others only by public open space, which is discussed below.

Hide Density

The perception of lower density can be achieved through a variety of design strategies.[66] Traffic reduction, compact building mass, street trees, gardens, green open spaces, and landscaping all contribute to the sense of lower density.[67] Garages off an alley and increased architectural detail may reduce perceived density.[68] Opportunities to personalize the home and landscape can also help.[69]

In the design of the dwelling unit itself, design can also obscure density.[70] The key is design action that makes the small household seem more spacious. In our own 500-square-foot home on a thirty-three by eighty foot lot (a net density of sixteen units per acre), the most effective strategies have been (1) claiming the attic, garage, and garage loft as living space, thereby enlarging the usable square footage to over 1,000 square feet (previously, the car occupied 880 square feet, more space than the three occupants had); (2) enlarging the kitchen windows and raising a shed roof to bring in more natural light, thereby making the entire yard and sky part of the kitchen;

Design can obscure density and make small houses seem spacious by claiming attic and garage spaces and enlarging windows with views to gardens, among other strategies.

Provide privacy

Hide density

Green the neighborhood

Acquire big nature

(3) creating small green gardens (these tiny gardens, called *tsubo niwa,* are widespread in Japan and extend small houses far beyond their size) that can be viewed from most rooms; (4) providing transom windows and partial openings from one room to another and that extend each room; and (5) making stained-glass windows to partially obscure the immediately adjacent houses while maintaining sunlight. There are also two private, carefully designed refuges and an exterior space left empty (we call it *ma,* or sacred emptiness). The emptiness makes it seem we have more space than we need. It is also flexible. It presently is being used to free-range our chickens for a few weeks and often is the location for large parties or temporary staging for house repairs and art projects. In the small yard, evergreen vines form each fence line, compacting the amount of space taken up for "green" privacy (living walls generally provide both privacy and green nature, lowering two aspects of perceived density in one space-saving action).

Green the Neighborhood

Providing neighborhood parks is one of the most important tradeoffs that prompt people to accept higher density,[71] and greenery throughout a neighborhood reduces information overload and stress, thereby lowering the sense of crowding.[72] The LIVES survey indicates an overwhelming preference, even among those who disdain density, for green neighborhoods. Creating a village green (85.9 percent prefer), small parks (84.2 percent prefer), and green courts and cul-de-sacs where children can play safely outdoors (80.5 percent prefer) and planting shade trees (74.6 percent) should persuade some to accept higher density.[73] Topography and water can also be used.[74] Density may be more desirable if housing has an overview of natural features.[75] The form of the landscape needs to vary, depending on the makeup of the community. The upper class typically prefers natural, unruly vegetation while the middle class prefers it manicured.[76] The strong preference for the natural over a manmade environment should generally guide the greening of the neighborhood to achieve increased density.[77]

Neighborhood greening reduces perceived density in another way. Often the greening projects are the initial efforts that community associations undertake, and they require collective action among neighbors. These actions change strangers into familiar faces, increase a sense of control, and through both familiarity and empowerment, reduce perceived density.[78]

Resilient Form

Acquire Big Nature

Closely associated with neighborhood greening, the provision of large, connected tracts of "natural" open space can both reduce perceived density and serve as a tradeoff to higher density.[79] Greenways and wildlife corridors provide recreation, wildlife viewing, and exercise; define neighborhood boundaries; and are associated with high-prestige residential addresses. Such large areas of nature are favored by 89.6 percent of homebuyers and shoppers, a definitive preference among all factors.[80] Since such acquisitions of large natural areas can generally be justified only in concert with compact residential development, providing large areas of nature seems the single most powerful tradeoff to increase density.

Access Transit

Increased density is acceptable when residences have ready access to public transportation. A rail station close by is most preferred[81] and seems to increase housing values.[82] Access to transit is the central tenet of Peter Calthorpe's transit-oriented development model. He calls for higher density around the transit stop, with an average walking distance of two thousand feet, a comfortable ten-minute walking distance.[83] Distance is of foremost importance, but the design of the experience of getting to transit is also critical. There must be a pleasant, safe walk or bike ride.[84] There should be convenient shopping and other everyday needs along the route; this reduces functional distance. If we can do multiple tasks on one walk, the total distance seems short. With useful and interesting things along a walk, we perceive that route as even shorter.[85]

A related transportation matter is wasteful streets and parking, which take up nearly half of the space in a city. For example, the reduction of a forty-foot-wide residential street to a still generous twenty-five feet could add one new dwelling unit for every block in my neighborhood. Every 160 feet of existing street would make a thirty by eighty foot lot, which is suitable for a small house and garage apartment. If that were done throughout the San Francisco Bay area, there would be no need to lose a single acre of prime agriculture or wildlife habitat at the suburban fringe in the next twenty-five years.

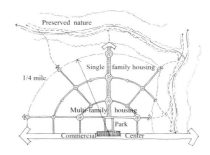

Access transit

Identify the block

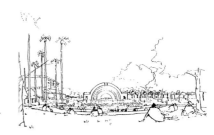

Create center

Identify the Neighborhood and the Block

When daily lives are filled with complexity, mobility, overstimulation, and uncertainty, perceived crowding skyrockets. To increase density, the neighborhood must provide a retreat.[86] Privacy, personalization, and greening contribute to this feeling of retreat. Creating clear, identifiable boundaries and maintaining an easily recognized character for the neighborhood are essential design strategies. A clear edge defining an identifiable district is essential in making the neighborhood legible.[87] Over 80 percent of Americans want a neighborhood with clear boundaries and a distinctive character, most notably like an old-fashioned Southern or New England town.[88] The boundary should define a distinct place that is within a district approximately half a mile across. The design of the neighborhood should evoke certainty, identity, familiarity, personalization, community, and control.

Even within a well-designed neighborhood there is a need for a recognizable articulation of space around the home and the homes of the closest neighbors. The block is the territory of most personally controlled publicness. The block of ten to thirty households is the fundamental unit of place-based civicness, face-to-face intimacy, psychological identity, social neighboring, and deliberative democracy.[89] The block serves as our tribal unit. Typically, the greening efforts mentioned above and other neighborhood improvements as well as NIMBY actions originate within the micro-neighborhood. These subdivisions within the neighborhood should be designed to provide a subtle distinctiveness, one from the other, while maintaining the overall character of the whole neighborhood.

Create the Center

For most Americans (85.9 percent), having a neighborhood center with park, shops, school, civic buildings, and places of worship is highly valued.[90] There is some public willingness to accept higher densities in return for, among other things, shops within the neighborhood.[91] The greater variety of stores, services, and civic facilities provided, the more acceptable density is.

There is a chicken-and-egg question here because density is more acceptable with nearby shopping, but there must be enough density to support those activities. So in retrofitting existing low-density suburbs where there is no center, poorly defined neighborhoods, little nature, and no public transit, you prescribe a holistic approach in which all of these design strategies are employed together, along with policy and funding that gives incentives to densification (such things as transit-efficient loans, low-interest loans for granny-flat conversions, and car-share programs). This comprehensive approach is the exception. Incremental change is more likely, and priority should go to whatever opportunity there is. If neighborhood greening is highly popular, pair that with city support for the additions of second units. If there is an outcry for better-connected wildlife habitat, pair the funding for needed open-space acquisitions with zoning that increases density at the strategic center of the neighborhood. This strategy is to create legitimate nexus and connect the provision of a desired change with increased density.

I Beg Your Pardon: I Never Promised You a Rose Garden

We must keep in mind that residential density is controlled basically through zoning. Although the design strategies I have described are essential in making density acceptable, zoning sets the fundamental ground rules and the absolute bottom line. In most suburbs, present regulations must be changed through a general plan, zoning, subdivision ordinances, use permits or a combination of these. Typically, residents resist this. In Berkeley, there are presently three separate cases where residents are seeking the opposite, fighting allowable moderate-density in-fill projects. All of these cases are located where higher density makes sense for the reasons stated above. One of these projects is a block away from my house. It is a four-story mixed-use project with thirty-five housing units and 5,200 square feet of ground-floor commercial space. The building has been designed by an accomplished developer and local architects with a history of projects that fit the context. It is planned on the site of a gas station that was abandoned for twenty years and where there is a cluster of existing neighborhood stores. With just a few more similar projects, this cluster could be transformed into a genuine neighborhood center. When someone spoke in favor of this project at a community meeting, neighbors were baffled why anyone would support density that they were certain was about to ruin the community. Most speakers were impassioned in their opposition to higher density. One neighborhood leader argued that the project should be defeated because the developer smokes cigars. He ignored the fact that this increased density will bring three more neighborhood shops within walking distance and save thirty acres of prime agricultural land in rural Contra Costa County. He probably did not know about the freezing quail either.

The residents who opposed the three infill projects concluded that they had spent too much time fighting density on a piecemeal basis and drafted a citizen initiative to limit all development in residential areas to a height of twenty-eight feet, thereby effectively freezing present density and precluding further in-fill.[92] After a contentious fight, their initiative failed. Increasing density is not going to be easy. But no one promised us a rose garden.[93]

A first order is to upgrade existing suburbs. For most low-density suburbs, the transition will be painful. Traffic will get worse before it gets better. Few shopping conveniences will be available until density demands them. It will require the very best of deliberative ecological democracy—complex reasoning and discussion about the importance of density that emerges from the grassroots. Within that context, small voices and changes will eventually cultivate density and smallness as virtues. Someone will add a garage apartment, doubling the density. Most neighbors do not notice. Others realize that they could do the same. A neighborhood transforms itself. In the meantime, holistic policy, funding, zoning, and design strategies should be pursued where there is an opportunity. For starters, a simple policy should be considered in every local jurisdiction. No new housing development anywhere in the country should be allowed to proceed unless it provides overall gross density of twelve units per acre. Farm housing will be exempt, but no other exceptions will be made.

In each design project, there are moments that density can be increased by making it fit so well that it is hidden from our perceived fears. This can happen by providing for privacy in small spaces, by greening the neighborhood by acquiring big nature, by accessing transit, by creating identity and control for the neighborhood, and by enhancing local centers. Each project we undertake, big or small, should contribute in some ways to increasing density and cultivating the culture that champions it. Keep in mind that the density needed to make more resilient form is not that dense. Generally, transit, neighborhood centers, and wildlife habitat can be supported with in-fill densities of ten to twenty dwelling units per acre—much of which can still be provided by carefully crafted, small, single-family homes and gardens. But considerably higher densities are also desirable to achieve resilience in many cases. Densities approaching fifty units per acre can provide spacious and gracious living. For example, neighborhoods of four-story Victorian row houses are often forty-eight units per acre and still provide private or shared gardens for most residents.[94] And as density is cleared of the charges wrongfully brought against it, more people are likely to acknowledge that they actually prefer densities of 100 units per acre and the truly urban amenities associated with resilient cities. This is where we promise the rose garden. It is a matter of perceiving density differently and choosing a new view of the best possible life we can achieve.

Limited Extent

A useful ecology lesson unfolds in the Lake Michigan dunes, where wood snails never leave the beech and maple forest. The wood snails thrive in the limited territory they occupy. They leave surrounding landscapes for other functions; the dunes ecosystem needs to sustain itself. The very same lesson can be found in cities with greenbelts that limit their outer boundaries. One such city, Greenbelt, Maryland, has been described as a particularly healthy place that is largely self-contained with unusually easy access to work, shopping, and open spaces.

Two Excellencies Make a Singular Resilience

For human habitation, the benefits in limiting the extent of land into which the city spreads are many. Resilience is increased by maintaining the functioning ecosystem and thereby regional biological diversity. This allows space for agricultural land and other functions that are necessary for supplying the city with food, clean air and water, and other resources, thereby making the city less susceptible to natural catastrophe and allowing a diverse economy—all the advantages of particularness that we have discussed. Other financial benefits accrue in savings from compact utility and service expansions. Limiting the extent of the city makes the city size comprehensible and reinforces identity and resident satisfaction. Limiting the extent of urban spread allows also for access to nearby nature and wilderness recreation. All of these have been described in some detail in chapters on Centeredness, Particularness, Selective Diversity, and Density and Smallness. Limited extent supports and, in turn, is supported by each of these.

Limited extent and density are inextricably bound as inseparable partners in resilient form. But unlike density, which is anathema to the majority of Americans, limiting the extent of cities has extraordinary, unrealized public support. In the LIVES survey discussed earlier, the single most strongly agreed on urban-design strategy was to create greenbelts between cities: 89.6 percent of those surveyed supported this action. Even among people who

Limited extent ensures two excellencies—
vibrant urbanity and accessible wild
nature—that create a singular resilience.

most prefer suburban living, 82.4 percent support greenbelts. For those who prefer more urban living, 97.9 percent would like to see more greenbelts between towns.[1] It is not merely that people are weary of subdivisions marching off endlessly. Rather, it is the recognition that there are two excellencies, the city and the countryside, "each indispensable, each different, both complementary, both life-enhancing."[2] Limiting the extent of continuous urban spread—whereby the boundary of the city is consciously controlled and surrounding agriculture and wilderness are protected—provides the two excellencies. The central point of limited extent is to maintain both the compact city and the countryside. In spite of this public desire and certainly because this desire has been overridden by other preferences, American cities have infrequently provided any restraint to their girth. Greenbelt, Maryland, is a midcentury exception, an outlier, and most of its green space has been developed over time.

From Settlement to Edge City and Fat Suburb

Growth for most American cities has followed one pattern—continuously expanding the periphery, preempting the edge, and pushing open space farther and farther from most people.[3] A small settlement of several hundred people expands outward to accommodate several thousand people and—if successful by American standards—hundreds of thousands and millions. Depending on the era, there may have been periods of densification in the central city and lately at the edge,[4] but the predominant pattern is low-density expansion at the edge.[5] This expansion has been fueled by antiurban sentiment, American preferences, government subsidies, policies, laws, and the highway and construction lobbies. Artificially undertaxed gas prices, fragmented local land-use decision making, and the combined forces of legal rights associated with private property and the windfall profit of land speculation add further incentive for cities to grow exclusively by spreading out at the edges.[6] Certainly, the prevailing cry that the city will die if it does not grow fulfilled popular pride in bigness.[7] Growth and expansion undoubtedly provided benefits for small towns, and outward growth makes sense for a very short period of time in the life of any city. Growing from five hundred to five thousand people allows some specialization, accumulated wealth, cultural organizations, and services that are infeasible for villages. But long after such advantages were exhausted, the spread continued—like a bulging waistline—and continues.

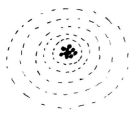

Concentric spread

Dense suburbs

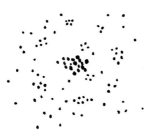

Thin spread

Three Questions of Size

Powerful forces fuel urban spread. It is difficult to pause and ask, "How big is enough?" But in an ecological democracy, this basic question requires a thoughtful answer. There are actually three significant questions of extent that affect resilience. First, how many people occupying how much land can any region support? Second, how many people or square miles make up the optimum city size? (Associated with this is another question: How can the extent be limited to support that optimum size?) Third, within a region where the population supersedes optimum city size, how big should the secondary cities be, and how should extent be limited between the various cities? These three questions might be thought of as the outer limit, the internal limit, and the minimum limit.

Appropriate Size: The Outer Limits of Regional Carrying Capacity

How many people occupying how much land any region can support is the most basic question of resilience. No region can be resilient if the demands of its population exceed the capacity of the environment to meet those demands.[8] Carrying capacity suggests that no region should exceed the ability to provide its own water, air, food, energy, forest, and other needed products; to guarantee safety from disasters; and to process its wastes within that region. This is what the wood snails in the forest of the Michigan dunes know that we do not seem to be able to learn. Few regions are able to do this. Consider water as an example. The World Watch Institute found that although three-fourths of all U.S. cities are in some way dependent on ground-water resources, "only three of the 35 largest—San Antonio, Miami and Memphis—can meet their needs solely from local supplies."[9] In California, water is the single most contested resource. Southern California does not have nearly enough to support its population; northern California has more and has long supplied the south through diversion projects, but now northern California is approaching its limit. Schemes abound to take more water south. A recent proposal would siphon water from the Gualala and Albion rivers into giant bags eight hundred feet long. These bags would be towed from the north coast to San Diego.[10] Such proposals have prompted many to seriously consider dividing California into several states based on regional watersheds. Within each region of the country, water is a critical limiting resource, but other critical factors vary, depending on soils, climate, and topography.

In recent years, one of the issues in the San Francisco Bay area is that its air pollution is pushed eastward by prevailing winds and decreases air quality for central-valley cities. Jurisdictions in both the San Joaquin and Sacramento valleys sued the State of California to force the San Francisco region to attend to its waste air before it moves into the valleys. Although there is still a debate over the significance of air pollution from San Francisco, the state assembly passed and the governor signed measures that force a more stringent smog-control program in the San Francisco Bay area.[11] In an era of specialized production, worldwide trade, and artificially cheap transportation, it may seem parochial to expect regions to attend to such problems, but generally, regional carrying capacity must set the parameters for a maximum population to attain resilience.

Appropriate Size: Internal Limits on Optimal City Size

The disadvantages of spreading population become apparent internally long before regional carrying-capacity thresholds are recognized. For example, the streets in a well-engineered city may have handled the traffic of a near exclusive automobile culture until the city approached fifty thousand people. But at that point, new highways to connect the various outlying parts of the sprawling city required destroying large swaths of the countryside for beltlines (beltlines are aptly named because they wrap around the waist of the spreading city). Viable inner-city neighborhoods were also needed for crosstown highways. These cross-town expressways often destroyed or divided poor neighborhoods and stream corridors, but all neighborhoods suffered severance. As the population grew beyond fifty thousand, the traffic system declined in quality even as more money was spent to make it work. By the time the girth reached thirty miles, traffic flow was hobbled; low-density spread had suffocated interior neighborhoods and gridlocked itself.

The spread city pattern at some point exceeds inefficiency and high cost. Spread causes widespread dysfunction.

So at what point should the extent of the city be limited for internal motivations? It is much easier to enclose broad limits than to be definitive—to say that five hundred people are too few and five million are too many. Aristotle argued that ten people were too few and a hundred thousand people

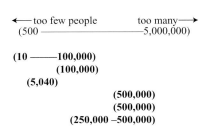

Ideal city population

too many to make a city.[12] The range of appropriate size is likely so great that it is political suicide to be precise.[13] One of the most thoughtful scientists I know reached the conclusion that Raleigh, North Carolina, was approaching its healthiest upper limit thirty years ago, with a population well below a hundred thousand people. He was an effective city council member but was soundly defeated in his bid for mayor, ending the most important discussion in the city's recent history. This makes me wonder if Plato was similarly ostracized when he advanced the idea that an ideal city would consist of only 5,040 citizens.[14]

In a lucid discussion about optimum city size, E. F. Schumacher constructed an economic logic by first bracketing the extremes. His economic analysis led him to conclude that cities of multimillions of people added nothing to those cities' real values but created major problems and human suffering. At the other extreme, he observed that most cities that achieved major advances in humankind in the past were very small compared to cities today. The accumulated wealth necessary to enrich human life is not nearly so much as typically projected. To illustrate, he showed how little philosophy, arts, and religion cost. Then he tackled the optimum size question directly. He stated that, "It is fairly safe to say that the upper limit of what is desirable for the size of a city is probably something of the order of half a million inhabitants."[15] *A Pattern Language* uses as its primary example a city of exactly this size—500,000 people.[16] Lynch states that the current thinking about optimal size puts the figure "somewhere between 250,000 and 500,000 persons."[17]

Schumacher's macro economic analysis can be done for any number of economic considerations—infrastructure cost, management costs, scientific advancement, or considerations like anomie, identity, health, and civic participation. If we take one previously poorly defined health measure—access to wild nature—that researchers have recently shown to be of critical importance in human development, stress reduction, and recovery from illness, we could develop a similar logic. Assume, as many researchers now do, that everyone needs access to an uninterrupted expanse of wild nature that defines the edge of the city, that is within two miles of home, and that is reached by a connected natural corridor no more than a quarter mile from home. This means that the wild nature that defines the city boundary can be reached in an easy fifteen-minute bike or bus ride, a twenty-minute job, or a forty-five-minute walk. Within this boundary, an urban land area of fifteen square miles in a compact city or thirty square miles for an elongated city could be accom-

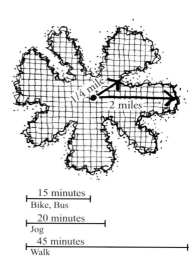

1/4 mile

2 miles

| 15 minutes |
| Bike, Bus |

| 20 minutes |
| Jog |

| 45 minutes |
| Walk |

Access to wild nature

modated. At a modest density of twenty housing units per net acre, with half the land for nonresidential purposes, a population of between 250,000 and 500,000 could be accommodated, depending on the form of the city.

The optimum population, even for this one measure, depends on many human variables (like homogeneity and density) and may be further limited by natural carrying capacity factors (like water supply and topography). However, generally, somewhere in the range of 250,000 to 500,000 people makes sense as a maximum population for a single city. Is that optimal? Certainly, that provides the upper limit, but many cities of less than a hundred thousand people score most strongly when a range of sustainability factors is considered. The optimal size varies somewhere between these brackets. I would use the 250,000 population as the maximum threshold for describing various design strategies that make cities more resilient.

Carrying capacity sets a cap on maximum population and the extent of land development within a region for that region to remain resilient. Cities do not need to be nearly as big as many have become to offer all the benefits associated with size. For many other reasons of health and well-being, limited city size is critical to resilience. We address the third question of minimum size when we consider the small city in regional context. Now let us reconsider how limited extent could be effected in megacities, in cities approaching 250,000 people, and in smaller cities.

Reconfiguring Megacities

About seventy cities in the United States already exceed 250,000 people. If optimal population size is smaller than that of these urban areas, what are the design strategies for such cities? A partial answer is that different cities have extraordinarily different functions and that for each dominant activity there is an appropriate size.[18] Variations in size add diversity to the overall union. But it seems more to the point of good city design that this bigness be reconfigured over time to break down the bigness. This is the lesson from most large organizations, public or private: "As soon as great size has been created, there is often a strenuous attempt to attain smallness within bigness."[19] "Break down bigness" should be the primary strategy for American megacities.[20] This is painful to do in cities that are already spread too far. The most cost-effective, multipurpose approach is to determine the natural systems that have been depressed in past city development and, over time, reestablish those natural patterns to subdivide a megacity into smaller, identifiable units that are separated by those natural features. Steam corridors and natural drainageways offer the most obvious framework for this. Efforts to do this are presently being implemented by unearthing buried creeks and undoing concrete flood-control projects. Breaking down bigness can also be achieved by reestablishing agricultural lands, urban forests, or wildlife corridors within megacities. In Los Angeles, this is being accomplished by the greening of the Los Angeles River and its multiple tributaries. In one visionary proposal a National Wildlife Refuge using the river as the primary framework will subdivide the city into 204 neighborhoods in twelve subwatershed jurisdictions to create habitat suitable for each district. The habitat will create green fingers that define communities, reduce flooding, improve water quality, provide recreation, and attract two hundred species of birds. Unfortunately, political jurisdictions usually do not follow the patterns of these natural systems. When political jurisdictions match the natural pattern, they foster an ecological democracy.

Another problem in reconfiguring existing cities in that present corridors may satisfy recreation or short-distance wildlife movement but are so thin that they do not provide enough space to fulfill the multiple purposes of the countryside—food production, core wildlife habitat, ground-water recharge, and the health benefits of exercise and stress reduction. This requires a more radical restructuring of existing cities—as Richard Register has proposed for the East Bay cities of the San Francisco Bay area. Beyond restoring creeks to provide green corridors, Register proposes relocating low-density housing from what was once prime productive agricultural land into denser nodal communities. His phased plan for Berkeley culminates 125 years from now in eleven distinct communities separated by at least two thousand feet of greenbelt and in some cases by five thousand feet of agricultural land.[21] In restructuring large cities, neighborhoods of approximately five thousand people should be separated one from another by no less than a hundred-foot natural corridor. Such a thin corridor can serve some but not all the purposes. To achieve maximum benefits, a fifteen-hundred-foot corridor is preferred. In disaggregated cities, communities of between a hundred thousand and five hundred thousand people should be separated from other communities by no less than a quarter-mile natural greenbelt. A ten-mile greenbelt between larger communities would achieve the multiple functions of the countryside but is an unrealistic goal when breaking down the bigness of existing cities.

To green the Los Angeles River, its vastness is broken into 204 neighborhoods, such as the Van Alden community, to satisfy the unique park needs of each locality and achieve the big vision.

Flood-water detention plan

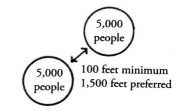

Neighborhood greenbelt widths

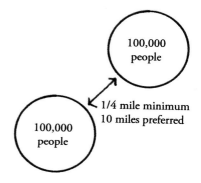

City greenbelt widths

5-15 Years   Create Centers

15- 20 Year   Centers Densifying

25- 90 Years   Pedestrian Network

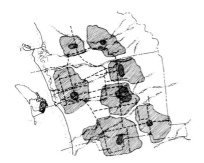

40-125 Years   Greenbelt Communities

Richard Register's plan to restructure
Berkeley reverses years of low-density
spread by densifying centers and eventually
creating communities that are separated by
creeks and productive agricultural lands.

Resilient Form

Inside and Outside

Compelling arguments for limiting extent are made in terms of access to nature and in terms of impact on ecological system and on costs of infrastructure. Underlying the human aspects of limited extent, however, is a fundamental psychological need for clarity of inside and outside. Inside and outside are essential for a sense of orientation, world view, relatedness, and healthy human development.[22] Donald Appleyard's study of perceptions of the environment concluded that the difference between insiders and outsiders was one of the most powerful forces in human development and habitation.[23] In nurturing resilient human beings, clarity of inside and outside may be as important as good diet and exercise. Inside and outside are distinguished at many levels, but in the design of the city, the boundaries between home and yard, neighborhood and urban nature, and city and countryside are most critical. In each, there is a contrast of built and unbuilt.

Providing the distinction between inside and outside requires a penetrable boundary and also enough of the outside to be experienced as a distinct territory, not just a buffer. In the same way that ten fruit trees in two rows may provide fruit but do not create an orchard, the greenbelt must have enough extent to be perceived as another landscape. This requires an edge and a distinct district beyond.[24] That is the basis of bounding neighborhoods with natural corridors of a minimum of a hundred feet and a preferred depth of fifteen hundred feet, depending on the ecological functions that the open areas serve. This is also the basis for separating the parts of megacities by at least quarter-mile greenbelts and preferably ten miles. The hundred-foot and quarter-mile corridors provide the edge; the fifteen-hundred-foot and ten-mile greenbelts create distinct districts that are essential to a clear experience of inside and out.

The active, face-to-face participation that is required in an ecological democracy requires small, distinct units that have clear inside and out and ecological context. Aristotle argued for small communities so that citizens could know each other personally and know each other's character and abilities.[25] Plato's ideal community of 5,040 people defined by natural boundaries is the largest unit that can provide an effective voice for most individuals and the opportunity to engage in the thoughtful decision making that is required in an ecological democracy. This is consistent with the

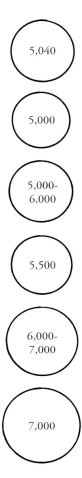

Ideal neighborhood size

research of Clarence Perry, who called for neighborhoods of between 5,000 and 6,000 people; Paul Goodman, who called for units of 5,500; Milton Kotler, who urged units of 6,000 to 7,000; and Chris Alexander, who prescribed units of 7,000 people—just some of the many who have reached similar conclusions.[26] The inside-outside distinction is fundamental because it facilitates participation; conveys a sense of possession, identity, and collective responsibility; is grounded in direct experience, realism, and depth of knowledge; and cultivates emotional attachments to people and place.[27]

Cities Approaching 250,000 People

In the United States today, there are approximately six hundred cities with populations of between 50,000 and 250,000. These cities have the best opportunity to limit their extent in a cost-effective manner. Relatively inexpensively they can (1) purchase the land and development rights or (2) transfer the rights necessary to formulate regional growth strategies and create boundaries in advance. These cities have a wide range of choices about how to grow. They can branch, expand, or replicate.[28] Creating these patterns in advance is less expensive than the land-use reallocation and purchase of already developed property that are required in megacities. In smaller cities, there are other obstacles to maintaining substantial natural boundaries, but that is changing as the public has become more aware of the need for limiting the extent of urban growth and more aware of possible solutions. In 2000, voters approved 400 of the 553 growth-related measures that were on ballots nationally.[29] In recent years, the measures for open-space acquisition and urban containment have passed at a rate of from 72 to 77 percent. In 1998 alone, such ballots set aside $7 billion for open-space land protection.[30]

Boulder, Colorado, population 94,673, is one of the most successful middle-sized cities in limiting its extent. Nearly fifty years ago, people in Boulder became concerned about the costs of sprawl. One of many cities that studied the impacts of carefully managed growth, it is one of few to adopt effective mechanisms for limiting extent. The city planned its infrastructure to restrict costly extensions of water service to outlying subdivisions. Fortunately and quite differently from many communities, the county government agreed with this strategy and supported it. Boulder adopted strategies to concentrate development within its boundaries and to support its downtown as the primary center.[31] Its efforts to keep the expanding governmental facilities downtown and to create affordable housing have been painful and heroic, requiring some of the best American examples of ecological democracy in action.[32]

Most relevant to this discussion is the greenbelt-acquisition program. Its specific purpose is to form a clear boundary between the developed city and the wildlands beyond. For over thirty years, the city has actively and systematically purchased key parcels of land to contain city growth. The money comes from a sales tax that is dedicated to open-space purchases and that has funded the purchase of 25,000 acres, creating "an extensive and relatively contiguous open space network" that may indeed preserve Boulder's spectacular natural setting.[33] One evaluation concluded, "Boulder's efforts are unique by American standards, resulting in a sharp and distinct separation between urban and rural/open space."[34]

Most middle-sized cities have employed variations of half a dozen city-design techniques to limit their extent. One is the urban-service boundary that Boulder applied, whereby public facilities that are essential to new development are provided for areas where the city wants to induce growth and are restricted in areas where growth is undesirable. Water, sewer, and transportation are most often used, but schools and other public facilities may also serve the purpose of directing growth. Restrictions on development on steep slopes, wetlands, or flood-prone areas are a second strategy for limiting extent. Typically, these restrictions do not create the desired distinct separation between urban and wild and do not encircle the entirety of the city.

Third, cluster development is effective in hiding development and providing scenic corridors. Clustering also provides some open space, but most often the clusters of development are on small properties, which produces pockets of sprawl without a distinct separation between urban and wild. Only when clusters are comprehensively planned do they create an open-space network.[35]

Fourth, growth-limit lines or urban-growth boundaries have received much deserved application. In 1973, Oregon, a state of 240 small- to middle-size cities, passed the best known urban-growth-boundary legislation. Portland was and continues to be one of the most livable cities, and the growth boundary seems to be helping maintain that quality and resilience.

A fifth means of limiting extent is the creation of agricultural-preservation zones that restrict the conversion of farmland to urban development. In Napa County, California, these zones have preserved the majority of Napa Valley for vineyards and wine making and created more compact cities and villages.

Sometimes a sixth technique is employed in concert with preservation zones to allow transferring the development rights from the preserved land to higher-density cores. The private-property owner sells his "transferred" rights to urbanize his land to a developer of a project in the city who is allowed to build more densely in a preferred location.

In a related seventh technique, farmland owners sell the rights to develop the farm to a land trust. Instead of transferring the rights elsewhere, the sale typically establishes a conservation easement on the property. Unless done within a preservation zone, neither transfers of development rights nor conservation easements are likely to create a continuous limited extent around a city.

The eighth method is to acquire land at the edge of the city's growth limit as dedicated open space. This is another approach that Boulder has used. Typically, to limit its extent successfully, the city will employ a number of these techniques, as Boulder has done.

Appropriate Size: Small Towns in Regional Form

Here we return to part of the third question about appropriate size. Within a region where the population supersedes optimum city size, how big should the secondary cities be, and how much space should be preserved between these cities and towns? An obvious next question is how big does a small town have to be to be resilient?

The sphere of regional influence of major American cities dominates the smaller towns and rural areas nearby. Even though these cities appear to control the region, they are, in fact, inextricably dependent on the towns around them. For any major city to gain the resilience of limited extent, it must have the cooperation of those around it. Regions with many fragmented local jurisdictions are less able to do so.[36] Boulder could never have created as much of its greenbelt as it has without the support of those living in the surrounding country. Limiting extent and directing growth to places that are most appropriate requires widespread agreement on a regional vision, one of the great challenges to any ecological democracy. Such an agreement depends on an acknowledgment of the regional interconnections (see the chapter on Connectedness), a willingness for each jurisdiction to do its share, a commitment to the fair distribution of public goods and liabilities, and the development of regional land-use and transportation plans that guarantee each jurisdiction—large or small—the surrounding open space that it needs to limit its extent. Otherwise fat-city spread will eventually envelop and devour smaller jurisdictions. In short, then, all the jurisdictions in the region are interdependent.[37]

But how much open space should be required between urbanized jurisdictions? As a general rule, even in the most extreme situation, there should never be less than a mile of undeveloped land—agriculture or wild open space—between any two cities. Some researchers list a more desirable eight to ten miles between small towns.[38] In most cases, the minimum distance between cities in a region will be dictated by the amount of land needed to supply water, food, and energy. The greenbelt, while never narrower than one mile, most often will be broader to produce what the region requires.

A related question concerns the optimal size of these small towns: how big must a small town be to be resilient? Generally, there should be variety and choice in the sizes of cities in a region. Some people prefer large cities, but most Americans would choose small towns if they could. Therefore, many small towns of varying sizes, separated by greenbelts, would satisfy a broad segment of Americans. However, for small towns to provide necessary everyday services, the population needs to be in the range of five thousand people. This provides the critical mass for a healthy nucleus of services necessary for daily life.[39] Otherwise, the long drives that are necessary for community services and grocery shopping will undermine regional resilience. Unless self-sufficient due to some unusual circumstance, small towns should be encouraged to develop to a minimum population of five thousand people. Cluster development of smaller populations may save visual corridors but adds little to overall resilience.

As an example, consider how the Honolulu metropolitan area has addressed these questions. Honolulu has confronted the problems of regional distribution with the advantage of a state land-use plan that sought to preserve much of Oahu's landscape beauty for ecological and cultural reasons and for the tourist economy.[40] The de facto regional plan has urbanized much of the south shore fairly densely while providing ready public access to beaches and mountains, then reversing the proportions of development on the north shore with a series of small villages interspersed in agricultural and natural areas. Dense Honolulu requires less land per resident than any other urban region in the United States.[41] One result is that Honolulu residents have the easiest access to wild nature of any major city in the country. Fortunate topography plays a key part. The ocean and steep interior mountains left Oahu with a small band of easily developed land on the south shore, which limited the extent of city spread.[42] The north shore has less limiting topography. Thousand of acres of rolling farmland rise from the coast to the distant mountains. Historically, the farmland, mostly in large corporate ownership, produced sugarcane and pineapples and provided a temporary greenbelt around distinct and bounded villages like Wailuea, Haleiwa, and Sunset Beach. No one imagined how temporary this greenbelt would be until these crops could be produced more cheaply in other parts of the world. As sugar mills closed, subdivisions and destination resorts were being proposed on agricultural land scattered throughout the north shore, but local residents wanted to maintain separate villages and the countryside. People in Honolulu also benefited from the open country of the north shore; it provided them variety and a change of pace from the city. "Keep the Country Country" became the rallying cry for a plan to concentrate growth within the existing villages and to preserve farmland through experimentation with new crops. The farmland provides greenbelts by separating the north-shore towns by between three and eight miles. Each village is less than five thousand people; with additional tourist business, a full range of daily services is available in Haleiwa. Villages are successfully limiting their outward expansion, allowing each to maintain its character and sacred places while growing and contributing to the overall quality of life for the metropolitan area. The rare region that has a diversity of city sizes and ample open space between, Honolulu's success in limiting the extent of urban expansion and concentrating habitation relies on fortuitous geography, a strong state land-use plan, and a single municipal government. Still, on the north shore, where geography is less limiting, preventing sprawl is an ongoing struggle. A citizenry that wants to maintain rural lifestyles is continually pitted against multinational corporations and large landowners who would make exceptions to growth containment to get their pet projects built.

The north shore of Oahu keeps the country country by directing growth to villages that are separated by agricultural lands and connected by bus. The permeable boundary is evident everywhere, from living gates to irrigation canals and sacred sites.

In other parts of the United States, particularly the southeast, communities have been as unsuccessful at limiting urban extents as Honolulu has been successful. In contrast to Honolulu, the southeast has weak land-use control, extremely fragmented governments, and few limits of geography to contain growth. In North Carolina, for example, no region of the state has been able to effectively control its extent. Fifty years ago, the state was made up of hundreds of farm market towns that were evenly spaced about thirty miles apart and separated by forest and farmland. Small towns were the pride of the state, a point of singular identity. Little was done to maintain them and much to undermine them. The state lost its identity in less than twenty-five years. From a state of small farming towns in 1950 (when only 33 percent lived in cities), North Carolina transformed into a suburban state by 1975 (when over half of the population lived in suburbs of larger cities).[43] Small towns lost population even as their counties grew. Most residential development was taking place outside incorporated areas.[44] The bulk of the state's new housing, by 1970 and continuing today, is scattered along state roads in the form of single-family and mobile homes on half-acre lots.[45] It is now estimated that the entire state will be totally developed and enveloped in exurban sprawl in less than seventy-five years.[46]

Haleiwa, Hawaii

Los Angeles, California

City without limits

Reseda-to-the-Sea freeway

Creating a Big Wild Greenbelt for Los Angeles

Given these difficulties, what is required, more precisely, to create the open space to contain a city and give natural form to a metropolitan region? Our firm has been involved in creating a greenbelt around Los Angeles since 1985. Our client has been the Santa Monica Mountains Conservancy, a state agency that originally was mandated to acquire land in the Santa Monica Mountains National Recreation Area. Although every region is different, this experience gives an overview of many of the issues to be faced elsewhere.

The idea of creating a greenbelt evolved as the Santa Monica Mountains Conservancy gained success in complex land acquisitions and political strategy and when research in conservation biology provided a scientific basis for the purchase of large land areas outside the original jurisdiction. Outright land purchase is the favored means of creating the Los Angeles boundary, often in concert with prohibition against steep-slope development, exactions, de facto transfer of development rights, and citizen protests against sprawl. The public has consistently voted for open-space bonds that have purchased much of the land.

Los Angeles may seem to be an unlikely place to be creating a greenbelt. Famous for its freeways and automobile culture, it is surprisingly dense and retains a largely functioning terrestrial ecosystem composed primarily of chaparral only fifteen minutes from downtown. This ecosystem still supports the full range of species, including mountain lions.

When we first began working for it, the Santa Monica Mountains Conservancy was in its infancy, and the greenbelt had not been envisioned. Each project consisted of creating a plan for small parcels that the Conservancy had purchased. Each master plan was negotiated through a participatory process that catered to residents in nearby neighborhoods. This fragmentary approach remains central to the Conservancy's success because local political support and stewardship are essential for plan approval, funding, and proper maintenance of this urban wilderness. Although today the Conservancy selects land acquisition based on a vision for a functioning ecosystem, each project is still planned with distinct local constituencies.

The creation of the greenbelt, now called Big Wild, advanced dramatically when we were doing the plan for one of these local fragments, Mulholland Gateway Park. That park consisted of a thousand acres in a few large parcels and bits and pieces along the ridge of the north slope of the Santa

Monica Mountains. My partner, Marcia McNally, insisted that the thousand acres were so fragmented that they had no ecological integrity. She argued that the parcel had to be planned within a bigger framework, hence the origin of Big Wild. She was clearly thinking outside the box. Each framework we drew led us to a bigger one until we had connected to the national forests that were two valleys away.

When we first began planning Mulholland Gateway Park, there was a serious conflict between two nearby neighborhood groups about a freeway that was being built through the park. Remember the lost mountain and the dirt contractor in the chapter on Connectedness? The battle over Reseda Ridge instigated this effort. At one meeting to discuss the freeway, a fistfight erupted between the wealthy pro- and con-freeway neighbors, indicating how emotional the park planning would be. Some neighborhoods had become overrun with traffic that cut through local streets when the freeways backed up. Because their neighborhood streets were unsuited for a high volume of fast traffic and had become dangerous by any measure, these residents strongly supported the freeway as a way to relieve congestion in their area. Other groups opposed the freeway on environmental grounds. As the grading for the freeway progressed, some beautiful mountain ridges were removed. Members of Earth First and other antifreeway groups chained themselves to bulldozers to stop further damage from being done by the freeway construction.

Two technical questions underlay the emotional conflict: would the new freeway improve traffic congestion, and would it negatively impact local biological diversity? We hired neutral experts to advise us.

The traffic consultant concluded that the new freeway could not alleviate traffic congestion. The new cross-mountain freeway in concert with the existing 405 freeway provided a capacity of 7,500 vehicles per hour, but there was a demand of over ten thousand trips per hour at rush hour. There were more than 2,500 people who desired to make trips at rush hour who could not. The new freeway would terminate on Sunset Boulevard, which was already near gridlock at peak hours. It would provide no relief from congestion for the neighborhood that so strongly supported it. Our traffic expert then began to work with the most impacted neighborhoods. They developed strategies to minimize the cut-through traffic using diverters and other traffic-control devices.

Earth First!

Freeway traffic invasion

Neighborhood gridlock

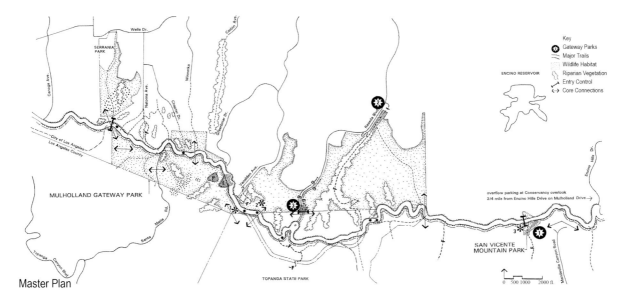

Master Plan

Although 1,000 acres seems like a large park, planner Marcia McNally insisted that it was so fragmented that it lacked ecological integrity and had to be considered in a bigger framework. That was the origin of Big Wild.

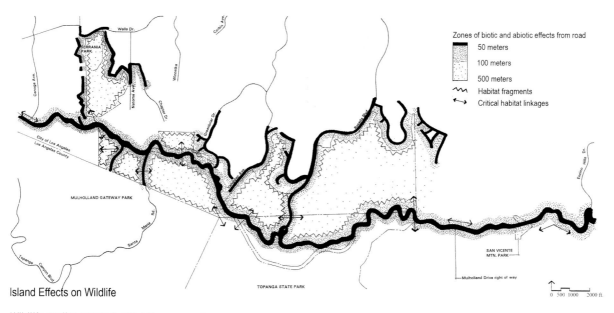

Island Effects on Wildlife

Wildlife studies concluded that the proposed freeway and associated road network would create island effects for key species and lead to local extinctions.

Meanwhile, the wildlife-habitat experts noted that the freeway would sever the most critical east-west wildlife corridor. They also discovered that a connector road was proposed along the primary wildlife corridor itself. Combined with several other roadway projects in the area, the freeway would lead to dramatic changes in species composition due to island effects. Large predators would be effectively eliminated from the eastern parts of the Santa Monica Mountains. Local extinctions of numerous species were projected if the roads were built as planned.

This was the first site-specific application of conservation biology principles in the Santa Monica Mountains. We did not know how to proceed, so we researched and translated into spatial form findings from various wildlife biologists. The literature gave some general guidance about wildlife-corridor geometry. Additional research provided specific spatial requirements for key species in the Santa Monica Mountains. Our wildlife biologists thought that a habitat for a healthy population of mountain lions would likely maintain the entire terrestrial ecosystem. That became a central goal in creating the greenbelt, and it was an idea bold enough to capture the imagination of Los Angeles citizens. Big Wild needed to be big for multiple reasons. Preliminary estimates suggested that 640,000 acres of diverse habitat are required for a sustainable population of mountain lions and that the freeway therefore should be stopped and a much bigger area acquired to maintain a balanced wildlife population.

At this point, McNally's vision for Big Wild acquired strong scientific support. In fact, her idea of Big Wild would need to become one of several core habitats of at least twenty thousand acres connected by generous corridors of native vegetation. These core habitats in the city, in turn, needed to be connected without interruption to much larger remote wildlands, including national forests. At that point, we drew a new plan that connected the habitat envisioned Big Wild.

In spite of the scientific logic, the Los Angeles City Council, after much debate, renewed its commitment to building the freeway. We realized the underlying political motivations. What had seemed to be an emotional battle between two neighborhoods was much more. Powerful political support for the freeway was coming from real estate developers, land owners, and even public agencies. All wanted the freeway built to provide access to lands on which they were speculating. Their combined political force in favor of the freeway seemed incontestable. Remember the power map discussed in the

Mountain Lion (640,000 acres)

Bobcat (21,000 acres)

Badger (13,000 acres)

Deer (7,000 acres)

Territories for sustainable populations

To maintain the top predators in the Los Angeles ecosystem required expansion of the Mulholland Gateway Park into a 20,000 acre Big Wild and connecting that to other core habitat.

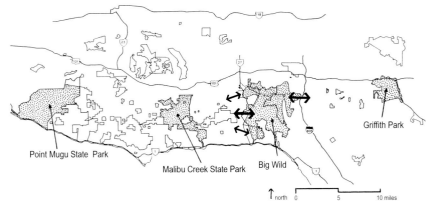

Point Mugu State Park

Malibu Creek State Park

Big Wild

Griffith Park

↑ north 0   5   10 miles

Bus tours

Citywide campaign of education

Experiencing Big Wild

chapter on Connectedness? The only strategy that anyone could imagine to counter their power was a citywide educational campaign to make more people aware of the extraordinary potential of Big Wild. From earlier research, we knew that people from all districts and social classes of Los Angeles valued the opportunities to be in nature and see wildlife and were willing to tax themselves to acquire the open space needed for natural areas. We assumed most people were unaware of the loss of wildlife that would occur if the freeways and development continued to fragment this link in the terrestrial ecosystem. Bus tours were planned to explain the findings from the wildlife and traffic studies on site where people could experience the implications. The bus tours were advertised in the *Los Angeles Times* and local city newspapers, through local civic groups, and from the mailing list of previous participants in the process. Hundreds of people participated in the tours. Half had never been to the Santa Monica Mountains area that was under threat. These first-time participants were important because they had no specific, narrow, vested interest in building or stopping the freeway. Therefore, their opinions represented broader, more general public interests. Simple diagrams of the traffic and wildlife studies and a scripted text supplemented the tour of key locations.

An overwhelming majority of these participants wanted to stop the freeway to create Big Wild. They were eager to participate in making this visionary plan a reality. A series of workshops followed to work out details of the plan. The Big Wild plan was presented to the Los Angeles City Council, and eventually the freeway was abandoned and Big Wild adopted.

Each part of the greenbelt has a similar story: A long fight to acquire land amid negotiations with landowners, developers, nearby residents, neighborhood associations, environmental, dog walking, and mountain-bike groups. The pace was too slow for Joe Edmiston, the executive director of the Santa Monica Mountains Conservancy. Over a period of years, Edmiston initiated a bolder strategy. He expanded his jurisdiction, engaged a broader constituency through hands-on experiences in the mountain eco-system, inserted defensible wildlife science into the public debate, and lengthened citizen visions beyond narrow neighborhood interests. Through legislation and joint powers agreements, his authority today extends throughout the mountains. His ability to cross traditionally rigid jurisdictional lines has been central to effectively acquiring the lands that are necessary to create functional wildlife corridors and complete the encircling greenway. He now intends to connect the greenway to related efforts in Orange County to provide core habitat and wildlife corridors to the national forests southeast of Los Angeles.

Across jurisdictional lines

To achieve educational goals, the Conservancy created the Mountains Education Program in 1989. Through interpretation of the mountain's resources, it has successfully sought to "form a community united by environmental stewardship."[47] Edmiston intends to introduce every Los Angeles child to the Santa Monica Mountains through outings and camping trips. Over fifteen thousand children and adults participate in the program each year.[48] Most become active in the urban wilderness projects.

Timely acquisitions

To attract more users to the greenbelt, gateway parks like the one created by the dirt contractor on Reseda Ridge (see the chapter on Connectedness) have been developed. This has successfully enlarged the use of the greenbelt. Women, who historically were afraid to use the natural parks by themselves, now report that they feel safe coming to these gateway parks alone. Teenagers regularly use the parks both to be in nature and to make out with boy- and girlfriends. Poor central-city youth and new immigrants from Central America and Asia have become regular visitors.

Nontraditional constituencies

The increase in nontraditional users, however, has created conflict with long-time urban-wilderness advocates. Traditionalists feel that the newcomers degrade the natural environment because of their concentrated use at gateway parks; social-class and racial divisions[49] have arisen because of conflicts over the provision of the grass lawns, shade trees, picnic areas, and rest rooms that are desired by newcomers. Lawsuits have led to exclusionary plans in some areas of Big Wild.

The bold vision for creating greenbelts that limit the extent of urbanization and shape the region must be implemented in increments people can experience and make meaningful.

The Los Angeles greenbelt

New top predator

In recent years, Edmiston has more consciously developed new constituencies for Big Wild among poor, central-city residents and new immigrants as some of the traditional constituents have become less supportive of greenway purchases. The strategies to do this include cooperative wilderness-education programs with public schools, overnight facilities for central-city families, urban wilderness parks in the poorest neighborhoods, and gateway parks with facilities for wildlife viewing. As a result, the essential support for the greenway has shifted from suburban neighborhoods to central-city districts. Surprisingly, the poorest ethnic neighborhoods have most consistently supported bond measures for Big Wild.

The effort to create the greenbelt around Los Angeles is ongoing. This effort has produced opportunities to have wilderness experiences every day. In turn, a large grassroots constituency has arisen to preserve enough habitat for the mountain lion and the entire chaparral ecosystem. Edmiston estimates that several more major bond issues will be needed to acquire the remaining critical pieces of the greenbelt.

Many lessons can be learned from the process of creating Big Wild. There has to be a bold vision for creating greenbelts that limit the extent of urbanization and give shape to the region. These visions must be more compelling than present city spread. And there must be an agency with region-wide authority and an ability to maintain cross-jurisdictional cooperation.

A well-informed public and an inclusive participatory process are essential for the implementation of any bold public action in the American landscape. Because the region is largely an abstraction to most people, each neighborhood parcel must be related to the overall plan. Continuing education must tie daily life to regional resilience.

In areas of extremely high real estate prices, it is possible to purchase greenbelt lands if multiple human needs are incorporated with the environmental actions. Of course, if the greenbelt had been implemented as part of the city plan proposed by the Olmsted firm nearly a century ago, it would have cost only a fraction of today's purchases. The total cost the firm projected is sometimes today spent on the purchase of a single parcel of land.[50]

Residents need high-quality ecological science that is synthesized from many fields and presented in a form that is spatially comprehensible for making decisions. The information, even about the most complex science, needs to be communicated so that ecological concepts relate to the everyday life patterns of the community. Only good, clear information that is relevant to the locality leads to informed judgments.

There is a potential to build a diverse and powerful constituency for limited extent via the broad desire of the American public to experience nature and wildlife. This constituency will, however, be constantly shifting as social conflicts are played out in the detail design of the greenbelt.

The Essential Scales for Governing Ecological Democracy

Although the focus throughout this book is on creating the urban form, governance cannot be avoided. Conclusions about good governance for ecological democracy become transparent here. Limited extent leads directly to questions about the appropriate scale of government. Limited extent cannot be achieved without changes in governance. It is clear that limited extent can be effectively implemented only with strong regional authority. This is the indication from Honolulu, the Pacific Northwest, and Los Angeles, where urban containment is working, and from other areas where there is no containment.[51] "Regional government" is seldom truly a regional government at present. It is either a consolidated government, like Honolulu, or a delegated authority from local governments that realize the need for cooperative regionwide decision making. De jure regional government is essential for providing the ecological framework for land use, to direct growth and connect habitat, to coordinate transportation and tax, and to distribute funds in such ways that centeredness, connectedness, and fairness are guaranteed and that particularness, diversity, and density, as well as limited extent, are cultivated.[52]

Simultaneously essential is legitimate neighborhood government. Face-to-face democracy provides direct access from the governed to the government and vice versa. It elevates our individual self-interests to a collective responsibility. Alexis de Tocqueville observed this happening in the New England town meeting.[53] Although some Americans "doubt that we have enough in common to be able mutually to discuss our central aspirations and fears,"[54] an ecological democracy depends on such sharing, mutual caring, and problem solving. Only the neighborhood provides the setting for such deliberation. Our present selfish political actions are motivated less by vested self-interest and more by government that is too far removed, professionalized local government, lack of control, and loss of general knowledge to think ecologically.[55] When city governments treat residents as children, we act as children. Neighborhood government alone offers the mechanism to overcome these problems. In the last thirty years, hundreds of cities have offered token authority to neighborhoods, but like "regional government," true authority at the neighborhood level has not been attained. City governments should be decentralized to neighborhood units. Authority over the content of daily life should be transferred from city government to these neighborhood governments. This is not a matter of simplistic local control but rather a reorganization of authority whereby the neighborhood assumes real power that is checked and balanced by the real power of regional government. City and county governments should be retired as neighborhoods and regions assume authority.

Although there will certainly be awkward transitions, this is not a radical idea. The roots are embedded in the tenth amendment of the U.S. Constitution, which divides powers between federal and state governments. The tension between the two—long ago expressed by Alexander Hamilton, an advocate for central authority, and John Calhoun, who wanted local authority—has served us well. Grassroots authority and ecologically based regional government provide parallel tension. This combination tempers the impulses of direct participation and regionally grounded science. These are the governmental bases for ecological democracy.

A Mollusk, a Crustacean, a Flat Worm, and Tocqueville

Limiting the extent of urbanization supports resilience in three ways that most impact city design. Limited extent guarantees that the total population and the area it requires for habitation does not exceed the capacity of the region to supply its needs. The metaphor of the Lake Michigan wood snail is most striking. The extent of habitat that the population occupies must be self-limiting, or land for other functions like food production, clean air and water, and wildlife will be overrun to the ruination of the region's resilience.

Limited extent can maintain city size at the optimum for human purposes, less than 250,000 total population, with open space of one quarter to ten miles, separating it from smaller towns, and green corridors of between a hundred and fifteen hundred feet separating neighborhoods within each city. Consciously limiting the size of the city thusly may be compared to the hermit crab that chooses a small shell because it well knows the needs of its own body.[56] We likewise limit the extent of our habitation because a city of less than 250,000 people best fits the needs of our human endeavors.

Limited extent provides the basis for distributing urbanized communities throughout the region. The planarium, a flat worm that can divide itself and regenerate new vital organs, never spreads into a bloated suburban planarium but limits its girth, producing small versions of itself with enough mass to be self-supporting. Big cities should do likewise, distributing population throughout small cities and towns in the region and decentralizing government into jurisdictions that allow deliberated democracy of the sort that Tocqueville observed centuries ago. At the same time, the regional counterpart that is grounded in an ecological setting needs authority to direct growth and limit extent.

Adaptability

Adaptability is the capacity of an ecosystem to adjust for changing conditions with a minimum of unhealthy stress or expenditure of essential resources. In natural systems, the persistence needed to remain healthy and evolve derives from adaptability by "maintaining flexibility above all else."[1] Adaptable cities may be achieved through human choices—by varying the uses of the environment, changing the form of natural systems, and altering the design of human-made systems. The focus here is city form and the elements of persistence.

In city design, flexibility is achieved by two primary means—an overall structure that accommodates change while maintaining its fundamental form and a detailed spatial configuration that is malleable enough to fit many functions over time.

Adaptable cities are designed so that many environments serve more than one purpose, connect things not originally thought to be connected, are suitable for new uses, are flexible but not entirely open-ended, and are suggested rather than dictatorial. Instead, cities presently are typically made up of highly specialized, single-purpose components (like highways, sewer plants, and research laboratories) with little flexibility and less adaptability. The trend toward ossified environments will have to be reversed to achieve resilience.[2]

What needs to be made more adaptable is city form, not the inhabitants. Humans are tremendously adaptable, but continuous forced adaptation creates undue stress and dysfunction. Humans "adapt at a price" that is evidenced by mental and emotional maladjustments, feelings of alienation, and physical illness.[3] Similarly, human conquest has stressed the natural environment beyond its capacity to rebound. The adaptable city responds to changing social needs without irreparable harm to human activity and ecological systems. An ecological democracy will require stressful changes in human values and lifestyles, such as reversing unhealthy status seeking and embracing density and smallness. City makers need to be selective about the

Tent camp after earthquake

stress that is generated, prioritize the critical actions that are necessary for resilient city form, and concomitantly reduce stress in other areas. Care must be taken not to force human adaptation so frequently and to such an extent that the associated stress—immediate, cumulative, or long term—undermines human well-being and leads to dysfunction. Likewise, care must be exercised not to unduly stress the natural ecosystem on which the city is dependent. Adaptable city form balances stress and necessary change.

Flexible City Form from Natural Process

Adaptability is provided, foremost, through particularness and limited extent, previously discussed. Where natural process directs city form, riparian corridors, steep slopes, aquifer recharge areas, forests, and wetlands reduce flood and landslide damage, provide clean drinking water and air, and remove toxic storm-water runoff, respectively, among other functions.[4] Additionally, these lands when left unbuilt accommodate multiple social demands that emerge over time. Observe how flexible open space is during a catastrophe. For example, after an earthquake, parks are transformed overnight into tent camps to provide temporary housing. Leftover urban open space, abandoned railroads, highway fragments, and vacant lots provide opportunities for adaptability.[5] The nature of urban open space allows more flexible use than the built environment. But resilient city design requires both adaptable landscapes and adaptable buildings. The peppered moth, adapting its color for camouflage in changing habitats, is figuratively and literally akin to urban parks or the warehouses that have been adapted to new uses in downtown Durham, North Carolina. Usually, a natural process creates the overall structure that accommodates change while maintaining fundamental city form, and the built landscape and architecture provide malleable detailed settings.

Durham, North Carolina

Landscapes of Adaptability

Some landscapes inherently are more adaptable than others. City landscapes that are large, open, and flat generally accommodate more uses than small, enclosed, and steeply sloped spaces. A large open space surrounded by an intricate permeable edge provides greater flexibility than one with a hard edge. When a large open space is subdivided, two spaces of different sizes afford more flexibility than two equally sized. An open space that is paired with its complementary and opposite space (for example, a large, flat space with smaller steeply sloped areas) is more adaptable than either alone.[6] A nodal landscape is more flexible than a linear one.

Among natural elements, grass, water, and sand are adaptive surfaces, but for different reasons. Grass allows a wide variety of activities; water and sand invite engagement and modification. Landscapes changed by temporal, seasonal, and climatic variations are more adaptable than ones that are unaffected by those forces. For example, deciduous trees typically create more adaptive landscapes than evergreens.

General, multipurpose landscapes are more flexible than specialized, single-purpose ones. Michael Hough concludes that single-purpose landscape solutions to problems tend to create additional problems.[7] Urban designer Robert Harris, one of the leading architects in revitalizing downtown Los Angeles, suggests that city makers follow this dictum: "We will abide no single-purpose plans." This applies to major public works like water and sewer infrastructure, open-space networks, and neighborhood parks.

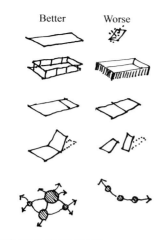

Better   Worse

Landscapes of adaptability

Because it is above ground, Kyoto's water-distribution system has always served many additional functions, such as cherry-blossom viewing, nature play, and local awareness of hydrological cycles.

Multipurpose action in the design of a major network—the drinking-water transportation system—makes Kyoto the finest city landscape I know. Instead of burying the infrastructure in pipes, Kyoto's water courses have historically been left open—moving water efficiently and providing identifiable boundaries between neighborhoods, places to play in nature, visual and sound delight, and a sense of connectedness throughout the city. The Philosopher's Walk, the most famous part of the system, transports water, provides a place for daily walks, and welcomes spring with cherry blossoms. But lesser known parts are equally multipurpose. I remember sketching in the far north of the city when a teenager stopped to watch me. After a few minutes of quiet, he said that the little canal I was painting had the purest water in all of Kyoto. He told me it was taken from his neighborhood in a two-meter channel to Shimagamo Shrine, four miles away, to be used in purification rituals. Along the route, it provides daily joy to neighbors. I was surprised that a teenager would be interested in the water system. Certainly, he would have been less aware if the channel had been culverted.

Do you know where your drinking water comes from? Do you know what direction it flows in your neighborhood or where the main channel of water is? Neither do I. It makes you wonder why engineers insist on putting water in pipes, diminishing the joy of water running free, disconnecting us from topography, and encouraging ignorance of place. Rigid, single-purpose infrastructure is one opportunity lost.

After many years of studying urban landscapes, Michael Laurie realized that multiple use is a matter of economy, providing value for money expended. At the small scale, these ideas might be translated into several design mandates. For example, landscapes with loose parts, like moveable chairs or play equipment, are preferred over landscapes with fixed parts. Furnishings that are suggestive are better than ones that are either too literal or too abstract. A seat wall that challenges kids to climb up and over, for example, performs better than a bench itself. Open-ended and incomplete landscapes encourage more uses than complete ones.[8] In the great Japanese treatise on aesthetics, Kenko declares, "Leaving something incomplete makes it more interesting and gives one the feeling that there is room for growth."[9]

The Method Day Care Center near North Carolina State University was highly successful because it was located along the daily walk of the designer. This made it easy for him to collect found objects and remains from construction sites and drop them in a pile in one corner of the playground.

Children were thrilled when surprise treasures appeared from time to time. The loose parts encouraged constructive and creative play.[10] The incompleteness fostered imaginative rearrangements by the children themselves and a greater variety of activities than any comparable play area I have ever studied. Such landscapes that are easily personalized, readily symbolically owned, and close to home are likely to be more adaptable.

Taking these criteria as a whole, the most sensible solution for urban open space is to create less defined and more flexible settings that are suitable for any recreational or social purpose that comes along.[11] Such landscapes can respond to the emerging social values, pleasures, and tastes of a more pluralistic society. Adaptable parks require a minimalist approach, resulting in a large, undifferentiated space that is surrounded by a rich edge of various surfaces, sun and shade, activities, and symbols—like Central Park in Davis, California (see the chapter on Centeredness). Laurie says that the edges of parks, like mantelpieces, support "an ever-changing set of objects, invitations, and memorabilia" and can be swept clear for special occasions or the inclusion of additional treasures.[12]

Emptiness

The undifferentiated landscape has double meaning in Japanese aesthetic thought that is pertinent to this discussion. The most sacred of ancient Shinto sites were often a clearing in the woods, a rock formation surrounded by a dense forest, or a climax tree that had outlived its surroundings and created its own overly shaded meadow. These landscapes were sensed as sacred, and no demarcation was necessary—no building, no *torii,* no *goheii,* no walls. Nothing marked them. The sites were left open. To the unfaithful, they were indistinguishable from the surrounding landscape. And the woods, many preserved as shrine forests today, served and serve many different functions in everyday life. They were and are managed to provide food and fiber, wildlife habitat, recreation, and worship. Unlike gods who dwell in abstracted, faraway places, Shinto gods, or Kami, inhabit these landscapes. A worshiper approaches the opening to communicate directly with the Kami. At ceremonial times, the site might be off limits to all except the high priestess.

Yoshida Kenko, the fourteenth-century Buddhist priest, had family ties to the Japanese court and hereditary Shinto priests. He described the essence

Method Day-Care Center

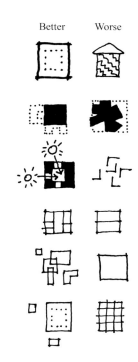

Flexible building form

of these seemingly vacant, unoccupied, open spaces in a classic line: "Emptiness accommodates everything."[13] From restricted high ritual to daily foraging and refuge for foxes, owls, tree spirits, and other apparitions, these undemarcated open spaces provide the utmost in adaptability and more. The more was detailed by Yamaguchi Sodo in a description of his rather empty natural abode in spring when he said, "True, there is nothing in it—there is everything!"[14] The emptiness of natural open space allows extraordinary adaptability and provides a repository of ritual and symbols— everything fundamental to a meaningful life. In the latter, emptiness fulfills our lives. This is the essence of open space. It requires a restraint that few designers attain. There is all too frequently the tendency to fill open space with stuff. This must be resisted not just for adaptability but for meaning as well. Keep open space open. Keep emptiness empty. Fill it only with meaning.

Landscape and Building

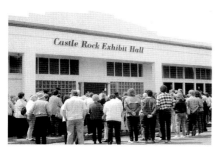

Ideas abound about how to make adaptable buildings. Invest more in the structure than in the finish of the building. Whether it is a repetitive modular structure with columns, a warehouse with alcoves, or a hand-sized building block, invest in the structure. Generally, start square or conventional, and let the building become unique over time, rather than vice versa. Generally, don't fall for the seeming adaptability of the office landscape or partition walls. Do provide thick outer walls and natural light to each room. Create a combination of small rooms, a few large rooms, and multiple rooms that are partially defined. Provide structure to grow upward by adding additional floors over time. Create fractal buildings that change as experienced from different distances and over time.

A warehouselike space exudes flexibility. Enrich the edges with columns or alcoves or a surrounding gallery. Supplement with attics, barns, garages, and other outbuildings.[15] The Castle Rock Exhibit Hall is one such building. Basically a large warehouse with columns, small rooms, and outbuildings, it had served diverse uses from feed store to auto repair shop. The people of Castle Rock, Washington, called the abandoned building a slum and hoped to raze it. Looking inside, the designers realized that the primary construction was still in excellent condition. This explained its ability to serve different functions over the years. After sensitive discussions led the community to realize that the building had at least one more life, plans were

Transforming the Keele building

drawn to accommodate the Exhibit Hall. Because of wise investment generations earlier, the building was readily converted to new purposes by community volunteers and only $11,000 in cash. Today it serves as a community center and museum, a repository of the suffering and heroism following the 1980 eruption of Mount Saint Helens.

Although perceived as a slum, the structure was sound and had accommodated many functions over the years. Its recent transformation to a civic exhibit hall cost only $11,000 and donated time.

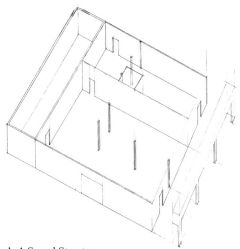

1. A Sound Structure

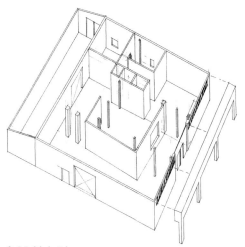

2. Multiple Lives

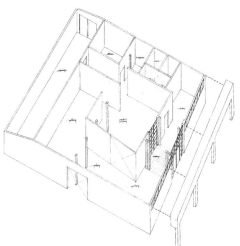

3. Exhibit Hall Plan

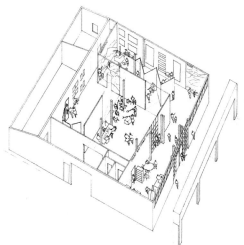

4. Reinhabited Place

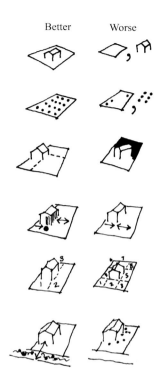

Building and landscape as one

That is a good start, but how does one make both the building and its landscape adaptable? Consider the open space and building as one. Organize a structure for the entirety. Again, invest in this overall structure rather than pretty stuff. A series of thoughtfully placed indoor-outdoor rooms is much more important than a lot of flowering shrubs filling the leftover spaces after a building has been plopped down on the site. Avoid odd-shaped, dark, and inaccessible spaces. The transition from inside to out should be through a thick ecotone where uses can be contested. Be sure the outdoor spaces are in scale with the likely functions; settings that are too big or too little are unusable. One sizeable indoor-outdoor space is more adaptable than many tiny ones. In most cases, microclimate and relationship to street are nearly deterministic in the use of outdoor space. An outdoor space that is too sunny or not sunny enough will almost never be used. A space too close or far away can preclude private or public interactions. On a small lot with limited outdoor space, arrange an outdoor service area to allow use of sidewalk and street as a spillover workshop.

There are a number of especially adaptable building and landscape arrangements: the Chinese courtyard, the street-to-alley shop house, the cloister garden, the one-sided zero lot line, the raked sand garden, and barnyard sheds. The Chinese courtyard compound provides living space for extended families in a U-shape around a large, multipurpose court extending to and capturing the street. The street-to-alley shop house typically is a long, narrow building, often with the roof and second-floor building extending over a multipurpose open space at the main street and a small garden at the back fronting on an alley or canal providing both land and water transport. Both the courtyard compound and the shop house create a larger open space of more flexible use by incorporating the street into the private domain.

The cloister garden provides a single, gracious, more private open space that is centrally located and accessible from all sides. Equal access invites different and multiple uses from the four directions; flexibility is increased because microclimate comfort can be attained by finding the appropriate side of the cloister for the time of day. This cloister concept is not restricted to formal religious or domestic architecture. The *zócalo* (town square) combines both in a civic place. A recent adaptation of this form at M Street Co-Housing in Davis, California, has created a multipurpose cloister garden in the interior of the residential block by removing fences that once marked private property lines. A larger more adaptable space results.

Building to the property line on one side eliminates the setback on that side—thus the one-sided zero-lot-line structure. The adjacent lot continues the patter. This aggregates otherwise small, unusable side-yard setbacks into a single, larger, more flexible open space. The raked-sand Japanese garden often employs a modified zero lot line. The building is constructed to one property line. A wall defines the garden on the opposite side. This creates a generous open space directly accessible from the building, as the Hojo Garden at Daisen-in or Ryoan-ji. The restricted use of these gardens today obscures their traditional multiple purposes from meditation to large ritual gatherings—all accommodated by the simple raked-sand surface in a sizeable space.

Barnyard buildings—for animals, for feed or equipment storage, for processing crops and firewood, for junk storage, and for workshops—typically cluster around a central open space and a partially enclosed swept yard. Separated by ten to a hundred feet, open sheds on most buildings create indoor-outdoor multipurpose workspaces—classic thick ecotones. The central yard, by virtue of its size, provides the most versatile space—for keeping newborn calves; repairing tractors; playing hide and seek, kick the can, and baseball; or making junk sculptures. This space between the buildings provides flexibility.[16]

These arrangements of buildings and landscape can easily be adapted to inspire multipurpose settings today. Each has a structure that organizes the building and landscape together. There is an investment in major open space with little wasted leftovers. The outdoor space is appropriately scaled and partially enclosed, allowing activity to extend conveniently from building to landscape through layers of climate control.

Priority Framework and Piecemeal Intricacy

At first glance, it seems that adaptability is derived from incrementalism, but in all the examples cited, there is both intricacy and a strong framework. Framework is fundamental to adaptability. Landscape architect Peter Walker refers to this as the structural base that is necessary before variation can occur. Framework is his internal order, objective visibility, and conceptual strength. These essential principles apply equally to designing gardens and to forming resilient cities.[17] Each site needs this order, but not nearly as much as the neighborhood and city need it. In fact, the structure of the site, if overemphasized, can call so much attention to an individual building that the overall community structure is subverted.

Classic adaptable arrangements

Unchanged structure

Priority framework

The framework changes little, if at all, but it holds together the change. Peppered moths may take on dramatically different colors in the dark and light settings of the polluted and healthy forests, but the overall form of the insect is not changed. Inspection of its bodies and wings immediately reveals that they are one species. The color modification, visually stunning, is superficial. The underlying structure is unchanged. A down-home version of this proclaims, "Blessed are the flexible, for they shall never be bent out of shape."[18] The priority framework has staying power. In the Castle Rock Exhibit Hall, which has undergone dramatic metamorphoses over the years, the well placed and unchanging columns and primary walls facilitate adaptability. This unchanging structure allows other changes to occur readily. The intelligent, unchanging enables change.

This framework is like a coat hanger that holds many varied items over time and, if well constructed, can support dozens of seemingly unrelated items at any one time. It accommodates changing needs but remains static. Habraken's architectural structures function this way as do clearly stated first principles for community action.

The framework is the skeletal system that gives overall form to the city.[19] The endoskeleton is an appropriate analogy. The endoskeleton allows growth, movement, and flexibility. And enclosed within the endoskeleton is marrow, essential to the production of blood cells. In this way, the framework is more than mere structure; it supports the vital essence of the city.

Establishing a well-recognized priority framework is essential to resilient cities. There are always many things to do, and they do not provide a clear sense of which are most important. The framework is a direct statement about what actions are most important for the general well-being of the city. Another difficulty is the crippling fear of solving a symptom and not a root problem—or worse, solving the wrong problems. Even when the relative importance of various actions is clear, attacking the most important problems may be politically infeasible. In those cases, unimportant matters may be legislated while difficult core issues are neglected. For example, air-quality regulations have forced dozens of minor actions, such as paving a few unpaved roadways because their dust pollutes the air but not addressing the most serious culprits in California air-quality problems, single-occupant automobiles. A priority framework helps ecologically thinking citizens focus on root causes.

Resilient Form

Jerry Brown concluded that air quality was simultaneously linked to the automobile, downtown revitalization, economic development, and the lack of housing near public transit in older California downtowns. When he was elected mayor of Oakland in 1998, he created a clear framework to attack core problems. He proposed to build housing for ten thousand new residents in downtown Oakland. This proposal, the 10K Initiative, creates a simple, imageable plan to attack multiple issues. Brown's comprehensive study found that eleven thousand new people could readily be housed without changing downtown height limits. Proposals to speed the approval process, improve the bus system, relax parking requirements, and invest in downtown open space were advanced, each to serve the primary housing objective.

To date, 2,465 housing units have been built or approved, and city officials expect that thirteen hundred planned units will be approved in the next year. This total would house six thousand people, the first such dramatic improvement in downtown stewardship in over fifty years. This would never have occurred if Brown had not seen the complex interconnections between housing, transit, the quality of downtown, and air pollution and developed a singular framework to which multiple objectives could be attached.[20]

What are the lessons here? With the best information at hand, determine the actions that are most essential—ones that would provide effective resilience on a number of fronts. Then establish a citywide priority framework that effects those actions. A framework that legislates a few most critical mandates is far more effective than one that legislates many secondary forces. Mandate as few actions as necessary, and mandate no more.

Because large natural systems, like river corridors and mountain ranges, provide the single most effective skeleton for urban adaptability, determining which should form the urban framework must be a first order of business. Cities that do this during initial development benefit most because that is when the cost to preserve necessary lands is cheapest. The lasting resilience saves millions of dollars in the long run. The early bird gets the worm, and the early bird with a visionary natural framework gets the most worms. Chicago, for example, continues to benefit from the open-space framework that was implemented in large part as a result of early plans. Chicago was still in its adolescence when Daniel Burnham reimagined its landscape—first in bold plans for the World's Columbian Exposition of 1893 and then in his Chicago plan of 1909. These, in concert with Dwight

Perkin's 1904 metropolitan parks plan, created not just a linear park along Lake Michigan but a water-based framework that exceeded utopian fiction. These plans shaped Chicago's city form. They are derived largely from the patterns of river and lakefront opportunities. Adding to its resilience over the last century, they make Chicago a splendid city today.[21]

Caspar, California, has recently taken similar actions. An old, north-coast logging town, Caspar was suddenly threatened when large agricultural holdings within the town went on the market. Citizens without a formal government joined together to determine a response to the real estate crisis. Through a year-long democratic process of community building, education, and prioritization, the Casparados, as they call themselves, created an inviolable open-space framework for their town. The skeletal plan clearly identified the structure that must be maintained. Their framework called for the public purchase of ecologically fragile lands surrounding Caspar Creek and the headlands above the ocean as first actions. The second part of the framework was the development of cattle lands in a way that aggregated development at the town center, maintained three important view sheds over farmland, and clustered development in villages at the edge of second-growth forests. The priority framework is composed of simple, imageable actions and nothing more: (1) create a backbone along the creek, terminating in the most sacred headlands and extending in armlike trails north and south; (2) make the center the heart of the community; and (3) save views by clustering new villages like old ones. The inviolable parts (the Caspar Creek corridor and headlands) provide access to nature, protect endangered salmon runs, and maintain locally endemic plant communities. The north-south trails along the pacific Coast extend links of a larger coastal-access system. Almost as important to residents was the enhancement of the town center as the heart of Caspar. Rather than deciding on a rigid, specific plan for the center, the Casparados were open to various ideas as long as they contributed to the center. They simply wanted more of a center. Their center expands from an existing cluster of stores, a church, and an abandoned school and is flexible enough to grow in several directions. As residents discovered during workshops and walking tours, the view sheds likewise can be pushed north and south, adjusting slightly to accommodate various locations that developers might propose for new neighborhoods. However, once located, local people wanted the new villages to be designed with a scale and setbacks that were similar to present development.

Resilient Form

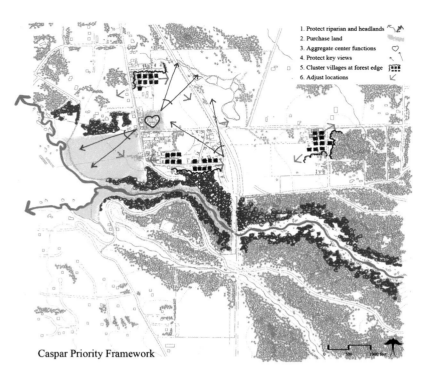

1. Protect riparian and headlands
2. Purchase land
3. Aggregate center functions
4. Protect key views
5. Cluster villages at forest edge
6. Adjust locations

Caspar Priority Framework

With simple inviolable priority actions and flexibility about their land-use decisions, Casparados have achieved all of their primary objectives in short order.

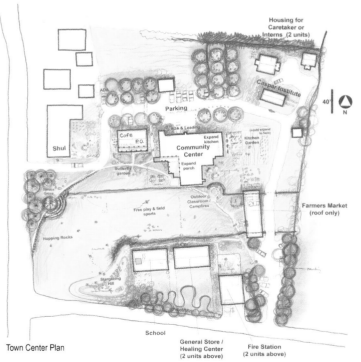

Town Center Plan

The Caspar town center also enjoys a simple fixed framework. A center was created by clustering buildings (uses to be determined) around a sunny car-free open space, keeping views and drainage east and west natural. Other decisions are negotiable.

Consensus democracy

The unanimous priority for Caspar Creek and the headlands allowed townspeople to acquire those most critical landscapes within two years. Then they purchased the old school building for a community center. Several development proposals are being considered. Because the framework is clear, there is great room for pliability regarding these individual projects. The community can readily horse trade with developers to enhance the town center and preserve strategic open space while achieving a wide variety of unexpected community benefits. They are negotiating a deal with one property owner to increase the number of housing units in his proposed village and to allow him to build additional commercial space. In return, he must locate new housing at the forest edge in a pattern like other houses in town, thereby protecting one of the most important views in perpetuity. The developer must donate land for the town green. His new commercial buildings will define one edge. This would complete a town square that clusters important community facilities in one place.

Following the dictum to control only what is most important, Caspar welcomes housing villages along various forest edges as long as views are protected and density and affordability are increased.

Resilient Form

Instead of fighting developers over every detail, the priority framework lets everyone know what the overall intention is. As long as the three main goals—backbone, heart, and views—are met, there is open-mindedness for on-site adjustments. This gives developers the flexibility to make projects feasible and enables the town to work for improvements like a school and community center, additional stores, a centrally located post office, a town square, and an agricultural institute. In Caspar's case, the natural systems—river, bluffs, and forest edges, along with a community center and view-sheds—create both a rigid skeleton and flexible arrangement of other lands. Only the most essential decisions were made.

Whereas Caspar's structure came from the natural landscape features, other frameworks derive from human modified systems (like fresh-water canals, forest preserves, and agricultural lands) or from repeated relationships (like cloister gardens, courtyard buildings, and shop houses). A freeway system, by the way, can never work as an effective framework for city form in an ecological democracy. In West Sacramento, California, existing irrigation channels form a logical framework. Because the irrigation system had a hierarchy of canal size based on water delivery, it readily divided the city form into flexible units for neighborhoods, recreation areas, school, other public facilities, and an agriculture greenbelt.

In Yountville, California, the priority framework repeats in fractals from regional landscape structure to rows of Chinese pistache trees. Extents of shady, enclosed spaces periodically opening to reveal dramatic views provide the organizing principle. Repeated at each scale, this makes Yountville's framework particularly memorable. The agricultural greenbelt encloses the town and provides views to surrounding mountains and outcrops. The vegetated walking routes restrict views, except at three major commercial and civic destinations that host community life. At these points, cooling shade opens suddenly to allow views to mountains east and west. At the Y intersection of the two major north-south streets, the center of town is enclosed with major buildings, special sacred places, trees, and focused views to spectacular hilltops. Within the town square, the same pattern is repeated. At this scale, the shady enclosure is formed by buildings at intimate distance; the views are confined to glimpses of the hills. Along the main streets, the framework of long, green, shady enclosures opening to a focused view of hills in the distance is repeated at the walking scale. The double rows of trees enclose the walker in dark green tunnels and protect her from the hot summer sun,

Yountville's framework is shaped by its topography and vegetation—from regional to urban-design scales—experienced as panoramic views of vineyards, enclosed allees, and glimpses to mountains at key points.

Landscape structure

Destination and host

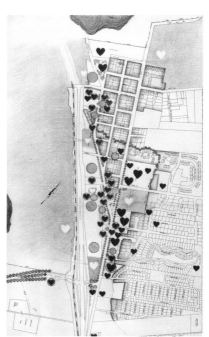

Special places

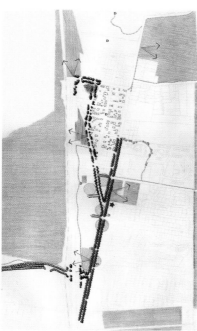

Key actions

Resilient Form

focusing the eye on the nearby, except at intersections and nodes where the eye sweeps over vineyard fragments to the hills east and west. In fall, when the trees turn stunningly red, the pistachios become the major visual attraction. The repeated framework is strong enough that the details of many ill-conceived decisions about building style, materials, subdivision layout, mass, and scale remain unified. The powerful visual framework is able to provide considerable flexibility and absorb architectural error in piecemeal building decisions.

In some cases, the priority framework is oriented toward policy rather than physical form. Seeking to achieve multiple purposes around a few priority actions in Curitiba, Brazil, Jaime Lerner committed to creating the world's best public bus system. His framework for the city sustains many other actions, including land-use planning and recycling. Curitiba is one of the few places where a transportation system humanely shapes the skeletal system of the city.

The danger of a priority framework is that if it is not well conceived and managed, it can calcify, producing large, rigid results. Any successful priority framework encourages multiple piecemeal intricacies—small actions of owners and volunteers who provide variety, local initiative, and innovations in sustainability. Intricacy increases opportunities for participation in decision making and expands ownership of those decisions. Whereas the framework evokes pride in a big vision, intricacy allows individual investments of finance and emotion, cultivating a stronger level of caring about place and community.

In the United States today, city design needs to provide both visionary frameworks and opportunities for small, flexible actions. Most cities lack and desperately need a carefully conceived overall framework that provides for long-term adaptability.

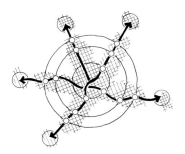

Curitiba, Brazil, bus framework

Continuous Experiment, Adaptive Management, and Windows of Opportunity

Adaptive cities can be changed when new knowledge allows better understanding of an aspect of resilience. Informed citizens, scientists, and city makers act today with the realization that we do not have sufficient knowledge of urban ecological workings. A line from a country song by Mickey Newbury describes our problem, "Time has a way of changing every day; truth has a way of changing all the time."[22] When maligned swamps became wetlands of international concern, we were confused, but city form changed. When housewives, a part of the shadow economy, joined the recognized workforce, we were confused, but city form changed. When ecological truths are debunked, we become befuddled. Centuries ago, the great Chinese philosopher Chuang Chou noted that "we may reckon that what man knows is less than what he doesn't know."[23] Recently, C. S. Holling referred to this as "the recognition of our ignorance."[24] I doubt that Holling knew Newbury or Chuang Chou's writings, but they share the same message. Some claim that the human capacity to comprehend and plan the resilient city has such limits that thinking too far ahead becomes a liability.[25] I disagree but am forewarned.

Much of what is known today about urban resilience was not known even a decade ago. For example, new scientific findings about the extent to which vegetation can mitigate the effects of urban heat sinks will significantly reconfigure city form. In Tokyo, this research has already changed city design. With urbanization, Tokyo's mean temperature has increased 5.2 degrees Fahrenheit five times faster than increases due to global warming. It has become an oven of asphalt, concrete, and black rooftops, with only 14 percent of the central city vegetated in cooling trees and grass. This dramatic rise in temperature has changed the local ecosystem, introducing new diseases and exotic plants, increasing deadly pollution, decreasing snowfall, and speeding the seasons. Cherry-blossom viewing, a seasonal celebration that is central to Japanese identity, frequently features only faded blooms. To mitigate the heat-sink effect, a new law requires that every new building on a plot over a quarter acre provide a roof garden of vegetation.[26]

The same emerging science is changing city form closer to home. In Chicago, where roofs and paved surfaces cover over half of the city, one strategy for reducing heat-island effects is to vegetate as much of those exposed surfaces as possible. If roof surfaces alone were greened, about 680 square kilometers, or 25 percent of the whole city, could be changed from a heat sink into a citywide cooling system.[27]

Applying emerging science about vegetation or hundreds of other discoveries through a public process is difficult because most of us are bogged down by information overload, lack a conceptual framework into which to place vital new findings, and view sustainable city forms with disfavor. Therefore, we need to structure attempts at sustainable design as experiments in which all of us are active participants: all of us are designers, citizen scientists, and ecologists.[28] This is fundamental for an ecological democracy to develop.

Adaptive management is a favored approach to ecological systems and potentially can be equally powerful when applied to cities. Simply put, adaptive management expects the unexpected because urban ecosystems change unpredictably and surprises are inevitable; city makers, by necessity, are continually adaptive.[29] Applying Holling's postulates to city design, we would expect that an urban crisis—a water, housing, or energy shortage or outdated recreation facilities or street-tree plans—occurs when a maturing city form becomes rigid, brittle, and inflexible. After a long period of unheeded warnings that the city needs to be restructured, a crisis hits dramatically and "unexpectedly," and leaders, citizens, designers, and scientists come together in an atypical period of mutual collaboration. Information is gathered and shared, and options are articulated and evaluated to solve the crisis.[30] People pay urgent attention to the problem for a short time and might bring about a significant adaptation in which the city or part of it is dramatically reconfigured.[31] Serious, often catastrophic matters can be crises that become windows of opportunity for adapting the city and making it significantly more resilient. Examples abound—cities that move out of flood plains after a disastrous flood,[32] that increase energy-conserving design after an economy-threatening shortage,[33] or that reengineer buildings after an earthquake.[34] In one dramatic example, the Loma Prieta earthquake in San Francisco weakened the Embarcadero Freeway, which had divided the city from its waterfront for nearly half a century. After much debate, the highway was permanently removed. Its destruction was hailed as the greatest urban-design improvement in recent San Francisco history. Sunlight now reaches pedestrians along its route. Such action would have been unthinkable before the crisis of the earthquake. City makers must be poised

Disaster as opportunity

to seize such windows of opportunity to make the urban habitat more resilient. To do so, the city landscape must be cultivated for adaptation beforehand, and designers must know what priority frameworks need to guide rebuilding.

In lieu of unpredictable crises, local participatory partnerships engage in ongoing adaptive management. One model that could be effective with modest adjustments is the U.S. Agricultural Extension Service, through which scientists work directly with farmers to apply scientific findings to crop production, soil erosion, and wildlife habitat management. Trial and error encourages innovations to be adopted at the grassroots.[35] An urban extension service would help citizens rehabilitate neighborhoods, expand urban agriculture, and reconstruct lost natural systems, among other things.

In recent years, hydrogeologist Matt Kondolf has done basic research on fluvial geomorphology and worked with citizen groups to improve salmon habitat in local streams. The latter depends on the former just as the Extension Service suggests. In one case, he and Lisa Kimbal found that rip-rap installed seventy years ago to stabilize a creek bank in John Muir Park was now a barrier to habitat improvement. At the time it was installed, the rip-rap was considered a scientifically justified engineering solution. Truth changes every day. This small case makes me wonder what actions will be needed seventy years from now to repair projects that I have carefully conceived.

Another worthy model is the Montana Study and Heritage Project, which was formed in 1945 to foster local study groups to research local culture and history. The group has worked continuously to study community problems and devise local solutions. It relies on citizen volunteers to research critical issues and develop alternatives, much like the League of Women Voters and like conflict resolution approaches do. The key is collaborative and joint fact finding. These approaches begin with the assumption that many serious disputes are caused by a lack of knowledge about the problem or disagreement about the facts. The solution is to have all the disagreeing parties work face to face to discover and synthesize the best factual information possible.[36]

One final model of note is the Citizen Science Program developed through the Sapsucker Center at Cornell University. That program trains lay people to monitor bird populations by teaching volunteers basic scientific methods. Citizen science efforts have led to important discoveries and multiple adaptive actions.[37] These programs suggest a formula for collective experimentation. The key is cross-sectoral grassroots groups in which scientists, citizens, policy makers, designers, and others exchange roles. They engage in joint problem identification and fact finding, scientific inquiry, the application of the discoveries to reconfigure city form, and ongoing evaluation to make further adjustments. To achieve resilient cities, we all must be part of the experiment.

Choice

Unlike the peppered moth, whose color changes allow it to blend into various forests, the adaptations that we make in the urban landscape are a matter of choice. Through participatory problem solving (like that used at the Agricultural Extension Service and the Montana Study and Heritage Project), joint fact finders and citizen scientists provide the public with a new ability to systematize complex urban ecology, make sense of it, grasp the entirety of it, and create a framework into which new information can be inserted and tested.[38] Otherwise, we have no way to engage in the discussion as informed citizens and to make choices about the future of our habitation. A flexible city requires us to use natural processes as an overall structure for city development. Within that framework, individual landscapes can be shaped to serve multiple purposes and to be adaptable over time. Metaphors like the "urban mantelpiece" and "emptiness" provide design inspiration for this appropriate city design. Similarly, buildings and their landscapes can be formed so that they are able to adapt to varying reuses. In all these actions, a skeletal framework that is relatively unchanging facilitates the metamorphosis of smaller parts of the city.

Impelling Form: "Make a City to Touch the People's Hearts"

Two hours away by bus and several worlds removed from the beaches of Waikiki, Ima Kamalani lived on a small parcel of land in the Haleiwa district of Honolulu. To be called "Uncle" by people in Haleiwa is the highest honor, and Kamalani was Uncle Ima. He took care of people, he stewarded them and the land, and he was an urban farmer who knew water, soil, and weather intimately by name and hand. He demonstrated by his practice that the frog does not drink up the pond in which he lives. He had a royal wisdom seasoned by the pain and joy of life and by choices made. He saw and understood things that the rest of us did not. I could never figure out if he was ahead of his time, of his time, or behind the times. But I listened when he spoke.

His landscape is as enigmatic and powerful as Ima himself, a secret natural garden within the city with magic powers. It is a productive yet fragile water-covered land fed by underground springs, which some say is the source of the sacred Kawaipuolo spring with the purest water that never ceases. This small wetland is less than one hundred feet behind Kam Highway, the main street that runs through Haleiwa, but it is hidden, unobserved by native and visitor alike. We met Uncle Ima when we were doing a plan for his community. Although he seldom attended workshops, we consulted him throughout our design process because he was a primary keeper of native wisdom.

To reach Ima's landscape, we took the back road by the icehouse, turned left on the road whose name no haole can pronounce, turned right on the road with no name whatsoever, and asked Annie if Ima was at home. He sometimes appeared and invited us to sit. We would then settle by the marsh in one of the outdoor rooms he had created for farming or resting, watching the wetland's birds, fish, and prawns. Ima grew lotus root (*hasu*) here. Ima and his landscape informed our design and nourished our minds and souls. His unselfish dreams and radical yet rooted visions inspired the plan we did for his town.

Sitting under a tent of coconut palms at the edge of the marsh, Ima one day demonstrated the correct way to grate coconut and weave *lauhala* (leaves of the hala tree). Then he told a story that I think was about the dangers of materialism. Ima once had cows, but they kept wandering into the cane fields and were hard to catch, and Ima had to pay fines for the damage that his cows did. More cows led to more profits but also more fines and worry. When someone offered to buy the cows, Ima traded them for two cases of beer. The buyer and seller shared the beer, and when the beer was gone, Ima nodded toward the cows and said to the buyer, "Now you catch them."

Ima did not drive. He used to have a car, but neighborhood kids would steal it and drive it on the sugar-cane haul roads until it ran out of gas. They would come to him and complain, "Uncle Ima, car won't go," and he would fetch the car. Once the kid thieves returned with only the steering wheel. He walked out, repaired the car, brought it back to Haleiwa, and gave it to the thieves. After that, the kids took care of the car.

There are lessons in the lotus. A lotus blossom is a special gift. He took Marcia by the hand and waded with her into the water to show her the correct way to pick the bloom. There are lessons in how the lotus grows. When one leaf curls and dies, a fish hides under it, which means that its root will soon be ready to harvest.

Seemingly out of the blue, Uncle Ima asked what project I was working on. A new lotus sprout broke the surface seeking the sun. I explained that I was writing about designing cities that support ecological democracy. He smiled a knowing smile that suggested that he knew exactly what I was writing. Balls of rainwater played a game on a lotus leaf that was two feet in diameter. Uncle Ima studied one drop chase another powered by gentle waves and gentle wind. A shift in wind direction completed the chase, and the two water balls became one. His intent gaze shifted from lotus leaf to my eyes as he softly commanded, "Make a city to touch the people's hearts."

I asked, "What do you mean, Uncle Ima?" He responded with silence that filled the wetland. He never told me what he meant directly. He didn't make me a list of principles. He only talked more story. Uncle Ima died while I was working on this book.

I pondered Uncle Ima's softly spoken command to "make a city to touch the people's hearts." What did he mean? He certainly understood that his community of Haleiwa faced wrenching changes as it transformed from a sugar-plantation economy and mentality to something unknown. Although he managed his own life and land based on his extensive, intimate knowledge of wetland ecology, Uncle Ima was keenly aware that his community did not. He worried that most young people in Haleiwa did not know much about their place. I think that's why he instructed us so diligently about the hydrological principles that are fundamental to any future habitation in Haleiwa and why he fretted over national legislation that he feared would threaten wetlands. He was quietly insistent that we keep those issues in mind during the planning effort. At the same time, he added firsthand instructions on the proper way to farm the lotus to maintain the natural functions of the wetland. Through our planning process, he observed how complex the future of his town would be, and he knew that creating enabling and resilient form were essential to any healthy future. He did not use those words, but he knew that making the changes necessary would be painful. Uncle Ima was warning me that an ecological democracy would have to be designed to be so joyful, fulfilling, meaningful, and inspiring that it would be the most desirable of all alternatives. Rather than being debilitated by the crises facing our cities and by our present inability to work together to solve them, citizens and designers need to fill the landscape with vision and delight while resupplying urbanity with enabling and resilient form. In short, Uncle Ima was saying that the future need not be a bitter pill to swallow if it is designed to awaken our hearts.

This is the essence of impelling form, which, by virtue of its design, is mindfully irresistible. It introduces needed innovations in acceptable ways. It convinces. It persuades. Impelling form contrasts with legislation that compels or forces us to live a certain way. To a rabbit hunter, impelling form is the carrot; compelling form is the stick. Ultimately, we must want to choose cities where ecological democracy can flourish. The impelling city persuades us to choose a life of ecological democracy, not merely because it is necessary or morally superior but because it is filled with joy, because it meets our needs and adds meaning to our lives, and because it inspires us to pursue our most noble values. Impelling form facilitates our understanding of alternatives, invites our participation, allows us control, and engages our imaginations and personal actions. To impel, the city must be made intelligently and deliciously beautiful.

Impelling form depends on many of the principles previously discussed. Choice impels; adaptability underlies impelling form. Sacredness, particularness, contrary status seeking, and limited extent all impel, as do centeredness and fairness. But to make our cities intelligently and deliciously beautiful, to make them mindfully irresistible, requires more than just these. In the five chapters in this section on impelling form, I introduce five principles that most directly create cities that provide joy and touch our hearts: everyday future, naturalness, inhabiting science, reciprocal stewardship, and pacing.

Everyday Future

Cities that support ecological democracy will be radically different from present ones, but the transition must accommodate everyday patterns of life. Alternatives that are shocking, that threaten security, or that upset basic needs will likely be rejected. Other than for provocation, there is no place for design that says, "Let them eat utopia." Nor is there a place for counterproductive or superficial changes, exterior decoration, or private jokes at public expense. Meaningful urban metamorphosis requires inspired everyday futures, which are defined as visionary ideas that are rooted in daily life and experience. Innovative transformations, even radical ones, that are recognizable and that accommodate and champion valued ways of living are more likely to be successfully implemented.[1] As action toward ecological democracy becomes more rapid and dramatic, city design needs to be more and more deeply grounded in everyday life. Familiarity supports metamorphosis to a different future.[2]

As a simple example, consider the restoration of Oakland's Courtland Creek. The Urban Creeks Council of California, a nonprofit organization that is committed to the natural restoration of city streams, commissioned Walter Hood to reclaim a badly abused section of the creek. Hood discovered that most neighbors feared the creek; they considered it a dump site. Indeed, the creek appeared to be a trash dump and not a stream. Most recreation occurred along streets and vacant rights-of-way that were adjacent to the creek. Rather than trying to force a purely ecological restoration plan, Hood meshed the daily-use patterns that were particular to these central-city residents with creek reclamation. He proposed that an active linear park should be created parallel to the creek. The budget had to be supplemented by city funds, most of which were spent on this park, with little money spent on Courtland Creek itself. Seeing no ecological benefit to the street park, some restoration purists objected, but the park plan was implemented along with minimal stream revegetation. Since its completion, residents most use the promenade formed by a double row of flowering fruit trees, a lawn adjacent to the linear walkway, and a garden of flowers and vegetables that they maintain. No significant increase in creek play has been observed, but the linear park generates so much activity that illegal dumping has been dramatically reduced. By championing everyday life, Hood's park protects the creek, accomplishing far more in ecological stream restoration than naturalistic improvements would have alone.

Everyday patterns suggested that an active linear park parallel to Courtland Creek was more likely to be valued by residents who feared the creek. The promenade is heavily used, and dumping in the creek has been reduced.

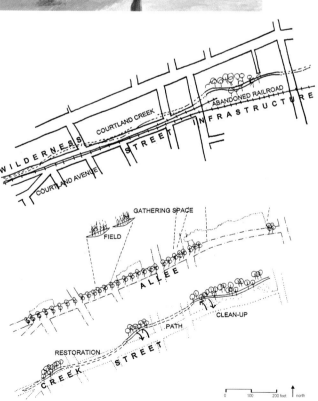

Impelling Form

Four design strategies are important for creating an inspired everyday future: design for what people do all day, integrate present experience with change, mark time, and inspire visionary futures by the everyday.

Designing for What People Do All Day

Designing any landscape requires knowing what people do there now and what they might do there in the future. Consider the activities that might occur along an urban stream like Courtland Creek, a larger one like Compton Creek (a major tributary of the Los Angeles River), or even the Los Angeles River itself. Where would you expect to see young children playing, swimming, wading, building dams, and catching salamanders; scientists sampling water quality; teens seeking privacy or sex; classes studying nature and watching birds; people hiking, biking, picnicking, fishing, reading, sunbathing, or practicing the saxophone; kids taking a shortcut and racing bikes, motorcycles, or stolen cars; people performing Christian baptisms, doing drug deals, engaging in prostitution, collecting native plant materials, and dumping industrial wastes, construction debris, a murder victim, or dead pit bulls? Knowing these patterns leads designers to fit the situation and to understand situations when no design is going to succeed. The designer learns about these patterns of activity through four strategies: reading the research on similar people and places, listening to people, observing carefully, and wearing the empathic shoes of others.[3]

An example is the work of Sydney Brower and others at the city of Baltimore's Department of Planning. Years ago, the planning staff was doing open-space improvements in the low-income Reservoir Hill area. Prior research suggested that central-city recreation occurred in developed playgrounds and parks. As a result, recreation improvements typically focused on parks. But the department's staff observed a distinctive pattern of everyday life in this neighborhood. Children played less in parks and playgrounds (10.5 percent) and more in streets, sidewalks, alleys, porches, and yards (89.5 percent). A quarter of teenage boys' recreation occurred in parks and playgrounds. Adult women recreated in parks and playgrounds less than 2 percent of the time. All groups recreated more around the home and nearby streets. Place-based research countered the prevailing literature. Consistent with local patterns, the planners proposed street-corner improvements, enlarging sidewalks to make places for sitting, congregating,

Everyday life

and playing street games, and for temporary vendors selling fish, fruit, vegetables, and ice cream. In some spots, they suggested mobile city services like bookmobiles, health screening, postal delivery, and telephones. The plans grew directly from the daily needs of the residents.[4] Observation of everyday urbanism is especially useful in the United States, where there are many variations from normative behavior of the dominant culture.[5]

Integrating Present Experience with Change

When new uses are anticipated and urban space is changed to accommodate those new uses, city makers often fail to integrate existing with future uses. There is a tendency to outlaw, segregate, or separate new uses; to divide existing space into distinct specialized territories to accommodate emerging activities; or to remove some facilities. Skateboarding, homeless camps, teenager hangouts, and dog walking are now commonplace urban-park uses that receive such outlaw treatment. It is wise to first try to integrate the emerging with present activities.[6]

Dana Park in Cambridge, Massachusetts, illustrates. Designed as a pleasure ground in the early era of park development, Dana Park originally provided only a place for strolling but had received additional uses during every new phase of park planning. Each new use was segregated by tall fences into separate areas for specialized activities.[7] By the 1970s, it was actually three separate parks—the outdated stroll garden that served no users well, a fenced and paved alleyway of play equipment, and an asphalt area with basketball hoops. Once an open space, it appeared chopped to pieces by a giant meat cleaver. Worse, it had become such a battleground between residents with different recreational needs that the police ordered its closure. The crisis that precipitated the closing was an escalating conflict between teens and parents with young children. These parents were newcomers to the neighborhood. There had long been conflict between teenagers and elderly citizens, but neither had power enough to force a successful resolution. The parents with young children felt threatened by the teenagers, many of whom were members of the Dana Park gang, which made the park its home and occupied the park nearly twenty-four hours a day. Parents who took their young children to the park for short visits had higher levels of income and education than the teens. Both the wealthier parents and the elderly wanted the teens out. In community meetings about park design, various outlaw

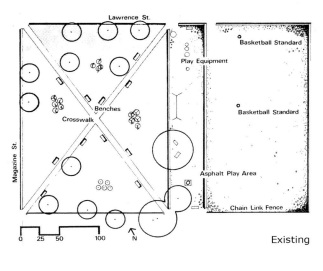

Existing

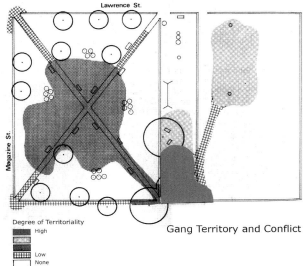

Gang Territory and Conflict

Degree of Territoriality

- High
- High
- Low
- None

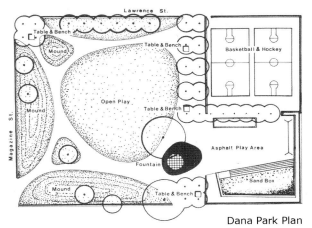

Dana Park Plan

The crosswalk design of Dana Park led to conflicts
with the local gang until the gang's territory was
studied and the park reshaped to meet gang
needs as well as those of the elderly and children.

and relocate schemes were put forward by adults. But the teens were adamant that they had no other place to go. The park fit their needs splendidly. They demanded a right to the park. The entirety of one meeting directed adult hostility toward the teens. Big Richie, the gang leader, remained silent. At the end of the meeting, he rose to speak, saying calmly and matter-of-factly, "If you don't include our needs, we will trash the place."

One member of the design team that had been doing behavior mapping at the park was a former professional basketball player who had grown up in the neighborhood. Because he was a homeboy and a hero to many teens, they slowly accepted him into their confidence. He listened intently. They admitted snatching purses and harassing young mothers. They even acknowledged sawing wood bench slats from underneath, hiding in the bushes, and waiting to see unsuspecting seniors crash through the last bits of wood to the ground. At the same time, the mapping uncovered distinct patterns of the gang's territory and revealed a relationship between the park layout and the conflict between the users. The conflicts were not random. They were concentrated in the field through which the stroll paths passed and in one end of the play-equipment alley. The teens conflicted with the elderly because the benches were located in the paths of field sports. The stroll garden layout with benches every twenty feet rendered any pickup games nearly impossible. The fenced play-equipment zone was the single best location for the teens to hang out because it allowed them a prospect, refuge, and ample space for working on cars and playing music in the spot that was most removed from surrounding residences. In that area, they conflicted with all other users, especially parents who brought their children to play on the play equipment. Through a series of community meetings, a plan evolved that eliminated the spatial basis of the social conflicts and integrated the new uses with existing ones. By moving sitting areas for the elderly to the side, relocating play equipment, and adding a multipurpose basketball and street-hockey court, designers resolved many of the conflicts without having to remove new or old uses. The teens remained the primary users. They dominated their turf, but seniors and young parents were accommodated with multiple sitting areas along the edges of a large open play space that was shared by all users. A variety of places for small children to play were integrated throughout the edges of the park. A recent renovation provides even more activities around the edges.

The conflicts between older and younger teens was another matter. The older teens wanted slightly younger ones around as an audience; in return, younger ones sought approval and social advancement. Paul Friedberg recognized this playground pattern in New York and often included two of the "best things" within easy view, separated by just enough distance to reduce physical bullying.[8] These cases suggest that although emerging uses may sometimes be incompatible with existing uses, we should try to integrate them—even conflicting ones—first.

Marking Time

The changes to our cities and lifestyles that are required to allow ecological democracy to flourish will often be threatening to the status quo. For most people, familiar landscapes, like neighborhoods and hometowns, that are often taken for granted become cherished, even beautiful, when threatened. A dramatically different future is easier to accept when the present everyday is acknowledged and marked in time. In this regard, city design shares much with the personal response to tragedies, whether family deaths or public assassinations, wars, terrorist bombings, floods, or famines. Only after these events are memorialized can we move forward. Although our lives will never be the same after such events, marking the event with a memorial frees us to embrace the future. The less traumatic changes needed in city design are similarly made easier by marking time. Five design strategies seem especially important—respecting context, remembering the past, making the future retro, overlaying history, and waiting over my dead body.

Sometimes all that is necessary to embrace a future that is vastly different than the present is to make that future fit the existing context. In neighborhood design, we have seen that higher density is much more acceptable to residents if it is housed in buildings that are in scale with present patterns. Residents will more readily accommodate three- or four-story buildings that are carefully crafted to respect an existing two-story neighborhood than they will accept eight- or ten-story projects.

In a case in Oley, Pennsylvania, Setha Low found that residents of the town, which had a long tradition of conservative German stone buildings, were willing to accept new purposes if the new construction maintained consistency of materials and details with the existing structures. Merely by

Marking historical details

The communal past

championing historical details, like window patterns and tiled roofs, a future of significant change could be accepted.

After the devastating earthquake in 2000, Taiwan towns faced uncertain futures. Many of them made memorials to the past before tackling the future. In one indigenous village, the earthquake destroyed communal washbasins that had been the center of community life. After much deliberation, residents decided that rebuilding the washbasins would be their first essential act, even though most households already had running water and many had washing machines. The washbasins symbolized not only the past but also a community solidarity that would be essential to face change and still preserve the town's culture. Remembering the communal past prepared residents for collective action. In fact, one restored washbasin became the primary meeting place, the setting for much deliberative democracy—first among women and then among members of the entire community as they mapped out plans for recovering from the tragedy.

In other cases, environmental changes may be accommodated only by reinventing the past or making a retro future. New Urbanist communities are sometimes criticized for calling up a romantic past with neocolonial buildings and dated architectural details, but living in higher-density mixed-use neighborhoods seems to be more acceptable when decorated in tradition. Eighty percent of people surveyed in a 1995 study favored the architectural styles of old-fashioned towns. Among people who disliked density, even more (nine out of ten) were attracted to New Urbanist neighborhoods by their old-timey Southern and New England styles. Those traditional towns were more popular than local regional styles. Similarly, those surveyed who otherwise disliked higher density were attracted by front porches and the trappings of the old-fashioned good life.[9] In spite of the fact that few people actually use porches as they do in Southern towns or lower-income communities, the criticism of New Urbanist architecture seems unwarranted. If meaningful change can be achieved by creating a retro future through harmless architectural details that appeal to romantic nostalgia, go for it.

A different design strategy for marking time is to create a plan for the future that is an overlay of the different designs and natural stages through which a site has evolved. In the design of Lafayette Square Park in Oakland, described in the chapter on Fairness, the plan accommodated many different demanding constituencies by including fragments of forms that existed

Impelling Form

in the park over the years—a formal crosswalk of the early pleasure-stroll-garden era, an observatory, and a collection of recreation services added willy-nilly starting in the 1930s. Activities that are desired by today's users, especially the near homeless and children, created additional pieces. The design team sifted through transparent overlays of the various eras and pulled out parts that recalled the past. Then they gave these fragments new functions dramatically different from their historic purposes. The outline of the observatory became a hillock in the new plan. Historic trees, remnants from every era, provide shade for hanging out, playing horseshoes, and relaxing. A playground snuggles into the clastic space of the historical crosswalks. Each marks a different era in the development of downtown Oakland and looks forward with a fresh and imaginative view.

Individuals, groups, or agencies may thwart significant transformations toward ecological democracy. When a citizen pronounces that a proposal might be good for the community but opposes it for personal reasons, he often uses the phrase "It will happen only over my dead body." If such a declaration is made by anyone powerful enough to block the proposal, time must be literally marked, as in suspending progress for a time while awaiting a new opportunity. The time is simply not right for a metamorphosis because it threatens some cherished aspect of everyday life or a powerful force that is intransigent. Wise designers learn that a seemingly trivial everyday pattern may embody meaning that is unknown to people until that pattern is menaced. Wise power brokers regroup.

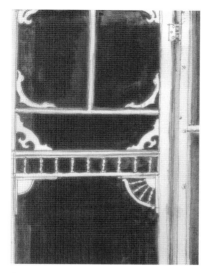

Old-timey style

Inspiring Visionary Futures with the Everyday

Given the self-preserving conservatism of everyday life, it may appear to be an oxymoron to suggest that bold futures can be inspired by daily spatial habits. The challenge for the designer is to uncover and give form to common patterns that are especially enabling, resilient, or impelling. Then she must create future-seeking plans based on those precedents. In most communities, there are at least some such patterns. For example, the washbasins that were rebuilt after the earthquake not only marked time but also eloquently expressed a centeredness that was fundamental to enabling form. In the case of Lafayette Square Park, the historic layering called out the particularness of the neighborhood and demonstrated how adaptable this open space had been over time.

Birmingham Street incorporates radical stormwater infiltration into carefully manicured gardens of native plants.

Name: William Thomas
Address: 102 Bluff Ave
Phone TE 9 5 6 2 9
Home Repair Skills: none

WHAT YOU THINK NEEDS TO BE DONE IN THIS NEIGHBORHOOD
1. we all work together
2. God love that
3.

Condemned housing

Mr. Thomas

Joan Nassauer's Birmingham Street project, which introduced a neighborhood storm-water infiltration system that would replace a system of piping runoff to Minnesota lakes, likewise was implemented only because she thoughtfully grounded her futuristic idea in the everyday lives of neighbors. She first listened and observed to understand the tidy, middle-class aesthetic that residents valued. She respected that order while interjecting native wetland and prairie plants in front-yard swales.[10] The rambunctious native plants are contained in recognizable "gardens" that are acceptable to the residents.[11] The "quietly radical scheme" satisfies storm-water management infrastructure needs at a reduced cost, enhances the neighborhood, and enriches plant-habitat diversity.[12]

It is much easier for a community to take bold action toward ecological democracy when there are homegrown precedents. Saul Alinsky warned organizers to avoid going outside the experience of the people who are being organized.[13] Finding local examples of enabling, resilient, and impelling form grounds the future in the experience of the community. This makes the future not only recognizable (I can see my place in it) but also a matter of identity and pride. This provides the basis for visionary futures that are socially acceptable, even desired.

When we began working with the residents of Chavis Heights in Raleigh, North Carolina, the city planned to demolish the neighborhood through an urban-redevelopment program. The city had concluded that the area was a slum with housing that was so deteriorated that it was beyond repair. The residents would have to be evicted, and the buildings removed. For most residents, this had been the only home they had ever known. Demolition and relocation seemed like a terrifying and depressing future.[14] Our initial study questioned the city's decision because we found housing conditions to be much better than the city had concluded. A power map would have helped us understand the city's intentions, but we didn't think of that approach at the time. It soon became clear that the city goal was not to improve the lives of Chavis Heights residents but was to respond to real estate, race, and suburban traffic needs. Chavis Heights was an old neighborhood that was adjacent to the downtown of Raleigh. It was immensely valuable real estate for downtown expansion but was occupied by relatively poor African Americans. Their removal would make room for office expansion and for a north-south highway that could bring suburban dwellers to the new offices.

Don Collins and I took on the task of making an alternative plan under the direction of a local community-development organization. Two years later, I moved into the neighborhood. At first, I was an object of suspicious curiosity, a racial oddity. Over time, however, I grasped firsthand the everyday patterns of people's lives that were particular to Chavis Heights. This information eventually gave birth to a radically new plan. It was based on a number of patterns that provided local precedents for enabling, resilient, and impelling form. Eight commonplace spatial behaviors were most important to the plan: narrow-street neighboring, porch neighboring, street play, corner hangout, street grid with variation, shotgun density, abandoned back yards, and car sharing and community self-help. The literature predicted the first three patterns. It told us that low-income communities use the street sides of their homes in striking contrast to middle-income neighborhoods, where backyard use dominates.[15] This pattern was reconfirmed by participant observation. Then we noticed that neighboring occurred in the streets themselves, which was not quite what was expected. Because the interior streets were only twenty to twenty-four feet wide with little traffic, the streets served as safe places to hang out and talk. There was also neighboring from porch to street and from porch to porch. Narrow streets and

Narrow-street neighboring

Porch neighboring

Street play

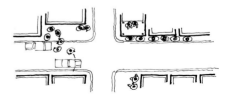

Corner hangout

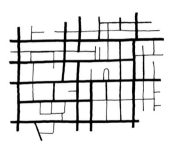

Varied street grid

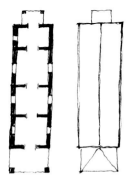

Shotgun density

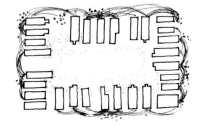

Abandoned backyards

Car sharing, self-help

minimum setbacks allowed easy eye contact and semipublic conversations from one porch to the facing one across the street, usually less than fifty feet away. Narrow streets and light traffic also invited street play. The most frequent activities were football, stickball, and stroll performances. Spring and fall afternoons were punctuated with choruses, as groups of young teens made their way home from school singing the latest popular songs.

At major intersections, small clusters of stores attracted older men and the unemployed to hang out, usually on the sidewalk, on a porch, or under an overhang. Youths would come and go, but this was adult male territory. The major streets were usually wider and generally formed a grid along arterials where buses ran. Within this arterial grid were the narrow streets with greater variety—dead ends, informal cul-de-sacs and turnarounds, wide spots, unpaved sections, and dropoffs.

Typical lots were long and narrow, sometimes as skinny as 20 feet by 120 feet. Most houses were rental shotguns, which are single-family dwellings with rooms lined up single file one after the other. You enter the front door and walk through each room to get to the next. Because doors align, you can, and people sometimes did, shoot a gun through the front door and out the back. Second units often aligned behind the main house. Net density was about fifteen units per acre, over three times the city average. Household size was twice the city average. Usually, a house of three to four rooms would be occupied by three generations of an extended family. Housing conditions varied. Half of the houses in some blocks were deteriorated beyond repair. In other blocks, most were repairable.

A striking pattern of everyday life was the lack of use of back yards. The literature suggested that would be the case, but the extent of back-yard abandonment was shocking. We observed that the back two-thirds of nearly every lot was overgrown and never used. The extent of vegetative succession ranged from five to thirty years, before which outbuildings and gardens had occupied the backs of the lots. Families associated gardening with impoverished oppression and were not interested in reestablishing urban farms. My instinct was to restore these unused backyards to intensive communal purposes, but residents set me straight about that. Overcoming my own impulses and following everyday patterns were key to developing a workable plan.

Because many families did not own cars, there was frequent car sharing. In the block where I lived, for example, Mr. Charlie's car was regularly used by six families for emergencies and for major grocery shopping. On Saturdays, the car would be repaired in the morning, and then we would load up for an excursion—a mixture of essential shopping, social occasion, and community building. Sharing resources extended to repairing each other's plumbing and appliances and to working on community self-help projects that employed a wide variety of construction skills.

These skills were especially important in the early phases of fighting the city plan to demolish the neighborhood. One strategy that the city used to bulldoze housing was enforcement of long overlooked building codes. City staff would "red tag" houses for minor code violations. Once labeled unfit for human habitation, eviction and demolition followed. Soon after this began, work parties were organized to make repairs before the city could evict the tenants. Student volunteers read the city reports, which detailed the required repairs for each house. Then they worked with a local contractor to prepare the work plans for targeted neighborhoods, matched needed repairs with appropriate skills within the community, and scheduled the workdays. Housing was repaired. Residents were empowered. Laborers were particularly pleased that the college students had to rely on them to figure out how to make repairs. No longer feeling helpless to stop the city clearance plan, residents turned their attention to a neighborhood-based plan to prevent the wholesale demolition.

The alternative plan emerged from the geometries of everyday lives. The contrast of intense use of the front porch and street and complete lack of use of the back of the lots was key. That contrast gave us an idea to counter the city's basic argument that there was no way to renew the neighborhood without evicting the residents and clearing the housing. The alternative plan created new streets into the neglected interiors of blocks. Reconfiguring property lines of abandoned backyards, new shotgun houses could be built facing the new streets. These would be sold or rented to residents who were facing eviction from the worst housing on the exterior of that block. Separate plans were made for dozens of blocks. In every block, we were able to provide enough housing so that no one would have to move from the block where he or she lived presently. This latter action was particularly important because the city had claimed that wholesale demolition was necessary because there was no way to revitalize the housing without moving large groups of people out of the area. The community plan proved that the primary public argument that the city had for neighborhood clearance was unfounded. Unspoken race, real estate, and traffic goals remained. But after

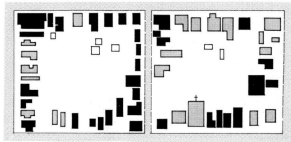

Existing Block Conditions

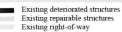
Existing deteriorated structures
Existing repairable structures
Existing right-of-way

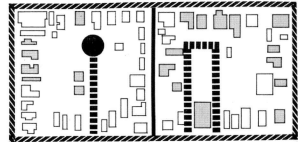

Block Rehabilitation: Phase One

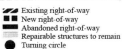
Existing right-of-way
New right-of-way
Abandoned right-of-way
Repairable structures to remain
Turning circle

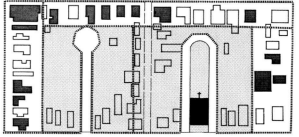

Block Rehabilitation: Phase Two

New streets into interior of blocks.
New houses constructed and sold
to residents in gray areas
Houses to be replaced

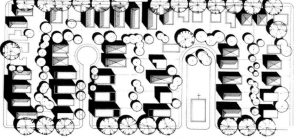

Block Rehabilitation: Phase Three

New structures

Rehabilitated structures moved
Rehabilitated structures

Abandoned backyards became new homes
on new streets in Chavis Heights, stopping
urban-renewal clearance, reinforcing
patterns of daily life, and allowing residents
to continue living on the same block.

numerous demonstrations in favor of the alternative plan and prolonged protests against the city plan, the city abandoned its goal to demolish Chavis Heights.

The city became reconciled to the fact that Chavis Heights would not be exploited for real estate interests. Official policy changed dramatically, leading to public support for in-fill housing, repairs to existing housing, and community improvements like parks, day-care centers, and job training programs, the highest priorities of local residents.

Emergency house repair

New housing

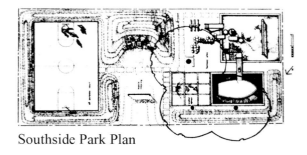

Southside Park Plan

After defeating urban renewal, residents organized to improve the community, repair housing, and create new housing and parks.

Southside Park

In the ten years that I worked with the community, we witnessed a transformation beyond our greatest expectations. The community's visionary plan saved the neighborhood and doubled the housing that was available to families of modest means. Residents created a new neighborhood landscape that was deeply embedded in a celebration of African American life in the urban South. They gained power and pride. They learned that there were many extraordinarily good things—like sharing and community self-help—in their neighborhood. They resisted unhealthy status. Even the most destructive north-south highway was eventually stricken from the city's transportation plan. Today new and revitalized parks and community facilities add livability. Housing rehabilitation continues, and recently built housing has attracted middle-class African Americans. Although still poor relative to the rest of the city, Chavis Heights has accomplished much of its vision, inspired directly by the geometry of its everyday life.

Everyday Lessons for Designers

The everyday patterns in the Chavis Heights neighborhood of Raleigh, North Carolina, stimulated a plan for the future that served the needs of the community and transformed the landscape so that an ecological democracy could flourish. In fact, the design of Chavis Heights embodies most of the principles of enabling and resilient form. The shared experience of the front-porch and street culture reinforces centeredness and sacredness. It incorporates many aspects of connectedness—perhaps most notably the use of the previously undiscovered resource of the abandoned back yards. The plan confronted environmental injustices and created a landscape of fairness. Residents resisted the derogatory description of their neighborhood as a slum. They insisted on maintaining their distinguished sense of community. I have never lived in a more mutually supportive neighborhood. The plan grew out of the particular characteristics of the culture and the landscape. It directly preserved cultural diversity that was threatened by modernization and cultural hegemony. It doubled density to over thirty units per net acre while maintaining a predominantly single-family atmosphere and did this primarily through smallness. The shotgun housing type, confronted with its disposability, proved to be adaptable. Attention to the everyday landscape underlies all of these accomplishments.

Design for everyday requires satisfying people's basic needs—fundamental things like security, new experience, response, and recognition.[16] It avoids pettiness that often accompanies the struggle for personal fulfillment. Dick Meier says that this is the process of drawing out of people their heroic insights and finding ways to implement them.[17]

In the design process, there are two fundamental actions necessary to achieve this. There has to be a clear statement of what people do and need. This is determined by reviewing existing research, by listening to people, by observing how people interact in and with their landscape, and by empathizing—putting oneself in others' shoes. Participant observation and other social spatial-analysis skills help in this endeavor. But stopping there leads to the fatal flaw of a consumer model that is antithetical to an ecological democracy. The second action is necessary to overcome this flaw. The everyday patterns must be integrated into a visionary future that is more than the sum of individual desires. This is typically done by a pattern maker—either professional designers, wise residents, or both. The first requires heightened social-research skills; the second creative form making. In fact, the two actions are mutually dependent. One cannot support ecological democracy without the other, and they can never be successfully married without a strong belief in people and in the power of design.

The design for the Ilan Performing Arts Center illustrates these two mutual actions. For many years, citizens of Ilan County in the Republic of China had wanted a community center where the many indigenous temporal arts could be performed and preserved. When the designers undertook the commission to create the center, the program seemed to dictate a standard theater. But the design team observed that the most exuberant and meaningful theater in Ilan was spontaneous street performances, which often attracted hundreds of people and stopped traffic. These performances—political rallies, weddings, business openings, funerals, and traditional arts—were a part of everyday life. The designers carefully recorded how these events occurred and what the essential spatial characteristics of each performance were. Street theater inspired the design of the National Center of Traditional Arts. At the site scale, the building complex reaches out to existing streets and a park, drawing city life into the center. The center's several buildings and sets create a street between the various parts. Informal amphitheaters and stages inconspicuously attach to buildings at various points. Breezeways and balconies provide circulation and viewing

Street performance

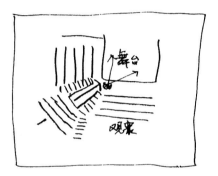

Extend the street inside

The Performing Arts Center is shaped to
extend spontaneous street-theater events
into the formal theater via a wide entry
promenade, a gracious front door and
lobby, and an oversized aisle to the stage.

Entry promenade

Formal performance

spots for impromptu performances. The main building provides the functions of a cultural arts center, yet it looks more like an oversized and refined street. The main entry and anteroom are large enough to accommodate street parades directly from the city into the building. The double-width main aisle encourages performances that flow from the city or stage and engage the audience. Unlike most contemporary theaters, the main stage thrusts into the audience, which helps create the interactive informality of the street. At the same time, the building contrasts sharply with the street. It is quietly detailed, is comfortably elegant, and formally focuses attention on the performance in ways that the street does not. The building captures the exuberance of the street and calms it to create activities that the city never before had. It does this through the two necessary actions—articulating how street performances presently occur every day and making these patterns into something much more via transcendent design. The building addresses all the points of an everyday future. It is designed for what people do presently, based on an unusually thorough behavior analysis. The design resists the typical urge to set a new building apart from its surroundings, like a jewel among swine; rather, the building integrates with its urban context. It knits present experience seamlessly into a different future. It marks time by respecting its surroundings. Above all, it shows a faith in people and in inspired design. And by this, it provides an impelling future.

Form follows the flow of everyday life. Even the form of a radical future follows the flow of everyday life.

Naturalness

Urban habitation must be filled with nature, which enhances our lives with the benefits of naturalness. We are ambivalent about city dwelling, but we have no mixed feelings about nature. We get great pleasure and a significant part of our identity from it. We like it large. We like it nearby. We embrace nature in many different ways. For example, almost all Americans participate in outdoor recreation. On any given weekend, as many as 78 percent of American households engage in gardening. In raw numbers, 109 million Americans participate in wildlife-related recreation. More than 76.5 million Americans watch wildlife, and 35.6 million fish. The National Wildlife Federation has over 4 million members.[1] All Americans do not enjoy nature the same way, and we do more than our share of nature exploitation and abuse. Still, nature is highly valued by most of us. Just why we cherish nature is explained today in terms of genetics (like biophilia), geography (like topophilia), culture, education (like the need to minimize damage to the environment for our own health), and psychology. It is likely all of these—and more.

In this section, we look primarily at the design aspects of feelings that are associated with nature. In this sense, naturalness is the affective domain, particularly the subconscious, emotional influences that nature has on human beings. Naturalness originates in feelings that are evoked by experiences with the nonhuman living world (like plants and wildlife) and the forces that make up that world (like earth, wind, and fire). Then naturalness creates in us, subconsciously, qualities that make us our most fully human selves. The emotions are typically expressed in simple terms such as "being in nature makes me feel good, healthy, joyful, free" or any number of other basic feelings. The qualities are profound—a sense of beauty, spontaneity, and relatedness. Naturalness refers to these emotions and basic human qualities that derive from experience with nature.

Naturalness keeps us healthy, stimulates joy and spontaneity, and nurtures natural citizenship.

In academic circles, the idea of nature is hotly debated. What is and is not natural? Is anything natural? The cultural construct of naturalness is more loaded than the construct of nature itself.[2] However, my interest is practical. From the user-needs perspective, it is possible to describe the outcomes without agreement about theoretical constructs and then to make the city in a way that touches people's hearts and endows us with more robust lives.

I look briefly at three of the many affective outcomes of human engagement with nature—health and healing (naturopathy), joy and spontaneity (naturism), and natural citizenship (naturalization). I also describe the landscape characteristics that are most essential to evoke good health, joy, and natural citizenship.

Naturopathy

The old-fashioned folk remedy for illness that is called *naturopathy* relies on sunshine, diet, and exercise in the out-of-doors to treat illness. Often met with skepticism from modern medicine, the healing power of nature is widely accepted in many parts of the world and increasingly acknowledged among skeptics. Consider this simple remedy. Did you ever visit a natural place when you were not feeling well and come away feeling better? If you can call to mind such experiences, you are among the majority of Americans who likewise report such naturopathic remedies. If you are skeptical, consider the poetic promise that only Edward Abbey could make.

Abbey, author of *The Monkey Wrench Gang* and inspiration to a generation of environmental activists, understood the health benefits of nature and had a spitefully humorous use for it. At an Earth First! rally, he cautioned ecological radicals not to burn themselves out trying to save the world. He urged that we not only fight for the land but also enjoy it by rambling and exploring the forests, the peaks, the rivers, and the air. He claimed that if we enjoy it, we will live longer, healthier lives. That would be a sweet victory over enemies of the land who, driven by spreadsheets and bank statements, destroy it from afar. If you experience the joys of nature, he promised, "You will outlive the bastards, the deskbound people with their hearts in a safety deposit box and their eyes hypnotized by desk calculators. I promise you this: you will outlive the bastards."[3]

When a person exclaims that being in nature makes her feel healthy, it is typically a pure emotional response, but increasingly it is backed by scientific evidence. Abbey was right: there is no doubt that experiencing nature helps keep us healthy, heals us when we are sick, shortens the time we are in the hospital for surgery, and diminishes the recurrence of illness.[4] Being in nature has the power to lower stress, combat mental fatigue, and make us less fearful.[5] Consider one example. For the 2 million children who are suffering from attention disorders in the United States, nature apparently helps them function better. Whereas present drug therapies do not change much long-term and have serious side effects and behavior modification is only partially successful, settings of natural greenery seem to reduce antisocial behavior and might relieve anxiety, low self-esteem, and depression. Rooms with windows help, open grass and big trees do more, and wild green places provide the most effective therapy.[6]

Hospitals today generally provide none of these. Mirroring trends in houses and cities, hospitals have become machines for sickness. The megahospital of technological intervention performs miracles of medicine but fails miserably in the forms of healing that many people need. This is beginning to change. Recent experiments to reintroduce natural healing (like the therapeutic Garden for Children designed by Douglas Reed in Wellesley, Massachusetts) blend nature and advanced technology. The grounds of

The Therapeutic Garden in Wellesley, Massachusetts, includes a gentle runnel of water making its way through landforms to help traumatized children express repressed feelings.

the Institute for Child and Adolescent Development were reconceived to create as much open space as possible. To help severely traumatized children express inner feelings through experiences in the landscape, Reed crafted settings that evoke security, exploration, seclusion, discovery, and risk taking. Each is expressed in an archetypal landform that is gently carved by water. A protected ravine, Reed reasoned, might evoke a sense of security. A small island might offer privacy and intimacy. A large, open space suggests recovery. Therapists recorded each child's activity on maps of the garden as a diagnostic tool to aid recovery. This also tested the assumptions of the designer until the garden was temporarily closed due to funding.[7]

The evidence from a wide range of carefully controlled medical experiments suggests that the experience of nature maintains and restores good health, largely through involuntary and unconscious responses. In varying ways, settings as diverse as gardens, parks, wilderness, rooms with windows for viewing nature, or rooms with potted plants have been reported as therapeutic.[8] Viewing nature restores our health. Active engagement with nature restores our health. And participation in designing and caring for these green environments restores our health.[9]

Historically, naturopathy begins with exposure to sunshine and good diet. To receive the full benefits of natural therapy today, we must consider the entire urban ecosystem—safe water, clean air, and the opportunity to view and actively engage trees, flowers, sky, butterflies, and other wildlife. For people to receive the maximum health benefits, the form of the city must be reordered to provide these therapeutic remedies in our everyday lives. When they are provided, we seem impelled to seek out those green places.

Naturism

In the same way that green landscapes convey healthfulness, nature evokes in us feelings of beauty, joy, spontaneity, and creativity. Nature can, if we are attuned to it, return us to our wild state, which seems essential for realizing our full potentials.[10] *Naturism* (literally, nudity) encompasses the sensory pleasures and associated actions that we derive from experiencing nature. Natural sensory stimulation—a fleeting view of a rainbow, the smell of wild ginger, the tickle of dandelion fluff on one's cheek, the taste of wild chanterelles, the sound of a waterfall—provides an immediate and unintentional delight. Have you seen adults, normally staid and structured, transformed by wind, water, or sand into, respectively, uninhibited kite-flying, fly-fishing, or sand-castle-building children? Do you ever wonder why sand prompts family members to bury their own alive? Or why wet snow compels us to shape obese fantasy characters? Or why a summer shower inspires us to soak ourselves splashing in mud puddles? Or why a grassy hill invites clumsy somersaults that end in a reversal of normalcy? This is the unexpectedly fun side of ecology. Most people don't think that science can be amusing and utterly delightful. This aspect of ecology makes one feel like a natural man or woman, as Carole King sings. Natural stimuli not only delight and amuse us but also free us from affectations and inhibitions, usually not as extreme as public nudity but often in ways contrary to expected behavior.

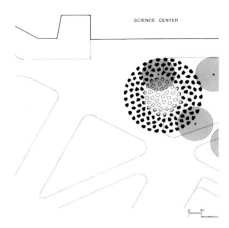

SCIENCE CENTER

This form of play is essential in normal child development. Natural environments stimulate fanciful role play and encourage children to explore the unknown in construction play and creative nonconventional thinking.[11] Although engagement with nature is among the most joyful kind of childhood play, important skills are also developed. It is equally valuable for adults to cultivate these skills of fanciful and divergent thinking, inventiveness, and spontaneous problem solving. These skills are quashed as we are socialized. But here I want to emphasize not the skills but the pure delight we gain from nature. Nature distracts us, puts us in the moment, amuses us, gratifies us, and pleasures us. It is relatively free entertainment from renewable resources.

In these instances, nature seems to reawaken our naivete and our primal spirits and often sparks delight, inquisitiveness, and reproduction. Such pure primitive emotion may be triggered by watching an amaryllis unfold with stunning color and geometry or making a cairn of rocks at the confluence of two mountain streams. Such pure emotion may be touched by

Elemental and changing with the seasons,
Tanner Fountain is mysterious and moving.

built landscapes that are elementally formed. Tanner Fountain, at Harvard University, is a simple circle of 159 rocks. Two feet wide and tall and four feet long, the boulders gather around an amorphous center and spread out in roughly concentric circles as ripples moving outward from a stone tossed into water. Yet in this case, the ripples are solid and unmoving, and the center is fluid and moving. In the center of the stones are jets of steam or misty water, depending on the season. Permanent rock takes the form of ephemeral water and vice versa, creating "a primordial focus of place."[12] Whether in its own summer mist or winter snow, with playing children or a solitary reader on a boulder, the place evokes a primal connection. Pete Walker, the landscape architect of Tanner Fountain, urges that gardens should be more than useful, more than beautiful: "I want them to be mysterious and moving."[13]

Similarly, the floating gardens that are attached to a hillock protruding from Sun Moon Lake in Taiwan are both mysterious and moving. The hillock clings to trees toppled by a deadly earthquake, and the floating gardens provide beauty and fish habitat. Such places, natural and built, evoke immense power to shape impelling cities.

The floating Lalu Garden marks a sacred site for native people of Sun Moon Lake. As the gardens grow, roots of the plants provide habitat for fish and food for the community.

Naturalization

Just as a person from another country can become a naturalized citizen, those who have been alienated from earth's wild processes can achieve full citizenship in the ecological world with all the rights and pleasures thereof by reacclimatizing, letting nature touch our hearts, and conforming to the ways of ecology—in short, by becoming naturalized. Becoming "renaturalized" might be more accurate given that *Homo sapiens* is not an alien species but for most of our existence has been integrally conformed to the ecologies around us.

Naturalization offers impelling benefits. We have already discussed that green cities can provide health, pleasure, and unconventional problem solving. Reacquainting ourselves with nature can also supply us with the ecological literacy that is necessary to better design our cities, but that is discussed later. Here I want to discuss three additional subconscious outcomes of naturalization that make us more fully human—fundamental character, art of dwelling, and civility.

There is disheartening evidence that our pursuit of individualism generally has not fulfilled us but rather has cast us adrift and filled us with insecurities that are calmed only by artificial material conformity.[14] Reflecting within the context of nature on ourselves and on the cities we make allows us to know who and where we are and what we most profoundly value.[15] As Utah author Terry Tempest Williams says about her Great Salt Lake, "I go to the lake for a compass reading, to orient myself once again in the midst of change."[16] Placing ourselves strips away layers of conditioned affectations and enables us to see our basic character, native disposition, and essential qualities. Experiences in nature are not only self-revealing but also empower us to act by reducing fear, increasing self-discipline, and building self-confidence.

Nature inspires artful creativity in dwelling. Whether art is a precise interpretation of nature or an expression of what nature is not, ecological forces play a major role in creative actions.[17] The Chinese poetry of Li Po, May dances, Japanese flower arrangements, and the paintings of Winslow Homer offer literal inspirations. The sculptural creations of British environmental artist Andy Goldsworthy use natural materials in ways that mimic their own patterns or other geometries of the wild landscape. Likewise, the creativity in each and every one of us, whether we think of our-

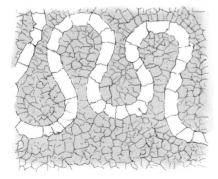

Goldsworthy inspiration

selves as artists or not, is aroused by the forces of nature. Think about a family that is walking in the autumn woods and collecting eye-catching treasures; suddenly its treasures inspire a Goldsworthy-like arrangement of orange, red, and gold. Think about a beach scene where otherwise sane adults are frantically searching for driftwood, rocks, rope, and other materials with which to build a wind and sun shelter. Burying a few large structural pieces makes the framework. A few stray pieces shoot upward to catch stars. A building emerges from the found objects, calming the wind and sun and gathering proclamations of self-satisfaction. The beach group breaks into dance and song. Nature stimulates art; art combines with need, a sense of play, and nature's resources to create dwelling.

With the professionalization of every aspect of life, however, art, building, and dwelling have become the exclusive realms of specialists, and few people today create, build, and dwell as part of their daily routines. This leads to incomplete human existence and is a source, unknown to us, of great dissatisfaction.[18] Anne Whiston Spirn simplifies this to a precise statement: "I am because I dwell; I dwell because I build."[19] We would be more fulfilled beings if art were a part of everyday life and integrated into the building of our habitation. This idea is reflected in the life of a chambered nautilus, which makes a beautiful house simply by living in it. Larry Halprin, many years ago, concluded that this integration was so essential that he created workshops to retrain people to reweave life, art, nature, and dwelling. Usually conducted on the beach, the workshops often resulted in extraordinary temporary structures of habitation and new self-awareness.[20] Nature stimulates art; art forms dwelling. The real benefit is that dwelling fulfills us in subconscious yet fundamental ways.

Nature makes us more civil. This may seem at odds with the previous discussion, which emphasizes the spontaneous and primitive. Yet shaping our lives to conform to nature or simply experiencing nature more increases our ability to listen to others, to empathize, and to be concerned about their needs as well as our own. This may be tied to relatedness or attention restoration. Exposure to green nature reduces our aggression and makes us less violent.[21] In a Chicago study, for example, residents who lived in "greener" surroundings reported fewer incivilities and less aggressive behavior.[22] Although these studies are far more cautious in their conclusions than I present here, it is reasonable to expect that the combined forces of increased use by legitimate users, the restorative aspects of greenery, and the awareness of

Stone in Aberdaron

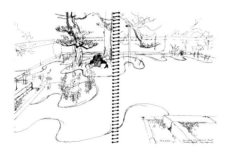

Accessible from home

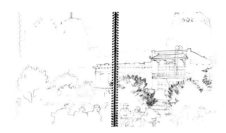

Neighborhood nature

City nature

Calm and restful

human interdependence that one gains from natural experiences would make us more collegial. This, in turn, would prepare us for more civil dialogue and problem solving with neighbors and strangers alike.

The Form to Arouse Naturalness

What form should the urban landscape take to give us the fullest impelling benefits of naturalness? The following design characteristics are most essential: access at home and nearby, restfulness, engaging distraction, spontaneous creativity, the elemental, the underdone, a perspective view, active and passive engagement, private and social settings, big and little areas, connectedness, tame and wild spaces.

First and foremost, to achieve the benefits of naturopathy, naturism, and naturalization, nature must be easily accessible every day. While offering the same benefits, faraway nature cannot provide the most essential aspects of naturalness. Nature must be in the home, surrounding the home, and within pleasant walking distance. Potted plants, pets, aquaria, green views from windows, and sunlit rooms—even cut flowers, paintings of nature, or miniature water fountains—are the first order. A place to sit immediately outside the home in the sunshine, breeze, or changing humidity, to feed birds, and to garden (if only in pots) is the next order. This need not be large; a balcony or steps will often suffice. In a San Francisco apartment complex with a limited budget, Clare Cooper Marcus specified a wall niche outside each person's entry door where shade plants might be kept. They became cherished moments of color. In Japan, the tiny garden (*tsubo-niwa*) provides this function, evoking the sensual pleasures of much larger wilderness in spaces that often are no larger than four square feet. I know a man in Japan whose garden consists of moss growing in discarded sardine cans. Small efforts evoke significant restorative and transformative powers. A view to a flowering tree from a window at home or work, for example, helps overcome weariness, even if experienced only subconsciously a dozen times a day. The refrain regarding nature must be to bring it on home—at home, school, and work. Make it close at hand. Access to an outdoor space for gardening or habitat creation may be essential for many people, depending on their life-cycle stage and predisposition (remember the three-quarters of American households who garden and the one-third who participate in wildlife-related recreation).

Impelling Form

The next order is the neighborhood landscape. For the mobility impaired, the very young, and the old, the landscape within a block of home—foundation plantings, lawn strips, street trees, a corner community garden, and neighbors' plants—forms the primary public landscape. There needs to be a public place to sit, surrounded by vegetation, within two hundred feet of every home. The subwatershed boundary of ravine, hilltop, or creek is the next order. As stated before, this nature should define neighborhood and be within a two-minute run or a five-minute walk (approximately a quarter mile) from any household. At the city scale, large urban wilderness should define the city edge; this nature should ideally be no further than a mile from any home. More likely, it may be two miles away, but never more, to be accessible for most people. Similarly, in the workplace, there needs to be interior greening and accessible green places for breaks and lunch.

To evoke naturalness, the character of the landscape should provide a calm and restful background. It should be unambiguously reassuring, easily legible, and positive. In spite of postmodern impulses, shocking landscapes of nature run amok almost always undermine naturalness. Tortured trees turned on their sides, concrete gardens without green, piercing geometries of natural objects disembodied are clever but provide few of the benefits of restoration. You may have heard of failures like the "garden" installation at a major hospital that provoked such fear that it was removed. For people under stress—patients, families, friends, and staff of hospitals—research has measured the need for unambiguously positive nature. Because hospitals are places of great anxiety, it makes sense to provide calming, restful, green oases there.[23] You might think that attention to restful nature is not important in other settings, but that is not the case. People go to most public landscapes for sun, fresh air, and restoration to combat mental fatigue and restore attention. Calming, restful green, as in the Olmsted tradition, may be boring to some designers, but people generally need naturalness more than they need increased stimulation.

While the restful green provides a calming background, other landscape elements must provide a natural distraction to achieve naturalness. Overcoming mental fatigue, for example, requires attention to be diverted from immediate problems by allowing it to focus unconsciously on some aspect of the natural environment. The ephemeral quality of the landscape—a sunflower newly in bloom, dappled sunlight on moss and stone, a mother mallard leading her ducklings to a first swim—restores us by this very power

Ephemeral distraction

Spontaneous interaction

Elemental

Simplicity

to capture our attention. By the arrangement of color, form, texture, space, light, shadow, and habitat, these ephemeral powers can be made present in varying forms throughout the day and year. Engaging distractions, like metaphorical specimen trees, need to be integrated within the overall embrace of restful green.

To achieve maximum health benefits, the urban landscape should be designed to invite spontaneous interactions with the natural environment and creative play. Sensual exploration must be prompted so that people are encouraged to touch, to smell, to stimulate the mind's eye to travel and investigate, to poke around, to make art with natural loose parts, and to participate in dance of one's own making.[24] Sand, rocks, water, dead leaves, limbs, woodpiles, forests, marshes, meadows, orchards, ponds, creeks, junk and compost piles, dump heaps and construction sites—all invite spontaneous engagement. These need to be more frequently available in the urban landscape. Landscapes that are too precious to be sensually embraced should be used sparingly.

Naturalness intertwines with the elemental. When people describe the essential characteristics of their favorite places, sunlight, sky, water, vegetative patterns, landforms, and rocks typically top their lists. One person recalled the discovery of what, as a child, had been the most enchanting place in his neighborhood. Tucked in a distant corner of a large, leftover wood lot, it was "a water hole banked by moss-covered mounds, hemlocks and yellow birch trees festooned with golden ruffles." The primal quality evoked such sentiment that he and his friends swore a pledge "to use the place for quiet, peaceful, loving thoughts," not an easy vow to keep as adolescent boys.[25] Landscapes of elemental forces—earth, air, fire, water, and life—touch us at a basic level in powerful ways. The force is greater without buildings or structures of any kind. Raw naked landscapes—a water hole with the ooze of life, a hilltop with a view and blustery wind, a deeply incised holler, a copse or a desert plain—are most elemental. Even small urban landscapes may have primal powers. This is the allure of the sheet of falling water in Paley Park in New York. The designer's task is to determine what elemental force a given sight has and to intensify that force. Every neighborhood should have some primal landscape. Not every neighborhood can have the moss-surrounded water hole, but every place should have some basic elements that arouse fundamental emotions.

Generally, the elemental landscape has greatest force when it is underdone. The power of basic elements lies in their simplicity, an unaffected elegance free of froufrou.

Naturalness is served by views that afford distant perspective. A prospect with refuge allowed early hominoids to escape large and fierce animals. Possibly genetically imprinted in all of us who survived, the classic prospect-refuge provides a broad view from a ridge top with the protection of canopy vegetation. This creates an enclosed space within a large, open space. An *aedicula* on a bare hilltop, a roof garden, a window in an attic, and a tree house are architectural parallels. In the urban landscape, the view from a hill, a niche on the edge of a steep slope, and a perch in a tree overlooking the street offer both a prospect (where one has an unimpeded opportunity to see out) and a refuge (where one has an opportunity to hide).[26] These views afford perspective and can help to get one's life under control during times of high stress. A panoramic view of one's neighborhood, city, or region provides pleasure and relatedness by seeing how usually unseen parts fit together.

Distant perspective

To achieve the full benefits of naturalness, people need to have opportunities for both active and passive engagement with the green environment. Nature is therapeutic whether we are consciously looking or subconsciously distracted while doing some other activity. Viewing might be considered the passive end of the scale, running through urban wilderness the active end of the scale, and many gradients come between. A healthy neighborhood provides choices—sitting outside, tending a garden, bird watching, fishing, playing among tunnels of tall grass, making a dam on a creek, catching tadpoles, building a tree fort, dancing in a meadow, and hiking. Strenuous exercise while viewing nature probably provides double benefits to health.[27] Because the benefits of naturalness vary depending on the degree of activity, it is essential to provide a full range of activities that are easily accessible in everyday life.

Passive and active engagement

Similarly, there need to be both social and private green settings. At first glance, the restorative experiences appear to call for solitary places. Psychological and physical healing are deeply personal matters that are experienced by the individual. While it is true that some restorative experiences occur in the privacy of the home, most people seek public outdoor places with private settings to relieve their stress.[28] This may be prompted, in part, by the need to get away from the source of the problem, which typically is in the home or at work. To achieve privacy, many people seek public green places

Tame to wild

that often are filled with anonymous people. Other benefits of naturalness occur in groups with family and friends. Social support, like nature, is therapeutic. In neighborhoods with limited natural spaces, only thoughtful, inventive design can provide a range of green settings from sociopetal to solitary.

Likewise, small and large areas of green provide for different aspects of naturopathy, naturism, and naturalization. Generally, the very old and very young need nature in small sizes and close to home. The critical design issue here is to make the city green only in ways that also facilitate higher density in the range of twenty to fifty units per acre. All too frequently, the expansion of urban green comes at the cost of sustainable density. Design that makes maximum effect of tiny green, like the Japanese *tsubo-niwa*'s green walls and roofs, can produce the benefits of naturalness without sacrificing density.[29] By providing small areas of nature near home and larger areas as natural boundaries, the conflict with density can be minimized. The large nature should form the boundaries of neighborhoods and cities primarily where ridges, stream corridors, or other ecological features define jurisdictions. In short, make small nature compact and big nature connected.

Open spaces should range from tame to wild. Generally, wild nature requires the large extent provided in greenbelts and distant national parks, but if habitat is carefully connected, the experience of wild nature can be brought within walking distance of each neighborhood, as in Honolulu and Kyoto (discussed earlier). But even in the city, the health benefits of wild nature can be achieved by creating wildlife habitat for patch species or using elemental landscape like water and sky. In tiny yards, neighbors can collectively create considerable habitat—say, for butterflies, by separately providing sun, larval food, flowers, mud, and water.

Some people prefer their nature tame, neat, and tidy or framed, which can readily be accomplished but may cause conflict in the public landscape with those who want their nature wild. In Los Angeles, one of the most contentious issues surrounding urban wilderness parks has repeatedly focused on the provision of irrigated lawns. It is nonnative and water consumptive but a critical ingredient for nontraditional wilderness users, including African Americans, some Hispanic and Asian Americans, lower-income people, teenagers, and new immigrants. Although I personally prefer wild nature, I have learned the importance of providing the full range. In one gateway park project, we used all native plants except lawn grasses in an effort to attract new users. A local environmental group sued and eventually obtained an injunction that stopped the project, but not before the grass had been installed. The gateway park, especially the grass area, is heavily used by an unusual diversity of people, but the lawn seems somewhat out of place amid the surrounding wild lands.

These eleven criteria guide design to achieve the benefits of naturopathy, naturism, and naturalization. We need nature every day—green, calming, distracting. We need it to evoke spontaneity and creative action. We need it elemental and understated. We need its views to put things in perspective. We need it active and passive, private and social, big and little, connected, tame and wild.

The Natural Park

The Natural Park in South Central Los Angeles illustrates many of the principles underlying naturalness. To most Americans, South Central is an unlikely place for a green park. Images of asphalt basketball courts and broken chain-link fences in an abandoned ghetto that was burned out during the Watts riots and the Rodney King uprising are more likely. Yes, the community still is recovering from the riots, and people there are poor. Nearly a third of the residents live below the poverty line, and more are unemployed. The few parks in South Central are paved because it has long been assumed that low-income minorities prefer recreation facilities to natural open space,[30] but that is an unfortunate stereotype.[31]

For over a decade, the Santa Monica Mountains Conservancy, the state agency that is creating the greenbelt around Los Angeles, has sponsored programs to take central-city youth to the urban wilderness in the mountains surrounding the city (see the chapter on Limited Extent). It was a once-in-a-lifetime experience, scary at first but exhilarating, but when students were back at home in South Central, the wilderness faded into a memory. For years, Conservancy director Joe Edmiston and I had talked about extending the surrounding greenbelt into the central city. Then Los Angeles city councilor Rita Walters challenged Edmiston by saying publicly that his greenbelt had never done anything for her constituency. That spurred the search for a potential nature park site in her district of South Central.[32] At the intersection of Slauson and Compton avenues was a pipe graveyard that was owned by Los Angeles Water and Power and was used to store the remains of bro-

Neighborhood context

Pipe graveyard

On-site workshop

ken utility projects. The eight-and-a-half-acre industrial wasteland was surrounded by warehouses, railroad tracks, neighborhoods, and a few stores. One outsider described the area as "block after block of concertina-wire-topped chain-link fence" and "graffiti-covered warehouse walls" with "bushels of broken glass."[33] But we saw potential there.

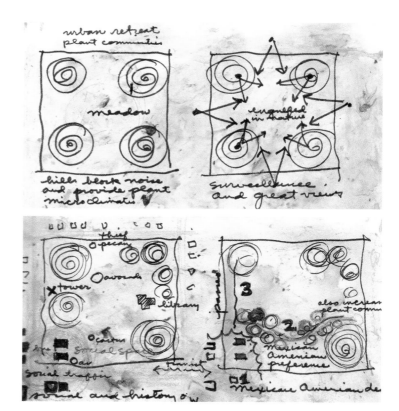

The concept for the Nature Park pursues social safety and urban wilderness adventure simultaneously with hills to create a cloistered meadow, a social center for the fearful, views for joy and surveillance, and a runnel of water supplying wetlands and arroyos.

After two years of negotiations, a lease was signed so that the site could be used for a park. During this time, community representatives proposed various uses. Some plans were dominated by ball courts and sports fields; others by naturalistic open space. Community meetings and door-to-door interviews produced skepticism and little feedback from residents. But when we took the plans to the Supermercado across the street from the proposed park, hundreds of people stopped to offer their opinions. More responded when plans were posted in other local stores. As community members began to trust the sincerity of the effort, more people from various cultures came to the meetings. The near unanimous priority of all residents—long-term African Americans and new immigrants from Asia, Mexico, and other Hispanic cultures who now form the largest population in the area—was safety. Park planning was frequently sidelined by outbursts against the lack of police patrols in South Central. Many feared that the park would become the battleground for the surrounding gangs. Edmiston and Walters promised the community that park rangers would be present full time, a ranger residence would be part of the design, and the entire park could be fenced. Only then did the discussion turn to other park matters. Some argued that there were already concrete playgrounds but no evidence of nature in the area.[34] Others retorted, "What do we need to see birds for? The kids want seesaws."[35] The most feared gangs sent word that they would respect a natural park. In the end, the community chose the greenest alternative. That was the origin of Parque Natural.

The design evolved from a number of factors. If a series of hills could be created around the perimeter of the park with a meadow in the center, a quiet green retreat maximizing therapeutic benefits and natural delights might result. The hills would also afford a perspective overview of the city that residents of the flatlands had never experienced. Various Southern California native plant communities could nestle into appropriate aspects. To provide surveillance into the park and green views for passersby, the hills were lowered at each midblock. The ranger residence, a nature center, and a community building were located at the corner of Slauson and Compton to reinforce the center of social activity near the busy Supermercado and other stores. The park buildings surround a *zócalo,* the traditional Mexican public courtyard. A path (*paseo*) connects to a pool of water via a stroll under sycamore trees. This side of the park is decidedly tame and familiar. There are places where older people can sit and watch. Benches and picnic areas for

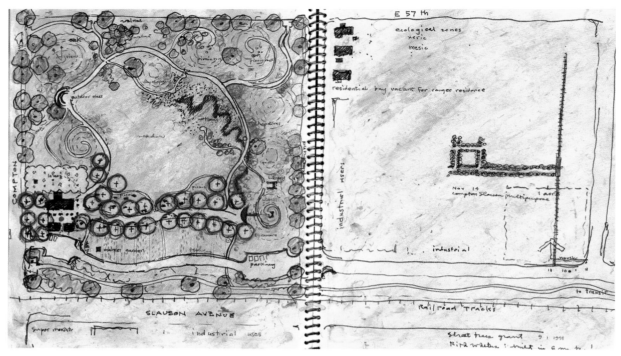

The social spine provides tame nature,
from the community center through a
sycamore *paseo* to a fountain. Topography
and water distribution shape the wild
nature of native plant associations from
marsh to xeric slopes.

The Sycamore *paseo*

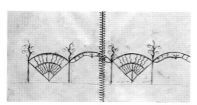

The social center

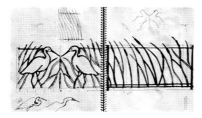

The evolution of the fence

Learn by doing

Somersault hill

Nature center

Community festival

large family groups are close by. After safety, residents called for these places where extended families could gather under a treed canopy, surrounded by green. They also wanted big, social spaces for outdoor fiestas, which occur around the buildings and *paseo*.

Beyond this social spine, the park becomes wilder. Community priorities included natural places for children to explore, a dry wash (arroyo), a marsh, a stream, and the miniature mountains casting this way and that, with habitats including oak woodlands, south-facing coastal chaparral, and fields of native grasses. Martha Maravilla, who runs the M&M Mini Market and Takeout across from the park, notes that the wild part is reminiscent of her homeland: "It's back to nature, the way it should be."[36] Sweeping, unruly plant communities and rolling hills surround elemental water, marsh, and meadow. There are spots for seclusion and quiet. There are also places to be alone but safely within the view of others. There are unmanicured natural delights and distractions that invite spontaneous play. Here youth "shed their sneakers, just to dance." Children play "steppingstones in the arroyo," fill squirt guns in the stream, and blast over the hills on scooters.[37] These engaging distractions of nature are supplemented by classes in which children use natural materials to make art. And nature-based art defines the edges of the park and social areas. Local artists shaped 2,400 linear feet of wrought iron into Gaudi-like organic forms and recognizable elements of the local ecosystem for perimeter fencing and gates. Artshare, a program to incubate the artist in everyone, engaged community members in making tiles and designing mosaic benches for an amphitheater that serves as an outdoor classroom. More than fifty community residents were hired during park construction, each adding his or her own creative energy. This artistic collective results in an eclectic aesthetic of incongruous elements, including the mini windmill that pumps the water for the arroyo, dwarf cannons, totem scarecrows, tiles, calligraphied quotes from George Washington Carver and the Huichol Indians, and some graffiti.[38] These personal artistic flourishes are still absorbed into the overall unity of the calming green. Local teenagers acknowledged this expression of their essential selves in the artistry of their park by naming it "o.g." for original.[39] The messiness and complete joy found in its naturalness and the local, grassroots art it has inspired make this truly an original. One former gang member sums it up: "It's real out here."[40]

Impelling Form

The dry arroyo

The riparian wood

Regional water flow

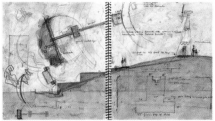

Irrigation and xeric habitats

Agricultural flow

Smallest runnel possible

This natural realness is startling. Only two years ago, this area was a near lifeless void. Today there is an abundance of wildlife—mostly insects, worms, and birds—that was unimaginable before. Still, the site is only a fragment. Its natural potential will be met only when this park joins the larger natural system. Planning is underway to connect the park via a greenbelt down Slauson Avenue to the light-rail station and to a restored Compton Creek. When completed, Parque Natural will be part of a continuous green swath that reaches to the Los Angeles River.

No studies have confirmed the trend, but residents comment about the park's restorative qualities. One contrasts it with frequent gunfire and police helicopters. The park is an antidote to harsh urbanity that creates anxiety, tension, stress, and fatigue. A teacher who brings his students to the park says that before the park was built, the only beauty in the neighborhood was reserved for restaurants and boxing centers.[41] The natural beauty and the opportunity for exercise in a safe place should improve health.

How safe is the park, given that it is the boundary for vicious and expanding gangs? A former gang member points out that before the park was built, this area was rough and frightening to most residents. He says that it is a crosscut for gang territory but predicts that gangs will respect the park.[42]

Water is moved by wind power along an agricultural runnel to the half-moon pool. Then a stream snakes its way through riparian zones to the dry arroyo—nature enough to lose oneself in the city.

Impelling Form

So far, the gang-bangers use the park but will not fight there.[43] Families with young children, the elderly, and the youth report that they feel safe there. Program directors have observed changes in the behavior of young people, who seem less aggressive and more courteous when they are at the park. One reports that the youth are more respectful.[44] Jorge Lopez, a leader on the local neighborhood park committee since the project was conceived, believes that the whole community is changing as a result of Parque Natural. He says that the neighborhood will "look out for itself more."[45] Whether or not the change will be lasting and transformative, the naturalness evoked by this green place is increasing the healing, joy, creativity, safety, and feelings of self-esteem and community in residents.

Naturalness Impels

Greening the city makes it impelling because nature evokes our most fully human selves. Naturalness nurtures good health and heals us when we are sick, fatigued, and stressed. Naturalness spurs us to play with reckless abandon, frees us from artificial affectations and inhibitions, instills in us divergent ways of thinking, and reawakens our naivete. Naturalness helps us discover our fundamental character (the "o.g." or original in ourselves and our community), introduces us to the chambered-nautilus-like art of dwelling, in which making art is integrated into everyone's everyday life and provokes relatedness and civility.

These benefits accrue through redesigning the city to provide significant doses of nature in everyday life. It must be nearby. It must be designed to be restful and to evoke overwhelmingly positive feelings and not increase anxiety. It must be formed to provide engaging natural distractions from overly artificial stimuli in everyday life. It must evoke dance, song, poetry, and creativity, which should be as much a part of life as breathing. Nature does this best if kept elemental and understated. Design of natural experiences must give perspective. There need to be settings for active, passive, private, and social relationships in nature. Nature must be big enough and interconnected to provide wildlife habitat and linear recreation, but it must be small enough to be close at hand without diminishing density. And there should be a range of encounters with nature form tame to wild. This combination gives us the most benefits and makes the city irresistible. Naturalness touches our hearts.

Inhabiting Science

A city will impel us only if we comprehend and truly understand it, know our place in it, and know how to be meaningfully engaged in the decisions that create it. Comprehension is joyful. It impels. Choice impels. But we have lost both.

The Japanese landscape scholar and community activist Nagahashi Tamesuke has a saying that appropriately describes our present situation: "A good man with bad information is a bad man." Today we as a society unquestionably lack the appropriate and relevant knowledge and skills that are necessary to design healthy cities. David Orr has labeled this ecological illiteracy.[1]

The urban ecology we inhabit is illegible to us.[2] Even though (and maybe because) there is far too much information available, we cannot read what is important. Our brains are filled with synthetic junk. We are likely to know corporate logos but almost nothing of our local flora and fauna.[3] Our affluence, technology, overspecialization, reliance on experts, globalization, loss of agricultural work, standardization, and mobility are at various times blamed for our ignorance of the ecology of locality. All of these undermine local knowledge that is grounded in a particular place. In the case of the latter, American mobility disrupts the understanding of an urban ecology that develops from close contact over a long period of time. This is in part because we are mostly recent immigrants. In new and unfamiliar territory, one must "learn to read the landscape inch by inch,"[4] but few of us take the time. If we don't take the time to comprehend the nuances of the landscape where we dwell, we are left with media slogans, dancing like sugar plums in our heads, to inform city making. We have become good people with bad information. It may be more accurate to say that the wrong information fills our heads or that our substantial knowledge does not prepare us for dwelling. The outcome of Nagahashi's homily is that we are unable to do right by ecological information. Instead, we act badly.

Habitation impels us only when we truly understand it, know how it works, know our place in it, and are engaged in making it.

Impelling Form

Urban Ecological Illiteracy

The result is that we are unable to make cities that nourish us. To the founders of our country, this represented a worrisome problem. Benjamin Franklin considered informed participation to be a moral imperative because each citizen's opinions were important. Others countered that widespread participation would not be well informed and that a truly democratic society would not act responsibly.[5] In the middle of this debate Thomas Jefferson argued persuasively that the only safe depository of power was the minds and hands of the people themselves. He particularly envisioned a nation of yeomen farmers whose knowledge was grounded in their land. To those elitists who considered the public too unenlightened to exercise power with prudence, he replied that the remedy was not to take authority from the people but to cultivate the public knowledge that is needed to make wise decisions.[6] John Adams spoke of this urgency in foretelling ways. He was certain that democracy could not be preserved unless the people had broad general knowledge.[7] Our most serious community problems today are consistently left unresolved by an uninformed public.[8]

The knowledge that must be cultivated to make prudent decisions about the form of our habitation might be labeled broadly as *urban ecology*— the interactive processes between organisms, whether people, algae, the city, or surrounding environments. Three forms of knowledge are critical—the understanding of ecological forces that comes from close contact and long experience with a place, a working awareness of the principles of urban ecological science, and a public language of both of the above that is suitable for shared decision making.

Knowledge from experience of place is often called *native wisdom.* This knowledge is alive, like the woods or a folk dance. People possessing native wisdom develop an unusual knowledge about natural and cultural processes that is rooted in a particular place and people.[9] It is inseparable from "the multiple tasks of living well in a specific place over a long period of time." Native wisdom is the "union between knowledge, livelihood, and living."[10] It is grounded in observation, sensing, and an awareness of kinship with the surrounding world. Native wisdom is a profound understanding of a place that comes from being truly of that place. In the United States, we generally think of native people, the Amish subculture, family farmers, and fishermen as natively wise. Dependent for survival on an intimacy with soils, water,

Native wisdom that comes from close
contact and long experience with a place
can be mentored.

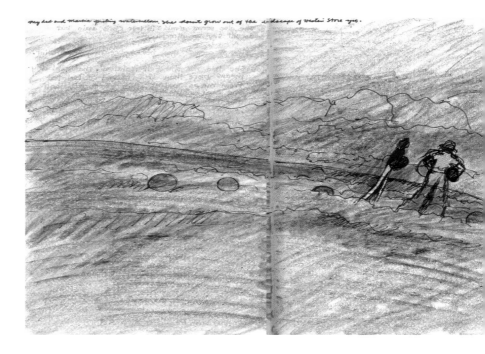

food webs, and the vagaries of weather, they develop both specialized and generalized knowledge of their localities. This understanding is driven by necessity and a sense of wonder rather than by a search for scientific knowledge.[11] Some scholars argue that although we are less directly dependent on ecological forces, "native wisdom is embedded in each person who strives every day for higher meaning in relationship to place."[12]

I personally believe, as David Orr has said, that most Americans have lost this wisdom and need to rediscover their urban ecological knowledge.[13] We are ignorant about the ecological processes and cultural nuances that underlie the places we live. In comparison to my cousin, Donald Hester, who has farmed all his life at Hester's Store, where we were raised, I remember almost nothing that is useful; he knows almost everything. I once knew more of the place, but I moved away forty years ago; the price of my mobility and independence is place illiteracy. For example, I recently was commiserating with Donald, who was complaining about the decline in North Carolina's quail population. I told him, "There can't be many quail because I haven't heard any calling all week." He looked at me with his forgiving look that belies his amazement at my stupidity and said, "But Randy, quail don't call this time of year." His rootedness has made him a repository of local knowledge not just about life cycles of birds but about most ecological processes. Similarly, people who live in a single urban neighborhood for their entire lives develop street smarts and intimacy with the natural and social nuances of their place. Most of us, however, have moved so often that we have lost our capacity to be natively wise. Further separated from natural processes by overly protective parents and technology, we must rediscover and recultivate local knowledge.

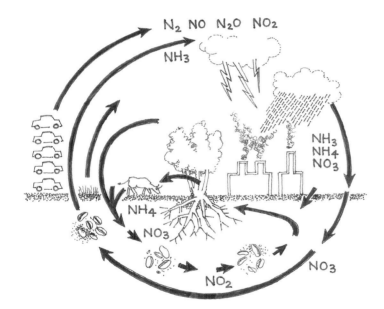

Urban ecological science

Public language

Another aspect of our reeducation is an understanding of the principles of urban ecological science. These principles are theoretical constructs that apply everywhere. In contrast to local knowledge, which grows from the grassroots, scientific principles are typically the domain of academic ecologists. They are developed through a rigorous search for knowledge, verified by experiment, and usually transferred through peer-reviewed papers and indoor classroom lectures. Fundamental ecological relationships have long been studied, but basic truths of ecology have not been, until recently, a central part of public education and mass culture. Most middle-age adult Americans never studied ecology in school. Although most of us adults are aware of environmental crises, we lack grounding in the fundamental principles of how ecological systems work. And those of us who are middle-age decision makers certainly do not have ecological truths at our intuitive fingertips; we learned math and science instead because of the cold war competition with Russia. So in most deliberations today, we have knee-jerk responses to ecological crises but little in the way of acculturated scientific judgment to guide us. Nitrogen, oxygen, and nutrient flows and the Allee and edge effects seem irrelevant. We recycle, but the idea of closed loops and waste as a resource is foreign to us. In many cases, faith in short-sighted science, technology, and experts undermined the ecological science that was available to us. When fundamentals of river hydrology, for example, conflict with engineering science, our generation almost always chooses engineering judgments.

Ecological principles that are related to cities are a slightly different matter. Until recently, natural ecologists paid little attention to the city; therefore, basic knowledge about the city as a natural ecosystem was typically unavailable. Some city makers have long tried to apply natural ecology findings to urban design (remember that Ian McHarg used Calhoun's rat studies to draw conclusions about people in central cities), but speculative cross-disciplinary efforts began in earnest only in the last three decades. As a result, few basic truths about urban ecology guide the theory of city design, much less the practice. For example, the need for moderate density, the urban counterpart of the Allee effect, was rediscovered only about twenty years ago. The relationship between health and nature was first medically tested a little over a decade ago. Even when new knowledge of urban ecology has been well tested, we are slow to accept it because new findings are often counter to powerful vested interests of science, professions, prior public investment, and public belief. But Robert Ryan has found encouraging evidence that the better we understand concepts, the more likely we are to support change in poor ecological practices.[14] This can be accomplished either by simplifying complex problems or by increasing the public capacity for complexity. Innovation diffusion suggests both may be successful strategies in creating the public language of ecological democracy.[15]

David Orr has shown that our ecological illiteracy stems from a number of forces. He notes that ecology requires broad thinking about how many things are connected to each other—"what is hitched to what." For scientists and the rest of us, this is nearly impossible in an age of specialization. Orr marvels that Rachel Carson wrote *The Silent Spring* because it required asking ecolate questions. Remember the lessons of connectedness? Relationships between chlorinated hydrocarbon pesticides and bird populations extended beyond conventional categories of inquiry. To discover the connections, Carson had to comprehend multiple, seemingly unrelated specialties—like farm practices, ornithology, and chemistry—of which scientists typically were ignorant.[16] They were blind to the relationships. Additionally, we frequently do not want to see the relationships because they unsettle accepted ways of living. In fact, Carson's own discovery about pesticides meant that the decline of birds was in large part due to widely practiced food production and our eating habits. "We have met the enemy and it is our ignorance," Pogo might have said. Webs of urban ecology lead back to our personal lifestyle choices, pointing fingers of unacknowledged responsibility at us. Urban ecology, then, is both incomprehensible and distasteful to us, further explaining our resistance to becoming ecologically literate. Wholeness of ecological thinking is likewise politically threatening, challenging every institution. Orr blames educators for their near exclusive emphasis on indoor education and city makers for the lack of natural places in cities, both contributors to ecological illiteracy.[17] For these reasons, we are unprepared to apply ecological principles to the creation of habitation.

Native Wisdom, Science, and the Language of Ecological Democracy

Some have suggested that native wisdom is more important than scientific principles,[18] but both are essential to impelling city form. Neither alone is complete. Thoreau described the fatal flaw in choosing one over the other. He compared the natively wise man—in his day, the locally wise were

Hands-on mentoring

Communicating science

Listening for values

considered unlearned—and the scientific man: "The knowledge of an un-learned man is living and luxuriant like a forest, but covered with mosses and lichens and for the most part inaccessible and going to waste; the knowledge of the man of science is like timber collected in yards for public works, which still supports a green sprout here and there, but even this is liable to dry rot."[19] Native wisdom is alive but inarticulate; scientific knowledge is useful but neutered and dead. Uncle Ima Kamalani was the rare person with both. He knew the water and soil of his Honolulu lotus farm personally by name and hand. He also understood the underlying hydrological principles so well that he could explain the ecology to others. And he freely shared both his na-tive and his scientific wisdom. Only in combination do native wisdom and science inform us with the public knowledge to make cities impelling.

In concert, native wisdom and principles of urban ecological science create a language of landscape that facilitates public discussion in a form that Jefferson envisioned.[20] This is a living vernacular language derived from an intimate experience of the nuances of specific places, made comprehensible by frameworks based on principles of interconnectivity and details of eco-logical science. In the past, we could not be good citizens without a language of democracy. Today we cannot be good citizens without a language of eco-logical democracy. The fifteen principles in this book provide the content of such a language regarding our habitation. But true citizenship needs to be informed not only by the biological ecology of place but also by the demo-cratic processes that we employ. Our language must include active and in-formed local participation that is far more respectful of and responsible to others than our self-serving process has been in the past. It must counter-balance the present language of exclusive individualism.[21] We must learn how to listen to and learn from one another. We must relearn how to par-ticipate, cooperate, and share values, just as we learn urban ecological aware-ness. Our language will then include old-fashioned civility, connectedness, newly minted public ecology, and civic environmentalism to create a re-sponsible, informed, strong democracy from the grass roots up.[22]

How Science Is Inhabited

One might logically ask what *inhabiting science* means. Couldn't this simply be called *urban ecological literacy?* Although it might be so labeled, I think that in designing the city we need to make both native wisdom and scientific principles parts of dwelling. Certainly dwelling is a requisite for native wisdom, but abstracted principles have more meaning when they too are integrated into everyday life. Inhabiting science is the act of making urban ecological principles a part of daily experience. Both consciously learned and subconsciously absorbed, these fundamentals become central to what we know and how we live. For many Americans, recycling has been incorporated into our awareness and daily lives. It is now second nature, not something we have to force ourselves to do or even go to much trouble to do. We do it because we know it is important and it is part of daily life. The goal of inhabiting science is that more complex and essential ecological processes will likewise inform how we design and dwell in our cities.

Learning about place-based ecology is straightforward. A stimulus, like watching a sunset or listening to a teacher, triggers either sensual experience or intellectual awareness, which in turn leads directly to pleasure or understanding, respectively. Then the process gets a bit more complicated because sensing and knowing are not neatly separate. Simply sensing often triggers greater awareness or knowing and intuitive understanding. And the more we know about a place or an ecological process, the more pleasure it gives us; the more pleasure we gain, the more attention we pay and learn. In addition, we retain more when the knowledge, even abstract principles, is aroused by both intellectual awareness and sensual experience simultaneously. This underlies hands-on learning and field experience versus classroom instruction.[23] Understanding—the goal of inhabiting science—may come from experiences that we are unconscious of or from focused, self-conscious instruction or from interactions between the two. Simplistically, we might say that native wisdom comes from unconscious experience and scientific knowledge comes from instruction. Although a fair generalization, it is almost never this simple. For example, my father, who was a locally wise farmer, certainly gained a large portion of his ecological knowledge from the direct experience of farming. Lessons he learned from eighty years of intimate dependence on the soil and weather at Hester's Store guided him. He contour plowed with an interior compass for precise elevation. His crop rows never flooded or broke, even in the most intense thunderstorms. His attention to erosion control made his land consistently productive. When I would cut a furrow divergent from the contour, he would poke fun saying that either the mule or I didn't have "it" in our bones. His implication was that he possessed the native wisdom for contour plowing as a matter of subconscious knowing. His

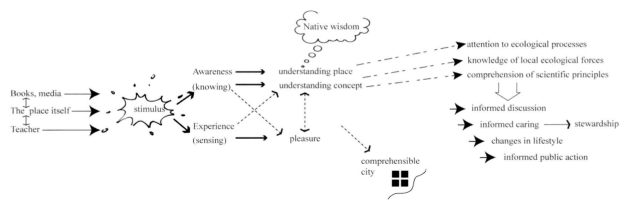

Both knowing and sensing are essential in developing an understanding of place and urban ecological science.

knowledge was derived largely from experience and classic local wisdom, but he, too, had received instruction from my grandfather, read about erosion control in *Progressive Farmer,* and surveyed crop acreages for the U.S. Department of Agriculture. The latter required special training in soil and watershed management and the use of transit, horizontal, and vertical angles in addition to the mathematics of plowing. Most native wisdom in the United States today is thus supplemented with instruction in the principles of practical ecology.

Simultaneous experience and instruction usually produce multiple outcomes—a greater appreciation for and attention to ecological processes, natural and urban; specific knowledge and wisdom about the local landscape and urban ecological forces; a working comprehension of scientific ecological principles; more informed discussion about local and regional policy, land use, and design; environment and community stewardship; changes in personal lifestyles; and more informed actions. These allow us to comprehend the city we inhabit, truly understand our place in it, and know how to shape its future meaningfully. This makes us more willing to change our lives to nourish ecological democracy.[24]

What We Need to Know

To those of us who are handicapped by urban ecological illiteracy (and that is most of us Americans), there seems to be an impossible amount to learn. In reality, what we need to know is aroused by our sense of wonder; we can learn first principles and then fill in the details as we dwell. As broad categories, the following provide a starting framework: the spatial and adjacency requirements for vital natural systems to function in the urban context; the basics of food production, nutrition, and health; plant and animal habitat needs, especially principles of conservation biology; the fifteen principles in this book for reforming the city; details of green materials and technologies of restoration; the maximum scale we can comprehend and plan; and processes of succession, metamorphosis, and change.

First, we must know what basic natural systems require to support the city. We might start with storm water and work backward to the watershed. As a public, we all must understand the amount of space that streams need to function healthfully, ebb, flow, carry nutrients and sediment, support aquatic flora and fauna, and flood. How does this system provide us with drinking water? How much do we want, and how much do we need? Who gets how much? How can our wastewater be appropriately cleaned? We need to understand the coefficient of run-off—how upstream development increases peak floods downstream, how destructive erosion can be slowed, where ground water is stored, and how permeable surfaces influence ground water and flooding. How do various land uses and practices impact water quality and quantity? We need to know the entirety of our watershed from headwaters to mouth. Yes, every one of us needs to know these things for an ecological democracy to flourish. Likewise, we should understand the sun and energy flows, the global impacts of the use of various energy sources, how the city can be formed to heat and cool itself naturally, and how global warming will change all of these. Similarly, we need to integrate nitrogen, oxygen, and carbon cycles into everyday experience. We should know nitrogen-fixing bacteria and earthworms like we know how to make change for a dollar and surf the Internet. In a cross-cultural study, people were asked what wild animals they most valued. At the top of the American list were large carnivores. The single most valued species among the Japanese sample was the earthworm. I was shocked by the "lowly" earthworm's status, but Japanese researchers assured me it was because the earthworm performs a vital function in creating soil. We need to truly comprehend these cycles, the various roles, and the environmental requirements of the forces that are vital to our lives.

Second, a basic knowledge of the web of food production, nutrition, and health is essential to public discussion of city design. Begin with the

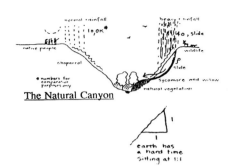

The Natural Canyon

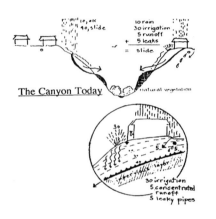

The Canyon Today

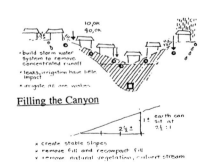

Filling the Canyon

Making complexity accessible

earthworm, nitrogen, oxygen, water, and carbon cycles. Add soil processes; the scale, crop rotation, diversity, and labor practices of farms; pesticides, fertilizers, and other growth stimulants; food processing, packaging, and transportation; and the elements of unique regional diets. Relate this to personal and community nutrition, health, and ultimately the number of people that the earth can support. At home, we need to know how much farmland to preserve for local food security. For many, the only prime agricultural land left in their regions is in backyards or on rooftops. How can this land be used effectively?

Third, to form healthier cities, we must apply concepts like trophic structure, limits of tolerance, and ecological pyramids. As one example that is related to pyramids, citizens need to know the singular value of wetland productivity to the food web and local economies. In the case of wetlands, this requires considerable reeducation because most of us in positions of power grew up thinking that wetlands were worthless swamps, a breeding ground of disease and pests. Beyond generational prejudices, we all need to understand conservation biology as it relates both to ecosystem and cultural diversity. Adequate core habitats, connecting corridors, and metapopulations are equally important to preserve indigenous cultures and wildlife.

Fourth, the fifteen principles described herein—from centeredness to pacing—translate ecological and democratic thinking into city form-making. They create a broad conceptual framework with practical applications. Some, like connectedness and particularness, are directly related to the hydrology, energy, nitrogen, and oxygen cycles. Others are more indirectly tied to ecological process. An example is the invisible relationship between density of urban residence and the preservation of wildlife habitat. Applied ecologist Bob Twiss argues that the most essential invisible connection is the link between transportation and land use. To be good citizens, we need to understand the concepts, the obvious and less obvious relationships, and the ways that these might be applied to reforming the city. These matters can no longer be the exclusive domain of professionals.

Fifth, we need a framework to make conserving, recycling, reusing, and auditing second nature to us. The details of city building are otherwise overwhelming. As lay people, we can't possibly know every green building material or the latest technology of reuse, but if we have an intellectual mechanism that scans the environment considering production impacts, closed loops, health risks, and long-term costs, we are likely to be able to ask the right question at the appropriate time: Is that wood certified sustainable? How does my city contribute to global warming? What was the health impact on the laborer who made that beautiful blue vinyl? What could be accomplished by reducing the width of every street by five feet? Could that reduce nonpoint-source pollution? Can wetlands really be restored? What is the total cost of a car, counting pollution and loss of community? Posing such questions strengthens an ecological democracy. Over time, the details may become second nature to us. We may start with a question that leads us to a better technical understanding of heat sinks. We incorporate that into our increasing local wisdom, learn more about strategic planting of urban grasslands and forests, and eventually change city design for cooling and cleansing.

Sixth, we need to comprehend fully that our ability to know is limited by scope and scale. Small-scale operations are less harmful to the world than large ones, but we are inclined by global economics to act on partial knowledge in making gigantic decisions far beyond our threshold of comprehension. These decisions produce second- and third-order effects that we cannot envision but that nonetheless destroy culture and the landscape.[25] Rob Thayer describes this with a metaphor: we can almost never understand because all we can see is the tip of the iceberg.[26] Wendell Berry argues that both our intelligence and responsibility are limited: "We are not smart enough or conscious enough or alert enough to work responsibly on a gigantic scale."[27]

Seventh, we need to comprehend change—geological, successional, decay, and metamorphosis. Change is fundamental to ecological systems. Change is difficult to comprehend and accept. It is disturbing. As a result, we want to freeze the world as it is. We must learn to discriminate about change to make changes that are essential to ecological democracy. And certainly, we need to comprehend change for the miraculous joys that metamorphosis presents us, the emergence of a wetwinged swallowtail from its decorated chrysalis or the loss of a tadpole's tail.

All of these forms of knowledge will help us make our lives and cities intelligible to us. They give us meaning, the capacity to participate, and possibly new native wisdom. It is vital that they become part of our experience and our education. But increased education can help only if it produces more wisdom.[28] Knowledge is the easy part. Wise action in reforming the city is what we ultimately seek.

Learning from the Urban Landscape

How one gets wisdom after accumulating knowledge is somewhat of a mystery to me. The ability to judge what is true, right, or the best course of action for one's community is a rare talent. Wisdom comes with experience, dwelling in a place over a long time, being especially attuned to and able to empathize with people and landscape, suffering, and having the capacity to separate nonsense from visionary insight. Wisdom requires knowledge and the capacity to process that knowledge through a special filter of goodness.

We get knowledge about dwelling, ecological processes, and city making from multiple sources. We learn conservation or slovenliness from our family and friends. We get urban ecological information from television and other media, textbooks, other books, and classroom instruction.[29] To gain the content for an ecological democracy to flourish will require singular changes in public education.[30] But other forces profoundly influence what we know about urban ecology. Where did we play as children? Did we have older mentors to provide role models for active engagement in discovering the world around us?[31] Supplemental activities—like good maps, neighborhood scavenger hunts, tours, camps, and environmental simulations—can instruct us as well.[32] One of my son's formative experiences was a day camp in which the children created their own ecological city, constitution, and governing body. This hands-on and integrated learning left lasting impressions.

Our primary interest, however, is how the physical environment instructs us. City designers create landscapes that, in turn, convey messages—intentional or unintentional. The landscape around us teaches. Michael Southworth put this to practice in Boston over two decades ago. He increased transparency to expose the processes that are going on in the city—processes of government, industry, ecology, and infrastructure—to make urbanity comprehensible. This he called the *educative city*. He said that if the interdependence of people and environment are made more explicit, the consequences of poor management are less likely to be overlooked: "Egregious mistakes could even be underscored. Solutions could be made known by exhibiting places where good environmental decisions have been made."[33] This is different than environmental education where a person instructs. The cityscape, in Southworth's designs, does the teaching itself.

Robin Moore and Herb Wong similarly created neighborhoods to reveal their ecologies in the commonplace landscapes of schoolyards and abandoned lots where processes of succession were readily apparent.[34] Artists Newton and Helen Harrison made ecological art that similarly exposed fragile ecosystems and endangered species. In recent years, this has been labeled *ecorevelatory design.*[35] Such city design seeks to both reveal and interpret cultural and ecological phenomena, processes, and relationships for the landscape to teach about itself.[36]

Three questions are central to this endeavor. First, do such landscapes add to our knowledge? Although there is little direct research about this, the answer appears to be yes but with limited impact.[37]

Second, do landscapes teach comparably to other forms of instruction, like reading books or going to camp? I don't think we know. It seems that a variety of means of urban ecological instruction are essential, among them early childhood exposure to nature, a mentor, and seminal books.[38] What can be read in books is inadequate by itself because, for many, concepts become meaningful only with firsthand experiences.[39] For childhood experience and mentorship, appropriate landscapes are a must.

Third, what makes a landscape appropriate for conveying urban ecological knowledge? Should the landscape be wild, romantically naturalistic, framed, aggressively interpreted, or deconstructed with its bowels exposed? There is no simple answer. Wild and naturalistic landscapes without any interpretive elaboration provide the rich environments needed for childhood experiences with a mentor. Such landscapes of earth, rock, greenery, water, and sky provide the equally important benefits of naturopathy, naturism, and naturalization discussed previously. Southworth cautioned that overly aggressive interpretation adds stress, increasing perceived density and thus undermining resilience. Quiet spaces, with no additional information, are as important as instruction, especially in the center of the city.[40] This suggests that in densifying neighborhoods, landscape revelation should be quiet, not anxiety provoking. This is true for neighborhoods and the everyday public landscape overall. Aggressively didactic landscape revelation should be situated in places where the public chooses to go, rather than must go, or in select public places where it serves its propaganda purposes most effectively.[41] Sparing propaganda is appropriate for a public that is rapidly losing its collective native wisdom. How this is designed is critical in the impelling city. Five forms of educative urban landscapes are most useful in nourishing an ecological democracy—discovery landscapes, cultivating landscapes, instructive landscapes, scientific landscapes, and argumentative landscapes.

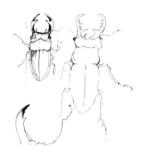

Direct discovery

Discovery Landscapes

Landscapes of discovery instruct when the participant seeks the lesson. Largely natural, utilitarian, or subtly manipulated, they are the least consciously revealed. I include four typologies of discovery landscapes—natural experience, transparent systems of pleasure, signifying features, and marks and indicators.

Relatively natural or even naturalistic landscapes invite discovery. These provide the "quiet" places for which Southworth called. If designed for legibility and exploration, they promote learning and provide the stress-reducing benefits of green nature. Learning is through personal discovery and mentoring. Terry Tempest Williams describes an example: "I find myself being mentored by the land once again, as two great blue herons fly over me. Their wings are slow, so slow that they remind me that, all around, energy is being conserved."[42] In this case, the wild landscape teaches the lesson of conserving energy. David Orr argues that in spite of more books about nature, ecoliteracy has diminished because there is less opportunity for the direct experience of nature. For him, the solution is "more urban parks, summer camps, greenbelts, wilderness areas, public seashores." He calls for dense, green cities with more trees and riverine open spaces.[43]

As people experience such places and understand their educational importance, they demand more places like them.[44] Thoreau urged this strategy. He realized that uninterpreted wild nature that is revealed only by discovery was by far the best teacher of ecological principles. In answering his own question of what made a city handsome, he concluded:

A river, with its waterfalls and meadows, a lake, a hill, a cliff or individual rocks, a forest, and ancient trees standing singly. Such things are beautiful; they have a high use which dollars and cents never represent. If the inhabitants of a town were wise, they would seek to preserve these things, though at a considerable expense; for such things educate far more than any hired teachers or preachers, or any at present recognized system of school education.[45]

To Thoreau and many scholars since, experience in relatively wild nature requires little artificial ecological revelation. In the design of the city, this provision of urban wilderness or even romantic nature is the single most important formula for conveying urban ecological wisdom. This reinforces the need for relatively wild nature that defines neighborhood boundaries no farther than a quarter mile from any household and that forms interconnected greenbelts that lead to a delimiting boundary within two miles of home. There may be ecorevelatory spots within these wildlands, but the education here comes primarily from sustained exploration.

In addition to natural landscapes, much can be discovered in manipulated but quietly transparent urban systems. I think again of the open-water diversions and rivers in Kyoto. A source of aesthetic pleasure, the water is directly yet gently educational.

Water is one of the easiest ways to reveal an ecosystem.[46] Water is a good choice educationally. An interconnected system, it reveals multiple fundamentals, like connectedness and particularness; has high value for discovery of plant and animal life; and invites participation. In Kyoto, the open waterways may be experienced by people who stroll along the Philosopher's Walk, may offer a child her first glimpse of a migratory bird, may surprise onlookers when an irrigation dike is opened to flood a rice field, may give lessons to children on biological diversity and water quality, and may allow other people to swim and fish. Vegetation, geology, and topography provide similar but generally less dramatic benefits.

The same is true for the built environment. Discovery through dwelling in neighborhoods that are designed by ecological principles is key. Living in a modestly dense community, with an active civic life, and with a center that can be walked to teaches ecological democracy by experience, pleasure, and reward. The liability in these transparent systems of pleasure is that we may only contemplate the surface. Complex aspects of water table, ground water, aquifer recharge, nonpoint source street contamination, and more interconnected built environment complexities like density and centeredness may remain undiscovered.

Another design strategy for discovery is to emphasize signifying features of the landscape. If the place is boggy, make it boggier. If the place has significant cuestas, dramatize the hard rock ridge by making gentle slopes gentler and abrupt cliffs more abrupt. If the landscape is merely flat, make its flatness a feature. Every site, even ones that at first seem plain, have particularness that can be instructive. The landscape feature and associated ecological phenomena chosen for emphasis should be relevant to the site and its region. It should be revealed honestly with little contrivance.[47] In the designs for Illinois homeplaces, Terry Harkness uses the very vocabulary of flatness

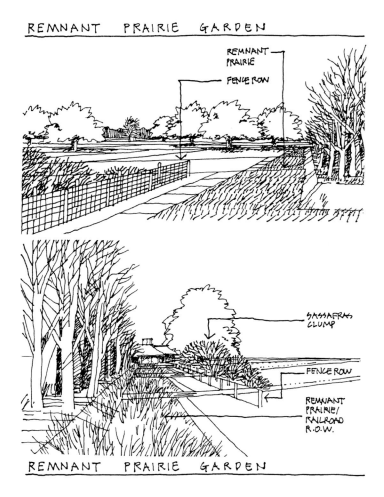

HORIZON GARDEN

HORIZON / DISTANCE / BACKGROUND

HORIZON FENCE

HORIZON GARDEN

Gardens unique to Illinois

Terry Harkness emphasizes the signifying features of Illinois landscapes—flatness, fence lines, and agricultural productivity—to invite discovery.

REMNANT PRAIRIE GARDEN

REMNANT PRAIRIE GARDEN

to advantage, emphasizing agricultural productivity, sparse fence and tree lines, and the horizon that the flatness provides. The result is both delight and an invitation to explore.[48] George Hargreaves's firm emphasizes landforms that draw attention to topography that would ordinarily be taken for granted. In urban environments, Linda Jewell similarly emphasizes landform, but for a different reason; she exaggerates the earth over parking structures because that is the location where below-ground concrete columns support the load of soil and trees. She creates a soothing sea of green with sculpted grass revealing the hidden underground structure. Nonaggressive revelations invite inquisitiveness and the joys of learning by further exploration.

Marks and indicators do the same and have the advantage of calling out more complex, unseen processes unobtrusively. A sign—"Flood Level February 1954"—high on the valley wall says a little and a lot.

Joe McBride marked a learning trail in Jackson Demonstration State Forest with four-inch numbers corresponding to a self-guided tour booklet. The small numbers can easily be ignored by the California hiker, can be puzzled over by the searching mind, or can instruct when connected to the booklet text.[49] Richard Hansen's watermarks at the Pueblo, Colorado, Nature Center does this with check dams, wetland pockets, and cottonwood zones to slow erosion, clean the water from parking lots, and restore lost vegetative habitats. His small granite markers with a bronze water-flow icon call attention to the restoration efforts they handsomely mark. They give order and make comprehensible invisible processes. They invite touch and intellectual inquiry, yet do not call out for attention. Subtle gestures delight.[50]

Mowers and markers

King Estate Park
Oakland, CA   Vegetation Zones Map

Goats mark Louise Mozingo's public park
in the fire-prone chaparral of Oakland,
California, creating fire breaks and calling
attention to the danger.

Inhabiting invisible process

Cultivating landscapes

Not all markers need to be numbers or posts. In Louise Mozingo's King Estates plan, goats grazing on overgrowth mark the landscape, drawing curious glances that inform the public about patterns of fire hazards in the chaparral landscape. In this case, the goats' diet reduces the fireload and creates firebreaks. A passerby may not know this immediately but is likely to ask.[51] All these landscapes invite learning, yet provide naturalistic benefits that serve many other urban ecological purposes. They are discovered. They delight, they distract, and they indirectly encourage density.

Cultivating Landscapes

Much of the loss of urban ecological literacy can be traced to urbanization and the decline of farming populations. In 1800, 94 percent of Americans lived in rural areas. Only 6 percent lived in cities with more than two thousand five hundred inhabitants. Even in small cities, farmland was part of everyday lives. Most survived only through knowledge of agricultural forces. By 1960, only 37 percent lived in rural areas; 63 percent lived in cities and had little access to farm enterprises. Just as wild nature teaches, so too does farming, and those with easy access to both are far more likely to learn competence and self-confidence regarding natural processes.[52] Farming requires an understanding of vital, complex, and invisible processes such as water, oxygen, nitrogen, and carbon cycles. In fact, most of what we need to know to design intelligent cities can be learned from farming. To teach urban ecological science, farms should be integrated into the everyday life of cities, not only to limit extent but to become part of dense neighborhoods, schoolyards, rooftops, balconies, and community gardens. For maximum return on the energy that is exerted in the pursuit of ecological knowledge, provide small, urban farms, and entice the public to grow food. Engage every child in her own food production. Learn from trial and error. Crops fail. They surprise. But the splendor of urban agriculture is that while we cultivate the land, the land cultivates our minds.

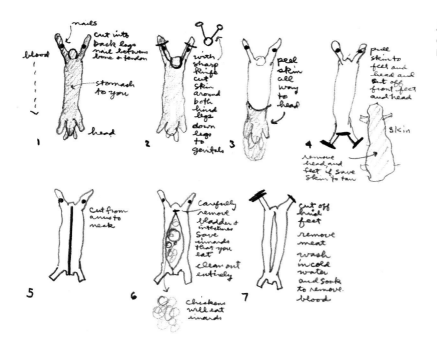

Almost all of what we need to know to design ecologically informed cities can be learned from farming.

Instructive Landscapes

The city is a museum—a repository of local history and of the ways that nature and culture have inspired or simply accommodated each other. Unfortunately, much of the most interesting and important kinds of knowledge of the city—especially the urban-ecology functions and principles—are hidden by blank concrete walls, segregated land uses, chain-link fences, and impenetrable, impervious paving. Frequently, they are guarded by armed patrols, surveillance cameras, and no-trespassing signs. Revealing the educative aspects of these urban ecological functions requires assertive design.

When he was incubating the educative city, Michael Southworth cited three hopeful examples—a program to take children to visit the parks in their city and region that they had never visited, an information center where a resident or visitor could go to learn about local attractions and events, and a school without walls that used the entire city as a classroom.[53] Each explored ways to learn more about natural and cultural processes. Each was program driven. Each was and is important. But it was his proposal for

Instructive urban landscapes

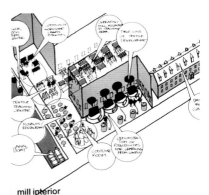

Revealing the hidden city

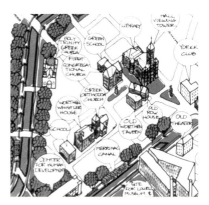

Walks that educate

transparency that provided ways to redesign the city so that a greater diversity of experience would be available to youth in their formative years. Hidden aspects of the city need to be revealed to prepare children to create cities where ecological democracy can flourish. These hidden aspects include city infrastructure (like water supply and circulation, storm water, sewer treatment, power, garbage, toxic-waste reuse, disposal, and transportation), work of all kinds (from faxing to animal slaughter, from food processing to manufacturing), government (and the relationships between public and private agencies and between the establishment and implementation of the public good), the natural processes in the city (how they function, have been compromised, and have been well managed), and proposals for the future of the city from individual buildings and open spaces to regional plans. One of Southworth's suggestions for revealing natural processes in the city was air-pollution monitors, like giant city clocks or thermometers, that turn black when critical thresholds of dangerous contaminants are superseded. Similar monitors could express vegetative and concrete influence on heat sinks, measure automobile emissions, and show noise levels.

Southworth revealed many of these hidden aspects of the city in the Lowell, Massachusetts, Discovery Network. Lowell had once been the innovative center of textile manufacturing but began a long decline after the Civil War when the textile mills moved south. By the time that he began working there, Lowell had lost its employment and its identity. Southworth had an idea to reverse the depressing trends. He proposed a network of walking trails along the canals of the city. From these trails, the past, present, and future of the city could be taught via historic buildings, the ruins of the textile industry, gas tanks, and other reminders of past employment, plus the canals themselves, which had been central to the textile industry. He called for restoring Francis Gate, the key site for water diversion and hydropower. He urged the creation of a museum to show how the textile operations two centuries before had worked. But the real discovery was to happen as one walked along the canals. The pieces of history revealed themselves to the pedestrian explorer. Even Southworth's proposal for boat tours on the canals and trips on the old trolley line were implemented after this Discovery Network was adopted as the first urban national park outside of Washington, DC. In the decades since Southworth's plan was implemented, Lowell has witnessed a difficult revitalization. It has gained new employment and identity. The educative city does far more than instruct.[54]

Lowell, Massachusetts, was redesigned as an educative city, and waterworks like Francis Gate were restored to provide water diversions with the hydropower that once was essential for textile manufacturing.

A number of educative design strategies are suggested by the above. Most urban infrastructure has central, nodal, and connecting facilities. Such facilities can be designed to encourage public access and provide hands-on information about water, sewer, power, and other processes. Tours to these places as part of school curricula and community events guarantee that the public receives instruction regarding vital services.

Another design strategy is to provide direct access to work by making peepholes into construction windows in blank walls and creating viewing areas at a safe distance for observing real work. These are especially critical today because children hardly ever have the opportunity to see the range of work that might serve as inspiration for career choices. This need not add more visual noise to already over stimulated urban environments but rather could provide layers that can be explored if desired. Similarly, if public monitors are placed in public places, they should focus on the most critical and particular ecological issues of the city; they should be a focal point, a landmark, even if they sometimes offer discouraging indicators of community well-being. These cautions are to prevent the city from being a machine for education.[55] For the most part, overt instruction should be a matter of choice—readily available and equally easily avoided. Transparency need not be dogmatic.

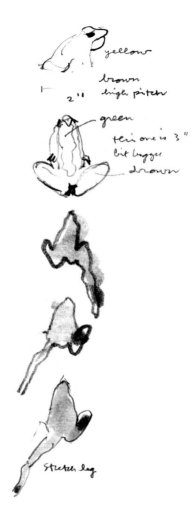

Landscapes for research

At every neighborhood center and other selected sites, mini libraries of public information should be provided about where and how urban ecological systems can be discovered and explored and how the public can access government processes and opportunities to participate and volunteer. This allows citizens to become interactive partners in every aspect of ecological democratic life.[56]

Scientific Landscapes

In most cities, some lands are set aside for research. These include experimental research plots for farms, industries, or universities; botanical gardens; arboreta; demonstration forests; weather stations; river, wetland, or prairie restoration projects; endangered-species habitats; and citizen science projects varying from water- and air-quality monitoring to breeding and migratory bird counts. In the home landscape, a windsock, rain gauge, or bulk atmospheric deposition sampler can be the basis of systematic scientific study.[57] These landscapes provide opportunities for people to learn careful observation, systematic research, data analysis, hypothesis testing, principles, and theory regarding the urban ecosystem. When these lands are nearby, the abstraction of science can be overcome by firsthand field experiences. Scientific landscapes can be inhabited in everyday life.

Monitoring local conditions makes scientific principles about the city comprehensible for its citizen scientists. These volunteers systematically gather scientific information for use in databanks or experiments organized by research institutions. Often they gather local data for grassroots activists and naturalists. In all cases, they inhabit science.

In Soquel Demonstration State Forest near San Jose, California, citizens and scientists are engaged in a whole range of such research—including studies of the impacts of woody debris on fish diversity, methods of erosion control on log roads, tree topping to create nest sites for birds of prey, horse logging, and aquatic-insect monitoring. The forest includes an outdoor school that is part of the county educational curriculum, a stewardship campus for adults, and facilities for traditional research and citizen science experiments. These facilities bring nearly every segment of the surrounding population to the forest for scientific study. The cumulative research gives citizens of the region an unusually complete understanding of the watershed. Public discussion about the management of the Soquel watershed has been raised to a particularly informed level. Forest practices, which often are hidden from public view, are consciously more visible.

Organized citizen research for public purposes is nothing new. It is well over a hundred years old, originating with volunteers who gathered weather data for national forecasting. In 1900, twenty-seven volunteers initiated the Audubon Christmas Bird Count, the longest continuous ornithological research project in our nation's history. Today over 52,000 volunteers participate. The Citizen Science program at Cornell University enlists twenty thousand volunteers in backyard bird counts. In other areas, volunteers engage in increasingly complex scientific work. Some band birds and butterflies; others do habitat analysis for quail populations and map wildlife corridors. Volunteers also monitor air and water quality in urban areas that are impacted by oil refineries. A 1993 survey identified over five hundred programs nationwide doing water-quality monitoring in rivers, lakes, wetlands, and wells.[58] The results of these projects are impressive in themselves, but the educational impact is central. Citizen volunteers not only make important contributions to science but also become advocates for better science, more informed decision making, and complex transjurisdictional thinking.[59]

For these reasons, there should be lands in every neighborhood that are designated for ongoing formal research and that are monitored by citizen scientists. At selected locations, stream-flow and water-quality gauges among others should become permanent interpretive installations. Scientific lands are appropriate places for assertive revelatory design, especially for phenomena that "are either too large, too small, too extensive, too complex, too fast, or too slow to be revealed by direct perceptual means."[60]

The outcomes of most city-design undertakings are uncertain. They should be viewed as experiments, and the public should be engaged over time in evaluating them.[61] Susan Galatowitsch argues that reforming the city is such a long-term endeavor that revelatory design should focus on process, not product. In her research on the restoration of sedge meadows at the Minnesota Landscape Arboretum, her design team divided the site into six blocks with different restoration treatments, which are visible to visitors from raised walkways. There are 120 poles that trace contour lines, marking one-foot intervals of topographic change and forming transects that are spaced thirty feet apart. These serve locational purposes for sampling stations and groundwater monitoring. By coloring the poles for contours differently, the design makes comprehensible the nuances of the topographic gradient and associated vegetation zonation.[62] The research site serves long-term experimental purposes as well as public-instruction goals. Research on residential density, habitat fragmentation, and biological diversity—which are among the most pressing issues but difficult to reveal—might be similarly conveyed to the public by ongoing experiments in urban neighborhoods.[63]

Argumentative Landscapes

Images of the civil rights movement—African Americans boycotting buses and marching, arms interlocked in solidarity, brutal police beatings, bombed churches, and the burials of innocents—provoked passionate public debate in the 1960s. When an invisible part of a culture forces itself into public view, there can be discomfort. Traditional power is threatened, and individual world orders are destabilized.

An early artwork by Helen and Newton Harrison, *Portable Fish Farm: Survival Piece #3,* challenged the supermarket mentality that divorces meat from the death of the animal. The art installation included a series of aquaria in which fish had grown to harvestable size. For the opening of the show, the Harrisons electrocuted, gutted, and served the fish to visitors. There was such an outcry against what sounded primitive, inhumane, or, at the least, distasteful that the British Parliament threatened to withdraw financial support for the British Art Council.[64] Whether the invisibility is a catfish, an oppressed minority group, or an abused ecosystem, its public visibility "challenges the authority of all dominant discourses." This is what ecorevelatory landscapes do that naturalistic landscapes do not.[65]

If there is grave injustice or an impending disaster, ecorevelation provides a wake-up call. It shocks. It provokes. To Patricia Phillips, "In its most promising manifestations, revelation invokes critical insight as a provocative agent."[66] The following design strategies are popular among designers who attempt to induce such aroused insight—exposed ruination, the visible "other," shifting, regional views, framed specimens, and unpleasant turbulence.

Usually, impending ecological disasters are not revealed in the landscape. They are hidden by design or complexity. But it is possible to memorialize ruination to heighten awareness to prevent similar calamity in the future. Aggressive revelation can focus attention on deadly contaminants hidden in soils, water, and air. Memorials concretize the previously uncomprehended.

The blast of methane burn-off from a towering smokestack serves as a daily reminder that a landfill must be carefully monitored. Rich Haag's remnant gas works in Seattle recall the poisoned site before and after remediation.

Quiet reminders of the prior lives of superfund sites alert Americans to past industrial dangers, but today's "high" technology industries poison the environment worldwide unchecked. Do we never learn, are these revelations too gentle or do argumentative landscapes have little effect? Enter the real provocateurs, like the Harrisons, whose in-your-face proposals raise issues of environmental disasters. Consider the artful crack in the Glen Canyon Dam created by Earth First! or Buster Simpson's River Rolaids, giant antacid tablets dumped into streams to absorb acid rain. Some of these installations are performance art; some become effective landscapes.[67] Their juxtaposition of beautiful and horrific, serene and gory, scream out the dangers of technology and industry.[68]

Environmental ruination that is caused by the cumulative impacts of the harmful habits of everyday life is a greater challenge. In these cases, industry is a culprit, but thoughtless consumers are coconspirators. It is difficult enough to effectively educate about distant corporate disasters, but when the public is largely to blame, education is doubly hard to swallow.[69] Such is the case regarding the impacts of the automobile. No single factor undermines environment and community more, but there has never been a public campaign to curb the car like there has been to stop cigarette smoking. "Why not?" asks artist Richard Register. His veggie car had its interior filled with soil and planted with flowers and vegetables and was parked at key locations, provoking interest and outrage in Berkeley. It stimulated debate about alternative transportation for over two decades. Similarly, the image of Stanley Marsh's *Cadillac Ranch,* a row of ten Cadillacs with their front bumpers buried in an old wheatfield outside Amarillo, Texas, evokes discomfort regarding our reliance on the car.

Just as society hides environmental unpleasantness such as clear cuts, nuclear plants, and junk yards, so too is human suffering kept out of sight and mind. For example, there is a homeless encampment in Osaka where thousands of day laborers live desperate lives in a modern nation. Most Japanese are unaware of the suffering because this district is secretly segregated. In most American cities, dispersal is the strategy for invisibility. In Mussolini's Italy, fake façades were required to keep poverty out of Hitler's view.

Argumentative Cadillacs

Sun setting

Earth rotating

Sun setting and earth rotating

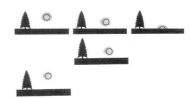

Combining science and experience

The suffering or different "other," however, is sometimes made visible in the landscape or art gallery by a conscious act. In *Urban Diaries: Improvisation in West Oakland, California,* Walter Hood proposes parks for the deviant and dispossessed who make up the urban ghetto, including parks for thieves and public houses for prostitution the size of bus stops along residential streets. Such strategies are tempered before construction, but the "other" has been made part of the discussion through gallery design.

Another strategy that is essential to wise comprehension is "shifting." Thoreau suggested standing on your head to see more completely.[70] He urged us to change our point of view, to shake ourselves out of habitual ways of thinking. He challenged us to see ourselves as sea slime.[71]

Paul Krapfel describes how our scientific understanding is diminished by habitual misperception. He starts by challenging the idea of the sun setting. Instead, one evening he saw the earth turning.[72] Designers may challenge similar long-held perceptions as did Cristo's running fence in Sonoma County, California. Krapfel, however, proposes other radical techniques that enable us to see through the eyes of other animals, to observe islands flow upstream, to watch edges dissolve into gradients.[73] He teaches us how to see clearly the misperceived ecological principle—the need for increased density—through a rolling Allee effect of foraging snow buntings.[74] Amid warnings not to obfuscate, not to confuse reality and fantasy, not to allow technology to blind us, Krapfel encourages individual responsibility for deeper knowledge in a world where the distinctions between reality, fantasy, myths, and science are murky at best.[75]

One of Krapfel's techniques makes the nearby comprehensible by contemplating the distant and vice versa. This is critical to placing oneself in one's region. He describes understanding distant and local patterns by observing the opposite: "Patterns fill the world with details. Different distances reveal different patterns. Right around me are small human-scale patterns; in the distance are larger patterns of rock layers, drainages, and vegetation. Usually I overlook these distant patterns; I lump them together into 'out there!' However, if I take the time I can interconnect near and distant patterns by shifting my focus back and forth between them. Nearby patterns give meaning to distant details which help reveal patterns too large to notice right around me."[76]

Designing places that afford a view of the region and neighborhood at the same time is essential to inhabiting science in a way that creates more re-

Impelling Form

silent cities.[77] Unseen patterns are made clear; invisible relationships are made comprehensible. Impacts of NIMBY actions may be seen in cumulative form. Ridgetop views and viewing towers prompt argumentative dialectics. They bring inquiring citizens "as close as possible to evolving processes" and enforce "multiple points of view."[78]

The framed specimen likewise provokes critical thinking. Chip Sullivan once did a series of gardens that were miniaturized to fit into Mason jars with tightly sealed lids. The jar gardens were all that remained of healthy landscapes that were long extinct.[79] An aged specimen tree surrounded by a fence conveys a similar message. Alan Sonfist's *Time Landscape,* a natural specimen surrounded by urbanity, evokes a sense of fragility, eliciting mental exploration. Its power is derived by the simplicity that framing endows.[80] Framing also allows easy comparison and contrast. It might be effectively used to create argumentative landscapes of fragmentation, island effects, and extinction.

A final discursive landscape strategy evokes unpleasant turbulence to point out the inherent change—often dramatic and unexpected, infrequently gentle and benign—that defines natural processes in the city.[81] Hurricanes, earthquakes, floods, and droughts create a dialogue that is unavailable to ecological designers. The uncertainty of their revelation gives them power. Matt Kondolf's description of "hungry" water dramatizes the effects of floods, dams, and sediment. He changes the discourse by his mere mention of the appetite of water.[82] Wise designers use disasters as an entree into comprehensive ecological action.

Specimen of extinction

LA96C

Perched high in the Santa Monica Mountains and surrounded by a wilderness that overlooked the City of Los Angeles were the remains of a military installation that from 1956 to 1968 was vital to the protection of the country. During the cold war, the most expensive military buildup ever undertaken shifted the balance of power back and forth between the United States and the Soviet Union. Both countries developed nuclear arsenals to attack each other and defensive systems to protect from such attacks. Soviet leader Nikita Krushchev threatened the United States, vowing that "History is on our side; we will bury you." This high mountain perch, with a military code name of LA96C, housed radar that scanned the skies around Los Angeles

Recalling the cold war

Restoring the tower

We will bury you

continuously to intercept Russian bombers that might attempt to destroy the city. Because of its height and 360-degree views, LA96C was ideal for radar. Nearby, in the San Fernando Valley, at LA96L, Nike missiles were kept at the ready. If the radar had ever detected a Russian invasion, missiles with a range of eighty-seven miles would have been launched from LA96L to demolish enemy planes before they could bomb the region.

To install the military base, the mountain tops were scalped of vegetation and flattened. Radar towers, computer-control buildings, barracks, and support facilities were built. The entire area was fenced and topped with concertina wire. A heavily guarded sentry post with a separately fenced corridor at the entry trapped intruders. The whole post was cordoned off from the outside world.

After the post was abandoned in 1968, classified elements were removed, and the remaining military facilities decayed. Native vegetation reinhabited the site. Control of the site transferred to the City of Los Angeles. A park replaced the military post. LA96C was renamed San Vicente Mountain Park, but in such a remote location, it was vandalized beyond recognition as a park. Only a hulking tower, fencing, and concrete bunkers survived. The city turned the site over to the Santa Monica Mountains Conservancy in the early 1990s and challenged it to maintain the open space.

By that time, the Conservancy was aggressively acquiring land to create the greenbelt around Los Angeles (see the chapter on Limited Extent). Priority acquisitions for wildlife habitat surrounded LA96C on three sides, making it an excellent location for a gateway to the urban wilderness and for a landscape full of discovery, instruction, and scientific study. The gateway could offer a new dimension to the urban-wilderness experience. By virtue of its history during the cold war, the destruction that the military had wrought on the mountain tops, and its extraordinary regional views, LA96C was a natural site for an argumentative landscape. It could teach many essential lessons through provocation. However, inhabiting science proved difficult.

First, the name—San Vicente Mountain Park versus LA96C—represented a struggle for dominance in the public discourse about the future of the park. The more they thought about it, the more central the military era seemed to Joe Edmiston, the executive director of the Santa Monica Mountains Conservancy, and to the designers. They preferred the name LA96C. At the outset, almost everyone else involved, including Edmiston's staff and the public, preferred San Vicente Mountain Park. Naming the park for a mountain that had been largely reduced to conglomerate fill by the military struck some as a romanticized fantasy, but most people who were involved wished to remove all traces of the military post and to naturalize the site. The neighbors wanted no development because they used the area for hiking and nature observation. They also wished to exclude broader public use, particularly minorities and teenagers, whom they blamed for previous vandalism.[83] Some hoped to remove all traces of the unsightly military structures; they considered them dangerous eyesores. Others erroneously argued that the fenced site blocked wildlife movement. For all these forces, the name San Vicente Mountain Park was a rallying cry to guide the design of a naturalistic park.

After the designers researched the history of the military installation, more people were attracted to the idea of retaining some reminders of that era. The history was fascinating, awful, personal, and paranoid. For example, radar structures and buildings at LA96C had not been camouflaged olive drab. Rather, they had been painted dazzling pastels and pale primaries, the colors of Los Angeles suburban homes and California pottery that were in vogue at the time. There was no need for camouflage because the Soviet bombs had primary targets in mind. Had the bombers advanced within eyesight of LA96C, Los Angeles would have already been destroyed. The isolated site was a lonely military assignment for anyone who expected to be living the sexy life that Hollywood projected to most Americans. A former

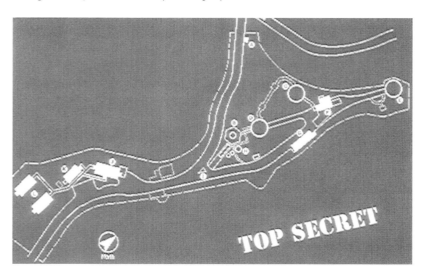

Military plans and interviews with personnel who once were stationed at LA96C revealed that life there was confined and fearful, which the design team conveyed in the new park.

The military layout was reconstructed both to provoke remembrance of the cold war and to create wildlife habitat.

Launch from LA96L

commander remembered that men felt like they were zoo animals who were locked inside the fences while abundant wildlife came to stare at them. Rattlesnakes, however, occupied the barracks buildings as if they were their home. Maybe they were. The public participants in the design process were intrigued with the stories and the details of the plan, especially the photographs and drawings of the military structures. The public began to favor the name LA96C, but today the park still has two names, a soothing naturalistic one and an argumentative historic one.

This division continued throughout the design process. Although the remains of the original military base accommodated all the anticipated gate-

Impelling Form

way park needs, powerful neighbors objected. The original sentry post, which had lost its roof and gates with time, could easily become the information center and gateway to urban wildlands. The concrete foundations where the barracks, latrine, and mess hall once stood could be used for the proposed ranger residence, public restrooms, and picnic structures. Walkways in abrupt geometries that connected the various radar towers could be reused. The one remaining alternate battery acquisition radar tower, although damaged, could be restored to give visitors a regional view that once was used to monitor the skies for enemy planes. By siting new structures chronologically, the military era could be revealed, providing a free history lesson. But neighbors wanted the military memory erased. Some wanted more nature. Some were skeptical of the safety of the historic fragments. As the design progressed, most acknowledged the good fit between old and new functions. Community and agency support for the military layout grew. However, the tower remained controversial. The design team (especially Bob Graves and his consultants) was convinced of the extraordinary educational value of the views from the tower. From this highest perch, almost the entire history of the development of Los Angeles could be comprehended, but the tower was dangerous and inaccessible. The designers developed multiple alternatives for repairing and making the tower accessible in a cost-effective manner. Eventually, neighbors relented, but they were adamant about the color. They wanted camouflaged colors that would blend the tower into the surroundings. One designer held out for a slightly gaudy pastel, one of the original colors of the military installation. No one else agreed.

The view of LA96C is the same for a mountain lion today as it was for a spy fifty years ago.

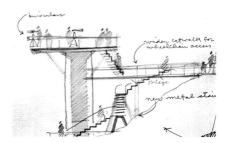

Tower concept

By using raw fencing to surround the park, the historical sense of military confinement is experienced—but with a new purpose as a reversed zoo in which the viewers are caged.

Although many residents wanted to remove the tower, it is the social center of the new park.

The color scheme that was adopted is a light sand, camouflaged but not drab. The interior cylinder of the tower is an intense cobalt blue.

The renovated tower provides breathtaking views, both pleasant and provocative. There is no didactic interpretation for anyone who simply wants to enjoy the view. For the inquisitive, a booklet titled *Restricted Use: Educational Operating Manual for LA96C* provides an abundance of aggressive and thought-provoking viewpoints about details of the cold war technology and its cost (the money to build LA96C alone could have created ten versions of the Parque Natural that is discussed in the chapter on Naturalness), the impacts of William Mulholland's water-diversion and freeway system on regional development, and the precise acreages that are needed to sustain native species. Site interpretation consists of signs based on military-era instructions that were posted around the military base. These offered explicit directions for how to operate equipment and what to do in case of attack. New signs explain precisely how the cold war proceeded and how Nike missiles were operated. They provide a sense of the military life at LA96C, including such details as the cactus gardens that the soldiers created. The entry signs offer contradictory messages of welcome in the biggest letters and prohibited entry in the subtext.

Each site decision was similarly decided through public discussions. The scalped mountaintops, which had been cleared for the military installa-

The tower provides great views to downtown Los Angeles, the San Fernando Valley, wildlife, and the regional ecosystem. It also is a backdrop for family photographs.

Interpretive signs are located where military instructions were necessary in case of attack. Today they explain the Nike missile systems and ecological requirements of locally cherished wildlife.

tion, remained, although a few people wanted to soften their abrupt angles. Participants concluded that revegetating with native plants would soon obscure most of the damage done by grading anyway. One slope, graded for a military road, remains unstable and suitable for instruction.

Fencing provoked similar discussions. Military enthusiasts and most of the design team wanted to restore the fencing that existed at LA96C. Along with the main tower, guard house, water tanks, and rigid concrete paths, intimidating ten-foot fencing with razor wire atop could evoke the sense of brutal enclosure—the zoolike isolation and lonely paranoia that the commander described—that typified these cold war military posts and the fear that debilitated America for over a decade. In Los Angeles and most major American cities, the cold war defined a generation, contributed to suburban decentralization in an effort to disperse primary targets, and focused education on narrow scientific disciplines, all forces that now must be reformed to create an ecological democracy. The designers felt that the lessons from this era should be maximized. The razor-topped fencing was far too unparklike for most people. It was unacceptable. Public agreement excluded concertina wire except in one location, and new fencing could not exceed six feet. At Nike sites, the entry enclosed a holding pen with ten-foot fences overlooked by armed guards where anyone who entered illegally could have been shot. Even as construction was underway, the Conservancy ordered the height of fencing on one side of the entry pen reduced to four feet for a scenic view. This compromised the confined feeling that visitors felt when entering the military holding pen.

The evaluations suggest that visitors are struck by the military history in spite of these compromises. The military past is primary. One former commander said it felt more like the military than when he was there. Teachers who have brought school children tout the educative value of the site. How much argumentative landscape is enough? Should the damage to the topography have been highlighted? Should the fencing have included razor wire? Or are such questions irrelevant to the public and of interest to only elite professionals?

Interpreting the military can be especially contentious. In this case, the public reached an easier consensus about assertively exposing regional growth patterns, threats to wildlife, habitat fragmentation, and island effects. Participants especially liked the metaphor of cold war personnel being in a zoo for the wild animals that surrounded them. Similarly, the revelatory interpretation about the effects of the unpaved part of Mulholland Drive along the ridge top and through key wildlife corridors was welcomed. This road is the largest visibly interpretive mark in the landscape, running over seven miles through otherwise native vegetation. It is powerfully conveyed in contrast with the surrounding landscape.

The public debate regarding the design of LA96C and subsequent evaluations inform strategies for inhabiting science. Exit surveys conclude that LA96C makes the effects of military history clear and that the tower view makes legible a region that is incomprehensible to most residents. Information at LA96C informs decision making about growth management and the multicounty greenbelt. How it ranks compared to other techniques for increasing debate about residential density, habitat fragmentation, and the greenbelt is less clear.

Educational experts think that the argumentative landscape has limited value compared to landscapes of discovery, cultivation, instruction, and science. While they agree that a variety of educational landscapes are essential for urban ecological literacy, they insist that natural and naturalistic places to discover with mentors near home should be the top priority in Los Angeles.

Recultivating native wisdom, learning principles of urban ecological design, and gaining the language and skills to work together are essential for creating cities where ecological democracy can flourish. We must consciously educate ourselves through all available channels and modify lifestyles and aspirations that render us illiterate. The landscape itself is a primary teacher in this arena. Urban wilderness and small agricultural endeavors in each neighborhood can cultivate local and scientific knowledge. Well-designed neighborhoods with centers, natural edges, and transit-friendly densities likewise teach essential lessons. These actions contribute to making the city comprehensible.

We know fairly well how to relearn the wisdom and gain the knowledge of urban ecology. We are beginning to understand some of what we must know—the natural systems in the city, food webs, plant and animal communities, conservation biology, the levels of density and centeredness that create stronger walking communities, the way to close loops, and realizing our limits. We can see that greater awareness of these will allow us to read and comprehend our habitation. We know that ecological science must be engaging, joyful, and integrated into everyday life for it to impel us. But we are just beginning to know the actions that are most essential to reinhabit science.

Reciprocal Stewardship

Whenever I run into friends in Haleiwa since Uncle Ima Kamalani died, the conversation always includes him. People remember him as a steward of the land that he owned and of the people who lived around him on the north shore of Oahu. Most do not use the word *stewardship* to describe him but instead say things like, "He sure knew how to take care of the land." That reminds me of his concern that the federal regulations protecting wetlands might be relaxed. Uncle Ima was certain that if the wetlands were developed, the whole north shore would soon have no drinking water or aquaculture. I never understood how he knew the details of both the local hydrogeology and the ongoing wetlands debate in Washington. I never saw him read a newspaper. But he knew aquifers like intimate friends, and he had made his community intimate friends of aquifers. They collectively worked to protect the aquifer-recharge areas.

Others remember how he would cook for everyone in his neighborhood, put people up when they were homeless, or help with community improvements: "Uncle Ima built the harbor, you know—worked on it for years." I then recall how he instructed us in making the long-range plan for Haleiwa. Uncle Ima was responsible for caring for the community, transmitting knowledge of the past, keeping the present in good working condition with his own hands, and watchfully supervising the future. He intuitively grasped the ultimate value of centeredness, sacredness, limited extent, and other aspects of a good city. And he understood they didn't just happen. He was diligent. He sacrificed for them over a long time. Someone else remembers him: "Ima knew how a community works, and it only works if we tend to it and each other. He really liked taking care of us."

Like other stewards, Uncle Ima's informed caring, which was grounded in an intimate knowledge of and love for his cultural and biological landscape, led him to take active responsibility for the people and the place around him. This is a logical outcome of naturalness and inhabiting science. Comprehending the interconnectedness of people and place spurs one to voluntary action far beyond narrowly defined self-interest. Community caring begets civic responsibility.

Stewardship improves the health of the participant, the community, and the larger urban ecology through an iterative process of reciprocity.

Stewarding and Stewarded

We might define *stewardship* today as actions taken to maintain, restore, and improve one's community, the landscape, and larger ecosystems. Informed by local wisdom and urban ecological principles, these actions are motivated by a sense of caring and civic responsibility. Individuals and groups on public or private lands may undertake acts to help other people and the environment. These may be voluntary or supported by legislation. Although it attends to the broader public interest, stewardship generally provides individual rewards of security, new experiences, responsiveness, and recognition. This explains why acts of stewardship, which seem on the surface to require personal sacrifice, are so impelling to Americans. The rewards of stewardship are great to the community, the landscape, and the individual. Accounts of stewardship activities—building houses through Habitat for Humanity, improving local schools through parent and teacher associations or 4-H projects, cleaning up despoiled beaches, and removing invasive plants to create wildlife habitat—make it difficult to assess who reaps the greatest benefits.[1] Although much of what they do is drudgery, stewards report being fulfilled just as much as the people, cities, and ecosystems they assist.

Recognizing these entwined mutual benefits, researchers recommend that at-risk and emotionally disturbed youth join ecological and human restoration programs. They argue that urban sites should be restored not for great improvement in biological diversity but rather for human health benefits.[2] Whether intentional or unconscious, stewardship programs result in improvements to the health of the participants, the community, and the larger urban ecology.[3]

Naive Stewardship Meets Freedom to Withdraw from Civic Life

Traditionally, a steward supervised the day-to-day operations of farm properties for a frequently absent landlord. The steward directed tenant laborers. A successful steward took good enough care of the laborers and the land to produce a profitable surplus. If continuously successful, the steward might receive favor from the landlord. This required constant presence in the landscape, considerable knowledge of natural processes and farm production, and attention to the health of workers and soil. The steward had fiduciary responsibility for the landlord's interests to keep the farm in good condition. He was both custodian and supervisor, a vital member of the farm society.[4] This resulted in iterative cycles of conservation and production, largely a closed loop of payoffs and penalties for the land, the laborers, the steward, and the landlord. Jefferson envisioned that this system would work even better for yeomen farmers.

By the time that I was growing up in Roxboro, North Carolina, where rolling hills and erosion created marginally profitable farms, stewardship was used primarily to describe the care that a small-farm owner afforded his land. A good steward husbanded every aspect of the family and property to make a living. Small contributions accrued to the overall health of streams, wildlife, and community. This was most notable in erosion control through contour plowing, strip cropping, and riparian buffers. My family took this seriously. Land was our servant, but we had to serve it in turn. Land was also a collective organism of workers, crops, fish, quail, turkey, earthworms, cows, chickens, foxes, and hawks. We represented the yeoman land stewards that Jefferson envisioned. Such naive stewardship, like primitive painting, is appealing because of the simple goodness it portrays. It depended and depends on a limited scale of farming and property ownership, rootedness in place, a basic understanding of land ecology, a balanced commitment to

Personal stewardship

Community stewardship

Hands-on stewardship

community and self, and modest monetary ambitions. This voluntary ethic worked for my father because he ascribed to these principles.

I was five years old when Aldo Leopold described stewardship in *A Sand County Almanac.* My father never read Leopold's book, but he and I debated the ideas starting in 1964 when I first read it and continuing even after his death. We still argue about the ideas. My father's grave marker commands, "Steward the Land."

Leopold stated one prevailing idea of stewardship: "That land is a community is the basic concept of ecology, but that land is to be loved and respected is an extension of ethics. That land yields a cultural harvest is a fact long known, but latterly often forgotten."[5] To Leopold, a land ethic required individual responsibility for the land's health. Humankind was not separate from the land but a plain member, a citizen of the community of land—all its plants, animals, soils, and water.[6] Dad agreed. He particularly liked the imagery of the latter. But he was skeptical of two of Leopold's ideas. Leopold argued that "land conservation based solely on economic self-interest" was and "is hopelessly lopsided." Dad believed that only stewardship and hard work had freed us from poverty and the land from ruin. Dad also disbelieved Leopold's argument that land not be considered property as women and slaves had been and land still is.[7] He had a violent reaction to this part because ownership of land shaped his personal identity and power, and he was racist enough to dislike the idea of emancipation, especially of his homeplace.

Recounting the changes that had freed women and slaves, Leopold foresaw the liberation of land as an "evolutionary possibility and an ecological necessity." He was willing to restrict private property rights as part of the struggle for survival.[8] The grand evolution that he foresaw—and that my father resisted—never materialized. There is little balance between private privileges and civic obligations in land ownership. In the United States, private-property rights rule. Today American landowners benefit from unfettered freedom compared to most other developed countries. In spite of Leopold's vision, land-use ethics are governed by short-term economic self-interest.[9] Land is less a community now than it was when Leopold voiced his ethic. Today land is above all else real estate.

The supremacy of private-property rights underlies privatization in every aspect of public life. These privileges facilitate the amassing of dangerously large amounts of capital in the hands of a few to do with as they will in the free market, regardless of the effects on what Leopold called the community of land. This, in turn, allows the upper echelons of American society who have accumulated the wealth to secede "from the civic life of their communities."[10] Declines in every public arena—education, transportation, and law enforcement—result, with some civic endeavors receiving only half the funding they did twenty-five years ago. A simultaneous rise in the quality of the private environment can be seen in dream homes and cars, private schools, gated communities, private entertainment centers, and private parks.[11] Although concentrated capital benefits the few at great expense to most of us, many genuine stewards support privatization because private property is so intertwined with individual freedom in American mythology. But this is not the sole deterrent to stewardship.

Ecological Necessity and Voluntary Stewardship

The unsuspecting stewardship that Thomas Jefferson imagined and that my father practiced does not serve today's circumstances. Dismissed as worse than naive, it is viewed as unsophisticated and childish. Some suggest it is time to abandon the "repetition of hackneyed platitudes about stewardship."[12] However, the staying power of the hackneyed platitudes underlie the value of stewardship. Like neighborhood and sense of community, stewardship continues to be offered up—sometimes naively, sometimes brilliantly—to solve our society's most vexing problems. The President's Council on Sustainability, for example, prescribed stewardship to make all of us, from individuals to corporations, take full responsibility for long-term consequences of waste, soil erosion, and urban sprawl and to conserve energy, limited natural resources, and farmland—a mind-boggling array of difficult issues.[13] We expect so much because stewardship addresses two fundamental issues. First, stewarding what Leopold called the "community" of land is now more than ever before an "ecological necessity." Second, voluntary actions, such as stewardship, are deeply ingrained in American visions of democracy and free will. The fact that we have *chosen* poor stewardship means we may *choose* better. Just as the core problem may lie in democracy, so too may the core solution. Creative solutions will emerge as ecological necessity becomes precisely understood and as freedom, the privileges of property, and legal controls are disentangled.

Consider the entanglements. The issue of private-property privileges has been misconstrued. The problem is not private lands. Public lands fare

Engagement

Spatial problem solving

little better because no one has assumed responsibility for the secondary side effects of short-term actions.[14] Both private ownership and the public commons can serve ecological democracy if the external costs of personal profit are borne by the profiteer.[15] The ecological tragedy for both the small, private property and the public commons occurs when Leopold's "community" of land is commodified by impersonal scale, placelessness, inattention to native wisdom, a lack of an agreed-on ethic governing community and self, and greed. When people are unfulfilled in their society, this is exacerbated.

Another entanglement surrounds the largely voluntary nature of stewardship, which often is used as an argument to reduce legislated controls on everything from air pollution to city design. Stewardship is no cure all. Powerful regulation is essential for an ecological democracy to flourish. Public support to encourage voluntary actions is likewise essential.

When presented choices, adequate information for evaluating, and a truly democratic forum in which to consider those choices, every local community with which I have worked has balanced the privileges of individuals with the needs of community. Some have been dominated by vested interests, some by community visionaries. Most have resulted in acts of stewardship that arise from shared values. This has been most apparent where there are small-property owners, long-term rootedness, collective local wisdom, a strong sense of community that acknowledges the importance of individuals, and a lack of unhealthy status seeking. However, these efforts would have been more successful and easier to sustain if there had been greater commitment to agreed-on civic obligations and less emphasis on private privileges. Compassion for both individuals and community would have also helped. Stewardship can be viewed as a thoughtful partnership ethic in which equal standing is respectfully acknowledged between humanity and nonhuman nature, between various people (women, youth, and the poor are not to be paternalized but acknowledged for the contributions they make), between individuals and community, and between regulations and voluntary actions.[16] In this sense, stewardship is a new ethic of caring action by various parties—from government to business and individuals—for local communities and ecosystems with a long-range goal of resilience.[17]

Many Places at the Table

We have become more self-conscious about stewardship. Appropriately labeled neostewardship diverges significantly from traditional stewardship. For most people, this is no longer a reflexive action to escape poverty or nourish neighbors. There are multiple new motivations. Today some become stewards to improve their neighborhoods. For the educated middle-class and disempowered youth, stewardship provides a means to do something personally about both global and local crises. Some pursue stewardship through lobbying for land-use reform or involvement in local planning efforts. To others, stewardship is a deliberate strategy to recruit workers for ecological conservation and urban-restoration projects, to replace agency staff after government layoffs, or to supplement funding through membership or estate donations. The latter have led to institutionalized stewardship among government, business, and nongovernmental organizations. Many are efforts to decentralize impersonal governmental services. Some are based on the belief that voluntary organizations can provide services better than government.[18]

Place inspiration

To counter the decline in local knowledge caused by placelessness and technology, many programs teach lost skills and build a constituency for public place. By learning the processes of locality from which they have become divorced and the skills to take positive action, participants are likely to volunteer to take care of their community and larger ecosystems.[19] Underlying these new efforts is the sense that modern, freedom-dominated, specialized people have become so independent of their localities that they suffer environmental anomie and do not actually know how to steward the ecosystem or public life in their community. Scientific understanding and shared experiences reunite people with other people in their community and the ecosystem within which they dwell.

Learning about place

Voluntary government

Every community-design process offers opportunities to reassociate people with locality and to engender stewardship. For many years, colleagues and I worked to create a design approach to maximize these benefits. The process consists of twelve interactive steps that develop place knowing, place understanding, place caring, and then action. It begins by listening to people and place.[20] Listening and setting goals increase participants' knowledge of their community. Making a comprehensive inventory, mapping, and introducing the community to itself expand knowledge and understanding of

This participatory process—in theoretical linearity and practical iteration—engenders community knowing, understanding, caring, and stewardship.

1 LISTENING
Place Knowing

2 SETTING GOALS
Place Knowing

3 MAPPING & INVENTORY
Place Knowing
Place Understanding

4 INTRODUCING THE COMMUNITY TO ITSELF
Place Knowing
Place Understanding

5 GETTING A GESTALT
Deep Place Understanding
Place Caring

6 DRAWING ANTICIPATED ACTIVITY SETTINGS
Deep Place Understanding

7 IDIOSYNCRASIES INSPIRE FORM
Deep Place Understanding

8 DEVELOPING A CONCEPTUAL YARDSTICK
Deep Place Understanding

9 SPECTRUM OF PLANS
Deep Place Understanding
Place Caring

10 EVALUATING COSTS & BENEFITS
Place Caring

11 TRANSFERRING RESPONSIBILITY
Place Caring
Hands-on stewardship

12 EVALUATION AFTER CONSTRUCTION
Deep Place Understanding

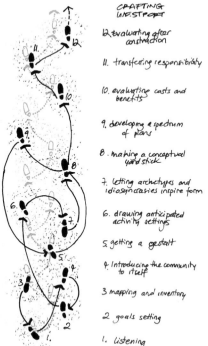

CRAFTING INVESTMENT

12 evaluating after construction

11. transferring responsibility

10. evaluating costs and benefits

9. developing a spectrum of plans

8. making a conceptual yard stick

7. letting archetypes and idiosyncrasies inspire form

6. drawing anticipated activity settings

5 getting a gestalt

4. Introducing the community to itself

3 mapping and inventory

2 goals setting

1. listening

Practical iteration

urban ecology. Getting a gestalt and making a spectrum of plans develop understanding and a sense of caring. Visualizing anticipated activity settings, seeing how local idiosyncrasies inspire form, and developing conceptual measures for comparison deepen understanding. Evaluating costs and benefits and transferring responsibility heighten citizen caring. This requires stewards to carry projects to successful conclusions. No city-design project is complete until a group is formalized to steward the place.[21]

This process nurtures stewardship. It does this by creating the forum for the participants and designers to learn from each other and the landscape. It is respectful of multiple points of view. It requires reaching out to nonparticipants who are critical to good stewardship—those with vested interests, the disenfranchised, those most directly affected by the project, leaders who are essential for funding or legislation, those with native wisdom or scientific information, those who are visionary without an axe to grind, and those who might volunteer for specific tasks to care for the project. These are vital participants, even if they might be reluctant at first. The process actively engages citizens in every step of city design. This includes studying the landscape firsthand. Residents can undertake tasks like analyzing ecological factors, behavior mapping, developing concepts, and making spatial layouts. They are more likely to take responsibility for a place if they have been involved in the totality of analysis and decision making.

Some designers argue that citizens are capable of setting goals and stating their wants but that the technical analysis and form making should be left to professionals. This is nonsense. Such exclusionary professionalism undermines the most impelling aspects of ecological democracy. To maximize stewardship, the design of every part of the city should provide opportunities for meaningful citizen involvement. There should be a place at the table for everyone to participate. This requires a diversity of table settings.

Making Places for Effective Stewardship

There needs to be a wide range of settings for people to engage in stewardship activities—in one's yard, in neighborhoods, on private farmland, in public wildlands, throughout a region, and in international flyways. Variety facilitates stewards of all persuasions and abilities.

Consider successful stewardship efforts from small to large scale. Most begin at home. The Grace Marchant Garden in San Francisco illustrates. In 1949, Marchant retired to Filbert and Napier Lane. Outside her window was a walkway. It had degenerated into a trash dump that was devoid of life. It discouraged neighborliness. Marchant spent the next thirty-three years cultivating a garden from this wasteland, engaging neighbors in her effort, and restoring wildlife habitat and beauty. She created a neighborhood group that continues to steward the place, celebrating her gift to the community long after her death. The garden is a magical setting that impels by evoking the joys of city living.[22]

In Eureka, California, wasted space was used for different purposes with similar stewardship outcomes. As Hmong refugees resettled to the United States after the Vietnam War, most had no access to farmland, which had been central to their seminomadic life in Laos. After bloodshed, refugee camps, and disquieting moves to America, over a thousand Hmong settled in Eureka. They had access to rivers, hunting, and fishing but no farmland. Deborah Giraud, a farm adviser for the University of California Cooperative Extension Service, created a garden partnership program, matching Hmong families with property owners in town who had underused backyards. These shared gardens allow Hmong to rekindle lost cultural practices and revitalize sterile land. Property owners in turn gain by giving; they often receive vegetables. Most important, they know that they are easing a difficult transition for the Hmong. In this case, the land, the Hmong, and the property owners nourish and are nourished by the program.[23]

Community gardens produce similar benefits in many American cities. Gardeners gain knowledge of soils, sun, and pests, as well as new friends and food. Derelict land gets needed attention. The nation's poorest, most disenfranchised communities take power by stewarding local community gardens.[24]

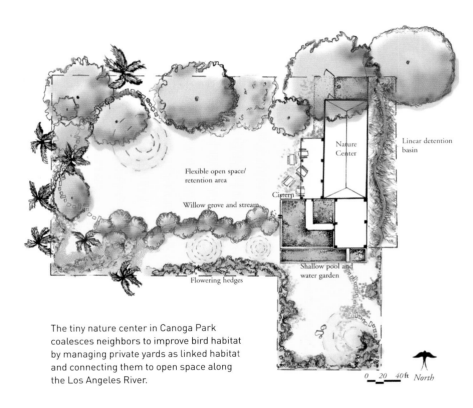

Connection to river

Neighborhood bird habitat

The tiny nature center in Canoga Park coalesces neighbors to improve bird habitat by managing private yards as linked habitat and connecting them to open space along the Los Angeles River.

In an institutionalized effort, the National Wildlife Federation Backyard Certification Program encourages homeowners to create wildlife habitats on their small properties. A family assesses the existing habitat in its backyard and develops a plan to upgrade it by providing more native vegetation, food, plants, water, and nesting material. Then the family receives a certificate. Over 26,000 households have been certified. The program has expanded to certify schools and towns.[25] Similar grassroots efforts have begun to coalesce neighbors to improve wildlife habitat cooperatively by managing private yards as a whole rather than as separate properties. These neighborhood plans provide more complete and connected habitat, especially useful for birds, butterflies, and other small animals.

Stewardship programs to restore larger ecosystems are noteworthy. The Bobwhite Brigade, created by Dale Rollins through the Texas Agricultural Extension Service, provides an intense five-day curriculum for high school youth, teaching quail biology, the impacts of nest predation, plant identification, radiotelemetry, habitat analysis and improvement, as well as hunting skills.[26] Graduates undertake community projects to improve quail habitat.

Many farmers and ranchers have voluntarily undertaken stewardship projects on their private lands, creating large acreages of wildlife habitat. The story of one Texas rancher illustrates. Sherman Hammond started building small humps in his roads to stop gullies and washes. The humps created spreader dams, holding scarce moisture for longer periods. With water, the grasses and forbs flourished. Hammond realized that this not only stopped erosion and created better grazing land but also made oases for wildlife, especially quail. He figures he has turned fourteen inches of annual rainfall into thirty inches of effective watering, creating over 33,000 acres of improved wildlife habitat by his personal actions.[27]

Public agencies from city governments to national parks depend on volunteers, like Friends of Runyon Canyon, for restoration activities. For example, during the last two decades, the Bosque del Apache Wildlife Refuge in New Mexico suffered reductions in staff and budgets. During that time, Phil Norton, superintendent of the Refuge, nurtured volunteer groups, who more than offset tight budgets. In 1986, there were only two volunteers; by 2000, there were forty and a friends group of six hundred members. Some of the stewards serve as roving naturalists and community ambassadors. Others harvest crops for winter feed for sandhill cranes and other migratory birds, remove exotic salt cedar (which has invaded riparian cottonwood

Snow geese, Bosque del Apache

Roving naturalists

Volunteer educators

Upper Chesapeake Bay watershed

Identifying sacred places

Informed and caring stewardship

communities), restore natural ecosystems, and create native gardens and viewing platforms.[28]

A similar story underlies a recent addition to the Golden Gate National Recreation Area. Once a wetland, which was replaced by a military base and paved airfield, Crissy Field has been recreated with a marsh inlet, native grasslands, and beach. Three thousand volunteers participated in the design process, cleared debris, propagated native plants, and removed nonnative plants to complete the hundred-acre urban restoration site.[29]

In many of these cases, volunteerism extends far from home to embrace faraway places. In a massive and long-term effort to restore the Chesapeake Bay, the volunteer group Bay Keepers maintains fish ladders for migratory species, raises oyster spat to repopulate beds, and plants and surveys underwater grasses.[30] Another program hundreds of miles from the Chesapeake Bay in Pennsylvania, Virginia, and Maryland identified locally sacred places in the upper watershed. Sacredness enhanced stewardship and improved the land-use practices that are essential to the bay's health.

A nonprofit group, Vermont Coverts, encourages landowners to manage private land as a shared regional resource. In spite of the lure of short-term profits from timber sales, many voluntarily chose to balance economic return with enhanced wildlife habitat, create scenic vistas, and improve recreational opportunities.[31] Some landowners coordinate timber cuts, mowing, and field cultivation to enhance wildlife habitat. In the past ten years, their cooperation has protected 110,000 acres in Vermont.[32] Land trusts nationwide have protected 14 million acres.[33] For all these stewards, the region has become the household for which they are responsible, an essential shift in our dwelling mindsets if we are to achieve ecological democracy. Ranging farther from the backyard, the Wildlands Project has initiated stewardship plans to create core wildlife habitats and corridors from Canada to Central America.[34]

Taken as a whole, these vignettes convey the wide range of opportunities that are available for volunteering in shaping the city and larger landscape. And these cases suggest general directions to cultivate stewardship through the design of the landscape.

By careful location based on everyday life patterns and intentional futures, places of stewardship can create center, limit extent, and express particularness essential to ecological democracy. Settings should be designed to offer hands-on learning regarding locality, hard physical labor, and occasions to restore damaged ecosystems. Urbanites typically lack these opportunities and derive a personal satisfaction from them that concretizes stewardship. To receive the maximum benefits, these sites should be located close to home. Design can encourage or inhibit acts of volunteerism. Those places that have a strong framework but that are not complete allow us to see an opportunity for our personal or group contributions. Small, identifiable, unfinished areas that need construction labor or maintenance invite participation. So does a clear definition of tasks and places where results of labor are immediately apparent.

Designers must make places that last, are adaptable, and work with natural processes. Low maintenance is essential, particularly in overall structure and daily upkeep. Places that are poorly conceived and constructed fall apart, invite abuse, and require constant repair. They discourage stewardship. Even if those places convey a sense of extreme need and pity, they debilitate rather than evoke positive action. Voluntary action is less rewarding when it constantly focuses on cleanup and repairs rather than on improvements and habitat restoration.

Urban landscapes should be designed to invite stewards to partner with others, cooperatively sharing expertise and labors. Projects that cross class, gender, generation, and ethnic divisions are especially valuable because they improve not only the urban ecology but also the capacity of the community to work together. And designers need to provide settings where milestones of stewardship activities can be celebrated and recognized.

Sorely needed are neighborhoods and buildings where people who want to conserve, reuse, and otherwise steward limited resources can test less consumptive lifestyles. Many well-intentioned lives are thwarted by barriers to environmental restoration created by previous city design. Removing hurdles to personal stewardship in the everyday landscape and making impelling alternatives are critical roles for designers.

The Garden Patch

Consider how design facilitates stewardship and associated goals in this example. The Garden Patch, a multipurpose youth-employment garden in the low-income, minority-dominated western part of Berkeley, California, is particularly instructive. It was begun by Laura Lawson in 1993 as an offshoot of Berkeley Youth Alternatives (BYA), a nonprofit center that for

thirty years has served children age six to eighteen who are at risk of dropping out of school or turning to violent crime. BYA provides after-school tutoring, mentoring, sports, counseling, job training, and employment. Among its innovative and time-tested programs is teen employment to do gardening and maintenance of parks in the city. That program, initiated twenty years ago, was among the first of its kind.

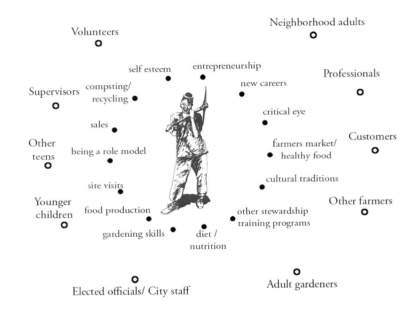

At the Garden Patch, Laura Lawson made sure that teenagers were central to decision making and action.

Garden Patch neighborhood

Impelling Form

When Lawson initiated the Garden Patch, a partnership with BYA was a logical choice, both programmatically and locationally. BYA is part of a neighborhood center consisting of Strawberry Creek Park, the original free-the-stream-from-the-culvert project, a senior center, a city public-works yard, a post office, a hardware store, a grocery, a bakery, and other stores serving primarily poorer African Americans, Hispanics, Anglo Americans, and recent Indian immigrants. By locating the garden here, Lawson could add to preexisting centeredness and create a place where many different groups might interact and possibly create cross-cultural partnerships.[35]

The design process engaged all the essential interests. It reached out to many who ordinarily would not be involved. Lawson knew that she wanted teenagers to be central to decision making and not just token window dressing at formal meetings, as is so often the case with youth in city design. The highest priority for these teens was job training and employment. To satisfy their needs, the major element of the design became a youth market garden where teen employees would be taught to grow vegetables, flowers, and plant starts. This later expanded to business training, marketing, and experiments in niche sales. BYA leaders wanted a children's garden where the very young would be taught nutrition through play with teen employees. Neighbors wanted individual garden plots. Others insisted that a tool shed, a greenhouse, an orchard, demonstration plots, a community gathering and classroom space, and a compost and service area were essential. A lot had to fit onto the site. Street and sun orientation dictated the placement of some things, but the primary framework was created by an axial path running the full length of the site. Completed in the first phase, it continuously provided a sense of order to the often disheveled garden during the first years when few areas were finished and various projects were under construction. The final design emerged after many meetings and workshops. The process enticed an unusually diverse group to volunteer to make the project a reality.

The half-acre site was an abandoned railroad right-of-way with gravel and bay mud compacted to concrete consistency. It supported no plant growth. Restoring this dead earth to productive agricultural land offered several opportunities for the stewardship that was desired by city dwellers. A dozen weekends of hard, physical labor were required to pickaxe the hardened earth. The hellish chore bonded all the volunteers—youth, neighbors, and staff. A new sense of community and lasting intergenerational and cross-cultural friendships grew from the labor. Double digging and horse

The Garden Patch had so many competing demands for space that it could easily have become a tossed salad, but the designer created a strong framework that gives it pleasing order.

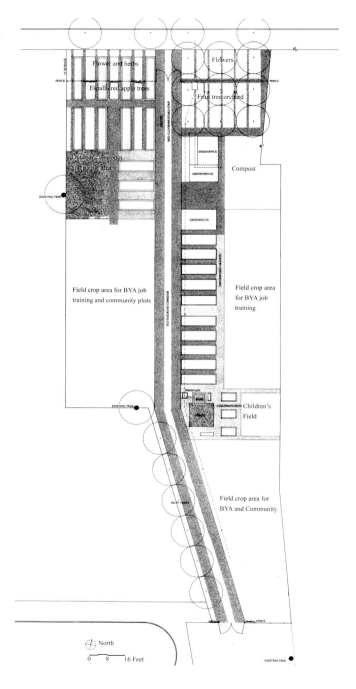

Flower and herbs

Flowers

Espaliered apple trees

Fruit tree orchard

SHED/OFFICE

Compost

GREENHOUSE

Outdoor classroom and picnic area

GREENHOUSE

EXISTING TREE

Field crop area for BYA job training and community plots

Field crop area for BYA job training

EXISTING TREE

FOUNTAIN

CHILDREN'S BEDS

Children's Field

Field crop area for BYA and Community

FRUIT TREES

North

0   8   16 Feet

EXISTING TREE

and rabbit manure amended the soil to make it marginally fertile. Every participant learned firsthand soil mechanics and nitrogen cycles. Science was inhabited and naturalness enjoyed beyond all expectation. Although not a critical ecosystem in the larger scheme of things, restoration of the half acre from sterile to fecund land was immensely rewarding and not forgotten by the workers.[36]

Lawson carefully cultivated volunteer stewards while subtly nurturing teenage leadership in all Garden Patch projects. She divided the various projects into bite-size undertakings with clear tasks. She paired teens with professionals to design and construct the main path, raised beds, tool shed, and entry. On completion, she organized a celebration to recognize everyone involved in each effort and invite new volunteers to take on the next facilities.

These early years provided the most effective employment training for the teenagers. They were involved in every aspect from planning and construction to food production and experiments in selling vegetables at a local farmers' market. With construction now complete, teenagers get more extensive management and marketing training but do not have the variety of work experiences. Nor do they get to work as equal partners with the early volunteers who were accomplished professionals and role models.[37]

Although the incremental construction engaged hundreds of volunteers and produced heart-warming partnerships with teens in leadership positions, the small Garden Patch staff suffered burnout. After the essential facilities were built, fewer community people volunteered. BYA staff assumed more responsibility. The lesson? Tangible projects were more engaging for

Before and after views show the dramatic improvement reciprocal stewardship fosters. The land is healthier, as are neighborhood residents and all who made the Garden Patch.

stewards than management and maintenance but presented a difficult coordination problem for a small staff. Generally, the facilities were designed to last. Lawson insisted on simple, well-crafted construction. That produced low maintenance and adaptable buildings and gardens. One exception is the children's garden, which was too complex and delicate. Parts of it fell apart and have been removed. But overall, the Garden Patch is well maintained. It is particularly attractive compared to many community gardens because Lawson attended the street façade with a vigorous orchard.

Although not self-supporting, the market garden has been unusually successful in teaching teenagers entrepreneurial skills. Marketing garden products was an untested area of youth services, so teens and staff have constantly tested innovative businesses, such as minicommunity-supported agriculture that delivers flower bouquets and baskets of organic produce. Another experiment provides vegetables to high-end restaurants, while yet another cross-markets with local businesses.[38]

Whereas in the first five years teenagers learned about city design and gardening, recent employees have learned business skills. Over a hundred teenagers have been employed in the intensive Garden Patch program, and many have graduated from high school, gone to college, or gotten quality jobs as a result. All indicate that they learned important lessons about responsibility, food production, and nutrition. A few, however, became teenaged parents or went to jail.[39]

Most impressive is the Garden Patch's web of stewardship. Lawson orchestrated a motley crew of disparate parts—a market garden for teens, community and demonstration plots for neighbors, a teaching garden, and a play space—into a workable whole. She also shepherded partnerships of mutual caring. Barren ground was stewarded and restored to exceptionally good health. Teens nurtured and were nurtured by the garden volunteers with whom they worked. The volunteers stewarded the teens, took personal responsibility for many of them, and saw the youths blossom. Volunteers also met other adults from other ethnicities and walks of life with whom they otherwise would never have become friends. From this, residents developed empathy for previous strangers in their community. This increased the capacity of neighborhood residents to work together.

Sensitivity to subtle differences between cultures and generations grew in fits and starts as people shared common ground. One Harvest Fair, an annual community celebration of the year's accomplishments, typified the line

Many of the at-risk teenagers who were stewarded through the Garden Patch graduated from high school or college and got jobs.

Teenagers also learned to eat more healthfully by replacing junk food with organically grown vegetables.

Crunchy granola or squash

that had to be walked to satisfy the various groups. Adults arranged to have a live bluegrass band that was popular with upper-class Berkeley volunteers. Adults regardless of ethnicity and class agreed. On the day of the event, the teens protested that the band was too "crunchy granola." A tense compromise was negotiated. Radio-produced hip-hop got equal time.[40] Respectful bargaining is required when many people have a place at the table.

Design for stewardship created a complex chain of interconnected neighbors, volunteers, employees, and youth. These partnerships of community—people, place, and the larger urban ecosystem—are powerful yet delicate. NASCAR champion Jeff Gordon noted that teamwork is the fuel that makes common people attain uncommon achievements. However, shared fuel is volatile; partnerships themselves have to be well stewarded.[41]

In terms of the goals of ecological democracy, stewardship efforts are most successful when they satisfy multiple purposes and are least successful when they focus on narrow, exclusive purposes.

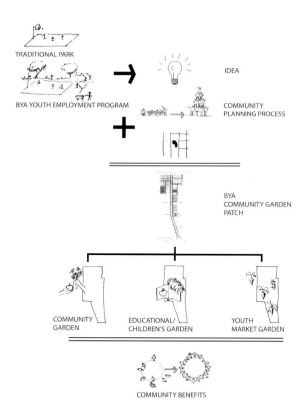

TRADITIONAL PARK

BYA YOUTH EMPLOYMENT PROGRAM

IDEA

COMMUNITY PLANNING PROCESS

BYA COMMUNITY GARDEN PATCH

COMMUNITY GARDEN

EDUCATIONAL/ CHILDREN'S GARDEN

YOUTH MARKET GARDEN

COMMUNITY BENEFITS

Active Responsibility

Stewardship has metamorphosed from the era of the yeoman farmer. We count on a revitalized sense of aggressive stewardship to counterbalance the harmful effects of individualism, selfishness, and greed. In present terms, stewardship expresses caring for community, including other people, plants, animals, soil, water, and air. Both a set of moral principles and a course of action, it requires active responsibility. Stewardship can guide our private daily lives, our volunteer activities, our engagement in public events, our professional behavior, and the design of the city.

In daily life, stewardship may be a matter of religious faith, ecological necessity, or both.[42] Either encourages us to conserve, to consume conscientiously, and to be voluntarily inconvenienced for family, community, and urban ecosystems.[43] For example, an active stewardship ethic might impel one to choose the inconvenience of driving less to reduce pollution, help clean the air, and enhance the local community. The ethic stimulates one to do such things even when others do not. This is difficult in circles where volunteerism is unfashionable. For example, did you ever notice that the only people who pick up trash are either those convicted of crimes or local do-gooders? Wendell Berry encourages us to gain the skills to live poorer than we do.[44] Of course, voluntary poverty enriches our lives.[45]

In public design, stewardship requires us to learn more about our locality, to gain generalized urban ecological knowledge about the big picture, and to act through connectedness. We must listen, empathize, and infect young generations with broad civic visions like those that Uncle Ima Kamalani championed. We have to both trust and be eternally vigilant. We risk being taken advantage of because others may not do their parts. Stewardship impels us to engage assertively, respectfully, and thoughtfully in public discussions about the future of our habitation and make difficult decisions, like limiting extent and creating centers. It urges us to embrace voluntary compliance with decisions made collectively, to legislate those most essential actions to achieve resilient regions, and to exercise focused civil disobedience when necessary. Democracy is not a spectator sport, and stewardship provides further arguments for neighborhood and regional governments to replace city and county governments.

Stewardship today expects more from professionals than specialized expertise. The practice of many professions lacks responsibility beyond

God of river stewardship

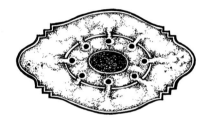

God and eight irrigation maidens

maximizing the efficiency of a single function that is disconnected from other systems. This specialization has created a moral loneliness with experts as out of control as protesting rioters.[46] Stewardship requires a general contextual knowledge and actions based on that knowledge. Such an ethic would certainly corral simpleminded entrepreneurs who become wealthy by greedy short-sightedness and meanspiritedness. The damage of such thinking—take Wal-Mart real estate strategies for example—is antithetical to stewardship. In this sense, the old saying "He made a killing" means just that—profiting greatly and causing the deaths of downtowns. Stewardship will be tested in countering such actions that diminish locality and undermine enabling, resilient, and impelling community form. More will be expected of business professionals and their designers.[47] The great modernist architect Philip Johnson noted that designers are all whores. The critical question is whose interest we will steward.

The River Tribunal of elder farmers meets weekly to resolve conflicts and steward the River Turia, Spain. The river god, eight irrigation maidens, and residents keep vigilant eyes on the deliberations.

Impelling Form

As we have seen, it is inadequate, for example, to design a likeable park. It is essential that park designers cultivate community-based "friends" groups who serve as long-term custodians of place. Stewardship requires much longer-term commitments on the parts of professionals themselves. We should live with every project and its impacts for many years, not a few months.

Stewardship changes the way that cities are designed—both the process and form. Designers can create and live in alternative neighborhoods where the conservation minded can test new lifestyles. Designers can make opportunities for caring action at multiple scales, from garden patches to transcontinental flyways. They can provide places for hands-on learning, physical labor, and ecosystem restoration. With a strong framework, the integrity of a site can be maintained, even as voluntary incrementalism completes the overall vision. Small identifiable projects can produce highly visible results that last. If designed to elicit involvement, such places can transform the public from passive viewers who might pass by and think, "How pretty!" to informed citizens who think, "Wow! I helped do that!"[48] Few have the broad vision needed to advance stewardship that considers a much larger, interconnected community, the design of which has impacts far from one's personal property or neighborhood. Reciprocal stewardship calls for city design that nourishes regional visions and transcontinental stewardship with bite-sized pieces for many participants.

Stewardship persuades by necessity and by the voluntary ring that it sounds. It is the only effective antidote to shortsighted greed that I know. Only reciprocal stewardship protects the sacred, comprehends naturalness, and champions density and limited extent. Caring actively for land, our locality, and other people, we reap extraordinary personal and public benefits.

Pacing

Urbanity is immensely more impelling when it is experienced at tempos that vary like the rhythms of life itself. Unfortunately, the pace of life today is monopolized by speed: Kwik Copy, Presto Prints, fast food, faster food, short exposure, instant access, and wireless mobility. Our cities are dominated by freeways and speedways and are stuck on full throttle. Every home appears an oxymoronic mobile home. We are constantly urged to keep up the pace or even ahead of time. With little effort, I can fly east across the Pacific Ocean and arrive before I left.

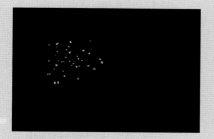

Light Speed and Snail's Pace

There is nothing inherently wrong with rapid urbanity. An essential part of culture, like the explosion of force in a hundred-yard dash, speed is part of the hustle. Speed fills a city with liveliness. To Louis, the trumpeter swan, the relative speed of Billings, Montana, made it teem with life, putting him in high spirits.[1] Speed makes the city alluring, animating, exhilarating, and stimulating.

Unfortunately, ungoverned speed becomes rushed. What was once exhilarating turns into a rat race, hurried and thoughtless. Hastiness breeds rashness, carelessness, and impatience; recklessness follows. Then there is the fallout from our perpetual swiftness. The detritus of the frenetic is the moribund with no vital force left.

Uncontrolled speed has usurped the great variety of tempos and rhythms, cornering the market of pace of life. Speed vilifies slowness. Slowness is viewed as tedious; it holds back progress. Slowness is pedestrian, in the mean sense of the word—dull, unimaginative, stupid. In a city of speed, there is no room for the pedestrian and certainly not the rambler, the saunterer, or the wanderer.

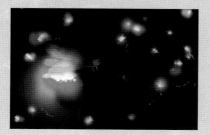

Last month, I went on a pilgrimage with a colleague to see fireflies in Taiwan. We were among the more than fifty thousand people who make the

Speed makes the city alluring and
exhilarating, but ungoverned speed
becomes hurried and thoughtless.

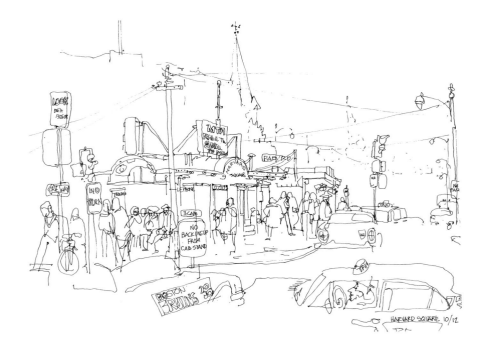

journey annually. On the bus from Hualien City to Liyu Lake, a Taiwanese
family of four was sitting in front of us. The parents were explaining the life
cycle of fireflies. The four-year-old little brother suddenly pronounced, "If
the world moves slower, we'd always be on holiday." I pondered the transla-
tion for the remainder of the trip. When we neared the bus stop, I asked the
little boy what would happen if the world went faster. His six-year-old sister
immediately answered for him, "The world will faint."

The ritual walk to see the fireflies was one of slowness, the tempo so
often slandered in an age of speed. For an hour, the procession moved at a
snail's pace up the dark mountain. I wondered why anyone would make
such a pilgrimage. But strangers talked to each other. When fireflies were
sighted in the distance, the procession quickened around a blind bend.
Sparkling brilliance emerged from the deep forest surrounding a mountain
stream. Thousands of fireflies filled the air in a dazzling slow-motion light
show. Our collective halt was followed by the silence of reverence. The silence lasted long enough to observe planets shifting overhead. When a firefly
flew into his range, however, the four-year-old squealed with unconstrained

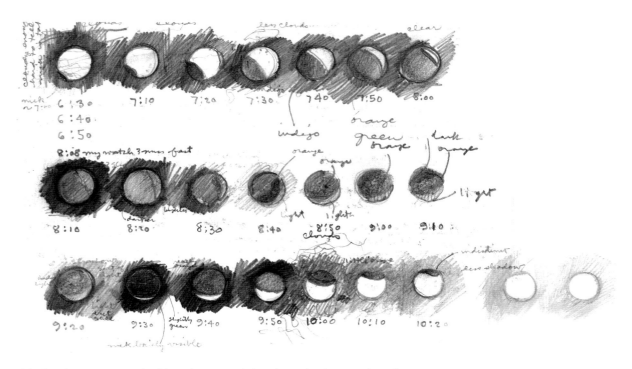

delight, the purest joy I had heard in years. The silence broken, spoken sharing followed. Why are there so many here in this one place? Can you distinguish the various species by the color of their lights? How exactly do their lights work? Why do some lights flash and others don't? Answers for all the questions abided somewhere in the group. I kept visualizing the magic lights. The children's comments filled my consciousness. I asked the children if I could quote them in my book. Their parents were pleased. Yes, the world is filled with holiday-like pleasures when the pace is varied and slower.

"Speed Kills" proclaimed the billboards of a driver-education campaign decades ago. The monopoly of speed has indeed taken a toll on the city. Frantic speed renders centeredness obsolete, precludes sacredness, transforms particularness into sameness, disconnects even as it deludes us into believing that it provides convenience over great distances. Frenzy makes it impossible to inhabit science, and the benefits of naturalness cannot be absorbed when hurried. Speed has no time for deliberative decision making. It debilitates ecological democracy.

If the world moves slower, we always would be on holiday.

An impelling city requires the full range of tempos—from the cinematic light speed to the snail's pace. There must be settings for the green flash, falling meteors, the hare, the tortoise, the slowpoke, and geological time. We need diversity of tempo, but mostly we need andantes and adagios. We need to demarcate space for careful observation, listening, unhurried conversation, chewing the cud, and deliberation. We need places for strolling, gazing, reflective meditation, and Noh theater. We need space to be still.[2] These must not be isolated events or special occasions in a landscape dominated by speed but rather a reversal that allows a calmer pace to permeate our cities and our lives. We will know that the transformation is complete when slow-pitch softball becomes the national sport.

Dwelling Pace

For calmness to permeate our cities, they must be redesigned to accommodate slower paces. Just as there are criteria for a dwelling place (we assume that the architect will provide a foundation that will be solid, a roof that keeps us dry, and walls to keep out the cold), so too should there be guidelines to design a dwelling pace.

Henry David Thoreau wrote that "Nothing can be more useful to a man" or a woman "than a determination not to be hurried."[3] Thoreau bespoke the essence of dwelling. To dwell is more than having an address. It means making a home as part of making a life. To dwell is also to hinder speed, to decide not to be rushed. This is the first presumption of designing dwelling pace. Design the household, neighborhood, connections, and workplace to support human efforts not to be hurried. Architects might start in the kitchen. Make it large; provide workplaces for every member of the family to share food preparation. Make a place for a round table where everyone can sit for meals face to face. Make the room sunny in the morning so that everyone will want to sit down for breakfast. Detail it richly enough that everyone will linger after dinner, even if they are not interested in the conversation. Extend this thinking throughout the house, garden, and neighborhood. Provide places for adults to loiter. Why should only teenagers and the unemployed hang out and loiter in the public landscape?

In a charrette for Adachi, Japan, children were redesigning their city. There were children from first grade to high school. When the youngest group made its presentation, its members apologized, saying, "We are just the little kids, but we will do our best." They then made a series of brilliant suggestions. One was to save small agricultural plots in town so that everyone could stop to pick strawberries for a snack on the way to and from school or work. Another was to make bookshelves at bus stops and fill them with library books so people would just stop, read, and talk to friends and strangers. They intended to change the overall tempo throughout their community. The Slow Food Movement is an attempt to do the same—to create a pace that penetrates every aspect of life in the city and spreads a sane rate for dwelling.

For years, residents of the north shore of Oahu have recognized that their pace of life is much slower than the rest of Honolulu. People in Haleiwa have designed their community to nourish a change in pace. From time to time, there is a "No Rush Rush" campaign to alert residents that certain projects are threatening their tempo. A freeway bypass stirred up No Rush Rush concerns as did proposals from major destination resorts. No Rush Rush was the response. For many years, residents fought a drive-through window at the local McDonald's because it threatened their ethic of taking longer to do things than seems necessary; they believe that a slow pace is good for the community. This is no indication that the community is dull, lacks energy, or is behind the times, characteristics often attributed to slowness. Indeed, Haleiwa is lively, energetic, and inventive. It is also humane and caring. People take time for their families and one another. They know a lot about their landscape. They enjoy life in a full and rich way. They dwell without rushing.

Their saying "No Rush Rush" serves them well in daily life and decision making. When our firm was there to do a community plan, we brought time-driven efficiency to the process. Local people appreciated the process and the organized steps that we used but not the fast pace. Uncle Ima said, "Whoa! Slow down. Talk story with us before we make a plan." That forced us to attend to local nuances and allowed residents more time to consider new information, to discuss its significance, and to give substantial feedback. Residents refused to rush city-design decisions. Proposals were debated at community meetings but only after thorough deliberation over shaved ice at Matsumotos and light beers at the Ice House, at luaus on Barney's beach, under the shade structure at Uncle Ima's, and in countless other places where informal story was talked. At a deliberate pace. Careful that everyone had his or her say. No Rush Rush.

No rush rush

Learning to walk

In every aspect of city design, tempo needs to encourage deliberate living. Process and form contribute to this. From the layout of a kitchen to the creation of strawberry fields and bookshelves at bus stops, design can change the rhythm of people's lives—to slow progress, to stop ill-founded freeways, to prevent the construction of dams. Slowing actions, whether reducing the speed of car traffic or reducing the impact of hungry water that dams would create, are noble pursuits of the city designer. If these are in a broader public interest and not merely NIMBY actions, professional designers should support and lead such activities. And in all cases, we should provide a process that allows slow deliberative democracy to reign.

Learning to Walk

Consider the most mundane aspect of speed. Americans once walked almost everywhere they went. Henry David Thoreau described walking as a gift from God. He argued that we are born walkers, not made—"*Ambulator nascitur, non fit.*"[4] We were a nation of walkers, a skill that was inherited and passed from generation to generation. People walked for transportation and for pleasure. But by 1850, Thoreau noticed that there were fewer walkers. Horses, carriages, and trains were faster. Walkers were rare. He was fearful that he and a friend were the only true walkers left.[5]

Walking has become more marginalized than Thoreau imagined. As speedy travel by automobile became dominant, places to walk fell into disuse—abandoned in favor of environments for the car. Today almost no one who counts walks to work, to shop, to see friends, or to worship. No one of importance wants to walk. Although some children and poor people still do as a matter of necessity, so few people with authority walk that the pedestrian environment is simply abandoned. The result is that Americans walk less and less. Many have forgotten how.

For us to derive pleasure from our cities, we must learn again how to walk. We may be born with the capacity to walk, but it takes practice. Walkers are born and made: "*Ambulator nascitur et fit cum practicus.*"

To want to walk, we need first to be aware of its benefits. As noted above, it offers pleasures that otherwise are missed. On my walk to school, for example, there are beauties unseen when I go faster. There is the section of sidewalk on Derby Street where residents added dozens of heart-shaped tiles to new pavement. There is the elderly man who sweeps the sidewalk in front of the elder-care facility nearly every morning. We say, "Good morning," and I admire his stewardship. There is the view back to the bay when I reach the block above Shattuck. There is the seasonal fragrance of pittosporum flowers. Beyond the pleasures, walking teaches us about our habitat. Frederick Law Olmsted noted that only by walking extensively through the southern states did he discover the clear connection between the exploitation of slaves and the ruination of southern soils. His observations were enabled by the slow pace of his travel and the careful study that walking allows. The book resulting from this educational journey influenced the move toward emancipation.[6] For us, the walking lessons are close to home but equally important to improving our neighborhoods. We learn things as mundane as where a stop sign could make children's walks to school safer or where underused properties might become a community garden. Walking extends the boundaries of the territory that we care about. Walking makes one feel equally at home everywhere one travels.[7] We become stewards of a vast landscape when that landscape is accessible by foot. Another major benefit of walking is that it is good for our health.[8] The following section considers this in more detail. In the design of cities, as has been pointed out in earlier chapters, walking is essential to maintain successful centeredness, limited extent, density, and smallness and to reverse harmful status seeking. As we learn about the benefits, Americans want to walk again.

There are considerable barriers to learning to walk. We have invested billions of public dollars in transportation infrastructure, mostly for cars, while destroying environments for people on foot. Places to walk are needed in every neighborhood, city, and region. These places must be safe and pleasant, well connected to centers and destinations, and accessible to both nature and social nodes. But first, we simply must acquire places where people can learn to walk. This requires public disinvestment in freeways, streets, parking lots, and other automobile-serving infrastructure and parallel investment to return streets to pedestrians, to acquire land and rights of way for walking, and to connect disconnected areas.

Slouching toward Obesity at Car Speed

The design of the city affects human health. We've observed this in dramatic form since the Middle Ages (see the chapter on Naturalness). Health officials conclude that many of the most serious chronic illnesses of our time are related to the content and arrangement of city form. Recent research ties illness caused by water pollution, food and soil contamination, and heat islands and even injuries from violent crime to the design of the urban ecology. Physical and mental illnesses from social isolation, diseases from air pollution, injuries from traffic accidents, stress-induced health problems, and maladies from lack of exercise are related to the shape of our habitation. These illnesses originate in pacing, the direct impacts of speed and the automobile and their indirect influences on city form. Consider these one at a time.

Lack of social contact increases risk of chronic stress, heart disease, and other illnesses. People with the weakest social ties have significantly higher death rates, possibly as great as three times higher than those who are socially integrated.[9] Although many other forces contribute to social isolation, city design is increasingly blamed. Segregated land uses and building design, inadequate public transportation, the demise of centers that provide locally accessible services, and loss of places to exercise all contribute to alienation. For many, especially the elderly, lack of physical access is one factor leading to illness and often death.[10]

City form of segregated land uses, a concomitant increase in the distance between home and work, and associated dependence on the automobile are responsible for the most of the smog that underlies 6 million asthma attacks per year in the United States.[11] City design encourages speeding, which creates a safety hazard for other drivers, occupants of cars, and pedestrians. Although Americans make fewer than 6 percent of their trips by foot, pedestrians account for 13 percent of traffic fatalities.[12] Pedestrian injuries and deaths occur most often where there are wide, heavily trafficked streets, no crosswalks, and a lack of spatial enclosure. All encourage speeding. These can no longer be dismissed as accidents. Pedestrians are at risk by design.

American city form increases stress. The hurried pace of life and long commute times create tension and impatience. Status seeking isolates individuals and adds anxiety about self-worth.

Lack of exercise has created an epidemic of chronic illnesses—heart disease and stroke, high blood pressure, colon cancer, anxiety, depression, type 2 diabetes, and obesity, among others. In concert with poor diet and genetic and environmental factors, physical inactivity has produced an obese nation in little more than fifty years. Nearly two-thirds of American adults are overweight or obese.[13] And we are getting fatter fast. In the last twenty years, obesity among adults has doubled; the number of overweight adolescents has tripled. Today approximately 300,000 deaths each year are associated with excess weight. One disputed study estimated 400,000 per year. This compares to 435,000 deaths each year associated with cigarette smoking. Health risks of obesity are overtaking those of smoking, drinking, and poverty.[14] The annual costs of physical inactivity and obesity in California alone are $24.6 billion.[15] Inactivity is the culprit. Lifestyles have changed from active to sedentary. Few do physical labor for a living. More of us sit to work. Nearly all of us drive to work and to almost everywhere else. Fifty years ago, daily tasks burned five hundred to a thousand calories. Today daily activities burn a fraction of that because people walk so seldom. Even children are driven everywhere; they walk or bike for about half as many of their trips today as they did twenty-five years ago.[16] Childhood obesity may shorten life expectancy by as much as five years.

It is easy but inaccurate to blame inactivity on laziness. Lifestyles of choice made us couch potatoes, but like many other things, we slouched into this lifestyle without much thought. We discarded active healthy lives without knowing the consequences. Had we done the necessary ecological thinking of interconnectedness, we would have observed a web of diet, work, personal transportation, exercise, and health much like a food web in a wild ecosystem. In this case, the car, nonnative and invasive, replaced the top predators, throwing this exercise web dangerously out of kilter. The entire habitat was rearranged to accommodate the car: centers were destroyed, distances between work and home extended, density diminished, and limited extent overcome. The city was fashioned in the image of the car.

If lack of exercise is causing diabetes, cancers, and heart disease, why don't we walk? Americans say that they do not exercise today due to the poor design of their neighborhoods. People want enjoyable scenery when they exercise. Few neighborhoods provide it. Worse is the lack of safe places to exercise. People worry about heavy and fast traffic, a lack of sidewalks, parks, natural open space, and trails, and empty sidewalks that make people feel vulnerable to crime (the underlying message is that there are more criminals than law-abiding exercisers on the streets). These are straightforward problems. Redesigning the city can encourage walking.

1980   Present

Decline in biking

Remedial and Preventive Prescriptions

We have rediscovered what the philosopher Chomei told us centuries ago: "To go on foot and do one's own work is the best path to strength and health."[17] Exercise, even daily tasks done on foot, can improve our health, make our hearts and psyches stronger, improve our productivity, and help us live longer. For example, consider the impact of exercise on type 2 diabetes. Sixteen million Americans have this obesity-related disease. Ten million more are at high risk to develop the disease. An epidemic is threatened. It costs $100 billion a year to treat. In one experiment, exercising two and a half hours per week at a brisk walk, taking classes in better nutrition, and reducing body weight by 7 percent cut type 2 diabetes by more than half for those most at risk. Exercise, diet, and weight loss are more effective at preventing the disease than present drug treatments.[18]

Pacing doesn't just make the city pleasant. Walking is essential if we are to have a population that is healthy enough to create an ecological democracy. Both require remedial and preventive prescriptions to redesign our communities. Guidelines for city design to encourage changes of tempo will be discussed in the following sections. These actions include enhancing the walking environment while curbing the car, creating pedestrian routes as symphonies so that public exercise becomes a daily routine and a community ritual, creating sequences with metamorphic power, and attending to the ground plane. I emphasize walking and other healthful transportation in the public outdoors, which provide benefits of exercise and naturalness while contributing to public life.

Pathfinders Curb the Car

The impacts of the car require the most direct remedial action. Even simple actions can return huge dividends. For example, vehicular traffic was consciously decreased in Atlanta during the 1996 Olympic games. Peak weekday morning car volume dropped 22.5 percent. This reduced ozone levels by 27.9 percent and the number of asthma medical attacks by 41.6 percent. By cutting car trips by one-fifth, asthma emergencies were cut by two-fifths.[19] Similar pedestrian safety and city-design benefits are attained when traffic is curbed.[20]

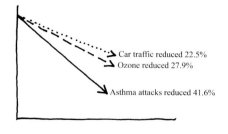

Car pollution and disease

The pedestrian environment has been neglected in direct proportion to the preponderance and speed of the automobile. Walking requires a relative diminishment of the car in terms of volume, speed, and dominating influence over land use and city design. In every local land-use and transportation decision in which modal priority is central (and that includes virtually every decision), preference must be given to the pedestrian. This may increase automobile congestion temporarily, but a hundred years of pedestrian bashing can be reversed only by favoring walkers, sometimes painfully for drivers.

This is not to suggest that we ban automobile use. Rather, pedestrians must take precedence to create a more humane urban pace. To accomplish this, city actions must improve the quality of the walking environment to equal or better the car environment. This intelligent strategy is being employed in several cities like Portland, where its Skinny Streets program and pedestrian plan make walking a priority.

To rectify the imbalance will require shifting public expenditures for highways, streets, and other car-related subsidies to projects that favor walkers. As an indication that this is beginning to happen, the governor of California has proclaimed that the primacy of the automobile in transportation planning is over in that state. In dedicating the Foothill Freeway east of Los Angeles, he declared that this would be the last freeway in California.[21] Freeway construction needs to be stopped, and those monies need to be directed toward pedestrian improvements. Likewise, steep increases in gasoline taxes should be earmarked for walking environments, including green streets, greenways, and urban forests to buffer air pollution. We must put our money where our feet might be.

Land-use and zoning changes can assist walking. As noted before, high-density housing produces a critical mass of people that can support mixed-use centers within walking distance of homes. Densities of only twenty units per acre support transit and justify a full range of daily shopping, services, and workplaces within pedestrian range. If centered, these facilities create destinations for multitask walking. This depends on limited extent, smallness, and mixed land uses. If parking and street requirements are reduced, the land saved at centers can be reallocated to concentrated building, outdoor places, and bicycle parking.

Another design imperative is to connect the pedestrian to the center and to open space. Fragments of pedestrian ways often are severed by busy streets or neglect. Fragments must be reconnected. To create walking routes where

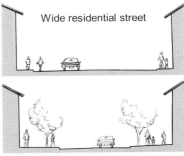

Wide residential street

Pedestrian scale street

Curb the car

there are few, the best approach is to start from the center, determine where most people walk presently, and create priorities based on existing everyday pedestrian patterns, density, and other indications of potential walking. Improve the top-priority walkways first, making them safe and irresistibly appealing. Lower the speed limit along those routes. Further decrease car speed by narrowing a few streets and planting tree lawns or medians heavily and continuously (this makes a pleasant place to walk and slows down drivers). A grid of streets with some intersections offset throughout a neighborhood also calms car speed and volumes. The grid spreads out the total volume, while the offsets and deflections reduce speed. This can be achieved with diverters, speed bumps, woornerfs (streets made primarily for pedestrians where cars enter only at low speed), and dead ends. Widen walkways to accommodate bikers. Keep modes in the same corridor rather than separating bikes from pedestrians or dividing pedestrians into parallel sidewalk and greenway routes. Although the idea of separate routes is appealing, there is usually not enough pedestrian demand for duplicative systems. When demand is low, both routes will be underused, unsafe, and often neglected. Prioritizing will create a few well-used walkways quickly and form the spine of the overall pedestrian system. Concentrating funds can make truly safe, appealing, and continuous routes by providing grade separation at major conflict points, neck-downs to ease pedestrian crossing at major intersections, marked and signaled crosswalks, lighting for nighttime and winter walking, generous landscaping, and places to linger. Be sure that surfaces are continuous and that curb cuts provide access for strollers, wheelchairs, and people with canes or infirmities. In concert, all of these actions will decrease the negative impacts of cars and restore the walking pace of everyday life.

Walking for exercise and recreation is likewise made more attractive by these changes, but there are additional considerations. Some people walk for health only in the company of others. Social centers should include routes with measured distances. Running tracks are great places to meet friends or support groups for exercising. Creating walking clubs may be a first-order action, even for city designers. Tree-lined tracks provide fuller health benefits. Periodic, even episodic pilgrimages might start at these community centers. Other exercisers want to do their walking in nature. Thoreau insisted that he needed the urban wild and lots of it. To preserve his health and spirits, he needed to saunter through woods and over hills and fields, absolutely free from all worldly engagements.[22] He felt that he really needed a walk in a wild landscape of a ten-mile radius, the limits of his afternoon meander on foot. An urban neighborhood that is bounded by stream corridors a quarter mile from the center and is connected to other open spaces could easily provide the ten-mile walks in nature that Thoreau demanded. Because pacing requires greenways for exercise and health, it adds criticality to previous goals to limit extent, maintain biological diversity, and facilitate naturalness.

Living Symphonic Sequences

To make pedestrian ways that are more than utilitarian alternatives to the car and to make the walking pace exhilarating, routes need to be designed to touch people's hearts. Splendid walks are sequences of related experiences with a melodic pattern. Like symphonies, they are carefully orchestrated and implemented. Great walking is performance art with a strong structure punctuated by lyrical variation.[23] There are logical orders of succession. There are beginnings, introductions to the main elements of the walk, and passages delineating transitions from home to block to neighborhood to major civic routes. Pace is varied to evoke thought or affective response. The route offers surprises, but fractal self-repetition maintains unity. The intensity of the walk builds to a crescendo or other highlight. There is an evocative aesthetic experience that is memorable. In the natural landscape, these elements are created by arranging eight elements including observer position (whether one is above or below a landscape); the degree of enclosure (how thoroughly does vegetation and topography create walls and canopy); the length of enclosure (the linear distance of the enclosure); sunlight and shade; color and texture; and details, like a flower in bloom or a sculptural tree. Of primary power is the ephemeral aspect of the landscape—wildlife, changing weather, or seasons.[24] In the cityscape, the elements, tempo, and potential surprises are determined largely by the combination of particular topography, vegetative mosaic, relationships of buildings to the landscape, and people themselves. Views from a high point, lower points with water, deep forests, or other distinctive features provide crescendos. They may be evoked by a single building that creates a landmark, a group of buildings that surround a social node, districts of distinctive building character, or dramatic edges between districts.[25] In the city, symphonic sequence combines natural elements into architectural form for powerful effect. Double rows of trees might serve an architectural purpose, such as creating axes that reach and paths that meander. Steps and grassy planes at regular intervals might provide changes of pace, different views, and social events. People can provide the crescendo, either as gatherings or expressions of uncommon friendliness. In Berkeley, for thirty years, Joseph Charles stood near the corner of Oregon and Martin Luther King Jr. streets every morning and waved to passersby, 36 million in all. He slowed the pace of rushing commuters with his "Have a good day."[26]

A well-designed walk is an extended harmonious composition of sensual movement. It is unforgettable; one never tires of it.[27] If this suggests a stroll garden, indeed, walks in the city should be as well composed and paced as a garden, like Katsura. Evoking its royal power and yet understated and contemplative, the walk is designed to delight senses, stimulate intellect, evoke poetic creativity, and stir the soul. The main path controls the visitor's experience—hiding a pond behind plants, revealing only its reflection, focusing the eye on a flower that distracts the viewer until another view unfolds around a bend, changing the pace with carefully placed stones that are far enough apart and interesting enough in arrangement to create a cautious pause until a breathtaking vista across multiple inlets is opened without warning. At every turn in the path and every rise in topography, the form of each rock and plant community, pavilion, and bridge has a purpose in the overall sequence. Certainly, the public urban landscape should not be as controlled as a private garden of Japanese royalty. But the lessons should not be discarded in designing urban walkways because the overall rules of creating visually unified, syncopated sequences apply equally to the experience of the city. Walks along the Seine River in Paris or down the Ramblas in Barcelona are exhilarating because these same principles are operating in each. The unifying tempo along the Seine is the pace of the water itself. It is both the background and the focal point as one strolls the Left Bank near the Île de la Cité. Handsome buildings, long and flowing, set a serious mood as backdrops. Bridges create divisions between musical movements. Tree-lined areas reflecting horizontal buildings serve as pauses between vistas or landmarks. The pace slows from relaxation and deep breaths and quickens as the leafy darkness reveals sunlight at the end of the treed tunnels, raising the expectation of the next landmark. Because I'm an infrequent visitor, the highlights are the most obvious. My pace quickens in anticipation of the light or shadow that will be playing on Notre Dame. Where the two flows converge below the island, a churning wake reunites the river. At this point

Impelling Form

Revealing slowly around

Exciting across

Up and over mystery

Walks in the city should be as well composed
as Katsura—delighting the senses and
evoking poetic creativity by changing the pace
of the stroll with topography, vegetation, and
points of interest.

Everyday walking

The sensation of space

of crescendo, the water is energetic in contrast to its reputation as pleasantly languid. Along the way, nodes of social celebration, music, and shopping stalls shift the tempo by their internal pacing, clearly secondary to the reflective river itself.

The main path of the Ramblas changes tempos, created by the degree of building enclosure and the number of trees and people that each section accommodates. In some sections, at certain times, the flow is leisurely; buildings project continuous façades. They wink and nod and quietly beckon, playing hide and seek with trees and passersby. A Gaudi building pleasantly surprises when a glimpse is revealed. Then there is a quickening of pace as store entrances become more frequent and sidewalks packed. A performer draws a gathering. At these points, everything else becomes background to the bustling celebratory crowd. There is no contemplation here. In contrast to the walk along the Seine where people view the river, here individuals create a flowing river of joyous humanity. Just as the intensity of the human river is about to overflow, it subsides into restaurants, bars, shops, and side streets.

Each of these informs us of important similarities and distinctions between symphonic and walking sequences. In these truly great walks, there is variation in tempo; the landscape lulls the walker, tantalizes, thrills, and reveals by twists and turns, ups and downs, that are harmonious in sequence. However, there are critical differences.

In music, drama, and dance, the audience is separated from the performers, participatory performances notwithstanding. In contrast, the walker is both active and passive as an audience and a primary performer—choosing where to walk, where to focus attention, when to stop, what details to notice. Even for the walker, however, choice is limited by paths, topography, vegetation, and water. At Katsura, the design manipulates every move; the Seine and Ramblas offer more choices. This makes the aesthetic experience of walking distinctly different from viewing both performing and two-dimensional arts. Walking provides multiple views of three-dimensional elements, whether buildings or landscape. This makes the experience a series of changing three-dimensional scenes, not gallery paintings. Erno Goldfinger described this as the sensation of space. He warned not to use two-dimensional painting criteria to design the landscape. Goldfinger's warning applies to the entire aesthetic experience of walking, with one exception. When the walker stops to focus attention on a distant view or a building façade, he may indeed see that scene as a painting composition. But this is a minor outlier because, by and large, the urban landscape is a three-dimensional sequence with changing perspectives of the elements. The walk surrounds us; it is never flat. Much of what is available to be experienced in a walking environment is unseen or unperceived consciously. There is far more information than we can process; therefore, we selectively choose what we consciously experience. More is experienced subliminally. Our attention is seldom firmly fixed, in contrast to gallery art or architectural façades, both of which the creator expects us to consciously study. On a walk, we may be altogether unaware of the orchestration of the sequence. Another distinction is that we respond to much of what is perceived on a walk differently than we respond to visual art because the landscape is living.[28]

Great walking experiences, then, are like symphonies but are distinctively different because we are not merely the audience; we are primary performers. It is a mistake to compare the aesthetic experience of walking to two-dimensional art because the landscape surrounds us, providing more information than we can consciously comprehend and far more that is subconsciously absorbed. Seldom static, walkers typically do not firmly fix their attention as people do on visual art. And our relationship to the living landscape further separates it from other arts. In sum, walking is its own art form—living symphonic sequences. Still, many walks are so dreadful that pedestrians resort to iPods to bring symphonic harmony to the landscape. When city paths are designed with spirit, the technology can be abandoned because the orchestra will play within the walker and the surrounding landscape itself.

For many years, Larry Halprin has applied the principles of living sequences to the design of urban landscapes. Borrowing from dance, he created scored walks that engage people to collaboratively make extraordinary public places.[29] He did one such plan based on dance scores with citizens in Yountville, California. He developed a framework for walking, including exercise, daily shopping, and school and special events, at multiple tempos and with various effects by capitalizing on the distinctive landscape of the central Napa Valley and surrounding hills. People remembered Halprin's scored walks twenty-five years later. They take unusual pride in their identity as a walking town. A recent town plan concretized that value, creating one primary promenade along the main street, using double rows of pistache trees to enclose walkers, both to protect them from summer heat and to create a

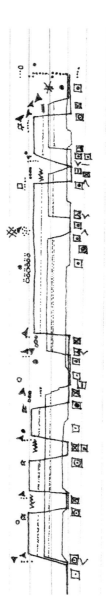

Scored symphonic walk

Pacing destination

Admiring pause

Halting beauty

memorable allée. The alternating spacing, fifteen feet on center, suggests two tempos—three quick syncopated paces or seven leisurely paces. From either direction, the tree-lined allée begins with views over vineyards to the hills beyond and proceeds across creeks into the village center. Where there is less visual interest, the enclosing allee simply provides rapid pacing. At social nodes, destinations, sacred places, and narrow views between buildings to the outlying mountains, the pace slows, and the pathways broaden to accommodate lingering. At three locations along the main promenade, remnant vineyards dedicated as agricultural open space, the pace stops for spectacular juxtapositions of built form and agricultural lands and a sense of connectedness to the regional agricultural landscape: places to pause and sit create rest and contemplation. In the center of the village, the tempo is faster, but this is relative. Magnitudes less intense than the Ramblas, it is the bustling social center of Yountville. A town square accommodates large public gatherings and eddies of daily newsing. Here rapid and slowest tempos combine. The quick marching allée of pistache trees and lingering public garden become one. This promenade is memorable because it is strongly unified by the double rows of trees that set a tempo that creates multiple internal rhythms. The blaze of fall color is unforgettable. Within the allee framework, the regional particularness of the town and landscape is revealed—clusters of buildings, vineyards, and hills. The walk is organized to dramatize each and weave them into harmony. It is a major attraction for local people, who walk more than twice as much as average Americans. The lesson from Yountville is fundamental. Every city can make great walking streets. One need not live in Kyoto, Paris, or Barcelona to have pedestrian routes that inspire people to walk, that are part of a new healthy community pride and identity, and that interpret the uniqueness of a place in ways that are both utilitarian and poetic.

Metamorphic Walks

My mother taught first grade for over thirty years and introduced hundreds of children to the magical processes of metamorphism and metamorphosis. She was enthusiastic about rocks, but she was passionate about insects and amphibians. Her classrooms extended outdoors and brought in every imaginable changing stage of larva, pupa, and adult. Once when she was explaining how tadpoles emerge from eggs, lose their tails, and become frogs, a tow-headed first grader was incredulous. My mother recalled the moment. When she said, "and they turn into frogs," Coleman's big blue eyes met hers and he shouted, "Miss Hester, you don't expect me to believe that, do you?" When I heard this story, Coleman was a graduate student studying with me. Both he and she remembered the scene precisely twenty years after it occurred. My mother always took her classes on metamorphosis walks with rewards for various life-cycle stages found. Those walks must have changed many lives.

Some walks indeed transform. They supersede the sublime living symphonic sequence. I have heard countless stories about life-changing judgments that were concluded on a long walk. Often these walks intentionally inspire. There are at least four types of walks designed to be transformative: journeys to sacred destinations, aimless wandering, routine routes, and walks without measure.

First, pilgrimages, like visiting Mecca, the Vatican, or the Parthenon, typically have a structured, geometric sequence toward a goal. The sando, the walk to Japanese religious sites, employs a sequence that heightens readiness for religious transcendence. In every case, the landscape is used to metamorphic advantage. The most powerful sando experiences involve a difficult uphill ascent that is graded to be even more strenuous than the natural topography suggests. Gateways mark increasingly sacred domains. Carefully orchestrated twists and turns reveal plateaus where one's breath is caught and, during the pause, attention is focused on a desired lesson. This is in addition to the pacing devices that are discussed in the previous section. By the time that the most sacred inner shrine is reached, often near but not at the mountaintop, exhaustion has readied the pilgrim for transformation.

The mountaintop itself has the power to help Americans metamorphose. When Martin Luther King Jr. proclaimed that he had been to the mountaintop, he followed with his declaration that he was ready for any challenge, even death.[30] The taxing process of reaching the mountaintop prepares us figuratively and literally for life's most difficult passages.

Mountaintops are only one of many metamorphic destinations. Walks to rivers, rushing streams, unusual geologic formations, and primal landscapes where biological metamorphosis occurs conspicuously can catalyze personal transformation. Thoreau concluded that when he needed to create himself anew, he sought the darkest wood, the thickest most interminable swamp. He also tried climbing a tall tree.[31] Daphne was transformed in a vast

Mom's metamorphic walks

Mountaintop pilgrimage

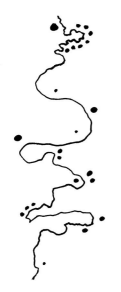

Aimless wandering

open field, circled by her pursuing lover until in desperation her white thighs grew bark, her arms became branches, her head and hair a cloud of leaves. She was laurel. Such dramatic archetypal landscapes invite mythic metamorphosis for gods and mortals undergoing life changes.[32]

Seeing change, whether a metamorphic rock form or a tadpole losing its tail, reminds us of our own need to grow. Whether a river that changes from side to side over geological time or an eel that wriggles past in an instant, transience inspires us to stop walking and leap into the darkness to a goal. The metamorphic landscape fills us with faith to metamorphose.[33]

The second category of metamorphic walks is aimless wandering. The archetype is the biblical story of the Jews wandering in the wilderness and gaining extraordinary revelations and insights. This wandering frees us from "all worldly engagements."[34] One becomes as vagrant as the meandering river. This is the essence of being equally at home everywhere.[35] Practical design applications include creating urban and wild places where such wandering can occur. There must be multiple paths and less orchestration than symphonic sequences. Aimless walking is facilitated by a lack of clear hierarchy and direction. The landscape may be illegible and disorienting. The design should help the wanderer become lost. Such places are important in the impelling city but should be provided with caution.

The third kind of transformative walk is routine. Typically to and from work or other frequently taken routes, they are as comfortable as a well-worn pair of shoes. Such walks allow the mind to disengage, become thoughtlessly thoughtful, and meditate unconsciously. After concentrated work, movement of one's legs stimulates the unthinking mind to flow in different directions.[36] For such endeavors, Thoreau prescribed walking like a camel, "which ruminates when walking."[37] Great discoveries and personal insights are stimulated by walks that are designed to have a simple, relaxing hierarchy of space, tempo that varies little, and unpronounced crescendos. Overorchestration for the camel walker is distracting. Ritual expectations, like daily social exchanges and seasonal changes, are welcome, but the overly dramatic is not. It is no accident that the great Japanese scholar Kitaro Nishida, who first integrated Eastern and Western thought, chose the route between home and Kyoto University that was later named for him, the Philosopher's Walk. It remains day in and day out meditatively simple—a simple tree-lined canal of water that quietly runs for several kilometers with little change in pacing.

Impelling Form

A fourth metamorphic travel is a walk without measure. People describe these as purposeful and Spartan—usually an out-and-back, unornamented course, like an abandoned railroad right-of-way, roadway, or other long, straight route through a starkly unchanging landscape. The walker with nagging problems or crisis walks at a brisk pace until the problem dissipates or a new course of action becomes clear. Sometimes this requires only several hundred feet of walking, sometimes four or five miles. The distance is never preset. You can't turn around until the solution is clearly visualized. One such walker in Fort Bragg, California, uses an abandoned logging road, part of a state beach. Perfectly straight, paralleling the Pacific Coast, the route is unchanging. Vegetation is sparse and monotonous. Sand stretches as far as he can see. The road vanishes into the horizon or is obscured by flowing sand, sea spray, or fog. His longest walk was nearly fourteen miles from Fort Bragg to Ten-Mile Beach and back. That was a complex problem, but he achieved a life-changing solution. The main design criteria for these walks is a long, perfectly straight way through an unadorned, simple, even severe landscape. The designer must be disciplined and restrained to create a stoic experience. These metamorphic walks, like the walk along the edge of Crissy Field in San Francisco rain, are rare treasures in any city. Never miss the opportunity to make one.

Walking without measure

Social promenade

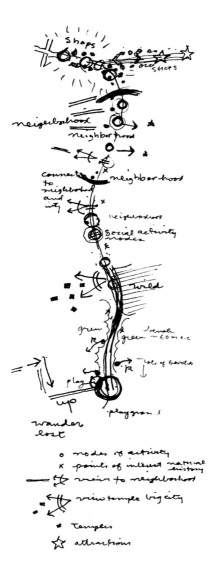

Philosopher's routine walk

Grounded

Mythic or mundane, the most essential aspect of walking is the ground plane. The design of the ground surface controls pace. Simplistically, create a wide, flat, or slightly downhill straight route, pave it with unadorned concrete, and you encourage rapid tempo. Narrow the route, twist the course uphill, roughen and vary the textures and spacing of the surfaces, and you slow the pace. Varying direction, material, and distance between steps vertically and horizontally forces the attention on the ground to avoid hazards and is a powerful means to control both the pace and what one sees, not just on the ground but all around. For example, when attention is fixed on steps with unfamiliar terrain, nothing can be casually viewed more than ten feet ahead. Hand and eye must be both firm and clever.[38] When the ground plane demands concentration, it is as effective as a wall at screening out the world.

Changing the amount of attention that the ground requires is the primary design tool for varying the pace of dwelling and orchestrating the experience of landscape. This is more than avoiding hazards. The ground plane ties us to the earth, forms our most basic relationship to the ecology of the landscape, gives us roots, and provides immense aesthetic pleasure.

Paving the walk makes a great deal of difference, not just in speed but also for ground-water infiltration. Pervious ground planes—like soil littered with fallen leaves, grass, sand, gravel, stones, or decomposed granite—replenish water tables and aquifers. Life emerges and invites kinship with the earth. Raw ground has textures and smells that are associated with earth dwelling. They turn to mud when wet. They require maintenance and stewardship and do not easily accommodate speed, heavy or intense human use, or large gatherings of people.

Impervious surfaces—like concrete, asphalt, brick, and other pavements—accommodate speed and heavy use. They divert water, changing local ecologies with dramatic impacts. Carefully crafted, they combine with pervious surfaces to welcome both continuous pedestrian use and ground-water infiltration. Most essential to urbanity, impervious walkways create enabling form. When designed for delight, paved ground surfaces can be so impelling that gathering and lingering is irresistible.

Laurie Olin's design for the Sixteenth Street mall in Denver created a ground plane that by itself bounds the space and makes an inviting gathering space of what is so often considered only a utilitarian exchange point. It

Laurie Olin's attention to the ground plane
changes a utilitarian streetscape into an
inviting gathering space.

serves pedestrians, bus exchanges, and lingering. For children, the pattern is
a hopscotch playground. For adults, it is art that hasn't been hung on a wall.

Paving provides artistry throughout significant expanses of some cities.
It calls out the particularness of the place and is a source of identity and
memory. Black and white stone fragments in Lisbon, Portugal, are formed
into sequential mosaics that lead the pedestrian through the most delightful
part of the city. Distinctive of the local geology, the contrasting colors call
out regional uniqueness. Patterning again creates ground art and makes an
unforgettable part of the city.

The design of the ground plane also delights when it turns pacing into
a ballet of movement. This is powerfully done in a variety of Japanese garden devices. Rhythm and direction created by the placement of carefully
chosen rocks guide one across a ground of pervious surfaces. This is the
method that is used at Katsura Imperial Villa. Each rock is worthy of inspection, as is the relationship of each to the next. The entirety of a series also
warrants study. The rocks are both visual music and walking surface. From
one perspective, the ground between, covered in moss, is an interval of negative space that is to be avoided in stepping. But careful viewing reveals that

Denver's Sixteenth Street Mall

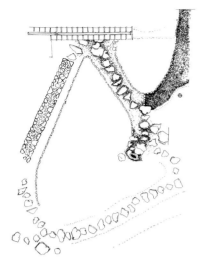

Rock walks, Katsura

Concrete turtles provide an adventurous crossing of the Kamo and Takano rivers and inspire the playful child even in adults.

the interval between rocks is itself finely crafted. One allows stepping but no infiltration; the other allows infiltration but no stepping. Both are firm and impel the eye.

Similarly arranged stones for crossing water add complexity. Water not only forbids stepping in the interval space but also creates tension between solid and liquid. The interplay of safety of terra firma and danger of transparent sea demands attention to each step and alerts and delights the senses. In Kyoto, this device extends into the public landscape, where stone turtles provide jumping stones across the Kamo River. These crossings transform everyone, young or old, expressive or reserved, into playful children. In this case, the ground plane is all that is needed to create unconstrained joy. Another device, the narrow wooden walkway (often no wider than twelve inches, joined at angles) makes an alternating rhythm over a pond or through an iris marsh. This draws undivided attention to the contrasting solid and vegetated liquid. Variations of this provide the delight of creek walking, crossing a bog by walking along fallen logs, traversing a wetland on a narrow boardwalk, or balancing while stepping along a diving board.

For city designers, the ground plane presents both a challenge and an opportunity. Because it is so often made for speed, it has come to be seen as a monotonous flat expanse of utility or (maybe more accurately) is not seen at all. The challenge is to reawaken city makers to its potential. The way that we treat the surface of the earth can alter the pace of life, can ground inhabitants in their places, can serve ecological purpose, and can provide beauty and identity. This requires design attention and resolve.

Impelling Form

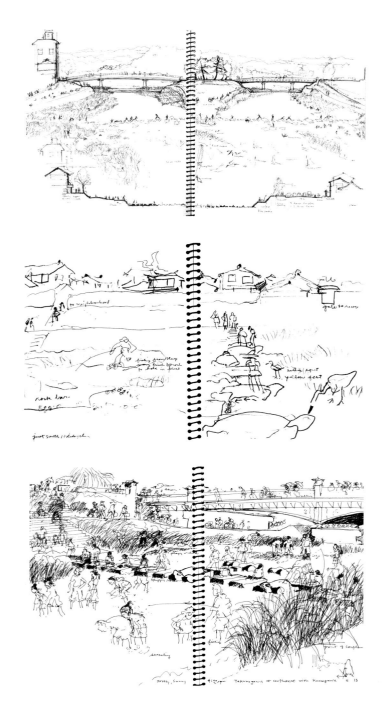

Walk All Over

In the study of pacing, we have observed that the tempo of American habitation is dysfunctionally dominated by the hurried and hasty. Swiftness has produced disastrous outcomes in our cities, not the least of which are disease-causing pollution, speedways, neighborhoods divided by freeways, and streets that pedestrians can cross only at considerable peril. Environments of speed replaced slower-paced dwelling. Pedestrian environments became neglected. Americans abandoned walking, undermining community and personal health. Increased obesity, heart diseases, and diabetes, among other illnesses of inactivity, resulted.

At this point, we can only imagine a world that turns more slowly and provides us with a holiday-like pace in our daily lives. However, when we change pace through the design of our habitation, we see immediate and dramatic benefits. The many impelling joys of sane tempo sing out. The paces of andantes and adagios encourage more deliberative decision making and appropriate denial of speedy but harmful projects. Freeways, dams, and other quick fixes are exposed. Andantes and adagios support enabling form, especially centeredness and associated socializing, lingering, hanging out, smelling the roses, tasting the strawberries, reading a library book at the bus stop, rambling, sauntering, and civic loitering. Slowness fosters naturalness and inhabits science. Essential design actions include curbing the car, making walkways in the spirit of living symphonic sequences, creating transcen-

Sequence of rapid nonspace

The walk between house and studio consisted of the shortest distance between doorways at such a rapid pace that it became nonspace.

Impelling Form

dent routes that are so evocative that they touch the soul, and forming the ground plane to dictate deliberate pacing that calls attention to the full richness of the earth.

Cities will be more impelling if we can walk all over them, even after midnight. This requires designers to provide safe and pleasant places to walk and exercise in every neighborhood. In each city-design decision, big or small, walkers should be given preference over the car. Speeds and volumes of car traffic should be decreased by design. Pedestrian ways must be multimodal to ensure the critical mass that is needed for social safety. They must be connected to centers and destinations and must access wild nature and social life within a brief walk. This requires better integrated and mixed land uses, higher density, and a decrease in distance between home, work, and daily needs.

The region should be accessible by foot, providing opportunities for ten- or twenty-mile walks and excursions of weeks or months. At the smallest scale of neighborhood and home, even utilitarian walking should provide unspeakable joy.

Recently, we confronted such a utilitarian space in our own small backyard. The former garage, now studio, is located about ten strides from the back door of our house. This is a trip someone in our household makes at least a dozen times each day, often many more. For years, this walk consisted of the shortest distance between two points, a functional and quick pace that rendered the walk nonspace. Then it occurred to us that this neglected path

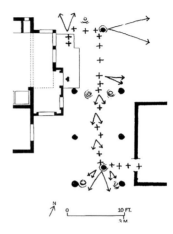

Sequence of pleasure

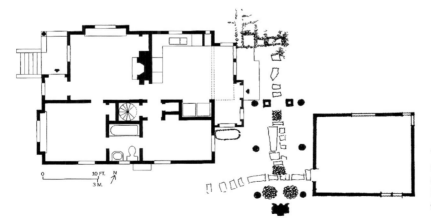

The redesigned path leads north to arrive south, encourages neighboring, forces the eye to the ground, and surprises with what is unseen during attentive stepping—a walk of pleasure.

North steps

Swaying fern

Sculpted third

Working-class east

The walk north steps down to a limestone post with sea-creature fossils and then to a sandstone landing that is generous enough to pause and comfortably turn east. The next three steps require focused downward attention—the narrowing sandstone, a small granite, a sculpted third, expecting a steadying hesitation.

0   3 inches

Red column south

Coral and Petoskey

Community god

Mothed lily

had the potential to change the most mundane daily route into a special event. We began to redesign the walk.

We made it indirect and varied the ground plane. To arrive southeast, the path now first leads north toward our neighbors, crossing a short, wooden stoop, down steps—one wood, one a recycled limestone fence post—to a sandstone landing with strawberries growing in the cracks and ferns swaying in a corner. This space, filled with treasured rocks, is shared with our neighbors. We talk to them more now. Then the path takes three steps east. Each step is over the intense smells of thyme. The three stones are placed far enough apart to require complete attention. The third is sculpted. It holds an inch of reflective water in a fold: the image in the water is interesting, but the step must be cautious to avoid the wet. This stone is large enough to stand on with both feet, pause, and look past firewood up through a walnut tree into the early morning sun. Then the path turns south across varied stones until one drops six inches to a point where the path is squeezed by three-foot-tall columns with two-foot rock capitals that invite touching and a pause. The pause directs my eye to a sign pointing east to my hometown, Hester's Store, 2,400 miles away. The smell of crushed pineapple mint acknowledges the entry to a short tunnel of six compactly spaced fig trees, dense with shade, dark purple with shadow. Smooth river rocks catch the eye. The path leads south six steps to bleached coral surrounded by orange sandstone. At the end of the eight-step tunnel is a large, red column that is so bright and mysterious in form that it continues to attract my attention after hundreds of trips. It draws me to the community god beside it. This forces me to alternate my focused eye on each step and back to the redness until I'm directly in front of the column. Here the path turns straight east toward the studio door, but I always linger because the end of the tunnel reveals, to the south, rock piles of multiple textures and colors, depending on the weather and, to the west, a tiny pond partly hidden by water irises. Goldfinches and chickadees attend me here. All call my observation away from the destination. I linger. A moth snuggles into the center of a lily. Finally, I turn and enter the studio.

The experience of the ground plane is primary but is reinforced by planting. It forms varied tempos of enclosure and opening, conceals features of the landscape until the right moment, provides detailed sensual delight, and creates wildlife habitat. The only full enclosure is the sunless tunnel of fig trees. Walls of honeysuckle, trumpet vine, iris, and jasmine make partial enclosures. These green walls direct the walker's eye, screen unsightly views, and hide sculptural elements and the pond until the walker finds an appropriate place to pause and contemplate them. Flowers change the walk with seasonal color and smells. When the wild irises are blooming, for example, I walk far out of the way for closer inspection. When the pond is alive with marsh marigolds, a detour through the water irises across rounded rocks that are awkwardly placed is required. The water plants also provide habitat for tadpoles and young fish, an irresistible attraction. The slower walk almost always includes a wildlife sighting. Red admirals, fritillaries, cabbage butterflies, skippers, hummingbirds, bushtits, mockingbirds, and squirrels are most frequent. Egrets, soaring hawks, painted ladies, and phoebes are so uncommon that their appearances make a crescendo that lingers for weeks.

By changing tempo, a five-second, hurried dash from house to studio was replaced with a thirty-second walk of pleasure. Our entire experience of daily life has been transformed. We dwell differently. The extended slow walk delights us at every turn. Such is the power of carefully attended pacing, in even the most unspectacular places.

The sandstone path leads to an intersection marked by bleached coral and Petoskey stones—inviting the weary to Oahu and Lake Michigan. An incised dragonfly, however, never flees one's approach—eastward to the studio, westward over the splendid curving flat rock, to unknown landscapes beyond.

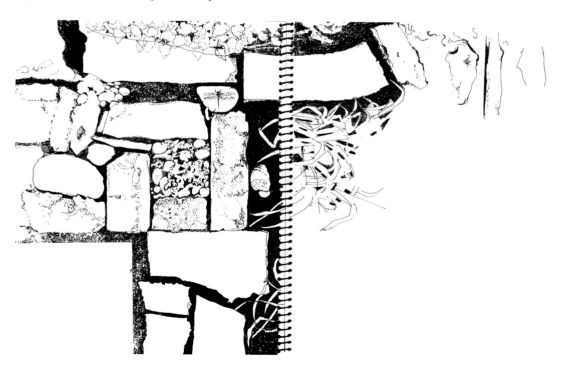

Epilogue

Writing this book reinforced my optimism. While I am overwhelmed by the despair around us and the meanness we confront in our habitation, ecological democracy takes root, sprouts, and blooms here and there. I have reported some of the cases. These convince me that partnered ecology and democracy offer us a lasting and fulfilling future. I have interwoven ecology and democracy into one theory of good city form. This intermixing forms my central thesis. With distance, it still rings true. I am equally convinced that healthy cities can be achieved only if they are shaped to gain enabling, resilient, and impelling form simultaneously. Our habitation must enable us to know and work with our neighbors. It must be resilient enough to endure. It must impel us by its beauty to fill our hearts with gladness. All three are essential. Without the others, any one is worthless.

Values are central to achieve this inseparable triumvirate. Until we refocus city making on things that really matter to people and help them uncover and concretize core values of dwelling, cities will be shaped by technology, real estate speculation, and misplaced status seeking. That is no way to make a good city. Therefore, sacredness, both worldly and spiritual, is the integer of the fifteen principles. Sacredness gives form to intense and abiding worth. This is the crux of my theory. Because limited extent, connectedness, centeredness, and particularness are urban patterns that are repeatedly associated with sacredness, they are the initiating forces of my ideas. These are most interrelated with other principles. These too continue to ring true.

Design theory, while speculative, seeks predictable orderliness through hierarchies like sentence structure or through simplicity like a single big bang. In my thesis, ranked classes are formed by centrality and degree of interconnectedness. Sacredness is the primary impetus but is no solitary big bang. This theory is messy—more like a mass of mating salamanders than a regression analysis. Each principle is a discrete amphibian subject to study as I have done, but the value of this theory lies in the entirety of the intertwined, squirming mass of fifteen principles. Each influences others to

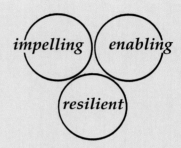

Essential form

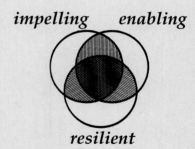

Simultaneous single objective

Sacredness, limited extent, connectedness, centeredness, and particularness are the initiating forces of the city form that supports ecological democracy.

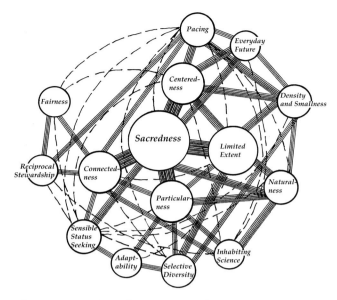

greater or lesser extents, but all act as one. Like salamanders that are drawn from multiple watersheds to one spot for the single purpose of mating, these principles form a thesis only when considered in the context of creating enabling, resilient, and impelling city form as a single objective.

This sounds too highfalutin given my ability. I still do not know with certainty how all the principles catalyze and influence each other. I am able to diagram only the most obvious relationships. Although the principles clearly serve primarily one master of the triumvirate, I have learned that their effects cross the arbitrary lines of enabling, resilient, and impelling form. Whether this is strength or weakness, I can't say for sure. Those smarter and more systematic than I will better understand how these principles interact and will answer if these are the best or fewest or even good principles to shape cities of ecological democracy.

For those of us who make cities, theory takes shape from intellectual inquiry and experience. We learn from success and failure. Why did this work and that fail? If something works, we keep doing it and it becomes a thesis. If it fails, we ponder it. Design theory adjusts to realities of implementation until that theory is meaningful. In retrospect, this is the strength of what I have written. The projects that I have studied have advanced small increments of ecological democracy. To be built, they had to be visionary yet practical enough to satisfy tax-weary publics, working drawings, contractors, and users. The theory that I advance is grounded in reflective city making. As such, it should be useful in everyday practice as a checklist. For public participants, it can serve to uncover what is being neglected in your own cities; it provides precedents for rallying imaginative local undertakings. For designers, it helps us think big and little at the same time. It helps take both corrective and inspirational city-making actions toward ecological democracy. It puts project design in an overall framework with a long-term vision. This helps us achieve influential results from small piecemeal efforts. And it encourages us to be playful even when tackling monstrous problems.

And yes, it is fearlessly optimistic. Optimism is essential in pursuing ecological democracy. Optimism will help us shape healthier places to dwell and create the most fulfilling lives we can achieve. And optimism will keep us cheerful along the way.

The principles as a collective theory help designers think big and small at the same time, which is essential for achieving ecological democracy.

Notes

Enabling Form: Introduction

1. Robert D. Putnam, *Bowling Alone: The Collapse and Revival of American Community* (New York: Simon and Schuster, 2000).

2. Percival Goodman and Paul Goodman, *Communitas: Means of Livelihood and Ways of Life* (New York: Columbia University Press, 1990).

3. Goodman and Goodman, *Communitas;* David Riesman, *The Lonely Crowd: A Study of the Changing American Character* (New Haven: Yale University Press, 1969); Mark Francis, Lisa Cashdan, and Lynn Paxon, *The Making of Neighborhood Open Spaces: Community Design, Development and Management of Open Spaces* (New York: City University of New York, Center for Human Environments, 1982); Allan B. Jacobs, *Making City Planning Work* (Chicago: American Society of Planning Officials, 1978).

4. Putnam, *Bowling Alone;* Richard Sennett, *The Fall of Public Man* (New York: Knopf, 1977).

5. Robert Gurwitt, "The Casparados," *Preservation* 52, no. 6 (2000): 38–45.

6. Roger Fisher, *Getting to Yes: Negotiating Agreement without Giving In* (Boston: Houghton Mifflin, 1981); Andre L. Delbecq, *Group Techniques for Program Planning: A Guide to Nominal Group and Delphi Processes* (Glenview: Scott, Foresman, 1975); Lawrence Susskind and Jeffrey Cruikshank, *Breaking the Impasse: Consensual Approaches to Resolving Public Disputes* (New York: Basic Books, 1987).

7. Randolph T. Hester Jr., "Participatory Design and Environmental Justice: Pas de Deux or Time to Change Partners?," *Journal of Architectural and Planning Research* 4, no. 4 (1987): 289–300, and "The Place of Participatory Design," in *Democratic Design in the Pacific Rim: Japan, Taiwan, and the United States* (22–41) ed. Randolph T. Hester Jr. and Corrina Kweskin (Mendocino: Ridge Times Press, 1999); Arthur M. Schlesinger Jr., *The Disuniting of America: Reflections on a Multicultural Society* (New York: Norton, 1993).

8. Hester, "Place of Participatory Design."

9. Edward C. Relph, *Place and Placelessness* (London: Pion, 1976) and *The Modern Urban Landscape* (London: Croom Helm, 1987).

10. Peter Calthorpe, *The Next American Metropolis: Ecology, Community and the American Dream* (New York: Princeton Architectural Press, 1993); Jane Jacobs, *The Death and Life of Great American Cities* (New York: Random

House, 1961); Randolph T. Hester Jr., *Neighborhood Space* (Stroudsburg: Dowden, Hutchinson & Ross, 1975).

11. Michael Southworth and Eran Ben-Joseph, *Streets and the Shaping of Towns and Cities* (New York: McGraw-Hill, 1997); Donald Appleyard, *Livable Streets* (Berkeley: University of California Press, 1981).

12. Simon Nicholson, *Community Participation in City Decision Making* (Milton Keynes: Open University Press, 1973); Robin C. Moore, *Childhood's Domain: Play and Place in Child Development* (London: Croom Helm, 1986).

13. William H. Whyte, *The Social Life of Small Urban Spaces* (Washington, DC: Conservation Foundation, 1980); Kevin Lynch, *Managing the Sense of a Region* (Cambridge: MIT Press, 1976) and *Good City Form* (Cambridge: MIT Press, 1981).

14. Appleyard, *Livable Streets.*

15. Moore, *Childhood's Domain;* Roger Hart, *Children's Experience of Place* (New York: Irvington, 1979) and *Children's Participation: The Theory and Practice of Involving Young Citizens in Community Development and Environment Care* (London: Earthscan, 1997); David W. Orr, *Ecological Literacy: Education and the Transition to a Postmodern World* (New York: State University of New York Press, 1992).

16. Milton Rokeach, *Beliefs, Attitudes, and Values: A Theory of Organization and Change* (San Francisco: Jossey-Bass, 1970).

Enabling Form: Centeredness

1. Relph, *Place and Placelessness;* Robert N. Bellah et al., *Habits of the Heart: Individualism and Commitment in American Life* (New York: Perennial, 1986); Hester, *Neighborhood Space;* Robert D. Putnam et al., *Making Democracy Work: Civic Traditions in Modern Italy* (Princeton: Princeton University Press, 1994); Judith E. Innes and David E. Booher, *Consensus Building as Role-Playing and Bricolage: Toward a Theory of Collaborative Planning* (Berkeley: Institute of Urban and Regional Development, University of California, 1997); Susskind and Cruikshank, *Breaking the Impasse.*

2. Lewis Mumford, *The City in History: Its Origins, Its Transformations, and Its Prospects* (New York: Harcourt, Brace, Jovanovich, 1961); Jacobs, *Death and Life;* Robert E. Park, Ernest W. Burgess, and Roderick D. McKenzie, *Human Communities: The City and Human Ecology* (Chicago: University of Chicago Press, 1967); Suzanne Keller, *The Urban Neighborhood: A Sociological Perspective* (New York: Random House, 1968); Clarence Perry, "The Neighborhood Unit: A Scheme of Arrangement for the Family-Life Community," in *Regional Survey of New York and Its Environs,* Vol. 7, *Neighborhood and Community Planning* (22–140) (New York: Committee on The Regional Plan of New York and Its Environs, 1929); Clarence Stein, *Toward New Towns in America* (Cambridge: MIT Press, 1966); Kevin Lynch, *The Image of the City*

(Cambridge: MIT Press, 1960) and *Good City Form* (Cambridge: MIT Press, 1981); John Simonds, *Landscape Architecture: A Manual of Site Planning and Design* (New York: McGraw-Hill, 1983).

3. Hester, *Neighborhood Space;* Simonds, *Landscape Architecture;* Perry, "Neighborhood Unit"; Andres Duany, Elizabeth Plater-Zyberk, and Alex Kreiger, *Towns and Town-Making Principles* (New York: Rizzoli, 1991); Marcia McNally, "On the Care and Feeding of the Grassroots," in *Democratic Design in the Pacific Rim: Japan, Taiwan, and the United States* (214–227), ed. Randolph T. Hester Jr. and Corrina Kweskin (Mendocino: Ridge Times Press, 1999).

4. Urban Ecology, *Blueprint for a Sustainable Bay Area* (Oakland: Urban Ecology, 1996), 64.

5. Hugh Sidey, "The Two Sides of the Sam Walton Legacy," *Time,* April 20, 1992, 50–52.

6. Urban Ecology, *Blueprint,* 56.

7. J. Douglas Porteous, *Environment and Behavior: Planning and Everyday Life* (Reading: Addison-Wesley, 1977), 72–83; Melvin M. Webber, "Order in Diversity: Community Without Propinquity," in *Cities and Space* (23–54), ed. L. Wingo (Baltimore: John Hopkins Press, 1963), "The Urban Place and the Nonplace Urban Realm," in *Explorations into Urban Structure* (79–153), ed. Melvin M. Webber (Philadelphia: University of Pennsylvania Press, 1964), and "Culture, Territoriality, and the Elastic Mile," *Papers and Proceedings of the Regional Science Association* 13 (1964): 59–69.

8. Svend Riemer, "Villagers in Metropolis," *British Journal of Sociology* 2, no. 1 (1951): 31–43; Richard Meier, *A Communications Theory of Urban Growth* (Cambridge: MIT Press, 1962).

9. Porteous, *Environment and Behavior,* 80.

10. Mark Francis, "Making a Community Place," in *Democratic Design in the Pacific Rim: Japan, Taiwan, and the United States* (170–177), ed. Randolph T. Hester Jr. and Corrina Kweskin (Mendocino: Times Press, 1999).

11. Herbert Gans, *The Urban Villagers: Group and Class in the Life of Italian-Americans* (New York: Free Press, 1962) and *People and Plans: Essays on Urban Problems and Solutions* (New York: Basic Books, 1968).

12. Michael D. Beyard and W. Paul O'Mara, *Shopping Center Development Handbook* (Washington, DC: Urban Land Institute, 1999), 12–13.

13. Perry, "The Neighborhood Unit"; Duany, Plater-Zyberk, and Kreiger, *Towns.*

14. Hester, *Neighborhood Space,* 99.

15. Ibid., 108.

16. Everett M. Rogers, *Diffusion of Innovations* (New York: Free Press, 1995); M. Tucker and T. L. Napier, "The Diffusion Task in Community Development," *Journal of the Community Development Society* 25, no. 1 (1994): 80–100.

17. Victor Steinbrueck, *Market Sketchbook* (Seattle: University of Washington Press, 1968).

18. Urban Ecology, *Blueprint,* 65.

19. Christopher Alexander et al., *A Pattern Language* (New York: Oxford University Press, 1977); Terrence Lee, "The Urban Neighborhood as a Sociospatial Schema," in *Environmental Psychology: Man and His Physical Setting* (349–369), ed. Harold M. Proshansky, William H. Ittelson, and Leanne G. Rivlin (New York: Holt Rinehard and Winston, 1970); Walter Hood, *Urban Diaries* (Washington, DC: Spacemaker Press, 1997).

20. Urban Ecology, *Blueprint,* 68–113; Randolph T. Hester Jr., "Life, Liberty and the Pursuit of Sustainable Happiness," *Places* 9, no. 3 (1995): 4–17.

21. H. Osmond, "Function as the Basis of Psychiatric Ward Design," *Mental Hospitals* (Architectural Supplement) 8 (1957): 23–29; M. P. Lawton, "The Human Being and the Institutional Building," in *Designing for Human Behavior: Architecture and the Behavioral Sciences* (60–71), ed. Jon T. Lang et al. (Stroudsburg: Dowden, Hutchinson and Ross, 1974); Robert Sommer, *Personal Space: The Behavioral Basis of Design* (Englewood Cliffs: Prentice-Hall, 1969); Whyte, *The Social Life of Small Urban Spaces.*

22. Delbecq, *Group Techniques;* Robert Sommer, "Small Group Ecology," *Psychological Bulletin,* no. 67 (1967): 145–152.

23. David Stea, "Space, Territoriality, and Human Movements," *Landscape* 15, no. 4 (1965): 13–16; Robert Sommer, "A Better World Not Utopia," keynote address, in *Proceedings of the International Association for the Study of the People and Their Physical Surroundings* (57–61) (West Berlin: I.A.P.S. [I.A.S.P.P.S.], 1984).

24. Hester, *Neighborhood Space,* 51, 57.

25. Robert Greese, *Jens Jensen* (Baltimore: John Hopkins University Press, 1992), 176–178.

26. Jan Gehl, *Life between Buildings* (New York: Van Nostrand Reinhold, 1987).

27. Hester, *Neighborhood Space,* 72.

28. Edward T. Hall, *The Hidden Dimension* (Garden City: Doubleday, 1966).

29. Community Development by Design, *Runyon Canyon Four: Cutout Workbook* (Berkeley: Community Development by Design, 1985).

30. Sommer, "Small Group Ecology," 147.

31. Ibid., 147–148.

32. Amos Rapoport, *House Form and Culture* (Englewood Cliffs: Prentice-Hall, 1969).

33. John Horton, *The Politics of Diversity: Immigration, Resistance, and Change in Monterey Park, California* (Philadelphia: Temple University Press, 1995).

Enabling Form: Connectedness

1. Eugene P. Odum, *Fundamentals of Ecology* (Philadelphia: Saunders, 1959); Paul Krapfel, *Shifting* (Cottonwood: Self-published, 1989); Michael Hough, *City Form and Natural Process* (New York: Van Nostrand Reinhold, 1984); Ian McHarg, *Design with Nature* (Garden City: Natural History Press, 1969).

2. Randolph T. Hester, Jr., *Community Design Primer* (Mendocino: Ridge Times Press, 1990); Michael Hough, *Out of Place: Restoring Identity to the Regional Landscape* (New Haven: Yale University Press, 1990); Tony Hiss, *The Experience of Place* (New York: Knopf, 1990).

3. Paul Hawken, *The Ecology of Commerce: A Declaration of Sustainability* (New York: HarperBusiness, 1993).

4. Vance O. Packard, *The Status Seekers* (New York: Pocket Books, 1967), 33.

5. Robert L. Thayer Jr., *Gray World, Green Heart: Technology, Nature, and the Sustainable Landscape* (New York: Wiley, 1994); Leo Marx, *The Machine in the Garden: Technology and the Pastoral Ideal in America* (Oxford: Oxford University Press, 2000).

6. Jane Smiley, *A Thousand Acres* (New York: Knopf, 1991); Rachel L. Carson, *Silent Spring* (New York: Houghton Mifflin, 1962).

7. Stewart S. Brand, *How Buildings Learn: What Happens After They're Built* (New York: Penguin, 1994); Wendell Berry, *The Unsettling of America: Culture and Agriculture* (New York: Avon, 1978); McHarg, *Design with Nature.*

8. Wenche E. Dramstad, James D. Olson, and Richard T. T. Forman, *Landscape Ecology Principles in Landscape Architecture and Land-Use Planning* (Washington, DC: Island Press, 1996); Nancy Jack Todd and John Todd, *From Eco-Cities to Living Machines: Principles of Ecological Design* (Berkeley: North Atlantic, 1994); Michael Bernick and Robert Cervero, *Transit Villages in the Twenty-first Century* (New York: McGraw-Hill, 1997); Randolph T. Hester Jr., "Community Design: Making the Grassroots Whole," *Built Environment* 13, no. 1 (1987): 45–60.

9. Hiss, *Experience,* 126–143.

10. Perry, "Neighborhood Unit," 23.

11. Allan Jacobs, Elizabeth Macdonald, and Yodan Rofe, *The Boulevard Book: History, Evolution, Design of Multiway Boulevards* (Cambridge: MIT Press, 2002).

12. Allan Jacobs, "Where the Freeway Meets the City," Paper presented at the University of California Transportation Center Symposium on the Art of Designing Bridges and Freeways, Berkeley, CA, September 20, 2002.

13. Kevin Lynch, *Wasting Away* (San Francisco: Sierra Club, 1990); Mira Engler, "Waste Landscapes: Permissible Metaphors in Landscape Architecture," *Landscape Journal* 14, no. 1 (1995): 10–25.

14. Hough, *City Form;* Thayer, *Gray World;* Ann Whiston Spirn, *The Granite Garden: Urban Nature and Human Design* (New York: Basic Books, 1984).

15. G. Mathias Kondolf, "Hungry Water: Effects of Dams and Gravel Mining on River Channels," *Environmental Management* 21, no. 4 (1997): 551–553.

16. Patricia L. Brown, "The Chroming of the Front Yard," *New York Times,* June 13, 2002, D1, D6.

17. Hart, *Children's Experience.*

18. Judy Corbett and Michael N. Corbett, *Designing Sustainable Communities: Learning from Village Homes* (Washington, DC: Island Press, 2000).

19. Greg Hise and William Deverell, *Eden by Design: The 1930 Olmsted-Bartholomew Plan for the Los Angeles Region* (Berkeley: University of California Press, 2000).

20. Community Development by Design, *Runyon Canyon One–Seven* (Berkeley: Community Development by Design, 1985).

21. Community Development by Design, *Runyon Canyon Master Plan and Design Guidelines* (Berkeley: Community Development by Design, 1986).

22. "Runyon Canyon Master Plan and Design Guidelines," *Landscape Architecture* 77, no. 6 (1987): 60–63.

23. *Landscape Journal,* Special issue on "Eco-Revelatory Design: Nature Constructed/Nature Revealed," ed. Brenda Brown, Terry Harkness, and Douglas Johnston (1998).

24. Orr, *Ecological Literacy.*

25. Hough, *City Form;* Frederick R. Steiner, *The Living Landscape: An Ecological Approach to Landscape Planning* (New York: McGraw-Hill, 1991).

26. Mathis Wackernagel and William E. Rees, *Our Ecological Footprint: Reducing Human Impact on the Earth,* New Catalyst Bioregional Series, no. 9 (Gabriola Island: New Society Publishers, 1996).

27. Urban Ecology, *Blueprint,* 28.

28. Rocky Mountain Institute, *Rocky Mountain Institute Newsletter* 5, no. 3 (1989).

29. Chip Sullivan, *Garden and Climate* (New York: McGraw-Hill, 2002); Joe R. McBride, "Urban Forestry: What We Can Learn from Cities around the World," Paper presented at the National Urban Forest Conference, 1999; Sim Van der Ryn, *The Toilet Papers: Designs to Recycle Human Waste and Water—Dry Toilets, Greywater Systems and Urban Sewage* (Santa Barbara: Capra, 1978); Sim Van der Ryn and Stuart Cowan, *Ecological Design* (Washington, DC: Island Press, 1996).

30. Lowell W. Adams and Louise E. Dove, *Wildlife Reserves and Corridors in the Urban Environment: A Guide to Ecological Landscape Planning and Resource Conservation* (Columbia: National Institute for Urban Wildlife, 1989).

31. Victoria Chanse and Randolph T. Hester Jr., "Characterizing Volunteer Involvement in Wildlife Habitat Planning," in *CELA 2002: Groundwork,* Proceeding of the Annual Meeting of the Council of Educators in Landscape Architecture, State University of New York, Syracuse, NY, September 25–28, 2002; Michael P. Moulton and James Sanderson, *Wildlife Issues in a Changing World* (Boca Raton: Lewis, 1999).

32. Todd and Todd, *Ecocities.*

33. Martin Luther King Jr., "Letter from Birmingham Jail," in *I Have a Dream: Writings and Speeches That Changed the World,* ed. James M. Washington (San Francisco: Harper, 1992), 85.

34. Randolph T. Hester Jr. et al., *Goals for Raleigh: Interview Results Technical Report One* (Raleigh: North Carolina State University, 1973); Nadine Cohodas, "Goals for Raleigh Issues Report," *News and Observer,* May 27, 1973, vi–l;

Michael J. Hall, "Goals for Raleigh: Coming Up with Answers," *Raleigh Times,* June 27, 1973, 9A.

35. Frank J. Smith and Randolph T. Hester Jr., *Community Goal Setting* (Stroudsburg: Dowden, Hutchinson & Ross, 1982).

36. Chanse and Hester, "Characterizing Volunteer Involvement."

37. Hester, *Neighborhood Space;* Karl Linn, "White Solutions Won't Work in Black Neighborhoods," *Landscape Architecture* 59, no. 1 (1968): 23–25; S. William Thompson, "Hester's Progress," *Landscape Architecture* 86, no. 4 (1996): 74–79, 97–99.

38. Hester, *Community Design Primer,* 84.

39. Victor Papanek, *Design for the Real World* (New York: Pantheon, 1971); Hough, *City Form,* 244–245.

40. Daniel Solomon, *Rebuilding* (New York: Princeton Architectural Press, 1992); Anne Vernez Moudon, *Built for Change: Neighborhood Architecture in San Francisco* (Cambridge: MIT Press, 1986).

41. Marc Treib, "A Constellation of Pieces," *Landscape Architecture* 92, no. 3 (2002): 58–67, 92.

42. Randolph T. Hester Jr., *Planning Neighborhood Space with People* (New York: Van Nostrand Reinhold, 1984).

43. Solomon, *Rebuilding;* Urban Ecology, *Blueprint,* 44.

44. Jacobs, Macdonald, and Rofe, *The Boulevard Book;* Calthorpe, *The Next American Metropolis;* Duany, Plater-Zyberk, and Kreiger, *Towns;* Anton C. Nelessen, *Visions for a New American Dream: Process, Principles, and an Ordinance to Plan and Design Small Communities* (Chicago: Planners Press, 1994); Allan B. Jacobs, *Great Streets* (Cambridge: MIT Press, 1993).

45. Louise P. Fortmann, "Talking Claims: Discursive Strategies in Contesting Property," *World Development* 23, no. 6 (1995): 1053–1063; Sally Fairfax et al., "The Federal Forests Are Not What They Seem: Formal and Informal Claims to Federal Lands," *Ecology Law Quarterly* 25, no. 4 (1999): 630–646; Elinor Ostrom, "Institutional Arrangements for Resolving the Commons Dilemma: Some Contending Approaches," in *The Question of the Commons: The Culture and Ecology of Communal Resources* (250–265), ed. Bonnie J. McCay and James M. Acheson (Tucson: University of Arizona Press, 1987) and *Governing the Commons: The Evolution of Institutions for Collective Action* (New York: Cambridge University Press, 1990).

46. Carol Kaesuk Yoon, "Aid for Farmers Helps Butterflies, Too," *New York Times,* July 9, 2002, Science, 1, 4.

47. Randolph T. Hester, Jr., "It's Just a Matter of Fish Heads: Using Design to Build Community," *Small Town* 24, no. 2 (1993): 4–13.

48. Roger Trancik, *Finding Lost Space: Theories of Urban Design* (New York: Van Nostrand Reinhold, 1986).

Enabling Form: Fairness

1. Michael Southworth, "City Learning: Children, Maps, and Transit," *Children's Environments Quarterly* 7, no. 2 (1990): 35–48.
2. Paul Davidoff, "Advocacy and Pluralism in Planning," *Journal of the American Institute of Planners* 31, no. 4 (1965): 331–338.
3. Gans, *Urban Villagers.*
4. Gans, *People and Plans.*
5. Hester, "Participatory Design," 289–300.
6. King, "Letter from Birmingham Jail," 91.
7. Lynch, *Good City Form.*
8. Anthony Downs, *New Visions for Urban America* (Washington, DC: Brookings Institution, 1994).
9. Hester, "Participatory Design."
10. Donald Appleyard et al., *A Humanistic Design Manifesto* (Berkeley: University of California, 1982); Leslie K. Weisman, *Discrimination by Design: A Feminist Critique of the Man-Made Environment* (Urbana: University of Illinois Press, 1992); Clare Cooper Marcus and Wendy Sarkissian, *Housing As If People Mattered: Site Design Guidelines for Medium-Density Family Housing* (Berkeley: University of California Press, 1986); Louise A. Mozingo, "Women and Downtown Open Spaces," *Places* 6, no. 1 (1989): 38–47.
11. Dolores Hayden, *Seven American Utopias: The Architecture of Communication Socialism, 1790–1975* (Cambridge: MIT Press, 1977).
12. Hester, "Participatory Design."
13. Southworth, "City Learning" and *Oakland Explorers: A Cultural Network of Places and People for Kids—Discovery Centers* (Berkeley: Institute of Urban and Regional Development, University of California, 1990).
14. "After Outcry: Greenwich Retreats from Beach Policy and Offers Daily Passes," *New York Times,* March 9, 2002, B15.
15. David Dowall, *The Suburban Squeeze: Land Conversion and Regulation in the San Francisco Bay Area* (Berkeley: University of California Press, 1984).
16. Richard C. Hatch, ed., *The Scope of Social Architecture* (New York: Van Nostrand Reinhold, 1984).
17. Peter Marcuse, "Conservation for Whom?," in *Environmental Quality and Social Justice in Urban America* (17–36), ed. James N. Smith (Washington, DC: Conservation Foundation, 1972); Sherry R. Arnstein, "A Ladder of Citizen Participation," *Journal of the American Institute of Planners* 35, no. 4 (1969): 216–224; Frances Fox Piven, "Whom Does the Advocate Planner Serve?" *Social Policy* 1, no. 1 (1970): 32–37.
18. Robert D. Bullard, *Dumping in Dixie: Race, Class, and Environmental Quality* (Boulder: Westview Press, 2000).
19. Patricia L. Brown, "A Park Offers Nature, Not Just Hoops," *New York Times,* December 28, 2000, F1.

20. Frances Kuo and William Sullivan, "Environment and Crime in the Inner City: Does Vegetation Reduce Crime?," *Environment and Behavior* 33, no. 3 (2001): 343–367.
21. Pyatok Architects, Inc., Gateway Commons housing project, Emeryville, California, <http://www.pyatok.com>.
22. Hester, *Community Design Primer,* 4.
23. Mozingo, "Women and Downtown."
24. Hester, *Community Design Primer.*
25. Dolores Hayden, *The Power of Place: Urban Landscapes as Public History* (Cambridge: MIT Press, 1995); Donna Graves, "Construction Memory: Rosie the Riveter Memorial, Richmond, California," *Places* 15, no. 1 (2002): 14–17.
26. Randolph T. Hester Jr. et al., *Our Children Need Open Space: Fruitvale Open Space Proposal* (Berkeley: Institute of Urban and Regional Development and Department of Landscape Architecture and Environmental Planning, June 1999), 1.
27. Hester, *Community Design Primer.*
28. Randolph T. Hester Jr. et al., *Learning about Union Point: Waterfront Park Site Environmental Analysis* (Berkeley: Institute of Urban and Regional Development, University of California, 1998), 15–17.
29. Union Point Park Partnership Team, *Union Point Park Master Plan* (October 1999).

Enabling Form: Sensible Status Seeking

1. Relph, *Place and Placelessness;* Dean MacCannell, *The Tourist: A New Theory of the Leisure Class* (New York: Schocken Books, 1989).
2. Bellah et al., *Habits of the Heart,* 148–149.
3. Paul Shepard, *Man in the Landscape: A Historic View of the Esthetics of Nature* (New York: Knopf, 1967) and *Thinking Animals: Animals and the Development of Human Intelligence* (New York: Viking, 1978); Rogers, *Diffusion.*
4. Berry, *Unsettling of America.*
5. Packard, *The Status Seekers.*
6. J. B. Jackson, "Other-Directed Houses," *Landscape* 6, no. 2 (1956): 29–35; Relph, *Place and Placelessness.*
7. Rogers, *Diffusion,* 160.
8. Randolph T. Hester Jr., "Womb with a View: How Spatial Nostalgia Affects the Designer," *Landscape Architecture* 69, no. 5 (1979): 475–481, 528.
9. Packard, *The Status Seekers,* 55.
10. Hester, *Neighborhood Space.*
11. Packard, *The Status Seekers,* 70.
12. Hester, "Life, Liberty," 9–10.
13. Jay Appleton, *The Experience of Landscape* (New York: Wiley, 1996).
14. Gans, *Urban Villagers;* Jacobs, *The Death and Life.*

15. *Unstrung Heroes,* dir. Diane Keaton, 93 min., Hollywood-Roth-Arnold, film, from the book by Franz Lidz.

16. Kenko, *Essays in Idleness: the Tsurezuregusa of Kenko,* trans. Donald Keene (Tokyo: Tuttle, 1997), 158.

17. Kathleen Norris, *Dakota: A Spiritual Journal* (New York: Houghton Mifflin, 1993), 169.

18. Relph, *Place and Placelessness;* J. B. Jackson, "The Westward-Moving House: Three American Houses and the People Who Live in Them," *Landscape* 2, no. 3 (1953): 8–21.

19. Hester, *Planning Neighborhood Space.*

20. Garrett Kaoru Hongo, *Volcano: A Memoir of Hawai'i* (New York: Vintage, 1996), 258.

21. William R. Morrish et al., *Planning to Stay: A Collaborative Project* (Minneapolis: Milkweed Editions, 1994).

22. E. F. Schumacher, *Small Is Beautiful: Economics As If People Mattered—Twenty-five Years Later . . . with Commentaries* (Vancouver: Hartley & Marks, 1999), 47–48.

23. Packard, *The Status Seekers,* 105; William H. Whyte, *The Organization Man* (New York: Simon and Schuster, 1972).

24. Packard, *The Status Seekers,* 54.

25. United States Census Bureau, *Statistical Abstract of the United States* (80th ed.) (Washington, DC: U.S. Census Bureau, 1960) and *Statistical Abstract of the United States* (120th ed.) (Washington, DC: U.S. Census Bureau, 2000).

26. Gyogy Kepes, ed., *Structure in Art and in Science* (New York: Braziller, 1965), i.

27. Chuang Chou, "Chuang Tzu," in *The Columbia Anthology of Traditional Chinese Literature: Translations from the Asian Classics* (45–57), ed. Victor Mair (New York: Columbia University Press, 1994), 46.

28. Schumacher, *Small Is Beautiful,* 49, 89, 206.

29. Alexander et al., *A Pattern Language;* Donald MacDonald, *Democratic Architecture: Practical Solutions to Today's Housing Crisis* (New York: Whitney Library of Design, 1996); Solomon, *Rebuilding;* Sam Davis, *The Architecture of Affordable Housing* (Berkeley: University of California Press, 1995); Michael Pyatok, "Martha Stewart vs. Studs Terkel? New Urbanism and Inner Cities Neighborhoods That Work," *Places* 13, no. 1 (2000): 40–43.

30. Martin H. Krieger, *What's Wrong with Plastic Trees? Artifice and Authenticity in Design* (Westport: Praeger, 2000).

31. Hester, *Neighborhood Space,* 38.

32. Kenko, *Essays in Idleness,* 137.

33. Robert L. Thayer Jr., "Conspicuous Non-Consumption: The Symbolic Aesthetics of Solar Architecture," in *Proceedings of the Eleventh Annual Conference of the Environmental Design Research Association* (Washington, DC: EDRA, 1980); Clare Cooper Marcus, *House as a Mirror of Self: Exploring the Deeper Meaning of Home* (Berkeley: Conari Press, 1995); Michael N. Cor-

bett, *A Better Place to Live: New Designs for Tomorrow's Communities* (Emmaus: Rodale Press, 1981).

34. Hester, *Planning Neighborhood Space,* 192–193.
35. Thayer, "Conspicuous Non-Consumption," 182.
36. Amos Rapoport, *Human Aspects of Urban Form: Toward a Man-Environment Approach to Urban Form and Design* (Oxford: Pergamon, 1977); Porteous, *Environment and Behavior.*
37. Edward J. Blakely and Mary Gail Snyder, *Fortress America: Gated Communities in the United States* (Washington, DC: Brookings Institutions Press, 1997).
38. Oscar Newman, *Community of Interest* (Garden City: Doubleday, 1980).
39. Rapoport, *Human Aspects.*
40. Packard, *The Status Seekers,* 16–17, 78.
41. Thayer, *Gray World;* and Berry, *Unsettling of America.*
42. Joan Iverson Nassauer, "Messy Ecosystems, Orderly Frames," *Landscape Journal* 14, no. 2 (1995): 161–170.
43. Tsutsumi Chunagon Monogatari, "The Lady Who Loved Insects," in *Anthology of Japanese Literature, from the Earliest Era to the Mid-nineteenth Century* (170–176), ed. Donald Keene (New York: Grove Press, 1960).
44. *Landscape Journal,* Special issue on "Eco-Revelatory Design"; Southworth, "City Learning," 35–48.
45. Louise A. Mozingo, "The Aesthetics of Ecological Design: Seeing Science as Culture," *Landscape Journal* 16, no. 1 (1997): 46–59; Nassauer, "Messy Ecosystems," 161–170.
46. Hester, *Neighborhood Space,* 180–181.

Enabling Form: Sacredness

1. Relph, *The Modern Urban Landscape.*
2. Gaston Bachelard, *The Poetics of Space,* trans. Maria Jolas (Boston: Beacon, 1969); Mircea Eliade, *Mystic Stories: The Sacred and the Profane* (New York: Columbia University Press, 1992).
3. Christopher Norberg-Schulz, *Genius Loci* (New York: Rizzoli, 1980).
4. William R. Lethaby, *Architecture, Nature and Magic* (London: Duckworth, 1956); Yi-Fu Tuan, *Cosmos and Heart: A Cosmopolite's Viewpoint* (Minneapolis: University of Minnesota Press, 1996).
5. Susanne K. Langer, *Feeling and Form: A Theory of Art* (New York: Scribner, 1953).
6. James Lovelock, *The Ages of Gaia: A Biography of Our Living Earth* (New York: Norton, 1995); Appleton, *The Experience of Landscape;* "Religion and Biodiversity," *Wild Earth* 6, no. 3 (Fall 1996); Marshall Berman, *All That Is Solid Melts into Air: The Experience of Modernity* (New York: Simon and Schuster, 1982); Mark Francis and Randolph T. Hester Jr., eds., *The Meaning of Gardens: Idea, Place, and Action* (Cambridge: MIT Press, 1990).

7. Langer, *Feeling and Form;* Tuan, *Cosmos;* Kent C. Bloomer and Charles W. Moore, *Body, Memory and Architecture* (New Haven: Yale University Press, 1977); Clare Cooper Marcus, "House as-Symbol-of-Self," *HUD Challenge* (U.S. Department of Housing and Urban Development) 8, no. 2 (1977): 2–4; Rapoport, *House Form and Culture;* Hayden, *The Power of Place.*

8. Marcus, "House as-Symbol-of-Self"; Kim Dovey, "Home: An Ordering Principle in Space," *Landscape* 22, no. 2 (1978): 27–30; D. G. Hayward, "Home as an Environmental and Psychological Concept," *Landscape* 20, no. 1 (1975): 2–9; Olivier Marc, *Psychology of the House* (London: Thomas and Hudson, 1977); Florence Ladd, "Residential History: You Can Go Home Again," *Landscape* 21, no. 2 (1977): 15–20.

9. Relph, *Place and Placelessness;* Yi-Fu Tuan, *Topophilia: A Study of Environmental Perception, Attitudes, and Values* (Englewood Cliffs: Prentice-Hall, 1974); Harold F. Searles, *Nonhuman Environment in Normal Development and in Schizophrenia* (New York: International Universities Press, 1960).

10. Rosabeth M. Kanter, *Commitment and Community* (Cambridge: Harvard University Press, 1972); Clare Cooper Marcus, "Designing for a Commitment to Place: Lessons from the Alternative Community Findhorn," in *Dwelling, Seeing, and Designing: Toward a Phenomenological Ecology* (299–330), ed. David Seamen (New York: State University of New York Press, 1993).

11. Randolph T. Hester Jr., "Subconscious Landscapes of the Heart," *Places* 2, no. 3 (1985): 13–16.

12. Hester, "Life, Liberty," 16; Lynch, *The Image of the City.*

13. Hester, "Life, Liberty," 16.

14. Hester, "The Place of Participatory Design."

15. Carl Jung, *Man and His Symbols* (Garden City: Doubleday, 1964).

16. Mark Riegner, "Toward a Holistic Understanding of Place: Reading a Landscape through Flora and Fauna," in *Dwelling, Seeing, and Designing: Toward a Phenomenological Ecology* (181–215), ed. David Seamon (New York: State University of New York Press, 1993).

17. Rogers, *Diffusion of Innovations.*

18. Lynch, *The Image of the City.*

19. Klara B. Kelley and Harris Francis, *Navajo Sacred Places* (Indianapolis: Indiana University Press, 1994).

20. Norris, *Dakota,* 165.

21. Kenko, *Essays in Idleness,* 181.

22. Isami Kinoshita, "The Apple Promenade," in *Democratic Design in the Pacific Rim: Japan, Taiwan, and the United States* (92–99), ed. Randolph T. Hester Jr. and Corrina Kweskin (Mendocino: Ridge Times Press, 1999).

23. Robert A. Ivy Jr., *Fay Jones* (New York: McGraw-Hill, 2001), 32–45.

24. Ann Whiston Spirn, *The Language of Landscape* (New Haven: Yale University Press, 1998).

25. Smith and Hester, *Community Goal Setting.*
26. Wendell Berry, *Continuous Harmony: Essays Cultural and Agricultural* (New York: Harcourt Brace Jovanovich, 1972).
27. Schumacher, *Small Is Beautiful,* 20.
28. Ibid., 74.

Resilient Form: Introduction

1. Virginia Morell, "The Variety of Life," *National Geographic* 195, no. 2 (1999): 24.
2. Tad Szulc, "Abraham Journey of Faith," *National Geographic* 200, no. 6 (2001): 110.
3. Shenglin Chang, "Real Life at Virtual Home: Silicon Landscape Construction in Response to Transcultural Home Identities," dissertation, University of California, Berkeley, 2000.
4. John Holtzclaw, "Northeast SF Factoids," memo to Paul Okamoto, September 22, 1995.
5. Barbara Taylor, *Butterflies and Moths* (New York: DK, 1996), 41.
6. Mary C. Comerio, *Disaster Hits Home: New Policy for Urban Housing Recovery* (Berkeley: University of California, 1998).
7. Rapoport, *House Form and Culture,* 57–58.
8. Corbett, *A Better Place;* McHarg, *Design with Nature.*
9. C. S. Holling, *Resilience and Stability of Ecological Systems* (Vancouver: Institute of Resource Ecology, University of British Columbia, 1973), 15.
10. Todd and Todd, *From Eco-Cities.*
11. Hester, "The Place of Participatory Design."
12. McHarg, *Design with Nature;* Carl Steinitz, *Defensible Processes for Regional Landscape Design* (Washington, DC: American Society for Landscape Architects, 1979); Philip H. Lewis Jr., *Tomorrow by Design: A Regional Design Process for Sustainability* (New York: Wiley, 1996); Julius Fabos, *Planning the Total Landscape: A Guide to Intelligent Land Use* (Boulder: Westview Press, 1978); Steiner, *The Living Landscape.*
13. Hough, *City Form;* Spirn, *The Granite Garden;* Dramstad, Olson, and Forman, *Landscape Ecology Principles;* Calthorpe, *The Next American Metropolis.*
14. Corbett, *A Better Place;* Joan Iverson Nassauer, *Placing Nature: Culture and Landscape Ecology* (Washington, DC: Island Press, 1997); Francis, Cashdan, and Paxon, *The Making of Neighborhood Open Spaces.*
15. John T. Lyle, *Regenerative Design for Human Development* (New York: Wiley, 1994) and *Design for Human Ecosystems: Landscape, Land Use, and Natural Resources* (New York: Van Nostrand Reinhold, 1985); Hester, *Neighborhood Space;* Patrick Condon and Stacy Moriarty, eds., *Second Nature: Adapting LA's Landscape for Sustainable Living* (Beverly Hills: TreePeople, 1999); J. William Thompson and Kim Sorvig, *Sustainable Landscape Construction: A Guide to*

Green Building Outdoors (Washington, DC: Island Press, 2000); and Morrish et al., *Planning to Stay.*

16. Todd and Todd, *From Eco-Cities;* R. Buckminster Fuller and Robert Marks, *The Dymaxion World of Buckminster Fuller* (Garden City: Anchor Books, 1973); R. Buckminster Fuller, *Pound, Synergy, and the Great Design* (Moscow: University of Idaho, 1977); Wes Jackson, *Becoming Native to This Place* (Washington, DC: Counterpoint, 1996); John Jeavons, *How to Grow More Vegetables and Fruits, Nuts, Berries, Grains, and Other Crops Than You Ever Thought Possible on Less Land Than You Can Imagine* (6th ed.) (Berkeley: Ten Speed Press, 2002).

17. Van der Ryn and Cowan, *Ecological Design;* William McDonough and Michael Braungart, *Cradle to Cradle: Remaking the Way We Make Things* (New York: North Point Press, 2002); Morrish et al., *Planning to Stay;* Carl Steinitz, *A Comparative Study of Resource Analysis Methods* (Cambridge: Department of Landscape Architecture Research Office, Harvard University, 1969); Randolph R. Croxton, "Sustainable Design Offers Key to Control," *Architectural Record* 185, no. 6 (1997): 76, 78.

18. Comerio, *Disaster,* 51, 56.

Resilient Form: Particularness

1. Rapoport, *House Form and Culture;* Jean-Paul Bourdier and Nezar AlSayyad, eds., *Dwellings, Settlements, and Tradition: Cross-Cultural Perspectives* (Lanham: University Press of America, 1989).

2. Charles Darwin, *On the Origin of Species by Means of Natural Selection* (Cambridge: Harvard University Press, 1964).

3. Jean Paul Bourdier, *Drawn from African Dwellings* (Bloomington: Indiana University Press, 1996).

4. Bourdier and AlSayyad, *Dwellings.*

5. Steinitz, *Defensible Processes;* Fabos, *Total Landscape;* John Radke, "The Use of Theoretically Based Spatial Decompositions for Constructing Better Datasets in Small Municipalities," paper, University of Michigan (1999) and "Boundary Generators for the Twenty-first Century: A Proximity-Based Classification Method," in *Department of City and Regional Planning Fiftieth Anniversary Anthology,* ed. John Landis (Berkeley: University of California, 1998).

6. Corbett, *A Better Place;* Lyle, *Regenerative Design.*

7. Corbett, *A Better Place;* Todd and Todd, *From Eco-Cities.*

8. Hough, *City Form.*

9. Dan Miller, "Making Money out of Thin Air," *Progressive Farmer* 117, no. 2 (2002): 14.

10. Douglas Jehl, "Development and Drought Cut Carolina's Water Supply," *New York Times,* August 29, 2002, 1, 16; Charles A. Flink and Robert Sears, *Greenways: A Guide to Planning, Design and Development,* (Washington, DC: Island Press, 1993).

11. Tamesuke Nagahashi et al., "Citizen Leap Participation or Government Led Participation: How Can We Find a Watershed Management Alternative for Yoshino River in Tokusima, Japan?," paper presented by the Kyoto University Team for Yoshino River Alternative at the Fourth Annual Pacific Rim Conference on Participatory Community Design, Hong Kong Polytechnic University, Hong Kong, December 2002.

12. McHarg, *Design with Nature,* 127; George Perkins Marsh, *Man and Nature,* ed. David Lowenthal (Cambridge: Harvard University Press, 1965).

13. McHarg, *Design with Nature,* 146.

14. Hough, *City Form.*

15. Tracy Rysavy, "Tree People," *Yes! A Journal of Positive Futures* no. 12 (2000): 19.

16. Sullivan, *Garden and Climate.*

17. John Liu, "The Tawo House," in *Democratic Design in the Pacific Rim: Japan, Taiwan, and the United States* (64–75), ed. Randolph T. Hester Jr. and Corrina Kweskin (Mendocino: Ridge Times, 1999).

18. Brand, *How Buildings Learn.*

19. David Abram, *The Spell of the Sensuous* (New York: Vintage, 1997).

20. Corbett, *A Better Place.*

21. Brand, *How Buildings Learn,* 132.

22. Hikaru Okuzumi, *The Stones Cry Out,* trans. by James Westerhoven (New York: Harcourt Brace, 1998).

23. Kenko, *Essays in Idleness,* 43.

24. Mimi Wagner and Peter F. Korsching, "Flood Prone Community Landscapes, The Application of Diffusion Innovations Theory and Community Design Process in Promoting Change," paper presented at the Society for Applied Sociology, Denver, Colorado, October 22–24, 1998, 3.

Resilient Form: Selective Diversity

1. Schlesinger, *The Disuniting of America.*

2. Schlesinger, *The Disuniting of America.*

3. Hawken, *The Ecology of Commerce,* 12.

4. Josh Sevin, "A Disappearing Act," *Grist Magazine,* February 23, 2000, accessed July 15, 2003, available at <http://www.gristmagazine.com/grist/counter022300.stm>; International Union for Conservation of Nature and Natural Resources (IUCN), "Species Extinction," IUCN Red List, n.d., accessed July 15, 2003, available at <http://iucn.org/themes/ssc> and <www.redlist.org>.

5. Don Hinrichsen, "Putting the Bite on Planet Earth: Rapid Human Population Growth Is Devouring Global Natural Resources," *International Wildlife* 24, no. 5 (1994): 39.

6. Virginia Morell, "The Sixth Extinction," *National Geographic* 195, no. 2 (1999): 46.

7. Paul A. Colinvaux, *Why Big Fierce Animals Are Rare: An Ecologist's Perspective* (Princeton: Princeton University Press, 1979), 195–197.

8. Dramstad, Olson, and Forman, *Landscape Ecology Principles.*

9. Jeffrey Hou, "From Activism to Sustainable Development: The Case of Chigu and the Anti-Binnan Movement," in *Democratic Design in the Pacific Rim: Japan, Taiwan, and the United States* (124–133), ed. Randolph T. Hester, Jr. and Corrina Kweskin (Mendocino: Ridge Times, 1999).

10. Joel L. Swerdlow, "Global Culture," *National Geographic* 196, no. 2 (1999): 2–5; "Vanishing Cultures," *National Geographic* 196, no. 2 (1999): 62–90; Hawken, *The Ecology of Commerce,* 136.

11. "Vanishing Cultures," *National Geographic.*

12. Frederick L. Olmsted, *The Slave States* (New York: Capricorn, 1959); Hester, *Neighborhood Space.*

13. Gans, *The Urban Villagers.*

14. Schlesinger, *The Disuniting of America.*

15. Nicholas Black Elk, with John G. Neihardt, *Black Elk Speaks: Being the Life Story of a Holy Man of the Oglala Sioux* (Lincoln: University of Nebraska Press, 1972), 9–10, 28; Rina Swentzell, "Conflicting Landscape Values," *Places* 7, no. 1 (1990): 19–27.

16. Calthorpe, *The Next American Metropolis,* xvi.

17. Hester, *Planning Neighborhood Space,* 50–51.

18. Hough, *City Form,* 250–251.

19. Relph, *Place and Placelessness;* MacCannell, *The Tourist.*

20. Berry, *A Continuous Harmony,* 67.

21. Van der Ryn and Cowan, *Ecological Design,* 23.

22. President's Council on Sustainable Development, *Sustainable America: A New Consensus for Prosperity, Opportunity, and a Healthy Environment* (Washington, DC: President's Council, 1996), 101–103.

23. Hawken, *The Ecology of Commerce,* 27.

24. Ibid., 146.

25. Ibid., xiii.

26. Ibid., 146.

27. Dramstad, Olson and Forman, *Landscape Ecology Principles,* 31.

28. Curtis Hayes, "No Fear of Change," *Farm Bureau News,* January 2002, 14.

29. McHarg, *Design with Nature,* 128.

30. Jacobs, *Death and Life.*

31. Peter Calthorpe, "The Region," in *The New Urbanism: Towards an Architecture of Community* (xi–xvi), ed. Peter Katz (New York: McGraw-Hill, 1994), xvi.

32. Andres Duany and Elizabeth Plater-Zyberk, "The Neighborhood, the District, and the Corridor," in *The New Urbanism: Towards an Architecture of Community* (xvii–xx), ed. Peter Katz, xvii–xx (New York: McGraw-Hill, 1994), xvii.

33. Duany and Plater-Zyberk, "The Neighborhood, the District, and the Corridor," xix.

34. Richard Register, *Ecocity Berkeley: Building Cities for a Healthy Future* (Berkeley: North Atlantic Books, 1987), 23.

35. Duany, Plater-Zyberk, and Kreiger, *Towns,* xix, 2.

36. Timothy Beatley and Kristie Manning, *Ecology of Place: Planning for Environment, Economy, and Community* (Washington, DC: Island Press, 1997), 63.

37. Porteous, *Environment and Behavior,* 75–76.

38. Rapoport, *Human Aspects,* 248–265.

39. Porteous, *Environment and Behavior,* 76.

40. Richard Sennett, *The Uses of Disorder: Personal Identity and City Life* (New York: Norton, 1992).

41. Rapoport, *Human Aspects,* 264.

42. Eduardo E. Lozano, *Community Design and the Culture of Cities* (Cambridge: Cambridge University Press, 1990), 144.

43. Odum, *Fundamentals,* 281.

44. Schumacher, *Small Is Beautiful,* 48.

45. King, "Letter from Birmingham Jail."

46. Jacobs, *Making City Planning Work;* Donald Appleyard, *Planning a Pluralist City: Conflicting Realities in Ciudad Guayana* (Cambridge: MIT Press, 1976).

47. Lynch, *The Image of the City.*

48. Rapoport, *Human Aspects,* 93; Urban Ecology, *Blueprint,* 18–29.

49. Rapoport, *Human Aspects,* 248–265.

50. Lozano, *Community Design,* 158.

51. David M. Halbfiner, "Yes in Our Backyards: A Shelter's New Value," *New York Times,* February 24, 2002, 26.

52. Rysavy, "Tree People," 19; McBride, "Urban Forestry," 106–109.

53. Relph, *Place and Placelessness;* MacCannell, *The Tourist.*

54. Porteous, *Environment and Behavior,* 278–286.

55. Richard Scarry, *What Do People Do All Day?* (New York: Random House, 1968).

56. Van der Ryn and Cowan, *Ecological Design,* 126.

57. Ibid., 126.

58. Beatley and Manning, *The Ecology of Place,* 62.

Resilient Form: Density and Smallness

1. Odum, *Fundamentals,* 217–221, 493.

2. Hinrichsen, "Putting the Bite," 41.

3. John G. Mitchell, "Urban Sprawl," *National Geographic* 200, no. 1 (2001): 43–73.

4. Reed F. Noss and Robert L. Peters, *Endangered Ecosystems: A Status Report on America's Vanishing Wildlife and Habitat* (Washington, DC: Defenders of Wildlife, 1995).

5. Kathrin D. Lassila, "The New Suburbanites: How America's Plants and Animals Are Threatened by Sprawl," *Amicus Journal* 21, no. 2 (1999): 18.

6. Roger Ulrich, "View through a Window May Influence Recovery from Surgery," *Science* 224 (1984), 420–421; Frances E. Kuo, William C. Sullivan, and Andrew Faber Taylor, "Coping with ADD: The Surprising Connection to Green Play Settings," *Environment and Behavior* 33, no. 1 (2001): 54–77 and "Views of Nature and Self-Discipline: Evidence from Inner City Children," *Journal of Environmental Psychology* 22, issues 1–2 (2002): 49–63.

7. Perry, "The Neighborhood Unit," 37.

8. Lozano, *Community Design,* 162–166.

9. Perry, "The Neighborhood Unit," 80.

10. Beyard and O'Mara, *Shopping Center Development Handbook,* 12–13; Calthorpe, *The Next American Metropolis,* 77, 82.

11. Bernick and Cervero, *Transit Villages,* 43, 64.

12. Urban Ecology, *Blueprint,* 86.

13. Bernick and Cervero, *Transit Villages,* 43.

14. Ibid., 98.

15. Ibid., 75.

16. Ibid., 82.

17. Calthorpe, *The Next American Metropolis,* 58.

18. Bernick and Cervero, *Transit Villages,* 83.

19. Calthorpe, *The Next American Metropolis,* 83–84.

20. Bernick and Cervero, *Transit Villages,* 83.

21. Lozano, *Community Design,* 158.

22. Calthorpe, *The Next American Metropolis,* 48.

23. Stephanie Mencimer, "The Price of Going the Distance," *New York Times,* April 28, 2002, 34.

24. Calthorpe, *The Next American Metropolis,* 30.

25. Urban Ecology, *Blueprint,* 111.

26. Ibid.

27. Richard J. Jackson and Chris Kochtitzky, *Creating a Healthy Environment: The Impact of the Built Environment on Public Health* (Washington, DC: Sprawl Watch Clearinghouse, 2001), 7.

28. Bernick and Cervero, *Transit Villages,* 44.

29. Rapoport, *Human Aspects,* 318.

30. American LIVES, Inc., "1995 New Urbanism Study: Revitalizing Suburban Communities," paper presented at the Urban Land Institute Seminar on Master Planned Communities 2000 and Beyond, November 2, 1995, 31.

31. Morton White and Lucia White, *The Intellectual versus the City: From Thomas Jefferson to Frank Lloyd Wright* (New York: Oxford University Press, 1977); R. E. Farris and H. W. Dunham, *Mental Disorders in Urban Areas* (Chicago: University of Chicago Press, 1939).

32. Randy Newman, "Baltimore," song, Warner Bros., 1978.

33. William H. Ittelson et al., *An Introduction to Environmental Psychology* (New York: Holt, Rinehart & Winston, 1974).

34. McHarg, *Design with Nature,* 193; J. B. Calhoun, "Population Density and Social Pathology," *Scientific American* 206 (1962): 139–148.

35. Lynch, *Good City Form.*

36. Rapoport, *Human Aspects,* 98.

37. Gans, *The Urban Villagers.*

38. Ittelson et al., *Environmental Psychology,* 256.

39. Rapoport, *Human Aspects,* 278.

40. Robert Cervero and Peter Bosselmann, *An Evaluation of the Market Potential for Transit-Oriented Development Using Visual Simulation Techniques* (Berkeley: Institute of Urban and Regional Development, University of California, 1994), 42.

41. Rapoport, *Human Aspects,* 201.

42. Ibid.

43. Ibid., 51.

44. Cervero and Bosselmann, *An Evaluation,* 73.

45. Horton, *The Politics of Diversity.*

46. American LIVES, "1995 New Urbanism Study," 30.

47. Ibid., 4.

48. Cervero and Bosselmann, *An Evaluation,* 73.

49. Rapoport, *Human Aspects,* 201.

50. Marcus and Sarkissian, *Housing As If People Mattered.*

51. Cervero and Bosselmann, *An Evaluation,* 73–74.

52. American LIVES, "1995 New Urbanism Study," 31–33.

53. Ibid., 31.

54. Rokeach, *Beliefs, Attitudes, and Values.*

55. Chanse and Hester, "Characterizing Volunteer Involvement."

56. Rapoport, *Human Aspects,* 200–201; Ittelson et al., *Environmental Psychology,* 151, 259.

57. Newman, *Community of Interest.*

58. American LIVES, "1995 New Urbanism Study," 31.

59. Marcus and Sarkissian, *Housing As If People Mattered.*

60. American LIVES, "1995 New Urbanism Study," 31.

61. Ibid.

62. Lloyd Bookout and James D. Wentling, "Density by Design," *Urban Land* 47, no. 6 (1988): 10–15.

63. Marcus and Sarkissian, *Housing As If People Mattered.*

64. Rapoport, *Human Aspects,* 330.

65. Hester, *Neighborhood Space,* 35.

66. Cervero and Bosselmann, *An Evaluation,* 5–6.

67. Rapoport, *Human Aspects,* 51, 61–62, 201.

68. Cervero and Bosselmann, *An Evaluation,* 6; Calthorpe, *The Next American Metropolis,* 87.

69. Marcus, "House –as-Symbol," 2–4.

70. J. Constantine, "Design by Democracy," *Land Development* 5, no. 1 (1992): 11–15.

71. Cervero and Bosselmann, *An Evaluation.*

72. Rachel Kaplan and Stephen Kaplan, *The Experience of Nature: A Psychological Perspective* (Cambridge: Cambridge University Press, 1989); Ulrich, "View," 420–421; Kuo, Sullivan, and Taylor, "Coping with ADD," 54–77.

73. American LIVES, "1995 New Urbanism Study," 31.

74. Rapoport, *Human Aspects,* 51, 61.

75. Sim Van der Ryn and William R. Boie, *Value Measurement and Visual Factors in the Urban Environment* (Berkeley: College of Environmental Design, University of California, 1963).

76. Rapoport, *Human Aspects,* 51.

77. David Lowenthal, "The American Scene," *Geographical Review* 58, no. 1 (1968): 61–88.

78. Francis, Cashdan, and Paxon, *The Making of Neighborhood Open Spaces.*

79. Chanse and Hester, "Characterizing Volunteer Involvement."

80. American LIVES, "1995 New Urbanism Study," 31.

81. Cervero and Bosselmann, *An Evaluation,* 73.

82. John Landis, Subharjit Guhathakurta, and Ming Zhang, *Capitalization of Transit Investments into Single-Family Home Prices: A Comparative Analysis of Five California Rail Transit Systems* (Berkeley: Institute of Urban and Regional Development, University of California, 1994), 619.

83. Calthorpe, *The Next American Metropolis,* 56.

84. Richard K. Untermann, *Accommodating the Pedestrian: Adapting Towns and Neighborhoods for Walking and Bicycling* (New York: Van Nostrand Reinhold, 1984).

85. Hester, *Planning Neighborhood Space,* 69.

86. Rapoport, *Human Aspects,* 207.

87. Lynch, *The Image of the City.*

88. American LIVES, "1995 New Urbanism Study," 31.

89. Alexander et al., *A Pattern Language;* Lee, "The Urban Neighborhood"; Hester, *Planning Neighborhood Space,* 39.

90. American LIVES, "1995 New Urbanism Study," 31.

91. Cervero and Bosselmann, *An Evaluation,* 73.

92. John Geluardi, "Officials Knock Down Building Height Initiative," *Berkeley Daily Planet,* July 25, 2002, 1, 6.

93. Joe South, "Rose Garden," song from *Introspection,* 1968, reissued by Raven Records, 2003.

94. Appleyard et al., *A Humanistic Design Manifesto.*

Resilient Form: Limited Extent

1. American LIVES, "1995 New Urbanism Study," 31.

2. McHarg, *Design with Nature,* 2.

3. Ibid., 57.

4. Joel Garreau, *Edge City: Life on the New Frontier* (New York: Doubleday, 1991).

5. Lozano, *Community Design;* Mumford, *The City in History.*

6. Beatley and Manning, *The Ecology of Place,* 41–42.

7. Schumacher, *Small Is Beautiful,* 46–56; Hawken, *The Ecology of Commerce,* 91–104.

8. Corbett, *A Better Place;* Todd and Todd, *From Eco-Cities;* Donella Meadows et al., *The Limits to Growth* (New York: Potomac Associates, 1972); Beryl L. Crowe, "The Tragedy of the Commons Revisited," *Science* 166 (1969): 1103–1107; Rene Dubos, "Half Truths about the Future," *Wall Street Journal,* May 8, 1981, 26.

9. Lester R. Brown and Jodi L. Jacobson, "The Future of Urbanization," *Urban Land* 46, no. 6 (1987): 4.

10. Mike Geniella, "Water Export Plan under Microscope," *Press Democrat* March 17, 2002, 1, 6–7.

11. "Last Gasp," *Fresno Bee* Special Report on Valley Air Quality, December 15, 2002, accessed July 16, 2003, available at <http://valleyairquality.com/special/valley_air/part1>; Andy Weisser, "American Lung Association Applauds Governor for Signing Important Smog Check II Bill," American Lung Association of California, September 27, 2003, accessed July 26, 2003, available at <http://www.californialung.org/press/020927smogcheckii.html>; Adelia Sabiston, "Meeting the Test: The Bay Area and Smog Check II," *Bay Area Monitor,* August/September 2002, accessed July 16, 2003, available at <http://www.bayareamonitor.org/aug02/test.html>; California State Assembly, AB 2637, accessed July 16, 2003, available at <http://www.leginfo.ca .gov/pub/01-02/bill/asm/ab_2601-2650/ab_2637_bill_20020927_cha>.

12. Aristotle, *Ethics, Nichomachean Ethics,* book 9, trans. J. A. K. Thomson (London: London Allen & Unwin, 1953).

13. Lynch, *Good City Form,* 241.

14. Plato, *The Republic* (Cambridge: Cambridge University Press, 2000), 119; Lozano, *Community Design;* Irving Hoch, "City Size Effects, Trends and Politics," *Science* 193, no. 3 (1976): 856–863; P. A. Stone, *The Structure, Size and Cost of Urban Settlements* (Cambridge: Cambridge University Press, 1973), 109–127; Dowall, *The Suburban Squeeze.*

15. Schumacher, *Small Is Beautiful,* 49.
16. Alexander et al., *A Pattern Language,* 4.
17. Lynch, *Good City Form,* 240.
18. Schumacher, *Small Is Beautiful,* 48.
19. Ibid., 47.
20. Appleyard et al., *A Humanistic Design Manifesto.*
21. Register, *Ecocity Berkeley,* 120–130; Alexander et al., *A Pattern Language,* 24–25.
22. Dovey, "Home"; Lynch, *The Image of the City;* MacCannell, *The Tourist;* Lowenthal, "The American Scene," 61–88.
23. Donald Appleyard, *Inside vs. Outside: The Distortions of Distance* (Berkeley: Institute of Urban and Regional Development, University of California, 1979), 307.
24. Lynch, *The Image of the City.*
25. Aristotle, *Politics* (Chicago: University of Chicago Press, 1984), 204–205.
26. Perry, "The Neighborhood Unit"; Alexander et al., *A Pattern Language,* 71–74; Goodman and Goodman, *Communitas;* Milton Kotler, *Neighborhood Government: The Location Foundations of Political Life* (New York: Bobbs-Merrill, 1969); Hester, *Neighborhood Space* and *Planning Neighborhood Space.*
27. Appleyard, *Inside vs. Outside,* 2, table 1.
28. Lozano, *Community Design.*
29. Mitchell, "Urban Sprawl," 65.
30. "The Race to Save Open Space," *Audubon* (March/April 2000): 69.
31. Beatley and Manning, *The Ecology of Place,* 45–46.
32. Mayor's Institute on City Design West, "1994 Institute Summary," paper presented at the College of Environmental Design, University of California, Berkeley, November 3–5, 1994.
33. Beatley and Manning, *The Ecology of Place,* 46, 48.
34. Ibid., 46.
35. Randall Arendt, "Principle Three," in *The Charter of the New Urbanism* (29–34), ed. Michael Leccese and Kathleen McCormick (New York: McGraw-Hill, 2000).
36. Eric Frederickson, "This Is Not Sprawl," *Architecture* 90, no. 12 (2001): 48.
37. Calthorpe, *The Next American Metropolis,* 51.
38. Alexander et al., *A Pattern Language,* 20.
39. Lozano, *Community Design.*
40. David L. Callies, *Preserving Paradise: Why Regulation Won't Work* (Honolulu: University of Hawaii Press, 1994).
41. Frederickson, "This Is Not Sprawl," 49.
42. Callies, *Preserving Paradise.*
43. Richard R. Wilkinson and Robert M. Leary, *Conservation of Small Towns* (Charleston: Coastal Plains Regional Commission, 1976), 7.
44. Ibid., 13.

45. Ibid., 15.

46. Ibid., 12.

47. Marcia McNally, "Making Big Wild," *Places* 9, no. 3 (1995): 44.

48. McNally, "Making Big Wild," 44.

49. Randolph T. Hester Jr., Nova J. Blazej, and Ian S. Moore, "Whose Wild? Resolving Cultural and Biological Diversity Conflicts in Urban Wilderness," *Landscape Journal* 18, no. 2 (1999): 137–146.

50. Hise and Deverell, *Eden by Design.*

51. Chris Lazarus, "LUTRAQ: Looking for a Smarter Way to Grow," *Earthword,* no. 4—Transportation (n.d.): 23–27; Donald Phares, "Bigger Is Better, or Is It Smaller? Restructuring Local Government in the St. Louis Area," *Urban Affairs Quarterly* 25, no. 1(1989): 5–17.

52. Calthorpe, *The Next American Metropolis.*

53. Larry Siedentop, *Tocqueville* (Oxford: Oxford University Press, 1994).

54. Bellah et al., *Habits of the Heart,* vi.

55. Alexander et al., *A Pattern Language,* 70–74; Hester, *Neighborhood Space;* Kotler, *Neighborhood Government.*

56. Kamo-no Chomei, *The Ten Foot Square Hut and Tales of the Heike,* trans. A. L. Sadler (Rutland: Tuttle, 1972), 17–18.

Resilient Form: Adaptability

1. Holling, *Resilience,* 1–23.

2. Sennett, *The Fall of Public Man,* 197–298.

3. Ittelson et al., *Environmental Psychology,* 264.

4. Hough, *City Form,* 94–95.

5. Trancik, *Finding Lost Space.*

6. Donlyn Lyndon and Charles W. Moore, *Chambers for a Memory Palace* (Cambridge: MIT Press, 1994), 53–78.

7. Hough, *City Form,* 94.

8. Hester, "Life, Liberty," 12; Michael Laurie, "The Urban Mantelpiece," *Landscape Design,* no. 216 (1992): 22.

9. Kenko, *Essays in Idleness,* 70.

10. Nicholson, *Community Participation.*

11. Laurie, "The Urban Mantelpiece," 22.

12. Ibid., 22.

13. Kenko, *Essays in Idleness,* xiii, 192.

14. Yamaguchi Sodo, in *Anthology of Japanese Literature, from the Earliest Era to the Mid-nineteenth Century,* ed. Donald Keene (New York: Grove Press, 1960), 385.

15. Lyndon and Moore, *Chambers for a Memory Place;* Brand, *How Buildings Learn;* Yasuhiro Endoh, "The Contemporary Meaning of Cooperative Housing: Case Study—M-Port (Kumamoto)," in *Democratic Design in the*

Pacific Rim: Japan, Taiwan, and the United States (178–191), ed. Randolph T. Hester Jr. and Corrina Kweskin (Mendocino: Ridge Times Press, 1999); Moudon, *Built for Change;* Alexander et al., *A Pattern Language;* Habraken, *Supports.*

16. Gehl, *Life between Buildings.*

17. Peter Walker, "A Personal Approach to Design," in *Peter Walker: Landscape as Art* (No. 85) (10–13), ed. Yoji Sasaki (Tokyo: Process Architecture, 1989), 10.

18. Cathy Newman, "Welcome to Monhegan Island, Maine. Now Please Go Away," *National Geographic* 200, no. 1 (2001): 108.

19. Habraken, *Supports.*

20. City of Oakland, *Report to the City Planning Commission,* September 1, 1999; Alex Greenwood and Patrick Lane, "Oakland's 10K Race for Downtown Housing," *Planning* 38, no. 8 (2002): 14–17.

21. John Zukowsky, "Introduction to Internationalism in Chicago Architecture," in *Chicago Architecture 1872–1922: Birth of a Metropolis* (15–26), ed. John Zukowsky (Munich: Prestel-Verlap, 1987); John E. Draper, "Paris by the Lake: Sources of Burnham's Plan of Chicago," in *Chicago Architecture 1872–1922: Birth of a Metropolis* (107–120), ed. John Zukowsky (Munich: Prestel-Verlap, 1987).

22. Mickey Newbury, "If you See Her," song, from *I Came to Hear the Music,* produced by Chip Young, 1974.

23. Chou, "Chuang Tzu," 46.

24. Holling, *Resilience,* 1–21.

25. Donald Schon, *The Reflective Practitioners* (New York: Basic Books, 1983).

26. James Brooke, "Heat Island Tokyo Is in Global Warming's Vanguard," *New York Times,* August 13, 2002, A3.

27. Hashem Akbari and Leanna Shea Rose, *Characterizing the Fabric of the Urban Environment: A Case Study of Metropolitan Chicago, Illinois,* Report LBNL-49275 (Berkeley: Lawrence Berkeley National Laboratory, October 2001).

28. Hester, "Life, Liberty," 15.

29. Lance H. Gunderson, C. S. Holling, and Stephen S. Light, eds. *Barriers and Bridges to the Renewal of Ecosystems and Institutions* (New York: Columbia University Press, 1995).

30. Randolph T. Hester, Jr., "Landstyles and Lifescapes: Twelve Steps to Community Development," *Landscape Architecture* 75, no. 1. (1985): 78–85; Scott T. McCreary, John K. Gamman, and Bennett Brooks, "Refining and Testing Joint Fact-Finding for Environmental Dispute Resolution: Ten Years of Success," *Mediation Quarterly* 18, no. 4 (2001): 329–348.

31. Gunderson, Holling and Light, *Barriers and Bridges.*

32. Wagner and Korsching, "Flood Prone Community Landscapes."

33. Timothy P. Duane, "Regulations Rationale: Learning from the California Energy Crisis," *Yale Journal on Regulation* 19, no. 2 (2002): 471–540.

34. Comerio, *Disaster Hits Home.*

35. Rogers, *Diffusion of Interventions.*

36. Hester, "Life, Liberty," 15; McCreary, Gamman, and Brooks, "Refining and Testing Joint Fact-Finding," 329–348; Susskind and Cruikshank, *Breaking the Impasse;* Innes and Booher, *Consensus Building* and *Planning Institutions in the Network Society: Theory for Collaborative Planning* (Berkeley: Institute of Urban and Regional Development, University of California, 1999).

37. Chanse and Hester, "Characterizing Volunteer Involvement."

38. Ittelson et al., *An Introduction to Environmental Psychology,* 97–98.

Impelling Form: Everyday Future

1. Rogers, *Diffusion of Innovations.*

2. Dovey, "Home," 27–30; Appleyard, *Inside vs. Outside;* Edward C. Relph, "Modernity and the Reclamation of Place," in *Dwelling, Seeing, and Designing: Toward a Phenomenological Ecology* (25–40), ed. David Seamon (New York: State University of New York Press, 1993); Randolph T. Hester Jr., "Sacred Structures and Everyday Life: A Return to Manteo, N.C.," in *Dwelling, Seeing, and Designing: Toward a Phenomenological Ecology* (271–297), ed. David Seamon (New York: State University of New York Press, 1993); Tuan, *Cosmos and Heart.*

3. Clare Cooper Marcus, *Easter Hill Village: Some Social Implications of Design* (New York: Free Press, 1975); Appleyard et al., *A Humanistic Design Manifesto;* Hester, *Community Design Primer;* John Zeisel, *Inquiry by Design: Tools for Environment-Behavior Research* (Cambridge: Cambridge University Press, 1987).

4. Hester, *Planning Neighborhood Space,* 19, 41; Sydney Brower, *Good Neighborhoods: A Study of Intown and Suburban Residential Environments* (Westport: Praeger, 1996).

5. John Chase, Margaret Crawford, and John Kaliski, eds., *Everyday Urbanism* (New York: Monacelli Press, 1999).

6. Galen Cranz, *The Politics of Park Design: A History of Urban Parks in America* (Cambridge: MIT Press, 1982).

7. Hester, *Neighborhood Space,* 34.

8. David Lowenthal, *The Past Is a Foreign Country* (Cambridge: Cambridge University Press, 1985); J. B. Jackson, *The Necessity for Ruins, and Other Topics* (Amherst: University of Massachusetts Press, 1980).

9. American LIVES, "1995 New Urbanism Study," 31.

10. Joan Iverson Nassauer, "Urban Ecological Retrofit," *Landscape Journal* (special issue on Eco-Revelatory Design) (1998): 15–17.

11. Brenda Brown, "Holding Moving Landscapes," *Landscape Journal* (special issue on Eco-Revelatory Design) (1998): 56.

12. Ibid.

13. Alinsky, *Rules for Radicals.*

14. Gans, *Urban Villagers* and *People and Plans.*

15. Hester, *Neighborhood Space,* 40.

16. Edmund H. Volkart, ed., *Social Behavior and Personality: Contributions of W. I. Thomas to Theory and Social Research* (New York: Social Science Research Council, 1951), 120–139.

17. Hester, *Community Design Primer,* 2.

Impelling Form: Naturalness

1. Rod Nash, *Wilderness in the American Mind* (New Haven: Yale University Press, 1967); Moulton and Sanderson, *Wildlife Issues in a Changing World,* 457; Francis and Hester, *The Meaning of Gardens,* 8; Chanse and Hester, "Characterizing Volunteer Involvement," 2–3.

2. Carolyn Merchant, *The Death of Nature: Women, Ecology, and the Scientific Revolution* (San Francisco: Harper & Row, 1980); Marx, *The Machine in the Garden;* Thayer, *Gray World;* Mozingo, "The Aesthetics of Ecological Design," 46–59; Nassauer, *Placing Nature.*

3. Edward Abbey, "Personal Bests," *Outside Magazine* (October 2001): 66.

4. Ulrich, "View through a Window," 420–421; Kaplan and Kaplan, *The Experience of Nature.*

5. Kaplan and Kaplan, *The Experience of Nature;* Clare Cooper Marcus and Marni Barnes, eds., *Healing Gardens: Therapeutic Benefits and Design Recommendations* (New York: Wiley, 1999); Frances E. Kuo and William C. Sullivan, "Aggression and Violence in the Inner City: Effects of Environment via Mental Fatigue," *Environment and Behavior* 33, no. 4 (2001): 543–571.

6. Kuo, Sullivan, and Taylor, "Coping with ADD," 54–77.

7. "Winning Big," *Landscape Architecture* 87, no. 11 (1997): 42–49.

8. Ulrich, "View through a Window"; Terry Hartig, M. Mang, and Gary W. Evans, "Restorative Effects of Natural Environment Experience," *Environment and Behavior* 23, no. 1 (1991): 3–26; B. Limprich, "Development of an Intervention to Restore Attention in Cancer Patients," *Cancer Nursing* 16 (1993): 83–92; Victoria I. Lohr, Caroline Pearson-Mims, and Georgia K. Goodwin, "Interior Plants May Improve Worker Productivity and Reduce Stress in a Windowless Environment," *Journal of Environmental Horticulture* 14, no. 2 (1996): 97–100.

9. Rachel Kaplan, Stephen Kaplan and Robert L. Ryan, *With People in Mind: Design and Management of Everyday Nature* (Washington, DC: Island Press, 1998).

10. Paul Shepard, *The Tender Carnivore and the Sacred Game* (New York: Scribner, 1973) and *Nature and Madness* (San Francisco: Sierra Club, 1982).

11. Robin Moore, "Plants as Play Props," *Children's Environments Quarterly* 6, no. 1 (1989): 3–6; Gary P. Nabham and Stephen Trimble, *The Geography of*

Childhood: Why Children Need Wild Places (Boston: Beacon, 1994); Hart, *Children's Experience of Place.*

12. Yoji Sasaki, ed., *Peter Walker: Landscape as Art,* No. 85 (Tokyo: Process Architecture, 1989), 94.

13. "Landscape as Art: A Conversation with Peter Walker and Yoji Sasaki," in *Peter Walker: Landscape as Art (No. 85)* (25–32), ed. Yoji Sasaki (Tokyo: Process Architecture, 1989), 32.

14. Bellah et al., *Habits of the Heart;* Studs Terkel, *American Dreams, Lost and Found* (New York: Pantheon, 1980) and *The Great Divide: Second Thoughts on the American Dream* (New York: Pantheon, 1988); Riesman, *The Lonely Crowd;* Whyte, *Organization Man.*

15. Ann Whiston Spirn, "The Poetics of City and Nature," *Landscape Journal* 7, no. 2 (1988): 109.

16. Terry Tempest Williams, *Refuge: An Unnatural History of Family and Place* (New York: Vintage, 1992), 75.

17. Susanne K. K. Langer, *Philosophy in a New Key: A Study in the Symbolism of Reason, Rite, and Art* (Cambridge: Harvard University Press, 1979); Rollo May, *The Courage to Create* (New York: Norton, 1975).

18. Bachelard, *The Poetics of Space;* Eliade, *Mystic Stories;* Martin Heidegger, "Building Dwelling Thinking," in *Poetry, Language, Thought* (New York: Harper & Row, 1971); Spirn, "The Poetics of City and Nature," 109, and *The Language of Landscape* (New Haven: Yale University Press, 1998); Charles W. Moore, Gerald Allen, and Donlyn Lyndon, *The Place of Houses* (New York: Holt, Rinehart and Winston, 1974).

19. Spirn, "The Poetics of City and Nature," 115.

20. Lawrence Halprin, *The RSVP Cycles: Creative Processes in the Human Environment* (New York: Braziller, 1969) and *The Sea Ranch: Diary of an Idea* (California: Comet Studios, 1995).

21. Kuo and Sullivan, "Aggression and Violence"; Steven Kaplan, "Mental Fatigue and the Designed Environment," in *Public Environments* (55–60), ed. J. Harvey and D. Henning (Edmond: Environmental Design Research Association, 1987).

22. Kuo and Sullivan, "Environment and Crime," 343–367.

23. Marcus and Barnes, *Healing Gardens.*

24. Nicholson, *Community Participation.*

25. Hester, "Womb with a View," 475–481, 528.

26. Appleton, *The Experience of Landscape.*

27. Marcus and Barnes, *Healing Gardens;* Rachel Kaplan, "The Nature of the View from Home: Psychological Benefits," *Environment and Behavior* 33, no. 4 (2001): 507–542; Linda Jewell, "The American Outdoor Theater: A Voice for the Landscape in the Collaboration of Site and Structure" in *Re-envisioning Landscape/Architecture,* ed. Catherine Spelman (Barcelona: Actar, 2003).

28. Clare Cooper Marcus and Carolyn Francis, eds., *People Places: Design Guidelines for Urban Open Space* (New York: Van Nostrand Reinhold, 1998).

29. Sheauchi Ching, Joe R. McBride, and Keizo Fukunari, "The Urban Forest of Tokyo," *Arboricultural Journal* 23 (2000): 379–392.

30. Linn, "White Solutions," 23–25.

31. Hester, *Neighborhood Space*.

32. Kim Sorvig, "The Wilds of South Central," *Landscape Architecture* 92, no. 4 (2002): 66–75.

33. Anne Canright, "Nature Comes to South Central L.A.," *California Coast and Ocean* 18, no. 1 (2002): 33–38.

34. Sorvig, "The Wilds of South Central," 70.

35. Patricia L. Brown, "A Park Offers Nature, Not Just Hoops," *New York Times,* December 28, 2000, F1, F9.

36. Brown, "A Park Offers Nature," F9.

37. Ibid.

38. Sorvig, "The Wilds of South Central," 70, 72.

39. Brown, "A Park Offers Nature," F1.

40. Ibid., F9.

41. Ibid.

42. Ibid.

43. Sorvig, "The Wilds of South Central," 75.

44. Ibid., 73–74.

45. Brown, "A Park Offers Nature," F9.

Impelling Form: Inhabiting Science

1. Orr, *Ecological Literacy.*

2. Lynch, *The Image of the City.*

3. Reed Noss, "A Citizen's Guide to Ecosystem Management," distributed as Wild Earth Special Paper #3 (Boulder: Biodiversity Legal Foundation, 1999).

4. Williams, *Refuge,* 10.

5. Hester, "The Place of Participatory Design."

6. Thomas Jefferson, "Letter to William Charles Jarvis, 28 September 1820," quoted in *Ecological Literacy: Education and the Transition to a Postmodern World* by David W. Orr (Albany: State University of New York Press, 1992), 77.

7. John Adams, "A Dissertation on the Canon and Feudal Law," 1765.

8. Duane, "Regulations Rationale," 471–540.

9. Randolph T. Hester Jr., "Native Wisdom amidst Ignorance of Locality," in *Building Cultural Diversity through Participation* (435–443), ed. John Liu (Taipei: Building and Planning Research Foundation, National Taiwan University, 2001), 435.

10. Orr, *Ecological Literacy,* 31–32.

11. Hough, *City Form,* 244–246; Orr, *Ecological Literacy,* 86–87.

12. John Liu, ed., *Building Cultural Diversity through Participation* (Taipei: Building and Planning Research Foundation, National Taiwan University, 2001), 451.

13. Orr, *Ecological Literacy,* 33.

14. Robert L. Ryan, "Magnetic Los Angeles: Planning the Twentieth-Century Metropolis [book review]," *Landscape Journal* 17, no. 1 (1998): 88–89; Robert L. Ryan and Mark Lindhult, "Knitting New England Together: A Recent Greenway Plan Represents Landscape Planning on a Vast Scale," *Landscape Architecture* 90, no. 2 (2000): 50, 52, 54–55.

15. Rogers, *Diffusion of Innovations.*

16. Orr, *Ecological Literacy.* 87.

17. Ibid., 88.

18. Ibid., 86.

19. Henry David Thoreau, *Journal,* as quoted in *Thoreau: A Book of Quotations* (Mineola: Dover, 2000), 6.

20. Spirn, *The Language of Landscape.*

21. Bellah et al., *Habits of the Heart.*

22. Hester, *Community Design Primer;* Daniel Kemmis, *The Good City and the Good Life* (Boston: Houghton Mifflin, 1995); Hiss, *The Experience of Place;* Benjamin Barber, *Strong Democracy: Participatory Politics for a New Age* (Berkeley: University of California Press, 1984); Dewitt John, *Civic Environmentalism* (Washington, DC: Congressional Quarterly Press, 1994); William A. Shutkin, *The Land That Could Be: Environmentalism and Democracy in the Twenty-first Century* (Cambridge: MIT Press, 2001).

23. Ervin H. Zube, J. L. Sell, and J. G. Taylor, "Landscape Perception: Research, Application and Theory" *Landscape Planning* 9, no. 1 (1982): 1–33; Relph, *Place and Placelessness;* David Seamon, "Phenomenology and Environmental Research," in *Advances in Environment, Behavior, and Design* (3–27), ed. Gary T. Moore and Ervin H. Zube (New York: Plenum Press, 1987).

24. Ryan, "Magnetic Los Angeles"; Ryan and Lindhult "Knitting New England Together."

25. Schumacher, *Small Is Beautiful,* 22.

26. Robert L. Thayer, Jr., "Landscape as an Ecologically Revealing Language," *Landscape Journal* (special issue on Eco-Revelatory Design) (1998): 118–129.

27. Wendell Berry, "The Futility of Global Thinking," *Harper's* 279, no. 1672 (1989): 22.

28. Schumacher, *Small Is Beautiful,* 61, 63–64.

29. Thayer, "Landscape as an Ecologically Revealing Language."

30. Michael Southworth, Susan Southworth, and Nancy Walton, *Discovery Centers* (Berkeley: Institute of Urban and Regional Development, University of California, 1990); Orr, *Ecological Literacy,* 97–124, 163–166; Shepard, *Thinking Animals,* 129; Gary Coates, *Alternative Learning Environments* (Stroudsburg: Dowden, Hutchinson & Ross, 1974).

31. Orr, *Ecological Literacy,* 88.

32. Denis Wood with John Fels, *The Power of Maps* (New York: Guilford Press, 1992); Southworth, "City Learning," 35–48; Peter Bosselmann and Kenneth H. Craik, *Perceptual Simulations of Environments* (Berkeley: Institute of Urban and Regional Development, University of California, 1987); Hester, *Community Design Primer.*

33. Michael Southworth, "The Educative City," in *Cities and City Planning* (19–29), ed. Lloyd Rodwin (New York: Plenum Press, 1981), 29.

34. Robin C. Moore and Herb H. Wong, *Natural Learning: The Life History of an Environmental Schoolyard: Creating Environments for Rediscovering Nature's Way of Teaching* (Berkeley: MIG Communications, 1997).

35. *Landscape Journal,* special issue on Eco-Revelatory Design: Nature Constructed/Nature Revealed, ed. Brenda Brown, Terry Harkness, and Douglas Johnston (1998): x–xvi; Terry Harkness, "Foothill Mountain Observatory: Reconsidering Golden Mountain," *Landscape Journal* (special issue on Eco-Revelatory Design) (1998): 42–45.

36. *Landscape Journal,* Special Issue on Eco-Revelatory Design, xvi.

37. Thayer, *Gray World,* 310–312.

38. Orr, *Ecological Literacy,* 88.

39. Ibid., 89.

40. Southworth, "Educative City," 27.

41. Ibid.

42. Terry Tempest Williams, *An Unspoken Hunger: Stories from the Field* (New York: Pantheon books, 1994), 12.

43. Orr, *Ecological Literacy,* 89.

44. Susan Galatowitsch, "Ecological Design for Environmental Problem Solving," *Landscape Journal* (special issue on Eco-Revelatory Design) (1998): 99.

45. Thoreau, *Journal.*

46. Thayer, "Landscape as an Ecologically Revealing Language," 129.

47. Galatowitsch, "Ecological Design," 99–100.

48. Terry Harkness, "Garden from Region," in *The Meaning of Gardens: Idea, Place, and Action* (110–119), ed. Mark Francis and Randolph T. Hester Jr. (Cambridge: MIT Press, 1990).

49. Joe McBride and Chris Reid, "Forest History Trail Guide" (California Department of Forestry and Fire Protection, 1991).

50. Richard Hansen, "Watermarks at the Nature Center," *Landscape Journal* (special issue on Eco-Revelatory Design) (1998): 21–23.

51. Mozingo, "The Aesthetics of Ecological Design," 46–59.

52. Orr, *Ecological Literacy,* 87–89.

53. Southworth, "The Educative City."

54. Michael Southworth and Susan Southworth, "The Educative City," in *Alternative Learning Environments* (274–281), ed. Gary Coates (Stroudsburg: Dowden, Hutchinson & Ross, 1974).

55. Southworth, "The Educative City," 26.

56. Carolyn Merchant, "Partnership with Nature," *Landscape Journal* (special issue on Eco-Revelatory Design) (1998): 69–71.

57. "The Wide World of Monitoring: Beyond Water Quality Testing," *Volunteer Monitor* 6, no. 1 (1994): 9.

58. Ibid., 4–5.

59. Chanse and Hester, "Characterizing Volunteer Involvement," 11.

60. Thayer, "Landscape as an Ecologically Revealing Language," 129.

61. Hester, *Neighborhood Space,* 162, and *Planning Neighborhood Space,* 163–167; Galatowitsch, "Ecological Design," 101–103.

62. Galatowitsch, "Ecological Design," 105.

63. Galatowitsch, "Ecological Design," 105; Thayer, "Landscape as an Ecologically Revealing Language," 129.

64. Newton Harrison, e-mail message to author, August 27, 2003.

65. Patricia Phillips, "Intelligible Images: The Dynamics of Disclosure," *Landscape Journal* (special issue on Eco-Revelatory Design) (1998): 109.

66. Phillips, "Intelligible Images," 117.

67. Gans, *People and Plans.*

68. Thayer, *Gray World.*

69. Timothy P. Duane, "Environmental Planning Policy in a Post Rio World," *Berkeley Planning Journal* 7 (1992): 27–47.

70. Thoreau, *Journal,* 2.

71. Henry David Thoreau, *Cape Cod,* as quoted in *Thoreau: A Book of Quotations* (Mineola: Dover, 2000), 41.

72. Krapfel, *Shifting.*

73. Krapfel, *Shifting; Landscape Journal* (special issue on Eco-Revelatory Design); Kristina Hill, "Rising Parks as Inverted Dikes," 35–37; Julie Bargmann and Stacy Levy, "Testing the Waters," 38–41; Terry Harkness, "Foothill Mountain Observatory: Reconsidering Golden Mountain," 42–45; Margaret McAvin with Karen Nelson, "Horizon Revealed and Constructed," 46–48; Catherine Howett, "Ecological Values in Twentieth-Century Landscape Design: A History and Hermeneutics," 80–98.

74. Krapfel, *Shifting;* Howett, "Ecological Values in Twentieth-Century Landscape Design," 83–85.

75. Thayer, "Landscape as an Ecologically Revealing Language," 119, and *Gray World,* 313, 321.

76. Krapfel, *Shifting,* 74.

77. Harkness, "Foothill Mountain," 42.

78. Phillips, "Intelligible Images," 116.

79. Sullivan, *Garden and Climate,* 226.

80. Thayer, *Gray World,* 317.

81. Frederick Turner, "A Cracked Case," *Landscape Journal* (special issue on Eco-Revelatory Design) (1998): 135.

82. Kondolf, "Hungry Water," 551–553.

83. Hester, Blazej, and Moore, "Whose Wild," 137–146.

Impelling Form: Reciprocal Stewardship

1. Chanse and Hester, "Characterizing Volunteer Involvement."

2. Terry Hartig, P. Bowler, and A. Wolf, "Psychological Ecology," *Restoration and Management News* 12, no. 2 (1994): 133–137.

3. Merchant, "Partnership with Nature."

4. Bob Scarfo, "Stewardship in the Twentieth Century," *Landscape Architectural Review* 7, no. 2 (1986): 13–15.

5. Aldo Leopold, *A Sand County Almanac, and Sketches Here and There* (New York: Oxford University Press, 1969), ix.

6. Leopold, *A Sand County Almanac,* 204, 221.

7. Ibid., 201–203.

8. Ibid., 202–203.

9. Ibid., 209.

10. Leopold, *Almanac,* 204, 221; Shutkin, *The Land That Could Be,* 41–44.

11. Shutkin, *The Land That Could Be,* 43–44.

12. Howett, "Ecological Values," 94.

13. President's Council on Sustainable Development, *Sustainable America,* 110–130.

14. Garrett Hardin, "The Tragedy of the Commons," *Science* 162 (1969): 1243–1248.

15. Bonnie J. McCay and James M. Acheson, "Human Ecology of the Commons," in *The Question of the Commons: The Culture and Ecology of Communal Resources* (1–34), ed. Bonnie J. McCay and James M. Acheson (Tucson: University of Arizona Press, 1987).

16. Merchant, "Partnership with Nature," 69–71.

17. Fern Heit Kamp, "Using Stewardship as a Guide for Planning," *Plan Canada* 36, no. 4 (1996): 28–30.

18. Robert Ogilvie, "Recruiting, Training, and Retaining Volunteers," in *Democratic Design in the Pacific Rim: Japan, Taiwan, and the United States* (243–249), ed. Randolph T. Hester Jr. and Corrina Kweskin (Mendocino: Ridge Times Press, 1999).

19. Chanse and Hester, "Characterizing Volunteer Involvement."

20. Hester, *Planning Neighborhood Space,* Chapter 5.

21. McNally, "On the Care and Feeding of the Grassroots."

22. Gray Brechin, "Grace Marchant and the Global Garden," in *The Meaning of Gardens: Idea, Place, and Action* (226–229), ed. Mark Francis and Randolph T. Hester Jr. (Cambridge: MIT Press, 1990).

23. Deborah D. Giraud, "Shared Backyard Gardening," in *The Meaning of Gardens: Idea, Place, and Action* (166–171), ed. Mark Francis and Randolph T. Hester Jr. (Cambridge: MIT Press, 1990).

24. Mark Francis, Lisa Cashdan and Lynn Paxon, *Community Open Spaces: Greening Neighborhoods through Community Action and Land Conservation* (Washington, DC: Island Press, 1984); Rebecca Severson, "United We Sprout: A Chicago Community Gardening Story," in *The Meaning of Gardens: Idea, Place, and Action* (80–85), ed. Mark Francis and Randolph T. Hester Jr. (Cambridge: MIT Press, 1990).

25. Chanse and Hester, "Characterizing Volunteer Involvement."

26. Larry D. Hodge, "Bobwhite Boot Camp: A Program to Teach Kids about Quails Is Flushed with Success," *Progressive Farmer* (March 1995): 38, 40.

27. Ibid.

28. U.S. Fish and Wildlife Service, "Bosque del Apache National Wildlife Refuge," 1999.

29. Chanse and Hester, "Characterizing Volunteer Involvement"; Crissy Field Center, "Crissy Field Fact Sheet: The Restoration," January 22, 2001.

30. Chanse and Hester, "Characterizing Volunteer Involvement."

31. Stephen Long, "Vermont Coverts Bring People Close to Their Neighbors . . . and to the Land," *Woodlands for Wildlife Newsletter* (1998): 28–32.

32. David Dobbs, "Private Property, Public Good," *Audubon* 100, no. 4 (1998): 120.

33. President's Council on Sustainable Development, *Sustainable America,* 112.

34. *Wild Earth,* 9, no. 2 (1999): inside cover.

35. Laura Lawson, "Linking Youth Training and Employment with Community Building: Lessons Learned at the BYA Garden Patch," in *Democratic Design in the Pacific Rim: Japan, Taiwan, and the United States* (80–91), ed. Randolph T. Hester Jr. and Corrina Kweskin (Mendocino: Ridge Times Press), 1999.

36. Lawson, "Linking Youth Training," 86.

37. Ibid., 85.

38. Laura Lawson and Marcia McNally, "Putting Teens at the Center: Maximizing Public Utility of Urban Space through Youth Involvement in Planning and Employment," *Children's Environments* 12, no. 2 (1995): 209–221.

39. Lawson, "Linking Youth Training," 90.

40. Laura Lawson, personal communication with author, May 22, 2002.

41. McNally, "On the Care and Feeding of the Grassroots."

42. Connie Barlow, "Because It Is My Religion," *Wild Earth* 6, no. 3 (1996): 5–11.

43. Duane Elgin, *Voluntary Simplicity: Toward a Way of Life That Is Outwardly Simple, Inwardly Rich* (New York: Morrow, 1981), 21–41.

44. Berry, "The Futility of Global Thinking," 19.

45. Henry David Thoreau, *Walden and Other Writings,* ed. Brooks Atkinson (New York: Modern Library, 2000).

46. Wendell Berry, *The Long-Legged House* (New York: Harcourt, Brace and World, 1969), 61.

47. Sidey, "The Two Sides of the Sam Walton Legacy."

48. Charles A. Lewis, "Gardening as Healing Process," in *The Meaning of Gardens: Idea, Place, and Action* (244–251), ed. Mark Francis and Randolph T. Hester Jr. (Cambridge: MIT Press, 1990), 248.

Impelling Form: Pacing

1. E. B. White, *The Trumpet of the Swan.*
2. Kenko, *Essays in Idleness,* 66–67.
3. Thoreau, *Journal,* 33.
4. Thoreau, "Walking," in *Walden and Other Writings,* 628.
5. Ibid., 628–629.
6. Olmsted, *The Slave States.*
7. Thoreau, "Walking," in *Walden and Other Writings,* 627.
8. Jackson and Kochtitzky, *Creating a Healthy Environment,* preface.
9. Carolyn R. Shaffer and Kristen Arundsen, "The Healing Powers of Community," *Utne Reader* 71 (1995): 64–65.
10. J. L. Gilderbloom and J. P. Markham, "Housing Quality among the Elderly: A Decade of Changes," *International Journal of Aging and Human Development* (1991); Marcus and Sarkissian, *Housing as If People Mattered.*
11. Jackson and Kochtitsky, *Creating a Healthy Environment,* 7.
12. Ibid., 11.
13. Ibid., 9.
14. State of California, "SB 1520 Child Obesity Prevention Fact Sheet" (Sacramento: State of California Senate Health Committee, Senator Deborah Ortiz, Chair, March 2002), 1–6.
15. Report to the Public Health Institute, funding provided by the U.S. Department of Agriculture through the California Nutrition Contracts #1003305 and #1002737, November 15, 2001.
16. Jackson and Kochtitsky, *Creating a Healthy Environment,* 8.
17. Chomei, *The Ten-Foot Square Hut,* 19.
18. Kenneth Chang, "Diet and Exercise Are Found to Cut Diabetes by Half," *New York Times,* August 9, 2001, A1.
19. M. S. Friedman et al., "Impact of Changes in Transportation and Commuting Behaviors during the 1996 Summer Olympic Games in Atlanta on Air Quality and Childhood Asthma," *Journal of American Medical Association* 285 (2001): 897–905.
20. Appleyard, *Livable Streets.*
21. James Sterngold, "Primacy of the Car Is Over, California Governor Declares," *New York Times,* August 21, 2001, A8.
22. Thoreau, "Walking," in *Walden and Other Writings,* 629.
23. Walker, "A Personal Approach to Design," 10.
24. R. B. Litton Jr., "Forest Landscape Description and Inventories: A Basis for Land Planning and Design," USDA Forest Service Research Paper PSW-49, 1968, 64.

25. Lynch, *The Image of the City.*

26. Douglas Martin, "Joseph Charles, Ninety-one: A Symbol of Street Corner Friendliness," *New York Times,* March 20, 2002, A25.

27. Lyndon and Moore, *Chambers for a Memory Palace;* Appleyard, *Livable Streets;* Appleyard, Lynch, and Myer, *The View from the Road.*

28. Appleton, *The Experience of Landscape;* Lovelock, *The Ages of Gaia.*

29. Halprin, *The RSVP Cycles.*

30. Martin Luther King Jr., "I See the Promised Land," in *I Have a Dream: Writings and Speeches That Changed the World* (193–203), ed. James M. Washington (San Francisco: Harper, 1992).

31. Thoreau, "Walking," in *Walden and Other Writings,* 247, 261.

32. Ovid, *Metamorphoses,* trans. Horace Gregory (New York: Signet, 2001), 46.

33. Thoreau, *Journal,* 42.

34. Thoreau, "Walking," in *Walden and Other Writings,* 629, 637.

35. Ibid., 627.

36. Thoreau, *Journal,* 26.

37. Thoreau, "Walking," in *Walden and Other Writings,* 631.

38. Ovid, *Metamorphoses,* 59.

References and Suggested Reading

Abbey, Edward. "Personal Bests." *Outside Magazine* (October 2001): 66.

Abram, David. *The Spell of the Sensuous.* New York: Vintage, 1997.

Adams, John. "A Dissertation on the Canon and Feudal Law." 1765.

Adams, Lowell W., and Louise E. Dove. *Wildlife Reserves and Corridors in the Urban Environment: A Guide to Ecological Landscape Planning and Resource Conservation.* Columbia: National Institute for Urban Wildlife, 1989.

"After Outcry: Greenwich Retreats from Beach Policy and Offers Daily Passes," *New York Times,* March 9, 2002, B15.

Akbari, Hashem, and Leanna Shea Rose. *Characterizing the Fabric of the Urban Environment: A Case Study of Metropolitan Chicago, Illinois,* Report LBNL-49275. Berkeley: Lawrence Berkeley National Laboratory, October 2001.

Alexander, Christopher, et al. *A Pattern Language.* New York: Oxford University Press, 1977.

Alinsky, Saul D. *Rules for Radicals: A Practical Primer for Realistic Radicals.* New York: Random House, 1971.

American LIVES, Inc. "1995 New Urbanism Study: Revitalizing Suburban Communities." Paper presented at the Urban Land Institute Seminar on Master Planned Communities 2000 and Beyond, November 2, 1995.

Appleton, Jay. *The Experience of Landscape.* New York: Wiley, 1996.

Appleyard, Donald. *Inside vs. Outside: The Distortions of Distance.* Berkeley: Institute of Urban and Regional Development, University of California, 1979.

———. *Planning a Pluralist City: Conflicting Realities in Ciudad Guayana.* Cambridge: MIT Press, 1976.

Appleyard, Donald, with M. Sue Gerson and Mark Lintell. *Livable Streets.* Berkeley: University of California Press, 1981.

Appleyard, Donald, Kevin Lynch, and John R. Myer. *The View from the Road.* Cambridge: MIT Press, 1964.

Appleyard, Donald, et al. *A Humanistic Design Manifesto.* Berkeley: University of California, 1982.

Arendt, Randall. "Principle Three." In *The Charter of the New Urbanism* (29–34). Edited by Michael Leccese and Kathleen McCormick. New York: McGraw-Hill, 2000.

Aristotle. *Ethics, Nichomachean Ethics.* Translated by J. A. K. Thomson. London: London Allen & Unwin, 1953.

———. *Politics.* Chicago: University of Chicago Press, 1984.

Arnstein, Sherry R. "A Ladder of Citizen Participation." *Journal of the American Institute of Planners* 35, no. 4 (1969): 216–224.

Bachelard, Gaston. *The Poetics of Space.* Translated by Maria Jolas. Boston: Beacon, 1969.

Bargmann, Julie, and Stacy Levy. "Testing the Waters." *Landscape Journal* (special issue on Eco-Revelatory Design) (1998): 38–41.

Barber, Benjamin. *Strong Democracy: Participatory Politics for a New Age.* Berkeley: University of California Press, 1984.

Barlow, Connie. "Because It Is My Religion." *Wild Earth* 6, no. 3 (1996): 5–11.

Beatley, Timothy, and Kristy Manning. *The Ecology of Place: Planning for Environment, Economy, and Community.* Washington, DC: Island Press, 1997.

Bellah, Robert N., et al. *Habits of the Heart: Individualism and Commitment in American Life.* New York: Perennial, 1986.

Berman, Marshall. *All That Is Solid Melts into Air: The Experience of Modernity.* New York: Simon and Schuster, 1982.

Bernick, Michael, and Robert Cervero. *Transit Villages in the Twenty-first Century.* New York: McGraw-Hill, 1997.

Berry, Wendell. *A Continuous Harmony: Essays Cultural and Agricultural.* New York: Harcourt Brace Jovanovich, 1972.

———. "The Futility of Global Thinking." *Harper's* 279, no. 1672 (September 1989): 16–19, 22.

———. *The Landscape of Harmony.* Madley: Five Seasons Press, 1987.

———. *The Long-Legged House.* New York: Harcourt, Brace and World, 1969.

———. *The Unsettling of America: Culture and Agriculture.* New York: Avon, 1978.

Beyard, Michael D., and W. Paul O'Mara. *Shopping Center Development Handbook.* Washington, DC: Urban Land Institute, 1999.

Black Elk, Nicholas, with John G. Neihardt. *Black Elk Speaks: Being the Life Story of a Holy Man of the Oglala Sioux.* Lincoln: University of Nebraska Press, 1972.

Blakely, Edward J., and Mary Gail Snyder. *Fortress America: Gated Communities in the United States.* Washington, DC: Brookings Institution Press, 1997.

Bloomer, Kent C., and Charles W. Moore. *Body, Memory and Architecture.* New Haven: Yale University Press, 1977.

Bookout, Lloyd, and James W. Wentling. "Density by Design." *Urban Land* 47, no. 6 (1988): 10–15.

Bosselmann, Peter, and Kenneth H. Craik. *Perceptual Simulations of Environments.* Berkeley: Institute of Urban and Regional Development, University of California, 1987.

Bourdier, Jean-Paul. *Drawn from African Dwellings.* Bloomington: Indiana University Press, 1996.

Bourdier, Jean-Paul, and Nezar AlSayyad, eds. *Dwellings, Settlements, and Tradition: Cross-Cultural Perspectives.* Lanham: University Press of America, 1989.

Brand, Stewart S. *How Buildings Learn: What Happens after They're Built.* New York: Penguin, 1994.

Brechin, Gray. "Grace Marchant and the Global Garden." In *The Meaning of Gardens: Idea, Place, and Action* (226–229). Edited by Mark Francis and Randolph T. Hester Jr. Cambridge: MIT Press, 1990.

Brooke, James. "Heat Island Tokyo Is in Global Warming's Vanguard." *New York Times,* August 13, 2002, A3.

Brower, Sydney. *Good Neighborhoods: A Study of Intown and Suburban Residential Environments.* Westport: Praeger, 1996.

Brown, Brenda. "Holding Moving Landscapes." *Landscape Journal* (special issue on Eco-Revelatory Design) (1998): 53–68.

Brown, Brenda, Terry Harkness, and Douglas Johnston, eds. "Eco-Revelatory Design: Nature Constructed/Nature Revealed." *Landscape Journal* (special issue) (1998).

Brown, Lester R., and Jodi L. Jacobson. "The Future of Urbanization." *Urban Land* 46, no. 6 (1987): 2–5.

Brown, Patricia L. "The Chroming of the Front Yard." *New York Times,* June 13, 2002, D1, D6.

———. "A Park Offers Nature, Not Just Hoops." *New York Times,* December 28, 2000, F1, F9.

Bullard, Robert D. *Dumping in Dixie: Race, Class, and Environmental Quality.* Boulder: Westview Press, 2000.

Calhoun, J. B. "Population Density and Social Pathology." *Scientific American* 206 (1962): 139–148.

California State Assembly. AB 2637, accessed July 16, 2003, available at <http://www.leginfo.ca.gov/pub/01-02/bill/asm/ab_2601-2650/ab_2637_bill_20020927>.

California State Senate. "SB 1520 Child Obesity Prevention Fact Sheet." Sacramento: State of California Senate Health Committee, March 2002.

Callies, David L. *Preserving Paradise: Why Regulation Won't Work.* Honolulu: University of Hawaii Press, 1994.

Calthorpe, Peter. *The Next American Metropolis: Ecology, Community and the American Dream.* New York: Princeton Architectural Press, 1993.

———. "The Region." In *The New Urbanism: Towards an Architecture of Community* (xi–xvi). Edited by Peter Katz. New York: McGraw-Hill, 1994.

Canright, Anne. "Nature Comes to South Central L.A." *California Coast and Ocean* 18, no. 1 (2002): 33–38.

Carson, Rachel L. *Silent Spring.* New York: Houghton Mifflin, 1962.

Cervero, Robert, and Peter Bosselmann. *An Evaluation of the Market Potential for Transit-Oriented Development Using Visual Simulation Techniques.* Berkeley: Institute of Urban and Regional Development, University of California, 1994.

Chang, Kenneth. "Diet and Exercise Are Found to Cut Diabetes by Half." *New York Times,* August 9, 2001, A1.

Chang, Shenglin. "Real Life at Virtual Home: Silicon Landscape Construction in Response to Transcultural Home Identities." Dissertation, University of California, Berkeley, 2000.

Chang, Shenglin, et al. *A Study of the Environmental and Social Aspects of the Taiwanese and US Companies in the Hsinchu Science-based Industrial Park.* Policy report for California Global Corporate Accountability Project. Berkeley: Nautilus Institute for Security and Sustainable Development and the Natural Heritage Institute and Human Rights Advocates, 2001.

Chanse, Victoria, and Randolph T. Hester Jr. "Characterizing Volunteer Involvement in Wildlife Habitat Planning." In *CELA 2002: Groundwork,* Proceedings of the Annual Meeting of the Council of Educators in Landscape Architecture, State University of New York, Syracuse, NY, September 25–28, 2002.

Chase, John, Margaret Crawford, and John Kaliski, eds. *Everyday Urbanism.* New York: Monacelli Press, 1999.

Ching, Sheauchi, Joe R. McBride, and Keizo Fukunari. "The Urban Forest of Tokyo." *Aboricultural Journal* 23 (2000): 379–392.

Chomei, Kamo-no. *The Ten-Foot Square Hut and Tales of the Heike.* Translated by A. L. Sadler. Rutland: Tuttle, 1972.

Chou, Chuang. "Chuang Tzu." In *The Columbia Anthology of Traditional Chinese Literature: Translations from the Asian Classics* (45–57). Edited by Victor Mair. New York: Columbia University Press, 1994.

Coates, Gary. *Alternative Learning Environments.* Stroudsburg: Dowden, Hutchinson & Ross, 1974.

Cohodas, Nadine. "Goals for Raleigh Issues Report." *News and Observer,* May 27, 1973, vi–l.

Colinvaux, Paul. *Why Big Fierce Animals Are Rare: An Ecologist's Perspective.* Princeton: Princeton University Press, 1979.

Comerio, Mary C. *Disaster Hits Home: New Policy for Urban Housing Recovery.* Berkeley: University of California Press, 1998.

Community Development by Design [Community Development Planning and Design]. *Restricted Use: Educational Operating Manual for LA96C: The Former U.S. Army NIKE Missile Control Reservation and the Present San Vicente Mountain Park, Gateway to Big Wild.* Berkeley: Community Development by Design, 1996.

———. *Runyon Canyon One: Summary of Listening.* Berkeley: Community Development by Design, 1985.

———. *Runyon Canyon Two: Goals, Objectives and Policies.* Berkeley: Community Development by Design, 1985.

———. *Runyon Canyon Three: Revisions to Goals, Objectives and Policies.* Berkeley: Community Development by Design, 1985.

———. *Runyon Canyon Four: Cutout Workbook.* Berkeley: Community Development by Design, 1985.

———. *Runyon Canyon Five: Environmental Analysis.* Berkeley: Community Development by Design, 1985.

———. *Runyon Canyon Six: She's a Hollywood Natural.* Berkeley: Community Development by Design, 1985.

———. *Runyon Canyon Seven: Program and Environmental Review.* Berkeley: Community Development by Design, 1985.

———. *Runyon Canyon Master Plan and Design Guidelines.* Berkeley: Community Development by Design, 1986.

———. "Runyon Canyon Master Plan and Design Guidelines." *Landscape Architecture* 77, no. 6 (1987): 60–63.

Condon, Patrick, and Stacy Moriarty, eds. *Second Nature: Adapting LA's Landscape for Sustainable Living.* Beverly Hills: TreePeople, 1999.

Constantine, J. "Design by Democracy." *Land Development* 5, no. 1 (1992): 11–15.

Corbett, Judy, and Michael N. Corbett. *Designing Sustainable Communities: Learning from Village Homes.* Washington, DC: Island Press, 2000.

Corbett, Michael N. *A Better Place to Live: New Designs for Tomorrow's Communities.* Emmaus: Rodale Press, 1981.

Cranz, Galen. *The Politics of Park Design: A History of Urban Parks in America.* Cambridge, MIT Press, 1982.

Crissy Field Center. "Crissy Field Fact Sheet: The Restoration." January 22, 2001.

Crowe, Beryl L. "The Tragedy of the Commons Revisited." *Science* 166 (1969): 1103–1107.

Croxton, Randolph R. "Sustainable Design Offers Key to Control." *Architectural Record* 185, no. 6 (1997): 76, 78.

Darwin, Charles. *On the Origin of Species by Means of Natural Selection.* Cambridge: Harvard University Press, 1964.

Davidoff, Paul. "Advocacy and Pluralism in Planning." *Journal of the American Institute of Planners* 31, no. 4 (1965): 331–338.

Davis, Sam. *The Architecture of Affordable Housing.* Berkeley: University of California Press, 1995.

Delbecq, Andre L. *Group Techniques for Program Planning: A Guide to Nominal Group and Delphi Processes.* Glenview: Scott, Foresman, 1975.

Derr, Mark. "Acrobatic Ape in Java is in High-Wire Scramble." *New York Times,* February 5, 2002, D5.

Dobbs, David. "Private Property, Public Good," *Audubon* 100, no. 4 (1998): 120.

Dovey, Kim. *Framing Places: Mediating Power in Built Form.* New York: Routledge, 1999.

———. "Home: An Ordering Principle in Space." *Landscape* 22, no. 2 (1978): 27–30.

Dowall, David. *Applying Real Estate Financial Analysis to Planning and Development Controls.* Berkeley: Institute for Urban and Regional Development, University of California, 1984.

———. *The Suburban Squeeze: Land Conversion and Regulation in the San Francisco Bay Area.* Berkeley: University of California Press, 1984.

Downs, Anthony. *New Visions for Urban America.* Washington, DC: Brookings Institution, 1994.

Dramstad, Wenche E., James D. Olson, and Richard T. T. Forman. *Landscape Ecology Principles in Landscape Architecture and Land-Use Planning.* Washington, DC: Island Press, 1996.

Draper, John E. "Paris by the Lake: Sources of Burnham's Plan of Chicago." In *Chicago Architecture 1872–1922: Birth of a Metropolis* (107–120). Edited by John Zukowsky. Munich: Prestel-Verlap, 1987.

Duane, Timothy P. "Environmental Planning Policy in a Post-Rio World." *Berkeley Planning Journal* 7 (1992): 27–47.

———. "Regulations Rationale: Learning from the California Energy Crisis." *Yale Journal on Regulation* 19, no. 2 (2002): 471–540.

Duany, Andres, and Elizabeth Plater-Zyberk. "The Neighborhood, the District, and the Corridor." In *The New Urbanism: Towards an Architecture of Community* (xvii–xx). Edited by Peter Katz. New York: McGraw-Hill, 1994.

Duany, Andres, Elizabeth Plater-Zyberk, and Alex Kreiger. *Towns and Town-Making Principles.* New York: Rizzoli, 1991.

Dubos, Rene. "Half Truths about the Future." *Wall Street Journal,* May 8, 1981, 26.

Edwards, Brian, and David Turrent, eds. *Sustainable Housing Principles and Practice.* New York: E&FN SPON, 2000.

Egan, Timothy. "Sprawl-Weary Los Angeles Builds Up and In." *New York Times,* March 10, 2002, 1, 30.

Elgin, Duane. *Voluntary Simplicity: Toward a Way of Life That Is Outwardly Simple, Inwardly Rich.* New York: Morrow, 1981.

Eliade, Mircea. *Mystic Stories: The Sacred and the Profane.* New York: Columbia University Press, 1992.

Endoh, Yasuhiro. "The Contemporary Meaning of Cooperative Housing: Case Study—M-Port (Kumamoto)." In *Democratic Design in the Pacific Rim: Japan, Taiwan, and the United States* (178–191). Edited by Randolph T. Hester Jr. and Corrina Kweskin. Mendocino: Ridge Times Press, 1999.

Engler, Mira. "Waste Landscapes: Permissible Metaphors in Landscape Architecture." *Landscape Journal* 14, no. 1 (1995): 10–25.

Fabos, Julius. *Planning the Total Landscape: A Guide to Intelligent Land Use.* Boulder: Westview Press, 1978.

Fairfax, Sally, et al. "The Federal Forests Are Not What They Seem: Formal and Informal Claims to Federal Lands." *Ecology Law Quarterly* 25, no. 4 (1999): 630–646.

Farris, R. E., and H. W. Dunham. *Mental Disorders in Urban Areas.* Chicago: University of Chicago Press, 1939.

"Finding Our Place." *Ecojustice Quarterly: Exploring Critical Issues of Ecology and Justice.* 14, no. 2 (1994).

Findley, Lisa. "Colorful License Plates Join Wood Shingles and Recycled Goods in the Hester/McNally House." *Architectural Record* 188, no. 7 (2000): 224–228.

Fisher, Roger. *Getting to yes: Negotiating Agreement without Giving In.* Boston: Houghton Mifflin, 1981.

Flink, Charles A., and Roberts Sears. *Greenways: A Guide to Planning, Design and Development.* Washington, DC: Island Press, 1993.

Flourney, W. L. *Capital City Greenway: A Report to the Council on the Benefits, Potential, and Methodology of Establishing a Greenway System in Raleigh.* Raleigh: n.d.

Forman, Richard T. T. *Landscape Ecology.* New York: Wiley, 1986.

Fortmann, Louise P. "Talking Claims: Discursive Strategies in Contesting Property." *World Development* 23, no. 6 (1995): 1053–1063.

Francis, Mark, Lisa Cashdan, and Lynn Paxon. *Community Open Spaces: Greening Neighborhoods through Community Action and Land Conservation.* Washington, DC: Island Press, 1984.

———. *The Making of Neighborhood Open Spaces: Community Design, Development and Management of Open Spaces.* New York: City University of New York, Center for Human Environments, 1982.

Francis, Mark. "A Case Study Method for Landscape Architecture." *Landscape Journal* 20, no. 1 (2001): 15–29.

———. "Making a Community Place: The Case of Davis' Central Park and Farmers' Market." In *Democratic Design in the Pacific Rim: Japan, Taiwan, and the United States* (170–177). Edited by Randolph T. Hester Jr. and Corrina Kweskin. Mendocino: Ridge Times Press, 1999.

Francis, Mark, and Randolph T. Hester Jr., eds. *The Meaning of Gardens: Idea, Place, and Action.* Cambridge: MIT Press, 1990.

Fredericksen, Eric. "This Is Not Sprawl." *Architecture* 90, no. 12 (2001): 48–49.

Friedman, M. S., et al. "Impact of Changes in Transportation and Commuting Behaviors during the 1996 Summer Olympic Games in Atlanta on Air Quality and Childhood Asthma." *Journal of the American Medical Association* 285 (2001): 897–905.

Fuller, R. Buckminster. *Pound, Synergy, and the Great Design.* Moscow: University of Idaho, 1977.

Fuller, R. Buckminster, and Robert Marks. *The Dymaxion World of Buckminster Fuller.* Garden City: Anchor Books, 1973.

Galatowitsch, Susan M. "Ecological Design for Environmental Problem Solving." *Landscape Journal* (special issue on Eco-Revelatory Design) (1989): 99–107.

Gans, Herbert J. *People and Plans: Essays on Urban Problems and Solutions.* New York: Basic Books, 1968.

———. *The Urban Villagers: Group and Class in the Life of Italian-Americans.* New York: Free Press, 1962.

Garreau, Joel. *Edge City: Life on the New Frontier.* New York: Doubleday, 1991.

Gehl, Jan. *Life between Buildings.* New York: Van Nostrand Reinhold, 1987.

Geluardi, John. "Officials Knock Down Building Height Initiative." *Berkeley Daily Planet,* July 25, 2002, 1, 6.

Geniella, Mike. "Water Export Plan under Microscope." *Press Democrat,* March 17, 2002, 1, 6–7.

Gilderbloom, J. L., and J. P. Markham. "Housing Quality among the Elderly: A Decade of Changes." *International Journal of Aging and Human Development* 46, no. 1 (1998): 71–90.

Giraud, Deborah D. "Shared Backyard Gardening." In *The Meaning of Gardens: Idea, Place, and Action* (166–171). Edited by Mark Francis and Randolph T. Hester Jr. Cambridge: MIT Press, 1990.

Gobster, Paul H., and R. Bruce Hull, eds. *Restoring Nature: Perspectives From the Social Sciences and Humanities.* Washington, DC: Island Press, 2000.

Goldberger, Paul. "Let Us Now Praise Famous Men [Samuel Mockbee]." *Architecture* 91, no. 3 (2002): 60–67.

Golden Gate Audubon Society. *The Gull* 87, no. 5 (2002).

Goodman, Percival, and Paul Goodman. *Communitas: Means of Livelihood and Ways of Life.* New York: Columbia University Press, 1990.

Graves, Donna. "Construction Memory: Rosie the Riveter Memorial, Richmond, California." *Places* 15, no. 1 (2002): 14–17.

Greenwood, Alex, and Patrick Lane. "Oakland's 10K Race for Downtown Housing." *Planning* 38, no. 8 (2002): 14–17.

Greese, Robert. *Jens Jensen.* Baltimore: John Hopkins University Press, 1992.

Gunderson, Lance H., C. S. Holling, and Stephen S. Light, eds. *Barriers and Bridges to the Renewal of Ecosystems and Institutions.* New York: Columbia University Press, 1995.

Gurwitt, Robert. "The Casparados." *Preservation* 52, no. 6 (2000): 38–45+.

Haag, Richard. "Eco-Revelatory Design: the Challenge of the Exhibit." *Landscape Journal* (special issue on Eco-Revelatory Design) (1998): 72–79.

Habraken, N. John. *Supports: An Alternative to Mass Housing.* New York: Praeger, 1972.

Halbfiner, David M. "Yes in Our Backyards: A Shelter's New Value." *New York Times,* February 24, 2002, 26.

Hall, Edward T. *The Hidden Dimension.* Garden City: Doubleday, 1966.

Hall, Michael J. "Goals for Raleigh: Coming Up with Answers." *Raleigh Times,* June 27, 1973, 9A.

Halprin, Lawrence. *Cities.* New York: Reinhold, 1963.

———. *The RSVP Cycles: Creative Processes in the Human Environment.* New York: Braziller, 1969.

———. *The Sea Ranch: Diary of an Idea.* Berkeley: Spacemaker, 2002.

Handy, Susan L., and Kelly J. Clifton. "Local Shopping as a Strategy for Reducing Automobile Travel." *Transportation* 28, no. 4 (2001): 317–346.

Hansen, Richard. "Watermarks at the Nature Center," *Landscape Journal* (special issue on Eco-Revelatory Design) (1998): 21–23.

Hardin, Garrett. "The Tragedy of the Commons." *Science* 162 (1968): 1243–1248.

Harkness, Terry. "Foothill Mountain Observatory: Reconsidering Golden Mountain." *Landscape Journal* (special issue on Eco-Revelatory Design) (1998): 42–45.

———. "Garden from Region." In *The Meaning of Gardens: Idea, Place, and Action* (110–119). Edited by Mark Francis and Randolph T. Hester Jr. Cambridge: MIT Press, 1990.

Hart, Roger. *Children's Experience of Place.* New York: Irvington, 1979.

———. *Children's Participation: The Theory and Practice of Involving Young Citizens in Community Development and Environmental Care.* London: Earthscan, 1997.

Hartig, Terry, P. Bowler, and A. Wolf. "Psychological Ecology." *Restoration and Management News* 12, no. 2 (1994): 133–137.

Hartig, Terry, M. Mang, and Gary W. Evans. "Restorative Effects of Natural Environment Experience." *Environment and Behavior* 23, no. 1 (1991): 3–26.

Hatch, C. Richard, ed. *The Scope of Social Architecture.* New York: Van Nostrand Reinhold, 1984.

Haupt, Hannah Beate, Joy Littell, and Sarah Solotaroff, eds. *The Environment.* Evanston: McDougal, Little, 1972.

Hawken, Paul. *The Ecology of Commerce: A Declaration of Sustainability.* New York: HarperBusiness, 1993.

Hayden, Dolores. *The Power of Place: Urban Landscapes as Public History.* Cambridge: MIT Press, 1995.

———. *Seven American Utopias: The Architecture of Communitarian Socialism, 1790–1975.* Cambridge: MIT Press, 1977.

Hayes, Curtis. "No Fear of Change." *Farm Bureau News,* January 2002, 14.

Hayward, D. G. "Home as an Environmental and Psychological Concept." *Landscape* 20, no. 1 (1975): 2–9.

Heidegger, Martin. "Building Dwelling Thinking." In *Poetry, Language, Thought.* New York: Harper & Row, 1971.

Helson, W. H., et al. *An Introduction to Environmental Psychology.* New York: Holt, Rinehart and Winston, 1974.

Hester, Randolph T., Jr. "The City of the Twenty-first Century." In *Make Our City Safe for Trees* (176–180). Edited by Phillip D. Rodbell. Washington, DC: American Forestry Association, 1990.

———. "Civic and Selfish Participation." Presented at the Yokohama Urban Design Forum. Yokohama, Japan, March 16–19, 1992.

———. "Community Design: Making the Grassroots Whole." *Built Environment* 13, no. 1 (1987): 45–60.

———. *Community Design Primer.* Mendocino: Ridge Times Press, 1990.

———. "It's Just a Matter of Fish Heads: Using Design to Build Community." *Small Town* 24, no. 2 (1993): 4–13.

———. "Landstyles and Lifescapes: Twelve Steps to Community Development." *Landscape Architecture* 75, no. 1 (1985): 78–85.

———. "Life, Liberty and the Pursuit of Sustainable Happiness." *Places* 9, no. 3 (1995): 4–17.

———. "Making a Place Clean Enough to be Happy and Dirty Enough to Be Happy." *Proceedings for Urban Ecology Sustainable City Proceedings.* 1994.

———. "Native Wisdom amidst Ignorance of Locality." In *Building Cultural Diversity through Participation* (435–443). Edited by John Liu. Taipei: Building and Planning Research Foundation, National Taiwan University, 2001.

———. *Neighborhood Space.* Stroudsburg: Dowden, Hutchinson & Ross, 1975.

———. "Participatory Design and Environmental Justice: Pas De Deux or Time to Change Partners?" *Journal of Architectural and Planning Research* 4, no. 4 (1987): 289–300.

———. "The Place of Participatory Design: An American View." In *Democratic Design in the Pacific Rim: Japan, Taiwan, and the United States* (22–41). Edited by Randolph T. Hester Jr. and Corrina Kweskin. Mendocino: Ridge Times Press, 1999.

———. *Planning Neighborhood Space with People.* New York: Van Nostrand Reinhold, 1984.

———. "Sacred Structures and Everyday Life: A Return to Manteo, N.C." In *Dwelling, Seeing and Designing: Toward a Phenomenological Ecology* (271–297). Edited by David Seamons. New York: State University of New York, 1993.

———. "Social Values in Open Space Design." *Places* 6, no. 1 (1989): 68–76.

———. "Subconscious Landscapes of the Heart." *Places* 2, no. 3 (1985): 10–22.

———. "Wilderness in L.A.?" *Urban Ecologist* no. 1 (1997): 6, 22.

———. "Womb with a View: How Spatial Nostalgia Affects the Designer." *Landscape Architecture* 69, no. 5 (1979): 475–481, 528.

Hester, Randolph T., Jr., Nova J. Blazej, and Ian S. Moore. "Whose Wild? Resolving Cultural and Biological Diversity Conflicts in Urban Wilderness." *Landscape Journal* 18, no. 2 (1999): 137–146.

Hester, Randolph T., Jr., et al. *Goals for Raleigh: Interview Results Technical Report One.* Raleigh: North Carolina State University, 1973.

Hester, Randolph T., Jr., with Marcia McNally. *The Language of Wildlands Appreciation: A Literature Review of Descriptions and Values.* Prepared for the Pacific Southwest Forest and Range Experiment Station. Berkeley: Department of Landscape Architecture and Environmental Planning, 1987.

Hester, Randolph T., Jr., et al. *Learning about Union Point: Waterfront Park Site Environmental Analysis.* Berkeley: Institute of Urban and Regional Development, University of California, 1998.

Hester, Randolph T., Jr., and Corrina Kweskin, eds. *Democratic Design in the Pacific Rim: Japan, Taiwan, and the United States.* Mendocino: Ridge Times Press, 1999.

Hester, Randolph T., Jr., et al. *Our Children Need Open Space: Fruitvale Open Space Proposal.* Berkeley: Institute of Urban and Regional Development and Department of Landscape Architecture and Environmental Planning, June 1999.

Hill, Kristina. "Rising Parks as Inverted Dikes." *Landscape Journal* (special issue on Eco-Revelatory Design) (1998): 35–37.

Hinrichsen, Don. "Putting the Bite on Planet Earth: Rapid Human Population Growth Is Devouring Global Natural Resources." *International Wildlife* 24, no. 5 (1994): 36–45.

Hise, Greg, and William Deverell. *Eden by Design: The 1930 Olmsted-Bartholomew Plan for the Los Angeles Region.* Berkeley: University of California Press, 2000.

Hiss, Tony. *The Experience of Place.* New York: Knopf, 1990.

Hoch, Irving. "City Size Effects, Trends and Politics." *Science* 193, no. 3 (1976): 856–863.

Hodge, Larry D. "Bobwhite Boot Camp: A Program to Teach Kids about Quail Is Flushed with Success." *Progressive Farmer* (March 1995): 38–40.

Holling, C. S. *Resilience and Stability of Ecological Systems.* Vancouver: Institute of Resource Ecology, University of British Columbia, 1973.

Holtzclaw, John. "Northeast SF Factoids." Memo to Paul Okamoto, September 22, 1995.

Hongo, Garret Kaoru. *Volcano: A Memoir of Hawai'i.* New York: Vintage, 1996.

Hood, Walter. *Urban Diaries.* Washington, DC: Spacemaker Press, 1997.

Horton, John. *The Politics of Diversity: Immigration, Resistance, and Change in Monterey Park, California.* Philadelphia: Temple University Press, 1995.

Hou, Jeffrey. "From Activism to Sustainable Development: The Case of Chigu and the Anti-Binnan Movement." In *Democratic Design in the Pacific Rim: Japan, Taiwan, and the United States* (124–133). Edited by Randolph T. Hester Jr. and Corrina Kweskin. Mendocino: Ridge Times Press, 1999.

———. "From Dual Disparities to Dual Squeeze: The Emerging Patterns of Regional Development in Taiwan." *Berkeley Planning Journal* 14 (2000): 4–22.

———. "Social, Intellectual, and Political Actions in Environmental Planning and Design: The Case of Anti-Binnan Movement in Chiku, Taiwan." Proceedings of the Thirty-first Annual Conference of the Environmental Design Research Association. San Francisco, CA, May 10–14, 2000, 19–25.

Hough, Michael. *City Form and Natural Process.* New York: Van Nostrand Reinhold, 1984.

———. *Out of Place: Restoring Identity to the Regional Landscape.* New Haven: Yale University Press, 1990.

Howett, Catherine. "Ecological Values in Twentieth-Century Landscape Design: A History and Hermeneutics." *Landscape Journal* (special issue on Eco-Revelatory Design) (1998): 80–98.

Innes, Judith E., and David E. Booher. *Consensus Building as Role-Playing and Bricolage: Toward a Theory of Collaborative Planning.* Berkeley: Institute of Urban and Regional Development, University of California, 1997.

———. *Planning Institutions in the Network Society: Theory for Collaborative Planning.* Berkeley: Institute of Urban and Regional Development, University of California, 1999.

International Union for Conservation of Nature and Natural Resources (IUCN). "Species Extinction." IUCN Red List, n.d., accessed July 15, 2003, available at <http://iucn.org/themes/ssc and www.redlist.org>.

Ittelson, William H., et al. *An Introduction to Environmental Psychology.* New York: Holt, Rinehart & Winston, 1974.

Ivy, Robert A., Jr. *Fay Jones.* New York: McGraw-Hill, 2001.

Jackson, J. B. *The Necessity for Ruins, and Other Topics.* Amherst: University of Massachusetts Press, 1980.

———. "Other-Directed Houses," *Landscape* 6, no. 2 (1956): 29–35.

———. "The Westward-Moving House: Three American Houses and the People Who Live in Them," *Landscape* 2, no. 3 (1953): 8–21.

Jackson, Richard J., and Chris Kochtitzky. *Creating a Healthy Environment: The Impact of the Built Environment on Public Health.* Washington, DC: Sprawl Watch Clearinghouse, 2001.

Jackson, Wes. *Becoming Native to This Place.* Washington, DC: Counterpoint, 1996.

Jacobs, Allan B. *Great Streets.* Cambridge: MIT Press, 1993.

———. *Looking at Cities.* Cambridge: Harvard University Press, 1985.

———. *Making City Planning Work.* Chicago: American Society of Planning Officials, 1978.

———. "Where the Freeway Meets the City." Paper presented at the University of California Transportation Center Symposium on the Art of Designing Bridges and Freeways, September 20, 2002.

Jacobs, Allan B., Elizabeth Macdonald, and Yodan Rofe. *The Boulevard Book: History, Evolution, Design of Multiway Boulevards.* Cambridge: MIT Press, 2002.

Jacobs, Jane. *The Death and Life of Great American Cities.* New York: Random House, 1961.

Jeavons, John. *How to Grow More Vegetables and Fruits, Nuts, Berries, Grains, and Other Crops Than You Ever Thought Possible on Less Land Than You Can Imagine* (6th ed.). Berkeley: Ten Speed Press, 2002.

Jefferson, Thomas. "Letter to William Charles Jarvis, 28 September 1820." Quoted in *Ecological Literacy: Education and the Transition to a Postmodern World* by David Orr. New York: State University of New York Press, 1992.

Jehl, Douglas. "Development and Drought Cut Carolina's Water Supply." *New York Times,* August 29, 2002, 1, 6.

Jewell, Linda. "The American Outdoor Theater: A Voice for the Landscape in the Collaboration of Site and Structure." In *Re-envisioning Landscape/Architecture.* Edited by Catherine Spelman. Barcelona: Actar Publications, 2003.

John, Dewitt. *Civic Environmentalism.* Washington, DC: Congressional Quarterly Press, 1994.

Jones, Tom. *Good Neighbors: Affordable Family Housing.* Melbourne: Images, 1995.

Jung, Carl G. *Man and His Symbols.* Garden City: Doubleday, 1964.

Kamp, Fern Heit. "Using Stewardship as a Guide for Planning." *Plan Canada* 36, no. 4 (1996): 28–30.

Kanter, Rosabeth M. *Commitment and Community.* Cambridge: Harvard University Press, 1972.

Kaplan, Rachel. "The Nature of the View from Home: Psychological Benefits." *Environment and Behavior* 33, no. 4 (2001): 507–542.

Kaplan, Rachel, and Stephen Kaplan. *The Experience of Nature: A Psychological Perspective.* Cambridge: Cambridge University Press, 1989.

Kaplan, Rachel, Stephen Kaplan, and Robert L. Ryan. "With People in Mind: Design and Management of Everyday Nature." *Places* 13, no. 1 (2000): 26–29.

———. *With People in Mind: Design and Management of Everyday Nature.* Washington, DC: Island Press, 1998.

Kaplan, Steven. "Mental Fatigue and the Designed Environment." In *Public Environments* (55–60). Edited by J. Harvey and D. Henning. Edmond: Environmental Design Research Association, 1987.

Katz, Peter. *The New Urbanism: Toward an Architecture of Community.* New York, NY: McGraw-Hill, 1994.

Keene, Donald, ed. *Anthology of Japanese Literature, from the Earliest Era to the Mid-nineteenth Century.* New York: Grove Press, 1960.

Keller, Suzanne. *Creating Community: The Role of Land, Space, and Place.* Cambridge: Lincoln Institute of Land Policy, 1986.

———. *The Urban Neighborhood: A Sociological Perspective.* New York: Random House, 1968.

Kelley, Klara B., and Harris Francis. *Navajo Sacred Places.* Indianapolis: Indiana University Press, 1994.

Kemmis, Daniel. *The Good City and the Good Life.* Boston: Houghton Mifflin, 1995.

Kenko. *Essays in Idleness: The Tsurezuregusa of Kenko.* Translated by Donald Keene. Tokyo: Tuttle, 1997.

Kepes, Gyogy, ed. *Structure in Art and in Science.* New York: Braziller, 1965.

Kilbridge, Maurice D., Robert P. O'Block, and Paul V. Teplitz. *Urban Analysis.* Cambridge: Harvard University Press, 1970.

King, Martin Luther, Jr. "I See the Promised Land." In *I Have a Dream: Writings and Speeches That Changed the World* (193–203). Edited by James M. Washington. San Francisco: Harper, 1992.

———. "Letter from Birmingham Jail." In *I Have a Dream: Writings and Speeches That Changed the World* (83–100). Edited by James M. Washington. San Francisco: Harper, 1992.

Kinoshita, Isami. "The Apple Promenade." In *Democratic Design in the Pacific Rim: Japan, Taiwan, and the United States* (92–99). Edited by Randolph T. Hester Jr. and Corrina Kweskin. Mendocino: Ridge Times Press, 1999.

Kondolf, G. Mathias. "Hungry Water: Effects of Dams and Gravel Mining on River Channels." *Environmental Management* 21, no. 4 (1997): 551–553.

Kotler, Milton. *Neighborhood Government: The Location Foundations of Political Life.* New York: Bobbs-Merrill, 1969.

Krapfel, Paul. *Shifting.* Cottonwood: Self-published, 1989.

Krieger, Martin H. *What's Wrong with Plastic Trees? Artifice and Authenticity in Design.* Westport: Praeger, 2000.

Kuhn, Richard G., Frank Duerden, and Karen Clyde. "Government Agencies and the Utilization of Indigenous Land Use Information in the Yukon." *Environments* 22, no. 3 (1994): 76–84.

Kuo, Frances E., and William C. Sullivan. "Aggression and Violence in the Inner City: Effects of Environment via Mental Fatigue." *Environment and Behavior* 33, no. 4 (2001): 543–571.

———. "Environment and Crime in the Inner City: Does Vegetation Reduce Crime?" *Environment and Behavior* 33, no. 3 (2001): 343–367.

Kuo, Frances E., William C. Sullivan, and Andrea Faber Taylor. "Coping with ADD: The Surprising Connection to Green Play Settings." *Environment and Behavior* 33, no. 1 (2001): 54–77.

———. "Views of Nature and Self-Discipline: Evidence from Inner City Children." *Journal of Environmental Psychology* 22, issues 1–2 (2002): 49–63.

Ladd, Florence. "Residential History: You Can Go Home Again." *Landscape* 21, no. 2 (1977): 15–20.

Landecker, Heidi. "Green Architecture: Recycling Redux." *Architecture* 80, no. 5 (1991): 90–94.

Landis, John, Subharjit Guhathakurta, and Ming Zhang. *Capitalization of Transit Investments into Single-Family Home Prices: A Comparative Analysis of Five California Rail Transit Systems.* Berkeley: Institute of Urban and Regional Development, University of California, 1994.

Landis, John, and Anupama Sharma. *First-Year Consolidated Plans in the Bay Area: A Review Document.* Berkeley: Bay Area Community Outreach Partnership, 1996.

"Landscape as Art: A Conversation with Peter Walker and Yoji Sasaki." In *Peter Walker: Landscape as Art (No. 85)* (25–32). Edited by Yoji Sasaki. Tokyo: Process Architecture, 1989.

Landscape Journal. Special issue on Eco-Revelatory Design: Nature Constructed/ Nature Revealed. Edited by Brenda Brown, Terry Harkness, and Douglas Johnston (1998).

Langer, Susanne K. *Feeling and Form: A Theory of Art.* New York: Scribner, 1953.

———. *Philosophy in a New Key: A Study in the Symbolism of Reason, Rite, and Art.* Cambridge: Harvard University Press, 1979.

Lassila, Kathrin D. "The New Suburbanites: How America's Plants and Animals Are Threatened by Sprawl." *Amicus Journal* 21, no. 2 (1999): 16–21.

"Last Gasp." Fresno Bee Special Report on Valley Air Quality. December 15, 2002. Accessed July 16, 2003. Available at <http://valleyairquality.com/special/valley_air/part1>.

Laurie, Michael. "The Urban Mantelpiece." *Landscape Design* no. 216 (1992): 21–22.

Lawson, Laura. "Linking Youth Training and Employment with Community Building: Lessons Learned at the BYA Garden Patch." In *Democratic Design in the Pacific Rim: Japan, Taiwan, and the United States* (80–91). Edited by Randolph T. Hester Jr. and Corrina Kweskin. Mendocino: Ridge Times Press, 1999.

Lawson, Laura, and Marcia McNally. "Putting Teens at the Center: Maximizing Public Utility of Urban Space through Youth Involvement in Planning and Employment." *Children's Environments* 12, no. 2 (1995): 209–221.

Lawton, M. P. "The Human Being and the Institutional Building." In *Designing for Human Behavior: Architecture and the Behavioral Sciences* (60–71). Edited by Jon T. Lang et al. Stroudsburg: Dowden, Hutchinson, and Ross, 1974.

Lazarus, Chris. "LUTRAQ: Looking for a Smarter Way to Grow." *Earthword,* no. 4—Transportation: 23–27.

Leccese, Michael, and Kathleen McCormick, eds. *Charter of the New Urbanism.* New York: McGraw-Hill, 2000.

Lee, Terrence. "The Urban Neighborhood as a Sociospatial Schema." In *Environmental Psychology: Man and His Physical Setting* (349–369). Edited by Harold M. Proshansky, William H. Ittelson, and Leanne G. Rivlin. New York: Holt, Rinehart and Winston, 1970.

Leopold, Aldo. *A Sand County Almanac, and Sketches Here and There.* New York: Oxford University Press, 1968.

Lethaby, William R. *Architecture, Nature and Magic.* London: Duckworth, 1956.

Lewis, Charles A. "Gardening as Healing Process." In *The Meaning of Gardens: Idea, Place, and Action* (244–251). Edited by Mark Francis and Randolph T. Hester Jr. Cambridge: MIT Press, 1990.

Lewis, Philip H., Jr. *Tomorrow by Design: A Regional Design Process for Sustainability.* New York: Wiley, 1996.

Limprich, B. "Development of an Intervention to Restore Attention in Cancer Patients." *Cancer Nursing* 16 (1993): 83–92.

Linn, Karl. "White Solutions Won't Work in Black Neighborhoods." *Landscape Architecture* 59, no. 1 (1968): 23–25.

Litton, R. B., Jr. "Forest Landscape Description and Inventories: A Basis for Land Planning and Design." USDA Forest Service Research Paper PSW-49, 1968.

Liu, John. "A Continuing Dialogue on Local Wisdom in Participatory Design." In *Building Cultural Diversity Through Participation,* edited by John Liu, 444–450. Taipei: Building and Planning Research Foundation, National Taiwan University, 2001.

———. "The Tawo House: Building in the Face of Cultural Domination." In *Democratic Design in the Pacific Rim: Japan, Taiwan, and the United States* (64–75). Edited by Randolph T. Hester Jr. and Corrina Kweskin. Mendocino: Ridge Times Press, 1999.

Liu, John, ed. *Building Cultural Diversity Through Participation.* Taipei: Building and Planning Research Foundation, National Taiwan University, 2001.

Lohr, Victoria I., Carolina Pearson-Mims, and Georgia K. Goodwin. "Interior Plants May Improve Worker Productivity and Reduce Stress in a Windowless Environment." *Journal of Environmental Horticulture* 14, no. 2 (1996): 97–100.

Long, Stephen. "Vermont Coverts Bring People Close to Their Neighbors . . . and to the Land." *Woodlands for Wildlife Newsletter* (1998): 28–32.

Lovelock, James. *The Ages of Gaia: A Biography of Our Living Earth.* New York: Norton, 1995.

Lowenthal, David. "The American Scene." *Geographical Review* 58, no. 1 (1968): 61–88.

———. *The Past Is a Foreign Country.* Cambridge: Cambridge University Press, 1985.

Lozano, Eduardo E. *Community Design and the Culture of Cities.* Cambridge: Cambridge University Press, 1990.

Lyle, John T. *Design for Human Ecosystems: Landscape, Land Use, and Natural Resources.* New York: Van Nostrand Reinhold, 1985.

———. *Regenerative Design for Sustainable Development.* New York: Wiley, 1994.

Lynch, Kevin. *Good City Form.* Cambridge: MIT Press, 1981.

———. *The Image of the City.* Cambridge: MIT Press, 1960.

———. *Managing the Sense of a Region.* Cambridge: MIT Press, 1976.

———. *Wasting Away.* San Francisco: Sierra Club, 1990.

Lyndon, Donlyn, and Charles W. Moore. *Chambers for a Memory Palace.* Cambridge: MIT Press, 1994.

MacCannell, Dean. *The Tourist: A New Theory of the Leisure Class.* New York: Schocken Books, 1989.

MacDonald, Donald. *Democratic Architecture: Practical Solutions to Today's Housing Crisis.* New York: Whitney Library of Design, 1996.

Maiklem, Lara, and William Lach, eds. *Ultimate Visual Dictionary of Science.* New York: DK Publishing, 1998.

Mair, Victor, ed. *The Columbia Anthology of Traditional Chinese Literature.* New York: Columbia University Press, 1994.

Marc, Olivier. *Psychology of the House.* London: Thomas and Hudson, 1977.

Marcus, Clare Cooper. "Designing for a Commitment to Place: Lessons from the Alternative Community Findhorn." In *Dwelling, Seeing, and Designing: Toward a Phenomenological Ecology* (299–330). Edited by David Seamen. New York: State University of New York Press, 1993.

———. *Easter Hill Village: Some Social Implications of Design.* New York: Free Press, 1975.

———. *House as a Mirror of Self: Exploring the Deeper Meaning of Home.* Berkeley: Conari Press, 1995.

———. "House as-Symbol-of-Self." *HUD Challenge* (U.S. Department of Housing and Urban Development) 8, no. 2 (1977): 2–4.

Marcus, Clare Cooper, and Wendy Sarkissian. *Housing as If People Mattered: Site Design Guidelines for Medium-Density Family Housing.* Berkeley: University of California Press, 1986.

Marcus, Clare Cooper, and Marni Barnes, eds. *Healing Gardens: Therapeutic Benefits and Design Recommendations.* New York: Wiley, 1999.

Marcus, Clare Cooper, and Carolyn Francis, eds. *People Places: Design Guidelines for Urban Open Space.* New York: Van Nostrand Reinhold, 1998.

Marcuse, Peter. "Conservation for Whom?" In *Environmental Quality and Social Justice in Urban America* (17–36). Edited by James N. Smith. Washington, DC: Conservation Foundation, 1972.

Marsh, George Perkins. *Man and Nature.* Edited by David Lowenthal. Cambridge: Harvard University Press, 1965.

Martin, Douglas. "Joseph Charles, Ninety-one: A Symbol of Street Corner Friendliness." *New York Times,* March 20, 2002, A25.

Martin, Frank E. "Field Trips into History: William Tishler, FASLA, Teaches Us the Cultural Values of Everyday Landscape." *Landscape Architecture* 92, no. 2 (2002): 80–81, 91.

Marx, Leo. *The Machine in the Garden: Technology and the Pastoral Ideal in America.* Oxford: Oxford University Press, 2000.

May, Rollo. *The Courage to Create.* New York: Norton, 1975.

Mayor's Institute on City Design West. "1994 Institute Summary." Paper presented at the College of Environmental Design, University of California, Berkeley, November 3–5, 1994.

McAvin, Margaret, with Karen Nelson. "Horizon Revealed and Constructed." *Landscape Journal* (special issue on Eco-Revelatory Design) (1998): 46–48.

McBride, Joe R. "Urban Forestry: What We Can Learn from Cities around the World." Paper presented at the National Urban Forest Conference, 1999.

McBride, Joe R., and Chris Reid. "Forest History Trail Guide." California Department of Forestry and Fire Protection, 1991.

McCamant, Katheryn, and Charles Durrent. *Cohousing: A Contemporary Approach to Housing Ourselves.* Berkeley: Habitat Press, 1988.

McCay, Bonnie J., and James M. Acheson. "Human Ecology of the Commons." In *The Question of the Commons: The Culture and Ecology of Communal Resources* (1–34). Edited by Bonnie J. McCay and James M. Acheson. Tucson: University of Arizona Press, 1987.

McCay, Bonnie J., and James M. Acheson, eds. *The Question of the Commons: The Culture and Ecology of Communal Resources.* Tucson: University of Arizona Press, 1987.

McCreary, Scott T., John K. Gamman, and Bennett Brooks. "Refining and Testing Joint Fact-Finding for Environmental Dispute Resolution: Ten Years of Success." *Mediation Quarterly* 18, no. 4 (2001): 329–348.

McCreary, Scott, et al. "Applying a Mediated Negotiation Framework to Integrated Coastal Zone Management." *Coastal Management* 29, no. 3 (2001): 183–216.

McDonough, William, and Michael Braungart. *Cradle to Cradle: Remaking the Way We Make Things.* New York: North Point Press, 2002.

McHarg, Ian. *Design with Nature.* Garden City: Natural History Press, 1969.

McLaren, Duncan. "Compact or Dispersed? Dilution is No Solution." *Built Environment* 18, no. 4 (1992): 268–284.

McNally, Marcia. "Making Big Wild." *Places* 9, no. 3 (1995): 38–45.

———. "On the Care and Feeding of the Grassroots." In *Democratic Design in the Pacific Rim: Japan, Taiwan, and the United States* (214–227). Edited by Randolph T. Hester Jr. and Corrina Kweskin. Mendocino: Ridge Times Press, 1999.

Meadows, Donella, et al. *The Limits to Growth.* New York: Potomac Associates, 1972.

Meier, Richard. *A Communications Theory of Urban Growth.* Cambridge: MIT Press, 1962.

Mencimer, Stephanie. "The Price of Going the Distance." *New York Times,* April 28, 2002, 34.

Merchant, Carolyn. *The Death of Nature: Women, Ecology, and the Scientific Revolution.* San Francisco: Harper & Row, 1980.

———. "Partnership with Nature." *Landscape Journal* (special issue on Eco-Revelatory Design) (1998): 69–71.

Miller, Dan. "Making Money out of Thin Air." *Progressive Farmer* 117, no. 2 (2002): 14–16.

Mitchell, John G. "Urban Sprawl," *National Geographic* 200, no. 1 (2001): 43–73.

Monogatari, Tsutsumi Chunagon. "The Lady Who Loved Insects." In *Anthology of Japanese Literature, from the Earliest Era to the Mid-nineteenth Century* (170–176). Edited by Donald Keene. New York, Grove Press, 1960.

Moore, Charles W., Gerald Allen, and Donlyn Lyndon. *The Place of Houses.* New York: Holt, Rinehart and Winston, 1974.

Moore, Robin C. *Childhood's Domain: Play and Place in Child Development.* London: Croom Helm, 1986.

———. "Plants as Play Props." *Children's Environments Quarterly* 6, no. 1 (1989): 3–6.

Moore, Robin C., and Herb H. Wong. *Natural Learning: The Life History of an Environmental Schoolyard: Creating Environments for Rediscovering Nature's Way of Teaching.* Berkeley: MIG Communications, 1997.

Morell, Virginia. "The Sixth Extinction." *National Geographic* 195, no. 2 (1999): 42–59.

———. "The Variety of Life." *National Geographic* 195, no. 2 (1999): 6–31.

Morrish, William R., et al. *Planning to Stay: A Collaborative Project.* Minneapolis: Milkweed Editions, 1994.

Moudon, Anne Vernez. *Built for Change: Neighborhood Architecture in San Francisco.* Cambridge: MIT Press, 1986.

Moulton, Michael P., and James Sanderson. *Wildlife Issues in a Changing World.* Boca Raton: Lewis, 1999.

Mozingo, Louise A. "The Aesthetics of Ecological Design: Seeing Science as Culture." *Landscape Journal* 16, no. 1 (1997): 46–59.

———. "Women and Downtown Open Spaces." *Places* 6, no. 1 (1989): 38–47.

Mumford, Lewis. *The City in History: Its Origins, Its Transformations, and Its Prospects.* New York: Harcourt, Brace, Jovanovich, 1961.

Nabham, Gary P., and Stephen Trimble. *The Geography of Childhood: Why Children Need Wild Places.* Boston: Beacon, 1994.

Nagahashi, Tamesuke, et al. "Citizen Leap Participation or Government Led Participation: How Can We Find a Watershed Management Alternative for Yoshino River in Tokushima, Japan?" Paper presented by the Kyoto University Team for Yoshino River Alternative at the Fourth Annual Pacific Rim Conference on Participatory Community Design, Hong Kong Polytechnic University, Hong Kong, December 2002.

Nasar, Jack L. *The Evaluative Image of the City.* Thousand Oaks: Sage, 1998.

Nash, Rod. *Wilderness in the American Mind.* New Haven: Yale University Press, 1967.

Nassauer, Joan Iverson. "Messy Ecosystems, Orderly Frames." *Landscape Journal* 14, no. 2 (1995): 161–170.

———. *Placing Nature: Culture and Landscape Ecology.* Washington, DC: Island Press, 1997.

———. "Urban Ecological Retrofit." *Landscape Journal* (special issue on Eco-Revelatory Design) (1998): 15–17.

Nelessen, Anton C. *Visions for a New American Dream: Process, Principles, and an Ordinance to Plan and Design Small Communities.* Chicago: Planners Press, 1994.

Newbury, Mickey. "If You See Her." Song from *I Came to Hear the Music,* produced by Chip Young, 1974.

Newman, Cathy. "Welcome to Monhegan Island, Maine. Now Please Go Away," *National Geographic* 200, no. 1 (2001): 92–109.

Newman, Oscar. *Community of Interest.* Garden City: Doubleday, 1980.

Newman, Randy. "Baltimore." Song. Warner Bros., 1978.

Nicholson, Simon. *Community Participation in City Decision Making.* Milton Keynes: Open University Press, 1973.

Norberg-Schulz, Christopher. *Genius Loci.* New York: Rizzoli, 1980.

Norris, Kathleen. *Dakota: A Spiritual Journey.* New York: Houghton Mifflin, 1993.

Noss, Reed F. "A Citizen's Guide to Ecosystem Management." Distributed as the Wild Earth Special Paper #3. Boulder, CO: Biodiversity Legal Foundation, 1999.

Noss, Reed F., and Robert L. Peters. *Endangered Ecosystems: A Status Report on America's Vanishing Wildlife and Habitat.* Washington, DC: Defenders of Wildlife, 1995.

Oakland, City of. *Report to the City Planning Commission.* September 1, 1999.

Odum, Eugene P. *Fundamentals of Ecology.* Philadelphia: Saunders, 1959.

Ogilvie, Robert. "Recruiting, Training, and Retaining Volunteers." In *Democratic Design in the Pacific Rim: Japan, Taiwan, and the United States* (243–249). Edited by Randolph T. Hester Jr. and Corrina Kweskin. Mendocino: Ridge Times Press, 1999.

Okuzumi, Hikaru. *The Stones Cry Out.* Translated by James Westerhoven. New York: Harcourt Brace, 1998.

Olmsted, Frederick L. *The Slave States.* New York: Capricorn, 1959.

Orr, David W. *Ecological Literacy: Education and the Transition to a Postmodern World.* Albany: State University of New York Press, 1992.

Osmond, H. "Function as the Basis of Psychiatric Ward Design." *Mental Hospitals* (Architectural Supp.) 8 (1957): 23–29.

Ostrom, Elinor. *Governing the Commons: The Evolution of Institutions for Collective Action.* New York: Cambridge University Press, 1990.

———. "Institutional Arrangements for Resolving the Commons Dilemma: Some Contending Approaches." In *The Question of the Commons: The Culture and*

Ecology of Communal Resources (250–265). Edited by Bonnie J. McCay and James M. Acheson. Tucson: University of Arizona Press, 1987.

Ovid. *Metamorphoses.* Translated by Horace Gregory. New York: Signet, 2001.

Packard, Vance O. *The Status Seekers.* New York: Pocket Books, 1967.

Papanek, Victor. *Design for the Real World.* New York: Pantheon, 1971.

Park, Robert E., Ernest W. Burgess, and Roderick D. McKenzie. *Human Communities: The City and Human Ecology.* Chicago: University of Chicago Press, 1967.

Perry, Clarence. "The Neighborhood Unit: A Scheme of Arrangement for the Family-Life Community." In *Regional Survey of New York and Its Environs.* Vol. 7, *Neighborhood and Community Planning* (22–140). New York: Committee on the Regional Plan of New York and Its Environs, 1929.

Phares, Donald. "Bigger Is Better, or Is It Smaller? Restructuring Local Government in the St. Louis Area." *Urban Affairs Quarterly* 25, no. 1 (1989): 5–17.

Phillips, Patricia. "Intelligible Images: The Dynamics of Disclosure." *Landscape Journal* (special issue on Eco-Revelatory Design) (1998): 109–117.

Phillips, Patrick. "Growth Management in Hardin Co., Kentucky: A Model for Rural Areas." *Urban Land* 46, no. 6 (1987):16–21.

Piven, Frances Fox. "Whom Does the Advocate Planner Serve?" *Social Policy* 1, no. 1 (1970): 32–37.

Plato. *The Republic.* Cambridge: Cambridge University Press, 2000.

Porteous, J. Douglas. *Environment and Behavior: Planning and Everyday Life.* Reading: Addison-Wesley, 1977.

President's Council on Sustainable Development. *Sustainable America: A New Consensus for Prosperity, Opportunity, and a Healthy Environment* (Washington, DC: President's Council, 1996).

Proshansky, Harold M., William H. Ittelson, and Leanne G. Rivlin. *Environmental Psychology.* New York: Holt, Rinehart and Winston, 1976.

Pukui, Mary Kowena, trans., with Laura C. S. Green. *Folktales of Hawai'i.* Honolulu: Bishop Museum Press, 1995.

Putnam, Robert D. *Bowling Alone: The Collapse and Revival of American Community.* New York: Simon and Schuster, 2000.

Putnam, Robert D., et al. *Making Democracy Work: Civic Traditions in Modern Italy.* Princeton: Princeton University Press, 1994.

Pyatok, Michael. "Martha Stewart vs. Studs Terkel? New Urbanism and Inner Cities Neighborhoods That Work." *Places* 13, no. 1 (2000): 40–43.

Pyatok Architects, Inc., Gateway Commons housing project, Emeryville, California, <http://www.pyatok.com>.

"The Race to Save Open Space." *Audubon* (March–April 2000): 69.

Radke, John. "Boundary Generators for the Twenty-first Century: A Proximity-Based Classification Method." *Department of City and Regional Planning Fiftieth Anniversary Anthology.* Edited by John Landis. Berkeley: University of California, 1998.

———. "The Use of Theoretically Based Spatial Decompositions for Constructing Better Datasets in Small Municipalities." Paper. University of Michigan, Ann Arbor, June 20, 1999.

Rapoport, Amos. *House Form and Culture.* Englewood Cliffs: Prentice-Hall, 1969.

———. *Human Aspects of Urban Form: Toward a Man-Environment Approach to Urban Form and Design.* Oxford: Pergamon, 1977.

———. "Toward a Redefinition of Density." *Environment and Behavior* 7, no. 2 (1975): 133–155.

Register, Richard. *Ecocity Berkeley: Building Cities for a Healthy Future.* Berkeley: North Atlantic Books, 1987.

———. *Ecocities: Building Cities in Balance with Nature.* Berkeley: Berkeley Hills Books, 2002.

Relph, Edward C. "Modernity and the Reclamation of Place." In *Dwelling, Seeing, and Designing: Toward a Phenomenological Ecology* (25–40). Edited by David Seamons. New York: State University of New York, 1993.

———. *The Modern Urban Landscape.* London: Croom Helm, 1987.

———. *Place and Placelessness.* London: Pion, 1976.

Report to the Public Health Institute. Funding provided by the U.S. Department of Agriculture through the California Nutrition Contracts #1003305 and #1002737, November 15, 2001.

Riegner, Mark. "Toward a Holistic Understanding of Place: Reading a Landscape through Flora and Fauna." In *Dwelling, Seeing, and Designing: Toward a Phenomenological Ecology* (181–215). Edited by David Seamon. New York: State University of New York Press, 1993.

Riemer, Svend. "Villagers in Metropolis." *British Journal of Sociology* 2, no. 1 (1951): 31–43.

Riesman, David. *The Lonely Crowd: A Study of the Changing American Character.* New Haven: Yale University Press, 1969.

Rocky Mountain Institute. *Rocky Mountain Institute Newsletter* 5, no. 3 (1989).

Rogers, Everett M. *Diffusion of Innovations.* New York: Free Press, 1995.

Rokeach, Milton. *Beliefs, Attitudes, and Values: A Theory of Organization and Change.* San Francisco: Jossey-Bass, 1970.

"Runyon Canyon Master Plan and Design Guidelines." *Landscape Architecture* 77, no. 6 (1987): 60–63.

Ryan, Robert L. "Magnetic Los Angeles: Planning the Twentieth-Century Metropolis." Book review. *Landscape Journal* 17, no. 1 (1998): 88–89.

Ryan, Robert L., and Mark Lindhult. "Knitting New England Together: A Recent Greenway Plan Represents Landscape Planning on a Vast Scale." *Landscape Architecture* 90, no. 2 (2000): 50, 52, 54–55.

Rysavy, Tracy. "Tree People." *Yes! A Journal of Positive Futures* no. 12 (2000): 19.

Sabiston, Adelia. "Meeting the Test: The Bay Area and Smog Check II." *Bay Area Monitor,* August/September 2002, accessed July 16, 2003, available at <http://www.bayareamonitor.org/aug02/test.html>.

Sadler, A. L., trans. *The Ten Foot Square Hut and Tales of the Heike.* Rutland: Tuttle, 1972.

Samuels, Sam H. "Making the Best of What Remains of Shrinking Habitats." *New York Times.* January 8, 2002, D5.

Sasaki, Yoji, ed., *Peter Walker: Landscape as Art (No. 85).* Tokyo: Process Architecture, 1989.

Scarfo, Bob. "Stewardship in the Twentieth Century." *Landscape Architectural Review* 7, no. 2 (1986): 13–15.

Scarry, Richard. *What Do People Do All Day?* New York: Random House, 1968.

Schlesinger, Arthur M., Jr. *The Disuniting of America: Reflections on a Multicultural Society.* New York: Norton, 1993.

Schon, Donald. *The Reflective Practitioners* (New York: Basic Books, 1983).

Schumacher, E. F. *Small Is Beautiful: Economics As If People Mattered—Twenty-five Years Later . . . with Commentaries.* Vancouver: Hartley & Marks, 1999.

Seamon, David. *Dwelling, Seeing, and Designing: Toward a Phenomenological Ecology.* New York: State University of New York Press, 1993.

———. "Phenomenology and Environmental Research." In *Advances in Environment, Behavior, and Design* (3–27). Edited by Gary T. Moore and Ervin H. Zube. New York: Plenum Press, 1987.

———. "A Singular Impact." *Environmental and Architectural Phenomenology Newsletter* 7, no. 3 (1996): 5–8.

Searles, Harold F. *Nonhuman Environment in Normal Development and in Schizophrenia.* New York: International Universities Press, 1960.

Sennett, Richard. *The Fall of Public Man.* New York: Knopf, 1977.

———. *The Uses of Disorder: Personal Identity and City Life.* New York: Norton, 1992.

Severson, Rebecca. "United We Sprout: A Chicago Community Gardening Story." In *The Meaning of Gardens: Idea, Place, and Action* (80–85). Edited by Mark Francis and Randolph T. Hester Jr. Cambridge: MIT Press, 1990.

Sevin, Josh. "A Disappearing Act." *Grist Magazine,* February 23, 2000, accessed July 15, 2003, available at <http://www.gristmagazine.com/grist/counter022300.htm>.

Shaffer, Carolyn R., and Kristen Arundsen. "The Healing Powers of Community," *Utne Reader* 71 (1995): 64–65.

Shepard, Paul. *Man in the Landscape: A Historic View of the Esthetics of Nature.* New York: Knopf, 1967.

———. *Nature and Madness.* San Francisco: Sierra Club, 1982.

———. *The Tender Carnivore and the Sacred Game.* New York: Scribner, 1973.

———. *Thinking Animals: Animals and the Development of Human Intelligence.* New York: Viking, 1978.

Shutkin, William A. *The Land That Could Be: Environmentalism and Democracy in the Twenty-first Century.* Cambridge: MIT Press, 2001.

Sidey, Hugh. "The Two Sides of the Sam Walton Legacy." *Time,* April 20, 1992, 50–52.

Siedentop, Larry. *Tocqueville.* Oxford: Oxford University Press, 1994.

Simonds, John. *Landscape Architecture: A Manual of Site Planning and Design.* New York: McGraw-Hill, 1983.

Smiley, Jane. *A Thousand Acres.* New York: Knopf, 1991.

Smith, Frank J., and Randolph T. Hester Jr. *Community Goal Setting.* Stroudsburg: Dowden, Hutchinson & Ross, 1982.

Sodo, Yamaguchi. In *Anthology of Japanese Literature, from the Earliest Era to the Mid-nineteenth Century.* Edited by Donald Keene. New York: Grove Press, 1960.

Solomon, Daniel. *Rebuilding.* New York: Princeton Architectural Press, 1992.

Sommer, Robert. "A Better World Not Utopia." Keynote address. In *Proceedings of the International Association for the Study of the People and Their Physical Surroundings* (57–61). West Berlin: I.A.P.S. [I.A.S.P.P.S.], 1984.

———. *Personal Space: The Behavioral Basis of Design.* Englewood Cliffs: Prentice Hall, 1969.

———. "Small Group Ecology." *Psychological Bulletin,* no. 67 (1967): 145–152.

Sorvig, Kim. "The Wilds of South Central." *Landscape Architecture* 92, no. 4 (2002): 66–75.

South, Joe. "Rose Garden." Song from *Introspection,* 1968, reissued by Raven Records, 2003.

Southworth, Michael. "City Learning: Children, Maps, and Transit." *Children's Environments Quarterly* 7, no. 2 (1990): 35–48.

———. "The Educative City." In *Cities and City Planning* (19–29). Edited by Lloyd Rodwin. New York: Plenum Press, 1981.

———. *Oakland Explorers: A Cultural Network of Places and People for Kids—Discovery Centers.* Berkeley: Institute of Urban and Regional Development, University of California, 1990.

Southworth, Michael, and Eran Ben-Joseph. *Streets and the Shaping of Towns and Cities.* New York: McGraw-Hill, 1997.

Southworth, Michael, with Susan Southworth. "The Educative City." In *Alternative Learning Environment* (274–281). Edited by Gary Coates. Stroudsburg: Dowden, Hutchinson & Ross, 1974.

Southworth, Michael, Susan Southworth, and Nancy Walton. *Discovery Centers.* Berkeley: Institute of Urban and Regional Development, University of California, 1990.

Spirn, Ann Whiston. *The Granite Garden: Urban Nature and Human Design.* New York: Basic Books, 1984.

———. *The Language of Landscape.* New Haven: Yale University Press, 1998.

———. "The Poetics of City and Nature: Toward a New Aesthetic for Urban Design." *Landscape Journal* 7, no. 2 (1988): 108–125.

Stapleton, Richard M. "Wild Times in the City." *Nature Conservancy* 45, no. 5 (1995): 10–15.

Stea, David. "Space, Territory, and Human Movements," *Landscape* 15, no. 4 (1965): 13–16.

Stein, Clarence. *Toward New Towns in America.* Cambridge: MIT Press, 1966.

Steinbrueck, Victor. *Market Sketchbook.* Seattle: University of Washington Press, 1968.

Steiner, Frederick R. *The Living Landscape: An Ecological Approach to Landscape Planning.* New York: McGraw-Hill, 1991.

Steinitz, Carl. *A Comparative Study of Resource Analysis Methods.* Cambridge: Department of Landscape Architecture Research Office, Harvard University, 1969.

———. *Defensible Processes for Regional Landscape Design.* Washington, DC: American Society for Landscape Architects, 1979.

Sterngold, James. "Primacy of the Car Is Over, California Governor Declares." *New York Times,* August 21, 2001, A8.

Stitt, Fred. *Ecological Design Handbook.* New York: McGraw-Hill, 1999.

Stone, P. A. *The Structure, Size and Cost of Urban Settlements.* Cambridge: Cambridge University Press, 1973.

Sullivan, Chip. *Garden and Climate.* New York: McGraw-Hill, 2002.

Susskind, Lawrence, and Jeffrey Cruikshank. *Breaking the Impasse: Consensual Approaches to Resolving Public Disputes.* New York: Basic Books, 1987.

Susskind, Lawrence, Paul F. Levy, and Jennifer Thomas-Larmer. *Negotiating Environmental Agreements: How to Avoid Escalating Confrontation, Needless Costs, and Unnecessary Litigation.* Washington, DC: Island Press, 2000.

Susskind, Lawrence, Mieke Van der Wansem, and Armand Ciccarelli. *Mediating Land Use Disputes: Pros and Cons.* Cambridge: Lincoln Institute of Land Policy, 2000.

Swentzell, Rina. "Conflicting Landscape Values." *Places* 7, no. 1 (1990): 19–27.

Swerdlow, Joel L. "Global Culture." *National Geographic* 196, no. 2 (1999): 2–5.

Szulc, Tad. "Abraham Journey of Faith." *National Geographic* 200, no. 6 (2001): 90–128.

Tangley, Laura. "Watching Birds—in the Field and on the Web." *National Wildlife* 39, no. 6 (2001): 14.

Taylor, Barbara. *Butterflies and Moths.* New York: DK, 1996.

Terkel, Studs. *American Dreams, Lost and Found.* New York: Pantheon, 1980.

———. *The Great Divide: Second Thoughts on the American Dream.* New York: Pantheon, 1988.

Thayer, Robert L., Jr. "Conspicuous Non-Consumption: The Symbolic Aesthetics of Solar Architecture." In *Proceedings of the Eleventh Annual Conference of the Environmental Design Research Association,* Washington, DC, 1980.

———. *Gray World, Green Heart: Technology, Nature, and the Sustainable Landscape.* New York: Wiley, 1994.

———. "Landscape as an Ecologically Revealing Language." *Landscape Journal* (special issue on Eco-Revelatory Design) (1998): 118–129.

Thompson, J. William. "Hester's Progress." *Landscape Architecture* 86, no. 4 (1996): 74–79, 97–99.

———. "Saving the Last Dance." *Landscape Architecture* 87, no. 12 (1997): 38–43.

Thompson, J. William, and Kim Sorvig. *Sustainable Landscape Construction: A Guide to Green Building Outdoors.* Washington, DC: Island Press, 2000.

Thoreau, Henry David. *Cape Cod,* as quoted in *Thoreau: A Book of Quotations.* Mineola: Dover, 2000.

———. *Journal,* as quoted in *Thoreau: A Book of Quotations.* Mineola: Dover, 2000.

———. *Walden and Other Writings.* Edited by Brooks Atkinson. New York: Modern Library, 2000.

Todd, Nancy Jack, and John Todd. *From Eco-Cities to Living Machines: Principles of Ecological Design.* Berkeley: North Atlantic, 1994.

Trancik, Roger. *Finding Lost Space: Theories of Urban Design.* New York: Van Nostrand Reinhold, 1986.

Treib, Marc. "A Constellation of Pieces." *Landscape Architecture* 92, no. 3 (2002): 58–67, 92.

Tuan, Yi-Fu. *Cosmos and Heart: A Cosmopolite's Viewpoint.* Minneapolis: University of Minnesota Press, 1996.

———. *Topophilia: A Study of Environmental Perception, Attitudes, and Values.* Englewood Cliffs: Prentice-Hall, 1974.

Tucker, M., and T. L. Napier. "The Diffusion Task in Community Development." *Journal of the Community Development Society* 25, no. 1 (1994): 80–100.

Turner, Frederick. "A Cracked Case." *Landscape Journal* (special issue on Eco-Revelatory Design) (1998): 131–140.

Ulrich, Roger. "View through a Window May Influence Recovery from Surgery." *Science* 224 (1984): 420–421.

Union Point Park Partnership Team. *Union Point Park Master Plan.* October 1999.

United States Census Bureau. *Statistical Abstract of the United States* (80th ed.). Washington, DC: U.S. Census Bureau, 1960.

———. *Statistical Abstract of the United States* (120th ed.). Washington, DC: U.S. Census Bureau, 2000.

United States Fish and Wildlife Service. "Bosque del Apache National Wildlife Refuge." 1999.

Unstrung Heroes. Directed by Diane Keaton, 93 min., Hollywood/Roth-Arnold, film. From the book by Franz Lidz.

Untermann, Richard K. *Accommodating the Pedestrian: Adapting Towns and Neighborhoods for Walking and Bicycling.* New York: Van Nostrand Reinhold, 1984.

Urban Ecology. *Blueprint for a Sustainable Bay Area.* Oakland: Urban Ecology, 1996.

Van der Ryn, Sim. *The Toilet Papers: Designs to Recycle Human Waste and Water— Dry Toilets, Greywater Systems and Urban Sewage.* Santa Barbara: Capra, 1978.

Van der Ryn, Sim, and William R. Boie. *Value Measurement and Visual Factors in the Urban Environment.* Berkeley: College of Environmental Design, University of California, 1963.

Van der Ryn, Sim, and Stuart Cowan. *Ecological Design.* Washington, DC: Island Press, 1996.

"Vanishing Cultures." *National Geographic* 196, no. 2 (199): 62–90.

Vente, Rolf E. *Urban Planning and High-Density Living: Some Reflections on Their Interrelationship.* Singapore: Chopman Enterprises, 1979.

Volkart, Edmund H., ed. *Social Behavior and Personality: Contributions of W. I. Thomas to Theory and Social Research.* New York: Social Science Research Council, 1951.

Wackernagel, Mathis, and William E. Rees. *Our Ecological Footprint: Reducing Human Impact on the Earth.* Gabriola Island: New Society Publishers, 1996.

Wagner, Mimi, and Peter F. Korsching. "Flood Prone Community Landscapes: The Application of Diffusion Innovations Theory and Community Design Process in Promoting Change." Paper presented at the Society for Applied Sociology, Denver, Colorado, October 22–24, 1998.

Walker, Peter. "A Personal Approach to Design." In *Peter Walker: Landscape as Art* (No. 85) (10–13). Edited by Yoji Sasaki. Tokyo: Process Architecture, 1989.

Walsh, Tom. "A Modest Proposal: Freeze the Urban Growth Boundary." *Earthword* no. 4—Transportation: 28–29.

Webber, Melvin M. "Culture, Territoriality, and the Elastic Mile." *Papers and Proceedings of the Regional Science Association* 13 (1964): 59–69.

———. "Order in Diversity: Community without Propinquity." In *Cities and Space* (23–54). Edited by L. Wingo. Baltimore: John Hopkins Press, 1963.

———. "The Urban Place and the Nonplace Urban Realm." In *Explorations into Urban Structure* (79–153). Edited by Melvin M. Webber. Philadelphia: University of Pennsylvania Press, 1964.

Weenig, Mieneke W. H., Taco Schmidt, and Cees J. H. Midden. "Social Dimensions of Neighborhoods and the Effectiveness of Information Programs." *Environment and Behavior* 22, no. 1 (1990): 27–54.

Weisman, Leslie K. *Discrimination by Design: A Feminist Critique of the Man-Made Environment.* Urbana: University of Illinois Press, 1992.

Weisser, Andy. "American Lung Association Applauds Governor for Signing Important Smog check II Bill." American Lung Association of California, September 27, 2002, accessed July 16, 2003, available at <http://www.californialung.org/press/020927smogcheckii.html>.

West, Troy. "Education in the 1970's: Teaching for an Altered Reality." *Architectural Record* 148, no. 4 (1970): 130.

White, E. B. *The Trumpet of the Swan.* New York: HarperCollins, 2000.

White, Morton, and Lucia White. *The Intellectual versus the City: From Thomas Jefferson to Frank Lloyd Wright.* New York: Oxford University Press, 1977.

Whyte, William H. *The Organization Man.* New York: Simon and Schuster, 1972.

———. *The Social Life of Small Urban Spaces.* Washington, DC: Conservation Foundation, 1980.

"The Wide World of Monitoring: Beyond Water Quality Testing." *Volunteer Monitor* 6, no. 1 (1994): 9.

Wild Earth (Citizen Science: Looking to Protect Nature). Vol. 11, no. 3/4 (2001–2002).

———. Inside cover. Vol. 9, no. 2 (1999).

———. (Religion and Biodiversity). Vol. 6, no. 3 (1996).

Wilkinson, Richard R., and Robert M. Leary. *Conservation of Small Towns: A Report on Community Development.* Charleston: Coastal Plains Regional Commission, 1976.

Williams, Terry Tempest. *Refuge: An Unnatural History of Family and Place.* New York: Vintage, 1992.

———. *An Unspoken Hunger: Stories from the Field.* New York: Pantheon, 1994.

Winn, Marie. *Red-tails in Love.* New York: Vintage, 1999.

"Winning Big." *Landscape Architecture.* 87, no. 11 (1997): 42–49.

Wood, Denis, with John Fels. *The Power of Maps.* New York: Guilford Press, 1992.

Wrenn, Douglas M. "Making Downtown Housing Happen." *Urban Land* 46, no. 1 (1987): 16–19.

Wright, Thomas K., and Ann Davlin. "Overcoming Obstacles to Brownfield and Vacant Land Redevelopment." *Land Lines,* 10, no. 5 (1998): 1–3.

Yoon, Carol Kaesuk. "Aid for Farmers Helps Butterflies, Too." *New York Times,* July 9, 2002, Science, 1, 4.

———. "Alien Invaders Reshape the American Landscape." *New York Times,* February 5, 2002, D1, D4.

Zeisel, John. *Inquiry by Design: Tools for Environment-Behavior Research.* Cambridge: Cambridge University Press, 1987.

Zube, Ervin H., J. L. Sell, and J. G. Taylor. "Landscape Perception: Research, Application and Theory." *Landscape Planning* 9, no. 1 (1982): 1–33.

Zukowsky, John, ed. *Chicago Architecture 1872–1922: Birth of a Metropolis.* Munich: Prestel-Verlap, 1987.

Zukowsky, John. "Introduction to Internationalism in Chicago Architecture." In *Chicago Architecture 1872–1922: Birth of a Metropolis* (15–26). Edited by John Zukowsky. Munich: Prestel-Verlag, 1987.

Image Credits

Cover painting by Nathaniel Hester, *They Missed the First Snowstorm of the Season but the View from the Top of the Mexican Pyramid Teotihuacan Wasn't That Great Anyhow—At Least Not on an Empty Stomach.* Oil on canvas. 64 x 64 inches. 2005. Private collection, Boston, Massachusetts.

Unless otherwise credited, illustrations were done by Randolph Hester, Rachel Berney, and Amy Dryden or by students and staff under my supervision at North Carolina State University, the University of California at Berkeley, Community Development by Design, and SAVE International.

Numerous graphics have been redrawn from others' work. These include the following:

Page 28: Siena time-of-day series, drawn from photographs in *Natural Light and the Italian Plaza,* Sandra Davis Lakeman.

Pages 30–31, 152, 155, 157, 158, 307: Diagrams, plans, and sections of Orchid Island, Matsu, and Lalu, from John Liu.

Page 53: Street neighboring, from *Livable Streets,* Donald Appleyard.

Page 59: Food web, from *Biology,* Ceci Starr and Ralph Taggart.

Page 87: Ladder of participation, from "A Ladder of Citizen Participation," Sherry Arnstein.

Page 99: Astoria, Oregon, Brian Scott.

Page 134: Thornhill Chapel, from *Fay Jones,* Robert A. Ivy Jr.

Page 147: Southern California watershed, *Design for Human Ecosystems,* John Lyle.

Page 154: Zero-runoff retrofit and gravel infiltration, from *Second Nature,* Patrick Condon and Stacy Moriarty, eds.

Page 154: Ground-water recharge, from *City Form and Natural Process,* Michael Hough.

Page 163: Sea Ranch plan, based on drawings by Jane Sheinman and Larry Halprin.

Page 168: Cherokee Town Relocation Plan, Mimi Wagner.

Page 189: Transit-oriented development and access to transit diagrams, from *The Next American Metropolis,* Peter Calthorpe.

Page 236: Berkeley over time, from *Eco-City Berkeley,* Richard Register.

Page 271: Curitiba bus routes, from *Our Ecological Footprint,* Mathis Wackernagel and William E. Rees.

Page 294: Chavis Heights, Don Collins.

Page 352: Sun setting, earth rotating, based on *Shifting,* Paul Krapfel.

Copyrighted graphics and projects include the following:

Pages 21, 33, 111: Neighborhood Space, Marge Smith.

Page 24: Central Park, Davis, California, Landscape architects Mark Francis and CoDesign/MIG.

Page 36: Yountville, Susi Marzoula.

Page 53: Octavia Boulevard, Allan Jacobs and Elizabeth Macdonald.

Pages 77, 82: Fairness diagrams, Mira Engler and Michael Boland.

Page 79: Bus Line 57, Michael Southworth.

Pages 80–81: Lafayette Square Park, Hood Design.

Page 84: Gateway Commons, Pyatok Architects, Inc.

Page 85: Chinatown, Mary Comerio.

Pages 92, 93: Union Point Park masterplans, EDAW, Mario Schjetnan Garduno, and Michael Rios.

Pages 105, 118–119, 121, 124–126, 128–129: Manteo illustrations and photos, Foster Scott, Aycock Brown, Jerry Blow, Brian Scott, Billie Harper, Patsy Eubanks, John Wilson, and Bill Parker.

Page 106: Small houses, Dan Solomon.

Page 110: Village Homes, zero-runoff swale photo, Rob Thayer.

Page 110: Village Homes Plan, Michael and Judy Corbett, plan courtesy of Judy Corbett.

Page 117: Canoe Etching, Manteo, North Carolina Archives.

Page 148: Raleigh and Piedmont Greenway diagrams, W. L. Flourney Jr. and Chuck Flink.

Pages 151, 153: Yoshino River, Tamesuke Nagahashi.

Page 161: Sea Ranch color sketch, Larry Halprin.

Pages 173, 175: Spoonbill photos, SAVE International, Jeff Hou.

Pages 211–214, 216, 220–221: Pasadena master plan, axonometrics adapted from Lyndon/Buchanan.

Page 218: Tiny Gardens (Small Gardens in the City), Garrett Eckbo student project at Harvard, 1937, Garrett Eckbo Collection (1990–1991), Environmental Design Archives, University of California, Berkeley.

Page 256: Tent camp in Golden Gate Park photo, Special Collections, Bancroft Library Collection, University of California, Berkeley.

Pages 280, 282: Courtland Creek, Hood Design.

Page 290: Birmingham Street photos, Chris Faust.

Pages 297–298: Ilan Performing Arts Center, John Liu.

Pages 300, 306: Tanner Fountain, Peter Walker and Associates.

Page 304: The Therapeutic Garden, Reed Hildebrand Associates Inc., Landscape Architecture.

Page 309: *Stone in Aberdaron,* Nathaniel Hester.

Pages 316, 320: The Natural Park, Larry Moss and Associates.

Page 342: Illinois Landscape Gardens, Terry Harkness.

Page 343: King Estate Park, Louise Mozingo.

Pages 346–347: Lowell, Massachusetts, illustrations, Michael Southworth and Susan Southworth, photo, Michael Southworth.

Page 351: Argumentative Cadillacs photo, Marshall Foster.

Page 353: Specimen of Extinction (garden in jar), Chip Sullivan.

Page 355: LA96C, Bob Graves.

Pages 376, 378–382: Garden Patch, Laura Lawson.

Page 384: River Tribunal, Sarah Minick.

Pages 401, 410: Katsura drawings, Kyoto University Library.

Page 403: Scored Symphonic Walk, Larry Halprin.

Page 409: Denver, Sixteenth Street Mall, Olin Partnership.

Index

Abbey, Edward, 303
Access, to nature. *See* Nature
Accessibility, 24–25, 77–78, 80, 82, 393, 413. *See also* Inaccessibility
Acropolis (Greece), 134–135
Activism, 18, 183, 245, 303, 351, 383–384
    citizen referendum, 150
    civil disobedience, 383
Actual distance, 25
Adachi, Japan, 390
Adams, John, 327
Adaptability, 143, 153–154, 255–275, 279, 289
    concept of, 255
    framework principles, 263–271
    and healthy change, 256, 337
    of urban systems, 265, 275
Adaptable cities, 255, 262
Adaptable landscape and building, 256, 260–261, 275, 380
    examples of, 262–263
    form of, 256–257
    multiuse, 263
Adaptive management, 272–275
    city form, 272
    partnerships, 274
    versus standard solutions, 274
Adjacency, guide for design, 75
Aesthetics, 104–105
Affordable housing, 84–85, 189, 192, 211–216, 239, 268. *See also* Low income
Agriculture
    community, 377 (*see also* Community garden)

Texas Agricultural Extension Service, 373
United States Agricultural Extension Service, 274–275
United States Department of Agriculture, 334
University of California Cooperative Extension Service, 371
    way of life, 371–372
Air quality, 148, 175, 264, 368
    volunteer monitoring, 348–349
Allée, 269–270, 403–404
Allee, W. C., 201
Allee principle/effect, 201, 205, 330, 330, 352
Alexander, Christopher, 238
Alinsky, Saul, 290
American cities, 117, 160, 171, 185. *See also* United States
    and cold war, 360
    density of, 205, 207–209, 222
    distinctiveness of, 172, 186
    diversity of, 171, 172, 197
    form of, 229, 233
    resilience of, 139, 143, 230, 238–252
    segregation of, 78, 196
American house, 106
American LIVES
    density study, 208–209, 217, 220
Americans. *See* United States
Appleyard, Donald, 237
Apollo Heights (Raleigh, NC), 108–109
Aquaculture, 174, 177–178, 180, 363
Aquifer, 363

Architecture, vernacular, 164
Aristotle, 231, 237
Arnstein, Sherry, 87
Astoria, Oregon, 97–100
Atlanta, Georgia, 396
Automobiles (private transportation)
    1996 Olympic Games, 396
    dependency on, 396
    disinvestment in, 204, 393, 396–397
    and health, 394, 396
    lack of access to, 79
Axis, design element, 29–30, 209, 377

Barriers
    economic, 80
    physical and psychological, 81
    to restoration, 375
    to walking, 393
"Baltimore," 206
Berkeley, CA, 114, 194, 223, 234, 236, 351, 375–382, 400
Berkeley Youth Alternative (BYA), 375–382
Berry, Wendell, 187, 383
Binnan industrial complex, 173–183
Biological diversity, 172–183
    benefits of, 179, 183, 197–199
    and citizen involvement, 277–279, 341, 350
    and city resilience, 179–180, 197
    and city/urban form, 172–173, 179, 201–202, 245
    in decline, 184,-185
    design for, 172–173, 183, 187, 197–199

in entire ecosystem, 180, 290
preserving, 182, 188, 197–199, 227,
   399
Biology, 190. *See also* Conservation
   biology; Ecological democracy
principles for design, 140, 143, 247
Biophilia, 301
Bioregion, 141–142, 147–148,
   150–151
Birds, 58–59, 75, 91, 234, 331, 341,
   349, 416. *See also* Black-faced
   spoonbill
Birmingham Street Project, 290
Black-faced spoonbill, 173, 183, 234
Blumenauer, Earl, 37
Boardwalk design, Manteo, 124–125,
   128–129, 133–134
Bobwhite Brigade, 373
Borneo, 184–185
Bosque del Apache National Wildlife
   Refuge, 373–374
Bosselmann, Peter, 209
Boston, MA, 338
   Common, 29
Boulder, CO, 130, 238–240
Boundaries
   natural, 127, 130, 133, 179–180,
      192, 227–229, 232–244, 314,
      341
   between neighborhoods, 217, 314
"Bowling alone," 15–16
Braude, Marvin, 67–69
Brower, Sydney, 283–284
Brown, Jerry, 265
Buchanan, Marvin, 209
Building form
   adaptable, 164, 256, 260–262
   appropriate, 266
   and center, 27, 266
   and climate, 29, 156, 163–164
   design standards of, 260
   flexible, 44, 256
   and multiuse, 263

standards, 186
typologies of adaptable, 262–263
Building inspired by nature, 309–310
Built form, 57, 266
   and experiential walking, 399
   town center, 269
Bullard, Robert, 82
Burnham, Daniel, 265
Burns, Paul, 71, 73

Caballero Canyon, 67–75
Calhoun, John, 207, 252
California Coastal Conservancy, 90,
   92
Calthorpe, Peter, 189, 204, 221
Cambridge, MA, 34, 101–103,
   284–287
Camogli, Italy, 130, 202
Carson, Rachel, 50
Carver, George Washington, 320
Carrying capacity
   development, 156
   regional/limited extent, 230–231,
      233, 253
Caspar, CA, 39, 266–269
Castle Rock, WA, 58, 260–261
Castle Rock Exhibit Hall, 260–261,
   264
Centeredness, 21–47, 227, 252, 259,
   289, 279, 363, 388, 393
   definition of, 21
   and density, 203, 341
Centering, 28, 143
Centers
   accessible, 24, 393
   and community life, 17–18, 21,
      24–25, 28, 266, 404
   connectivity of, 393, 413
   decentralizing (sprawl), 22
   design of (criteria), 23–32, 27, 42
   and ecological democracy, 341
   and identity, 21, 127
   location of, 25, 44, 239

loss of, 29, 105, 128
mixed-use, 21, 46
multiuse, 21, 23–24, 25, 29
neighborhood, 203, 222, 224, 393
new, making of, 31, 266, 374
and public buildings (form), 29
recurring, 127–129
and rituals, 40
and sacred structure, 127, 133
and scale, 32
town planning, 266–269
traditional, 21, 29
typologies, 29, 31–32, 35
Central Park (Davis, CA), 24, 29, 46,
   259
Central Park (New York, NY), 29
Cevero, Robert, 204, 209
Chaos theory, 190–191
Chapel Hill, NC, 165
Charles, Joseph, 400
Chavis Heights (Raleigh, NC),
   291–296
Cherokee, Iowa, 168–169
Chesapeake Bay, 374
Chicago, IL, 265–266
Chigu Lagoon, 182
Ch'ien, T'ao, 133
Children
   and ecological democracy, 346
   health and nature, 303–304, 314
   learning in landscape, 112–114, 259,
      338–339, 345
   and nature play, 320–322, 410–411
   redesigning a city, 390–391
China, 29–30, 173
Chinatown, 67, 85, 186
Chomei, Kamo-no, 396
Chou, Chuang, 107, 272
Christmas, William (Raleigh
   Greenway), 149
Citizen involvement, 55–56, 60, 77,
   274–275, 348, 371, 383
City Beautiful, 209–210, 213

City design. *See also* Design with
nature
adaptable form, 255, 273 (*see also*
Adaptability)
approach to, 17, 51, 62, 65, 117,
127, 363
appropriate, 141, 147
and automobile, 393
and community life, 60, 105
for daily activities, 85, 283–284
and delight, 279
and diversity, 173, 191, 194, 197
as ecorevelatory, 339
and equity, 77–80
evaluating over time, 349
and everyday future, 281, 287–289
and exercise, 395, 404
and food web, 335
and health, 393–394, 404 (*see also*
Health)
and integration of uses, 284–287
memorializing change, 287–289
and pace of life, 387–388, 392
and public discussion, 335
and resource consumption, 57, 65,
273
Schumacher's principles of, 107
and speed, 394, 410
and status seeking, 111
and stewardship, 384–385
urban farm, 57, 380
for walking, 399–400
and wild nature, 340
City form. *See also* City design; Design
with nature
adaptable, 165–166, 255, 262, 272
adaptive management of, 272
and automobile, 394
and community, 17–18, 61, 138
and connectedness, 51
cultural complexity of, 186
density of, 209–216
diversity of, 171–172, 179–183, 233

divided by transportation, 52
ecological democracy of, 77
ecological principles of, 330–331
and fairness, 78
framework of, 264
and global warming, 272
growth of, 202
healthy, 264, 305, 279, 336, 394
lack of diversity, 184–185
and limited extent, 152, 227–229,
231–253
and lifestyle, 305
and natural patterns, 59, 148–169,
233–234, 256
and nature, 56, 140–143, 179–183
and particularness, 104, 145, 160,
172
preservation of, 121
and resilience, 139, 274
and sacredness, 135
Schumacher's principles (for size),
232
and services and resources, 148, 213
and status seeking, 98
and stewardship, 384–385
sustainable, 179, 272
traditional, 145, 147
and values, 17–18, 104
by watershed, 149
City life, 17, 190
City making, knowledge sources, 338
Cityscape, designed for walking,
399–400
City size, 230–232, 238–243
Ciudad Rodrigo (Spain), 135
Civic
amenities, 213
center and redevelopment, 214–215,
265
mindedness, 17, 32, 46
space and recreation, 216–217
Civic engagement, 21, 197, 383
Civic responsibility

community caring, 363–364
community commitment, 368
habitat preservation, 374
versus individualism, 383
land ownership, 366
Civil Rights Movement, 350
Cloister concept, 262
Cohousing (M Street), 262
Collins, Don, 291
Columbia River, 58, 65, 97, 99
Commons, 29, 109, 367–368
Community building capacity, 38,
135, 142
Community centers, 22, 29, 32, 36,
42, 44–46, 261, 317–318, 348
Caspar, 266–269
Westport, 44
Yountville, 36, 269–271, 404
Community development, 98, 139,
291–296
Community garden, 29–30, 39, 61,
80, 344, 371–372, 375–383
The Garden Patch, 375–383
Community life
dealing with change, 278, 288–296
and density, 218
expression of, 30, 118, 125, 127
fulfilling, 19
landscape structure, 269
and local solution, 274
nurturing it, 363
and pace of life, 391, 404
patterns of, 154
social space of, 33, 118, 125
and stewardship, 365
Community planning and design
balance of community and individual, 368
collective framework, 118–131,
133–134, 274–275, 320, 368,
391
exchange of local knowledge, 370
increased awareness, 125, 369

methodology, 317
preservation of cultural diversity, 185
process of, 15, 29, 91–95, 101–102, 118–131, 133–134, 317
sacred structure, 120
to stimulate stewardship, 369–370
success of, 370
and teens, 92–95, 375–383
Community rituals, 22, 37–47, 91, 120, 159–160, 320
affected by global warming, 272
Connectedness, 49–76, 241, 245, 248, 252, 341. *See also* Inter-connectedness
and built form, 143, 168–169
definition of, 49–50
design approach, 50, 59, 159
design for, 19, 46, 97, 99, 112
disconnection, 66, 388
invisible, 54–55, 58, 331, 336, 353
local knowledge, 277–279
making visible, 56, 58, 63, 65
park design, 322, 66–75
planning and design decisions, 49–50
reconnecting systems and networks, 56, 393
sacred structure, 127, 133
systemic, 60
Conservation biology, 174, 179, 197–198, 244, 247, 335–336
Conservationists, 63
Conservation lands, 173, 183
Conservation of resources. *See* Resources
Conservation strategy, 64
Conspicuous nonconsumption, 110–111
Consumption, 100, 110, 173
Corbett, Michael, 110–111, 140
Cornell University, Citizen Science Program, 274, 349
Coulter, Malcolm, 174

Courtland Creek Park (Oakland, CA), 281–282
Cowlitz River, 58–59
Crissy Field, 374, 407
Cristo, Running Fence (Sonoma County, CA), 352
Cultural diversity, 172, 184–187, 197–199, 336
civil rights, 350
park design, 317–320
Cumulative impacts, 351, 353
Curitiba, Brazil, 271
Cycles. *See* Ecological, processes

Daily experience
and center, 127
and ecological processes, 335
informal, 35, 37, 43
with nature, 18, 182
and pace of life, 412
Daily life
and city form, 30, 42, 46, 78, 191–192, 203, 222, 393
community, 27, 29, 101, 269–270, 291–292
ecological concepts/science in, 251, 277–279, 348
and everyday future, 281–282, 287–289
and exercise, 396
and farming, 344
and house form, 78, 154–160, 192
incorporating activities of, 25, 269
particularness of, 132, 269
patterns as guides for design, 291–299
and resource consumption, 153–154, 333
routes and walking, 393, 396–397, 403–404, 413–417
and sacredness, 120, 122, 126, 135
and stewardship, 374–375
and water system, 258

Dam, 150–153, 175, 353
Dangermond, Jack, 147
Darwin, Charles, 145
Davis, CA, 24–29, 110–111, 259, 262
Decentralization, 21–22. *See also* Centers
Deliberative decision making, 388, 391, 412
Democracy, 16, 21, 29, 77, 112, 139, 252, 288, 327, 332, 367, 383
Democratic design, 32, 141, 156, 197
Density, 143
affective, 207–209
and amenities, 211–216, 221–22
benefits of, 224, 341
and citizen science research, 350
concentrated and resilience, 201–203
conspiracy against, 205–207, 218, 224
design strategies for, 215, 218–219, 221–223, 314
and housing, 209–214, 219, 287–288, 292
increasing, 204–205, 218, 221, 268, 314
and lifestyle, 208–209
and limited extent, 227, 229–230, 233, 252
measurable, 207–209
and nature, 220–221
and new urbanism, 63, 189–190, 209, 218, 288
perceived, 207–209, 219–220, 221–225
and privacy, 218–219
and proximity to walk, 397, 413
retrofitting for, 222–223
social factors, 207–208, 222
trade-offs, 209, 215–220, 287–288, 314, 339, 344
and transportation, 204, 221, 397
typologies of, 214

Density, low, 203, 205–206, 222. *See also* Suburban development; Suburbs
  cold war, 360
  and health costs, 205
  preference for, 208–209, 217
  subsidized, 206, 215
  supported by designers, 207
Density and smallness, 143, 201, 225, 227, 255, 393
Design, public, 32, 35, 109, 124–125, 128–129, 133–134, 410
Designers
  cautions for, 27–28, 78, 84, 100, 114, 122, 186, 207, 289, 353
  principles/considerations, 39–40, 50, 58, 61, 100, 134, 139, 146, 180, 186, 207, 255–256, 283–284, 289, 338, 392
  role of/philosophy, 25, 62, 77–78, 101, 111, 127, 146, 160–161, 274, 297, 312, 375, 384–385, 410
Design with nature, 55–56, 137–143, 151, 155, 194, 256, 305, 279, 330
Design principles, 19, 51, 113–114, 140–143, 218–219, 221–223, 283, 287, 332, 336, 340, 397, 413
Design process, 69, 77–78, 100, 118–131, 135, 297–299, 356–359
Detroit, MI, 63
Development. *See also* Urban development
  guidelines for, 215
  rate of and diversity, 202
Diversity. *See also* Biological diversity; Cultural diversity; Selective diversity; Social diversity
  and center, 23
  of community, 196, 199, 315–323
  community activities, 23–24, 31, 39–40, 248–249

as design principle, 141, 187, 191–192, 197–199, 252
  ecological, 336
  enough, 190–195
  healthy cities, 140, 171, 202
  idea and concept of, 31, 171
  index of, 190–191
  loss of, 188
  scale of, 191
  seeding, 196–199
  versus unity, 194–195
Discrimination, 24. *See also* Exclusivity; Fairness; Inclusivity
Duany, Andres, 189. *See also* New urbanism
Duomo Cathedral (Florence, Italy), 134–135
Durham, NC, 138, 256

Earth First!, 245, 303, 351
Earthquakes
  Kobe, 142
  Lalu Garden, 307
  Loma Prieta, San Francisco, 54, 273–274
Ecoilliteracy, 17, 82, 325, 328–331, 334
Ecoliteracy, 18, 50, 113, 130, 308, 327, 331–332
Ecological
  art, 309, 339
  citizenship, 308
  context and design, 27, 110–111, 137, 149, 159, 165–166, 237, 245, 333
  education, 183, 274, 248–251, 330–331, 338, 348–351, 373–374
  health, 16, 304–305
  knowledge, 333, 340, 372, 383
  lessons, 278
  processes (natural processes), 328–330, 333, 335–338, 343, 346, 365

science (*see* Inhabiting science; Science)
Ecological democracy
  actions to create, 26, 234, 239–241, 255, 281, 287, 296–297, 334, 337, 339, 341, 346, 348, 360, 374
  and connectedness, 75, 171
  and daily life, 38, 154, 333
  deterrents to, 289
  examples of, 29, 31, 46, 216
  and fairness, 95
  and health, 396
  and identity, 32, 104
  inclusive, 273
  in neighborhood, 16, 32
  and participation, 237–238, 252
  and particularness, 94–95
  principles of, 19, 37, 46, 60, 63, 77, 117, 197, 230, 278
  and public language, 331–332
  and sacredness, 131–135
  scale for, 251–252
  versus speed, 388
  and status seeking, 98
  and stewardship, 371, 380
Ecological thinking, 18, 59–60, 131, 264, 272, 383, 395
Ecology, 27, 59, 189
  of commerce, 187
  and emotional responses, 305–307
  land, 365–366
  transparent process, 338
Economic
  activity and centers, 21
  barriers to inclusiveness, 80
  cost of preservation, 265
  development and species, 63, 70
  place-based development, 65, 98, 177, 278–279
Economy
  diversified, 187
  global, 60, 197–199, 337

local, 175–183, 187, 336
of multiuse landscape, 258
of necessity, 153
place-based, 145
real estate, 366
regional, 187, 197–198
and resilience, 137, 171–172, 177,
    187, 199, 227
of scale, 188
Ecorevelatory, 49–50, 58, 141–142,
    290, 340–341, 350–351
    design, 339, 342–343, 349
    King Estate Park (Oakland, CA),
        343–344
    Lowell, Massachusetts, Discovery
        Network, 346–347
    water system, 341
Ecosystems, 55, 140, 190–191, 244
    adaptable and health, 255, 273
    aeolian, 198–199
    decline of and sprawl, 202
    Los Angeles, 274–250
    urban and human health, 305
Ecotourism, 178–183
Edmiston, Joe, 249–250, 315, 317
Education. See Ecological, education
Educative city, 338, 345, 346
Elderly. See Seniors
Enabling
    community, 16, 18, 24, 29, 43, 78,
        105, 185
    design principles, 19
    form, 16–19, 24, 143, 289–291,
        296, 279, 412
    resilience, 142–143
    sacredness, 123, 135
Enclaves, 97, 104, 191
Environmental impact
    assessment, 175
    statement, 59, 173–174, 183
Environmental justice, 77, 85–86, 92
Environments, restorative, 313–315,
    322

Everyday future, 279, 281–299
    design strategies, 283
Everyday life. See Daily life
Everyday urbanism, 28, 152, 284
Everyday walk, 406
Evora, Portugal, 130, 146
Exclusivity, 40, 78, 80, 111, 371

Fairness, 19, 60, 77–95, 139, 142,
    252, 288, 279
The Fall of Public Man, 16
Farmer's market, 24, 31–32, 37,
    379–381. See also Marketplaces;
    Urban form
Farming, farmland. See Agriculture
Feng shui, 29
Flood control, 56, 149–153, 165–166,
    168–169, 234, 353. See also
    Stormwater runoff
Flooding, 54, 149–151, 168–169. See
    also Stormwater runoff
Flournoy, William, 149
Fluvial geomorphology, 274
Food web, 57, 75
Footprints, 57–58, 75
Fort Bragg, CA, 407
Framework(s)
    and adaptability, 263–271
    for city form, 269, 332, 335
    conceptual and science, 273
    for design, 55, 130, 133, 151, 171,
        178–179, 245, 251, 336, 353,
        377–378
    landscape as, 269–270, 275
    priority, 263–271, 274
    and stewardship capacity, 375, 385
Francis, Mark, 24
Franklin, Benjamin, 327
Freeway, 185, 231, 412
    divisive highway, 66, 149, 185
    fights and conflicts, 245–248, 291,
        295–296, 391
    subsidy and true costs, 204, 397

Friedberg, Paul, 287
Friedman, Terry, 69
Fruitvale district (Oakland, CA),
    87–95
Fruitvale Recreation and Open Space
    Initiative, 87–88, 90–93. See also
    Park design; Union Point Park
Functional distance, 23, 25

Galatowitsch, Susan, 349–350
Gans, Herbert, 207
Garden Patch, The (Berkeley, CA),
    375–383
Gas Works Park (Seattle, WA), 351
Gateway Commons, 83–84. See also
    Affordable housing; Low income
Gaudi building, 402
Gestalt, 122, 127, 132–133, 135
Geographic Information Systems
    (GIS), 147
Geologic time, 165–167, 406
Giraud, Deborah, 371
Globalization, 186
Global warming
    city form, 272, 337
    mitigation of, 272
Glocalization, 51, 60–61, 186. See also
    Mutualism
Golden Gate National Recreation
    Area, 374
Goldsworthy, Andy, 308–309
Goodman, Paul, 238
Gordon, Jeff, 382
Government, 251–253, 346
    transparent process, 338
Grassroots, 64, 90, 150, 185, 250,
    252, 274
    cross-sectional, 274–275
    democracy, 29, 224, 332
    knowledge and science, 330
Graves, Bob, 357
Greenbelt, 148, 221, 227–228,
    236–237, 240–241, 253, 314

boundary, 269
LA Big Wild Greenbelt, 244–251, 354
trade-off for density, 216–218, 314
Greenbelt, MD, 130, 227, 229
Greenburgh, NY, 192
Greenfields, 79
Green materials/construction/technologies, 177, 335–336
Ground plane (experience of), 408–411, 413–417
Guided fantasy technique, 101–102
Guyton, Tyree, 63

4–H projects, 364
Habitat. *See also* Wildlife habitat
citizen science research, 350
core habitat of species, 58, 180–183, 247, 336
and endangered species, 180
impact of urban form on, 179–183, 185, 202, 335
loss of, 58, 61, 172, 174, 202
nearby and neighborhood, 314, 417
preservation of, 59
requirements, 178, 180
stakeholders, 61
Habitat for Humanity, 364
Habitation
building dwelling, 309, 338
discovery in, 341
form of, 160, 184, 207
human and cultural preservation, 184
human development, 237
human and ecological, 77, 137–138, 172–173, 201, 277–279, 331
Habraken, N. John, 264
Haleiwa, HI (Oahu), 130–131, 164, 242, 277–279, 363, 391
Halprin, Lawrence, 161–163, 309, 403
Halsband, Frances, 209
Hamilton, Alexander, 252

Hansen, Richard, 343
Haran, Turkey, 137–138, 145, 147, 184
Hargreaves, George, 342
Harkness, Terry, 341–342
Harris, Robert, 257
Harrison, Helen, 339, 350
Harrison, Newton, 339, 350
Harrison, Shelby, 52
Harvard Law School Child Care Center, 101–103
Harvard Square (Cambridge, MA), 103
Harvard University, 307
Hawaii (island of), 198–199
Hawken, Paul, 187
Health, 337
and art in everyday life, 309
and automobile reduction, 396
benefits of nature, 232–233, 314
and city form, 394
and community gardens, 380–381
and density, 201–202
and design of city, 393–394
and ecological vulnerability, 191
and exercise, 393–396, 398
and human adaptation, 256
and interactions with natural environments, 312–315, 320–323
and local capital, 198–199
and low density, 205
and natural and human systems, 140, 256, 335
naturopathy, 302–305
obesity, 394–396
and pace of life, 391, 393, 412
and social interaction, 398
and spontaneity, 312
Health, mental
city form, 394
experiencing nature, 309, 311–315
landscape character, 311
prospect-refuge, 313
Health care, modern and naturopathy, 303

Heat island effect and mitigation, 272–273
The Heidelberg Project, 63
Hester, Donald, 328–329
Hester, Nathaniel, 163–164, 338
Hester, Randolph T., Jr., 291–296
Hester, Randolph T., Sr., 333–334
Hester's Store (NC), 328, 333–334, 416
Heterogeneity, 111, 172, 186–187, 190–191
Highways. *See* Freeway
Hills, Angus, 147
Historic preservation legislation, 122
Hmong people, 184, 371–372
Holiday, Leland, 63
Holling, C. S., 272–273
Hollywood, CA, 15–18
Homogeneity, 186, 190–191, 196
Hong Kong, China, 130
Honolulu, HI (Oahu), 130, 241–243, 251, 277, 314, 332, 391
Hood, Walter, 80–81, 281, 352
Hough, Michael, 140, 257
House and form, 150, 154–160
Housing design
density of, 160, 204, 209–210, 219, 222
diversity of, 210, 191, 196, 197–198
in downtown, 209–213, 265
inclusive, 83–84
low-income, 84
mixed-income, 197–198, 210, 212–214
mixed-use, 160, 191
natural features, 150, 220, 268
place-based, 141, 268, 287–288
slowness, 390, 397
for stormwater, 290
as strategy, 209–210
user specific, 85
for walking, 397

Hsin Chu City, Taiwan, 137, 187
Huichol Indians, 320
Huan-chi, Su, 175, 177, 183
Hurricanes
    Hugo, 138, 142–143
    Katrina, 79, 143, 146
Hydrological cycles, 54–56, 70, 146,
    151, 165–166, 257, 335, 343,
    363. *See also* Rivers
Hydrological principles, 332, 277–279

Identity
    collective, 97, 133, 227, 238
    community, 97, 103, 109, 133, 224,
        278, 290
    facilitated by design, 32
    formation of, 132
    local, 17, 21–22, 133, 153, 186
    loss of local, 17, 21–22, 97, 105,
        243
    and mobility, 105
    rootedness, 21–22, 27, 186
    and tourism, 186
    and urban form, 22, 138–139, 403
Ilan Performing Arts Center (China),
    297–299
Illinois, 265–266, 341–342
Immigrants, 90–91, 104, 185, 250,
    314, 377
    ways of life, 371–372
Impelling
    form and design, 19, 143, 277–279,
        289–291, 323, 331, 339, 390,
        413
    form and legislation, 279
    stewardship, 364
Inaccessibility. *See also* Accessibility
    design in, 79
    patterns of, 25, 79
    and preservation, 185
    of public resources, 88, 90, 92, 97
    rectified, 83–84
Inclusion. *See* Inclusivity

Inclusivity
    and centers, 24
    and city design, 78
    as design goal, 32
    generating mutualism, 31
    of local knowledge, 125, 387
    and park design, 73, 80–81, 84, 90,
        128
    planning process, 18, 80
Industry
    green, 177
    and species habitat, 174–183
    as tourist attraction, 65, 97
    transitioning land uses, 88, 315
    transparent process, 338
Infrastructure. *See also* Development
    amenities and benefits of, 290
    compact service expansion of,
        227–239
    costs of, 237, 290
    transparent process of, 338, 346
    and transportation (public), 393
Inhabiting science, 56, 113, 279,
        325–361, 363
    definition of, 333
    and transparent processes, 338
    understanding, 325–326, 333, 378
Institute for Children and Adolescent
        Development, 304
Integration. *See also* Segregation
    concept of, 24
    and housing design, 83–84
    and land use, 83–84
    of multifunctional systems, 140
    of social classes, 172, 190
Interaction. *See also* Sociofugal;
        Sociopetal
    and center, 21, 29
    daily, 29, 35–37, 222, 394, 406
    democratic, 34
    design for, 18, 32, 35–37, 44, 222,
        377, 398
    diagram of, 33

and health, 394, 398
    microcenters of, 34
    and sociopetal design, 21, 32,
        34–37
Interconnectedness. *See also*
        Connectedness
    of everything, 49
    and impelling form, 332
    interdependent adjacencies, 52
    in landscape, 49
    of materials and city form, 57
    of networks and cycles, 335–336
    of people and place, 363, 382
    and redevelopment, 265
    and resilient form, 140–143
Interdependent adjacencies
    and connectedness, 51
    and design form, 51–52
    diagram of, 52
    and responsible city management,
        338
    rules of, 187
International Rivers Network, 61
International Union of Conservation,
    174
Interviews, information gathering,
    118
Island effect, 185

Jackson Demonstration State Forest,
    343
Jacobs, Allan, 54, 106–107, 209, 211
Japan, 131, 134, 173, 184, 192–194,
    310, 390, 410–411
    ecological literacy, 335
Japanese gardens, 263, 409–410
Jefferson, Thomas, 327, 332, 365,
    367
Jefferson Park, 34
Jensen, Jens, 33
Jewell, Linda, 342
John Muir Park, 274
Jones, Fay, 134

Kamalani, Ima, 277–279, 332, 363, 383

Kamo River, 410–411

Katsura Imperial Villa (Japan), 400–401, 409–410

Keller, Suzanne, 21

Kenko, Yoshida, 258–259

King, Martin Luther, Jr., 60, 78, 405

King, Rodney, uprising, 315

King Estate Park (Oakland, CA), 343–344

Knowledge, evolution of ecological, 272

Kobe, Japan, 142

Kondolf, G. Mathias, 274, 353

Korea, 173

Kotler, Milton, 238

Krapfel, Paul, 352

Ku Klux Klan, 78

Kyoto, Japan
    cityscape, 257–258
    landscape, 134, 256
    neighborhoods, 258, 192–194, 314, 404
    sacredness, 133
    Shugakuin, 192–194
    water system, 257–258, 341, 410–411

LA96C Park (Los Angeles, CA), 353–361

Lafayette Park (Oakland, CA), 80–81

Lalu Garden, 307

Land
    ecology, 365
    liberation of, 365
    ownership and identity, 363, 366–367
    as real estate, 366
    stewardship, 366

Land ethic, 366, 368, 385

Landscape. *See also* Sacred landscapes
    adaptive, 29, 151–153, 256–259

argumentative landscapes, 339, 350–353, 361

bioregion, 148

capacity to change behavior, 111, 142

commonplace, 338–339

cultivating, 339, 344

cultural and biological, 363

discovery, 339–344

diversified economy, 187

educative/instructive, 338–340, 345–348, 353–361

ephemeral, 399, 416

everyday, 109, 269

healthy, 112–113

imbued/embodied, 130–131, 134, 198–199, 259

metamorphic, 406

military, reused, 353–361

multiuse versus single use, 257–258, 275

open-ended design of, 258–259

particularness, 145

productive, 29, 140, 146, 375–383

with a range of tempos, 388, 400, 402

reforming, 66, 69–75, 141, 249

scientific, 339, 348–350

and status seeking, 98

sterile versus dirty, 112

structure and framework, 194, 269–270, 404

three-dimensional, 402

and transcendence, 405

undervalued, 113

urban and delight, 312, 279

urban form, 18, 142, 269, 275

urban and naturalness, 310–315

valued, 109, 130–131

wild, 339–340, 344

Landscape ecology, 51, 180, 188, 256, 261, 336
    and cities, 330–331

Landslides, 55–56, 71

Land use
    balanced, 191
    compatibility of, 190
    conflict of, 187–288
    diversity of, 172, 189
    integrated, 83–84, 111, 188, 413
    limited extent, 241–243, 251
    and location of center, 27
    and mixed use, 188–189
    natural processes, 335
    patterns and geologic actions, 165–166
    segregated, 78–79, 188, 191
    transportation, 336

Lasack, Ed, 71, 73, 75

Las Cruces, NM, 131

Laurie, Michael, 258

Lawson, Laura, 375, 377, 379–381

Leopold, Aldo, 366, 368

Lerner, Jaime, 271

Lessons
    of nature, 277–279
    of poverty, 104–105

Letters from Birmingham Jail, 60, 78

Lewis, Phil, 147

Limited extent, 62, 143, 227–254, 256, 279, 315, 354, 363, 393, 397, 399. *See also* Carrying capacity; City design; City form; Nature; Regional form
    benefits of, 227–229, 232–233, 234–237, 239, 242, 248–250, 252–253
    and identity, 227, 374
    and nature/recreation, 227
    need for cooperation among cities, 240
    population limits, 230–233, 236–238, 253

Lipkis, Andy, 154

Lisbon, Portugal, 409

Liu, John, 158

Livable cities, 206

Local culture and ecology
    and design, 91–95
    ignored, 172
    and instruction, 30, 39
    patterns of, 61, 147, 162
Local government
    role in design, 29, 183
Locality
    collective experience, 21, 27,
        277–279, 374
    inspires building form, 27, 147
    paving, 409
    planning process, 18, 21, 277–279
    stewardship, 383
Local knowledge. *See also* Native wisdom
    concept of, 16
    as focus of center, 27, 46
    fostered through good design, 25,
        109
    gathered through walking, 392–393
    informs necessity, 104
    inspiring form, 27, 30, 104,
        145–147, 149, 165–166, 199,
        337, 369
    loss of and city design, 17, 22, 369
    of nature and ecology, 140,
        165–166, 277–279, 329–330,
        363, 365
    and planning process, 18, 277–279
    sacredness, 125, 199
    stewardship capacity, 369–370
    undermined, 325
Local wisdom. *See* Local knowledge;
    Native wisdom
Los Angeles, CA, 15, 82, 147, 154,
    204, 257, 314, 397
    Big Wild Greenbelt, 244–251
    LA96C Park, 353–361 (*see also* San
        Vicente Mountain Park)
    LA River and neighborhood plan-
        ning, 234–235, 320, 372
    Mulholland Gateway Park,
        244–245, 248

Runyon Canyon, 55, 66–75
Pasadena, 209–218
Santa Monica Mountains, 244–245,
    247–249, 353
San Vicente Mountain Park,
    353–361 (*see also* LA96C Park)
Low, Setha, 287
Low income. *See also* Affordable housing
    density in neighborhood, 191
    exclusionary zoning, 191
    highway impacts, 231
    nature (or park) access, 248–250,
        314–323
    neighborhood gangs, 317, 322–323
    neighborhoods, 78–94, 100–101
    redevelopment impacts, 291–296
Lowell, Massachusetts, Discovery
    Network, 346–347
Lyle, John, 140–141
Lynch, Kevin, 232
Lyndon, Donlyn, 209, 211, 215

Macdonald, Elizabeth, 54
Manteo, NC, 118–131, 133–134. *See
    also* Fairness; Sacredness
    boardwalk design, 124–125,
        128–129, 133–134
    Jules's Park, 105, 120
    mapping injustices, 86
Mapping
    behavior, 39, 118, 126, 128, 286,
        297, 299, 371
    distribution of resources, 83–84, 100
    environmental aspects and natural
        patterns, 60, 161–162, 370
    GIS (computer), 147
    and holistic site analysis, 62
    injustices, 85–87, 90
    inventory, 369
    legibility of, 80
    limits of traditional, 128
    McHargian, 146–147
    natural patterns, 163

opportunities, 89
power, 66–69, 75, 87, 291
to reveal for discussion, 85–87, 90,
    126
sacred structure, 119–120, 128, 133
specie needs, 175
with youth, 80
Marcus, Clare Cooper, 310
Marsh, Stanley, Cadillac Ranch, 351
Marketplaces, 32. *See also* Farmer's
    market
Masai, 138, 143
Masayoshi, Himeno, 150
Matsu Island, China
    community ritual, 39, 46
    design process, 32
    diagram of, 30
    natural boundary, 130
    town center, 28, 30
Mauna Kea, HI, 198–199
McBride, Joe, 343
McHarg, Ian, 139–140, 146–147, 330
McNally, Marcia, 209, 245–247, 278
Mecca, 405
Megacity, 233, 237
Meier, Richard, 297
Memorial Park (Pasadena, CA), 213–
    216
Method Day Care Center, 258–159
Military base, 353–361
Mixed-use
    commercial space, 192
    density, 207–209
    healthy cities, 189–195, 397
    neighborhood diversity, 197–198,
        221–222
    strategies, 189, 210–211
Mobility, 17, 21, 98, 105
Monarch Butterfly Biosphere Preserve,
    The, 63–64
Monkey Wrench Gang, The, 303
Montana Study and Heritage Project,
    274–275

Moore, Robin, 114
Mount Kurama, 131–132
Mount Saint Helens, 58, 260
Mount Vernon, WA, 38, 130
    Skagit River, 165–168
Mozingo, Louise, 85, 343–344
Mulholland, William, 359
Mulholland Gateway Park, 244–245,
    248
Mumford, Lewis, 21
Mutualism, 60–62
    coalition of, 60–62
    developed in planning process, 69,
        75
    and glocalization, 51
    lack of, 66
    social and city design, 60

Napa, CA. *See also* Yountville, CA
    natural boundary, 130, 137, 240
NASCAR, 382
Nassauer, Joan, 290
National Taiwan University, 177, 183
National Trust for Historic
        Preservation, 21
National Wildlife Federation, 301
National Wildlife Federation Backyard
        Certification Program, 373
National Wildlife Refuge, 234,
        373–374
Native American, 184
Native plant communities, 73, 75, 88,
        165–166, 194, 247, 290, 314,
        317–318, 320
Native wisdom, 327–328, 333–334,
        337. *See also* Local knowledge
    city form, 331–333
    ecological principles, 364
    land ethic, 368
    loss of, 329–331
Natural citizenship, 302
Natural disasters, 145–146, 353
    adaptability, 256, 273, 307

botulism outbreak, 180
Cherokee river flooding, 168–169
ecological, 330, 350
flooding, 54, 149–151, 168–169
Hurricane Hugo, 138, 142–143
Hurricane Katrina, 79, 143, 146
Kobe earthquake, 142
landslides, 55–56, 71
limited through resilience, 227
Loma Prieta, San Francisco earth-
        quake, 54, 273–274
Mount Saint Helens volcano, 58
and opportunities for city design,
        273
Taiwan earthquake, 288
Yoshino river flooding, 149–151
Natural environment, 306. *See also*
        Nature
Naturalization, 302, 308–310, 315
Naturalness, 27, 279, 301–324, 359,
        363, 388, 393
    concept of, 301
    and creativity, 308, 323
    design characteristics of, 310–315
    and elemental forces, 312, 323
    evoking, 311
    examples of, 315–323
    and human emotion, 301–303, 305
    nurtures good health, 323
Natural Park (South Central Los
        Angeles, CA), The, 315–323
Natural process
    creating structure, 149–154,
        165–169, 256, 275
    directing city form, 256
    experiencing, 17, 353
    as factor that informs design,
        161–163, 156
Natural therapy, 305
Nature
    access to, 201
    academic versus practical, 302
    design aspects of feelings, 301–324

and emotional response, 301–303,
        305–307
ephemeral, 311, 399, 416
and everyday life, 311–315, 323
health of and city form, 305
and human well being, 24, 140,
        202, 301–305, 308–309,
        311–315, 330, 340
inspiring creativity, 308
and mental restoration, 311
and modern medicine, 303
multiple scales of, 313–314
nearby, 227, 232, 237, 242, 248,
        250, 310, 313, 317, 341, 371,
        416–417
in neighborhood, 26, 103, 234, 311
observation of, 91
people's experiences of, 24, 112,
        301, 303, 305, 309
and play, 17, 103, 257, 316–317
and self-awareness, 308
therapeutic, 313–315
urban wilderness, 311, 314, 316,
        340, 344
Nature, experience of, 112, 301, 303,
        305, 399
    emotional response to, 301–302,
        305–307, 323
    impelling, 310
    self-awareness, 308, 311
    health, 311–312, 323
Naturism, 302, 305–307, 310, 315
    definition of, 305
Naturopathy, 302–305, 310, 315
Neighborhood
    amenities, 222
    boundaries between, 217, 221–222,
        258
    center, 203, 222, 224, 377, 399
    and citizen science, 349
    conflicts between groups, 245
    density and public transportation,
        204

design and exercise, 395
divided by highways, 52, 54
form and renewable resources, 110, 140
greening, 220–222, 224, 234–235, 314, 398–399
identity, 222–224
improvement, 369, 371, 393
integrated versus segregated, 189–190, 196, 205
lack of cooperation in, 66
low-income, 78–94, 100–101, 291–296, 315, 372, 377
mixed-use, 188–190, 197–198, 204, 215
nature, design guidelines, 311
parks, 213–214, 220, 313–323, 372
quarter-mile radius, 25, 189, 203, 295, 311, 341, 399
real-estate development, 66, 67–69
reknitting, 54
and resilient form, 140, 252
services, 104, 192, 203–204, 222
slowness, 390
size of, 192, 203
walkable, 192, 203, 413
Neighboring. *See also* Working together
enabled through design, 18–19, 53
and working together, 15, 291–296, 371
Neighbors
division of, 66
knowing through planning, 15–16
Networks
closing the loop of, 65
and effects on city development, 51, 54–55
essential for good city form, 51
and healthy cities, 140, 258
irrigation and city form, 269
irrigation and park design, 321
making visible, 56, 258
multiuse, 257

natural, 54–55, 148
reconnecting, 56
walking, 393
Newbury, Mickey, 272
Newman, Randy, 206–207
New Orleans, LA, 146
Newsing at the post office, 38–39
New urbanism, 63, 189–190, 209, 218, 288
NIMBY, 16, 84, 222, 353, 392
Nishida, Kitaro, 406
North Carolina, 60–61, 108–109, 130, 138, 148–149, 151, 164–165, 256, 365
lack of limited extent, 243
quail/farming, 328–329
State University, 258
Norton, Phil, 373

Oahu, HI, 131, 242, 363, 417. *See also* Haleiwa; Honolulu
Oakland, CA, 83, 130, 265
Courtland Creek Park, 281–283
King Estate Park, 343–344
Lafayette Square, 288–289
Port of Oakland, 90
Union Point Park, 87–95
Observation
by designer, 161–163
of participant, 291, 297
of site, 161–163
through walking, 392–393, 413–417
Octavia Boulevard, 53–54
Okuzumi, Hikaru, 164
Olin, Laurie, 408–409
Olmsted, Frederick L., 207, 393
firm, 251
tradition, 311
Open space
adaptability of, 256–257
and density, 213–216, 221–222
distribution of, 87–88, 229, 239–242

and emptiness, 259–260
and health, 303–304, 399
inventory of, 87, 103
linear systems, 149
natural, 221, 259–260
need for, 87, 92–93
preservation of, 268
regional system, 148, 239–240, 251
urban and flexible, 258–259, 274
wild and tame, 314
Orchid Island, 154–160
Orientation of centers, 27–28, 30
Orr, David, 325, 327, 331, 340
Osaka, Japan, homeless encampment, 351

Pace of life, 387
dwelling, 390–392, 408
fast, 388, 392, 412
range of tempos, 391, 399–400, 402, 417
slow, 390, 400
Pacific coast, 407
Pacing, 279, 387–412
ground plane, 408–411
Palley Park, NY, 312
Park design
amenity, 213, 316–317
city form, 266
democratic, 81
exclusion, 81
integration of uses, 284–287, 315, 317, 322
master plan, 90, 244
park planning, 87, 249
precedents, 288–289
principles of naturalness, 317
redesigning of, 80–81, 213
safety, 317–318, 320, 322–323
schools, 89–90
urban national park, 346–347
user needs, 73, 81, 91–95, 315
water features, 321–322

Park planning, 316–317
  employment, 320
Parthenon, 405
Participation, public, 28, 56, 82,
  91–95, 117
Participation, informed/democratic,
  327, 332, 337, 341
Participatory design process, 370
  and fairness, 90–91, 94–95
  inclusive planning, 18, 251, 377
  in park planning, 15, 56, 244–251,
    286–287, 317, 320, 356–361
  roundtable movement, 32
  sacred structure, 120, 122–123
  status seeking, 181
  transparent, 95
Particularness, 100, 137, 143,
  145–170, 227, 256, 279, 341,
  388
  benefits of, 169, 227
  centers, 29, 100, 266–271
  definition of, 145
  design examples of, 145, 289
  ignorance of, 146
  and sacred structure, 127, 133,
    132–133
Partnerships. *See* Mutualism
  community, 371–372, 377, 382
  participatory, 274
  unlikely planning, 94, 274,
    377–378
Pasadena, CA, 209–218
Pattern Language, A, 232
Patterns
  of activity, 38
  behavior, 128
  community, 132, 154
  of conserving, recycling, and repair-
    ing, 147, 152, 154
  daily life, 27, 132, 154, 289, 291
  design with ecological, 146, 151 (*see
    also* Design with nature)
  economic, 21

hydrologic, 149–151
idiosyncratic, 152, 161–162, 169,
  185, 391
inaccessibility, 25, 79
land use and geologic, 165–166
local activity and environment, 24
natural, 148, 151, 161–162
regional, 146, 149–151
sacred structure, 133
social, 29, 126
suburban, 59
traditional and modern, 158–159
traditional settlement, 145, 147,
  156
unhealthy versus productive,
  114–115
vegetation, 73, 75, 151
visible and invisible, 123, 353 (*see
  also* Connectedness)
wildlife inspire city form, 52, 59
Paving, surface
  affecting walking experience,
    408
  as art, 409
  impervious and pervious, 408
Pedestrian
  environment, 408–409
  movement and design standards,
    24–25, 52–54, 110, 413
  routes and health, 404, 413
  safety and transportation, 394,
    396–398, 413
Penan people, 184–185
Perceived distance, 25
Perkin, Dwight, 265–266
Perry, Clarence, 203, 237
Philippines, 173
Phillips, Patricia, 350
Philosopher's walk, 258, 341,
  406–407
Piazza del Campo, Siena, 27–28, 36,
  46
Piedmont Greenway, 148

Pike Place Market (Seattle, WA),
  31–32
Pilgrimage, 387–388, 405–406
Place-based design, 145
  Astoria, 97, 100
  benefits of, 169
  Caspar town center, 266–269
  design process of Sea Ranch, 163
  Mauna Kea, 198–199
  reflects place centered life, 22
  Tawo house, 156
  threatened by technology, 22
Placelessness, 17, 22, 50, 97,
  368–369, 384–385
Planners. *See also* Designers
  directives for diverse economies, 188
  who prey on communities, 97
Plater-Zyberk, Elizabeth, 189. *See also*
  New urbanism
Plato, 232, 237
Politics (political), 247, 252
Pollution, 145, 148, 337, 368. *See also*
  Air quality
  air pollution, 148, 231, 264, 368
  global warming, 272
  and health, 394
  and low density, 205
  of low income neighborhoods, 82,
    188, 190
  superfund site, 190
Population, growth and sustainability,
  173, 179
Portable Fish Farm: Survival Piece #3,
  350
Portland, Oregon, 239, 251, 397
  Skinny Streets Program, 397
Postmodernity, 39
Poverty, lessons of, 104–105
Power, 60, 77, 350
  elemental landscape, 312
Power map, 66–69, 75, 87. *See also*
  Mapping
Preservation

growth-management techniques, 240, 242
of landscape or wilderness, 67, 107, 173, 266
through legislation, 122, 363–364, 368
of local place, 118–131, 133–134, 126, 266
role of federal government, 363
and sacredness, 135
viewsheds, 266–268
way of life, 118–131, 133–134, 266
of wetlands and habitat, 176–183, 363
Private property rights, 363, 368
and privilege, 366–368
Privatization of public life, 366–368
Problem solving
accurate framework for, 264–265
democratic, 197, 274
holistic, 62
innovative, 63–64, 71, 279, 306, 373
participatory, 274–275
resourceful, 64
and shared experience, 16, 18, 274
through stewardship, 367–368
walking, 406
Property ownership, 365–367
managed as public resource, 374
Prospect-refuge, 313
Protest, 77–78, 82, 177, 191, 295, 303
Psychology
environmental, 32, 303–305
gestalt, 127
health, 27, 58, 313
natural therapy, 305
Public art, 24, 30, 63
Portable Fish Farm: Survival Piece #3, 350
Public debate, 249
Public decision making, 78. *See also* Participatory design process

uninformed public, 327
youth, 377
Public facilities, for prestige, 109
Public life, decline of, 366–367
Public transportation, 79–80, 83, 271
and density, 201, 204, 221, 397
investing in, 204, 393
Putnam, Robert, 16
Pyatok, Mike, 83–84
Pyramids (Egypt), 134

Quality of life, 58, 107, 118, 125
Quarter-mile radius, 25, 189, 203, 295, 311, 341, 399

Racism, 78, 315, 366
Radke, John, 147
Raleigh, NC, 60–61, 130
Apollo Heights, 108–109
Chavis Heights, 291–296
city size, 232
Raleigh Greenway, 148–149, 151
Ramblas, Barcelona, 400, 402, 404
Rapoport, Amos, 207
Rauschenberg, Robert, 63
Real estate development, conflict with, 66, 67–69
Recreation, 227, 234, 281, 283
facilities, 88–90, 149
Recycling, 49, 51, 104, 140–141, 153–154
and design, 51–52, 65, 189
Redevelopment
adaptability, 260–261
of African American community (Chavis Heights), 291–296
and cultural diversity, 185
and density, 223–224
of downtown, 209–218, 265
of Hood River, 65
industrial wasteland, 315–316, 377
riverfront plaza in Lawrence, Kansas, 32

of urban and low income areas, 291–296, 315
of waterfront, 97–99, 118–131, 133–134
Reed, Douglas, 303–304
Regional
cross-jurisdictional planning/authority, 249–252
ecological education, 348
form, 149–150, 230–231, 233, 240–253, 336
growth and planning, 60, 177–183, 251
landscape as framework, 169, 171
mixed-use, 189
sense of, 352
trail, 88, 92
Register, Richard, 189–190, 234, 236, 351
Renewable resources, 110, 145–146, 159–160, 189
Renewal, urban, 78, 100, 185
Reseda Ridge (CA), 66–75
Reseda Ridge Park (CA), 69, 73
Resilience
and design, 19
and development, 142, 184, 227, 272
and diversity, 172, 179, 187
efficient, 187, 196
form, 289–291, 296, 279
and lack of diversity, 196
and natural factors, 142
principles of, 140–143
sociological principles of, 142–143
Resources
conservation of, 65, 147, 152, 169, 172, 227, 367, 375, 383
consumption of, 97, 110, 230, 375
design for conservation of, 110–111
distribution of, 85, 241, 253
exploited, 64
inventory of, 100, 103

linking, 88–89
local, 147
natural, 179
public, 82, 107
renewable, 110, 145–146, 159–160, 189
unequal distribution of, 78, 82, 87, 90
Restoration
  and daily life influences, 281
  design goal of, 69–75
  economy of, 70
  and human health, 365
  of vacant land, 375–380
Riparian
  and city form, 256
  management, 165–166, 168, 274
  system, 54–55, 58, 274
  zone, 58
Rivers
  Cherokee River, 168–169
  Columbia River, 58, 65, 97, 99
  Cowlitz River, 58–59
  hydrology, 330
  Kamo River, 410–411
  River Tribunal, The, 384
  Seine River, 400, 402, 404
  Skagit River, 165–168
  Takano River, 410–411
Rollins, Dale, 373
Roof garden, 272–273, 336, 344
Rootedness, 21–22, 98, 105, 186, 329, 365, 368
Rootlessness, 17. *See also* Mobility
Roxboro, NC, 365
Runyon Canyon
  Friends of, 55, 373
Runyon Canyon Park, 55–56
Ryan, Robert, 331

Sacred landscapes
  capacity to legitimize place, 122–123
  community connections, 130–131, 134

context of, 117–118
emptiness and Shinto shrines, 259–260
Manteo, 118–131, 133–134
Mauna Kea, 198–199
Sacredness, 19, 100, 117–136, 142, 279, 363, 388
  expression of human values, 117
  preservation of and trade-offs, 123
Sacred structure, 119–124, 127
Sand County Almanac, A, 366
Sando, 405
San Francisco, 64, 221, 371, 407
  air pollution, 231
  density, 201, 205
  earthquakes, 54, 256, 273
  freeway battle, 54
  natural boundary, 130
  nearby nature, 310
  and resilient form, 137
  watershed, 147
San Jose, CA
  Soquel Demonstration State Forest, 348–349
Santa Monica Mountains, 244–245, 247–249, 353
Santa Monica Mountains Conservancy, 67, 71, 73, 75, 244, 249, 315
San Vicente Mountain Park, 353–361 (*see also* LA96C Park)
SAVE (Spoonbill Action Voluntary Echo), 173–183
Scale
  appropriate for goals, 32, 188
  for creating connectedness, 58
  of design, 141, 251
  and framework, 269–271
  governing ecological democracy, 251–252
  impersonal, 368
  micro and macro, 22, 146–147, 152, 352

of neighborhood, 22, 32
and quality of life, 107
regional, 146
of systems, 141
Scarry, Richard, 196
Schumacher, E. F., 107, 188, 232
Science. *See also* Ecological, processes; Inhabiting science
  astronomy, 198–199
  citizen science, 348–350
  citizen science program, 274
  conceptual framework, 273
  ecological, 251
  habitat (reserved for research), 348–350
  narrow, 360
  naturism, 305
  shared experience, 369
  Soquel Demonstration State Forest, 348–349
  spatial principles, 182
  urban ecological principles, 330–332, 335, 341, 343, 345, 361
Sea Ranch (CA), 161–163
Seasonal change, 166–167, 404, 406, 416–417
  and global warming, 272
Seattle, WA, 31
  Gas Works Park, 351
Segregated
  districts versus mixed use, 190
  land use, 188
  land use and automobile dependency, 394
  neighborhood, 205
  pollution, 394
  single-use purpose, 27, 188 (*see also* Designers, cautions for)
Segregation. *See also* Integration
  in cities, 80
  and city form, 78
  and designers, 111
  social, 190

and special interest, 22
Seine River, Paris, 400, 402, 404
Selective diversity, 143, 171–199, 202, 227
Sennet, Richard, 16
Seniors
    housing design for, 85, 155
    and nature, 314
    park design for, 91, 284–287
Sense of community, 15, 18, 21, 39, 367–368
Setagaya, Japan, 108–109
Shared destiny, 49, 60
Shared experience
    and center, 21–22
    design for, 21, 36–37
    loss of, 17
    and problem solving, 16, 18
    science, 369
Shared interests, 21, 27, 75. *See also* Mutualism; Shared experience; Working together
Shared values, 15, 117, 368, 370, 374. *See also* Values
Shinto, 131–132, 259–260
Shugakuin, Kyoto, 192–194
Siena, Italy, 27–28, 36
Silent Spring, 50, 331
Simone, Nina, 206
Site analysis. *See* Mapping
Sixteenth Street Mall (Denver), 408–409
Skagit River Valley, 38, 165–167
Slowness, 387–388, 412–413, 417
    and community life, 391, 412
    design for/guidelines for, 388, 390
    and health, 391
    and observation, 392–393
Smallness, 107, 218, 397
Smiley, Jane, 50
Social capital, 21, 38
Social diversity, 184–185, 188, 190, 196, 315–323

Social environments, 16, 118–131, 134, 318–319
    health, 394, 398
Social segregation versus integration, 190
Sociofugal, 33, 44
Sociopetal, 32–36
    benefits of, 33
    and community interaction, 22, 33–34, 36–37, 40
    and design, 32–34, 40
    patterns of, 39
    Piazza del Campo, Siena, 36
    space, 33–34, 36, 40, 44
Sodo, Yamaguchi, 260
Solomon, Dan, 63, 106–107
Sonfist, Alan, 353
Soquel Demonstration State Forest (San Jose, CA), 348–349
Southworth, Michael, 79–80, 338–340, 345–347
Spanish Speaking Unity Council, 87, 90–94
Spartan, 407
Specialization, 17, 104
Species
    diversity, 58–59, 244
    dominant/subordinate, 191
    endangered, 63, 173–183
    extinction, 172–183, 202, 246
    intricate connections, 59
    protection and economic development, 63, 173–175
    survival, 58
    vegetation mosaic supports, 75
Speed
    benefits and costs, 388
    design to slow, 391–392, 394, 398, 410
    pace, 412
Spirn, Anne Whiston, 309
Sprawl, 22, 202, 216
Standards

building, 186
engineering, 110, 149, 274
Standardization of American values, 117
Status seeking. *See also* Symbolic ownership
    community improvement, 98
    destructive, 19, 100, 109, 188, 393
    healthy forms of, 100–115, 279
    misguided, 97–100, 104, 107
    and sacred places, 122
    sensible, 19, 97–115, 100, 142, 218
    status, 98, 106–107, 109, 255
    and sterile versus happy, 112
Steinbrueck, Victor, 31
Steinitz, Carl, 147
Steward
    farmer, 365
    land, 277–279, 363, 365–366
    neighborhoods, 371, 393
    people, 56, 75, 277–279
Stewardship. *See* Symbolic ownership
    active, 383–385
    definition of, 363–364
    design to encourage, 374–375, 382
    ecological health, 364, 383
    ecological necessity of, 367–368, 385
    and everyday patterns, 374, 393
    and habitat, 348, 373–374
    historical context of, 365
    and human health, 364–365
    institutional/programs for, 364–365, 369, 373–382, 385
    landscape, 149
    local wisdom, 109, 140, 149, 365, 374
    naïve, 365–367
    neo- versus traditional, 369
    opportunities for, 369, 371, 375, 385
    park planning, 90, 244
    as partnership, 368

personal, 366, 375

public place, 28, 109

reciprocal, 56, 61, 279, 363–385

rewards of, 364, 384–385

Stormwater runoff. *See also* Flood
control

control of and recreation, 88,
149–153

dispersal of, 56

in the landscape, 54–55

and natural drainage, 110–111

and residential design, 290

Strawberry Creek Park, 376

Street design

as boulevard, 54

and everyday route, 221

green, 88, 397

narrow, 221, 291–296, 337,
397–398

neighborhood, 291–292

and opportunity from natural disaster, 273

for pedestrians, 52–53, 215, 393,
398

Stress. *See* Health, mental

Stuttgart, Germany, 145, 148–149

Subdivision, 17, 59, 222

Suburban development

low density, 201–202, 206, 224,
243

required density, 203

Suburbs, 59, 79, 194, 205, 209, 217,
222, 224, 229

Sullivan, Chip, 353

Sun Moon Lake (Taiwan), 307

Survey, 101, 120

Sustainability

framework and ecological systems,
273

and growth pattern, 151

and interdependent adjacencies, 51

President's Council on
Sustainability, 367

and resilient form, 138–139, 172,
233

of urban form and biological diversity, 179

Sustainable

design and adaptive approach, 273

happiness, 107, 137

materials (green), 337

population size, 179, 247

Symbolic ownership, 25, 28, 109,
383

Symphonic sequence for walking,
399–400, 402, 405, 408–409,
412

Systems, 140–141, 256. *See also*
Networks; Todd, John; Todd,
Nancy

Tainan City, Taiwan, 137, 174,
177–178

Tainan County, spoonbills, 173–183

Taipei, landscape theater, 184

Taiwan, 137, 173–183, 388

carbon dioxide emissions, 175

Lalu Garden, 307

national government, 177, 183

Takano River, Japan, 194, 410–411

Tamesuke, Nagahashi, 325

Tanner Fountain, 300, 306–307

Tawo people, 154–160, 185

Technology

American values, 17, 351

appropriate or place-based, 146,
152

computer mapping, 163

green, 335–336

impacts on community life, 22, 37,
369

place-based thinking, 50

quick fix, 55, 412

removal from natural world, 325

urban development, 173, 177, 179

Thayer, Robert, 111, 337

Therapeutic Garden for Children
(Wellesley, MA), 303–304

Thinking outside the box, 245

Thoreau, Henry David, 331–332, 340,
352, 390, 392, 405–406

Thorncrown Chapel (Arkansas), 134

Thousand Acres, A, 50

Tocqueville, Alexis de, 252–253

Tokushima, Japan, 149–153. *See also*
Yoshino River

Todd, John, 141, 196–197

Todd, Nancy, 141

Tokyo, Japan, 272

Topophilia, 118, 301

Tourism

economy, 195, 241–242

local industry, 65, 97–98, 118–120,
122

in Manteo, 118–120, 122

sustainable, 195

Yountville, 195

Trade-offs, 119–120, 123. *See also*
Density

Transit Oriented Development, 189,
221

Transportation. *See also* Street design

alternative, 351

connective systems, 52, 397

costs of, 231

costs of car, 337, 351

design and fairness, 79, 231

design for resilience/open space,
241

divisive highway, 66, 149, 185

environment, 392

and land use, 336

networks that divide, 52, 60

public, 79–80, 83, 201, 204, 221,
271

restoration of, 69–75

street design, 52

subsidy and true costs, 204

Treepeople, 154

Tsen-wen Estuary (Tainan County), 173–183
Tsurezuregusa, The, 104–105
Twiss, Bob, 336

Union Point Park (CA), 90–95
United Nations, 183
United States
    bottom up and top down, 185
    city form and culture, 112, 185, 284, 392–393
    city form and flexible frameworks, 271
    ecological literacy, 330, 334–337, 372
    form of human habitation, 173
    health care, 303
    loss of biodiversity, 173, 202
    and native wisdom, 146, 327, 329, 333, 335
    and pace of life, 412
    and pollution, 351
    and recreation, 301
    recycling in, 330, 333
    and refugee settlements, 371–372
    rural living in, 344
    stewardship in, 364, 372
    and transportation, 204
Urban Creeks Council of California, 281
Urban development
    disruptive, 58
    and global warming, 272
    limits to, 137
    mitigation of, 272
    and need to create habitats, 59
    pressure and species needs, 174–176, 202
    and resilience, 137, 139
Urban Diaries: Improvisation in West Oakland, California, 352
Urban farming, 29, 57, 104, 189. *See also* Community garden

Urban form. *See* City form
Urban ecology, 52, 59, 138–139, 145, 275, 330, 332, 344
    definition of, 327
    and design, 345, 394
    effects of human actions, 331, 365
    learning, 338–339
    principles of, 330–332, 335, 341, 343, 345, 361
    unintelligible to us, 325, 328–329
Urban growth, 139, 177
    managed, 238–240, 251
    rate of and loss of diversity, 202
Urbanization. *See* Development; Urban development
Urban Land Institute, The, 25, 203
User needs
    and city design, 283–284
    and housing design, 85, 219
    and park design, 91–95, 249, 288–289
    and park design conflicts, 284–287

Values
    of community and built environment, 17–18, 24, 27, 135, 171
    conscious and unconscious, 123
    developing shared, 332
    and local and economic development, 120–121, 123–124, 126
    reflecting social class, 114
    shared and sacredness, 117
Van der Ryn, Sim, 141, 196–197
Vatican, 405
Venice, Italy, 130
Vermont, state of, 21
Vernacular architecture, 164
Village Homes (Davis, CA), 110–111
Violence, domestic, 82
Vision
    of everyday, 289–296
    redevelopment framework, 264
    of Tsen-wen Estuary, 177

Voluntary ethic, 366, 383
Volunteering
    diverse opportunities for, 369, 371, 375
    diverse population of, 380
    economic benefit of, 373
    incrementalism of, 385
    and National Wildlife Refuge, 373–374
    and necessity of agencies, 373
    organizations, 364–365, 369, 373
    and restoration efforts, 374–375, 377, 379
    and scientific monitoring, 348–349

Walkable, 413
    downtown, 215
    neighborhood, 192, 203
    proximity, 30, 397
Walking
    as aesthetic experience, 401–403, 408–409
    decline of, 392
    fosters stewardship, 392–393
    without measure, 407
    metamorphic, 404–407
    scored, 403
    tempo, 402, 404, 408, 417
    transformative, 405
    transformative, design for, 406–407
    utilitarian vs. experiential, 412–417
Walking distance, 392, 397, 413
    centers, 21, 25, 215, 221, 269
    design-based on, 397, 413
    to nature, 313–314
Walking environment, 392, 400
    and everyday patterns, 398, 413
    examples of, 397
    experiential, 393, 399, 403, 408
    funding for, 397
    guidelines for, 396–397, 399–401
Waller, Peter, 83–84, 263, 307
Walters, Rita, 315, 317

Wandering, aimless, 406
Washington Environmental Yard
      (Berkeley, CA), 113–114
Waste
      pattern of disposal, 82
      Todd, John, 196
      toxic, 82
      treatment of, 196
Waterfront development, 97, 118
Water quality/quantity, 335, 341
      protection of, 363
      volunteer monitoring, 348–349
Water resources, in California, 230
Watershed
      connecting through design, 55
      and design, 234
      disruptions of, 70
      erosion of, 179
      limit to habitation, 156
      planning and management,
         150–152, 157, 175
      restoration, 71
      Soquel, 348–349
Watts riots, 315
Webs, 54–57. *See* Ecological, processes
Westport, CA, 41–45, 130
Wetlands, 150, 278–279, 336
      habitat, 177–183
      preservation of, 173–183, 363
      RAMSAR, 183
      restoration, 337, 374
What Do People Do All Day?, 196
Wilderness, 227–229, 244, 249, 311
      preserves, 173, 182
      urban, 311, 314, 316, 340, 344 (*see
         also* Greenbelt)
Wildlife
      coalitions, 61
      corridors, 221, 336, 361
      in everyday life, 182
      failure to preserve, 63
      patterns inspire city form, 59,
         233–234

population, 247
preservation of, 67, 248–249, 336
refuges, 61, 234, 373–374
viewing, 183, 58, 91, 301
Wildlife habitat. *See also* Habitat
      city form, 51, 58–59, 224, 248,
         250, 354, 356
      in everyday life, 103, 321
      and farming stewardship, 373
      impacts of urban development on,
         244–250
      improvement programs, 373–374
      loss of, 106
      management, 274
      and neighborhood planning,
         372–373
      Olmsted plan, 55
      requirements of, 247
      threatened by highway, 66
Wildlands Project, 374
Williams, Terry Tempest, 340
Wong, Herbert, 338
Working together
      capacity to, 17–18, 21–22, 64, 142
      diversity, 111
      enabled by, 135
      encouraged through place, 32
      inability to, 66
      to solve problems, 18, 274–275,
         292–296, 279
World Watch Institute, 230
Wright, Frank Lloyd, 207

Yoshino River, 149–154
Young, Zell, 165–166
Yountville, CA
      community center, 35, 404
      landscape as framework, 269–271,
         403
      tourism, 195
      walking in, 403
Youth
      daily life, 292

and design, 91–95, 283, 377
ecological democracy, 346
employment, 62–63, 375–381
involvement, 80, 91–95
park access/use, 82, 249, 284–287
public transit, 80, 91

Zero-lot line, 263
Zoning
      city shaping, 186, 195, 210
      for density, 210, 223
      for habitat preservation, 59, 88
      inclusive, 52
      mixed-use, 188, 210
      protection of place through, 122,
         194
      separates uses, 52, 78
      single-use, 188, 191
      for walking environment, 397